Beginning Java 8 APIs, Extensions, and Libraries

Swing, JavaFX, JavaScript, JDBC, and Network Programming APIs

Kishori Sharan

Beginning Java 8 APIs, Extensions and Libraries: Swing, JavaFX, JavaScript, JDBC and Network Programming APIs

ISBN-13 (pbk): 978-1-4302-6661-7

ISBN-13 (electronic): 978-1-4302-6662-4

Publisher: Heinz Weinheimer
Lead Editor: Steve Anglin
Development Editor: Matthew Moodie
Technical Reviewers: Jeff Friesen
Editorial Board: Steve Anglin, Mark Beckner, Ewan Buckingham, Gary Cornell, Louise Corrigan, James T. DeWolf, Jonathan Gennick, Robert Hutchinson, Michelle Lowman, James Markham, Matthew Moodie, Jeff Olson, Jeffrey Pepper, Douglas Pundick, Ben Renow-Clarke, Dominic Shakeshaft, Gwenan Spearing, Matt Wade, Steve Weiss
Coordinating Editor: Anamika Panchoo
Copy Editor: Mary Behr
Compositor: SPi Global
Indexer: SPi Global
Artist: SPi Global
Cover Designer: Anna Ishchenko

Distributed to the book trade worldwide by Springer Science+Business Media New York, 233 Spring Street, 6th Floor, New York, NY 10013. Phone 1-800-SPRINGER, fax (201) 348-4505, e-mail orders-ny@springer-sbm.com, or visit www.springeronline.com. Apress Media, LLC is a California LLC and the sole member (owner) is Springer Science + Business Media Finance Inc (SSBM Finance Inc). SSBM Finance Inc is a Delaware corporation.

For information on translations, please e-mail rights@apress.com, or visit www.apress.com.

Apress and friends of ED books may be purchased in bulk for academic, corporate, or promotional use. eBook versions and licenses are also available for most titles. For more information, reference our Special Bulk Sales–eBook Licensing web page at www.apress.com/bulk-sales.

Any source code or other supplementary material referenced by the author in this text is available to readers at www.apress.com. For detailed information about how to locate your book's source code, go to www.apress.com/source-code/.

To
My parents, Ram Vinod Singh and Pratibha Devi

Contents

About the Author xxi

About the Technical Reviewer xxiii

Acknowledgments xxv

Foreword xxvii

Introduction xxix

■Chapter 1: Introduction to Swing 1

What Is Swing? 1

The Simplest Swing Program 3

Components of a JFrame 7

Adding Components to a JFrame 8

Some Utility Classes 12

    The Point Class 12

    The Dimension Class 13

    The Insets Class 13

    The Rectangle Class 13

Layout Managers 14

    FlowLayout 15

    BorderLayout 21

    CardLayout 23

    BoxLayout 26

    GridLayout 30

    GridBagLayout 32

    SpringLayout 49

GroupLayout 56

The null Layout Manager 66

Creating a Reusable JFrame 67

Event Handling 69

Handling Mouse Events 76

Summary 79

■Chapter 2: Swing Components 81

What Is a Swing Component? 81

JButton 86

JPanel 90

JLabel 91

Text Components 93

JTextComponent 95

JTextField 97

JPasswordField 101

JFormattedTextField 102

JTextArea 105

JEditorPane 108

JTextPane 113

Validating Text Input 121

Making Choices 122

JSpinner 129

JScrollBar 131

JScrollPane 133

JProgressBar 135

JSlider 136

JSeparator 137

Menus 137

JToolBar 146

JToolBar Meets the Action Interface 148

JTable 149

JTree 155

JTabbedPane and JSplitPane 160

Custom Dialogs 162

Standard Dialogs 166

File and Color Choosers 172

    JFileChooser 172

    JColorChooser 176

JWindow 177

Working with Colors 177

Working with Borders 178

Working with Fonts 181

Validating Components 183

Painting Components and Drawing Shapes 184

Immediate Painting 189

Double Buffering 189

JFrame Revisited 190

Summary 192

■Chapter 3: Advanced Swing 195

Using HTML in Swing Components 195

Threading Model in Swing 196

Pluggable Look and Feel 205

Skinnable Look-and-Feel 210

Drag and Drop 219

Multiple Document Interface Application 227

The Toolkit Class 230

Decorating Components Using JLayer 232

Translucent Windows 239

Shaped Window 245

Summary 248

■**Chapter 4: Applets** **249**

What Is an Applet? 249

Developing an Applet...250

Writing an Applet..250

Deploying an Applet 252

    Creating the HTML Document..252

    Deploying Applets in Production 254

    Deploying Applets for Testing 254

Installing and Configuring Java Plug-in 255

    Installing the Java Plug-in...255

    Opening the Java Control Panel..255

    Configuring Java Plug-in 257

Viewing an Applet..260

Using the appletviewer to Test Applets 260

Using the codebase Attribute 262

    Example 1 262

    Example 2 263

    Example 3 263

The Life Cycle of an Applet...264

    The init() Method 264

    The start() Method 264

    The stop() Method..265

    The destroy() Method 265

Passing Parameters to Applets 266

Publishing the Applet's Parameter Information..269

Publishing the Applet's Information 270

Other Attributes of the <applet> Tag..270

Using Images in an Applet..272

Playing Audio Clips in an Applet 273

Interacting with the Applet's Environment 274

Communion of Applet, HTML, and JavaScript 275

Packaging Applets in Archives 278

The Event Dispatching Thread and Applets..278

Painting in Applets 280

Is the Java Code Trusted? 280

Security Restrictions for Applets...284

Signing Applets 287

    Step 1: Developing an Applet.. 287

    Step 2: Packaging Class Files into a JAR File 288

    Step 3: Generating Private/Public Key Pair.. 288

    Step 4: Signing the JAR File 288

    Step 5: Creating the HTML File 289

    Step 6: Viewing the Signed Applet.. 289

Summary..291

■Chapter 5: Network Programming...293

What Is Network Programming? 293

Network Protocol Suite 295

IP Addressing Scheme...297

    IPv4 Addressing Scheme 298

    IPv6 Addressing Scheme 300

Special IP Addresses 302

    Loopback IP Address 302

    Unicast IP Address... 303

    Multicast IP Address 303

    Anycast IP Address 303

    Broadcast IP Address... 304

    Unspecified IP Address... 304

Port Numbers 304

Socket API and Client-Server Paradigm 305

    The Socket Primitive...307

    The Bind Primitive 307

    The Listen Primitive 307

    The Accept Primitive 308

    The Connect Primitive...308

    The Send/Sendto Primitive 309

    The Receive/ReceiveFrom Primitive 309

    The Close Primitive 309

Representing a Machine Address 309

Representing a Socket Address 311

Creating a TCP Server Socket 312

Creating a TCP Client Socket...317

Putting a TCP Server and Clients Together..319

Working with UDP Sockets...319

Creating a UDP Echo Server 322

A Connected UDP Socket..327

UDP Multicast Sockets 327

URI, URL, and URN 330

URI and URL as Java Objects...333

Accessing the Contents of a URL 337

Non-Blocking Socket Programming 345

Socket Security Permissions..356

Asynchronous Socket Channels 357

    Setting Up an Asynchronous Server Socket Channel 359

    Setting up an Asynchronous Client Socket Channel 365

    Putting the Server and the Client Together...369

Datagram-Oriented Socket Channels 370

    Creating the Datagram Channel 371

    Setting the Channel Options 371

    Sending Datagrams 372

Multicasting Using Datagram Channels 376

    Creating the Datagram Channel 376

    Setting the Channel Options 376

    Binding the Channel 376

    Setting the Multicast Network Interface 377

    Joining the Multicast Group 378

    Receiving a Message 379

    Closing the Channel 379

Further Reading 382

Summary 382

■Chapter 6: JDBC API 385

What Is the JDBC API? 385

System Requirements 386

Types of JDBC Drivers 386

    JDBC Native API Driver 387

    JDBC-Net Driver 387

    JDBC Driver 387

A Brief Overview of Java DB 387

    Java DB Installation Files 387

    Configuring Java DB 388

    Running the Java DB Server 388

Creating a Database Table 393

    Oracle Database 394

    Adaptive Server Anywhere Database 394

    SQL Server Database 394

    DB2 Database 394

MySQL Database 395

Java DB Database.. 395

Connecting to a Database 395

Obtaining the JDBC Driver.. 396

Setting up the CLASSPATH 396

Registering a JDBC Driver 396

Setting the jdbc.drivers System Property 397

Loading the Driver Class.. 397

Using the registerDriver() Method 397

Constructing a Connection URL 398

Establishing the Database Connection 402

Setting the Auto-Commit Mode 406

Committing and Rolling Back Transactions...406

Transaction Isolation Level 407

Dirty Read.. 407

Non-Repeatable Read.. 407

Phantom Read 408

JDBC-Types-to-Java-Types Mapping 409

Knowing About the Database 412

Executing SQL Statements 414

Results of Executing a SQL Statement 415

Using the Statement Interface.. 416

Using the PreparedStatement Interface 422

CallableStatement Interface 425

Processing Result Sets...437

What Is a ResultSet?.. 437

Getting a ResultSet.. 442

Getting the Number of Rows in a ResultSet 448

Bidirectional Scrollable ResultSets.. 451

Scrolling Through Rows of a ResultSet 453

Knowing the Cursor Position in a ResultSet 456

Closing a ResultSet 456

Making Changes to a ResultSet 457

Inserting a Row Using a ResultSet 457

Updating a Row Using a ResultSet 460

Deleting a Row Using a ResultSet 462

Handling Multiple Results from a Statement 463

Getting a ResultSet from a Stored Procedure 464

MySQL Database 465

Adaptive Server Anywhere Database 466

Oracle Database 466

SQL Server Database 466

DB2 Database 467

Java DB Database 467

ResultSetMetaData 472

Using RowSets 474

Working with a Large Object (LOB) 500

Retrieving LOB Data 502

Creating a LOB Data 504

Batch Updates 511

Savepoints in a Transaction 517

Using a DataSource 520

Retrieving SQL Warnings 522

Enabling JDBC Trace 522

Summary 523

■Chapter 7: Java Remote Method Invocation 525

What Is Java Remote Method Invocation? 525

The RMI Architecture 526

Developing an RMI Application 528

Writing the Remote Interface...528

Implementing the Remote Interface 529

Writing the RMI Server Program..531

Writing the RMI Client Program 534

Separating the Server and Client Code 536

Generating Stub and Skeleton..536

Running the RMI Application 537

Running the RMI Registry...537

Running the RMI Server...538

Running an RMI Client Program 539

Troubleshooting an RMI Application 540

java.rmi.StubNotFoundException 540

java.rmi.server.ExportException 540

java.security.AccessControlException 541

java.lang.ClassNotFoundException..541

Debugging an RMI Application 542

Dynamic Class Downloading...543

Garbage Collection of Remote Objects...545

Summary..548

■Chapter 8: Java Native Interface 549

What Is the Java Native Interface?...549

System Requirements 550

Getting Started with the JNI 551

Writing the Java Program..551

Compiling the Java Program 554

Creating the C/C++ Header File 554

Writing the C/C++ Program 556

Creating a Shared Library 557

Running the Java Program 560

Native Function Naming Rules 561

Data Type Mapping 563

Using JNI Functions in C/C++ 565

Working with Strings 565

Working with Arrays 568

Accessing Java Objects in Native Code 573

Getting a Class Reference 573

Accessing Fields and Methods of a Java Object/Class.. 574

Creating Java Objects 579

Exception Handling 581

Handle the Exception in Native Code.. 582

Handling the Exception in Java Code 583

Throwing a New Exception from Native Code 583

Creating an Instance of the JVM 584

Synchronization in Native Code... 589

Summary... 590

Chapter 9: Introduction to JavaFX.. 591

What Is JavaFX? 591

The History of JavaFX.. 593

System Requirements 593

The JavaFX Runtime Library 594

JavaFX Source Code.. 594

Your First JavaFX Application 594

Creating the HelloJavaFX Class 594

Overriding the start() Method 595

Showing the Stage 595

Launching the Application 596

Adding the main() Method 598

Adding a Scene to the Stage 598

Improving the HelloFX Application 600

The Life Cycle of a JavaFX Application 602

Terminating a JavaFX Application 604

What Are Properties and Bindings? 604

Properties and Bindings in JavaFX 605

Using Properties in JavaFX Beans 608

Handling Property Invalidation Events 612

Handling Property Change Events 615

Property Bindings in JavaFX 617

Observable Collections 623

Event Handling 627

Event Processing Mechanism 628

Creating Event Filters and Handlers 631

Registering Event Filters and Handlers 631

Layout Panes 636

Controls 642

Using 2D Shapes 648

Drawing on a Canvas 652

Applying Effects 654

Applying Transformations 656

Animation 659

Using the Timeline Animation 662

FXML 665

Printing 670

Summary 675

■Chapter 10: Scripting in Java 677

What Is Scripting in Java? 677

Executing Your First Script 678

Using Other Scripting Languages 680

Exploring the javax.script Package 683

The ScriptEngine and ScriptEngineFactory Interfaces 683

The AbstractScriptEngine Class 684

The ScriptEngineManager Class 684

The Compilable Interface and the CompiledScript Class 684

The Invocable Interface 684

The Bindings Interface and the SimpleBindings Class 684

The ScriptContext Interface and the SimpleScriptContext Class 684

The ScriptException Class 685

Discovering and Instantiating ScriptEngines 685

Executing Scripts 686

Passing Parameters 687

Passing Parameters from Java Code to Scripts 688

Passing Parameters from Scripts to Java Code 690

Advanced Parameter Passing Techniques 691

Bindings 691

Scope 693

Defining the Script Context 693

Putting Them Together 697

Using a Custom ScriptContext 703

Return Value of the eval() Method 705

Reserved Keys for Engine Scope Bindings 707

Changing the Default ScriptContext 707

Sending Scripts Output to a File 708

Invoking Procedures in Scripts 710

Implementing Java Interfaces in Scripts 713

Using Compiled Scripts 717

Using Java in Scripting Languages 719

    Declaring Variables.. 719

    Importing Java Classes.. 720

    Creating and Using Java Objects... 723

    Using Overloaded Java Methods 724

    Using Java Arrays 725

    Extending Java Classes Implementing Interfaces 729

    Using Lambda Expressions.. 731

Implementing a Script Engine 732

    The Expression Class.. 733

    The JKScriptEngine Class.. 738

    The JKScriptEngineFactory Class 740

    Preparing for Deployment.. 742

    Packaging the JKScript Files 742

    Using the JKScript Script Engine 742

The jrunscript Command-line Shell... 745

    The Syntax... 745

    Execution Modes of the Shell 746

    Listing Available Script Engines... 748

    Adding a Script Engine to the Shell 748

    Using Other Script Engines 748

    Passing Arguments to Scripts.. 748

The jjs Command-Line Tool 749

JavaFX in Nashorn 753

Summary... 757

Index... 759

About the Author

Kishori Sharan is a Senior Software Consultant at Doozer, Inc. He holds a Master of Science in Computer Information Systems from Troy State University in Montgomery, Alabama. He is a Sun Certified Java Programmer and Sybase Certified PowerBuilder Developer Professional. He specializes in developing enterprise applications using Java SE, Java EE, PowerBuilder, and Oracle database. He has been working in the software industry for over 16 years. He has helped several clients migrate legacy applications to the Web. He loves writing technical books in his free time. He maintains his web site at `www.jdojo.com` where he posts blogs on Java and JavaFX.

About the Technical Reviewer

Jeff Friesen is a freelance tutor, author, and software developer with an emphasis on Java, Android, and HTML5. In addition to writing several books for Apress and serving as a technical reviewer for other Apress books, Jeff has written numerous articles on Java and other technologies for JavaWorld (www.javaworld.com), informIT (www.informit.com), java.net, SitePoint (www.sitepoint.com), and others. Jeff can be contacted via his web site at tutortutor.ca.

Acknowledgments

My heartfelt thanks are due to my father-in-law, Mr. Jim Baker, for displaying extraordinary patience in reading the initial draft of the book. I am very grateful to him for spending so much of his valuable time teaching me quite a bit of English grammar that helped me produce better material.

I would like to thank my friend Richard Castillo for his hard work in reading my initial draft of the book and weeding out several mistakes. Richard was instrumental in running all examples and pointing out errors.

My wife, Ellen, was always patient when I spent long hours at my computer desk working on this book. She would happily bring me snacks, fruit, and a glass of water every 30 minutes or so to sustain me during that period. I want to thank her for all of her support in writing this book. She also deserves my sincere thanks for letting me sometimes seclude myself on weekends so I could focus on this book.

I would like to thank my family members and friends for their encouragement and support for writing this book: my elder brothers, Janki Sharan and Dr. Sita Sharan; my sister and brother-in-law, Ratna and Abhay; my nephews Babalu, Dabalu, Gaurav, Saurav, and Chitranjan; my friends Shivashankar Ravindranath, Kannan Somasekar, Mahbub Choudhury, Biju Nair, Srinivas Kakkera, Anil Kumar Singh, Chris Coley, Willie Baptiste, Rahul Jain, Larry Brewster, Greg Langham, Ram Atmakuri, LaTondra Okeke, Rahul Nagpal, Ravi Datla, Prakash Chandra, and many more friends not mentioned here.

My sincere thanks are due to the wonderful team at Apress for their support during the publication of this book. Thanks to Anamika Panchoo, the Senior Coordinating Editor, for providing excellent support and for being exceptionally patient with me when I asked her so many questions in the beginning, Thanks to Matthew Moodie and Jeff Friesen for their technical insights and feedback during the editing process. My heartfelt thanks go to Jeff for his diligence in reviewing the book and pointing out technical errors. He did not stop at just pointing out the errors; he also included the solution in his comments that helped me save time. Last but not least, my sincere thanks to Steve Anglin, the Lead Editor at Apress, for taking the initiative for the publication of this book.

Foreword

I recently had the privilege of tech reviewing Kishori Sharan's *Beginning Java 8 APIs, Extensions, and Libraries* book, which continues on from his *Beginning Java 8 Language Features* book by covering more advanced Java APIs. Within this volume, you learn about Swing, applets, network programming, JDBC, remote method invocation, the Java Native Interface, JavaFX, and Java's scripting framework.

This book offers a wealth of detail. For example, in his chapter on JDBC, Kishori covers result sets along with row sets, which derive from result sets, and which you might expect to see covered in a book focused on enterprise Java. Kishori also provides decent coverage of Java's Swing user interface API while not shying away from the modern JavaFX alternative.

As I recommended in my forward to this book's predecessor, I believe that *Beginning Java 8 APIs, Extensions, and Libraries* definitely deserves a place on your bookshelf.

—Jeff Friesen
August/2014

Introduction

How This Book Came About

My first encounter with the Java programming language was during a one-week Java training session in 1997. I did not get a chance to use Java in a project until 1999. I read two Java books and took a Java 2 Programmer certification examination. I did very well on the test, scoring 95 percent. The three questions that I missed on the test made me realize that the books I read did not adequately cover all of the details on all of the necessary Java topics. I made up my mind to write a book on the Java programming language. So I formulated a plan to cover most of the topics that a Java developer needs understand to use the Java programming language effectively in a project, as well as to get a certification. I initially planned to cover all essential topics in Java in 700 to 800 pages.

As I progressed, I realized that a book covering most of the Java topics in detail could not be written in 700 to 800 hundred pages; one chapter that covered data types, operators, and statements spanned 90 pages. I was then faced with the question, "Should I shorten the content of the book or include all the details that I think a Java developer needs?" I opted for including all the details in the book, rather than shortening the content to keep the number of pages low. It has never been my intent to make lots of money from this book. I was never in a hurry to finish this book because that rush could have compromised the quality and the coverage of its contents. In short, I wrote this book to help the Java community understand and use the Java programming language effectively, without having to read many books on the same subject. I wrote this book with the plan that it would be a comprehensive one-stop reference for everyone who wants to learn and grasp the intricacies of the Java programming language.

One of my high school teachers used to tell us that if one wanted to understand a building, one must first understand the bricks, steel, and mortar that make up the building. The same logic applies to most of the things that we want to understand in our lives. It certainly applies to an understanding of the Java programming language. If you want to master the Java programming language, you must start by understanding its basic building blocks. I have used this approach throughout this book, endeavoring to build each topic by describing the basics first. In the book, you will rarely find a topic described without first learning its background. Wherever possible, I have tried to correlate the programming practices with activities in our daily life. Most books about the Java programming language either do not include any pictures at all or have only a few. I believe in the adage, "A picture is worth a thousand words." To a reader, a picture makes a topic easier to understand and remember. I have included plenty of illustrations in this book to aid readers in understanding and visualizing concepts. Developers who have little or no programming experience can have difficulty putting things together to make a complete program. Keeping them in mind, the book contains over 216 complete Java programs that are ready to be compiled and run.

I spent countless hours doing research for this book. My main sources of research were the Java Language Specification, white papers and articles on Java topics, and Java Specification Requests (JSRs). I also spent quite a bit of time reading the Java source code to learn more about some of the Java topics. Sometimes it took a few months to research a topic before I could write the first sentence on it. It was always fun to play with Java programs, sometimes for hours, to add them to the book.

Structure of the Book

This is the third book in the three-book Beginning Java series. This book contains 10 chapters. The chapters cover the Java libraries and extensions such as Swing, JavaFX, Nashorn, Java Native Interface, network programming, etc. If you have intermediate level Java experience, you can pick up chapters in any order. The new features of Java 8 are included wherever they fit in the chapter. The Nashorn script engine, which was added in Java 8, is covered in depth.

Audience

This book is designed to be useful for anyone who wants to learn the Java programming language. If you are a beginner with little or no programming background in Java, you are advised to read the companion books, *Beginning Java 8 Fundamentals* and *Beginning Java 8 Language Features*, before reading this book.

If you are a Java developer with an intermediate or advanced level of experience, you can jump to a chapter or a section in a chapter directly.

If you are reading this book to get a certification in the Java programming language, you need to read almost all of the chapters, paying attention to all of the detailed descriptions and rules. Most of the certification programs test your fundamental knowledge of the language, not advanced knowledge. You need to read only those topics that are part of your certification test. Compiling and running over 216 complete Java programs will help you prepare for your certification.

If you are a student who is attending a class in the Java programming language, you should read the chapters of this book selectively. You need to read only those chapters that are covered in your class syllabus. I am sure that you, as a Java student, do not need to read the entire book page by page.

How to Use This Book

This book is the beginning, not the end, of gaining knowledge of the Java programming language. If you are reading this book, it means you are heading in the right direction to learn the Java programming language, which will enable you to excel in your academic and professional career. However, there is always a higher goal for you to achieve and you must constantly work hard to achieve it. The following quotations from some great thinkers may help you understand the importance of working hard and constantly looking for knowledge with both your eyes and mind open.

> *The learning and knowledge that we have is, at the most, but little compared with that of which we are ignorant.*

> —Plato

> *True knowledge exists in knowing that you know nothing. And in knowing that you know nothing, that makes you the smartest of all.*

> —Socrates

Readers are advised to use the API documentation for the Java programming language as much as possible while using this book. The Java API documentation is where you will find a complete list of everything available in the Java class library. You can download (or view) the Java API documentation from the official web site of Oracle Corporation at `www.oracle.com`. While you read this book, you need to practice writing Java programs yourself. You can also practice by tweaking the programs provided in the book. It does not help much in your learning process if you just read this book and do not practice by writing your own programs. Remember that "practice makes perfect," which is also true in learning how to program in Java.

Source Code and Errata

Source code and errata for this book may be downloaded from www.apress.com/source-code.

Questions and Comments

Please direct all your questions and comments for the author to ksharan@jdojo.com.

■ ■ ■

## CHAPTER 1

Introduction to Swing

In this chapter, you will learn

- What Swing is
- The difference between a character-based interface and a graphical user interface
- How to develop the simplest Swing program
- What a JFrame is and how it is made up of different components
- How to add components to a JFrame
- What a layout manager is and different types of layout managers in Swing
- How to create reusable frames
- How to handle events
- How to handle mouse events and how to use the adapter class to handle mouse events

What Is Swing?

Swing provides graphical user interface (GUI) components to develop Java applications with a rich set of graphics such as windows, buttons, checkboxes, etc. What is a GUI? Before I define a GUI, let me first define a user interface (UI). A program does three things:

- Accepts inputs from the user
- Processes the inputs, and
- Produces outputs

A user interface provides a means to exchange information between a user and a program, in terms of inputs and outputs. In other words, a user interface defines the way the interaction between the user and a program takes place. Typing text using a keyboard, selecting a menu item using a mouse, or clicking a button can provide input to a program. The output from a program can be displayed on a computer monitor in the form of character-based text, a graph such as a bar chart, a picture, etc.

You have written many Java programs. You have seen programs where users had to provide inputs to the program in the form of text entered on the console, and the program would print the output on the console. A user interface where the user's input and the program's output are in text form is known as a *character-based user interface*. A GUI lets users interact with a program using graphical elements called *controls* or *widgets*, using a keyboard, a mouse, and other devices.

Figure 1-1 shows a program that lets users enter a person's name and date of birth (DOB), and save the information by using the keyboard. It is an example of a character-based user interface.

```
Please enter person details
Name:John Jacobs
DOB:01/12/1971
Enter S to Save and E to exit without saving:S
```

Figure 1-1. *An example of a program with a character-based user interface*

Figure 1-2 lets the user perform the same actions, but using a graphical user interface. It displays six graphical elements in a window. It uses two labels (Name: and DOB:), two text fields where the user will enter the Name and DOB values, and two buttons (Save and Close). A graphical user interface, compared to a character-based user interface, makes the user's interaction with a program easier. Can you guess what kind of application you are going to develop in this chapter? It will be all about GUI. GUI development is interesting and a little more complex than character-based program development. Once you understand the elements involved in GUI development, it will be fun to work with it.

Figure 1-2. *An example of a program with a graphical user interface*

This chapter attempts to cover the basics of GUI development using Swing's components and top-level containers. Care has been taken to explain GUI-related details for those programmers who might not have used any programming languages/tools (e.g. Visual C++, Visual Basic, VB.NET, or PowerBuilder) to develop a GUI before. If you have already used a GUI development language/tool, it will be easier for you to understand the materials covered in this chapter. Swing is a vast topic and it is not possible to cover every detail of it. It deserves a book by itself. In fact, there are a few books in the market dedicated to only Swing.

A *container* is a component that can hold other components inside it. A container at the highest level is called a *top-level container*. A JFrame, a JDialog, a JWindow, and a JApplet are examples of top-level containers. A JPanel is an example of a simple container. A JButton, a JTextField, etc. are examples of components. In a Swing application, every component must be contained within a container. The container is known as the component's parent and the component is known as container's child. This parent-child relationship (or container-contained relationship) is known as *containment hierarchy*. To display a component on the screen, a top-level container must be at the root of the containment hierarchy. Every Swing application must have at least one top-level container. Figure 1-3 shows the containment hierarchy of a Swing application. A top-level container contains a container called "Container 1," which in turn contains a component called "Component 1" and a container called "Container 2," which in turn contains two components called "Component 2" and "Component 3."

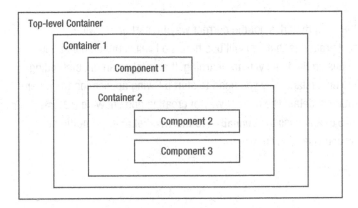

Figure 1-3. *Containment hierarchy in a Swing application*

The Simplest Swing Program

Let's start with the simplest Swing program. You will display a JFrame, which is a top-level container with no components in it. To create and display a JFrame, you need to do the following:

- Create a JFrame object.

- Make it visible.

To create a JFrame object, you can use one of the constructors of the JFrame class. One of the constructors takes a string, which will be displayed as the title for the JFrame. Classes representing Swing components are in the javax.swing package, so is the JFrame class. The following snippet of code creates a JFrame object with its title set to "Simplest Swing":

```
// Create a JFrame object
JFrame frame = new JFrame("Simplest Swing");
```

When you create a JFrame object, by default, it is not visible. You need to call its setVisible(boolean visible) method to make it visible. If you pass true to this method, the JFrame is made visible, and if you pass false, it is made invisible.

```
// Make the JFrame visible on the screen
frame.setVisible(true);
```

That is all you have to do to develop your first Swing application! In fact, you can wrap the two statements, to create and display a JFrame, into one statement, like so:

```
new JFrame("Simplest Swing").setVisible(true);
```

■ **Tip** Creating a JFrame and making it visible from the main thread is not the correct way to start up a Swing application. However, it does not do any harm in the trivial programs that you will use here, so I will continue using this approach to keep the code simple to learn, so you can focus on the topic you are learning. It also takes an understanding of event-handling and threading mechanisms in Swing to understand why you need to start a Swing application the other way. Chapter 3 explains how to start up a Swing application in detail. The correct way of creating and showing a JFrame is to wrap the GUI creation and make it visible in a Runnable and pass the Runnable to the invokeLater() method of the javax.swing.SwingUtilities or java.awt.EventQueue class as shown:

```
import javax.swing.JFrame;
import javax.swing.SwingUtilities;
...
SwingUtilities.invokeLater(() -> new JFrame("Test").setVisible(true));
```

Listing 1-1 has the complete code to create and display a JFrame. When you run this program, it displays a JFrame at the top-left corner of the screen as shown in Figure 1-4. The figure shows the frame when the program was run on Windows XP. On other platforms, the frame may look a little different. Most of the screenshots for the GUIs in this chapter were taken on Windows XP.

Listing 1-1. Simplest Swing Program

```java
// SimplestSwing.java
package com.jdojo.swing;

import javax.swing.JFrame;

public class SimplestSwing {
        public static void main(String[] args) {
                // Create a frame
                JFrame frame = new JFrame("Simplest Swing");

                // Display the frame
                frame.setVisible(true);
        }
}
```

This was not very impressive, was it? Do not despair. You will improve this program as you learn more about Swing. This was just to show you the tip of the iceberg of what Swing offers.

You can resize the JFrame shown in the Figure 1-4 to make it bigger. Place your mouse pointer on any of the four edges (left, top, right, or bottom) or any of the four corners of the displayed JFrame. The mouse pointer changes its shape to a resize pointer (a line with arrows at both ends) when you place it on the JFrame's edge. Then just drag the resize mouse pointer to resize the JFrame in the direction you want to resize it.

Figure 1-4. *The Simplest Swing frame*

Figure 1-5 shows the resized JFrame. Note that the text "Simplest Swing" that you passed to the constructor when you created the JFrame is displayed in the title bar of the JFrame.

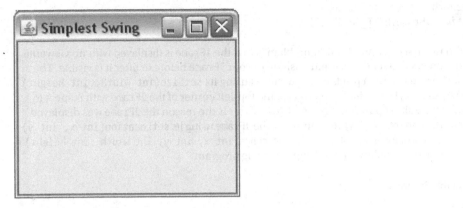

Figure 1-5. *The Simplest Swing frame after resizing*

How do you exit a·Swing application? How do you exit when you run the program listed in Listing 1-1? When you click the close button in the title bar (right-most button on the title bar with an X), the JFrame is closed. However, the program does not exit. If you are running this program from a command prompt, the prompt does not return when you close the JFrame. You will have to force exit the program, for example, by pressing Ctrl + C if you are running it from a command prompt on Windows. So, how do you exit a Swing application? You can define one of the four behaviors of a JFrame to determine what happens when the JFrame is closed. They are defined in the javax.swing.WindowsConstants interface as four constants. The JFrame class implements the WindowsConstants interface. You can reference all these constants using JFrame.CONSTANT_NAME syntax (or you can use the WindowsConstants.CONSTANT_NAME syntax). The four constants are

- DO_NOTHING_ON_CLOSE: This option does not do anything when the user closes a JFrame. If you set this option for a JFrame, you must provide some other way to exit the application, such as an Exit button or an Exit menu option in the JFrame.

- HIDE_ON_CLOSE: This option just hides a JFrame when the user closes it. This is the default behavior. This is what happened when you clicked the close button from the title bar to close the program listed in Listing 1-1. The JFrame was just made invisible and the program was still running.

- DISPOSE_ON_CLOSE: This option hides and disposes of the JFrame when the user closes it. Disposing a JFrame releases any operating system-level resources used by it. Note the difference between HIDE_ON_CLOSE and DISPOSE_ON_CLOSE. When you use the option HIDE_ON_CLOSE, a JFrame is just hidden, but it is still using all the operating system resources. If your JFrame is hidden and shown very frequently, you may want to use this option. However, if your JFrame consumes many resources, you may want to use the DISPOSE_ON_CLOSE option, so the resources may be released and reused while it is not being displayed.

- EXIT_ON_CLOSE: This option exits the application. Setting this option works when a JFrame is closed, as if System.exit() has been called. This option should be used with some care. This option will exit the application. If you have more than one JFrame or any other type of window displayed on the screen, using this option for one JFrame will close all other windows. Use this option with caution as you may lose any unsaved data when the application exits.

You can set the default close behavior of a JFrame by passing one of the four constants to its setDefaultCloseOperation() method as shown:

```
// Exit the application when the JFrame is closed
frame.setDefaultCloseOperation(JFrame.EXIT_ON_CLOSE);
```

You solved one problem with the first example. Another problem is that the JFrame is displayed with no viewable area. It displays only the title bar. You need to set the size and position of your JFrame before or after it is visible. The size of a frame is defined by its width and height in pixels that you can set using its setSize(int width, int height) method. The position is defined by the (x, y) coordinates in pixels of the top-left corner of the JFrame with respect to the top-left corner of the screen. By default, its position is set to (0, 0) and this is the reason the JFrame was displayed at the top-left corner of the screen. You can set the (x, y) coordinates of the JFrame using its setLocation(int x, int y) method. If you want to set its size and its position in one step, use its setBounds(int x, int y, int width, int height) method instead. Listing 1-2 fixes these two problems in the Simplest Swing program.

Listing 1-2. Revised Simplest Swing Program

```java
// RevisedSimplestSwing.java
package com.jdojo.swing;

import javax.swing.JFrame;

public class RevisedSimplestSwing {
        public static void main(String[] args) {
                // Create a frame
                JFrame frame = new JFrame("Revised Simplest Swing");

                // Set the default close behavior to exit the application
                frame.setDefaultCloseOperation(JFrame.EXIT_ON_CLOSE);

                // Set the x, y, width and height properties in one go
                frame.setBounds(50, 50, 200, 200);

                // Display the frame
                frame.setVisible(true);
        }
}
```

■ **Tip**   You can position a JFrame in the center by calling its setLocationRelativeTo() method with a null argument.

Components of a JFrame

You displayed a JFrame in the previous section. It looked empty; however, it was not really empty. When you create a JFrame, the following things are automatically done for you:

- A container, which is called a *root pane*, is added as the sole child of the JFrame. The root pane is a container. It is an object of the JRootPane class. You can get the reference of the root pane by using the getRootPane() method of the JFrame class.

- Two containers called *glass pane* and *layered pane* are added to the root pane. By default, the glass pane is hidden and it is placed on top of the layered pane. As the name suggests, the glass pane is transparent, and even if you make it visible, you can see through it. The layered pane is named as such because it can hold other containers or components in its different layers. Optionally, a layered pane can hold a menu bar. However, a menu bar is not added by default when you create a JFrame. You can get the reference of the glass pane and the layered pane by using the getGlassPane() and getLayeredPane() methods of the JFrame class, respectively.

- A container called a *content pane* is added to the layered pane. By default, the content pane is empty. This is the container in which you are supposed to add all your Swing components, such as buttons, text fields, labels, etc. Most of the time, you will be working with the content pane of the JFrame. You can get the reference of the content pane by using the getContentPane() method of the JFrame class.

Figure 1-6 shows the assembly of a JFrame. The root pane, layered pane, and glass pane cover the entire viewable area of a JFrame. The viewable area of a JFrame is its size minus its insets on all four sides. Insets of a container consist of the space used by the border around the container on four sides: top, left, bottom, and right. For a JFrame, the top inset represents the height of the title bar. Figure 1-6 depicts the layered pane smaller than the size of the root pane for better visualization.

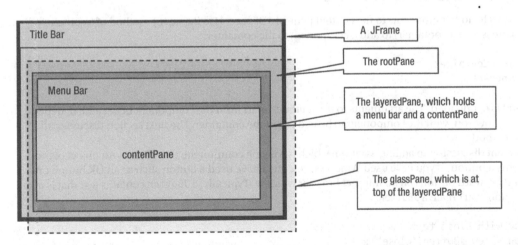

Figure 1-6. *The making of a JFrame*

Are you confused? If you are confused with all the panes of a JFrame, here is a simpler explanation. Think of a JFrame as a picture frame. A picture frame has a glass cover, and so does a JFrame, in the form of a glass pane. Behind the glass cover, you place your picture. That is your layered pane. You can place multiple pictures inside one picture frame. Each picture will make up one layer behind the glass cover. As long as one picture is not fully overlapped by another, you can view it wholly or partly. All pictures taken together in different layers form the layered pane of your picture frame. The picture layer, which is farthest from the glass cover, is your content pane. Usually your picture frame contains only one picture in it. So does the layered pane; by default, it contains one content pane. The picture in the picture frame is the content of interest and paintings are placed there. So is the case with the content pane; all components are placed in the content pane.

The containment hierarchy of a JFrame is listed below. A JFrame is at the top of the hierarchy, and the menu bar (it is not added by default; it is shown here for completeness) and the content pane are at the bottom of the containment hierarchy.

```
JFrame
        root pane
                glass pane
                layered pane
                        menu bar
                        content pane
```

If you are still not able to understand all of the "pains" (read panes) of a JFrame, you can revisit this section later. For now, you have to understand only one pane of the JFrame, and that is the content pane, which holds the Swing components of a JFrame. You should add all components you want to add to a JFrame to its content pane. You can get the reference of the content pane as follows:

```
// Create a JFrame
JFrame frame = new JFrame("Test");

// Get the reference of the content pane
Container contentPane = frame.getContentPane();
```

Adding Components to a JFrame

This section explains how to add components to the content pane of a JFrame. Use the add() method of a container (note that a content pane is also a container) to add a component to the container.

```
// Add aComponent to aContainer
aContainer.add(aComponent);
```

The add() method is overloaded. The arguments to the method, apart from the component being added, depend on other factors such as how you want the component to be laid out in the container. The next section discusses all versions of the add() method.

I will limit the current discussion to adding a button, which is a Swing component, to a JFrame. An object of the JButton class represents a button. If you have used Windows, you must have used a button such as an OK button on a message box, Back and Forward buttons on an Internet browser window. Typically, a JButton contains text that is also called its label. This is how you create a JButton:

```
// Create a JButton with Close text
JButton closeButton = new JButton("Close");
```

To add closeButton to the content pane of a JFrame, you have to do two things:

- Get the reference of the content pane of the JFrame.

  ```
  Container contentPane = frame.getContentPane();
  ```

- Call the add() method of the content pane.

  ```
  contentPane.add(closeButton);
  ```

That is all it takes to add a component to the content pane. If you want to add a JButton using one line of code, you can do so by combining all three statements into one, like so:

```
frame.getContentPane().add(new JButton("Close"));
```

The code to add components to a JFrame is shown in Listing 1-3. When you run the program, you get a JFrame as shown in the Figure 1-7. Nothing happens when you click the Close button because you have not yet added any action to it.

Listing 1-3. Adding Components to a JFrame

```java
// AddingComponentToJFrame.java
package com.jdojo.swing;

import javax.swing.JFrame;
import javax.swing.JButton;
import java.awt.Container;

public class AddingComponentToJFrame {
        public static void main(String[] args) {
                JFrame frame = new JFrame("Adding Component to JFrame");
                frame.setDefaultCloseOperation(JFrame.EXIT_ON_CLOSE);
                Container contentPane = frame.getContentPane();

                // Add a close button
                JButton closeButton = new JButton("Close");
                contentPane.add(closeButton);

                // set the size of the frame 300 x 200
                frame.setBounds(50, 50, 300, 200);
                frame.setVisible(true);
        }
}
```

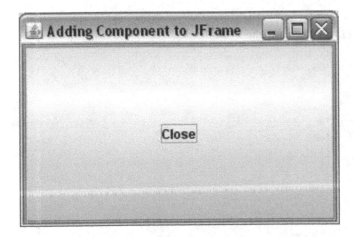

Figure 1-7. *A JFrame with a JButton with Close as its text*

The code did its job of adding a JButton with the Close text to the JFrame. However, the JButton looks very big and it fills the entire viewable area of the JFrame. Note that you have set the size of the JFrame to 300 pixels wide and 200 pixels high using the setBounds() method. Since the JButton fills the entire JFrame, can you set the JFrame's size little smaller? Alternatively, can you set the size for the JButton itself? Both suggestions are not going to work in this case. If you want to make the JFrame smaller, you need to guess how much smaller it needs to be made. If you want to set the size for the JButton, it will fail miserably; the JButton will always fill the entire viewable area of the JFrame. What is going on? To get a complete understanding of what is going on, you need to read the next section about the layout manager.

Swing provides a magical and quick solution to the problem of computing the size of the JFrame and JButton. The pack() method of the JFrame class is that magical solution. The method goes through all the components you have added to the JFrame and decides their preferred size and sets the size of the JFrame just enough to display all the components. When you call this method, you do not need to set the size of the JFrame. The pack() method will calculate the size of the JFrame and set it for you. To fix the sizing problem, remove the call to the setBounds() method and add a call to the pack() method instead. Note that the setBounds() method was setting the (x, y) coordinates for the JFrame too. If you still want to set the (x, y) coordinates of the JFrame to (50, 50), you can use its setLocation(50, 50) method. Listing 1-4 contains the modified code and Figure 1-8 shows the resulting JFrame.

Listing 1-4. Packing All Components of a JFrame

```
// PackedJFrame.java
package com.jdojo.swing;

import javax.swing.JFrame;
import java.awt.Container;
import javax.swing.JButton;

public class PackedJFrame {
        public static void main(String[] args) {
                JFrame frame = new JFrame("Adding Component to JFrame");
                frame.setDefaultCloseOperation(JFrame.EXIT_ON_CLOSE);

                // Add a close button
                JButton closeButton = new JButton("Close");
                Container contentPane = frame.getContentPane();
                contentPane.add(closeButton);

                // Calculates and sets appropriate size for the frame
                frame.pack();

                frame.setVisible(true);
        }
}
```

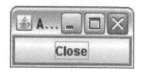

Figure 1-8. Packed JFrame with a JButton

So far, you have been successful in adding one JButton to a JFrame. Let's add another JButton to the same JFrame. Call the new button helpButton. The code will be similar to Listing 1-4, except that this time you will add two instances of the JButton class. Listing 1-5 contains the complete program. Figure 1-9 shows the result when you run the program.

Listing 1-5. Adding Two Buttons to a JFrame

```java
// JFrameWithTwoJButtons.java
package com.jdojo.swing;

import javax.swing.JFrame;
import java.awt.Container;
import javax.swing.JButton;

public class JFrameWithTwoJButtons {
        public static void main(String[] args) {
                JFrame frame = new JFrame("Adding Component to JFrame");
                frame.setDefaultCloseOperation(JFrame.EXIT_ON_CLOSE);

                // Add two buttons - Close and Help
                JButton closeButton = new JButton("Close");
                JButton helpButton = new JButton("Help");
                Container contentPane = frame.getContentPane();
                contentPane.add(closeButton);
                contentPane.add(helpButton);
                frame.pack();
                frame.setVisible(true);
        }
}
```

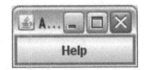

Figure 1-9. A JFrame with two buttons: Close and Help. Only the Help button is visible

When you added the Help button, you lost the Close button. Does this mean that you can add only one button to a JFrame? The answer is no. You can add as many buttons to a JFrame as you want. So, where is your Close button? You need to understand the layout mechanism of a content pane before I can answer this question.

A content pane is a container. You add components to it. However, it hands over the task of laying out all components within it to an object known as a *layout manager*. A layout manager is simply a Java object whose sole job is to determine the position and size of components within a container. The example in Listing 1-5 was carefully chosen to introduce you to the concept of the layout manager. Many types of layout managers exist. They differ in the way they position and size components within the container.

By default, the content pane of a JFrame uses a layout manager called BorderLayout. Only the Help button was displayed in the previous example because of the way the BorderLayout lays out the components. In fact, when you added two buttons, the content pane received both of them. To confirm that both buttons are still there in the content pane, add the following snippet of code at the end of the main() method in Listing 1-5 that displays the number of components that the content pane has. It will print a message on the standard output: "Content Pane has 2 components." Each container has a getComponents() method, which returns an array of components added to it.

```
// Get the components added to the content pane
Component[] comps = contentPane.getComponents();

// Display how many components the content pane has
System.out.println("Content Pane has " + comps.length + " components.");
```

With this background, it is time to learn various layout managers. You will solve the puzzle of the missing Close button when I discuss the BorderLayout manager in a later section. But before I discuss the various layout managers, I will introduce you to some utility classes that are frequently used when working with Swing applications.

■ **Tip**   A component can be added to only one container at one time. If you add the same component to another container, the component is removed from the first container and added to the second one.

Some Utility Classes

Before you start developing some serious Swing GUIs, it is worth mentioning some utility classes that are used frequently. They are simple classes. Most of them have some properties that can be specified in their constructors, and have getters and setters for those properties.

The Point Class

As the name suggests, an object of the Point class represents a location in a two-dimensional space. A location in a two-dimensional space is represented by two values: an x coordinate and a y coordinate. The Point class is in the java.awt package. The following snippet of code demonstrates its use:

```
// Create an object of the Point class with (x, y) coordinate of (20, 40)
Point p = new Point(20, 40);

// Get the x and y coordinate of p
int x = p.getX();
int y = p.getY();

// Set the x and y coordinate of p to (10, 60)
p.setLocation(10, 60);
```

The main usage of the Point class in Swing is to set and get the location (x and y coordinates) of a component. For example, you can set the location of a JButton.

```
JButton closeButton = new JButton("Close");

// The following two statements do the same thing.
// You will use one of the following statements and not both.
closeButton.setLocation(10, 15);
closeButton.setLocation(new Point(10, 15));

// Get the location of the closeButton
Point p = closeButton.getLocation();
```

The Dimension Class

An object of the Dimension class wraps the width and height of a component. The width and height of a component are collectively known as its size. In other words, an object of the Dimension class is used to represent the size of a component. You can use an object of the Dimension class to wrap any two arbitrary integers. However, in this chapter, it will be used in the context of the size of a component. The class is in the java.awt package.

```
// Create an object of the Dimension class with a width and height of 200 and 20
Dimension d  = new Dimension(200, 20);

// Set the size of closeButton to 200 X 20. Both of the statements have the same efecct.
// You will use one of the following two statements.
closeButton.setSize(200, 20);
closeButton.setsize(d);

// Get the size of closeButton
Dimension d2 = closeButton.getSize();
int width = d2.width;
int height = d2.height;
```

The Insets Class

An object of the Insets class represents spaces that are left around a container. It wraps four properties named top, left, bottom, and right. Their values represent the spaces left on the four side of a container. The class is in the java.awt package.

```
// Create an object of the Insets class
// using its constructor Insets(top, left, bottom, right)
Insets ins = new Insets(20, 5, 5, 5);

// Get the insets of a JFrame
Insets ins = frame.getInsets();
int top = ins.top;
int left = ins.left;
int bottom = ins.bottom;
int right = ins.right;
```

The Rectangle Class

As its name suggests, an instance of the Rectangle class represents a rectangle. It is in the java.awt package. You can define a rectangle in many ways. A Rectangle is defined by three properties:

- (x, y) coordinates of the upper-left corner
- Width
- Height

You can think of a Rectangle object as a combination of a Point object and a Dimension object; the Point object holds the (x, y) coordinates of the upper left corner and the Dimension object holds the width and height. You can create an object of the Rectangle class by specifying different combinations of its properties.

```
// Create a Rectangle object whose upper-left corner is at (0, 0)
// with width and height as zero
Rectangle r1 = new Rectangle();

// Create a Rectangle object from a Point object with its width and height as zero
Rectangle r2 = new Rectangle(new Point(10, 10));

// Create a Rectangle object from a Point object and a Dimension object
Rectangle r3 = new Rectangle(new Point(10, 10), new Dimension(200, 100));

// Create a Rectangle object by specifying its upper-left corner's
// coordinate at (10, 10) and width as 200 and height as 100
Rectangle r4 = new Rectangle(10, 10, 200, 100);
```

The Rectangle class defines many methods to manipulate a Rectangle object and to inquire about its properties, such as the (x, y) coordinate of its upper-left corner, width, and height.

An object of the Rectangle class defines the location and size of a component in a Swing application. The location and size of a component are known as its bounds. Two methods, setBounds() and getBounds(), can be used to set and get the bounds of any component or container. The setBounds() method is overloaded and you can specify x, y, width, and height properties of a component, or a Rectangle object. The getBounds() method returns a Rectangle object. In Listing 1-2, you used the setBounds() method to set the x, y, width, and height of the frame. Note that the "bounds" of a component is a combination of its location and its size. The combination of the setLocation() and setSize() methods will accomplish the same as the setBounds() method does. Similarly, you can use the combination of getLocation() (or, getX() and getY()) and getSize() (or, getWidth() and getHeight()) instead of using the getBounds() method.

Layout Managers

A container uses a layout manager to compute the position and size of all its components. In other words, the job of a layout manager is to compute four properties (x, y, width, and height) of all components in a container. The x and y properties determine the position of a component within the container. The width and height properties determine the size of the component. You might ask, "Why do you need a layout manager to perform a simple task of computing four properties of a component? Can't you just specify these four properties in the program and let the container use them for displaying the components?" The answer is yes. You can specify these properties in your program. If you do that, your component will not be repositioned and resized when the container is resized. In addition, you will have to specify the size of the component for all platforms on which your application will run because different platforms render components a little differently. Suppose your application displays text in multiple languages. The optimal size for a JButton, say a Close button, will be different in different languages and you will have to calculate the size of the Close button in each language and set it, depending on the language the application is using. However, you do not have to take all of these into consideration if you use a layout manager. The layout manager will do these simple, though time-consuming, things for you.

Using a layout manager is optional. If you do not use a layout manager, you are responsible for computing and setting the position and size of all components in a container.

Technically, a layout manager is an object of a Java class that implements the LayoutManager interface. There is another interface called LayoutManager2 that inherits from the LayoutManager interface. Some of the layout manager classes implement the LayoutManager2 interface. Both interfaces are in the java.awt package.

There are many layout managers. Some layout managers are simple and easy to code by hand. Some are very complex to code by hand and they are meant to be used by GUI builder tools such as NetBeans. If none of the available layout managers meet your needs, you can create your own. Some useful layout managers are available for free on the Internet. Sometimes you need to nest them to get the desired effects. I will discuss the following layout managers in this section:

- FlowLayout
- BorderLayout
- CardLayout
- BoxLayout
- GridLayout
- GridBagLayout
- GroupLayout
- SpringLayout

Every container has a default layout manager. The default layout manager for the content pane of a JFrame is BorderLayout, and for a JPanel, it is FlowLayout. It is set when you create the container. You can change the default layout manager of a container by using its setLayout() method. If you do not want your container to use a layout manager, you can pass null to the setLayout() method. You can use the getLayout() method of a container to get the reference of the layout manager the container is currently using.

```
// Set FlowLayout as the layout manager for the content pane of a JFrame
JFrame frame - new JFrame("Test Frame");
Container contentPane = frame.getContentPane();
contentPane.setLayout(new FlowLayout());

// Set BorderLayout as the layout manager for a JPanel
JPanel panel = new JPanel();
panel.setLayout(new BorderLayout());

// Get the layout manager for a container
LayoutManager layoutManager = container.getLayout()
```

Starting from Java 5, the calls to add() and setLayout() methods on a JFrame are forwarded to its content pane. Before Java 5, calling these methods on a JFrame would throw a runtime exception. That is, from Java 5, the two calls frame.setLayout() and frame.add() will do the same as calling frame.getContentPane().setLayout() and frame.getContentPane().add(). It is very important to note that the getLayout() method of a JFrame returns the layout manager of the JFrame and not its content pane. To avoid this trouble of asymmetric call forwarding (some calls are forwarded and some not) from the JFrame to its content pane, it is better to call the content pane's methods directly rather than calling them on a JFrame.

FlowLayout

The FlowLayout is the simplest layout manager in Swing. It lays out the components horizontally, and then vertically. It lays the components in the order they are added to the container. When it is laying the components horizontally, it may lay them left to right, or right to left. The horizontal layout direction depends on the orientation of the container. You can set the orientation of a container by calling its setComponentOrientation() method. If you want to set the orientation of a container and all its children, you can use the applyComponentOrientation() method instead. Here is a snippet of code that sets the orientation of a container:

```
// Method - 1
// Set the orientation of the content pane of a frame to "right to left"
JFrame frame = new JFrame("Test");
Container pane = frame.getContentPane();
pane.setComponentOrientation(ComponentOrientation.RIGHT_TO_LEFT);

// Method - 2
// Set the orientation of the content pane and all its children to "right to left"
JFrame frame = new JFrame("Test");
Container pane = frame.getContentPane();
pane.applyComponentOrientation(ComponentOrientation.RIGHT_TO_LEFT);
```

If your application is multilingual and the component orientation will be decided at runtime, you may want to set the components locale and orientation in a more generic way rather than hard-coding it in your program. You can globally set the default locale for all Swing components in your application like so:

```
// "ar" is used for Arabic locale
JComponent.setDefaultLocale(new Locale("ar"));
```

When you create a JFrame, you can get the component's orientation according to the default locale and set it to the frame and its children. This way, you do not have to set the orientation for every container in your application.

```
// Get the default locale
Locale defaultLocale = JComponent.getDefaultLocale();

// Get the component's orientation for the default locale
ComponentOrientation componentOrientation = ComponentOrientation.getOrientation(defaultLocale);

// Apply the component's default orientation for the whole frame
frame.applyComponentOrientation(componentOrientation);
```

A FlowLayout tries to place all components into one row, giving them their preferred size. If all components do not fit into one row, it starts another row. Every layout manager has to compute the height and width of the space where it needs to lay out all components. A FlowLayout asks for width, which is the sum of the preferred widths of all components. It asks for height, which is the height of the tallest component in the container. It adds extra space to the width and height to account for horizontal and vertical gaps between the components. Listing 1-6 demonstrates how to use a FlowLayout for the content pane of a JFrame. It adds three buttons to the content pane. Figure 1-10 shows the screen with three buttons using the FlowLayout.

Listing 1-6. Using a FlowLayout Manager

```
// FlowLayoutTest.java
package com.jdojo.swing;

import java.awt.Container;
import java.awt.FlowLayout;
import javax.swing.JButton;
import javax.swing.JFrame;
```

```java
public class FlowLayoutTest {
    public static void main(String[] args) {
        JFrame frame = new JFrame("Flow Layout Test");
        frame.setDefaultCloseOperation(JFrame.EXIT_ON_CLOSE);

        Container contentPane = frame.getContentPane();
        contentPane.setLayout(new FlowLayout());

        for(int i = 1; i <= 3; i++) {
            contentPane.add(new JButton("Button " + i));
        }

        frame.pack();
        frame.setVisible(true);
    }
}
```

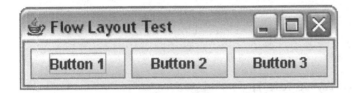

Figure 1-10. *Three buttons in a JFrame with a FlowLayout Manager*

When you expand the frame horizontally, the buttons are displayed as shown in Figure 1-11.

Figure 1-11. *After the JFrame using a FlowLatout has been expanded horizontally*

By default, a FlowLayout aligns all components in the center of the container. You can change the alignment by calling its setAlignment() method or passing the alignment in its constructor, like so:

```java
// Set the alignment when you create the layout manager object
FlowLayout flowLayout = new FlowLayout(FlowLayout.RIGHT);

// Set the alignment after you have created the flow layout manager
flowLayout.setAlignment(FlowLayout.RIGHT);
```

The following five constants are defined in the FlowLayout class to represent the five different alignments: LEFT, RIGHT, CENTER, LEADING, and TRAILING. The definitions of the first three constants are obvious. The LEADING alignment may mean either left or right; it depends on the orientation of the component. If the component's orientation is RIGHT_TO_LEFT, the LEADING alignment means RIGHT. If component's orientation is LEFT_TO_RIGHT, the LEADING alignment means LEFT. Similarly, TRAILING alignment may mean either left or right. If the component's orientation is RIGHT_TO_LEFT, the TRAILING alignment means LEFT. If component's orientation is LEFT_TO_RIGHT, the TRAILING alignment means RIGHT. It is always a good idea to use LEADING and TRAILING instead of RIGHT and LEFT, so you do not have to worry about the orientation of your component.

You can set the gaps between two components either in the constructor of the FlowLayout class or using its setHgap() and setVgap() methods. Listing 1-7 has the complete code that adds three buttons to a JFrame. The content pane uses a FlowLayout with the LEADING alignment and the JFrame's orientation is set to RIGHT_TO_LEFT. When you run the program, the JFrame will look as shown in Figure 1-12.

Listing 1-7. Customizing a FlowLayout

```java
// FlowLayoutTest2.java
package com.jdojo.swing;

import java.awt.ComponentOrientation;
import java.awt.Container;
import java.awt.FlowLayout;
import javax.swing.JButton;
import javax.swing.JFrame;

public class FlowLayoutTest2 {
        public static void main(String[] args) {
                int horizontalGap = 20;
                int verticalGap = 10;
                JFrame frame = new JFrame("Flow Layout Test");
                frame.setDefaultCloseOperation(JFrame.EXIT_ON_CLOSE);

                Container contentPane = frame.getContentPane();
                FlowLayout flowLayout =
                new FlowLayout(FlowLayout.LEADING, horizontalGap, verticalGap);
                contentPane.setLayout(flowLayout);
                frame.applyComponentOrientation(
                        ComponentOrientation.RIGHT_TO_LEFT);

                for(int i = 1; i <= 3; i++) {
                    contentPane.add(new JButton("Button " + i));
                }

                frame.pack();
                frame.setVisible(true);
        }
}
```

Figure 1-12. *A JFrame having three buttons and a customized FlowLayout*

You must remember that a FlowLayout tries to lay out all components in only one row. Therefore, it does not ask for a height that will fit all components. Rather, it asks for the height of the tallest component in the container. To demonstrate this subtle point, try adding 30 buttons to the JFrame so they all do not fit into one row. The following snippet of code demonstrates this:

```
JFrame frame = new JFrame("Welcome to Swing");
frame.setDefaultCloseOperation(JFrame.EXIT_ON_CLOSE);
frame.getContentPane().setLayout(new FlowLayout());

for(int i = 1; i <= 30; i++) {
        frame.getContentPane().add(new JButton("Button " + i));
}

frame.pack();
frame.setVisible(true);
```

The JFrame is shown in Figure 1-13. You can see that not all 30 buttons are displayed. If you resize the JFrame to make it bigger in height, you will be able to see all the buttons, as shown in Figure 1-14. The FlowLayout hides the components that it cannot display in one row.

Figure 1-13. *A JFrame with 30 buttons. Not all buttons are displayed*

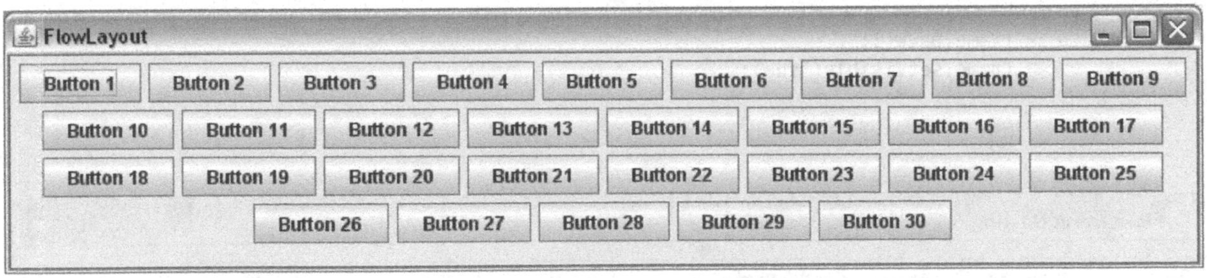

Figure 1-14. *A JFrame with 30 buttons after it is resized*

There is a very important implication of the feature of the FlowLayout where it tries to lay out all components in only one row. It asks for the height just enough to display the tallest component. If you nest a container with a FlowLayout manager inside another container that also uses a FlowLayout manager, you will never see more than one row in the nested container. Just to demonstrate this, add 30 instances of the JButton to a JPanel. A JPanel is an empty container with a FlowLayout as its default layout manager. Set the layout manager of the content pane of the JFrame to a FlowLayout and add the JPanel to the content pane of the JFrame. This way, you have the container JPanel with a FlowLayout nested within another container (a content pane), with a FlowLayout. Listing 1-8 contains the complete program to demonstrate this. When you run the program, the resulting JFrame is shown in Figure 1-15. You will always see only one row of buttons even if you resize the JFrame to make it bigger in height.

Listing 1-8. Nesting FlowLayout Managers

```java
// FlowLayoutNesting.java
package com.jdojo.swing;

import java.awt.FlowLayout;
import javax.swing.JButton;
import javax.swing.JFrame;
import javax.swing.JPanel;

public class FlowLayoutNesting {
        public static void main(String[] args) {
                JFrame frame = new JFrame("FlowLayout Nesting");
                frame.setDefaultCloseOperation(JFrame.EXIT_ON_CLOSE);

                // Set the content pane's layout to FlowLayout
                frame.getContentPane().setLayout(new FlowLayout());

                // JPanel is an empty container with a FlowLayout manager
                JPanel panel = new JPanel();

                // Add thirty JButtons to the JPanel
                for(int i = 1; i <= 30; i++) {
                        panel.add(new JButton("Button " + i));
                }

                // Add JPanel to the content pane
                frame.getContentPane().add(panel);

                frame.pack();
                frame.setVisible(true);
        }
}
```

Figure 1-15. *A nested FlowLayout always display only one row*

I would like to finish the discussion about FlowLayout with a note that it has very limited use in a real world applications because of the limitations discussed in this section. It is typically used for prototyping.

BorderLayout

The BorderLayout divides a container's space into five areas: north, south, east, west, and center. When you add a component to a container with a BorderLayout, you need to specify to which of the five areas you want to add the component. The BorderLayout class defines five constants to identify each of the five areas. The constants are NORTH, SOUTH, EAST, WEST, and CENTER. For example, to add a button to the north area, you write

```
// Add a button to the north area of the container
JButton northButton = new JButton("North");
container.add(northButton, BorderLayout.NORTH);
```

The default layout for the content pane of a JFrame is a BorderLayout. Listing 1-9 contains the complete program that adds five buttons to the content pane of a JFrame. The resulting JFrame is shown in Figure 1-16.

Listing 1-9. Adding Components to a BorderLayout

```java
// BorderLayoutTest.java
package com.jdojo.swing;

import java.awt.BorderLayout;
import javax.swing.JFrame;
import java.awt.Container;
import javax.swing.JButton;

public class BorderLayoutTest {
    public static void main(String[] args) {
        JFrame frame = new JFrame("BorderLayout Test");
        frame.setDefaultCloseOperation(JFrame.EXIT_ON_CLOSE);
        Container container = frame.getContentPane();

        // Add a button to each of the five areas of the BorderLayout
        container.add(new JButton("North"), BorderLayout.NORTH);
        container.add(new JButton("South"), BorderLayout.SOUTH);
        container.add(new JButton("East"), BorderLayout.EAST);
        container.add(new JButton("West"), BorderLayout.WEST);
        container.add(new JButton("Center"), BorderLayout.CENTER);

        frame.pack();
        frame.setVisible(true);
    }
}
```

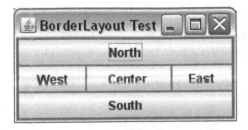

Figure 1-16. *Five areas of the BorderLayout*

You can add at most one component to one area of a BorderLayout. You may leave some areas empty. If you want to add more than one component to an area of a BorderLayout, you can do so by adding those components to a container, and then adding that container to the desired area.

The five areas in a BorderLayout (north, south, east, west, and center) are fixed in direction and are not dependent on the orientation of components. Four more constants exist to specify areas in a BorderLayout. These constants are PAGE_START, PAGE_END, LINE_START, and LINE_END. The PAGE_START and PAGE_END constants are the same as the NORTH and SOUTH constants, respectively. The LINE_START and LINE_END constants change their positions depending on the orientation of the container. If the container's orientation is left to right, LINE_START is the same as WEST, and LINE_END is the same as EAST. If the container's orientation is right to left, LINE_START is the same as EAST, and LINE_END is the same as WEST. Figure 1-17 and Figure 1-18 depict the differences in positioning of the areas of a BorderLayout with different component orientations.

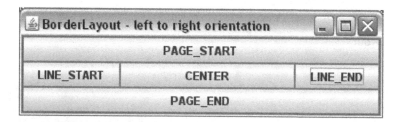

Figure 1-17. *A BorderLayout's areas when the container's orientation is left to right*

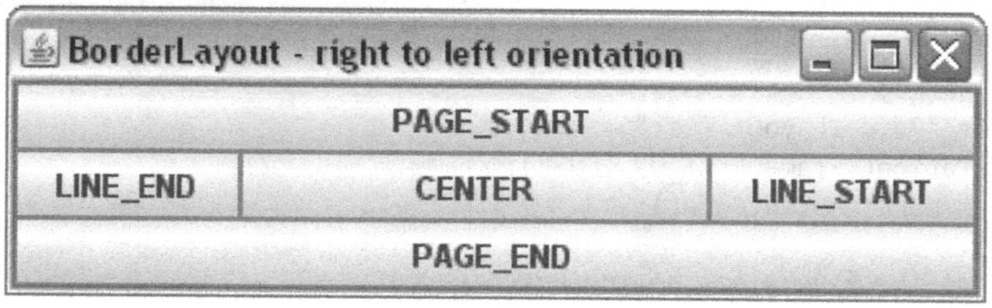

Figure 1-18. *A BorderLayout's areas when the container's orientation is right to left*

If you do not specify the area for a component, it is added to the center. The following two statements have the same effect:

```
// Assume that the container has a BorderLayout
// Add a button to the container without specifying the area
container.add(new JButton("Close"));

// The above statement is the same as the following
container.add(new JButton("Close"), BorderLayout.CENTER);
```

I have already stated that you can add at most five components to a BorderLayout, one in each of the five areas. What happens if you add more than one component to the same area of a BorderLayout? That is, what happens if you write the following code?

```
// Assume that container has a BorderLayout
container.add(new JButton("Close"), BorderLayout.NORTH);
container.add(new JButton("Help"), BorderLayout.NORTH);
```

You will find that the north area of the BorderLayout displays only one button: the button that was added to it last. That is, the north area will only display the Help button. This is what happened in Listing 1-5. You added two buttons called Close and Help to the content pane of the JFrame. Since you did not specify the area of the BorderLayout in which you wanted to add them, both of them were added to the center area. Since you can have only one component in each area of a BorderLayout, the Help button replaced the Close button. This is the reason that you did not see the Close button when you ran the program in Listing 1-5. To fix this problem, specify the areas for both buttons when you add them to the container.

■ **Tip** If you are missing some components in a BorderLayout managed container, make sure that you have not added more than one component in the same area. If you add components to a BorderLayout mixing the area constants, the PAGE_START, PAGE_END, LINE_START, and LINE_END constants take precedence over the NORTH, SOUTH, EAST, and WEST constants. That is, if you add two components to a BorderLayout using add(c1, NORTH) and add(c2, PAGE_START), c2 will be used, not c1.

How does a BorderLayout compute the size of the components? It computes the size of the components based on the area in which they are placed. It respects the preferred height of the component in north and south. However, it stretches the component's width horizontally according to the available space in north and south. That is, it does not respect the preferred width of the components in north and south. It respects the preferred width of the components in east and west and gives them height necessary to fill the entire space vertically. The component in the center area is stretched horizontally as well as vertically to fit the available space. That is, the center area does not respect its component's preferred width and height.

CardLayout

The CardLayout lays out components in a container as a stack of cards. Like a stack of cards, only one card (the card at the top) is visible in a CardLayout. It makes only one component visible at a time. You need to use the following steps to use a CardLayout for a container:

- Create a container such as a JPanel.

  JPanel cardPanel = new JPanel();

- Create a CardLayout object.

  CardLayout cardLayout = new CardLayout();

- Set the layout manager for the container.

  cardPanel.setLayout(cardLayout);

- Add components to the container. You need to give a name to each component. To add a JButton to the cardPanel, use the following statement:

  cardPanel.add(new JButton("Card 1"), "myLuckyCard");

  You have named your card myLuckyCard. This name can be used in the show() method of the CardLayout to make this card visible.

- Call its next() method to show the next card.

  cardLayout.next(cardPanel);

The CardLayout class provides several methods to flip through components. By default, it shows the first component that was added to it. All flipping-related methods take the container it manages as its argument. The first() and last() methods show the first and the last card, respectively. The previous() and next() methods show the previous and the next card from the card currently being shown. If the last card is showing, calling the next() method shows the first card. If the first card is showing, calling the previous() method shows the last card.

Listing 1-10 demonstrates how to use a CardLayout. Figure 1-19 shows the resulting JFrame. When you click the Next button, the next card is flipped. The program adds two JPanels to the content pane of the JFrame. One JPanel, buttonPanel, has the Next button, and it is added to the south area of the content pane. Note that, by default, a JPanel uses a FlowLayout.

Listing 1-10. The CardLayout in Action

```java
// CardLayoutTest.java
package com.jdojo.swing;

import java.awt.Container;
import javax.swing.JFrame;
import java.awt.CardLayout;
import javax.swing.JPanel;
import javax.swing.JButton;
import java.awt.Dimension;
import java.awt.BorderLayout;

public class CardLayoutTest {
    public static void main(String[] args) {
        JFrame frame = new JFrame("CardLayout Test");
        frame.setDefaultCloseOperation(JFrame.EXIT_ON_CLOSE);
        Container contentPane = frame.getContentPane();

        // Add a Next JButton in a JPanel to the content pane
        JPanel buttonPanel = new JPanel();
        JButton nextButton = new JButton("Next");
        buttonPanel.add(nextButton);
        contentPane.add(buttonPanel, BorderLayout.SOUTH);

        // Create a JPanel and set its layout to CardLayout
        final JPanel cardPanel = new JPanel();
        final CardLayout cardLayout = new CardLayout();
        cardPanel.setLayout(cardLayout);

        // Add five JButtons as cards to the cardPanel
        for(int i = 1; i <= 5; i++) {
            JButton card = new JButton("Card " + i);
            card.setPreferredSize(new Dimension(200, 200));
            String cardName = "card" + 1;
            cardPanel.add(card, cardName);
        }

        // Add the cardPanel to the content pane
        contentPane.add(cardPanel, BorderLayout.CENTER);
```

```
                // Add an action listener to the Next button
                nextButton.addActionListener(e -> cardLayout.next(cardPanel));

                frame.pack();
                frame.setVisible(true);
        }
}
```

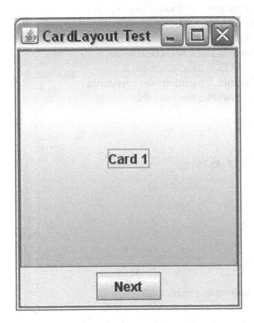

Figure 1-19. *A CardLayout in action. Click the Next JButton to flip through the cards*

The program adds an action listener to the Next button. I have not discussed how to add an action listener to a button yet. It is necessary to see the CardLayout in action. I will discuss how to add an action to a button in detail in the event handling section. For now, it is sufficient to mention that you need to call the addActionListener() method of the JButton class to add an action listener to it. This method accepts an object of type ActionListener interface and has one method called actionPerformed(). The code in the actionPerformed() method is executed when you click the JButton. The code that flips the next card is the call to the cardLayout.next(cardPanel) method. The ActionListener interface is a functional interface and you can use a lambda expression to create its instance, like so:

```
// Add an action listener to the Next JButton to flip the next card
nextButton.addActionListener(e -> cardLayout.next(cardPanel));
```

■ **Tip** A CardLayout is not used very often because all but one component are hidden from the user. A JTabbedPane, which is easier to use, provides functionality similar to a CardLayout. I will discuss the JTabbedPane in Chapter 2. A JTabbedPane is a container, not a layout manager. It lays out all components as tabs and lets the user switch between those tabs.

BoxLayout

The BoxLayout arranges components in a container either horizontally in one row or vertically in one column. You need to use the following steps to use a BoxLayout in your program:

- Create a container, for example, a JPanel.

  ```
  JPanel hPanel = new JPanel();
  ```

- Create an object of the BoxLayout class. Unlike other layout managers, you need to pass the container to the constructor of the class. You also need to pass the type of box you are creating (horizontal or vertical) to its constructor. The class has four constants: X_AXIS, Y_AXIS, LINE_AXIS, and PAGE_AXIS. The constant X_AXIS is used to create a horizontal BoxLayout that lays out all components from left to right. The constant Y_AXIS is used to create a vertical BoxLayout that lays out all components from top to bottom. The other two constants, LINE_AXIS and PAGE_AXIS, are similar to X_AXIS and Y_AXIS. However, they use the orientation of the container in laying out the components.

  ```
  // Create a BoxLayout for hPanel to lay out
  // components from left to right
  BoxLayout boxLayout = new BoxLayout(hPanel, BoxLayout.X_AXIS);
  ```

- Set the layout for the container.

  ```
  hPanel.setLayout(boxLayout);
  ```

- Add the components to the container.

  ```
  hPanel.add(new JButton("Button 1"));
  hPanel.add(new JButton("Button 2"));
  ```

Listing 1-11 uses a horizontal BoxLayout to display three buttons, as shown in Figure 1-20.

Listing 1-11. Using a Horizontal BoxLayout

```java
// BoxLayoutTest.java
package com.jdojo.swing;

import java.awt.Container;
import javax.swing.JFrame;
import javax.swing.JButton;
import javax.swing.JPanel;
import javax.swing.BoxLayout;
import java.awt.BorderLayout;

public class BoxLayoutTest {
    public static void main(String[] args) {
        JFrame frame = new JFrame("BoxLayout Test");
        frame.setDefaultCloseOperation(JFrame.EXIT_ON_CLOSE);
        Container contentPane = frame.getContentPane();

        JPanel hPanel = new JPanel();
        BoxLayout boxLayout = new BoxLayout(hPanel, BoxLayout.X_AXIS);
        hPanel.setLayout(boxLayout);
```

```
        for(int i = 1; i <= 3; i++) {
                hPanel.add(new JButton("Button " + i));
        }

        contentPane.add(hPanel, BorderLayout.SOUTH);
        frame.pack();
        frame.setVisible(true);
    }
}
```

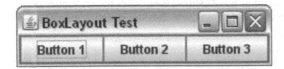

Figure 1-20. *A JFrame with a horizontal BoxLayout with three buttons*

A BoxLayout tries to give the preferred width to all components in a horizontal layout and the preferred height in a vertical layout. In a horizontal layout, the height of the tallest component is given to all other components. If it cannot adjust the height of a component to match the tallest component in the group, it aligns the component horizontally along the center. You can change this default alignment by setting the component's alignment or the container alignment by using the setAlignmentY() method. In a vertical layout, it tries to give the preferred height to all components, and tries to make the size of all components the same width as the widest component. If it cannot make all components have the same width, it aligns them vertically along their centerlines. You can change this default alignment by changing either the component's alignment or the container's alignment using the setAlignmentX() method.

The javax.swing package contains a Box class that makes using a BoxLayout easier. A Box is a container that uses a BoxLayout as its layout manager. The Box class provides static methods to create a container with a horizontal or vertical layout. The methods createHorizontalBox() and createVerticalBox()create a horizontal and vertical box, respectively.

```
// Create a horizontal box
Box hBox = Box.createHorizontalBox();

// Create a vertical box
Box vBox = Box.createVerticalBox();
```

To add a component to a Box, use its add() method, like so:

```
// Add two buttons to the horizontal box
hBox.add(new JButton("Button 1"));
hBox.add(new JButton("Button 2"));
```

The Box class also allows you to create invisible components and add them to a box, so you can adjust spacing between two components. It provides four types of invisible components:

- Glue

- Strut

- Rigid Area

- Filler

A glue is an invisible, expandable component. You can create horizontal and vertical glues using the createHorizontalGlue() and createVerticalGlue() static methods of the Box class. The following snippet of code uses horizontal glue between two buttons in a horizontal box layout. You can also create a glue component using the createGlue() static method of the Box class that can expand horizontally as well as vertically.

```
Box hBox = Box.createHorizontalBox();
hBox.add(new JButton("First"));
hBox.add(Box.createHorizontalGlue());
hBox.add(new JButton("Last"));
```

The buttons with a glue in between look as shown in Figure 1-21. Figure 1-22 shows them after the container is expanded horizontally. Notice the horizontal empty space between the two buttons, which is the invisible glue that has expanded.

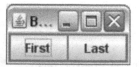

Figure 1-21. *A horizontal box with two buttons and a horizontal glue between them*

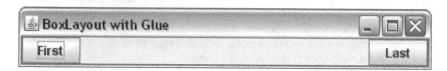

Figure 1-22. *A horizontal box with two buttons and a horizontal glue between them after resizing*

A strut is an invisible component of a fixed width or a fixed height. You can create a horizontal strut using the createHorizontalStrut() method that takes the width in pixels as an argument. You can create a vertical strut using the createVerticalStrut() method that takes the height in pixels as an argument.

```
// Add a 100px strut to a horizontal box
hBox.add(Box.createHorizontalStrut(100));
```

A rigid area is an invisible component that is always the same size. You can create a rigid area by using the createRigidArea() static method of the Box class. You need to pass a Dimension object to it to specify its width and height.

```
// Add a 10x5 rigid area to a horizontal box
hBox.add(Box.createRigidArea(new Dimesnion(10, 5)));
```

A filler is an invisible custom component that you can create by specifying your own minimum, maximum, and preferred sizes. The Filler static nested class of the Box class represents a filler.

```
// Create a filler, which acts like a glue. Note that the glue is
// just a filler with a minimum and preferred size set to zero and
// a maximum size set to Short.MAX_VALUE in both directions
```

```
Dimension minSize = new Dimension(0, 0);
Dimension prefSize = new Dimension(0, 0);
Dimension maxSize = new Dimension(Short.MAX_VALUE, Short.MAX_VALUE);
Box.Filler filler = new Box.Filler(minSize, prefSize, maxSize);
```

You can get a very powerful layout by nesting boxes with a horizontal and vertical BoxLayout. The Box class provides convenience methods to create glue, strut, and rigid areas. However, they are all objects of the Box.Filler class. When the minimum and preferred sizes are set to zero, and the maximum size to Short.MAX_VALUE in both directions, a Box.Filler object acts as a glue. When the maximum height of a glue is set to zero, it acts like a horizontal glue. When the maximum width of a glue is set to zero, it acts like a vertical glue. You can create a horizontal strut using the Box.Filler class by using its minimum and preferred sizes of a specified width and zero height, and a maximum size as the specified width and Short.MAX_VALUE height. Can you think of a way to create a rigid area using the Box.Filler class? All sizes (minimum, preferred, and maximum) will be the same for a rigid area. The following snippet of code creates a rigid area of 10x10:

```
// Create a 10x10 rigid area
Dimension d = new Dimension(10, 10);
JComponent rigidArea = new Box.Filler(d, d, d);
```

Listing 1-12 demonstrates how to use the Box class and glue. Figure 1-23 shows the resulting JFrame after you expand it horizontally. When the HFrame is opened, there is no gap between the Previous and Next buttons.

Listing 1-12. A BoxLayout Using the Box Class and Glue

```
// BoxLayoutGlueTest.java
package com.jdojo.swing;

import java.awt.Container;
import javax.swing.JFrame;
import javax.swing.JButton;
import javax.swing.Box;
import java.awt.BorderLayout;

public class BoxLayoutGlueTest {
        public static void main(String[] args) {
                JFrame frame = new JFrame("BoxLayout with Glue");
                frame.setDefaultCloseOperation(JFrame.EXIT_ON_CLOSE);

                Container contentPane = frame.getContentPane();
                Box hBox = Box.createHorizontalBox();
                hBox.add(new JButton("<<First"));
                hBox.add(new JButton("<Previous"));
                hBox.add(Box.createHorizontalGlue());
                hBox.add(new JButton("Next>"));
                hBox.add(new JButton("Last>>"));

                contentPane.add(hBox, BorderLayout.SOUTH);
                frame.pack();
                frame.setVisible(true);
        }
}
```

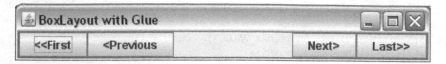

Figure 1-23. *A BoxLayout with glue*

GridLayout

A GridLayout arranges components in a rectangular grid of equally sized cells. Each component is placed in exactly one cell. It does not respect the preferred size of the component. It divides the available space into equally sized cells and resizes each component to the cell's size.

You can specify either the number of rows or the number of columns in the grid. If you specify both, only the number of rows is used, and the number of columns is computed. Suppose ncomponents is the number of components added to the container, and nrows and ncols are the specified number of rows and columns. If nrows is greater than zero, the number of columns in the grid is computed using the following formula:

```
ncols = (ncomponents + nrows - 1)/nrows
```

If nrows is zero, the number of rows in the grid is computed using the following formula:

```
nrows = (ncomponents + ncols - 1)/ncols
```

You cannot specify a negative number for nrows or ncols, and at least one of them must be greater than zero. Otherwise, a runtime exception is thrown.

You can create a GridLayout using one of the following three constructors of the GridLayout class:

- GridLayout()

- GridLayout(int rows, int cols)

- GridLayout(int rows, int cols, int hgap, int vgap)

You can specify the number of rows, the number of columns, a horizontal gap, and a vertical gap between two cells in the grid. You can also set these properties using the methods setRows(), setColumns(), setHgap(), and setVgap().

The no-args constructor creates a grid of one row. The number of columns is the same as the number of components added to the container.

```
// Create a grid layout of one row
GridLayout gridLayout = new GridLayout();
```

The second constructor creates a GridLayout by a specified number of rows or columns.

```
// Create a grid layout of 5 rows. Specify 0 as the number of columns.
// The number of columns will be computed.
GridLayout gridLayout = new GridLayout(5, 0);
```

```
// Create a grid layout of 3 columns. Specify 0 as the number of rows.
// The number of rows will be computed.
GridLayout gridLayout = new GridLayout(0, 3);
```

```
// Create a grid layout with 2 rows and 3 columns. You have specified
// a non-zero value for rows, so the value for columns will be ignored.
// It will be computed based on the number of components.
GridLayout gridLayout = new GridLayout(2, 3);
```

The third constructor lets you specify the number of rows or the number of columns, and horizontal and vertical gaps between two cells. You can create a GridLayout of three rows with a horizontal gap of 10 pixels and a vertical gap of 20 pixels between cells, as shown:

```
GridLayout gridLayout = new GridLayout(3, 0, 10, 20);
```

Listing 1-13 demonstrates how to use a GridLayout. Note that you do not specify in which cell the component will be placed. You just add the component to the container and the layout manager decides the placement.

Listing 1-13. Using GridLayout

```
// GridLayoutTest.java
package com.jdojo.swing;

import java.awt.GridLayout;
import javax.swing.JPanel;
import java.awt.BorderLayout;
import javax.swing.JFrame;
import java.awt.Container;
import javax.swing.JButton;

public class GridLayoutTest {
    public static void main(String[] args) {
        JFrame frame = new JFrame("GridLayout Test");
        frame.setDefaultCloseOperation(JFrame.EXIT_ON_CLOSE);
        Container contentPane = frame.getContentPane();

        JPanel buttonPanel = new JPanel();
        buttonPanel.setLayout(new GridLayout(3,0));

        for(int i = 1; i <= 9 ; i++) {
            buttonPanel.add(new JButton("Button " + i));
        }

        contentPane.add(buttonPanel, BorderLayout.CENTER);
        frame.pack();
        frame.setVisible(true);
    }
}
```

Figure 1-24 shows a container with a GridLayout that has three rows and nine components. Figure 1-25 shows a container with a GridLayout that has three rows and seven components. If you resize the container with a GridLayout, all components will be resized and they will be of the same size. Try resizing the JFrame by running the program in Listing 1-13.

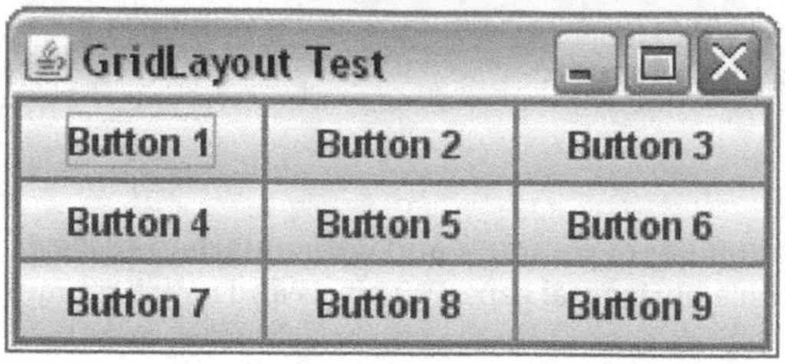

Figure 1-24. A GridLayout with three rows and nine components

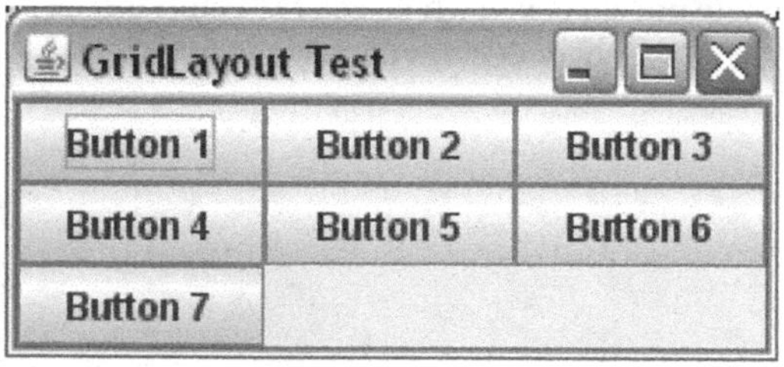

Figure 1-25. A GridLayout with three rows and seven components

A GridLayout is a simple layout manager to code by hand. However, it is not very powerful, for two reasons. First, it forces each component to have the same size, and second, you cannot specify the row and column number (or exact location) of a component in the grid. That is, you can only add a component to the GridLayout. They will be laid out horizontally, and then vertically in the order you add them to the container. If the container's orientation is LEFT_TO_RIGHT, components are laid out from left-to-right, and then top-to-bottom. If the container's orientation is RIGHT_TO_LEFT, components are laid out from right-to-left, and then top-to-bottom. One good use of the GridLayout is to create a group of buttons of the same size. For example, suppose you add two buttons with the text OK and Cancel to a container and want them to have the same size. You can do this by adding the buttons to a container managed by a GridLayout layout manager.

GridBagLayout

The GridBagLayout lays out components in a grid of rectangular cells arranged in rows and columns similar to the GridLayout. However, it is much more powerful than the GridLayout. Its power comes with an added complexity in its usage. It is not as easy to use as the GridLayout. There are so many things you can customize in the GridBagLayout that it becomes hard to learn and use all of its features quickly.

It lets you customize many properties of the components, such as size, alignment, expandability, etc. Unlike the GridLayout, all cells of the grid do not have to be of the same size. A component does not have to be placed exactly in one cell. A component can span multiple cells horizontally as well as vertically. You can specify how a component inside its cell should be aligned.

The GridBagLayout and GridBagConstraints classes are used while working with a GridBagLayout layout manager. Both classes are in the java.awt package. An object of the GridBagLayout class defines a GridBagLayout layout manager. An object of the GridBagConstraints class defines constraints for a component in a GridBagLayout. The constraints of a component are used to lay out the component. Some of the constraints include the component's position in the grid, width, height, alignment inside the cell, etc.

The following snippet of code creates an object of the GridBagLayout class and sets it as the layout manager for a JPanel:

```
// Create a JPanel container
JPanel panel = new JPanel();

// Set GridBagLayout as the layout manager for the JPanel
GridBagLayout gridBagLayout = new GridBagLayout();
panel.setLayout(gridBagLayout);
```

Let's use GridBagLayout in the simplest form: create a frame, set the layout for its content pane to GridBagLayout, and add nine buttons to the content pane. This is accomplished in Listing 1-14. Figure 1-26 shows the screen you get when you run the program.

Listing 1-14. *A GridBagLayout Used in Its Simplest Form*

```java
// SimplestGridBagLayout.java
package com.jdojo.swing;

import javax.swing.JFrame;
import java.awt.Container;
import javax.swing.JButton;
import java.awt.GridBagLayout;

public class SimplestGridBagLayout {
    public static void main(String[] args) {
        String title = "GridBagLayout in its Simplest Form";
        JFrame frame = new JFrame(title);
        frame.setDefaultCloseOperation(JFrame.EXIT_ON_CLOSE);
        Container contentPane = frame.getContentPane();
        contentPane.setLayout(new GridBagLayout());

        for(int i = 1; i <= 9; i++) {
            contentPane.add(new JButton("Button " + i));
        }
        frame.pack();
        frame.setVisible(true);
    }
}
```

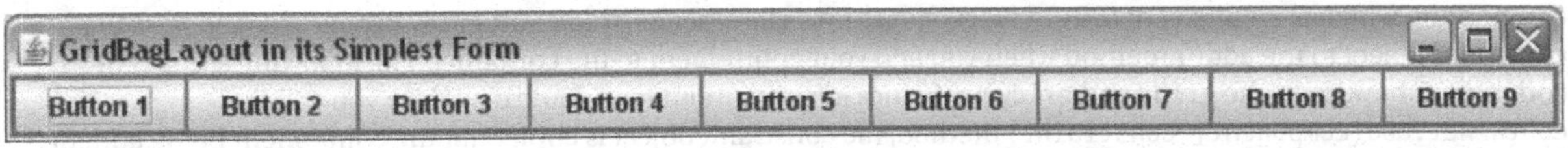

Figure 1-26. *Nine buttons in a GridBagLayout*

At first, it seems that a GridBagLayout behaves like a FlowLayout. The effect is the same as if you used a FlowLayout. However, a GridBagLayout is not the same as a FlowLayout, although it has the ability to work like a FlowLayout. It is much more powerful (and error prone too!) than a FlowLayout. When you added nine buttons, you did not specify their cells. You used the contentPane.add(Component c) method to add the buttons. The result was that it placed one button after another in a single row.

You can specify the cell in which a component in a GridBagLayout should be placed. To specify the cell for a component, you need to call the add(Component c, Object constraints) method, where the second argument is an object of the GridBagConstraints class. If you do not specify the constraints object for a component in a GridBagLayout, it places the component in the *next cell*. The next cell is the cell after the cell that was used to place the previous component. If you do not use constraints for any components in a GridBagLayout, all components are placed in one row, as shown in Figure 1-26. I will discuss more about this when I cover the gridx and gridy properties of a GridBagConstraints object.

Let's set the record straight for the GridBagLayout by showing that it is really a grid layout and that it places components in a grid of cells. To prove this, you will display nine buttons in the previous example in a grid of cells with three rows and three columns. This time, there will be only one difference: you will specify the position of the cell in the grid for the buttons. The combination of the row number and column number denotes the position of a cell in the grid. All properties for the components and its cells are specified using an object of the GridBagConstraints class. It has many public instance variables. Its gridx and gridy instance variables specify the column number and row number of a cell, respectively. The first column is denoted by gridx = 0, the second column by gridx = 1, and so on. The first row is denoted by gridy = 0, the second row by gridy = 1, and so on.

Which one is the first cell in a grid—the upper-left corner, the upper-right corner, the lower-left corner, or the lower-right corner? It depends on the orientation of the container. If the container uses the LEFT_TO_RIGHT orientation, the cell in the upper-left corner of the grid is the first cell. If the container uses the RIGHT_TO_LEFT orientation, the cell in the upper-right corner of the grid is the first cell. Table 1-1 and Table 1-2 show the cells with their corresponding gridx and gridy values in a GridBagLayout with different container orientations. These tables show only nine cells. A GridBagLayout is not limited to having only nine cells. You can have as many cells as you want. To be exact, you can have a maximum of Integer.MAX_VALUE number of rows and columns, which you will never use in any application for sure.

Table 1-1. *Values of gridx and gridy for Cells in a Container With LEFT_TO_RIGHT Orientation*

gridx=0, gridy=0	gridx=1, gridy=0	gridx=2, gridy=0
gridx=0, gridy=1	gridx=1, gridy=1	gridx=2, gridy=1
gridx=0, gridy=2	gridx=1, gridy=2	gridx=2, gridy=2

Table 1-2. *Values of gridx and gridy for Cells in a Container with RIGHT_TO_LEFT Orientation*

gridx=2, gridy=0	gridx=1, gridy=0	gridx=0, gridy=0
gridx=2, gridy=1	gridx=1, gridy=1	gridx=0, gridy=1
gridx=2, gridy=2	gridx=1, gridy=2	gridx=0, gridy=2

Setting the gridx and gridy properties of a component is easy. You create a constraint object for your component, which is an object of the GridBagConstraints class; set its gridx and gridy properties; and pass the constraint object to the add() method when you add your component to the container. The following snippet of code shows how to set the gridx and gridy properties in a constraint for a JButton. When you call the container.add(component, constraint) method, the constraint object is copied for the component being added, so that you can change some of its properties and reuse it for another component. This way, you do not have to create a new constraint object for each component you add to a GridBagLayout. However, this approach is error prone. You may set a constraint for a component and forget to change that when you reuse the constraint object for another component. So, be careful when you reuse a constraint object.

```
// Create a constraint object
GridBagConstraints gbc = new GridBagConstraints();

// Set gridx and gridy properties in the constraint object
gbc.gridx = 0;
gbc.gridy = 0;

// Add a JButton and pass the constraint object as the
// second argument to the add() method.
container.add(new JButton("B1"), gbc);

// Set the gridx property to 1. The gridy property
// remains as 0 as set previously.
gbc.gridx = 1;

// Add another JButton to the container
container.add(new JButton("B2"), gbc);
```

Listing 1-15 demonstrates how to set gridx and gridy values (or cell number) for a component. Figure 1-27 shows the JFrame that you get when you run the program.

Listing 1-15. Setting gridx and gridy Properties for Components in a GridBagLayout

```java
// GridBagLayoutWithgridxAndgridy.java
package com.jdojo.swing;

import java.awt.GridBagLayout;
import java.awt.Container;
import javax.swing.JFrame;
import javax.swing.JButton;
import java.awt.GridBagConstraints;

public class GridBagLayoutWithgridxAndgridy {
    public static void main(String[] args) {
        String title = "GridBagLayout with gridx and gridy";
        JFrame frame = new JFrame(title);
        frame.setDefaultCloseOperation(JFrame.EXIT_ON_CLOSE);

        Container contentPane = frame.getContentPane();
        contentPane.setLayout(new GridBagLayout());

        // Create an object for GridBagConstraints to set
        // the constraints for each JButton
        GridBagConstraints gbc = new GridBagConstraints();

        for(int y = 0; y < 3; y++) {
            for(int x = 0; x < 3; x++) {
                gbc.gridx = x;
                gbc.gridy = y;
                String text = "Button (" + x + ", " + y + ")";
                contentPane.add(new JButton(text), gbc);
            }
        }
```

```
        frame.pack();
        frame.setVisible(true);
    }
}
```

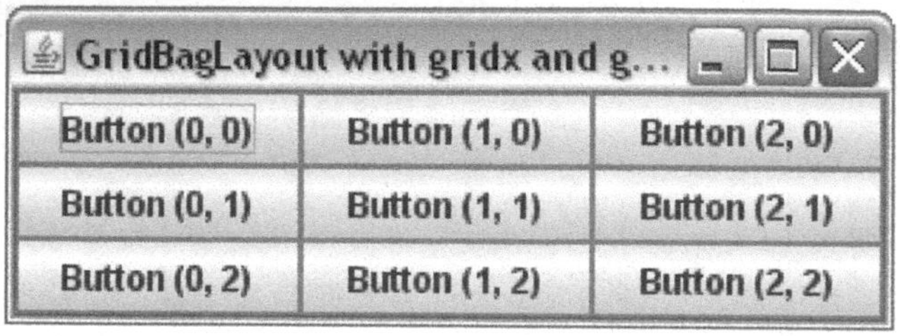

Figure 1-27. *A GridBagLayout with nine buttons*

You can specify other constraints for a component using a GridBagConstraints object. All constraints in a GridBagConstraints object are set using one of the instance variables listed in Table 1-3. The class also defines many constants such as RELATIVE, REMAINDER, etc. Note that all instance variables are in lowercase.

Table 1-3. *Instance Variables of the GridBagConstraints Class*

Instance Variable	Default Value	Possible Values	Usage
gridx gridy	RELATIVE	RELATIVE An integer	Column number and row number of the cell in the grid in which the component is placed.
gridwidth gridheight	1	An integer RELATIVE REMAINDER	Number of grid cells used to display the component.
fill	NONE	BOTH HORIZONTAL VERTICAL NONE	Specifies how the component will fill the cell(s) allotted to it in the grid.
ipadx ipady	0	An integer	Specifies the internal padding of a component that is added to its minimum size. A negative integer is allowed, which will decrease the minimum size of the component.
insets	(0,0,0,0)	An Insets object	Specifies the external padding between edges of the components and its cell in the grid. Negative values are allowed.

(continued)

Table 1-3. (*continued*)

Instance Variable	Default Value	Possible Values	Usage
anchor	CENTER	CENTER, NORTH, NORTHEAST, EAST, SOUTHEAST, SOUTH, SOUTHWEST, WEST, NORTHWEST, PAGE_START, PAGE_END, LINE_START, LINE_END, FIRST_LINE_START, FIRST_LINE_END, LAST_LINE_START, LAST_LINE_END, BASELINE, BASELINE_LEADING, BASELINE_TRAILING, ABOVE_BASELINE, ABOVE_BASELINE_LEADING, ABOVE_BASELINE_TRAILING, BELOW_BASELINE, BELOW_BASELINE_LEADING, BELOW_BASELINE_TRAILING	Where in the display area the component is placed.
weightx weighty	0.0	A positive double value	How the extra space (horizontally and vertically) is distributed among the grid cells when the container is resized.

The following sections discuss the effects of each constraint in detail.

The gridx and gridy Constraints

The gridx and gridy constraints specify the cell in the grid in which the component is placed. A component can occupy multiple cells horizontally as well as vertically. All the cells that a component occupies, when taken together, are known as the display area of the component.

Let's have a precise definition of the gridx and gridy constraints. They specify the starting cell of the display area of a component. By default, each component occupies only one cell. I will discuss how to make a component occupy multiple cells in the next section when I discuss the gridwidth and gridheight constraints. Please refer to Listing 1-15 for more details on setting gridx and gridy constraints values for a component.

You can specify a RELATIVE value for either or both gridx and gridy constraints. If you specify the values for gridx and gridy (an integer greater than or equal to zero), you decide where the component will be placed. If you specify either or both constraint values as RELATVE, the layout manager will determine the value for gridx and/or gridy. If you read the API documentation for the GridBagLayout class, the description of the RELATIVE value for gridx and/or gridy is not very clear. All it says is that when you specify the value for gridx and/or gridy as RELATIVE, the component will be placed next to the component that was added before this component. This description in the API documentation is as clear as mud! The following paragraphs will describe setting the values for gridx and gridy in full detail with examples.

Case #1

You have specified values for both gridx and gridy. This is the case of absolute positioning in the grid. Your component is placed according to the value of gridx and gridy that you have specified. You have already seen an example of this kind in Listing 1-15.

Case #2

You have specified a value for gridx and you have set the value for gridy to RELATIVE. In this case, the layout manager needs to determine the value for gridy. Let's look at an example. Assume that you have three buttons to place in the grid, and you have a container object whose layout manager is set to a GridBagLayout. The following snippet of code adds the three buttons to the grid. Figure 1-28 shows the screen with three buttons.

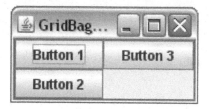

Figure 1-28. *Specifying gridx and Setting gridy to RELATIVE*

```
GridBagConstraints gbc = new GridBagConstraints();
JButton b1 = new JButton("Button 1");
JButton b2 = new JButton("Button 2");
JButton b3 = new JButton("Button 3");

gbc.gridx = 0;
gbc.gridy = 0;
container.add(b1, gbc);

gbc.gridx = 0;
gbc.gridy = GridBagConstraints.RELATIVE;
container.add(b2, gbc);

gbc.gridx = 1;
gbc.gridy = GridBagConstraints.RELATIVE ;
container.add(b3, gbc);
```

There is no confusion about the placement of the button b1 because you have specified both gridx and gridy values. It is placed in the first row (gridy = 0) and first column (gridx = 0).

For button b2, you have specified gridx = 0. You want it to be placed in the first column and the result is the same as you expected. You have specified gridy as RELATIVE for b2. This means that you are telling the GridBagLayout to find an appropriate row for b2 by placing it in the first column (gridx = 0). Since the first row is already occupied by b1 in the first column, the next row available for b2 is the second row and it is placed there.

You have set gridx = 1 for the button b3. This means that it should be placed in the second column. You have specified its gridy as RELATIVE. It means that the layout manager needs to find a row for it in the second column. Since the very first row does not have any component placed in the second column, the layout manager places it in the first row. Where will b3 be placed if you had specified its gridx as 0? Apply the same logic again. Since the first column already had b1 and b2 in the first row and the second row, respectively, the only next row available for b3 is the third row and the layout manager would place it just below b2.

Case #3

You have specified a value for gridy and you have set the value for gridx to RELATIVE. In this case, the layout manager needs to determine the value for gridx. That is, based on the specified value of the row number, the layout manager has to determine its column number. Figure 1-29 shows the three buttons laid out when you use the following snippet of code. The logic to lay out the buttons this way is the same as in the previous example, except that this time the layout manager decides the column numbers for b2 and b3 instead of their row numbers.

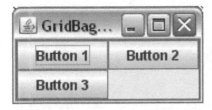

Figure 1-29. *Specifying gridy and setting gridx to RELATIVE in a GridBagLayout*

```
gbc.gridx = 0;
gbc.gridy = 0;
container.add(b1, gbc);

gbc.gridx = GridBagConstraints.RELATIVE;
gbc.gridy = 0;
container.add(b2, gbc);

gbc.gridx = GridBagConstraints.RELATIVE;
gbc.gridy = 1;
container.add(b3, gbc);
```

Case #4

This is the last of the four possibilities in which you specify both gridx and gridy as RELATIVE. The layout manager has to determine the row number as well as the column number for the component being added. It will determine the row number first. The row for the component will be the current row. Which row is the current row? By default, the first row (gridy = 0) is the current row. When you add a component, you can also specify its gridwidth constraint. One of its values is REMAINDER, which means that this is the last component in the row. If you add a component to the first row with its gridwidth set to REMAINDER, the second row becomes the current row. Once the layout manager determines the row number for a component, which is the current row, it will place the component in the column next to the last component added in that row. The default value for gridx and gridy is RELATIVE. Now you can understand why Listing 1-14 placed all buttons in the first row, which used RELATIVE as gridx and gridy for all buttons, by default. Since the default gridwidth is 1, the first row was always the current row. Whenever you added a button, the first row (the current row) was assigned as its row and its column was the next to the last button added in that row. Let's have some examples in which you will set both gridx and gridy to RELATIVE.

Example 1:

The following snippet of code lays out the buttons as shown in Figure 1-30:

```
gbc.gridx = 0;
gbc.gridy = 0;
container.add(b1, gbc);
```

```
gbc.gridx = GridBagConstraints.RELATIVE;
gbc.gridy = GridBagConstraints.RELATIVE;
container.add(b2, gbc);

gbc.gridx = GridBagConstraints.RELATIVE;
gbc.gridy = 1;
container.add(b3, gbc);
```

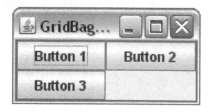

Figure 1-30. *Specifying Both gridx and gridy as RELATIVE*

You used absolute positioning for b1 by specifying its gridx = 0 and gridy = 0. It resulted in placing b1 in the first row and the first column. You have specified both gridx and gridy for b2 as RELATIVE. The layout manager has to determine the row number and the column number for b2. It looks at the current row, which is the first row by default. Therefore, it sets b2's row number to 0. It finds that there is already one component (b1) placed in the first column. Therefore, it sets the next column, which is the second column, for b2. And here you see b2 placed in the first row and the second column. It is simple to understand the placement of b3. Since you have specified its gridy = 1, it is placed in the second row. Its gridx is RELATIVE and since the first column is available in the second row, it is placed in the first column.

Example 2:

The following snippet of code lays out the buttons as shown in Figure 1-31. Note that the b1 button is placed in the center of its available space, which is the default behavior. You can customize the placement of a component inside its allocated space using the anchor property that I will discuss shortly.

Figure 1-31. *Specifying gridx and gridy as RELATIVE with gridwidth as REMAINDER*

```
gbc.gridx = 0;
gbc.gridy = 0;
gbc.gridwidth = GridBagConstraints.REMAINDER;// Last component in the row
container.add(b1, gbc);
```

```
gbc.gridx = GridBagConstraints.RELATIVE;
gbc.gridy = GridBagConstraints.RELATIVE;
gbc.gridwidth = 1; // Reset to the default value
container.add(b2, gbc);

gbc.gridx = GridBagConstraints.RELATIVE; gbc.gridy = 1;
container.add(b3, gbc);
```

You specified gridx = 0 and gridy = 0 for b1. This time, you specified gridwidth for b1 as REMAINDER. This means that b1 is the last component in the first row. Since this is the only component added to the first row, it becomes the first and the last component in this row. After b1 is added with its gridwidth as REMAINDER, the second row becomes the current row. For b2, gridx and gridy are set to RELATIVE. The layout manager will set the second row (gridy = 1) as its row number. Since there is no component placed in the second row before b2, it will be the first one in the row. This results in placing b2 in the second row and the first column. Note that you set the value for gridwidth to 1 for b2 and b3. Determining the position of b3 is simple. Since you specified its gridy to 1 (the second row), it is placed in the second row. Its gridx is RELATIVE. Since b2 is already in the first column, it is placed in the second column.

The gridwidth and gridheight Constraints

The gridwidth and gridheight constraints specify the width and height of the display area of a component, respectively. The default value for both is 1. That is, by default, a component is placed in one cell. If you specify gridwidth = 2 for a component, its display area will be two cells wide. If you specify gridheight = 2 for a component, its display area will be two cells high. If you have worked with HTML tables, you can compare gridwidth with colspan and gridheight with rowspan properties of a cell of an HTML table.

You can specify two predefined constants for gridwidth and gridheight. They are REMAINDER and RELATIVE. The REMAINDER value for gridwidth means that the component will span from its gridx cell to the remainder of the row. In other words, it is the last component in the row. The REMAINDER value for the gridheight indicates that it is the last component in the column. The RELATIVE value for gridwidth indicates that the width of the display area of the component will be from its gridx to the second last cell in the row. The RELATIVE value for gridheight indicates that the height of the display area of the component will be from its gridy to the second last cell. Let's take an example of each kind for gridwidth. You can extend this concept for gridheight. The only difference is that the gridwidth affects the width of a component's display area, whereas the gridheight affects the height.

The following snippet of code adds nine buttons to a container—three in the first row and six in the second row:

```
// Expand the component to fill the whole cell
gbc.fill = GridBagConstraints.BOTH;

gbc.gridx = 0;
gbc.gridy = 0;
container.add(new JButton("Button 1"), gbc);

gbc.gridx = 1;
gbc.gridy = 0;
gbc.gridwidth = GridBagConstraints.RELATIVE;
container.add(new JButton("Button 2"), gbc);

gbc.gridx = GridBagConstraints.RELATIVE; gbc.gridy = 0;
gbc.gridwidth = GridBagConstraints.REMAINDER;
container.add(new JButton("Button 3"), gbc);
```

```
// Reset gridwidth to its default value 1
gbc.gridwidth = 1;

// Place six JButtons in second row
gbc.gridy = 1;
for(int i = 0; i < 6; i++) {
        gbc.gridx = i;
        container.add(new JButton("Button " + (i + 4)), gbc);
}
```

The very first statement is new to you. It sets the fill instance variable of GridBagConstraints to BOTH, which indicates that the components added to cells will be expanded in both directions (horizontally and vertically) to fill the entire cell area. I will discuss this in more detail later. The first button is placed in the first row and the first column.

The second button is placed in the first row and the second column. Its gridwidth is set to RELATIVE, which means it will span from the second column (gridx = 1) to the second to last column in the row. Which column is the last column in the first row? You do not know yet. You must look at all components that are added to a GridBagLayout to find out the maximum number of rows and columns in the grid. For now, you know that the second button starts in the second column, but you do not know in which column it will end (or up to what column it will extend).

Let's look at the third button. You have specified its gridy = 0, which means that it should be placed in the first row. You have set its gridx to RELATIVE, which means that it will be placed after the second button in the first row. You have set its gridwidth value as REMAINDER, which means this is the last component in the first row. There is an interesting point to note. The second button will expand as needed from the second column to the second to last column. You are saying that the third button is the last component in the first row and it should occupy the rest of the cells. The result is that there will always be only one cell (the last cell) left for the third button because of the *greedy* value of RELATIVE for the gridwidth of the second button.

In the second row, you have added six buttons. The total number of cells in each row is decided by the maximum number of columns in a row. Therefore, each row (first and second) will have six cells. You have set the gridwidth to its default value of 1, so each button in the second row will occupy only one cell. In the first row, the first button occupies one cell, the third one occupies one cell, and the second one occupies the remaining four, as shown in Figure 1-32.

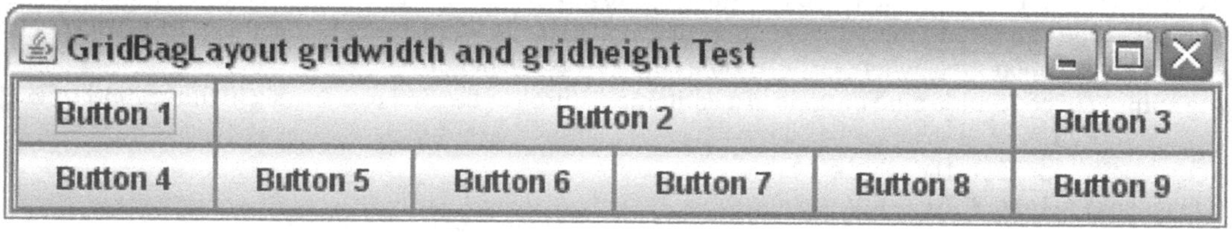

Figure 1-32. *Specifying gridwidth and gridheight*

The fill Constraint

A GridBagLayout gives the preferred width and height to each component. The width of a column is decided by the widest component in the column. Similarly, the height of a row is decided by the highest component in the row. The fill constraint value indicates how a component is expanded horizontally and vertically when its display area is bigger than its size. Note that the fill constraint is only used when the component's size is smaller than its display area.

The fill constraint has four possible values: NONE, HORIZONTAL, VERTICAL, and BOTH. Its default value is NONE, which means "do not expand the component." The value HORIZONTAL means "expand the component horizontally to fill its display area." The value VERTICAL means "expand the component vertically to fill its display area." The value BOTH means "expand the component horizontally and vertically to fill its display area."

The following snippet of code adds nine buttons to a grid of three rows and three columns, as shown in Figure 1-33.

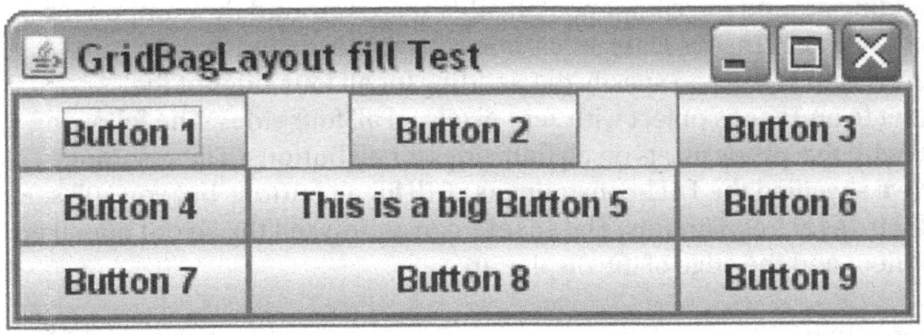

GridBagLayout fill Test

Button 1	Button 2		Button 3
Button 4	This is a big Button 5		Button 6
Button 7	Button 8		Button 9

Figure 1-33. Specifying the fill constraint for a component in a GridBagLayout

```
gbc.gridx = 0; gbc.gridy = 0;
container.add(new JButton("Button 1"), gbc);
gbc.gridx = 1; gbc.gridy = 0;
container.add(new JButton("Button 2"), gbc);
gbc.gridx = 2; gbc.gridy = 0;
container.add(new JButton("Button 3"), gbc);

gbc.gridx = 0; gbc.gridy = 1;
container.add(new JButton("Button 4"), gbc);
gbc.gridx = 1; gbc.gridy = 1;
container.add(new JButton("This is a big Button 5"), gbc);
gbc.gridx = 2; gbc.gridy = 1;
container.add(new JButton("Button 6"), gbc);

gbc.gridx = 0; gbc.gridy = 2;
container.add(new JButton("Button 7"), gbc);
gbc.gridx = 1; gbc.gridy = 2;
gbc.fill = GridBagConstraints.HORIZONTAL;
container.add(new JButton("Button 8"), gbc);
gbc.gridx = 2; gbc.gridy = 2;
gbc.fill = GridBagConstraints.NONE;
container.add(new JButton("Button 9"), gbc);
```

The fifth button decides the width of the second column because it is the widest JButton in that column. Note the empty space in the second column of the first row. It has empty space because for the second button the fill value is NONE, which is the default and the second button was not expanded to take the entire width of its display area. It was left to its preferred size. Look at the eighth button. You specified that it should expand horizontally, and it did so to match the width of its display area.

The ipadx and ipady Constraints

The ipadx and ipady constraints are used to specify internal padding for a component. They increase the preferred size and the minimum size of the component. By default, both constraints are set to zero. Negative values are allowed. The negative value for these constraints will decrease the component's preferred and minimum size. If you specify the value for ipadx, the component's preferred and minimum width will be increased by 2*ipadx. Similarly, if you specify the value for ipady, the component's preferred and minimum height will be increased by 2*ipady. These options are rarely used. The values for ipadx and ipady are specified in pixels.

The insets Constraints

The insets constraint specifies the external padding around the component. It adds spaces around the component. You specify the insets value as an object of the java.awt.Insets class. It has one constructor called Insets(int top, int left, int bottom, int right). You can specify the padding for all four sides of the component. By default, the value for insets is set to an Insets object with zero pixels on all four sides. The following snippet of code adds nine buttons in a 3X3 grid with five pixels insets on all four sides for all buttons. The resulting layout is shown in Figure 1-34. Note that you have specified the fill constraint as BOTH for all buttons but you still see the gap between adjacent buttons because of their insets constraints. The insets constraints tell the layout manager to leave a space between the edge of the component and the edge of the display area.

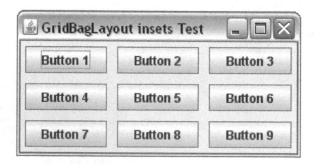

Figure 1-34. *Specifying insets for components in a GridBagLayout*

```
gbc.fill = GridBagConstraints.BOTH;
gbc.insets = new Insets(5, 5, 5, 5);
int count = 1;
for(int y = 0; y < 3; y++) {
        gbc.gridy = y;
        for(int x = 0; x < 3; x++) {
                gbc.gridx = x;
                container.add(new JButton("Button " + count++), gbc);
        }
}
```

The anchor Constraint

The anchor constraint specifies where a component should be placed within its display area when its size is smaller than that of its display area. By default, its value is set to CENTER, which means that the component is centered within its display area.

There are many constants defined in the GridBagConstraints class that can be used as a value for the anchor constraint. All constants can be categorized in three categories: absolute, orientation-based, and baseline-based.

The absolute values are NORTH, SOUTH, WEST, EAST, NORTHWEST, NORTHEAST, SOUTHWEST, SOUTHEAST, and CENTER. Figure 1-35 shows how a component is placed inside a cell with different absolute anchor values. Note that all nine components in the figure have their fill constraint set to NONE.

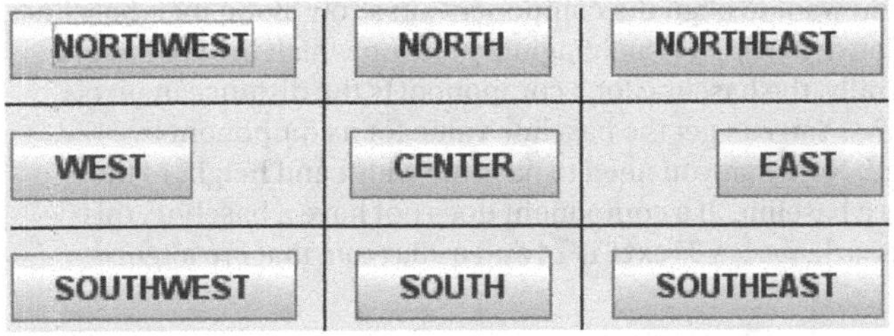

NORTHWEST	NORTH	NORTHEAST
WEST	CENTER	EAST
SOUTHWEST	SOUTH	SOUTHEAST

Figure 1-35. *Absolute anchor values and their effects on component location in the display area*

The orientation-based values are used based on the ComponentOrientation property of the container. They are PAGE_START, PAGE_END, LINE_START, LINE_END, FIRST_LINE_START, FIRST_LINE_END, LAST_LINE_START, and LAST_LINE_END. Figure 1-36 and Figure 1-37 show the effects of using orientation-based anchor values when the container's orientation is set to LEFT_TO_RIGHT and RIGHT_TO_LEFT. You may notice that the orientation-based values adjust themselves according to the orientation used by the container.

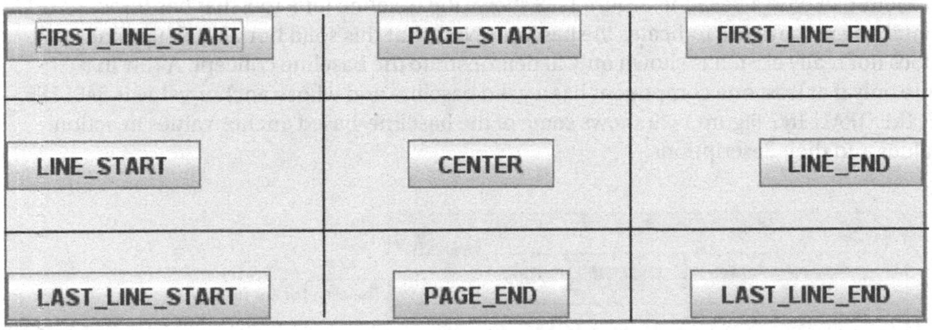

FIRST_LINE_START	PAGE_START	FIRST_LINE_END
LINE_START	CENTER	LINE_END
LAST_LINE_START	PAGE_END	LAST_LINE_END

Figure 1-36. *Orientation-based anchor values and their effects when the container's orientation is LEFT_TO_RIGHT*

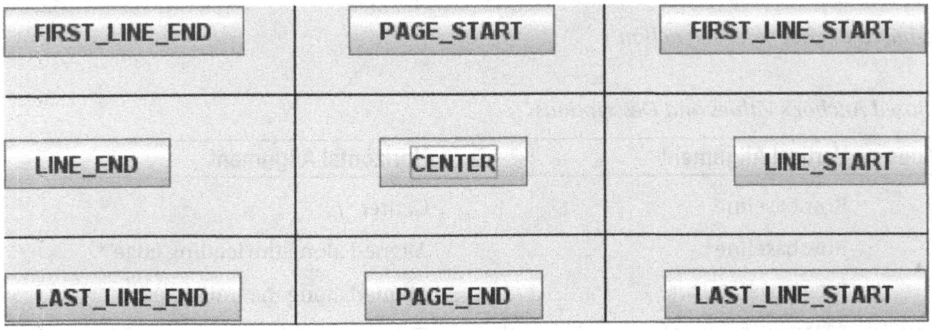

FIRST_LINE_END	PAGE_START	FIRST_LINE_START
LINE_END	CENTER	LINE_START
LAST_LINE_END	PAGE_END	LAST_LINE_START

Figure 1-37. *Orientation-based anchor values and their effects when the container's orientation is RIGHT_TO_LEFT*

The baseline-base anchor's values are used when you want to align the components in a row along their baseline. What is the baseline of a component? The baseline is relative to text. It is an imaginary line on which the characters of the text rest. A component may have a baseline. Generally, the baseline for a component is the distance in pixels between its top edge and the baseline of the text it displays. You can get the baseline value for a component by using its getBaseline(int width, int height) method. Note that you need to pass the width and height of the component to get its baseline. Not every component has a baseline. If a component does not have a baseline, this method returns –1. Figure 1-38 shows three components, a JLabel, a JTextField and a JButton, that are aligned along their baseline in a row in a GridBagLayout.

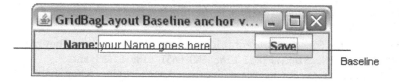

Figure 1-38. *A JLabel, a JTextField, and a JButton aligned along their baselines*

Each row in a GridBagLayout can have a baseline. Figure 1-38 shows the baseline for a row that has three components. A solid horizontal line in the figure indicates the baseline. Note that this solid horizontal baseline is an imaginary line and it does not really exist. It is shown only to demonstrate the baseline concept. A row in a GridBagLayout has a baseline only if at least one component has a valid baseline and whose anchor value is BASLINE, BASELINE_LEADING, or BASELINE_TRAILING. Figure 1-39 shows some of the baseline-based anchor values in action. Table 1-4 lists all possible values and their descriptions.

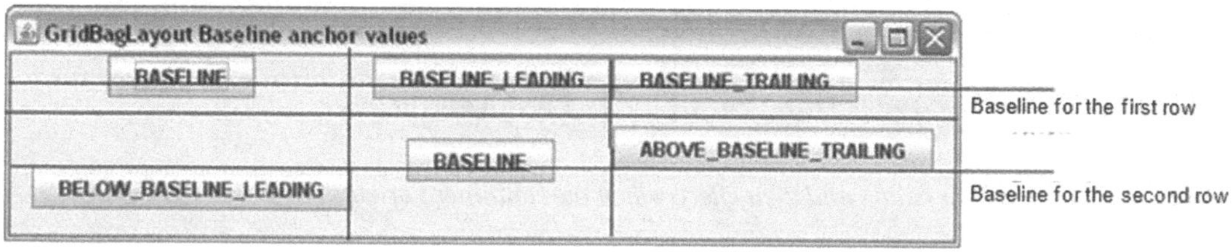

Figure 1-39. *Some baseline-based anchor values in action*

Table 1-4. *List of Baseline-Based Anchor's Values and Descriptions*

Baseline-Based Anchor Values	Vertical Alignment	Horizontal Alignment
BASELINE	Row baseline	Center
BASELINE_LEADING	Row baseline	Aligned along the leading edge**
BASELINE_TRAILING	Row baseline	Aligned along the trailing edge***
ABOVE_BASELINE	Bottom edge touches baseline of the starting row	Center
ABOVE_BASELINE_LEADING	Bottom edge touches baseline of the starting row*	Aligned along the leading edge**
ABOVE_BASELINE_TRAILING	Bottom edge touches baseline of the starting row	Aligned along the trailing edge***

(continued)

Table 1-4. (*continued*)

Baseline-Based Anchor Values	Vertical Alignment	Horizontal Alignment
BELOW_BASELINE	Top edge touches baseline of the starting row*	Center
BELOW_BASELINE_LEADING	Top edge touches baseline of the starting row	Aligned along the leading edge**
BELOW_BASELINE_TRAILING	Top edge touches baseline of the starting row*	Aligned along the trailing edge***

starting row: The phrase "starting row" applies only when a component spans multiple rows. Otherwise, read it as the row in which the component is placed. If a row has no baseline, the component is vertically centered
**Leading edge is left edge for LEFT_TO_RIGHT orientation and right edge for RIGHT_TO_LEFT orientation*
***Trailing edge is right edge for LEFT_TO_RIGHT orientation and left edge for RIGHT_TO_LEFT orientation*

The weightx and weighty Constraints

The weightx and weighty constraints control how the extra space in the container is distributed among rows and columns. The default values for weightx and weighty are zero. They can have any non-negative value.

Figure 1-40 shows a JFrame using the GridBagLayout with nine buttons. Figure 1-41 shows the same JFrame expanded horizontally and vertically.

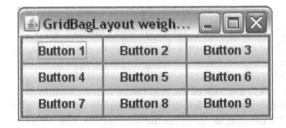

Figure 1-40. A JFrame with a GridBagLayout having nine buttons with no extra spaces

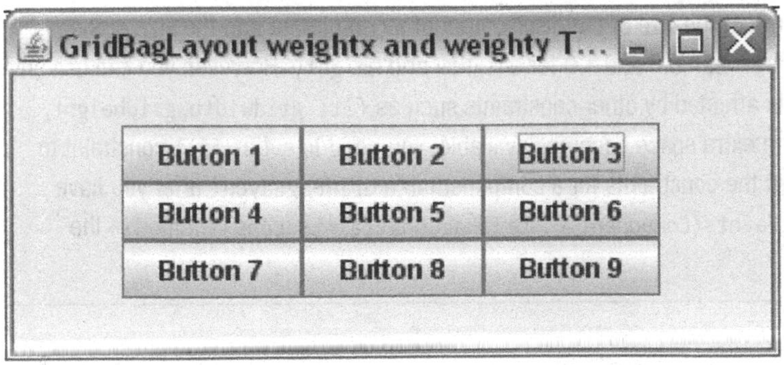

Figure 1-41. A JFrame with a GridBagLayout having nine buttons after resizing

47

Notice the extra spaces generated around the group of buttons. You have set the fill constraint as BOTH for all buttons, so all buttons represent the grid of cells in the GridBagLayout. The weightx and weighty constraints were left to their default values of zero. When all the components have their weightx and weighty constraints set to zero, any extra space in the container appears between the edge of the container and the edge of the grid of cells.

The weightx value determines the distribution of extra horizontal space among the columns, whereas the weighty value works on distributing the extra vertical space among rows. If all components have the same weightx and weighty, extra space is distributed equally among them. Figure 1-42 shows all nine buttons when their weightx and weighty are set to 1.0. You could have set any positive values for weightx and/or weighty. As long as they are the same for all components, extra space will be distributed equally among them.

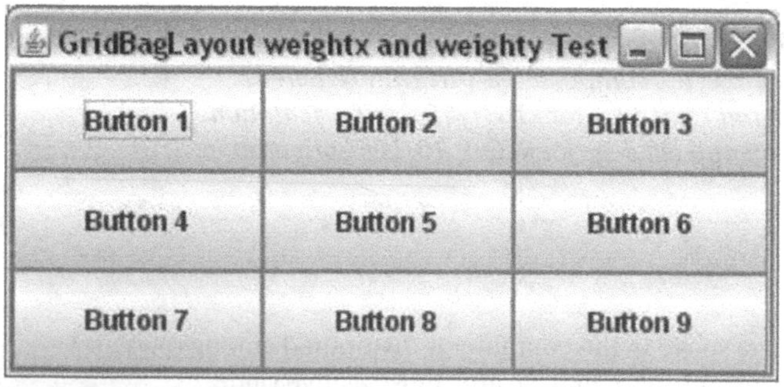

Figure 1-42. *A JFrame with a GridBagLayout having nine buttons after resizing. All buttons have their weightx and weighty set to 1. Extra space is distributed among the display area of all buttons equally*

Here is how the extra space for each column is computed based on the weightx values. Suppose a container with a GridBagLayout is expanded horizontally to make ES pixels of additional space available. Suppose there are three columns in the grid with three rows. The layout manager will find the maximum value of weightx value for the components in each column. Suppose cwx1, cwx2, and cwx3 are the maximum values for weightx for column 1, column 2, and column 3, respectively. Column 1 will get (cwx1 * ES)/(cwx1 + cwx2 + cwx3) amount of the additional space. Column 2 will get (cwx2 * ES)/(cwx1 + cwx2 + cwx3) amount of the additional space. Column 3 will get (cwx3 * ES)/(cwx1 + cwx2 + cwx3) amount of the additional space. It is necessary to compute the extra space given to a column by using the maximum weightx value in that column to maintain the grid of cells. The computation for distributing extra vertical space among the cells using weighty is similar

---

■ **Tip** The weightx and weighty constraints affect the size of the display area of a component and the size of the component itself. It is customary to use a value between 0.0 and 1.0 for weightx and weighty. However, you can use any non-negative value. The size of the component is affected by other constraints such as fill, gridwidth, gridheight, etc. If you want your component to expand as the extra space becomes available, you need to set its fill constraint to HORIZONTAL, VERTICAL, or BOTH. You can also set the constraints for a component in a GridBagLayout after you have added it to the container by using the setConstraints(Component c, GridBagConstraints cons) method of the GridBagLayout class.

SpringLayout

An instance of the SpringLayout class in the javax.swing package represents a SpringLayout manager. Recall that the job of a layout manager is to compute four properties (x, y, width, and height) of components in a container. In other words, it is responsible for positioning the components inside the container and computing their size. A SpringLayout manager represents these four properties of a component in terms of springs. It is cumbersome to code by hand. It is meant for GUI builder tools. I will cover the basics of this layout in this section by hand-coding some simple examples.

What is a spring? In the context of a SpringLayout manager, you can think of a spring the same way as a mechanical spring, which can be stretched, compressed, or stay in its normal state. An object of the Spring class represents a spring in a SpringLayout. A Spring object has four properties: minimum, preferred, maximum, and current value. You can think of these four properties as its four types of length. A spring has its minimum value when it is most compressed. In its normal state (neither compressed nor stretched), it has its preferred value. In its most stretched state, it has its maximum value. Its value at any given point in time is its current value. When the minimum, preferred, and maximum values of a spring are the same, it is known as a *strut*.

How do you create a spring? The Spring class has no public constructors. It contains factory methods to create springs. To create a spring or strut from scratch, you can use its overloaded constant() static method. You can also create a spring using the width or height of a component. The minimum, preferred, and maximum values of the spring are set from the corresponding values of the width or height of the component

```
// Create a strut of 10 pixels
Spring strutPadding = Spring.constant(10);

// Create a spring having 10, 25 and 50 as its minimum,
// preferred, and maximum value respectively.
Spring springPadding = Spring.constant(10, 25, 50);

// Create a spring from the width of a component named c1
Spring s1 = Spring.width(c1);

// Create a spring from the height of a component named c1
Spring s2 = Spring.height(c1);
```

The Spring class has some utility methods that let you manipulate spring properties. You can create a new spring by adding two springs using the sum() method, like so:

```
// Assuming that s1 and s2 are two springs
Spring s3 = Spring.sum(s1, s2);
```

The computation sum is not performed at the time the statement is executed. Rather, the spring s3 stores the references of s1 and s2. Whenever s1, s2, or both change, the value for s3 is computed. In this case, s3 behaves as if you have connected springs s1 and s2 in series.

You can also create a spring by subtracting one spring from another. However, you do not have a method named subtract(). There is a method called minus() that gives you the negative of a spring. You can use the combination of the sum() and minus() methods to perform a subtraction, like so:

```
// Perform s1 - s2, which is the same as s1 + (-s2)
Spring s4 = Spring.sum(s1, Spring.minus(s2));
```

To get the maximum of two springs s1 and s2, you can use Spring.max(s1, s2). Note that there is no corresponding method called min(). However, you can simulate it by using the combination of the minus() and max() methods, like so:

```
// Minimum of 2 and 5 is the minus of the maximum of -2 and -5.
// To get the minimum of two spring s1 and s2, you can use minus
// of maximum of -s1 and -s2
Spring min = Spring.minus(Spring.max(Spring.minus(s1), Spring.minus(s2)));
```

You can also get a fraction of another spring using the scale() method. For example, if you have a spring s1 and you want to create a spring that is 40% of its value, you can do so by passing 0.40f as the second argument to the scale() method, like so:

```
String fractionSpring = Spring.scale(s1, 0.40f);
```

■ **Tip** You cannot change the minimum, preferred, and maximum values of a spring after you have created it. You can set its current value by using its setValue() method.

You just had a great deal of discussion about springs. It is time to see them in action. How do you add a component to a container with a SpringLayout? In the simplest form, you use the add() method of the container to add a component. Listing 1-16 sets the layout for the content pane of a JFrame to a SpringLayout and adds two buttons to it. Figure 1-43 shows the JFrame when you run the program.

Listing 1-16. The Simplest SpringLayout

```
// SimplestSpringLayout.java
package com.jdojo.swing;

import java.awt.Container;
import javax.swing.JFrame;
import javax.swing.SpringLayout;
import javax.swing.JButton;

public class SimplestSpringLayout {
    public static void main(String[] args) {
        JFrame frame = new JFrame("Simplest SpringLayout");
        frame.setDefaultCloseOperation(JFrame.EXIT_ON_CLOSE);
        Container contentPane = frame.getContentPane();

        // Set the content pane's layout as SpringLayout
        SpringLayout springLayout = new SpringLayout();
        contentPane.setLayout(springLayout);

        // Add two JButtons to the content pane
        JButton b1 = new JButton("Button 1");
        JButton b2 = new JButton("Little Bigger Button 2");
        contentPane.add(b1);
        contentPane.add(b2);
```

```
            frame.pack();
            frame.setVisible(true);
        }
}
```

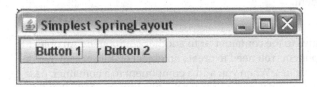

Figure 1-43. *The JFrame when you run the SimplestSpringLayout class*

Figure 1-43 shows that you see only the title bar of the JFrame. When you expand the JFrame, you see the screen as shown in Figure 1-44. Note that both of your buttons are in the JFrame. However, they overlap. The simplest SpringLayout example may be the simplest to code; however, it is not that simple to see the result.

Figure 1-44. *After expanding the JFrame when you run the SimplestSpringLayout class*

So, what was wrong with your simplest SpringLayout example? I mentioned that a SpringLayout was hard to hand code and you saw it now! You used the pack() method on the frame to give it an optimal size. But your frame is shown with no display area. When you use a SpringLayout, you must specify the x, y, width, and height for all components and the container. It is too much work for developers, and this is why I stated that this layout manager is meant for a GUI builder, not for coding by hand.

Let's examine the screens shown in Figure 1-43 and Figure 1-44 one more time. You see that the container got a position (x and y) and the buttons got size (width and height). A JFrame is displayed at (0, 0) by default, and this is how you see the position for the container (in fact, your container is a content pane). Buttons get their default minimum, preferred, and maximum size (all set to the same value) and this is how you see the buttons after you expand the screen. By default, a SpringLayout positions all components at (0, 0) within the container. In this case, both buttons are positioned at (0, 0). To fix this problem, specify the x, y, width, and height of two buttons and the content pane.

A SpringLayout uses constraints to arrange components. An object of the Constraints class, which is a static inner class of the SpringLayout class, represents constraints for a component and the container. A Constraints object lets you specify x, y, width, and height of a component using its methods. All four properties must be specified in terms of a Spring object. When you specify these properties, you need to specify them using one of the constants defined in the SpringLayout class, listed in Table 1-5.

Table 1-5. *List of Constants Defined in the SpringLayout Class*

Constant Name	Description
NORTH	It is synonymous with y. It is the top edge of the component.
WEST	It is synonymous with x. It is the left edge of the component.
SOUTH	It is the bottom edge of the component. Its value is the same as NORTH + HEIGHT.
EAST	It is the right edge of the component. It is the same as WEST + WIDTH.
WIDTH	The width of the component.
HEIGHT	The height of the component.
HORIZONTAL_CENTER	It is the horizontal center of the component. It is the same as WEST + WIDTH/2.
VERTICAL_CENTER	It is the vertical center of the component. It is the same as NORTH + HEIGHT/2.
BASELINE	It is the baseline of the component.

You can set the x and y constraints of a component relative to the container or to another component. An object of the Constraints class specifies the constraints for a component. You need to create an object of the SpringLayout. Constraints class and use its methods to set the constraints' values. When you add a component to a container, pass this constraint object to the add() method. Listing 1-17 sets the x and y constraints for the two buttons. Note that the values (10, 20) and (150, 20) are specified in terms of Spring objects and they are measured from the edges of the content pane. Figure 1-45 shows the screen when you run the program and after you expand the JFrame.

Listing 1-17. Setting x and y Constraints for Components

```java
// SpringLayout2.java
package com.jdojo.swing;

import javax.swing.SpringLayout;
import java.awt.Container;
import javax.swing.JFrame;
import javax.swing.JButton;
import javax.swing.Spring;

public class SpringLayout2 {
    public static void main(String[] args) {
        JFrame frame = new JFrame("SpringLayout2");
        frame.setDefaultCloseOperation(JFrame.EXIT_ON_CLOSE);
        Container contentPane = frame.getContentPane();

        // Set the content pane's layout to a SpringLayout
        SpringLayout springLayout = new SpringLayout();
        contentPane.setLayout(springLayout);

        // Add two JButtons to the content pane
        JButton b1 = new JButton("Button 1");
        JButton b2 = new JButton("Little Bigger Button 2");
```

```
        // Create Constraints objects for b1 and b2
        SpringLayout.Constraints b1c = new SpringLayout.Constraints();
        SpringLayout.Constraints b2c = new SpringLayout.Constraints();

        // Create a Spring object for y value for b1 and b2
        Spring yPadding = Spring.constant(20);

        // Set (10, 20) for (x, y) for b1
        b1c.setX(Spring.constant(10));
        b1c.setY(yPadding);

        // Set (150, 20) for (x, y) for b2
        b2c.setX(Spring.constant(150));
        b2c.setY(yPadding);

        // Use the Constraints object while adding b1 and b2
        contentPane.add(b1, b1c);
        contentPane.add(b2, b2c);

        frame.pack();
        frame.setVisible(true);
    }
}
```

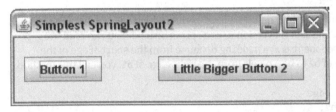

Figure 1-45. *After expanding the JFrame when the (x, y) are set for two buttons*

You have not fixed the size of the JFrame yet. When you run the program, the JFrame is still displayed with no display area. At least the two buttons are not overlapping this time. You picked an arbitrary value of 150 pixels as the value of x for b2. That is, the left edge of b2 is 150 pixels from the left edge of the content pane. There is a way to specify that the left edge of b2 should be at a specified distance from the right edge of b1. To achieve this, you need to add b1 to the container first. When you add a component to the container, SpringLayout associates a Constraints object to the component, irrespective of whether you pass a constraints object to the add() method of the container or not. You can get the constraint for any edge for a component using the getConstraint(String edge, Component c) method of the SpringLayout class. The following snippet of code does the same. It sets (x, y) for b1 to (10, 20) and sets (x, y) for b2 to (b1's right edge + 5, 20). If you replace the code for adding two buttons in Listing 1-17 with the following snippet of code, b2 will appear 10 pixels right of b1:

```
// Create a Spring object for y value for b1 and b2
Spring yPadding = Spring.constant(20);

// Set (10, 20) for (x, y) for b1
b1c.setX(Spring.constant(10));
b1c.setY(yPadding);
```

```
// Add b1 to the content pane first
contentPane.add(b1, b1c);

// Now query the layout manager for b1's EAST constraint,
// which is the right edge of b1
Spring b1Right = springLayout.getConstraint(SpringLayout.EAST, b1);

// Add a 5-pixel strut to the right edge of b1 to define the
// left edge of b2 and set it using setX() method on b2c
Spring b2Left = Spring.sum(b1Right, Spring.constant(5));
b2c.setX(b2Left);
b2c.setY(yPadding);

// Now add b2 to the content pane
contentPane.add(b2, b2c);
```

There is an easier and more intuitive way to set the constraints for components in a SpringLayout. First, add all components to the container without worrying about their constraints and then define the constraints using the putConstraint() method of the SpringLayout class. Here are two versions of the putConstraint() method:

- void putConstraint(String targetEdge, Component targetComponent, int padding, String sourceEdge,Component sourceComponent)

- void putConstraint(String targetEdge, Component targetComponent, Spring padding, String sourceEdge, Component sourceComponent)

The first version uses a strut. The third argument (int padding) defines a fixed spring, which will behave as a strut (a fixed distance) between the edges of two components. The second version uses a spring instead. You can read the method description as, "The targetEdge of the targetComponent is at a padding distance from the sourceEdge of the sourceComponent." For example, if you want the left edge of b2 to be 5 pixels from the right edge of b1, you call this method:

```
// Set b2's left edge 5 pixels from b1's right edge
springLayout.putConstraint(SpringLayout.WEST, b2, 5,
                           SpringLayout.EAST, b1);
```

To set the left edge of b1 (left edge defines the x value) 10 pixels from the left edge of the content pane, you use

```
springLayout.putConstraint(SpringLayout.WEST, b1, 5,
                           SpringLayout.WEST, contentPane);
```

Let's go back to the sizing problem of your JFrame when you call its pack() method. You need to set the position for the bottom and right edges for the content pane so that the pack() method will resize it correctly. You set its bottom edge to 10 pixels below the bottom edge of b1 (or b2, whichever is the closest to its bottom edge). In this example, both are at the same distance from the bottom edge of the content pane. You set its right edge 10 pixels from the right edge of b2, which is the rightmost JButton in the content pane. The following snippet of code does this:

```
// Set the bottom edge of the content pane
springLayout.putConstraint(SpringLayout.SOUTH, contentPane, 10,
                           SpringLayout.SOUTH, b1);

// Set the right edge of the content pane
springLayout.putConstraint(SpringLayout.EAST, contentPane, 10,
                           SpringLayout.EAST, b2);
```

Listing 1-18 contains the complete program and Figure 1-46 shows the JFrame when you run the program.

Listing 1-18. Using the putConstraint() Method of the SpringLayout Class

```java
// NiceSpringLayout.java
package com.jdojo.swing;

import javax.swing.JFrame;
import java.awt.Container;
import javax.swing.SpringLayout;
import javax.swing.JButton;

public class NiceSpringLayout {
        public static void main(String[] args) {
                JFrame frame = new JFrame("SpringLayout2");
                frame.setDefaultCloseOperation(JFrame.EXIT_ON_CLOSE);
                Container contentPane = frame.getContentPane();

                // Set the content pane's layout to a SpringLayout
                SpringLayout springLayout = new SpringLayout();
                contentPane.setLayout(springLayout);

                // Create two JButtons
                JButton b1 = new JButton("Button 1");
                JButton b2 = new JButton("Little Bigger Button 2");

                // Add two JButtons without using any constraints
                contentPane.add(b1);
                contentPane.add(b2);

                // Now add constraints to both JButtons
                // Set x for b1 as 10
                springLayout.putConstraint(SpringLayout.WEST, b1, 10,
                                        SpringLayout.WEST, contentPane);
                // Set y for b1 as 20
                springLayout.putConstraint(SpringLayout.NORTH, b1, 20,
                                        SpringLayout.NORTH, contentPane);

                // Set x for b2 as 10 from the right edge of b1
                springLayout.putConstraint(SpringLayout.WEST, b2, 10,
                                        SpringLayout.EAST, b1);
                // Set y for b1 as 20
                springLayout.putConstraint(SpringLayout.NORTH, b2, 20,
                                        SpringLayout.NORTH, contentPane);

                /* Now set height and width for the content pane as the bottom
                   edge of b1 + 10 and right edge of b2 + 10. Note that source
                   is b1 for content pane's height and b2 for its width
                */
```

```
            // Set the bottom edge of the content pane
            springLayout.putConstraint(SpringLayout.SOUTH, contentPane, 10,
                                   SpringLayout.SOUTH, b1);

            // Set the right edge of the content pane
            springLayout.putConstraint(SpringLayout.EAST, contentPane, 10,
                                   SpringLayout.EAST, b2);

            frame.pack();
            frame.setVisible(true);
        }
}
```

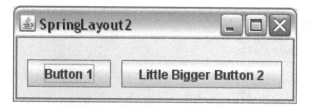

Figure 1-46. *Nice SpringLayout with the JFrame sized automatically*

SpringLayout is a very powerful layout to mimic many complex layouts. The following snippet of code has some more examples. The comments explain what it is supposed to do.

```
// Place a JButton b1 horizontally centered at the top of the content pane, you
// would set its constraints as below. Replace HORIZONTAL_CENTER with
// VERTICAL_CENTER to center the JButton vertically
springLayout.putConstraint(SpringLayout.HORIZONTAL_CENTER, north, 0,
                       SpringLayout.HORIZONTAL_CENTER,
                       contentPane);

// You can set the width of two JButtons, b1 and b2, to be the same by
// assigning the maximum width to the both of them. Assuming that you have
// already added b1 and b2 JButtons to the container
SpringLayout.Constraints b1c = springLayout.getConstraints(b1);
SpringLayout.Constraints b2c = springLayout.getConstraints(b2);

// Get a spring that represents the maximum of the width of b1 and b2,
// and set that spring as width for both b1 and b2
Spring maxWidth = Spring.max(b1c.getWidth(), b2c.getWidth());
b1c.setWidth(maxWidth);
b2c.setWidth(maxWidth);
```

GroupLayout

The GroupLayout is in the javax.swing package. It is meant to be used by GUI builders. However, it is easy enough to be hand-coded as well.

A GroupLayout uses the concept of a group. A group consists of elements. An element of a group may be a component, a gap, or another group. You can think of a gap as an invisible area between two components.

You must understand the concept of groups before using a GroupLayout. There are two types of groups:

- Sequential group
- Parallel group

When the elements in a group are placed in series, one after another, it is called a *sequential group*. When the elements in a group are placed in parallel, it is called a *parallel group*. A parallel group aligns its elements in one of the four ways—baseline, centered, leading, and trailing. In a GroupLayout, you need to define the layout for each component twice—once along the horizontal axis and once along the vertical axis. That is, you need to specify separately how all components form a group horizontally and vertically. Let's look at some examples of groups. Figure 1-47 shows a group of two components.

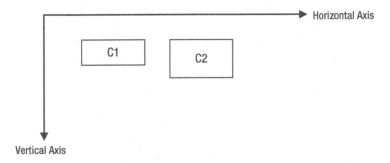

Figure 1-47. *Two components, C1 and C2, form a sequential group along the horizontal axis and a parallel group along the vertical axis*

In Figure 1-47, the two axes have been shown only for discussion purpose and they are not part of the layout. Components are placed one after another (left to right), forming a sequential group along the horizontal axis. They form a parallel group along the vertical axis. Along the vertical axis, in the parallel group, the two components are aligned along their top edges. If you have a problem visualizing the sequential and parallel groups along the horizontal and vertical axes, you can redraw Figure 1-47 as Figure 1-48. The two dashed arrows in the horizontal direction (left to right) represent C1 and C2 when you visualize their grouping in the horizontal direction. You can see that two arrows are in series and therefore C1 and C2 form a sequential group along the horizontal axis. The two dashed arrows in the vertical direction (top to bottom placed left of the component C1) represent C1 and C2 when you visualize them along the vertical axis. You can see that these two arrows are not in series. Rather, they are in parallel. Therefore, C1 and C2 form a parallel group along the vertical axis. You need to figure out the alignment for a parallel group. In this case, C1 and C2 are aligned along their top edges, which is called *leading alignment* in the GroupLayout terminology.

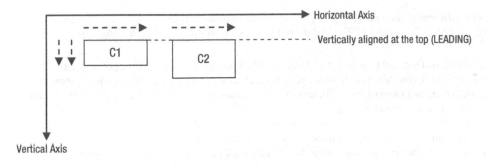

Figure 1-48. *Groupings for components C1 and C2*

What are the other possible alignments for C1 and C2? There are four possible alignments in a parallel group: baseline, centered, leading, and trailing. If the parallel group occurs along the vertical axis, all four types of alignment are possible. If the parallel group occurs along the horizontal axis, only three alignments (centered, leading, and trailing) are possible. Along the vertical axis, leading is the same as top edge, trailing is the same as bottom edge. Along the horizontal axis, leading is left edge if the component orientation is LEFT_TO_RIGHT, and it is right edge if the component orientation is RIGHT_TO_LEFT. Figure 1-49 and Figure 1-50 show the possible alignments along the vertical and horizontal axes. The alignment is shown by dashed lines. Note that along the vertical axis, the alignment line is horizontal and along horizontal axis, it is vertical. The four constants in the GroupLayout.Alignment enum, LEADING, TRAILING, CENTER, and BASELINE, are used to represent the four alignment types.

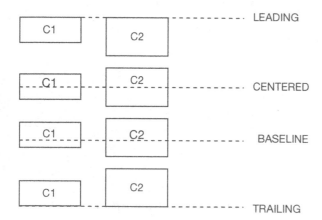

Figure 1-49. *The four possible alignments in a parallel group along the vertical axis in a group*

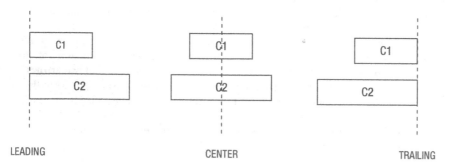

Figure 1-50. *The three possible alignments in a parallel group along the horizontal axis in a group for component orientation of LEFT_TO_RIGHT. For RIGHT_TO_LEFT orientation, LEADING and TRAILING will swap edges*

How do you create sequential and parallel groups for a GroupLayout? The GroupLayout class contains three inner classes: Group, SequentialGroup, and ParallelGroup. Group is an abstract class and the other two classes are inherited from the Group class. You do not have to create an object of these classes directly. Rather, you use the factory methods of the GroupLayout class to create their objects.

The GroupLayout class provides two separate methods to create groups: createSequentialGroup()and createParallelGroup(). It is obvious from the name of these methods the kind of groups they create. Note that you need to specify the alignment for a parallel group. The createParallelGroup() method is overloaded. The version with no arguments defaults the alignment to LEADING. Another version lets you specify the alignment. Once you have a group object, you can add components, gaps, and groups to it using its addComponent(), addGap(), and addGroup() methods, respectively.

How do you use the GroupLayout manager? Here are the steps you need to follow to use a GroupLayout. Assume that you have to place two buttons in a JFrame, as shown in Figure 1-51.

Figure 1-51. *The simplest GroupLayout in which two buttons are placed side by side*

Assume that the JFrame is named frame and the two JButtons are named b1 and b2. First, you need to create an object of the GroupLayout class. It contains only one constructor that takes the container reference as an argument. This means that you need to get the reference to the container for which you want to create the GroupLayout, before you can create an object of the GroupLayout class.

```
// Get the reference of the container
Container contentPane = frame.getContentPane();

// Create a GroupLayout object
GroupLayout groupLayout = new GroupLayout(contentPane);

// Set the layout manager for the container
contentPane.setLayout(groupLayout);
```

Second, you need to create the group of components along horizontal axis (called horizontal group) and set that group to the GroupLayout using the setHorizontalGroup() method. Note that a group can be sequential or parallel along any axis—horizontal and vertical. In your case, two buttons, b1 and b2, form a sequential group along the horizontal axis.

```
// Create a sequential group
GroupLayout.SequentialGroup sGroup = groupLayout.createSequentialGroup();

// Add two buttons to the group
sGroup.addComponent(b1);
sGroup.addComponent(b2);

// Set the horizontal group for the GroupLayout
groupLayout.setHorizontalGroup(sGroup);
```

You can combine all steps into one, like so:

```
groupLayout.setHorizontalGroup(groupLayout.createSequentialGroup()
                                        .addComponent(b1)
                                        .addComponent(b2));
```

Finally, create the group of components along the vertical axis (called vertical group) and set that group to the GroupLayout using the setVerticalGroup() method. Two buttons form a parallel group along vertical axis. You can accomplish this as follows:

```
groupLayout.setVerticalGroup(
        groupLayout.createParallelGroup(GroupLayout.Alignment.BASELINE)
                .addComponent(b1)
                .addComponent(b2));
```

■ **Tip** In a GroupLayout, you do not add a component to the container using its add() method. Rather, you add a component to a group along the horizontal and vertical axes and add the group to the GroupLayout using the setHorizontalGroup() and setVerticalGroup() methods.

Listing 1-19 demonstrates how to use a GroupLayout to display two buttons side by side in a JFrame. When you run the program, the JFrame is displayed as shown in Figure 1-51. I will discuss more complex examples shortly.

Listing 1-19. The Simplest GroupLayout

```java
// SimplestGroupLayout.java
package com.jdojo.swing;

import java.awt.Container;
import javax.swing.JFrame;
import javax.swing.JButton;
import javax.swing.GroupLayout;

public class SimplestGroupLayout {
        public static void main(String[] args) {
                JFrame frame = new JFrame("Simplest GroupLayout");
                frame.setDefaultCloseOperation(JFrame.EXIT_ON_CLOSE);
                Container contentPane = frame.getContentPane();

                // Create an object of the GroupLayout class for contentPane
                GroupLayout groupLayout = new GroupLayout(contentPane);

                // Set the content pane's layout to a GroupLayout
                contentPane.setLayout(groupLayout);

                // Add two JButtons to the content pane
                JButton b1 = new JButton("Button 1");
                JButton b2 = new JButton("Little Bigger Button 2");

                groupLayout.setHorizontalGroup(
                        groupLayout.createSequentialGroup()
                        .addComponent(b1)
                        .addComponent(b2));
```

```
            groupLayout.setVerticalGroup(
                    groupLayout.createParallelGroup(GroupLayout.Alignment.BASELINE)
                            .addComponent(b1)
                            .addComponent(b2));

            frame.pack();
            frame.setVisible(true);
    }
}
```

A GroupLayout has two more features that are worth discussing:

- It lets you add a gap between two components.

- It lets you specify the resizing behaviors for the components, gaps, and groups.

You can think of a gap as an invisible component. There are two types of gaps: the gap between two components, and the gap between a component and the container. You can add a gap between two components using the addGap() method of the Group class. You can add a rigid gap as well as a flexible gap (as a spring). A rigid gap is fixed in size. A flexible gap has a minimum, a preferred, and a maximum size, and it acts like a spring when the container is resized. To add a rigid gap of 10 pixels between b1 and b2 in your previous example, you set up your horizontal group like so:

```
groupLayout.setHorizontalGroup(groupLayout.createSequentialGroup()
                                .addComponent(b1)
                                .addGap(10)
                                .addComponent(b2));
```

There are three ways to add gaps between two components. They are based on the gap size and their ability to resize.

- You can add a rigid gap between two components using the addGap(int gapSize).

- You can add a flexible (spring-like) gap between two components, which has a minimum, a preferred, and a maximum size, using the addGap(int min, int pref, int max) method. To add a flexible gap with 5, 10, and 50 as the minimum, preferred, and maximum size respectively, you set up your horizontal group like so:

```
groupLayout.setHorizontalGroup(groupLayout.createSequentialGroup()
                                .addComponent(b1)
                                .addGap(5, 10, 50)
                                .addComponent(b2));
```

- You can add a preferred gap between two components. In this case, you have the option to specify the size of the gap or let the layout manager compute it for you. However, you must specify the way in which these two components are related as far as this gap is concerned. There are three kinds of such gaps: RELATED, UNRELATED, and INDENT. If you are adding a preferred gap between a label and its corresponding field, you add a RELATED gap between them. For example, if you have a login form, and you want to add a preferred gap between "User ID:" and the text field to enter the user id, you add a RELATED gap between them. You use an UNRELATED gap when two components belong to different groups. When you are adding a gap just to indent a component, you add an INDENT gap. Three types of gaps are represented by three constants,

RELATED, UNRELATED and INDENT, defined in the LayoutStyle.ComponentPlacement enum. Use the addPreferredGap() method to add a preferred gap. The following snippet of code adds a RELATED preferred gap between b1 and b2:

```
groupLayout.setHorizontalGroup(
groupLayout.createSequentialGroup()
        .addComponent(b1)
        .addPreferredGap(LayoutStyle.ComponentPlacement.RELATED)
        .addComponent(b2));
```

You need to use the addContainerGap() method of the GroupLayout.SequentialGroup class to add a gap between edges of a component and a container. The method is overloaded. It also lets you specify the preferred and maximum size of the gap.

Setting hard-coded gaps may create problems when you run your application on different platforms. This is the reason that the GroupLayout has two methods that let you specify that you want the GroupLayout to compute the preferred gaps depending on the platform your application is running on. To let the GroupLayout compute and set the gaps between two components, you need to call its setAutoCreateGaps(true) method. To let it compute and set gaps between components and the container edges, you need to call its setAutoCreateContainerGaps(true) method. By default, the auto-computing of gaps is disabled. Replace the statement

```
// Create an object of the GroupLayout class
GroupLayout groupLayout = new GroupLayout(contentPane);
```

in Listing 1-19 with the following statements

```
// Create an object of the GroupLayout class and setup gaps
GroupLayout groupLayout = new GroupLayout(contentPane);
groupLayout.setAutoCreateGaps(true);
groupLayout.setAutoCreateContainerGaps(true);
```

Now, the JFrame will look as shown in Figure 1-52. You can see that the layout manager added the necessary gaps for you.

Figure 1-52. *The simplest GroupLayout with auto gaps enabled*

A GroupLayout respects the minimum, preferred, and maximum size of a component. When the container is resized, the layout manager asks the components for their sizes and resizes them accordingly. However, you can override this behavior by using the addComponent(Component c, int min, int pref, int max) method that lets you specify the minimum, preferred, and maximum size of a component. You need to understand the meaning of the two constants defined in the GroupLayout class. They are DEFAULT_SIZE and PREFERRED_SIZE. They can be used for the min, pref, and max arguments in the addComponent() method. DEFAULT_SIZE means that the layout manager should ask the component for this size type and use it. PREFERRED_SIZE means that the manager should use the component's preferred size. For example, if you want the JButton b2 in your previous example to expand (by default, a JButton has the same min, pref, and max size), you add it to the horizontal group like so:

```
groupLayout.setHorizontalGroup(groupLayout.createSequentialGroup()
          .addComponent(b1)
          .addComponent(b2,
                    GroupLayout.PREFERRED_SIZE,
                    GroupLayout.PREFERRED_SIZE,
                    Integer.MAX_VALUE));
```

By specifying PREFERRED_SIZE as the minimum size and preferred size, you are telling the layout manager that b2 should not be shortened below its preferred size. Integer.MAX_VALUE as its maximum size tells the layout manager that it can expand it infinitely. To make a component not resizable, you can use all three of its sizes the same as GroupLayout.PREFERRED_SIZE.

You can nest groups in a GroupLayout. Let's look at a layout of four buttons named b1, b2, b3, and b4 as shown in Figure 1-53.

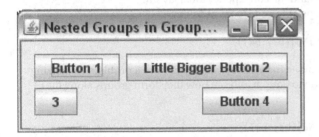

Figure 1-53. *Nested groups in GroupLayout*

Let's look at components layout along horizontal axis. You can see two parallel groups (b1, b3) and (b2, b4) and these two groups are placed sequentially. Let's use PG and SG to represent parallel and sequential groups, respectively, in the pseudo code. Note that in PG(b1, b3), the components are aligned along the LEADING edge (here, the left edge) and in PG(b2, b4), they are aligned along the TRAILING edge (here, the right edge). Let's insert the alignment to your pseudo code and the groups will look like this: PG[LEADING](b1, b3) and PG[TRAILING](b2, b4). I have made up this syntax for the purpose of discussing this example. You will see the Java code shortly. If you have a problem visualizing the arrangement, you can refer to Figure 1-54, where each button has been shown by an arrow along the horizontal axis.

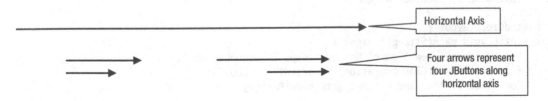

Figure 1-54. *Four buttons represented by four arrows along horizontal axis*

The arrows are aligned the same as the buttons. You can observe that arrows for b1 and b3 are parallel, and that the arrows for b2 and b4 are parallel. If you visualize the two parallel groups, you can observe that these two groups make up one sequential group along the horizontal axis. To help you visualize this final arrangement, the arrow arrangements have been refined in Figure 1-55.

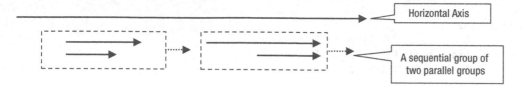

Figure 1-55. *Four buttons represented by four arrows along horizontal axis*

Each parallel group is shown inside a dashed rectangle. The arrow coming out of the dashed rectangle shows that these groups are sequential along the horizontal axis. It may take a while to understand these parallel and sequential arrangements of components along an axis. Once you get it, it will be quite easy to use a GroupLayout in a complex scenario. Most likely, you will be using a GUI builder tool to arrange your components, and you won't care about the complexity of the groups. However, it always helps to understand the concept behind a layout.

To finalize this discussion along the horizontal axis, the pseudo code looks as follows:

```
Horizontal Group = SG(PG[LEADING](b1, b3), PG[TRAILING](b2, b4))
```

Similarly, you can visualize the grouping arrangements along the vertical axis. If you have a problem visualizing this, you can draw all four buttons as arrows pointing from top to bottom and see how they form groups along the vertical axis. Here is the vertical groupings arrangement:

```
Vertical Group = SG(PG[BASELINE](b1, b2), PG[BASELINE](b3, b4))
```

Now, it is easy to translate the pseudo code into Java code, as shown in Listing 1-20.

Listing 1-20. Nested Groups in GroupLayout

```java
// NestedGroupLayout.java
package com.jdojo.swing;

import java.awt.Container;
import javax.swing.JFrame;
import javax.swing.JButton;
import javax.swing.GroupLayout;
import static javax.swing.GroupLayout.Alignment.*;

public class NestedGroupLayout {
        public static void main(String[] args) {
                JFrame frame = new JFrame("Nested Groups in GroupLayout");
                frame.setDefaultCloseOperation(JFrame.EXIT_ON_CLOSE);
                Container contentPane = frame.getContentPane();

                // Set the content's pane layout to GroupLayout
                GroupLayout groupLayout = new GroupLayout(contentPane);
                groupLayout.setAutoCreateGaps(true);
                groupLayout.setAutoCreateContainerGaps(true);
                contentPane.setLayout(groupLayout);
```

```
// Add four JButtons to the content pane
JButton b1 = new JButton("Button 1");
JButton b2 = new JButton("Little Bigger Button 2");
JButton b3 = new JButton("3");
JButton b4 = new JButton("Button 4");

groupLayout.setHorizontalGroup(
        groupLayout.createSequentialGroup()
        .addGroup(groupLayout.createParallelGroup(LEADING)
                .addComponent(b1)
                .addComponent(b3))
        .addGroup(groupLayout.createParallelGroup(TRAILING)
                .addComponent(b2)
                .addComponent(b4))
);

groupLayout.setVerticalGroup(
        groupLayout.createSequentialGroup()
        .addGroup(groupLayout.createParallelGroup(BASELINE)
                .addComponent(b1)
                .addComponent(b2))
        .addGroup(groupLayout.createParallelGroup(BASELINE)
                .addComponent(b3)
                .addComponent(b4))
);

frame.pack();
frame.setVisible(true);
    }
}
```

How do you make the sizes of two components the same? Let's try to make b1 and b3 the same size. You need to consider two things when making a component resizable. First, you need to consider the resizable behavior of the group. Second, you need to consider the resizable behavior of the components inside the group. The size of a parallel group is the size of the largest element. If you consider PG{LEADING}(b1, b3), the width of this group would be the size of b1 because b1 is the largest component in this group. By default, a JButton has a fixed size. To make b3 stretch to the size of the group (which is the size of b1), you must add it to the group specifying that it can expand as addComponent(b3, GroupLayout.DEFAULT_SIZE, GroupLayout.DEFAULT_SIZE, Integer.MAX_VALUE). This will force b3 to stretch to the same size as its group, which in turn is the same as the b1 width. If two components are not in the same parallel group, to make them the same size, you can use the linkSize() method of the GroupLayout class. When you use the linkSize() method to make components the same size, the components become non-resizable irrespective of their minimum, preferred, and maximum size.

```
// Make b1, b2, b3 and b4 the same size
groupLayout.linkSize(b1, b2, b3, b4);

// Make b1 and b3 the same size horizontally
groupLayout.linkSize(SwingConstants.HORIZONTAL, new Component[]{b1, b3});
```

You can also make a group resizable when you create a parallel group using the createParallelGroup(GroupLayout.Alignment a, boolean resizable) method. If you place resizable components in a resizable group, the group will resize when you resize the container, which in turn makes the components resize.

The null Layout Manager

By now, you may have realized that a layout manager handles the positioning and resizing of components within a container. If a container is resized, the layout manager will take care of repositioning and resizing of the components within it. If you do not want to have a layout manager, you lose this benefit and you are responsible for positioning and resizing of all components within a container. It is simple to tell a container that you do not want a layout manager. Just set the layout manager to null, like so:

```
// Do not use a layout manager for myContainer
myContainer.setLayout(null);
```

You can set the layout manager of a JFrame's content pane to null, like so:

```
JFrame frame = new JFrame("No Layout Manager Frame");
Container contentPane = frame.getContentPane();
contentPane.setLayout(null);
```

The phrase "null layout manager" simply means that there is no layout manager. It is also known as absolute positioning. Note that your program may run on different platforms. The size of components may differ when they are displayed on different platforms, and your null layout manager cannot account for this inconsistency. When you are using a null layout manager, make sure that your component's size is big enough to be displayed properly on all platforms.

Listing 1-21 uses a null layout manager for the content pane of a JFrame. It adds two buttons to it. It also sets the position and size of buttons and JFrame using the setBounds() method. Figure 1-56 shows the resulting JFrame.

Listing 1-21. Using a null Layout Manager

```
// NullLayout.java
package com.jdojo.swing;

import javax.swing.JFrame;
import java.awt.Container;
import javax.swing.JButton;

public class NullLayout  {
        public static void main(String[] args) {
                JFrame frame = new JFrame("Null Layout Manager");
                frame.setDefaultCloseOperation(JFrame.EXIT_ON_CLOSE);
                Container contentPane = frame.getContentPane();
                contentPane.setLayout(null);

                JButton b1 = new JButton("Small Button 1");
                JButton b2 = new JButton("Big Big Big Button 2...");
                contentPane.add(b1);
                contentPane.add(b2);

                // Must set (x, y) and (width, height) of components
                b1.setBounds(10, 10, 100, 20);
                b2.setBounds(120, 10, 150, 20);
```

```
        // Must set the size of JFrame, because it uses a null layout.
        // Now, you cannot use the pack() method to compute its size.
        frame.setBounds(0, 0, 350, 100);
        frame.setVisible(true);
    }
}
```

Figure 1-56. *A JFrame using a null layout manager*

Note that the labels for buttons are not displayed fully. This is one of the problems that you will face when using a null layout manager. If you try to resize the JFrame at runtime, you will notice that the buttons are not resized automatically, as they would have been if you had used a layout manager. A layout manager computes the size of a JButton based on the platform, its text, and font whereas with a null layout manager you are supposed to compute (most of the time, you just guess) the button's size considering all these factors. It is not good practice in Java to use a null layout manager, except when you are prototyping or learning the null layout manager.

Creating a Reusable JFrame

In previous sections, you created a JFrame by instantiating the JFrame class and you used the main() method of the class to write the code to build the GUI. The JFrames in your examples were not reusable. So far, you were fine because the Swing programs were simple and their sole purpose was to display some components in a JFrame. As you start writing more complex Swing programs, this way of programming is not going to work well. For example, suppose you want to make a JButton in a JFrame invisible or disabled after the JFrame is displayed. Since you have been declaring all your JButtons as local variables inside the main() method, you will not have access to their references once the main() method has finished executing. To make your JFrame reusable and keep the references of the components added to the JFrame handy, so you can refer to them later, you need to change the approach of creating a JFrame.

Here is your new approach to creating a JFrame. You create your own class, inheriting it from the JFrame class as shown:

```
public class CustomFrame extends JFrame {
        // Code for CustomFrame goes here
}
```

All your components are declared as instance variables in your custom class, as shown:

```
public class CustomFrame extends JFrame {
        // Declare all components in the JFrame as instance variables
        JButton okButton - new JButton("OK");
        JButton cancelButton = new JButton("Cancel");
}
```

You have an `initFrame()` method to add components to the `JFrame`'s content pane. You call this method from the constructor of your custom `JFrame`. The method `initFrame()` is not required by Java. It is just your convention for writing code for your Swing applications. To display your `JFrame`, you instantiate your class and make it visible. This approach has similar code, arranged differently, so you can write some more serious Swing programs. Listing 1-22 accomplishes the same thing as the code in Listing 1-19.

Listing 1-22. Creating a Cutom JFrame

```java
// CustomFrame.java
package com.jdojo.swing;

import javax.swing.JFrame;
import javax.swing.GroupLayout.Alignment;
import javax.swing.JButton;
import java.awt.Container;
import javax.swing.GroupLayout;

public class CustomFrame extends JFrame {
        // Declare all components as instance variables
        JButton b1 = new JButton("Button 1");
        JButton b2 = new JButton("Little Bigger Button 2");

        public CustomFrame(String title) {
                super(title);
                initFrame();
        }

        // Initialize the frame and add components to it.
        private void initFrame() {
                this.setDefaultCloseOperation(JFrame.EXIT_ON_CLOSE);
                Container contentPane = this.getContentPane();
                GroupLayout groupLayout = new GroupLayout(contentPane);
                contentPane.setLayout(groupLayout);

                groupLayout.setHorizontalGroup(
                        groupLayout.createSequentialGroup()
                                .addComponent(b1)
                                .addComponent(b2)
                );

                groupLayout.setVerticalGroup(
                        groupLayout.createParallelGroup(Alignment.BASELINE)
                                .addComponent(b1)
                                .addComponent(b2)
                );
        }
```

```
        // Display the CustomFrame
        public static void main(String[] args) {
                CustomFrame frame = new CustomFrame("Custom Frame");
                frame.pack();
                frame.setVisible(true);
        }
}
```

Event Handling

What is an event? The literal meaning of an event is

"An occurrence of something at a specific point in time."

The meaning of an event in a Swing application is similar. An event in Swing is an action taken by a user at a particular point in time. For example, pressing a button, pressing a key down/up on the keyboard, and moving the mouse over a component are events in a Swing application. Sometimes the occurrence of an event in Swing (or any GUI-based application) is also known as "triggering an event" or "firing an event." When you say that a clicked event has occurred on a button, you mean that the button has been pressed using the mouse, the spacebar, or by any other means your application allows you to press a button. Sometimes you can use the phrase "clicked event has been triggered or fired on a button" to mean the same that the button has been pressed.

When an event occurs, you want to respond to the event. Taking an action in a program is nothing but executing a piece of code. Taking an action in response to the occurrence of an event is called *event handling*. The piece of code that is executed when an event occurs is called an *event handler*. Sometimes an event handler is also called an *event listener*.

How you write an event handler depends on the type of event and the component that generates the event. Sometimes the event handler is built into a Swing component, and sometimes you need to write the event handler yourself. For example, when you press a JButton, you need to write the event handler yourself. However, when you press a letter key on the keyboard when the focus is in a text field, the corresponding letter is typed in the text field because of the key pressed event has a default event handler that is supplied by Swing.

There are three participants in an event:

- The source of the event

- The event

- The event handler (or the event listener)

The source of an event is the component that generates the event. For example, when you press a JButton, the clicked event occurs on that JButton. In this case, the JButton is the source of the clicked event.

An event represents the action that takes place on the source component. An event in Swing is represented by an object that encapsulates the details about the event such as the source of the event, when the event occurred, what kind of event occurred, etc. What is the class of the object that represents an event? It depends on the type of the event that occurs. There is a class for every type of event. For example, an object of the ActionEvent class in the java.awt.event package represents a clicked event for a JButton.

I will not discuss all types of events in this chapter. I will list the important events for a component when I discuss components in Chapter 2. This section will explain how to handle any type of event in a Swing application.

An event handler is the piece of code that is executed when an event occurs. Like an event, an event handler is also represented by an object, which encapsulates the event handling code. An object of what class represents an event handler? It depends on the type of event that the event handler is supposed to handle. An event handler is also known as an event listener because it listens for the event to occur in the source component. I will use the phrases "event handler" and "event listener" interchangeably in this chapter. Typically, an event listener is an object that implements a specific interface. The specific interface an event listener has to implement depends on the type of event it will listen for. For example, if you are interested in listening for a clicked event of a JButton (to rephrase, if you are interested in handling the clicked event of a JButton), you need an object of a class that implements the ActionListener interface, which is in the java.awt.event package.

Looking at the descriptions of the three participants of an event handling, it seems you need to write a lot of code to handle an event. Not really. Event handling is easier than it seems. I will list the steps to handle an event, followed by an example of how to handle the clicked event of a JButton. Here are the steps to handle an event. These steps apply to handle any kind of event on any Swing component.

- Identify the component for which you want to handle the event. Assume that you have named the component as sourceComponent. So your event source is sourceComponent.

- Identify the event that you want to handle for the source component. Assume that you are interested in handling Xxx event. Here Xxx is an event name that you will have to replace by an event name that exists for the source component. Recall that an event is represented by an object. The Java naming convention for event classes comes to your rescue in identifying the name of the class whose object represents Xxx event. The class whose object represents Xxx event is named XxxEvent. Usually the event classes are in the java.awt.event and javax.swing.event package.

- It is time to write an event listener for the Xxx event. Recall that an event listener is nothing but an object of a class that implements a specific interface. How do you know what specific interface you need to implement in your event listener class? Here again, the Java naming convention comes to your rescue. For Xxx event, there is an XxxListener interface that you need to implement in your event listener class. Usually the event listener interfaces are in the java.awt.event and javax.swing.event package. The XxxListener interface will have one or more methods. All methods for XxxListener take an argument of type XxxEvent because these methods are meant to handle an XxxEvent. For example, suppose you have an XxxListener interface that has a method named aMethod() as

  ```
  public interface XxxListener {
      void aMethod(XxxEvent event);
  }
  ```

- Your event listener class will look as follows. Note that you will be creating this class.

  ```
  public class MyXxxEventListener implements XxxListener {
      public void aMethod(XxxEvent event) {
          // Your event handler code goes here
      }
  }
  ```

- You are almost done. You have identified the event source, the event you are interested in, and the event listener. There is only one thing missing. You need to let the event source know that your event listener is interested in listening to its Xxx event. This is also known as registering an event listener with the event source. You register an object of your event listener class with the event source. In your case, you will create an object of the MyXxxEventListener class.

  ```
  MyXxxEventListener myXxxListener = new MyXxxEventListener();
  ```

- How do you register an event listener with the event source? Here again, the Java naming convention comes in handy. If a component (an event source) supports an Xxx event, it will have two methods, addXxxListener(XxxListener l) and removeXxxListener(XxxListener l).

When you are interested in listening for an Xxx event of a component, you call the addXxxListener() method, passing an event listener as an argument. When you do not want to listen for Xxx event of a component anymore, you call its removeXxxListener() method. To add your myXxxListener object as the Xxx event listener for sourceComponent, you write

```
sourceComponent.addXxxListener(myXxxListener);
```

That is all you need to do to handle an Xxx event. It may seem that you have to perform many steps to handle an event. However, that is not the case. You can always avoid writing a new event listener class, which implements the XxxListener interface by using an anonymous inner class, which implements the XxxListener interface. For example, you could have written the above pieces of code in two statements, like so:

```
// Create an event listener object using an anonymous inner class
XxxListener myXxxListener = new XxxListener() {
        public void aMethod(XxxEvent event) {
                // Your event handler code goes here
        }
};

// Add the event listener to the event source component
sourceComponent.addXxxListener(myXxxListener);
```

If the listener interface is a functional interface, you can use a lambda expression to create its instance. Your XxxListener is a functional interface because it contains only one abstract method. You can avoid creating the bulky anonymous class and rewrite the above code as follows:

```
// Add the event listener using a lambda expressions
sourceComponent.addXxxListener((XxxEvent event) -> {
        // Your event handler code goes here
});
```

I have discussed enough theories about handling events. It is time to look at an example. Add an event listener to a JButton, and then add a JButton with text Close to a JFrame. When the JButton is pressed, the JFrame is closed and the application exits. A JButton generates an Action event when it is pressed. Once you know the name of the event, which is Action in this case, you just need to replace Xxx in the previous generic example with the word Action. You will come to know the class and method names you need to use to handle the Action event of JButton. Table 1-6 compares the names of classes/interfaces/method used to handle Action event for a JButton to that of generic names I had used in the discussion.

Table 1-6. *A Comparison Between Generic Event Handlers With Action Event Handlers for a JButton*

Generic Event Xxx	Action Event for JButton	Comments
XxxEvent	ActionEvent	An object of ActionEvent class in java.awt.event package represents Action event for JButton.
XxxListener	ActionListener	An object of a class that implements ActionListener interface represents Action event handler for a JButton.
addXxxListener (XxxListener 1)	addActionListener (ActionListener 1)	The addActionListener() method of a JButton is used to add a listener for its Action event.
removeXxxListener (XxxListener 1)	removeActionListener (ActionListener 1)	The removeActionListener() method of JButton is used to remove a listener for its Action event.

The `ActionListener` interface is simple. It has one method called `actionPerformed()`. The interface declaration is as follows:

```
public interface ActionListener extends EventListener {
        void actionPerformed(ActionEvent event);
}
```

All event listener interfaces inherit from the `EventListener` interface, which is in the `java.util` package. The `EventListener` interface is a marker interface, and it does not have any methods. It just acts as the ancestor for all event listener interfaces. When a `JButton` is pressed, the `actionPerformed()` method of all its registered Action listeners is called.

Using a lambda expression, here is how you add an `Action` listener to a `JButton`:

```
// Add an ActionListener to closeButton
closeButton.addActionListener(e -> System.exit(0));
```

Listing 1-23 displays a `JFrame` that contains a `JButton`. It adds an `Action` listener to the `JButton`. The `Action` listener simply exits the application. Clicking the Close button in the `JFrame` will close the application.

Listing 1-23. A JFrame with a Close JButton With an Action

```
// SimplestEventHandlingFrame.java
package com.jdojo.swing;

import java.awt.FlowLayout;
import javax.swing.JFrame;
import javax.swing.JButton;

public class SimplestEventHandlingFrame extends JFrame {
        JButton closeButton = new JButton("Close");

        public SimplestEventHandlingFrame() {
                super("Simplest Event Handling JFrame");
                this.initFrame();
        }

        private void initFrame() {
                this.setDefaultCloseOperation(EXIT_ON_CLOSE);

                // Set a FlowLayout for the content pane
                this.setLayout(new FlowLayout());

                // Add the Close JButton to the content pane
                this.getContentPane().add(closeButton);

                // Add an ActionListener to closeButton
                closeButton.addActionListener(e -> System.exit(0));
        }
}
```

```java
    public static void main(String[] args) {
        SimplestEventHandlingFrame frame =
            new SimplestEventHandlingFrame();
        frame.pack();
        frame.setVisible(true);
    }
}
```

Let's have one more example of adding an Action listener to JButton. This time, add two buttons to a JFrame: a Close button and another to display the number of times it is clicked. Every time the second button is clicked, its text is updated to show the number of times it has been clicked. You need to use an instance variable to maintain the click count. Listing 1-24 contains the complete code. Figure 1-57 shows the JFrame when it is displayed and after the counter button has been clicked three times.

Listing 1-24. A JFrame With Two Buttons With Actions

```java
// JButtonClickedCounter.java
package com.jdojo.swing;

import javax.swing.JFrame;
import java.awt.FlowLayout;
import java.awt.event.ActionEvent;
import javax.swing.JButton;
import java.awt.event.ActionListener;

public class JButtonClickedCounter extends JFrame {
    int counter;
    JButton counterButton = new JButton("Clicked #0");
    JButton closeButton = new JButton("Close");

    public JButtonClickedCounter() {
        super("JButton Clicked Counter");
        this.initFrame();
    }

    private void initFrame() {
        this.setDefaultCloseOperation(EXIT_ON_CLOSE);

        // Set a FlowLayout for the content pane
        this.setLayout(new FlowLayout());

        // Add two JButtons to the content pane
        this.getContentPane().add(counterButton);
        this.getContentPane().add(closeButton);

        // Add an ActionListener to the counter JButton
        counterButton.addActionListener(new ActionListener() {
            public void actionPerformed(ActionEvent event) {
                // Increment the counter and set the JButton text
                counter++;
                counterButton.setText("Clicked #" + counter);
            }
        });
```

```
                    // Add an ActionListener to closeButton
                    closeButton.addActionListener(new ActionListener() {
                            public void actionPerformed(ActionEvent event) {
                                    // Exit the application, when this button is pressed
                                    System.exit(0);
                            }
                    });
            }

    public static void main(String[] args) {
            JButtonClickedCounter frame = new JButtonClickedCounter();
            frame.pack();
            frame.setVisible(true);
    }
}
```

Figure 1-57. *A JFrame when it is displayed and after the counter JButton is clicked three times*

Figure 1-58 shows the class diagram for the classes and interfaces involved in handling the Action event.

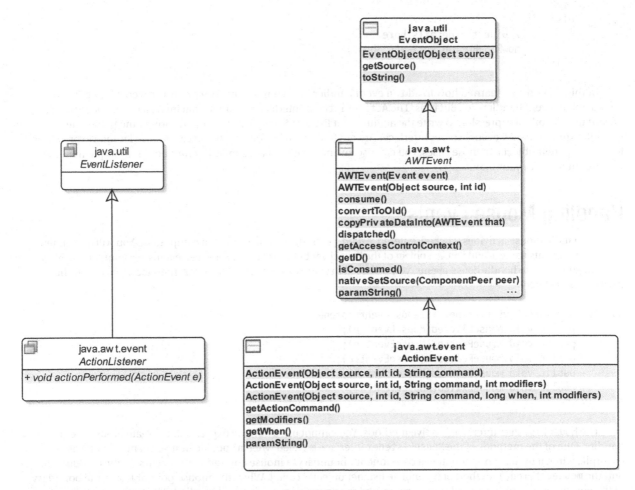

Figure 1-58. *A class diagram for classes and interfaces realted to Action Event*

Note that you do not create an object of the ActionEvent class. The JButton, when pressed, creates an object of the ActionEvent class, and passes it to the actionPerformed() method of your event handler object. The getActionCommand() method of the ActionEvent returns, by default, the text of the JButton. You can explicitly set the action command text for a JButton using its setActionCommand() method. The getModifiers() returns the state of the modifier keys such as Shift, Ctrl, Alt held down during the action event. A modifier key is a key on the keyboard that is meaningful only when used in combination with other keys. The paramString() method returns a string describing the action event. It is usually used for debugging purposes.

One of the uses of the getActionCommand() method is to take some action, depending on the text displayed on the JButton. For example, you may have a JButton that is used to show or hide some details on the screen. Suppose you want to display the text of a JButton as Show or Hide. You can write its Action listener as follows:

```
JButton showHideButton = new JButton("Hide");
showHideButton.addActionListener(e -> {
        if (e.getActionCommand().equals("Show")) {
                // Show the details here...
                showHideButton.setText("Hide");
        }
```

```
        else {
                // Hide the details here...
                showHideButton.setText("Show");
        }});
```

In this section, you learned how to add an event handler for a component. The examples were simple. They added action event handlers to JButtons. The ActionListener interface is a functional interface and you took advantage of lambda expression to write the action event listener. Swing was developed a long time before the lambda expressions. All event listener interfaces are not functional interfaces, so you cannot use lambda expressions for creating their objects. In those cases, you can use an anonymous class, a member inner class, or implement the listener interface in your main class.

Handling Mouse Events

You can handle mouse activities (clicked, entered, exited, pressed, and released) on a component. You will experiment with mouse events using a JButton. An object of the MouseEvent class represents a Mouse event on a component. Now, you can guess that to handle Mouse events, you will need to work with the MouseListener interface. Here is how the interface is declared:

```
public interface MouseListener extends EventListener {
        public void mouseClicked(MouseEvent e);
        public void mousePressed(MouseEvent e);
        public void mouseReleased(MouseEvent e);
        public void mouseEntered(MouseEvent e);
        public void mouseExited(MouseEvent e);
}
```

The MouseListener interface has five methods. You cannot use a lambda expression to create mouse event handler. One of the methods of the MouseListener interface is called when a specific mouse event occurs. For example, when a mouse pointer enters a component's boundary, a mouse entered event occurs on the component, and the mouseEntered() method of the mouse listener object is called. When the mouse pointer leaves the boundary of the component, a mouse exited event occurs, and the mouseExited() method is called. The names of other methods are self-explanatory.

The MouseEvent class has many methods that provide the details about a mouse event:

- The getClickCount() method returns the number of clicks a mouse made.

- The getX() and getY() methods return the x and y positions of the mouse with respect to the component when the event occurs.

- The getXOnScreen() and getYOnScreen() methods return the absolute x and y positions of the mouse at the time the event occurs.

Suppose you are interested in handling only two kinds of mouse events for a JButton: the mouse entered and mouse exited events. The text of the JButton changes to describe the event. The mouse event handler code is as follows:

```
mouseButton.addMouseListener(new MouseListener() {
        @Override
        public void mouseClicked(MouseEvent e) {
                // Nothing to handle
        }
```

```java
    @Override
    public void mousePressed(MouseEvent e) {
            // Nothing to handle

    }

    @Override
    public void mouseReleased(MouseEvent e) {
            // Nothing to handle
    }

    @Override
    public void mouseEntered(MouseEvent e) {
            mouseButton.setText("Mouse has entered!");
    }

    @Override
    public void mouseExited(MouseEvent e) {
            mouseButton.setText("Mouse has exited!");
    }
});
```

In this code, you provided an implementation for all five methods of the MouseListener interface even though you were interested in handling only two kinds of mouse events. You left the body of three methods empty.

Listing 1-25 demonstrates the mouse entered and exited event for a JButton. When the JFrame is displayed, try moving your mouse in and out of the boundary of the JButton to change its text to indicate the appropriate mouse event.

Listing 1-25. Handling Mouse Events

```java
// HandlingMouseEvent.java
package com.jdojo.swing;

import java.awt.FlowLayout;
import javax.swing.JFrame;
import javax.swing.JButton;
import java.awt.event.MouseListener;
import java.awt.event.MouseEvent;

public class HandlingMouseEvent extends JFrame {
        JButton mouseButton = new JButton("No Mouse Movement Yet!");

        public HandlingMouseEvent() {
                super("Handling Mouse Event");
                this.initFrame();
        }

        private void initFrame() {
                this.setDefaultCloseOperation(EXIT_ON_CLOSE);
                this.setLayout(new FlowLayout());
                this.getContentPane().add(mouseButton);
```

```
                // Add a MouseListener to the JButton
                mouseButton.addMouseListener(new MouseListener() {
                        @Override
                        public void mouseClicked(MouseEvent e) {
                        }

                        @Override
                        public void mousePressed(MouseEvent e) {
                        }

                        @Override
                        public void mouseReleased(MouseEvent e) {
                        }

                        @Override
                        public void mouseEntered(MouseEvent e) {
                                mouseButton.setText("Mouse has entered!");
                        }

                        @Override
                        public void mouseExited(MouseEvent e) {
                                mouseButton.setText("Mouse has exited!");
                        }
                });
        }

        public static void main(String[] args) {
                HandlingMouseEvent frame = new HandlingMouseEvent();
                frame.pack();
                frame.setVisible(true);
        }
}
```

Do you always have to provide implementation for all event-handling methods of an event listener interface, even though you are not interested in all of them? No, you do not. Swing designers thought of this inconvenience and devised a way to avoid this. Swing includes a convenience class for some XxxListener interfaces. The class is named XxxAdapter. I will call them *adapter classes*. An XxxAdapter class is declared abstract and it implements the XxxListener interface. The XxxAdapter class provides empty implementation for all methods in the XxxListener interface. The following snippet of code shows the relationship between an XxxListener interface having two methods m1() and m2() and its corresponding XxxAdapter class.

```
public interface XxxListener {
        public void m1();
        public void m2();
}

public abstract class XxxAdapter implements XxxListener {
        @Override
        public void m1() {
                // No implementation provided here
        }
```

```
        @Override
        public void m2() {
                // No implementation provided here
        }
}
```

Not all event listener interfaces have corresponding adapter classes. The event listener interface, which declares more than one method, has a corresponding adapter class. For example, you have an adapter class for the MouseListener interface that is called MouseAdapter. What good will the MouseAdapter do for you? It can save you a few lines of unnecessary code. If you only want to handle a few of the mouse events, you can create an anonymous inner class (or regular inner class) that inherits from the adapter class and overrides the only methods that are of interest to you. The following snippet of code rewrites the event handler used in Listing 1-28 using the MouseAdapter class:

```
mouseButton.addMouseListener(new MouseAdapter() {
        @Override
        public void mouseEntered(MouseEvent e) {
                mouseButton.setText("Mouse has entered!");
        }

        @Override
        public void mouseExited(MouseEvent e) {
                mouseButton.setText("Mouse has exited!");
        }
});
```

You may notice that you did not have to worry about three other methods of the MouseListener interface because the MouseAdapter class provided empty implementation for you.

There is no adapter class named ActionAdapter for the ActionListener interface. Can you guess why there is no ActionAdapter class? Since the ActionListener interface has only one method in it, providing an adapter class will not save any keystrokes for you.

Note that using an adapter class to handle an event has no special advantage, except for saving some keystrokes. However, it does have a limitation. If you want to create an event handler by using the main class itself, you cannot use an adapter class. Typically, your main class is inherited from the JFrame class and Java does not allow you to inherit a class from multiple classes. So you cannot inherit your main class from the JFrame class as well as the adapter class. If you are using an adapter class to create an event handler, you must use either an anonymous inner class or a regular inner class.

Summary

Swing is a widget toolkit to develop Java applications with GUIs. Most classes used in developing Swing applications are in the javax.swing package. A GUI consists of several parts; each part represents a graphic that displays information to the user and lets them interact with the application. Each part in a Swing-based GUI application is called a component that is a Java object. A component that can contain other components is called a container. Containers and components are arranged to form a parent-child hierarchy. Components are contained within a container that, in turn, can be contained within another container. Two types of containers exist: top-level containers and non-top-level containers. A top-level container is not contained within another container and it can be displayed directly on the desktop. For example, an instance of the JFrame class represents a top-level container, which is a window that can have a title bar, a menu bar, a border, and other components. An instance of the JButton class represents a component.

A top-level container consists of many layers such as root pane, layered panes, a glass pane, and a content pane. Components are added to the content pane.

Swing provides layout managers that are responsible for laying out components in a container. A layout manager is an object that is responsible for determining the position and size of components to be displayed in a container. Each container has a default layout manager. For example, BorderLayout is the default layout manager for a JFrame. You can use the setLayout() method of the container to set a different layout manager. If the layout manager of a component is set to null, no layout manager is used and you are responsible for laying out the components in a container.

FlowLayout is the simplest of all layout managers that lays out components horizontally, and then vertically. BorderLayout divides the container's space into five areas (north, south, east, west, and center) that can be used to lay out components. CardLayout lays out components in a container as a stack of cards in which only one component is visible at a time. BoxLayout arranges components in a container either horizontally in one row or vertically in one column. GridLayout arranges components in a rectangular grid of equally sized cells placing each component in exactly one cell. GridBagLayout lays out components in a grid of rectangular cells arranged in rows and columns where each component occupies one or multiple cells. SpringLayout lays out components by defining constraints between their edges; constraints are defined in terms of springs. GroupLayout lays out components by forming sequential and parallel groups of components.

An event indicates a user action, for example, clicking of a button by the user. Users interact with Swing component through events. Taking an action in a program in response to an event is called event handling. There are three participants in an event: the event source, the event, and the event handler. The source of an event is the component that generates the event. The event is represented by an object that encapsulates the details of the user's action that led to the occurrence of the event. The event handler is an instance of a specific interface that is executed in response to the occurrence of the event. Components that let you handle events contain methods to add and remove event handlers. The classes, interfaces, and methods used in event handling follow a naming convention that makes names easy to remember.

CHAPTER 2

■ ■ ■

Swing Components

In this chapter, you will learn

- What Swing components are
- Different types of Swing components
- How to validate input in a text component
- How to use menus and toolbars
- How to edit tabular and hierarchical data using JTable and JTree components
- How to use custom and standard dialogs
- How to customize a component's properties such as colors, borders, fonts, etc.
- How to paint components and how to draw shapes
- Immediate painting and double buffering

What Is a Swing Component?

Swing provides a huge set of components to build GUIs. In Java programs, a Swing component is an instance of the JComponent class. The JComponent class is in the javax.swing package and it serves as the base class for all Swing components. Its class hierarchy is shown in Figure 2-1.

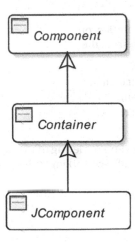

Figure 2-1. *The class hierarchy for the JComponent class*

The JComponent class inherits from the java.awt.Container class, which in turn inherits from the java.awt.Component class. JComponent is an abstract class. You cannot instantiate it directly. You must use one of its subclasses, such as JButton, JTextField, etc.

As the JComponent class inherits from the Container class, every JComponent can also act as a container. For example, a JButton can act like a container for another JButton or other JComponents. You would not use (or need) a JComponent as a container unless a JComponent such as a JPanel has been provided by the Swing library to be used as a container. However, this hierarchy allows you to write code like this:

```
JButton btn = new JButton("Container JButton");
btn.setLayout(new FlowLayout());
btn.add(new JButton("Container JButton. Do not use."));
```

The JComponent class, as a base class for all Swing components, provides the following basic functionalities that are inherited by all Swing components. I will discuss these features in detail later in this chapter.

- It provides support for tool tips. A tool tip is short text that is displayed when the mouse pointer is paused on a component for a certain period of time.

- It provides support for a pluggable look and feel. All aspects of a component related to how it looks (painting and layout) and how it feels (responding to the user's interaction with a component such as event handling) is handled by a UI delegate object. Like the JComponent class, ComponentUI in the javax.swing.plaf package is the base class used as a UI delegate object. Each descendant of JComponent uses a different kind of UI delegate object, which is derived from the ComponentUI class. For example, a JButton uses ButtonUI, a JLabel uses LabelUI, and a JToolTip uses ToolTipUI as a UI delegate.

- It provides support for adding a border around a Swing component. The border can be any one of the predefined types (Line, Bevel, Titled, Etched, etc.) or a custom border type.

- It provides support for accessibility. Accessibility of an application is the degree to which it can be used by people with varying abilities and disabilities. For example, it has features that can display text in a bigger font size for vision-impaired users. This book does not cover the Java Accessibility API.

- It provides support for double buffering that facilitates smooth on-screen painting. When a component is erased and painted on-screen, a flicker may occur. To avoid any flickering, it provides an off-screen buffer. The erasing and repainting (updating a component) is done in an off-screen buffer, and the off-screen buffer is copied to on-screen.

- It provides binding of a key on the keyboard to a Swing component. You can bind any key on the keyboard with an ActionListener object to a component. When that key is pressed, the actionPerformed() method of the associated ActionListener is called.

- It provides support for laying out the component when a layout manager is used. It contains methods to get and set the minimum, preferred, and maximum size of a component. The three different type size settings for a JComponent serves as a hint to a layout manager in deciding the size of the JComponent.

It allows associating multiple arbitrary properties (key-value pairs) to a Swing component and retrieving those properties. The putClientProperty() and getClientProperty() methods of the JComponent allows working with component properties.

Table 2-1 lists some of the commonly used methods of the JComponent class that are available to be used in all Swing components.

Table 2-1. *Commonly Used Methods of the JComponent Class and Their Descriptions*

Method Name	Description
`Border getBorder()`	Returns the border of the component or `null` if the component has no border.
`void setBorder(Border border)`	Sets the border for the component.
`Object getClientProperty(Object key)`	Returns the value associated with the specified key. The value must have been set using the `putClientProperty (Object key, Object value)` method.
`void putClientProperty(Object key, Object value)`	Adds an arbitrary key-value pair to the component.
`Graphics getGraphics()`	Returns the graphics context object for the component, which can be used to draw on the component.

`Dimension getMaximumSize()`
`Dimension getMinimumSize()`
`Dimension getPreferredSize()`
`Dimension getSize(Dimension d)`
`void setMaximumSize(Dimension d)`
`void setMinimumSize(Dimension d)`
`void setPreferredSize(Dimension d)`
`void setSize(Dimension d)`
`void setSize(int width, int height)`
	Gets/sets the maximum, minimum, preferred, and actual size of the component. When you call the `getSize()` method, you can pass a `Dimension` object and the size will be stored in it and the same object is returned. This way, the method may avoid creating a new `Dimension` object. If you pass `null`, it creates a `Dimension` object, stores the actual size in it, and returns that object.

`String getToolTipText()`	Returns the tool tip text for this component.
`void setToolTipText(String text)`	Sets the tool tip text, which is displayed when mouse pointer pauses on the component for a specified amount of time.
`boolean isDoubleBuffered()`	Returns `true` if the component uses double buffering. Otherwise, it returns `false`.
`void setDoubleBuffered(boolean db)`	Sets if the component should use double buffering to paint or not.
`boolean isFocusable()`	Returns `true` if the component can gain focus. Otherwise, it returns `false`.
`void setFocusable(boolean focusable)`	Sets if the component can gain focus or not.
`boolean isVisible()`	Returns `true` if the component is visible. Otherwise, it returns `false`.
`void setVisible(boolean v)`	Sets the component visible or invisible.
`boolean isEnabled()`	Returns `true` if the component is enabled. Otherwise, it returns `false`.
`void setEnabled(boolean e)`	Enables or disables the component. A component is enabled by default. An enabled component responds to the user inputs and generates events.

(*continued*)

Table 2-1. (*continued*)

Method Name	Description

`boolean requestFocus(boolean temporary)`
`boolean requestFocusInWindow()`
`boolean requestFocusInWindow(boolean temporary)`
	Both `requestFocus()` and `requestFocusInWindow()` methods request that the component should get the input focus. You should use the `requestFocusInWindow()` method instead of the `requestFocus()` method because its behavior is consistent across all platforms. The boolean argument indicates if the request is temporary. These methods return `false` if the request is guaranteed to fail. They return `true` if the request will succeed unless it is vetoed.

`boolean isOpaque()`	Returns `true` if the `JComponent` is opaque. Otherwise, it returns `false`.
`void setOpaque(boolean opaque)`	Sets the opacity of the `JComponent`. If a `JComponent` is opaque, it will paint every pixel within its bounds. If it is non-opaque, it may paint some or no pixels in its bounds, allowing the pixels behind it to show through. By default, the `JComponent` class sets this value to `false`, making it transparent. However, the default value for opacity for its subclasses depends on the look and feel, and the specific component.

Table 2-2 lists some of the commonly used events that are available for all Swing components. Each Swing component also supports some specialized events. I will explain those specialized events when I discuss those components. Note that all the events listed in the table follow the XxxEvent class, XxxListener interface, XxxAdapter abstract class, and addXxxListener() method naming convention unless noted otherwise. That is, to handle Xxx event for a component, you need to call its addXxxListener(XxxListener l) method and pass object of a class that implements an XxxListener interface. All the methods in an XxxListener interface accept an argument of the type XxxEvent. If there is more than one method in XxxListener, there is a corresponding XxxAdapter abstract class that implements the XxxListener interface and it provides empty implementations for the XxxListener methods.

Table 2-2. *Some Commonly Used Events Available for All Swing Components*

Event Class Name	Event Listener Interface	Description

`ComponentEvent`	`ComponentListener`
	
	Methods:
	`componentShown()`
	`componentHidden()`
	`componentResized()`
	`componentMoved()`
		The event occurs when a component's visibility, size, or location is changed.

`FocusEvent`	`FocusListener`
	
	Methods:
	`focusGained()`
	`focusLost()`
		The event occurs when a component gains or loses the focus.

(*continued*)

Table 2-2. (*continued*)

Event Class Name	Event Listener Interface	Description
KeyEvent	KeyListener Methods: keyPressed() keyReleased() keyTyped()	The event occurs when the component has the focus and a key on the keyboard is pressed, released, or typed. The key pressed and released events are triggered when you press or release any key on the keyboard. The key typed event is triggered only when a Unicode character is typed. For example, when you type character 'a' on the keyboard, a key pressed, a key typed, and a key released event are triggered in sequence.
MouseEvent	MouseListener Methods: mousePressed() mouseReleased() mouseClicked() mouseEntered() mouseExited()	The mouse pressed, released, and clicked events are triggered when the mouse is pressed, released, and clicked on a component. When a mouse enters the component's bound, a mouse entered event is triggered. A mouse exited event is triggered when a mouse leaves the component's bounds. Note that the MouseAdapter class implements three interfaces: MouseListener, MouseMotionListener, and MouseWheelListener (see two more mouse events below).
MouseEvent	MouseMotionListener Methods: mouseDragged() mouseMoved() **Note:** It uses a MouseEvent object as an argument in the event methods. There is no corresponding MouseMotionEvent class.	A mouse dragged event is triggered when you drag the mouse over a component by pressing a mouse button. The mouse dragged event continues to trigger even if the mouse leaves the component until the mouse button is released. The mouse moved event is triggered when you move the mouse over a component, but no mouse button is pressed. You can use either the MouseAdapter or MouseMotionAdapter abstract class to write your listener object for this event.
MouseWheelEvent	MouseWheelListener Method: mouseWheelMoved()	A mouse wheel moved event is triggered if the wheel of the mouse is rotated when the component is in focus. If a mouse does not have a wheel, this event is not triggered.

In the beginning, Java provided the AWT (**A**bstract **W**indow **T**oolkit) for building a GUI. All AWT components were in the java.awt package and they used peers to handle how they worked. If you create a button using AWT, there is a corresponding button created by the operating system, which is called the *peer*, to handle most of how the AWT button works. Because of the fact that each AWT component has a peer, AWT components are called *heavyweight* components.

Swing became part of the Java class library in JDK 1.2 as an alternative to AWT. Most of the Swing components do not use peers, and hence, they are called *lightweight* components. For every AWT component, you will find a corresponding Swing component. Swing provides some additional components that are not present in AWT such as JTabbedPane. Swing components have their names prefixed with a J. For example, to use a button component, AWT provides a Button class and Swing provides a JButton class. To display a decorated window, AWT provides a Frame class and Swing provides a JFrame class. Some components in Swing are still heavyweight components. After all, basic

GUI capabilities are always provided by the operating system. All top-level containers in Swing (JFrame, JDialog, JWindow, and JApplet) are heavyweight components, and they have peers. Swing components, other than top-level containers, are lightweight components. Swing's lightweight components use their heavyweight containers' area to paint. Swing's lightweight components are written in Java.

The main disadvantage of AWT is that a GUI may look different on different operating systems. AWT supports features that are available on all platforms. Because of their dependence on operating system peers, AWT can provide only rectangular components. None of these limitations exist with Swing lightweight components. In Swing, you can have a component of any shape because Swing paints lightweight components using Java code. Swing offers pluggable look and feel, so that you are not limited to seeing GUI components only in the way the operating system paints them. It is not advisable to mix Swing and AWT components in the same application, although it is allowed. Mixing them may result in problems that are hard to debug. This book covers only Swing.

In the next sections, I will discuss several Swing components in detail.

JButton

A JButton is also known as a *push button* or a *command button*. The user presses or clicks a JButton to perform an action. Typically, it displays text that describes the action it performs when it is clicked. The text is also known as the *label*. A JButton also supports displaying an icon. You can use one of the constructors listed in Table 2-3 to create an instance of a JButton.

Table 2-3. *Constructors of the JButton Class*

Constructor	Description
JButton()	Creates a JButton without any label or icon.
JButton(String text)	Creates a JButton and sets the specified text as its label.
JButton(Icon icon)	Creates a JButton with an icon and no label.
JButton(String text, Icon icon)	Creates a JButton with the specified label and icon.
JButton(Action action)	Creates a JButton with an Action object. You will have an example of using an Action object for a JButton later in this section.

You can create a JButton with its text as Close, like so:

```
JButton closeButton = new JButton("Close");
```

To create a JButton with an icon, you need to have an image file. An icon is a fixed-sized image. An object of a class that implements the javax.swing.Icon interface represents an icon. Swing provides a very useful ImageIcon class that implements the Icon interface. You can create an icon in your program using the ImageIcon class from an image file or a URL that contains a GIF, JPEG, or PNG image. The following snippet of code shows how to create buttons with icons:

```
// Create icons
Icon previousIcon = new ImageIcon("C:/images/previous.gif");
Icon nextIcon = new ImageIcon("C:/images/next.gif");

// Create buttons with icons
JButton previousButton = new JButton("Previous", previousIcon);
JButton nextButton = new JButton("Next", nextIcon);
```

It is advised that you use a forward slash (/) in the file path in the constructor of the ImageIcon class. The file path you specify is converted to a URL and the forward slash works on all platforms. This file path example (C:/images/next.gif) is for the Windows platform. Figure 2-2 shows a JFrame with three buttons. Two buttons have icons and one has only text.

Figure 2-2. *Buttons with an icon and text, and with only text*

There is only one event for a JButton that you will be using in your Java program most of the time. It is called the ActionEvent. It is triggered when you click the JButton. The ActionListener interface is a functional interface and it contains only one method called actionPerformed(ActionEvent e). You can use a lambda expression to represent an ActionListener. Here is how you add code using a lambda expression for the ActionEvent for a closeButton:

```
closeButton.addActionListener(() -> {
    // The code to handle the action event goes here
});
```

A JButton supports keyboard *mnemonic*, which is also known as a *keyboard shortcut* or *keyboard indicator*. It is a key that, when pressed, activates the JButton if the focus is in the window that contains the JButton. The mnemonic key is often pressed in combination with a modifier key such as an Alt key. The modifier key is platform-dependent; however, it is usually an Alt key. For example, suppose you set the C key as a mnemonic for a Close JButton. When you press Alt + C, the Close JButton is clicked. If the character that is represented by the mnemonic key is found in the JButton text, its first occurrence is underlined.

The following snippet of code sets C as a mnemonic key for a Close JButton:

```
// Set the 'C' key as mnemonic key for closeButton
closeButton.setMnemonic('C');

// You can also use the following code to set a mnemonic key.
// The KeyEvent class is in the java.awt.event package.
closeButton.setMnemonic(KeyEvent.VK_C);
```

The code shows two methods to set the mnemonic key. The second method can be used when you do not use a character key as a mnemonic key. For example, if you want to set the F3 key as a mnemonic key, you can use the KeyEvent.VK_F3 constant using the second method. Figure 2-3 shows the Close JButton in which the first character of the text is underlined. When you press Alt + C, the Close JButton is activated (the same as if you clicked it with the mouse). Table 2-4 shows commonly used method in the JButton class.

Figure 2-3. *A Close button with C as its keyboard mnemonic*

Table 2-4. *Commonly Used Methods of the JButton Class*

Method	Description
`Action getAction()`	Returns the `Action` object associated with the `JButton`.
`void setAction(Action a)`	Sets an `Action` object for the `JButton`. When this method is called, all properties for the `JButton` are refreshed from the specified `Action` object. If there was an `Action` object already set, the new one replaces the old one. The new `Action` object is registered as an `ActionListener`. Any other `ActionListener` registered with the `JButton` using `addActionListener()` method remains registered.
`Icon getIcon()`	Returns the `Icon` object associated with the `JButton`.
`void setIcon(Icon icon)`	Sets an icon for the `JButton`.
`int getMnemonic()`	Returns the keyboard mnemonic for this `JButton`.
`void setMnemonic(int n)` `void setMnemonic(char c)`	Sets the keyboard mnemonic for the `JButton`.
`String getText()`	Returns the text for the `JButton`.
`void setText()`	Sets the text for the `JButton`.

Let's use an `Action` object to create a `JButton`. So far, you have seen that a `JButton` has only four commonly used properties: text, icon, mnemonic, and action listener. Using these properties of a `JButton` is easy and straightforward. How does using an `Action` object help you deal with a `JButton`? Let's take an example where you have a button, say `Close`, placed in different areas of the window, say different tab pages. If the button is placed four times on a window, and all of them have to look and behave the same, an `Action` object will help you write the code for the `Close` button only once and use it at multiple times.

An `Action` object encapsulates the state and the behavior of a button. You set the text, icon, mnemonic, tool tip text, other properties, and the `ActionListener` in an `Action` object, and use the same `Action` object to create all instance of the `JButton`. One obvious benefit of doing this is that if you want to enable/disable all four JButtons, you do not need to enable/disable all of them separately. Rather, you set the `enabled` property in the `Action` object and it will enable/disable all of them. Let's extend this usage to the menu item and tool bar. It is common to provide a menu item, a tool bar item, and a button to perform the same action in a window. In such cases, you create all three of them (a menu item, a tool bar item and a button) using the same `Action` object to keep their states synchronized. Now you can realize the benefits of an `Action` object is in reusing the code and keeping the state of multiple components synchronized.

`Action` is an interface. The `AbstractAction` class provides the default implementation for the `Action` interface. `AbstractAction` is an abstract class. You need to inherit your class from it. Listing 2-1 defines a `CloseAction` inner class, which inherits from the `AbstractAction` class.

Listing 2-1. Using an Action Object to Create and Configure a JButton

```java
// ActionJButtonTest.java
package com.jdojo.swing;

import java.awt.FlowLayout;
import javax.swing.JFrame;
import javax.swing.JButton;
import java.awt.event.ActionEvent;
import javax.swing.AbstractAction;
import javax.swing.Action;
import java.awt.Container;
```

```java
public class ActionJButtonTest extends JFrame {
        // Inner Class starts here
        public class CloseAction extends AbstractAction {
                public CloseAction() {
                        super("Close");
                }

                @Override
                public void actionPerformed(ActionEvent event) {
                        System.exit(0);
                }
        } // Inner Class ends here

        JButton closeButton1;
        JButton closeButton2;
        Action closeAction = new CloseAction(); // See inner class above

        public ActionJButtonTest() {
                super("Using Action object with JButton");
                this.initFrame();
        }

        private void initFrame() {
                this.setDefaultCloseOperation(EXIT_ON_CLOSE);
                this.setLayout(new FlowLayout());
                Container contentPane = this.getContentPane();

                // Use the same closeAction object to create both Close buttons
                closeButton1 = new JButton(closeAction);
                closeButton2 = new JButton(closeAction);

                contentPane.add(closeButton1);
                contentPane.add(closeButton2);
        }

        public static void main(String[] args) {
                ActionJButtonTest frame = new ActionJButtonTest();
                frame.pack();
                frame.setVisible(true);
        }
}
```

The ActionJButtonTest class creates an Action object, which is of type CloseAction, and uses it to create two buttons, closeButton1 and closeButton2. The CloseAction class sets the text to Close, and in its actionPerformed() method, it simply exits the application. Figure 2-4 shows the JFrame that you get when you run the program. It shows two Close buttons. Clicking either of them will call the actionPerformed() method of the Action object and that will exit the application.

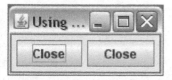

Figure 2-4. *Two Close buttons created using the same Action object*

If you want to set any property for the JButton while using the Action object, you can do so by using putValue(String key, Object value) method of the Action interface. For example, the following snippet of code sets the tool tip text and mnemonic key for the object closeAction:

```
// Set the tool tip text for the Action object
closeAction.putValue(Action.SHORT_DESCRIPTION, "Closes the application");

// Set the mneminic key for the Action object
closeAction.putValue(Action.MNEMONIC_KEY, KeyEvent.VK_C);
```

■ **Tip**   If you use an Action object to configure a JButton, and later change a property for the JButton directly, the changed property will be in effect until you change that property in the Action object again. Suppose you have created two Close buttons using a CloseAction object. If you call closeButton1.setText("Exit"), the first button will display the text as Exit. If you call closeAction.putValue(Action.NAME, "Close/Exit"), both buttons will display the text as Close/Exit.

JPanel

A JPanel is a container that can contain other components. You can set its layout manager, border, and background color. Typically, you use a JPanel to group related components and add it to another container such as to a content pane of a JFrame. Note that a JPanel is a container, but not a top-level container, whereas a JFrame is a top-level container. Therefore, you cannot display a JPanel by itself in a Swing application, unless you add it to a top-level container. Sometimes, a JPanel is inserted between two components to create a gap. You can also use a JPanel as a canvas for drawing such as for drawing lines, rectangles, circles, etc.

The default layout manager for a JPanel is FlowLayout. Note that the default layout manager of the content pane of a JFrame is a BorderLayout. You have the option to specify its layout manager in the constructor of the JPanel class. You can change its layout manager after you create it by using its setLayout() method. Table 2-5 lists the constructors of the JPanel class.

Table 2-5. *Constructors for the JPanel Class*

Constructor	Description
JPanel()	Creates a JPanel with FlowLayout and double buffering.
JPanel(boolean isDoubleBuffered)	Creates a JPanel with FlowLayout and the specified double buffering flag.
JPanel(LayoutManager layout)	Creates a JPanel with the specified layout manager and double buffering.
JPanel(LayoutManager layout, boolean isDoubleBuffered)	Creates a JPanel with the specified layout manager and double buffering flag.

The following snippet of code shows how to create a JPanel with a BorderLayout and add four buttons to it. Note that the buttons are added to the JPanel, which in turn is added to the content pane of a JFrame. You can also add a JPanel to another JPanel to create a nested, complex components layout.

```
// Create a JPanel and four buttons
JPanel buttonPanel = new JPanel(new BorderLayout());
JButton northButton = new JButton("North");
JButton southButton = new JButton("South");
JButton eastButton = new JButton("East");
JButton westButton = new JButton("west");

// Add buttons to the JPanel
buttonPanel.add(northButton, BorderLayout.NORTH);
buttonPanel.add(southButton, BorderLayout.SOUTH);
buttonPanel.add(eastButton, BorderLayout.EAST);
buttonPanel.add(westButton, BorderLayout.WEST);

// Add the buttonPanel to the JFrame's content pane assuming that
// the content's pane layout is set to a BorderLayout
contentPane.add(buttonPanel, BorderLayout.SOUTH);
```

JLabel

As the name suggest, a JLabel is a label used to identify or describe another component on the screen. It can display text, an icon, or both. Typically, a JLabel is placed next to (to the right or left) or at the top of the component it describes. Figure 2-5 shows a JLabel with its text set to Name:, which is an indicator for the user that he is supposed to enter a name in the field that is placed next to it.

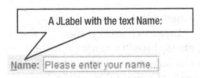

Figure 2-5. *A JLabel component with the text Name: and the mnemonic set to N*

Another common use of a JLabel is to display an image. Swing does not include a component such as a JImage to display an image. You need to use a JLabel with an Icon to display an image. Table 2-6 lists the constructors of the JLabel class.

Table 2-6. *Constructors of the JLabel Class*

Constructor	Description
JLabel()	Creates a JLabel with an empty string as its text and no icon.
JLabel(Icon icon)	Creates a JLabel with an icon and an empty string as its text.
JLabel(Icon icon, int horizontalAlignment)	Creates a JLabel with an icon and the specified horizontal alignment. A JLabel is aligned vertically in the center inside its display area. You can specify its horizontal alignment in its display area as one of the following constants defined in the SwingConstants class: LEFT, CENTER, RIGHT, LEADING, or TRAILING.
JLabel(String text)	Creates a JLabel with the specified text. This is the most commonly used constructor. It is aligned in the center vertically and with the leading edge horizontally inside its display area. The leading edge is determined by the component's orientation.
JLabel(String text, Icon icon, int horizontalAlignment)	Creates a JLabel with the specified text, icon, and horizontal alignment.
JLabel(String text, int horizontalAlignment)	Creates a JLabel with the specified text and horizontal alignment.

The following snippet of code shows some examples of how to create a JLabel:

```
// Create a JLabel with a Name: text
JLabel nameLabel = new JLabel("Name:");

// Display an image warning.gif in a JLabel
JLabel warningImage = new JLabel(new Icon("C:/images/warning.gif"));
```

A JLabel does not generate any interesting events. However, it has some useful methods that you can use to customize it. You will use three of its methods very frequently: setText(), setDisplayedMnemonic(), and setLabelFor(). The setText() method is used to set the text for the JLabel. The setDisplayedMnemonic() method is used to set a keyboard mnemonic for the JLabel. If the keyboard mnemonic is a character that occurs in the text of the JLabel, that character is underlined to give a hint to the user. The setLabelFor() method accepts a reference to another component and it indicates that this JLabel describes that component. The two methods - setDisplayedMnemonic() and setLabelFor() work in tandem. When the mnemonic key for the JLabel is pressed, the focus is set to the component that was used in the setLabelFor() method. The JLabel shown in Figure 2-5 has its mnemonic set to the character N and you can see that the character N in its text is underlined. When the user presses Alt + N, the focus will be set to the JTextField that is displayed to the right of the JLabel. The following snippet of code shows how to create the component arrangements shown in Figure 2-5:

```
// Create a JTextField where the user can enter a name
JTextField nameTextField = new JTextField("Please enter your name...");

// Create a JLabel with N as its mnemonic and nameTextField as its label-for component
JLabel nameLabel = new JLabel("Name:");
nameLabel.setDisplayedMnemonic('N');
nameLabel.setLabelFor(nameTextField);
```

```
// Add name label and field to a container, say a contentPane
contentPane.add(nameLabel);
contentPane.add(nameTextField);
```

There are other methods defined in the JLabel class that let you set/get its alignments inside the display area and its text inside its bounds. If you look at a JLabel component's features, you will find that it exists only to describe another component—a truly altruistic component!

Text Components

In simple terms, you can define text as a sequence of characters. Swing provides a rich set of features to work with text. Figure 2-6 shows a class diagram for classes representing text components in Swing.

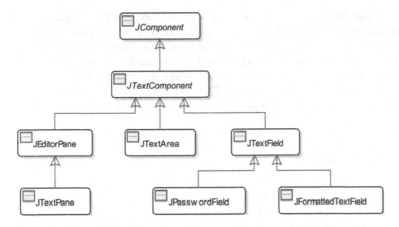

Figure 2-6. *A class diagram for text-related components in Swing*

Swing provides so many text-related features that it has a separate package, javax.swing.text, which contains all text related classes. The JTextComponent class is in the javax.swing.text package. The rest of the classes are in the javax.swing package.

There are different Swing components to work with different kinds of text. We can categorize the text components based on two criteria: the number of lines in text and the type of text they can handle. Based on the number of lines of text that a text component can handle, you can further categorize them as follows:

- Single-line text component

- Multiline text component

A single line text component is designed to handle one line of text, for example, a user name, a password, a birth date etc. Instances of the JTextField, JPasswordField, and JFormattedTextField classes represent single-line text components.

A multiline text component is designed to handle multiple lines of text, for example, comments, the description of an item in a store, a document, etc. Instances of the JTextArea, JEditorPane, and JTextPane classes represent multiline text components.

Based on the type of the text that a text component can handle, you can categorize text components as follows:

- Plain text component

- Styled text component

The style of text (or parts of text) is the way the text is displayed, such as bold, italic, underlined, etc., font, and color. In the context of a text component, a plain text means that the entire text contained in the text component is displayed using only one style. JTextField, JPasswordField, JFormattedTextField, and JTextArea are examples of plain text components. That is, you cannot display multiline text in a JTextArea in which some parts of the text is in boldface font and others not. You can display either the entire text in a JTextArea in boldface font or the entire text in a regular font. Note that plain text does not mean that text cannot have a style. It means that there is only one style that applies to the entire text (all characters comprising the text).

In styled text, you can apply different styles to different parts of the text. In styled text, some part of the text can be in boldface (or italic, bigger font size, underlined, etc.) and some part not in boldface. JEditorPane and JTextPane are examples of styled components.

All Swing components, including Swing text components, are based on a model-view-controller (MVC) pattern. An MVC pattern uses three components: a model, a view, and a controller. The model is responsible for storing the contents (the text). The view is responsible for displaying the contents. The controller is responsible for responding to user actions. Swing combines the view and the controller into one object called the UI, which is responsible for displaying the content and reacting to the user's actions. It keeps the model separate and it is represented by an instance of the Document interface, which is in the javax.swing.text package. The model of a text component is sometimes also referred to as its *document*. Figure 2-7 depicts the different parts of a Swing text component.

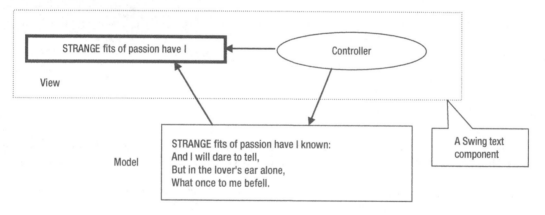

Figure 2-7. *Components of the model-view-controller pattern for Swing text components*

Note that the view may not always display the entire contents of a text component. In Figure 2-7, the model contains four lines of the part of a poem by William Wordsworth, whereas the view displays only some words from the first line.

Swing provides a default implementation of the Document interface, which makes is easy for developers to work with commonly used text types. When you use a text component, it creates an appropriate model (sometimes I will refer to it as a document in the discussion) for you, which is suitable to store the content of the text component. Figure 2-8 shows a class diagram for the Document interface, plus related classes and interfaces. All classes and interfaces shown in the figure are in the javax.swing.text package.

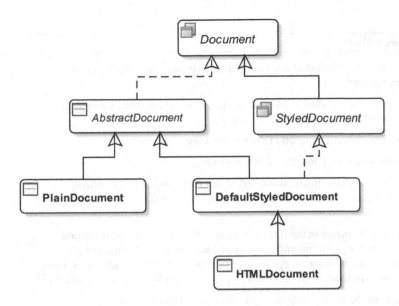

Figure 2-8. *A class diagram for the document interface and related interfaces and classes*

You can set the model for a text component using the setDocument(Document doc) method. The getDocument() method returns the model for a text component.

By default, JTextField, JPasswordField, JFormattedTextField, and JTextArea use an instance of the PlainDocument class as their models. If you want to customize the models for these text components, you need to create a class inheriting from the PlainDocument class and override some of the methods.

The model for JEditorPane and JTextPane depends on the content type that is being edited and/or displayed. The position of the characters in a text component uses a zero-based index. That is, the first character in the text occurs at index 0.

JTextComponent

JTextComponent is an abstract class. It is the ancestor of all Swing text components. It includes common functionalities that are available to all text components. Table 2-7 lists some commonly used methods of text components that are included in the JTextComponent class.

Table 2-7. *Commonly Used Methods in the JTextComponent Class*

Method	Description
Keymap addKeymap(String name, Keymap parentKeymap)	Adds a new keymap to the keymap hierarchy of the component.
void copy()	Copies the selected text to the system clipboard.
void cut()	Moves the selected text to the system clipboard.
Action[] getActions()	Returns the command list for the text editor.
Document getDocument()	Returns the model for the text component.
Keymap getKeymap()	Returns the currently active keymap for the text component.

(continued)

Table 2-7. (*continued*)

Method	Description
static Keymap getKeymap (String keymapName)	Returns the keymap associated with this document with the name keymapName.
String getSelectedText()	Returns the selected text in the component. It returns null if there is no selected text or the document is empty.
int getSelectionEnd()	Returns the end position of the selected text.
int getselectionStart()	Returns the start position of the selected text.
String getText()	Returns the text that is contained in this text component. It returns the text contained in the model of the component and not what is displayed by the view.
String getText(int offset, int length) throws BadLocationException	Returns a portion of the text contained in the text component starting at the offset position and number of characters equal to the length. It throws BadLocationException if offset or length is invalid. For example, if a text component contains Hello as its text, getText(1,3) will return ell.
TextUI getUI()	Returns the user-interface factory for the text component.
boolean isEditable()	Returns true if the text component is editable. Otherwise, returns false.
void paste()	Transfers the content of the system clipboard to the text component model. If text is selected in the component, the selected text is replaced. If there is no selection, the content is inserted before the current position. If the system clipboard is empty, it does nothing.
void print()	It displays a print dialog and lets you print the content of the text component without a header and footer. This method is overloaded. Other versions of this method provide more functionality to print the content of a text component.

void read(Reader source, Object description) throws IOException	Reads the content from the source stream into the text component, discarding the component's old content. The description is an object that describes the source stream. For example, to read the text of file test.txt into a JTextArea named ta you would write
	
	`FileReader fr = new FileReader("test.txt");`
	`ta.read(fr, "Hello");`
	`fr.close();`

void replaceSelection(String newContent)	Replaces the selected content with the newContent. If there is no selected content, it inserts the newContent. If newContent is null or an empty string, it removes the selected content.
void select(int start, int end)	Selects the text between the start and end positions.
void selectAll()	Selects all text in a text component
void setDocument(Document doc)	Sets the document (that is, the model) for the text component.
void setEditable(boolean editable)	Sets a text component as editable if editable is true. If editable is false, sets the text component as non-editable.
void setKeymap(Keymap keymap)	Sets the keymap for the text component.

(*continued*)

Table 2-7. (*continued*)

Method	Description
void setSelectionEnd(int end)	Sets the end position of selection.
void setSelectionStart(int start)	Sets the start position of selection.
void setText(String newText)	Sets the text of the text component.
void setUI(TextUI newUI)	Sets new UI for the text component.
void updateUI()	Reloads the pluggable UI for the text component.

void write(Writer output)	Writes the contents of the text component to a stream defined by output. For example, to write the text of a JTextArea named ta into a file named test.txt, you would write
	
	FileWriter wr = new FileWriter("test.txt");
	ta.write(wr);
	wr.close();

The most commonly used methods of text components are getText() and setText(String text). The getText() method returns the contents of a text component as a String, and the setText(String text) method sets the content of a text component specified in the argument.

JTextField

A JTextField can handle (display and/or edit) one line of plain text. You can create a JTextField in a number of different ways using its constructors. Its constructors accept a combination of

- A string
- The number of columns
- A Document object

The string specifies the initial text. The number of columns specifies the width. The Document object specifies the model. The default value for the initial text is null, the number of columns is zero, and document (or model) is an instance of the PlainDocument class.

If you do not specify the number of columns, its width is determined by the initial text. Its preferred width will be wide enough to display the entire text. If you specify the number of columns, its preferred width will be wide enough to display as many m characters in the current font of the JTextField as the specified number of columns. Table 2-8 lists constructors of the JTextField class.

Table 2-8. *Constructors of the JTextField Class*

Constructor	Description
JTextField()	Creates a JTextField with default values for initial text, number of columns, and document.
JTextField(Document document, String text, int columns)	Creates a JTextField with the specified document as its model, text as its initial text, and columns as its number of columns.
JTextField(int columns)	Creates a JTextField with the specified columns as its number of columns.
JTextField(String text)	Creates a JTextField with the specified text as its initial text.
JTextField(String text, int columns)	Creates a JTextField with the specified text as its initial text and columns as its number of columns.

The following snippet of code creates many instance of JTextField using the different constructors:

```
// Create an empty JTextField
JTextField emptyTextField = new JTextField();

// Create a JTextField with an initial text of Hello
JTextField helloTextField = new JTextField("Hello");

// Create a JTextField with the number of columns of 20
JTextField nameTextField = new JTextField(20);
```

How many characters can you enter in a JTextField? There is no limit to the number of characters that you can enter in a JTextField. If you want to limit the number of characters in a JTextField, you need to customize its model. Note that the model of the JTextField stores its contents. Before you see a custom model in action, let's see the power of separating the model and the view for a text component in Swing.

Let's create two instances of JTextField named name and mirroredName. You will set the model for mirroredName to be the same as that of name. You are doing a very simple thing. You are using the same model for both text fields. This makes both fields as mirror fields of each other. If you enter text in one of them, the same text is automatically displayed for you in the other. How does this happen? When you enter text in a JTextField, its model is updated. Any update in its model sends a notification to its views (in this case, the two components act as views) to update themselves. Since two text fields are two views with the same model, any update in the model (through either of the text fields) will send a notification to both text fields, and both will update their views to display the same text.

Listing 2-2 demonstrates how to share a model between two text fields. Run this program and enter some text in either of the text fields. You will see that the other text field is updated simultaneously with the same text.

Listing 2-2. Mirroring a JTextField by Sharing Its Model With Another JTextField

```
// MirroredTextField.java
package com.jdojo.swing;

import javax.swing.JFrame;
import javax.swing.JTextField;
import javax.swing.JLabel;
import java.awt.GridLayout;
import java.awt.Container;
import javax.swing.text.Document;

public class MirroredTextField extends JFrame {
        JLabel nameLabel = new JLabel("Name:") ;
        JLabel mirroredNameLabel = new JLabel("Mirrored Name:") ;
        JTextField name = new JTextField(20);
        JTextField mirroredName = new JTextField(20);

        public MirroredTextField() {
                super("Mirrored JTextField");
                this.initFrame();
        }

        private void initFrame() {
                this.setDefaultCloseOperation(EXIT_ON_CLOSE);
                this.setLayout(new GridLayout(2, 0));
```

```
                Container contentPane = this.getContentPane();
                contentPane.add(nameLabel);
                contentPane.add(name);
                contentPane.add(mirroredNameLabel);
                contentPane.add(mirroredName);

                // Set the model for mirroredName to be the same
                // as name's model, so they share their content's storage.
                Document nameModel = name.getDocument();
                mirroredName.setDocument(nameModel);
        }

        public static void main(String[] args) {
                MirroredTextField frame = new MirroredTextField();
                frame.pack();
                frame.setVisible(true);
        }
}
```

To have your own model for a JTextField, you need to create a new class. The new class can either implement the Document interface or inherit from the PlainDocument class. The latter approach is easier and most commonly used. Listing 2-3 contains the code for a LimitedCharDocument class, which inherits from the PlainDocument class. You can use this class as a model for a JTextField when you want to limit the number of characters in a JTextField. By default, it lets a user enter an unlimited number of characters. You can set the number of allowed characters in its constructor.

Listing 2-3. A Class That Represents a Plain Document With a Limited Number of Characters

```
// LimitedCharDocument.java
package com.jdojo.swing;

import javax.swing.text.PlainDocument;
import javax.swing.text.BadLocationException;
import javax.swing.text.AttributeSet;

public class LimitedCharDocument extends PlainDocument {
        private int limit = -1; // < 0 means an unlimited characters

        public LimitedCharDocument() {
        }

        public LimitedCharDocument(int limit) {
                this.limit = limit;
        }

        @Override
        public void insertString(int offset, String str, AttributeSet a)
                                throws BadLocationException {
                String newString = str;
                if (limit >=0 && str != null) {
                        // Check for the limit
                        int currentLength = this.getLength() ;
```

```
                int newTextLength = str.length();
                if (currentLength + newTextLength > limit) {
                        newString = str.substring(0, limit - currentLength);
                }
        }

        super.insertString(offset, newString, a);
    }
}
```

The code of interest in the LimitedCharDocument class is the insertString() method. The Document interface declares an insertString() method. The PlainDocument class provides the default implementation. The LimitedCharDocument class overrides the default implementation and checks whether the inserted string will exceed the number of characters allowed. If the inserted string exceeds the maximum number of characters allowed, it chops off the extra characters. If you set the limit to a negative number, an unlimited number of characters are allowed. At the end, the method simply calls its implementation in the PlainDocument class to execute the real action.

The insertString() of the model is called every time a text is inserted into the JTextField. This method gets the following three arguments:

- int offset: It is the position where the string is inserted in the JTextField. The first character is inserted at offset 0, the second at offset 1, and so on.

- String str: It is the string that is inserted into the JTextField. When you enter a text in a JTextField, the insertString() method is called for each character you enter and this argument will contain only one character. However, when you paste text into a JTextField or use its setText() method, this argument may contain more than one character.

- AttributeSet a: The attributes that have to be associated with the inserted text.

You can use the LimitedCharDocument in your code as follows:

```
// Create a JTextField, which will only allow 10 characters
Document tenCharDoc = new LimitedCharDocument(10);
JTextField t1 = new JTextField(tenCharDoc, "your name", 10);
```

There is another way to set a document for a JTextField. You need to create a new class inheriting from JTextField and override its createDefaultModel() method. It is declared protected in the JTextField class, and by default, it returns a PlainDocument. You can return an instance of your custom document class from this method. The code for your custom JTextField would look as follows:

```
public class TenCharTextField extends JTextField {
        @Override
        protected Document createDefaultModel() {
                // Return a document object that allows maximum 10 characters
                return new LimitedCharDocument(10);
        }

        // Other code goes here
}
```

You can use an instance of the TenCharTextField class whenever you need a JTextField with a capacity of ten characters.

The createDefaultModel() method is called from the constructor in the JTextField class. Therefore, you should not pass an argument to your custom JTextField and use that argument's value to construct the model in the createDefaultModel() method in your class. For example, the following snippet of code will not produce the desired result:

```
static class LimitedCharTextField extends JTextField {
        private int maxChars = -1;

        public LimitedCharTextField(int maxChars) {
                this.maxChars = maxChars;
        }

        protected Document createDefaultModel() {
                /* Wrong use of maxChars!!! By the time this method is called,
                   maxChars will have its default value of zero. This method will be
                   called from the constructor of the JTextField class and at that time
                   the constructor for this class would not start executing.
                */
                return new LimitedCharDocument(maxChars);
        }
}
```

Sometimes, you may want to force the user to enter text in a text field in a specific format, such as entering a date in mm/dd/yyyy format or entering digits only. This is possible using a custom model for the JTextField component. Swing contains another text component called JFormattedTextField that lets you set the format for a text field. A JFormattedTextField makes the job a lot easier if you need a component that should allow a user to add text in a specific format. I will discuss JFormattedTextField shortly.

JPasswordField

A JPasswordField is a JTextField, except that it allows hiding the actual characters being displayed in the field. For example, when you are using a login form to enter your password, you do not want others looking over your shoulders to see your password on the screen. By default, it displays an asterisk (*) character for each actual character in the field. This is called the echo character. The default echo character also depends on the look-and-feel used for the application. You can set your own echo character by using its setEchoChar(char newEchoChar) method.

The JPasswordField class has the same set of constructors as the JTextField class. You can use a combination of the initial text, the number of columns, and a Document object to create a JPasswordField object.

```
// Create a password field 10 characters wide
JPasswordField passwordField = new JPasswordField(10);
```

The getText() method for JPasswordField has been deprecated for security reasons. You should use its getPassword() method instead, which returns an array of char. You should reset all the elements in the char array to zero value after you are done using it. The following snippet of code shows how to validate a password entered in a JPasswordField:

```
// Get the password entered in the field
char c[] = passwordField.getPassword();

// Suppose you have the correct password in a string.
// Usually, you will get it from a file or database
String correctPass = "Hello";
```

```
// Do not convert your password in c[] to a String. Rather, convert the correctPass
// to a char array. Or, better you would have correctPass as char array in the first place.
char[] cp = correctPass.toCharArray();

// Use the equals() method of the java.util.Arrays class to compare c and cp for equality
if (Arrays.equals(c, cp)) {
        // The password is correct
}
else {
        // The password is incorrect
}

// Null out the password that you have in the char arrays
Arrays.fill(c, (char)0);
Arrays.fill(cp, (char)0);
```

You can set an echo character of your choice using the setEchoChar() method as follows:

```
// Set # as the echo character
password.setEchoChar('#');
```

You can use a JPasswordField as a JTextField by setting its echo character to zero as follows:

```
// Set the echo character to 0, so the actual password characters are visible.
passwordField.setEchoChar((char)0);
```

■ **Tip**　You need to set the echo character of a JPasswordField to a character value whose ASCII value is zero so the JPasswordField will show the actual characters. If you set the echo character to 'o' (ASCII value of 48), the actual password will not be displayed. Rather, a 'o' character will be echoed for each actual character.

JFormattedTextField

A JFormattedTextField is a JTextField with the following two additional capabilities:

- It lets you specify the format in which the text will be edited and/or displayed.

- It also lets you specify a format when the value in the field is null.

In addition to the getText() and setText() methods, which let you get and set the text in the field, the JFormattedTextField offers two new methods called getValue() and setValue(), which let you work with any type of data instead of just text.

The JFormattedTextField comes preconfigured to work with three kinds of data: numbers, dates, and strings. However, you have the ability to format any object to be displayed in this field. You can set the format for a JFormattedTextField in many ways using its different constructors, which are listed in Table 2-9.

Table 2-9. *Constructors of the JFormattedTextField Class*

Constructor	Description
JFormattedTextField()	Creates a JFormattedTextField with no formatter. You need to use its setFormatterFactory() or setValue() method to set a formatter.
JFormattedTextField(Format format)	Creates a JFormattedTextField and it will use the specified format to format the text in the field.
JFormattedTextField(JFormattedTextField.AbstractFormatter formatter)	Creates a JFormattedTextField with the specified formatter.
JFormattedTextField(JFormattedTextField.AbstractFormatterFactory factory)	Creates a JFormattedTextField with the specified factory.
JFormattedTextField(JFormattedTextField.AbstractFormatterFactory factory, Object initialValue)	Creates a JFormattedTextField with the specified factory and the specified an initial value.
JFormattedTextField(Object value)	Creates a JFormattedTextField with the specified value. The field will configure itself to format the value based on the class of the value. If a null is passed as the value, the field has no way to know which type of value it needs to format and it will not attempt to format the value at all.

It is necessary to understand the difference between format, formatter, and formatter factory. A java.text.Format object defines the format of an object in a string form. That is, it defines how an object looks as a string; for example, a date object in mm/dd/yyyy format would look like 07/09/2008.

A formatter is represented by a JFormattedTextField.AbstractFormatter object and it uses a java.text.Format object to format an object. Its job is to convert an object to a string and a string back to an object.

A formatter factory is a collection of formatters. A JFormattedTextField uses a formatter factory to get a formatter of a specific type. A formatter factory object is represented by an instance of the JFormattedTextField.AbstractFormatterFactory class.

The following snippet of code configures dobField to format the text in it as a date in the current locale format:

```
JFormattedTextField dobField = new JFormattedTextField();
dobField.setValue(new Date());
```

The following snippet of code configures a salaryField to display a number in the current locale format:

```
JFormattedTextField salaryField = new JFormattedTextField();
salaryField.setValue(new Double(11233.98));
```

You can also create a JFormattedTextField with a formatter. You need to use the DateFormatter, NumberFormatter, and MaskFormatter classes to format a date, a number, and a string, respectively. These classes are in the javax.swing.text package.

```
// Have a field to format a date in mm/dd/yyyy format
DateFormat dateFormat = new SimpleDateFormat("mm/dd/yyyy");
DateFormatter dateFormatter = new DateFormatter(dateFormat);
dobField = new JFormattedTextField(dateFormatter);
```

```
// Have field to format a number in $#0,000.00 format
NumberFormat numFormat = new DecimalFormat("$#0,000.00");
NumberFormatter numFormatter = new NumberFormatter(numFormat);
salaryField = new JFormattedTextField(numFormatter);
```

You need to use a mask formatter to format a string. A mask formatter uses the special characters listed in Table 2-10 to specify a mask.

Table 2-10. *Special Characters Used to Specify a Mask*

Character	Description
#	A number
?	A letter
A	A letter or a number
*	Anything
U	A letter, with lowercase characters mapped to their uppercase equivalents
L	A letter, with uppercase characters mapped to their lowercase equivalents
H	A hexadecimal digit (A-F, a-f, 0-9)
'	A single quote. It is an escape character that is used to escape any of the special formatting characters.

To let the user enter a social security number in the ###-##-#### format, you create a JFormattedTextField as follows. Note that the constructor, MaskFormatter(String mask), throws a ParseException.

```
MaskFormatter ssnFormatter = null;
JFormattedTextField ssnField = null;
try {
        ssnFormatter = new MaskFormatter("###-##-####");
        ssnField = new JFormattedTextField(ssnFormatter);
}
catch (ParseException e) {
        e.printStackTrace();
}
```

When you use a mask formatter, you are forced to use only as many characters as you have specified in the mask. All non-special characters (see Table 2-10 for the list of special characters) are displayed as they appear in the mask. A placeholder (a space by default) is displayed for each special character in the mask. For example, if you specify the mask as "###-##-####", the JFormattedTextField displays "   - -   " as the placeholder. You can also specify a placeholder character for special characters using the setPlaceHolderCharacter(char placeholder) method of the MaskFormatter class. To display 000-00-0000 in a SNN field, you need to use '0' as a placeholder character for the mast formatter, as shown:

```
ssnFormatter = new MaskFormatter("###-##-####");
ssnFormatter.setPlaceholderCharacter('0');
```

You can use the setFormatterFactory() method of JFormattedTextField to change the formatter after you have created the component. For example, to set a date format to a JFormattedTextField named payDate, after you have created it, you write

```
DateFormatter df = new DateFormatter(new SimpleDateFormat("mm/dd/yyyy"));
DefaultFormatterFactory dff = new DefaultFormatterFactory(df, df, df, df);
dobField.setFormatterFactory(dff);
```

A JFormattedTextField lets you specify four types of formatters:

- A *null formatter*: It is used when the value in the field is null.

- An *edit Formatter*: It is used when the field has focus.

- A *display Formatter*: It is used when the field does not have focus and it has a non-null value.

- A *default Formatter*: It is used in the absence of any of the above three formatters.

You can specify all four formatters by using a formatter factory in the constructor of the JFormattedTextField class or calling its setFormatterFactory() method. An instance of the JFormattedTextField. AbstractFormatterFactory abstract class represents a formatter factory. The javax.swing.text. DefaultFormatterFactory class is an implementation of the JFormattedTextField.AbstractFormatterFactory class. When you specify a formatter, the same formatter is used in place of four formatters. When you specify a formatter factory, you have the ability to specify different formatters for four different situations.

Suppose you have a JFormattedTextField named dobField to display a date. When this field has focus, you want to let the user edit the date in the format mm/dd/yyyy (e.g. 07/07/2008). When it does not have focus, you want to display a date in the mmmm dd, yyyy (e.g. July 07, 2008) format. The following snippet of code will do the job:

```
DateFormatter df = new DateFormatter(new SimpleDateFormat("mmmm dd, yyyy"));
DateFormatter edf = new DateFormatter(new SimpleDateFormat("mm/dd/yyyy"));
DefaultFormatterFactory ddf = new DefaultFormatterFactory(df, df, edf, df);
dobField.setFormatterFactory(ddf);
```

If you have configured the JFormattedTextField to format a date, you can use its getValue() method to get a Date object. The getValue() method's return type is Object and you will need to cast the returned value to the type Date. You can place the cursor in the month, day, year, hour, minute, and second parts of the date value in the field and use up/down arrow key to change that specific part. If you want to overwrite the value in the field as you type, you need to set the formatter in overwrite mode by using the method setOverwriteMode(true).

Another advantage of using a JFormattedTextField is to set a limit on the number of characters that can be entered in a field. Recall that you achieved this by using a custom document for a JTextField in the previous section. You can achieve the same by setting a mask formatter. Suppose you want to let the user enter a maximum of two characters in a field. You can accomplish this as follows:

```
JFormattedTextField twoCharField = new JFormattedTextField(new MaskFormatter("**"));
```

JTextArea

A JTextArea can handle multiline plain text. Most often, when you have multiline text in a JTextArea, you will need scrolling capabilities. A JTextArea does not provide scrolling by itself. Rather, you need to get help from another Swing component called JScrollPane when you need to have scrolling capability for any Swing component.

You can specify the number of rows and columns for a JTextArea that are used to determine its preferred size. The number of rows is used to determine its preferred height. If you set the number of rows to N, it means that its preferred height will be set to display N number of lines of text in the current font settings. The number of columns is used to determine its preferred width. If you set the number of columns to M, it means that its preferred width is set to M times the width of the character m (lowercase M) in the current font settings.

A JTextArea provides a number of constructors to create a JTextArea component using a combination of the initial text, the model, the number of rows, and the number of columns as arguments, as shown in Table 2-11.

Table 2-11. *Constructors of the JTextArea Class*

Constructor	Description
JTextArea()	Creates a JTextArea with a default model, initial string as null, and rows/columns as zero.
JTextArea(Document doc)	Creates a JTextArea with the specified doc as its model. Its initial string is set to null, and rows/columns to zero.
JTextArea(Document doc, String text, int rows, int columns)	Creates a JTextArea with all its properties (model, initial text, rows, and column) as specified in its arguments.
JTextArea(int rows, int columns)	Creates a JTextArea with a default model, initial string as null, and the specified rows/columns.
JTextArea(String text)	Creates a JTextArea with the specified initial text. A default model is set and rows/columns are set to zero.
JTextArea(String text, int rows, int columns)	Creates a JTextArea with the specified text, rows, and columns. A default model is used.

The following snippet of code creates many instances of JTextArea using different initial values:

```
// Create a blank JTextArea
JTextArea emptyTextArea = new JTextArea();

// Create a JTextArea with 10 rows and 50 columns
JTextArea commentsTextArea = new JTextArea(10, 50);

// Create a JTextArea with 10 rows and 50 columns with an initial text of "Enter resume here"
JTextArea resumeTextArea = new JTextArea("Enter resume here", 10, 50);
```

It is very important to remember that when you work with a JTextArea, most often your text size will be bigger than its size on the screen and you will need a scrolling capability. To add the scrolling capability to a JTextArea, you need to add it to a JScrollPane, and add the JScrollPane to the container, not the JTextArea. The following snippet of code demonstrates this concept. It is assumed that you have a JFrame named myFrame whose content pane's layout is set to BorderLayout and you want to add a scrollable JTextArea in the center region.

```
// Create JTextArea
JTextArea resumeTextArea = new JTextArea("Enter resume here", 10, 50);

// Add JTextArea to a JScrollPane
JScrollPane sp = new JScrollPane(resumeTextArea);

// Get the reference of the content pane of the JFrame
Container contentPane = myFrame.getContentPane();

// Add the JScrollPane (sp) to the content pane, not the JTextArea
contentPane.add(sp, BorderLayout.CENTER);
```

Table 2-12 has some of the commonly used methods of a JTextArea. Most of the time, you will use its setText(), getText(), and append() methods.

Table 2-12. *Commonly Used Methods of JTextArea*

Method	Description
void append(String text)	Appends the specified text to the end of the JTextArea.
int getLineCount()	Returns the number of lines in the JTextArea.
int getLineStartOffset(int line) throws BadLocationException int getLineEndOffset(int line) throws BadLocationException	Returns the start and end offset (also called position, which is zero based) for a specified line number. Throws an exception if the line number is out of range. This method is useful when you combine it with the getLineCount() method. You can parse the text contained in the JTextArea line by line using these three methods inside a loop.
int getLineOfOffset(int offset) throws BadLocationException	Returns the line number in which the specified offset occurs.
boolean getLineWrap()	Returns true if line wrapping has been set. Otherwise, it returns false.
int getTabSize()	Returns the number of characters used for a tab. By default, it returns 8.
boolean getWrapStyleWord()	Returns true if word wrapping has been set to true. Otherwise, it returns false.
void insert(String text, int offset)	Inserts the specified text at the specified offset. If the model is null or the specified text is empty or null, calling this method has no effect.
void replaceRange(String text, int start, int end)	Replaces the text between the start and end positions with the specified text.
void setLineWrap(boolean wrap)	Sets the line-wrapping policy for the JTextArea. If line-wrapping is set to true, a line is wrapped if it does not fit into the width of the JTextArea. If it is set to false, lines are not wrapped even though it is longer than the width of the JTextArea. By default, it is set to false.
void setTabSize(int size)	Sets the number of characters that a tab will expand to the specified size.
void setWrapStyleWord(boolean word)	Sets the word-wrapping style when line wrapping is set to true. When it is set to true, the line wraps at a word boundary. Otherwise, the line wraps at a character boundary. By default, it is set to false.

JTextArea uses configurable policies for wrapping lines and words in its displayable area. If the line wrapping is set to true and a line is longer than the width of the component, the line will be wrapped. By default, the line wrapping is set to false. The line wrapping is set using the setLineWrap(boolean lineWrap) method.

A line can wrap at a word boundary or at a character boundary, which is determined by the word wrapping policy. The word wrapping policy is set using the setWrapStyleWord(boolean wordWrap) method. Calling this method takes effect only if the setLineWrap(true) is called. That is, a word wrapping policy defines the details of the line wrapping policy. Figure 2-0 shows three JTextArea components displayed in a JFrame.

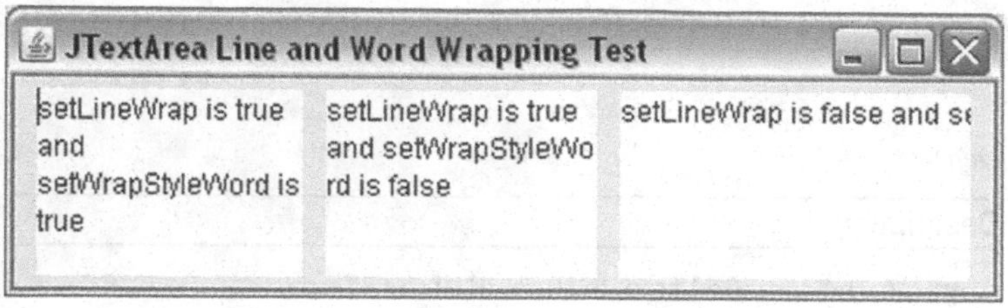

Figure 2-9. *The effects of line and word wrapping in a JTextArea*

For the three JTextArea components in the figure (left to right), the line wrapping and word wrapping settings are (true, true), (true, false) and (false, true). The first one wrapped the line at the word boundaries. The second one wrapped the lines at a character boundary. The third one did not wrap the line at all and you are not able to view the entire text in its width. Note that each of the three JTextArea components were added to the JFrame without adding it to a JScrollPane.

JEditorPane

A JEditorPane is a text component that is designed to handle different kinds of text. By default, it knows how to handle plain text, HTML, and Rich Text Format (RTF). Although it is designed to edit and display many types of content, it is primarily used to display an HTML document, which contains only basic HTML elements. The support for RTF content is very basic.

A JEditorPane handles a specific type of content using a specific EditorKit object. If you want to handle new types of content in this component, you will need to create a custom EditorKit class, which is a subclass of the javax.swing.text.EditorKit class. If you are using this component only to display HTML content, you do not need to worry about an EditorKit; the component will handle the EditorKit related functionalities for you. It takes only one line of code to use a JEditorPane to display a HTML page, as shown:

```
// Create a JEditorPane to display yahoo.com web page
JEditorPane htmlPane = new JEditorPane("http://www.yahoo.com");
```

Note that some of the constructors of the JEditorPane class throw an IOException. When you specify a URL, you must use the full form of the URL, starting with the protocol. You can let JEditorPane know what type of an EditorKit it needs to install to handle its content in the following three different ways:

- By calling the setContentType(String contentType) method

- By calling the setPage(URL url) or setPage(String url) method

- By calling the read(InputStream in, Object description) method

JEditorPane is preconfigured to understand three types of contents: text/plain, text/html, and text/rtf. You can use the following code to display the text Hello, using the <h1> tag in HTML:

```
htmlPane.setContentType("text/html");
htmlPane.setText("<html><body><h1>Hello</h1></body></html>");
```

When you call its setPage() method, it uses an appropriate EditorKit to handle the content provided by the URL. In the following snippet of code, the JEditorPane uses an EditorKit depending on the content type:

```
// Handle an HTML Page
editorPane.setPage("http://www.yahoo.com");
```

```
// Handle an RTF file. When you use a file protocol, you may use three slashes instead of one
editorPane.setPage("file:///C:/test.rtf");
```

The JEditorPane reads the contents from a stream into the editor pane. If its editor kit is already set to handle the HTML content and the specified description is of type javax.swing.text.html.HTMLDocument, the content will be read as HTML. Otherwise, the content will be read as plain text.

When you work with an HTML document, you may want to navigate to a different page when you click a hyperlink. In order to use a hyperlink, you need to add a hyperlink listener to the JEditorPane, and in the hyperlinkUpdate() method of the event listener, navigate to the new page using the setPage() method. One of the three type of actions, ENTERED, EXITED, and ACTIVATED, on a hyperlink triggers the hyperlinkUpdate() method. The ENTERED event occurs when the mouse enters a hyperlink area, the EXITED event occurs when the mouse leaves the hyperlink area, and the ACTIVATED event occurs when a hyperlink is clicked. Make sure you check for an ACTIVATED event in the hyperlinkUpdate() method in your hyperlink listener when you want to navigate to another page using a hyperlink. The following snippet of code uses a lambda expression to add a HyperlinkListener to a JEditorPane:

```
editorPane.addHyperlinkListener((HyperlinkEvent event) -> {
        if (event.getEventType() == HyperlinkEvent.EventType.ACTIVATED) {
                try {
                        editorPane.setPage(event.getURL());
                }
                catch (IOException e) {
                        e.printStackTrace();
                }
        }
});
```

If you want to know when a new page is loaded in the JEditorPane, you need to add a property change listener to listen to its property change event and to check if the property with the name page has changed. Listing 2-4 contains the complete code that uses a JEditorPane as a browser to view a web page. When you run the program, you can enter a web page address in the URL field and press the Enter key (or press the Go button), and the browser will display the contents of the new URL. You can also click a hyperlink in the contents to navigate to another web page. The code is simple and contains enough comments to assist you in understanding the program logic.

Listing 2-4. An HTML Browser Using the JEditorPane Component

```
// HTMLBrowser.java
package com.jdojo.swing;

import javax.swing.JFrame;
import java.awt.Container;
import javax.swing.JLabel;
import javax.swing.JScrollPane;
import javax.swing.Box;
import javax.swing.JEditorPane;
import javax.swing.JTextField;
import javax.swing.JButton;
import java.awt.BorderLayout;
import java.net.URL;
import javax.swing.event.HyperlinkEvent;
import java.beans.PropertyChangeEvent;
import java.net.MalformedURLException;
import java.io.IOException;
```

```java
public class HTMLBrowser extends JFrame {
        JLabel urlLabel = new JLabel("URL:");
        JTextField urlTextField = new JTextField(40);
        JButton urlGoButton = new JButton("Go");
        JEditorPane editorPane = new JEditorPane();
        JLabel statusLabel = new JLabel("Ready");

        public HTMLBrowser(String title) {
                super(title);
                initFrame();
        }

        // Initialize the JFrame and add components to it
        private void initFrame() {
                this.setDefaultCloseOperation(JFrame.EXIT_ON_CLOSE);
                Container contentPane = this.getContentPane();
                Box urlBox = this.getURLBox();
                Box editorPaneBox = this.getEditPaneBox();

                contentPane.add(urlBox, BorderLayout.NORTH);
                contentPane.add(editorPaneBox, BorderLayout.CENTER);
                contentPane.add(statusLabel, BorderLayout.SOUTH);
        }

        private Box getURLBox() {
                // URL Box consists of a JLabel, a JTextField and a JButton
                Box urlBox = Box.createHorizontalBox();
                urlBox.add(urlLabel);
                urlBox.add(urlTextField);
                urlBox.add(urlGoButton);

                // Add an action listener to urlTextField, so when the user enters a url
                // and presses the enter key, the appplication navigates to the new URL.
                urlTextField.addActionListener(e -> {
                        String urlString = urlTextField.getText();
                        go(urlString);
                });

                // Add an action listener to the Go button
                urlGoButton.addActionListener(e -> go());

                return urlBox;
        }

        private Box getEditPaneBox() {
                // To display HTML, you must make the editor pane non-editable.
                // Otherwise, you will see an editable HTML page that doesnot look nice.
                editorPane.setEditable(false);

                // URL Box consists of a JLabel, a JTextField and a JButton
                Box editorBox = Box.createHorizontalBox();
```

```java
        // Add a JEditorPane inside a JScrollPane to provide scolling
        editorBox.add(new JScrollPane(editorPane));

        // Add a hyperlink listener to the editor pane, so that it
        // navigates to a new page, when the user clicks a hyperlink
        editorPane.addHyperlinkListener((HyperlinkEvent event) -> {
                if (event.getEventType() == HyperlinkEvent.EventType.ACTIVATED) {
                        go(event.getURL());
                }
                else if (event.getEventType() == HyperlinkEvent.EventType.ENTERED) {
                        statusLabel.setText("Please click this link to visit the page");
                }
                else if (event.getEventType() == HyperlinkEvent.EventType.EXITED) {
                        statusLabel.setText("Ready");
                }
        });

        // Add a property change listener, so  we can update
        // the URL text field with url of the new page
        editorPane.addPropertyChangeListener((PropertyChangeEvent e) -> {
                String propertyName = e.getPropertyName();
                if (propertyName.equalsIgnoreCase("page")) {
                        URL url = editorPane.getPage();
                        urlTextField.setText(url.toExternalForm());
                }
        });

        return editorBox;
}

// Navigates to the url entered in the URL JTextField
public void go() {
        try {
                URL url = new URL(urlTextField.getText());
                this.go(url);
        }
        catch (MalformedURLException e) {
                setStatus(e.getMessage());
        }
}

// Navigates to the specified URL
public void go(URL url) {
        try {
                editorPane.setPage(url);
                urlTextField.setText(url.toExternalForm());
                setStatus("Ready");
        }
        catch (IOException e) {
                setStatus(e.getMessage());
        }
}
```

```
        // Navigates to the specified URL specified as a string
        public void go(String urlString) {
                try {
                        URL url = new URL(urlString);
                        go(url);
                }
                catch (IOException e) {
                        setStatus(e.getMessage());
                }
        }

        private void setStatus(String status) {
                statusLabel.setText(status);
        }

        public static void main(String[] args) {
                HTMLBrowser browser = new HTMLBrowser("HTML Browser");
                browser.setSize(700, 500);
                browser.setVisible(true);

                // Let us visit yahoo.com
                browser.go("http://www.yahoo.com");
        }
}
```

The following are the important parts of the program:

- The getURLBox() method packs a JLabel, a JTextField, and a JButton in a horizontal box, and it is added to the north region of the frame. It adds an action listener to the JTextField and to the JButton, so that when a user presses the Enter key or the Go button after typing the new URL, the browser navigates to the new URL.

- The getEditPaneBox() method packs a JEditorPane inside a JScrollPane and it is added in the center region of the frame. It also adds a hyperlink listener and a property change listener to the JEditorPane. The hyperlink listener is used to navigate to a URL when the user clicks a hyperlink. It also displays an appropriate help message in the status bar when the mouse enters and exits a hyperlink area.

- A JLabel is used to display a brief message in the south area of the frame.

- The go() method has been overloaded and its main job is to navigate to a new page using the setPage() method.

- The main() method is used for testing. It displays Yahoo's home page in the browser.

As an assignment, you can add the Back and Forward buttons to the browser to let the user navigate back and forth between the already visited web pages.

■ **Tip** In order to display an HTML page in a nice format, you need to make the JEditorPane non-editable by calling its setEditable(false) method. You should not use a JEditorPane to display all kinds of HTML pages because it does not handle all kinds of different things that can be embedded in an HTML page. Rather, you should only use it to display HTML pages that contain basic HTML content, such as an HTML help file for your application.

JTextPane

The JTextPane class is a subclass of the JEditorPane class. It is a specialized component to handle the styled document with embedded images and components. You can set attributes for characters and paragraphs. If you want to display an HTML, RTF, or plain document, the JEditorPane is your best choice. However, if you need the rich set of functionalities provided by a word processor to edit/display styled text, you need to use the JTextPane. It is a mini word processor. It always works with a styled document, even if its contents are plain text. It is not possible to discuss all of its features in this section; it deserves a small book by itself. I will touch upon its features, such as setting styled text, embedding images, and components.

A JTextPane uses a styled document, which is an instance of the StyledDocument interface. The StyledDocument interface inherits the Document interface. DefaultStyledDocument is an implementation class for the StyledDocument interface. A JTextPane uses a DefaultStyledDocument as its default model. A document in a Swing text component consists of elements that are organized in a tree-like structure. The top element is called the root element. An element in a document is an instance of the javax.swing.text.Element interface.

A plain document has a root element. The root element can have multiple child elements. Each child element consists of one line of text. Note that in a plain document, all characters in the document have the same attributes (or formatting style).

A styled document has a root element, which is also known as a section. The root element has branch elements, which are also known as paragraphs. A paragraph has character runs. A character run is a set of contiguous characters that share the same attributes. For example, the "Hello world" string defines one character run. However, the "Hello **world**" string defines two character runs. Note that the word "**world**" is in boldface font and "Hello" is not. That is why they define two different character runs. In a styled document, a paragraph ends with a newline character unless it is the last paragraph, which need not end in a newline. You can define attributes at the paragraph level, such as indenting, line spacing, text alignment, etc. You can define attributes at character run level, such as font size, font family, bold, italics, etc. Figure 2-10 and Figure 2-11 show the structures of a plain document and a styled document, respectively.

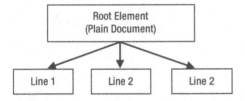

Figure 2-10. *Structure of a plain document*

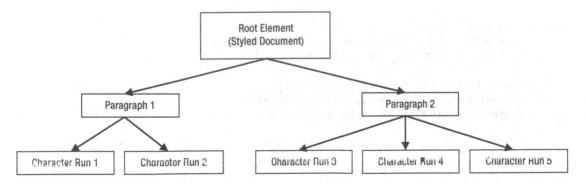

Figure 2-11. *Structure of a styled document*

The program in Listing 2-5 develops a basic word processor using a JTextPane. It lets you edit text and apply styles such as bold, italics, color, and alignment to the text.

Listing 2-5. A Simple Word Processor Using JTextPane and JButtons

```java
// WordProcessor.java
package com.jdojo.swing;

import javax.swing.JFrame;
import java.awt.Container;
import javax.swing.JTextPane;
import javax.swing.JButton;
import java.awt.BorderLayout;
import javax.swing.JPanel;
import javax.swing.text.StyledDocument;
import javax.swing.text.BadLocationException;
import javax.swing.text.Style;
import javax.swing.text.StyleContext;
import javax.swing.text.StyleConstants;
import java.awt.Color;

public class WordProcessor extends JFrame {
        JTextPane textPane = new JTextPane();

        JButton normalBtn = new JButton("Normal");
        JButton boldBtn = new JButton("Bold");
        JButton italicBtn = new JButton("Italic");
        JButton underlineBtn = new JButton("Underline");
        JButton superscriptBtn = new JButton("Superscript");
        JButton blueBtn = new JButton("Blue");
        JButton leftBtn = new JButton("Left Align");
        JButton rightBtn = new JButton("Right Align");

        public WordProcessor(String title) {
                super(title);
                initFrame();
        }

        private void initFrame() {
                this.setDefaultCloseOperation(JFrame.EXIT_ON_CLOSE);
                Container contentPane = this.getContentPane();

                JPanel buttonPanel = this.getButtonPanel();
                contentPane.add(buttonPanel, BorderLayout.NORTH);
                contentPane.add(textPane, BorderLayout.CENTER);

                this.addStyles(); // Add styles to the text pane for later use
                insertTestStrings(); // Insert some texts to the text pane
        }
```

```java
    private JPanel getButtonPanel() {
        JPanel buttonPanel = new JPanel();
        buttonPanel.add(normalBtn);
        buttonPanel.add(boldBtn);
        buttonPanel.add(italicBtn);
        buttonPanel.add(underlineBtn);
        buttonPanel.add(superscriptBtn);
        buttonPanel.add(blueBtn);
        buttonPanel.add(leftBtn);
        buttonPanel.add(rightBtn);

        // Add ation event listeners to buttons
        normalBtn.addActionListener(e -> setNewStyle("normal", true));
        boldBtn.addActionListener(e -> setNewStyle("bold", true));
        italicBtn.addActionListener(e -> setNewStyle("italic", true));
        underlineBtn.addActionListener(e -> setNewStyle("underline", true));
        superscriptBtn.addActionListener(e -> setNewStyle("superscript", true));
        blueBtn.addActionListener(e -> setNewStyle("blue", true));
        leftBtn.addActionListener(e -> setNewStyle("left", false));
        rightBtn.addActionListener(e -> setNewStyle("right", false));

        return buttonPanel;
    }

    private void addStyles() {
        // Get the default style
        StyleContext sc = StyleContext.getDefaultStyleContext();
        Style defaultContextStyle = sc.getStyle(StyleContext.DEFAULT_STYLE);

        // Add some styles to the document, to retrieve and use later
        StyledDocument document = textPane.getStyledDocument();
        Style normalStyle = document.addStyle("normal", defaultContextStyle);

        // Create a bold style
        Style boldStyle = document.addStyle("bold", normalStyle);
        StyleConstants.setBold(boldStyle, true);

        // Create an italic style
        Style italicStyle = document.addStyle("italic", normalStyle);
        StyleConstants.setItalic(italicStyle, true);

        // Create an underline style
        Style underlineStyle = document.addStyle("underline", normalStyle);
        StyleConstants.setUnderline(underlineStyle, true);

        // Create a superscript style
        Style superscriptStyle = document.addStyle("superscript", normalStyle);
        StyleConstants.setSuperscript(superscriptStyle, true);

        // Create a blue color style
        Style blueColorStyle = document.addStyle("blue", normalStyle);
        StyleConstants.setForeground(blueColorStyle, Color.BLUE);
```

```java
                // Create a left alignment paragraph style
                Style leftStyle = document.addStyle("left", normalStyle);
                StyleConstants.setAlignment(leftStyle, StyleConstants.ALIGN_LEFT);

                // Create a right alignment paragraph style
                Style rightStyle = document.addStyle("right", normalStyle);
                StyleConstants.setAlignment(rightStyle, StyleConstants.ALIGN_RIGHT);
        }

        private void setNewStyle(String styleName, boolean isCharacterStyle) {
                StyledDocument document = textPane.getStyledDocument();
                Style newStyle = document.getStyle(styleName);
                int start = textPane.getSelectionStart();
                int end = textPane.getSelectionEnd();
                if (isCharacterStyle) {
                        boolean replaceOld = styleName.equals("normal");
                        document.setCharacterAttributes(start, end - start,
                                                        newStyle, replaceOld);
                }
                else {
                        document.setParagraphAttributes(start, end - start, newStyle, false);
                }
        }

        private void insertTestStrings() {
                StyledDocument document = textPane.getStyledDocument();
                try {
                        document.insertString(0, "Hello JTextPane\n", null);
                }
                catch (BadLocationException e) {
                        e.printStackTrace();
                }
        }

        public static void main(String[] args) {
                WordProcessor frame = new WordProcessor("Word Processor");
                frame.setSize(700, 500);
                frame.setVisible(true);
        }
}
```

The word processor program is little lengthy. However, it does simple, repetitive things. I have broken the program's logic down into smaller pieces for easier understanding. The intent of this program is to show a JTextPane where a user can edit text and apply styles to the text using some buttons

There are eight buttons. Five of them are used to format text: normal, bold, italic, underline, and superscript. The Blue button is used to set the text color to blue. The last two buttons, Left Align and Right Align, are used to set the paragraph alignment to left and right.

What is a style and how do you set a style to text and a paragraph? In simple terms, a style is a collection of attributes (name-value pairs). It is simple to set the style; however, you need to write a few lines of code to have the style itself. You add styles to the document of a JTextPane and to the JTextPane itself. You need to use the addStyle(String styleName, Style parent) method of the StyledDocument class. It returns a Style object. The parent argument can be null. If it is not null, unspecified attributes are resolved in the parent style. Once you have a style object, you can use a setXxx() method of the StyleConstants class to set the appropriate attributes in that style. If you are confused, here is a recap.

Think of a style as a table with two columns: name and value. The addStyle() method of the StyledDocument class returns an empty style (meaning an empty table). By using the setXxx() methods of StyleConstants, you are adding new rows to the style (that is, to the table). Once you have at least one row in the table (that is, at least one style attribute defined), you can apply that style to characters or paragraphs depending on the type of the style. Note that you can have an empty style. An empty style may be used to remove all current styles from a range of characters or from a paragraph. The following snippet of code creates two styles: the first one is bold and second one is bold + italic. If you apply the first style to text, it will format the text in boldface font. If you apply the second style to a text, it will format the text in boldface font and italic. Note that you are setting the parent style to null.

```
// Get the styled document from the text pane
StyledDocument document = textPane.getStyledDocument();

// Add an empty style named "bold" to the document
Style bold = document.addStyle("bold", null);

// Add bold attribute to this style
StyleConstants.setBold(bold, true);

// From this point on, you can use the bold style

// Let's create a bold + italic style called boldItalic.
// Add an empty style named boldItalic to the document
Style boldItalic = document.addStyle("boldItalic", null);

// Add bold and italic attributes to the boldItalic style
StyleConstants.setBold(boldItalic, true);
StyleConstants.setItalic(boldItalic, true);

// From this point on, you can use the boldItalic style
```

You may need the reference of the style object after you add it to a StyledDocument. You can retrieve the reference of the same style by using its getStyle(String styleName) method.

```
// Get the bold style from document
Style myBoldStyle = document.getStyle("bold");
```

Once you have a Style object, you can use the setCharacterAttributes(int offset, int length, AttributeSet s, boolean replace) and setParagraphAttributes (int offset, int length, AttributeSet s, boolean replace) methods of the StyledDocument class to set the style to a character range or to a paragraph. If the replace argument is specified as true, any old style for that range will be replaced with the new one. Otherwise, the new style is merged with the old one.

```
// Suppose a text pane has more than five characters in it.
// Make the first three characters bold
document.setCharacterAttributes(0, 3, bold, false);
```

A `StyleContext` object defines a pool of styles for their efficient use. You can get the default collection of styles as follows:

```
StyleContext sc = StyleContext.getDefaultStyleContext();
Style defaultContextStyle = sc.getStyle(StyleContext.DEFAULT_STYLE);

// Let's add a default context style as normal style's parent.
// We do not add any extra attribute to normal styles
StyledDocument document = textPane.getStyledDocument();
Style normal = document.addStyle("normal", defaultContextStyle);
```

Table 2-13 contains a list of important methods with their descriptions, which may assist you in understanding the code in Listing 2-5. Figure 2-12 shows how the simple word processor looks like after you enter **E = mc²** in it.

Table 2-13. *Methods of the WordProcessor Class With Their Descriptions*

Method	Description
initFrame()	Initializes the frame by adding components to it and setting the default behavior of the JFrame.
getButtonPanel()	Returns a JPanel, which contains all JButtons for formatting. It also adds action listeners to all JButtons.
addStyles()	It adds styles to the document. The default context style is named "normal" and it is used as the parent for all other styles. Styles such as bold, italic, etc., are character level styles, whereas left and right are paragraph level styles. These styles are retrieved from the document for using them in the setNewStyle() method.
setNewStyle()	It sets the style to a character range or a paragraph range as indicated by its isCharacterStyle argument. Note that if you set the "normal" style, you replace the entire style by this style. Otherwise, you merge the style. This logic is determined by the following statement: `boolean replaceOld = styleName.equals("normal");`
insertTestStrings()	Inserts a string to the JTextPane's document using the insertString() method.
main()	Creates and displays the word processor frame.

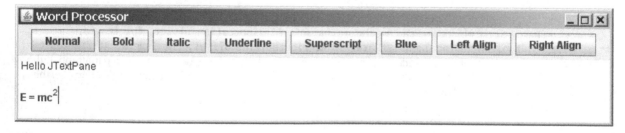

Figure 2-12. *A simple word processor using a JTextPane and JButtons*

The word processor does not have a save feature. In a real world application, you would prompt the user for a location and the name of the saved file. The following snippet of code saves the contents of the JTextPane to a file named test.rtf in the current working directory:

```
// Save the contents of the textPane to a file
FileWriter fw = new java.io.FileWriter("test.rtf");
textPane.write(fw);
fw.close();
```

The write() method of JTextPane writes the text contained in its document as plain text. If you want to save the formatted text, you need to use an RTFEditorKit object as its editor kit, and use that editor kit's write() method to write to a file. The following snippet of code shows how to save formatted text in a JTextPane using an RTFEditorKit object. Note that RTFEditorKit contains a read() method to read the formatted text back to a JTextPane.

```
// Set an RTFEditorKit to a JTextPane right after you create it
JTextPane textPane = new JTextPane();
textPane.setEditorKit(new RTFEditorKit());

// Other code goes here

// Save formatted text from the JTextPane to a file
String fileName = "test.rtf";
FileOutputStream fos = new FileOutputStream(fileName);
RTFEditorKit kit = (RTFEditorKit)textPane.getEditorKit();
StyledDocument doc = textPane.getStyledDocument();
int len = doc.getLength();
kit.write(fos, doc, 0, len);
fos.close();
```

■ **Tip** If you want to save icons and components added to a JTextPane, you need to serialize the document object of a JTextPane to a file, and load it back to display the same contents.

You can add any Swing components and icons to a JTextPane. It is just a matter of wrapping a component or an icon in a style, and using that style in the insertString() method. The following snippet of code shows how to add a JButton and an icon to a JTextPane:

```
// Add a Close button to our document
JButton closeButton = new JButton("Close");
closeButton.addActionListener(e -> System.exit(0));

Style cs = doc.addStyle("componentStyle", null);
StyleConstants.setComponent(cs, closeButton);

// Insert the component at the end of the text.
try {
        document.insertString(doc.getLength(), "Close Button goes", cs);
}
catch (BadLocationException e) {
        e.printStackTrace();
}
```

Adding an icon to a JTextPane is similar to adding a component to it, except that you use the setIcon() method of the StyleConstants class instead of the setComponent() method and an ImageIcon object instead of a component, as shown:

```
// Add an icon to a JTextPane
StyleConstants.setIcon(myIconStyle, new ImageIcon("myImageFile"));
```

■ **Tip** You can also use the insertComponent(Component c) and insertIcon(Icon g) methods of a JTextPane to insert a component and an icon into it, respectively.

You can take a look at the element structures of a JTextPane document by using the dump(PrintStream p) method of the AbstractDocument class. The following snippet of code displays the dump on the standard output:

```
// Display the document structure on the standard output
DefaultStyledDocument doc = (DefaultStyledDocument)textPane.getStyledDocument();
doc.dump(System.out);
```

The following is the dump of a JTextPane's document with text, as shown in Figure 2-12. It gives you an idea about the structure of a styled document.

```
<section>
  <paragraph
    resolver=NamedStyle:default {bold=false,name=default,foreground=sun.swing.PrintColorUIResource
[r=51,g=51,b=51],family=Dialog,FONT_ATTRIBUTE_KEY=javax.swing.plaf.FontUIResource[family=Dialog,
name=Dialog,style=plain,size=12],size=12,italic=false,}
  >
    <content>
      [0,16][Hello JTextPane
]
  <paragraph
    resolver=NamedStyle:default {bold=false,name=default,foreground=sun.swing.PrintColorUIResource
[r=51,g=51,b=51],family=Dialog,FONT_ATTRIBUTE_KEY=javax.swing.plaf.FontUIResource[family=Dialog,
name=Dialog,style=plain,size=12],size=12,italic=false,}
  >
    <content>
      [16,17][
]
  <paragraph
    resolver=NamedStyle:default {bold=false,name=default,foreground=sun.swing.PrintColorUIResource
[r=51,g=51,b=51],family=Dialog,FONT_ATTRIBUTE_KEY=javax.swing.plaf.FontUIResource[family=Dialog,
name=Dialog,style=plain,size=12],size=12,italic=false,}
  >
    <content
      bold=true
      name=bold
      resolver=NamedStyle:normal {name=normal,resolver=AttributeSet,}
```

```
>
    [17,21][E=mc]
  <content
    bold=true
    name=bold
    resolver=NamedStyle:normal {name=normal,resolver=AttributeSet,}
    superscript=true
  >
    [21,22][2]
  <content>
    [22,23][
]
<bidi root>
  <bidi level
    bidiLevel=0
  >
    [0,23][Hello JTextPane

E=mc2
]
```

Validating Text Input

You have seen examples of validating text input in a text component: using a custom model and using a JFormattedTextField. You can attach an input verifier object to any JComponent, including a text component. An input verifier object is simply an object of a class, which inherits from the abstract class named InputVerifier. The class is declared as shown:

```
public abstract class InputVerifier {
        public abstract boolean verify(JComponent input);

        public boolean shouldYieldFocus(JComponent input) {
                return verify(input);
        }
}
```

You need to override the verify() method of the InputVerifier class. The verify() method contains the logic to verify the input in the text field. If the value in the text field is valid, you return true from this method. Otherwise, you return false. When the text field is about to lose focus, the verify() method of its input verifier is called. The text field loses focus only if its input verifier's verify() method returns true. The setInputVerifier() method of a text component is used to attach an input verifier. The following snippet of code sets an input verifier to an area code field. It will keep the focus in this field until the user enters a three-digit numeric area code. It lets the user navigate to another field if the field is empty.

```
// Create an area code JTextField
JTextField areaCodeField = new JTextField(3);

// Set an input verifier to the area code field
areaCodeField.setInputVerifier(new InputVerifier() {
```

```
public boolean verify(JComponent input) {
        String areaCode = areaCodeField.getText();
        if (areaCode.length() == 0) {
                return true;
        }
        else if (areaCode.length() != 3) {
                return false;
        }

        try {
                Integer.parseInt(areaCode);
                return true;
        }
        catch(NumberFormatException e) {
                return false;
        }
    }
});
```

You can set an input verifier to any JComponent using the setInputVerifier() method. Typically, it is used only for text fields. As a good GUI design practice, you should add some visual hints about the valid input values, so the user can understand what kind of values are expected in the field. For example, you may want to add a label for the area code field with a text "Area Code (three digits):" or display an error message when the user enters an invalid value in the field. If there is no visual clue about the valid values for the field with an input verifier, users will be stuck in the field without knowing what kind of value to enter.

Making Choices

Swing provides the following components that let you make a selection from a list of choices:

- JToggleButton
- JCheckBox
- JRadioButton
- JComboBox
- JList

The number of choices available to select from a list may vary from 2 to N, where N is a number greater than 2. There are different ways to make a selection from the list of choices:

- The selection may be mutually exclusive. That is, the user can only make one selection from the list of choices. In mutually exclusive choices, if the user changes the current selection, the previous selection is automatically deselected. For example, the list of gender selection with three choices of Male, Female, and Unknown is mutually exclusive. The user must only select one of the three choices, but not two or more of them at the same time.

- There is a special case of selection where the number of choice N is 2. In this case, the choices are of type boolean: true or false. Sometimes they are also referred to as a Yes/No choice, or an On/Off choice.

- Sometimes the user can have multiple selections from a list of choices. For example, you may present the user with a list of hobbies and the user can choose more than one hobby from the list.

Swing components provide you with the ability to present different kinds of choices to the user and let the user select zero, one, or multiple choices. Figure 2-13 shows the Swing components with four season names: Spring, Summer, Fall, and Winter. The figure shows the look of the five different types of Swing components that can be used for selecting choices from a list. Some of the components shown in this figure may not be the appropriate way for the choices it displays. For example, even though it is possible to use a group of checkboxes to display a list of mutually exclusive choices, it is not a good GUI practice. When choices are mutually exclusive, a group of radio buttons is considered more appropriate than a group of checkboxes.

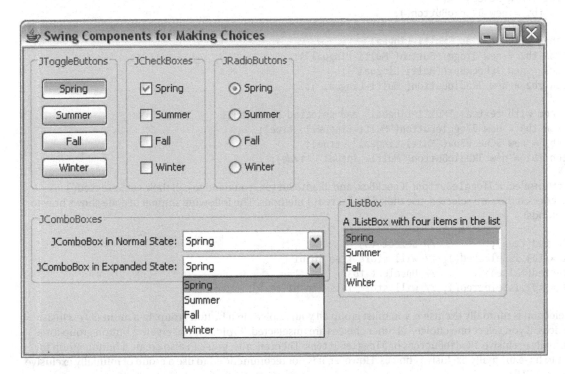

Figure 2-13. *Swing components to make a selection from a list of choices*

A JToggleButton is a two-state button. The two states are *selected* and *unselected*. When you press the toggle button, it toggles between being depressed and undepressed. Depressed is its selected state and undepressed is its unselected state. Note that a JButton is different from a JToggleButton in the way it works and in its usage. A JButton is pressed only when mouse is pressed over it, whereas a JToggleButton toggles between depressed and undepressed states. A JButton is used to initiate an action whereas a JToggleButton is used to select a choice from a list of possible choices. Typically, a group of JToggleButtons is used to let the user select one choice from a list of mutually exclusive choices. One JToggleButton is used when the user has a boolean choice where he needs to indicate true or false (or, Yes or No). The depressed state indicates the choice of true and the undepressed state indicates the choice of false.

A JCheckBox also has two states: *selected* and *unselected*. A group of JCheckBoxes is used when the user can select zero or more choices from a list of two or more choices. One JCheckBox is used when the user has a boolean choice to indicate true or false.

A JRadioButton also has two states: *selected* and *unselected*. A group of JRadioButtons is used when there is a list of two or more mutually exclusive choices and the user must select one choice. A JRadioButton is never used as a standalone component for making a choice from two boolean choices of true and false. It is always used in a group of two or more. A JCheckBox (not a JRadioButton) should be used when you have to let the user select between two boolean choices, true or false.

Constructors for JToggleButton, JCheckBox, and JRadioButton let you create them using a combination of different arguments. You can use a combination of an Action object, a string label, an icon, and a boolean flag (to indicate if it is selected by default) to create them. By default, JToggleButton, JCheckBox, and JRadioButton are unselected. The following snippet of code shows some of the ways to create them:

```java
// Create them with no label and no image
JToggleButton tb1 = new JToggleButton();
JCheckBox cb1 = new JCheckBox();
JRadioButton rb1 = new JRadioButton();

// Create them with text as "Multi-Lingual"
JToggleButton tb2 = new JToggleButton("Multi-Lingual");
JCheckBox cb2 = new JCheckBox("Multi-Lingual");
JRadioButton rb2 = new JRadioButton("Multi-Lingual");

// Create them with text as "Multi-Lingual" and selected by default
JToggleButton tb3 = new JToggleButton("Multi-Lingual", true);
JCheckBox cb3 = new JCheckBox("Multi-Lingual", true);
JRadioButton rb3 = new JRadioButton("Multi-Lingual", true);
```

To select/unselect a JToggleButton, JCheckBox, and JRadioButton, you need to call their setSelected() methods. To check if they are selected, use their isSelected() methods. The following snippet of code shows how to use these methods:

```java
tb3.setSelected(true);         // Select tb3
boolean b1 = tb3.isSelected(); // will store true in b1
tb3.setSelected(false);        // Unselect tb3
boolean b2 = tb3.isSelected(); // will store false in b2
```

If the selection is mutually exclusive, you must group all your choices in a button group. In a mutually exclusive group of choices, if you select one choice, all other choices are unselected. Typically, you create a button group for a group of mutually exclusive JRadioButtons or JToggleButtons. Theoretically, you can also create a button group for JCheckBoxes to have mutually exclusive choices. However, it is not recommended to use a group of mutually exclusive JCheckBoxes in a GUI.

An instance of the ButtonGroup class represents a button group. You can add and remove a JRadioButton or JToggleButton to a button group by using its add() and remove() methods, respectively. Initially all members of a button group are unselected. To form a button group, you need to add all mutually exclusive choice components to an object of the ButtonGroup class. You do not add (in fact, you cannot add) a ButtonGroup object to a container. You must add all choice components to the container. Listing 2-6 contains the complete code that shows a group of three mutually exclusive JRadioButtons.

Listing 2-6. A Group of Mutually Exclusive Three Choices Represented By Three JRadioButtons

```java
// ButtonGroupFrame.java
package com.jdojo.swing;

import java.awt.BorderLayout;
import java.awt.Container;
import javax.swing.Box;
import javax.swing.ButtonGroup;
import javax.swing.JFrame;
import javax.swing.JRadioButton;
```

```java
public class ButtonGroupFrame extends JFrame {
    ButtonGroup genderGroup = new ButtonGroup();
    JRadioButton genderMale = new JRadioButton("Male");
    JRadioButton genderFemale = new JRadioButton("Female");
    JRadioButton genderUnknown = new JRadioButton("Unknown");

    public ButtonGroupFrame() {
        this.initFrame();
    }

    private void initFrame() {
        this.setTitle("Mutually Exclusive JRadioButtons Group");
        this.setDefaultCloseOperation(EXIT_ON_CLOSE);

        // Add three gender JRadioButtons to a ButtonGroup,
        // so they become mutually exclusive choices
        genderGroup.add(genderMale);
        genderGroup.add(genderFemale);
        genderGroup.add(genderUnknown);

        // Add gender radio button to a vertical Box
        Box b1 = Box.createVerticalBox();
        b1.add(genderMale);
        b1.add(genderFemale);
        b1.add(genderUnknown);

        // Add the vertical box to the center of the frame
        Container contentPane = this.getContentPane();
        contentPane.add(b1, BorderLayout.CENTER);
    }

    public static void main(String[] args) {
        ButtonGroupFrame bf = new ButtonGroupFrame();
        bf.pack();
        bf.setVisible(true);
    }
}
```

A JComboBox<E> is another type of Swing component that lets you make one selection from a list of choices. Optionally, it can include an editable field that lets you type a new choice value. The type parameter E is the type of the elements it contains. You can use a JComboBox instead of a group of JToggleButtons, JCheckBoxes, or JRadioButtons when the space on the screen is limited. You save space on the screen using a JComboBox. However, the user has to perform two clicks to make a selection. First, the user has to click on the arrow button to display the list of choices in a drop-down list, and then he has to click on a choice from the list. The user can also use up/down arrow keys on the keyboard to scroll through the list of choices and select one when the component is in focus. You can create a JComboBox by passing the list of choices in one of its constructors, as shown:

```java
// Use an array of String as the list of choices
String[] sList = new String[]{"Spring", "Summer", "Fall", "Winter"};
JComboBox<String> seasons = new JComboBox<>(sList);
```

```
// Use a Vector of String as the list of choices
Vector<String> sList2 = new Vector<>(4);
sList2.add("Spring");
sList2.add("Summer");
sList2.add("Fall");
sList2.add("Winter");
JComboBox<String> seasons2 = new JComboBox<>(sList2);
```

You can create a JComboBox with no choices and afterwards add choices to it by using one of its methods. It also includes methods to remove a choice from the list and get the value of the selected choice. Table 2-14 shows a list of commonly used methods of the JComboBox class.

Table 2-14. *Commonly Used Methods of the JComboBox class*

Method	Description
void addItem(E item)	Adds an item as a choice in the list. The toString() method on the added object is called and the returned string is displayed as a choice.
E getItemAt(int index)	Returns the item at the specified index from the list of choices. The index starts at zero and ends at the size of the list minus one. If the specified index is out of bound, it returns null.
int getItemCount()	Returns the number of items in the list of choices.
int getSelectedIndex()	Returns the index of the selected item. It returns –1, if the selected item is not in the list. Note that for an editable JComboBox, you can type in a new value in the field and that may not exist in the list of choices. In this case, this method will return –1. It also returns –1 if there is no selection.
Object getSelectedItem()	Returns the currently selected item. Returns null if there is no selection.
void insertItemAt(E item, int index)	Inserts the specified item at the specified index in the list.
boolean isEditable()	Returns true if the JComboBox is editable. Otherwise, it returns false. By default, a JComboBox is non-editable.
void removeAllItems()	Removes all items from the list.
void removeItem(Object item)	Removes the specified item from the list.
void removeItemAt(int index)	Removes the item at the specified index.
void setEditable(boolean editable)	If the specified editable argument is true, the JComboBox is editable. Otherwise, it is non-editable. The user can type in a value in an editable JComboBox, which is not in the list of choices. Note that the new typed in value is not added to the list of choices.
void setSelectedIndex(int index)	Selects the item at the specified index in the list. If the specified index is –1, it clears the selection. If the specified index is less than –1 or greater than the size of the list minus 1, it throws an IllegalArgumentException.
void setSelectedItem(Object item)	Selects the item in the field. If the specified item exists in the list, it is always selected. If the specified item does not exist in the list, it is selected in the field only if the JComboBox is editable.

If you want to be notified when an item is selected or deselected in the JComboBox, you can add an item listener to it. An item listener is notified whenever an item is selected or deselected. Note that when you change a selection in a JComboBox, it fires the deselected item event followed by a selected event. The following snippet of code shows how to add an item listener to a JComboBox. You can use the getItem() method of the ItemEvent class to find out which item has been selected or deselected.

```
String[] sList = new String[]{"Spring", "Summer", "Fall", "Winter"};
JComboBox<String> seasons = new JComboBox<>(sList);

// Add an item listener to the combobox
seasons.addItemListener((ItemEvent e) -> {
        Object item = e.getItem();
        if (e.getStateChange() == ItemEvent.SELECTED) {
                // Item has been selected
                System.out.println(item + " has been selected");
        }
        else if (e.getStateChange() == ItemEvent.DESELECTED) {
                // Item has been deselected
                System.out.println(item + " has been deselected");
        }
});
```

A JList<T> is another Swing component that displays a list of choices and lets you select one or more choices from that list. The type parameter T is the type of elements it contains. A JList differs from a JComboBox mainly in the way it displays the list of choices. A JList can show multiple choices on the screen whereas a JComboBox shows the list of choices when you click the arrow button in it. In this sense, a JList is an expanded version of a JComboBox. A JList can display a list of choices in one column or multiple columns. You can create a JList the same way you create a JComboBox, as shown:

```
// Create a JList using an array
String[] items = new String[]{"Spring", "Summer", "Fall", "Winter"};
JList<String> list = new JList<>(items);

// Create a JList using a Vector
Vector<String> items2 = new Vector<>(4);
items2.add("Spring");
items2.add("Summer");
items2.add("Fall");
items2.add("Winter");
JList<String> list2 = new JList<>(items2);
```

A JList does not have scrolling capability. You must add it to a JScrollPane and add the JScrollPane to the container to get the scrolling capability, like so:

```
myContainer.add(new JScrollPane(myJList));
```

You can configure the layout orientation of a JList to arrange the list of choices in three ways:

- Vertical
- Horizontal Wrapping
- Vertical Wrapping

In a vertical arrangement, which is the default, all items in a JList are displayed using one column and multiple rows.

In a horizontal wrapping, all items are arranged in a row and multiple columns. However, if not all items can fit into a row, new rows are added to display them as necessary. Note that the item can flow horizontally left-to-right or right-to-left depending on the orientation of the component.

In a vertical wrapping, all items are arranged in a column and multiple rows. However, if all items cannot fit into a column, new columns are added to display them as necessary.

You can use the setVisibleRowCount(int visibleRows) method of the JList class to set the number of visible rows you would prefer to see in the list without a need to scroll. When you set the number of visible rows to zero or less, the JList will decide the number of visible rows based on width/height of the field and its layout orientation. You can set its layout orientation using its setLayoutOrientation(int orientation) method, where orientation value could be one of the three constants defined in the JList class: JList.VERTICAL, JList.HORIZONTAL_WRAP, and JList.VERTICAL_WRAP.

You can configure the mode of selection for a JList using its setSelectionMode(int mode) method. The mode value could be one of the following three values. The mode values are defined as constants in the ListSelectionModel interface.

- SINGLE_SELECTION

- SINGLE_INTERVAL_SELECTION

- MUTIPLE_INTERVAL_SELECTION

In a single selection mode, you can only select one item at a time. If you change your selection, the previously selected item will be deselected.

In a single interval selection mode, you can select multiple items. However, the items selected must always be contiguous. Suppose you have ten items in a JList and you have selected the seventh item. Now you can select the sixth item or the eighth item in the list, but not any other items. You can keep selecting more contiguous items. You can use the combination of Ctrl key or Shift key and the mouse to make contiguous selections.

In a multiple interval section, you can select multiple items without any restrictions. You can use the combination of Ctrl key or Shift key and the mouse to make selections.

You can add a list selection listener to a JList, which will notify you when a selection is changed. The valueChanged() method of ListSelectionListener is called when a selection is changed. This method may also be called multiple times in the middle of one selection change. You need to use the getValueIsAdjusting() method of the ListSelectionEvent object to make sure that selection changing is finalized, as shown in following snippet of code:

```
myJList.addListSelectionListener((ListSelectionEvent e) -> {
        // Make sure selection change is final
        if (!e.getValueIsAdjusting()) {
                // The selection changed logic goes here
        }
});
```

Table 2-15 lists the commonly used methods of the JList class. Note that a JList does not have a direct method to give you the size of the list (the number of choices in a JList). As every Swing component uses a model, so does a JList. Its model is an instance of the JListModel interface. To know the size of the list of choices of a JList, you need to call the getSize() method of its model, like so:

```
int size = myJList.getModel().getSize();
```

Table 2-15. *Commonly Used Methods of the JList Class*

Method	Description
void clearSelection()	Clears the selection made in the JList.
void ensureIndexIsVisible(int index)	Makes sure the item at the specified index is visible. Note that to make an invisible item visible, the JList must be added in a JScrollPane.
int getFirstVisibleIndex()	Returns the smallest visible index. If there is no visible item or list is empty, it returns –1.
int getLastVisibleIndex()	Returns the largest visible index. If there is no visible item or list is empty, it returns –1.
int getMaxSelectionIndex()	Returns the largest selected index. Returns –1 if there is no selection.
int getMinSelectionIndex()	Returns the smallest selected index. Returns –1 if there is no selection.
int getSelectedIndex()	Returns the smallest selected index. If JList selection mode is single selection, it returns the selected index. Returns –1 if there is no selection.
int[] getSelectedIndices()	Returns the indices of all selected items in an int array. The array will have zero elements if there is no selection.
E getSelectedValue()	Returns the first selected item. If the JList has single selection mode, it is the value of the selected item. Returns null if there is no selection in the JList.
List<E> getSelectedValuesList()	Returns a list of all the selected items in increasing order based on their indices in the list. It there is no selected item, an empty list is returned.
boolean isSelectedIndex(int index)	Returns true if the specified index is selected. Otherwise, it returns false.
boolean isSelectionEmpty()	Returns true if there is no selection in the JList. Otherwise, it returns false.
void setListData(E[] listData) void setListData(Vector<?> listData)	Sets the new list of choices in the JList.
void setSelectedIndex(int index)	Selects an item at the specified index.
void setSelectedIndices(int[] indices)	Selects items at the indices in specified array
void setSelectedValue(Object item, boolean shouldScroll)	Selects the specified item if it exists in the list. Scrolls to the item to make it visible if the second argument is true.

JSpinner

A JSpinner component combines the benefits of a JFormattedTextField and an editable JComboBox. It lets you set a list of choices in a JComboBox, and at the same time, you can also apply a format to the displayed value. It shows only one value at a time from the list of choices. It lets you enter a new value. The name "spinner" comes from the fact that it lets you spin up or down through the list of choices by using up and down arrow buttons. One thing that is special about the list of choices in a JSpinner is that it must be an ordered list. Figure 2-14 shows three JSpinners that are used to select a number, a date, and a season value.

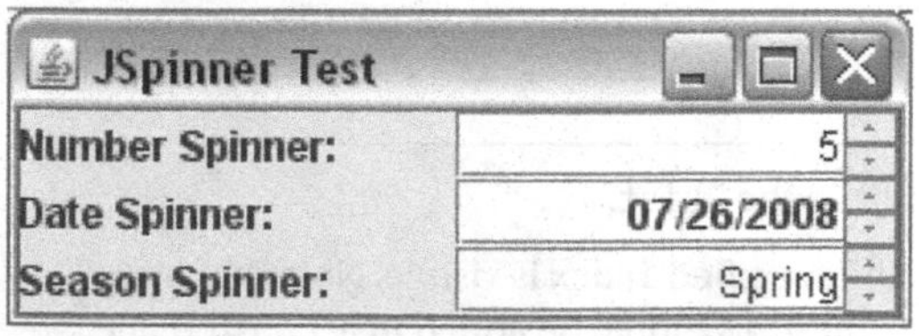

Figure 2-14. JSpinner components in action

Since a JSpinner provides the spinning capability to a variety of list of choices, it depends heavily on its model for its creation. In fact, you must provide a model for the JSpinner in its constructor unless you want a trivial JSpinner with just a list of integers. It supports three different kinds of ordered lists of choices: a list of numbers, a list of dates, and a list of any other objects. It provides three classes to create a model of three different kinds of lists:

- SpinnerNumberModel

- SpinnerDateModel

- SpinnerListModel

A spinner model is an instance of the SpinnerModel interface. It defines the getValue(), setValue(), getPreviousValue(), and getNextValue() methods to work with values in the JSpinner. All these methods work with objects of the Object class.

The SpinnerNumberModel class provides a model for a JSpinner that lets you spin through an ordered list of numbers. You need to specify the minimum, maximum, and current values in the list. You can also specify the step value that is used to step through the number list when you use up/down buttons of a JSpinner. The following snippet of code creates a JSpinner with a list of numbers from 1 to 10. It lets you spin through the list in steps of 1. The current value for the field is set to 5. The SpinnerNumberModel class also has methods that let you get/set different values for the spinner model after you create it.

```
int minValue = 1;
int maxValue = 10;
int currentValue = 5;
int steps = 1;
SpinnerNumberModel nModel = new SpinnerNumberModel(currentValue, minValue, maxValue, steps);
JSpinner numberSpinner = new JSpinner(nModel);
```

The SpinnerDateModel class provides a model for a JSpinner that lets you spin through an ordered list of dates. You need to specify the start date, the end date, the current value, and the step. The following snippet of code creates a JSpinner to spin through a list of dates from January 1, 1950 to December 31, 2050 in steps of one day at a time. The current system date is set as the current value for the field.

```
Calendar calendar = Calendar.getInstance();
calendar.set(1950, 1, 1);
Date minValue = calendar.getTime();
calendar.set(2050, 12, 31);
Date maxValue = calendar.getTime();
Date currentValue = new Date();
int steps = Calendar.DAY_OF_MONTH; // Must be a Calendar field
SpinnerDateModel dModel = new SpinnerDateModel(currentValue, minValue, maxValue, steps);
dateSpinner = new JSpinner(dModel);
```

Note that the date value will be displayed in the default locale format. The step value is used when you use the getNextValue() method on the model. A JSpinner with a list of dates lets you spin through any of the displayed date fields by highlighting a part of the date field and using the up/down button. Suppose the date format that your JSpinner uses is mm/dd/yyyy. You can place your cursor in the year part of the field (yyyy) and use up/down buttons to step through the list based on the year.

The SpinnerListModel class provides a model for a JSpinner that lets you spin through an ordered list of objects. You just specify an array of objects or a List object, and the JSpinner will let you spin through the list as it appears in the array or the List. The returned String from the toString() method of the object in the list is displayed as the value in the JSpinner. The following snippet of code creates a JSpinner to display a list of four seasons:

```
String[] seasons = new String[] {"Spring", "Summer", "Fall", "Winter"};
SpinnerListModel sModel = new SpinnerListModel(seasons);
listSpinner = new JSpinner(sModel);
```

A JSpinner uses an editor object to display the current value. It has the following three static inner classes to display three different kinds of ordered lists:

- JSpinner.NumberEditor

- JSpinner.DateEditor

- JSpinner.ListEditor

If you want to display a number or a date in a specific format, you need to set a new editor for the JSpinner. The editor classes for the number and date editors let you specify the formats. The following snippet of code sets the number format as "00", so numbers 1 to 10 are displayed as 01, 02, 03...10. It sets the date format to mm/dd/yyyy.

```
// Set the number format to "00"
JSpinner.NumberEditor nEditor = new JSpinner.NumberEditor(numberSpinner, "00");
numberSpinner.setEditor(nEditor);

// Set the date format to mm/dd/yyyy
JSpinner.DateEditor dEditor = new JSpinner.DateEditor(dateSpinner, "mm/dd/yyyy");
dateSpinner.setEditor(dEditor);
```

■ **Tip**   You can use the getValue() method defined of a JSpinner or SpinnerModel to get the current value in the JSpinner as an Object. SpinnerNumberModel and SpinnerDateModel define the getNumber() and getDate() method that return the Number and Date objects, respectively.

JScrollBar

If you want to view a component that is bigger than the available space, you want to use a JScrollBar or a JScrollPane component. I will discuss the JScrollPane in the next section. A JScrollBar has an orientation property that determines whether it is displayed horizontally or vertically. Figure 2-15 depicts a horizontal JScrollBar.

Figure 2-15. *A horizontal JScrollBar*

A `JScrollBar` is made up of four parts: two arrow buttons (one at each end), a knob (also known as a thumb), and a track. When the arrow button is clicked, the knob moves on the track towards the arrow button. You can drag the knob towards either end with the help of a mouse. You can also move the knob by clicking on the track.

You can customize various properties of a `JScrollBar` by passing their values in its constructor or by setting them after you create it. Table 2-16 lists some commonly used properties and methods to manipulate them.

Table 2-16. *Commonly Used Properties of a JScrollBar and Methods to Get/Set Those Properties*

Property	Method	Description
Orientation	getOrientation() setOrientation()	Determines whether the `JScrollBar` is horizontal or vertical. Its value could be one of the two constants, `HORIZONTAL` or `VERTICAL`, which are defined in the `JScrollBar` class.
Value	getValue() setValue()	The position of the knob is its value. Initially, it is set to zero.
Extent	getVisibleAmount() setVisibleAmount()	It is the size of the knob. It is expressed in proportion to the size of the track. For example, if the track size represents 150 and you set the extent to 25, the knob size will be one sixth of the track size. Its default value is 10.
Minimum Value	getMinimum() setMinimum()	The minimum value that it represents. The default value is zero.
Maximum Value	getMaximum() setMaximum()	The maximum value that it represents. The default value is 100.

The following snippet of code demonstrates how to create a `JScrollBar` with different properties:

```
// Create a JScrollBar with all default properties. Its orientation
// will be vertical, current value 0, extent 10, minimum 0, and maximum 100
JScrollBar sb1 = new JScrollBar();

// Create a horizontal JScrollBar with default values
JScrollBar sb2 = new JScrollBar(JScrollBar.HORIZONTAL);

// Create a horizontal JScrollBar with a current value of 50,
// extent 15, minimum 1 and maximum 150
JScrollBar sb3 = new JScrollBar(JScrollBar.HORIZONTAL, 50, 15, 1, 150);
```

The current value of a `JScrollBar` can be set only between its minimum and (maximum – extent) value. A `JScrollBar` by itself does not add any value to a GUI. All it has are some properties. You can add an `AdjustmentListener` to a `JScrollBar` that is notified when its value changes.

```
// Add an AdjustmentListener to a JScrollBar named myScrollBar
myScrollBar.addAdjustmentListener((AdjustmentEvent e) -> {
        if (!e.getValueIsAdjusting()) {
                // The logic for value changed goes here
        }
});
```

It is not simple to use a JScrollBar to scroll through a component that is bigger in size than its display area. You need to write a significant amount of code to achieve that task if you ever want to use a JScrollBar alone. A JScrollPane makes this task easier. It takes care of the scrolling without writing any extra code.

JScrollPane

A JScrollPane is a container that can hold and display up to nine components, as shown in Figure 2-16. It uses its own layout manager that is an object of the class JScrollPaneLayout.

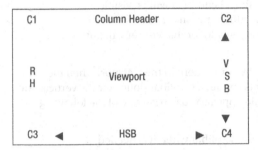

Figure 2-16. *The components of a JScrollPane*

The nine components that a JScrollPane manages are two JScrollBars, a viewport, a row header, a column header, and four corners.

- *Two JScrollBars*: In the diagram, the two scrollbars are named HSB and VSB. They are two instances of the JScrollBar class: one horizontal and one vertical. A JScrollPane will create and manage the two JScrollBars for you. You do not need to write any code for that. The only things you need to indicate are whether you want them or not, and when you want them to appear.

- *A Viewport*: The viewport is the area where a JScrollPane displays the scrollable component such as a JTextArea. You can think of a viewport as a peephole through which you view the component by scrolling up/down and right/left using scrollbars. A viewport is a Swing component. An object of the JViewport class represents a viewport component. A JViewport is simply a wrapper for a Swing component to implement a scrollable view of that component. The JScrollPane creates a JViewport object for your component and uses it internally.

- *Row and Column Headers*: The row header is abbreviated as RH in the diagram. Row/Column headers are two optional viewports you can use in a JScrollPane. When you use the horizontal scrollbar, the column header scrolls with it horizontally. When you use the vertical scrollbar, the row header scrolls with it vertically. A good use of row/column headers is to display horizontal and vertical rulers for a picture or drawing in the viewport. Typically, you do not use row/column headers.

- *Four Corners*: Four corners can exist in a JScrollPane. A corner exists when two components meet vertically. The four corners are named C1, C2, C3, and C4 in the diagram. These are not the names given to the corners by the JScrollPane. I gave them a name for the discussion purpose. The corner C1 exists if you add a row header and a column header. The corner C2 exists if you add a column header and the vertical scrollbar is visible. The corner C3 exists if you add a row header and the horizontal scrollbar is visible. The corner C4 exists if both horizontal and vertical scrollbars are visible. You can add any Swing component as a corner component. The only limitation is that you cannot add the same component in more than one corner. Note that adding a corner component does not guarantee that it will be visible. A corner component will be visible in a corner only if that corner exists according to the rules discussed. For example, if you add a corner component for the C4 corner, it will be visible only if both scrollbars, horizontal and vertical, are visible. If either or both scrollbars are not visible, the corner C4 does not exist and the component that you add for that corner will not be visible.

A scrollbar in a direction (horizontal or vertical) is needed to view the component in the viewport when the component's size is bigger than the JScrollPane size. A JScrollPane lets you set a scrollbar policy for the vertical and horizontal scrollbars. A scrollbar policy is a rule to control when it should appear. You can set one of the following three scrollbar policies:

- *Show as needed*: It means that a JScrollPane should show the scrollbar when it is needed. A scrollbar is needed when the component in the viewport in a direction, horizontal or vertical, is bigger than its display area. It is up to the JScrollPane to decide when a scrollbar is needed, and if it is needed, it will make the scrollbar visible. Otherwise, it will make the scrollbar invisible.

- *Show Always*: It means that a JScrollPane should always show the scrollbar.

- *Show Never*: It means that a JScrollPane should never show the scrollbar.

The scrollbar polices are defined by six constants in the ScrollPaneConstants interface. Three constants are for a vertical scrollbar and three are for a horizontal scrollbar. The JScrollPane class implements the ScrollPaneConstants interface. So you can also access these constants using the JScrollPane class. The constants that define scrollbar policies are XXX_SCROLLBAR_AS_NEEDED, XXX_SCROLLBAR_ALWAYS, and XXX_SCROLLBAR_NEVER, where you need to replace XXX with VERTICAL or HORIZONTAL, depending on which scrollbar's policy you are referring to. The default value of the scrollbar policy for both vertical and horizontal scrollbars is "Show as needed". The following snippet of code demonstrates how to create a JScrollPane with different options:

```
// Create a JScrollPane with no component as its viewport and
// with default scrollbars policy as "As Needed"
JScrollPane sp1 = new JScrollPane();

// Create a JScrollPane with a JTextArea as its viewport and
// with default scrollbars policy as "As Needed"
JTextArea description = new JTextArea(10, 60);
JScrollPane sp2 = new JScrollPane(description);

// Create a JScrollPane with a JTextArea as its viewport and
// both scrollbars policy set to "show always"
JTextArea comments = new JTextArea(10, 60);
JScrollPane sp3 = new JScrollPane(comments,
                        JScrollPane.VERTICAL_SCROLLBAR_ALWAYS,
                        JScrollPane.HORIZONTAL_SCROLLBAR_ALWAYS);
```

As noted before, when you add a component to a JScrollPane, you add the JScrollPane to the container, not the component. The viewport of a JScrollPane keeps the reference to the component you add to the JScrollPane. You get the reference of the component in a JScrollPane by querying its viewport as shown:

```
// Get the reference to the viewport of the JScrollPane sp3
JViewport vp = sp3.getViewport();

// Get the reference to the comments JTextArea added
// to the JScrollPane, sp3, using its viewport reference
JTextArea comments1 = (JTextArea)vp.getView();
```

If you create a JScrollPane without specifying the component for its viewport, you can add a component to its viewport later using its setViewportView() method as shown:

```
// Set a JTextPane as the viewport component for sp3
sp3.setViewportView(new JTextPane());
```

JProgressBar

A JProgressBar is used to display the progress of a task. It has an orientation, which can be horizontal or vertical. It has three values associated with it: the current value, the minimum value, and the maximum value. You can create a progress bar as shown:

```
// Create a horizontal progress bar with current, minimum, and maximum values
// set to 0, 0, and 100, respectively.
JProgressBar hpBar1 = new JProgressBar();

// Create a horizontal progress bar with current, minimum, and maximum values
// set to 20, 20, and 200, respectively.
JProgressBar hpbar2 = new JProgressBar(SwingConstants.HORIZONTAL, 20, 200);

// Create a vertical progress bar with current, minimum, and maximum values
// set to 5, 5 and 50, respectively.
JProgressBar vpBar1 = new JProgressBar(SwingConstants.VERTICAL, 5, 50);
```

As the task progresses, you need to set the current value for the progress bar using its setValue(int value) method to indicate the progress. The component will update itself visually to reflect the new value. The progress is reflected differently depending on the look and feel of the application. Sometimes a solid bar is used is show the progress and sometimes solid rectangles are used to show the progress. You can use the getValue() method to get the current value.

You can also display a string that describes the progress bar's current value using the setStringPainted() method. Passing true to this method displays the string value and passing false does not display the string value. The string to be painted is specified by calling the setString(String s) method.

Sometimes the current value of the progress of a task is unknown or indeterminate. In such cases, you cannot set the current value for the progress bar. Rather, you can indicate to the user that the task's execution is in progress. You can set a progress bar in an indeterminate mode using its setIndeterminate() method. Passing true to this method places the progress bar in an indeterminate mode and passing false places the progress bar in a determinate mode. A JProgressBar component displays an animation to indicate its indeterminate state.

Figure 2-17 shows a JFrame with two JProgressBars. The horizontal JProgressBar is in determinate mode and it displays a string to describe the progress. The vertical JProgressBar has been placed in an indeterminate mode; note the solid rectangular bar in the middle that is displayed as an animation.

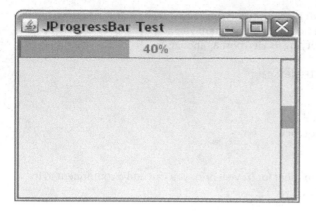

Figure 2-17. *JProgressBars in action*

JSlider

A JSlider lets you select a value graphically from a set of values between two integers by sliding a knob along a track. It has four important properties: an orientation, a minimum value, a maximum value, and a current value. The orientation determines whether it is displayed horizontally or vertically. You can use SwingConstants.VERTICAL and SwingConstants.HORIZONTAL as valid values for its orientation. The following snippet of code creates a horizontal JSlider with the minimum value of 0, the maximum value of 10, and the current value set to 5:

```
JSlider points = new JSlider(0, 10, 5);
```

You can get the current value of a JSlider using its getValue() method. Typically, the user sets the current value of a JSlider by sliding the knob right/left for the horizontal JSlider and up/down for the vertical one. You can also set its value programmatically by using its setValue(int value) method.

You can display the minor and major ticks on a JSlider. You need to set the interval at which these ticks need to be displayed, and call its method to enable the tick paintings, as shown:

```
points.setMinorTickSpacing(1);
points.setMajorTickSpacing(2);
points.setPaintTicks(true);
```

You can also display the labels showing values along the track in a JSlider. You can display standard labels or custom labels. The standard labels will display the integer values along the track. You can call its setPaintLabels(true) method to display the integer values at major tick spacing. Figure 2-18 shows a JSlider with ticks and standard labels.

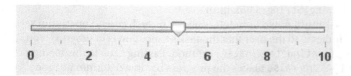

Figure 2-18. *A JSlider component with minimum = 0, maximum = 10, current value = 5, minor tick spacing = 1, major tick spacing = 2, tick painting enabled, and showing standard labels*

JSlider also lets you set custom labels. A label on a JSlider is displayed using a JLabel component. You need to create a Hashtable with value-label pairs and use its setLabelTable() method to set the labels. A value-label pair consists of an Integer-JLabel pair. The following snippet of code sets the label Poor for value 0, Average for value 5, and Excellent for value 10. Setting a label table does not display the labels. You must call the setPaintLabels(true) method to display them. Figure 2-19 shows a JSlider with custom labels produced by the following snippet of code:

```
// Create the value-label pairs in a Hashtable
Hashtable labelTable = new Hashtable();
labelTable.put(new Integer(0), new JLabel("Poor"));
labelTable.put(new Integer(5), new JLabel("Average"));
labelTable.put(new Integer(10), new JLabel("Excellent"));

// Set the labels for the JSlider and make them visible
points.setLabelTable(labelTable);
points.setPaintLabels(true);
```

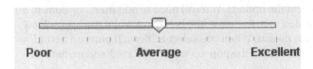

Figure 2-19. *A JSlider with custom labels*

JSeparator

A JSeparator is a handy component when you want to add a separator between two components or two groups of components. Typically, a JSeparator is used in a menu to separate groups of related menu items. You can create a horizontal or a vertical JSeparator by specifying its orientation. You can use it anywhere you would use a Swing component.

```
// Create a horizontal separator
JSeparator hs = new JSeparator(); // By default, the type is horizontal

// Create a vertical separator
JSeparator vs = new JSeparator(SwingConstants.VERTICAL);
```

A JSeparator will extend itself to fill the size provided by the layout manager. You can use the setOrientation() and getOrientation() methods to set and get the orientation of the JSeparator.

Menus

A menu component is used to provide a list of actions to the user in a compact form. You can also provide a list of actions by using a group of JButtons, where each JButton represents an action. It is a matter of preference to use a menu or a group of JButtons to present a list of actions. However, there is a noticeable advantage to using a menu; it uses much less space on the screen compared to a group of JButtons. A menu uses less space by folding (or nesting) a group of options under another option. For example, if you have used a file editor, the options such as New, Open, Save, and Print are nested under a top-level File menu option. A user needs to click the File menu to see the list of options that are available under it. Typically, in case of a group of JButtons, all JButtons are visible to the user all the time, and it is easy for users to know what actions are available. Therefore, there is a little tradeoff between the amount of space and usability when you decide to use a menu or JButtons.

There is another kind of menu called a *pop-up menu*. It does not take any space on the screen at all. Usually, it is displayed when the user clicks the right mouse button. It disappears as soon as the user makes a choice or clicks the mouse outside the displayed pop-up menu area. It is a super compact menu component. However, it makes it difficult for the user to know that any options are available. Sometimes, a text message is displayed on the screen stating that the user needs to right click to view the list of available options. An object of the JPopupMenu class represents a pop-up menu in Swing. Now let's see menus in action.

Creating and adding a menu to a JFrame is a multistep process. The following steps describe the process in detail.

Create an object of the JMenuBar class and add it to a JFrame using its setJMenuBar() method. A JMenuBar is an empty container that will hold a list of menu options, and each option in a JMenuBar represents a list of options.

```
// Create a JMenuBar and set it to a JFrame
JMenuBar menuBar = new JMenuBar();
myFrame.setJMenuBar(menuBar);
```

At this point, you have an empty JMenuBar associated with a JFrame. Now, you need to add the list of options, also called top-level menu options, to the JMenuBar. An object of the JMenu class represents a list of options. A JMenu is also an empty container that can hold menu items that represent the options. You will need to add menu options to a JMenu. A JMenu does not always display the options that are added to it. Rather, it displays them when the user selects the JMenu. This is where you get the compactness when you use menus. When you select a JMenu, it pops up a window that displays the options contained in it. Once you select an option from the pop-up window or click somewhere outside the JMenu, the pop-up window disappears.

```
// Create two JMenu (or two top-level menu options):
// File and Help, and add them to the JMenuBar
JMenu fileMenu = new JMenu("File");
JMenu helpMenu = new JMenu("Help");
menuBar.add(fileMenu);
menuBar.add(helpMenu);
```

At this point, your JFrame will display a menu bar at its top area with two options called File and Help, as shown in Figure 2-20. If you select or click File or Help, nothing happens at this point.

File   Help

Figure 2-20. *A JMenuBar With Two JMenu Options*

Let's add some options to your JMenu. You want to display three menu options under File and they are New, Open, and Exit. You want to add a separator (a horizontal line as a divider) between the Open and Exit options. An object of the JMenuItem class represents an option inside a JMenu.

```
// Create menu items
JMenuItem newMenuItem = new JMenuItem("New");
JMenuItem openMenuItem = new JMenuItem("Open");
JMenuItem exitMenuItem = new JMenuItem("Exit");

// Add menu items and a separator to the menu
fileMenu.add(newMenuItem);
fileMenu.add(openMenuItem);
fileMenu.addSeparator();
fileMenu.add(exitMenuItem);
```

At this point, you have added three JMenuItems to the File menu. When you click the File menu, it will display the options shown in Figure 2-21. You can scroll through options under the File menu by using down/up arrow key on the keyboard or select one of them by using the mouse. When you select any one of the options under the File menu, nothing happens because you have not added any actions to them.

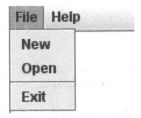

Figure 2-21. *A File JMenu with three options*

You may want to have two suboptions under a menu item such as under the New option. That is, the user can create two different things, Policy and Claim, and you want those two options available under the New option. You not trying to nest options within an option. The File menu is an instance of the JMenu class, which represents a list of options, and you want to add a New menu that should also display a list of options. You can do this easily. The only thing you need to understand is that a JMenu represents a list of options, whereas a JMenuItem represents only one option. You can add a JMenuItem or JMenu to a JMenu. To achieve this, you need to make a little modification to the snippet of code shown earlier. Now the New menu will be an instance of the JMenu class, not the JMenuItem class. You will add two JMenuItems to the New menu. The following snippet of code will do the job:

```
// New is a JMenu - a list of options
JMenu newMenu = new JMenu("New");
JMenuItem policyMenuItem = new JMenuItem("Policy");
JMenuItem claimMenuItem = new JMenuItem("Claim");
newMenu.add(policyMenuItem);
newMenu.add(claimMenuItem);

JMenuItem openMenuItem = new JMenuItem("Open");
JMenuItem exitMenuItem = new JMenuItem("Exit");

fileMenu.add(newMenu);
fileMenu.add(openMenuItem);
fileMenu.addSeparator();
fileMenu.add(exitMenuItem);
```

Now, the menu is displayed as shown in Figure 2-22. When you select the File menu, the New menu displays an arrow next to it indicating that it has sub menus. When you select the New menu, it displays the two submenus labeled Policy and Claim.

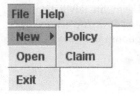

Figure 2-22. *Nesting menus*

There is no limit on the number of levels a menu can be nested. However, more than two levels of nesting is not considered good GUI practice because the user would have to drill down several levels just to get to the available options.

The final piece to make menus work is to add actions to the menu items. You can add action listeners to a JMenuItem. The associated action listener is notified when the user selects the JMenuItem. The following snippet of code adds an action listener to the Exit menu item that will exit the application:

```
// Add an action listener to the Exit menu item
exitMenuItem.addActionListener(e -> System.exit(0));
```

Now you have added an action to the Exit menu item. If you select it, the application will exit. Similarly, you can add action listeners to other menu items to perform actions when they are selected.

You can enable/disable a menu using the setEnabled() method. Although it is possible to make a menu visible/invisible, it is not good practice to do it. It makes it hard for a user to learn an application. If you keep all menu options available (either in an enabled or disabled state) all the time, the user will be able to work with the application faster by knowing where the menu options are located. If you make menu options visible/invisible, the locations of the menu options keep changing and the user will have to pay more attention to the location of menu options each time he wants to use them.

You can also assign shortcuts to menu options. You can use the setMnemonic() method to add a shortcut to a menu item by specifying a shortcut key. You can invoke the action represented by that menu item by pressing a combination of the Alt key and the shortcut key. Note that the menu item must be visible for its mnemonic to work. For example, if you have a mnemonic (the N key) set for a New menu option, you must select the File menu so the New menu option is visible, and press Alt + N to invoke the action represented by the New menu item.

If you want to invoke the associated action to a menu item irrespective of whether it is visible or not, you need to set its accelerator key by using the setAccelerator() method. The following snippet of code sets the E key as a mnemonic and Ctrl + E as an accelerator for the Exit menu option:

```
// Set E as mnemonic for Exit menu and Ctrl + E as its accelerator
exitMenuItem.setMnemonic(KeyEvent.VK_E);
KeyStroke cntrlEKey = KeyStroke.getKeyStroke(KeyEvent.VK_E, ActionEvent.CTRL_MASK);
exitMenuItem.setAccelerator(cntrlEKey);
```

Now you can invoke the Exit menu option in two ways: you can press Alt + E key combination when it is visible, or you can press Ctrl + E keys combination any time.

You can use a pop-up menu, which is displayed on demand. The creation of a pop-up menu is similar to a JMenu. You need to create an instance of the JPopupMenu class, which represents an empty pop-up menu container, and then add instances of JMenuItem to it. You can also have nested menus in a pop-up menu, as you had in a JMenu.

```
// Create a popup menu
JPopupMenu popupMenu = new JPopupMenu();

// Create three menu items for our popup menu
JMenuItem popup1 = new JMenuItem("Poupup1");
JMenuItem popup2 = new JMenuItem("Poupup2");
JMenuItem popup3 = new JMenuItem("Poupup3");

// Add menu items to the popup menu
popupMenu.add(popup1);
popupMenu.add(popup2);
popupMenu.add(popup3);
```

Since a pop-up menu does not have a fixed location and it is displayed on demand, you need to know where to display it and when to display it. You need to use its show() method to display it at a location. The show() method takes three arguments: the invoker component whose space will be used to display the pop-up menu, plus x and y coordinates on the invoker component where it will be displayed.

```
// Display the popup menu
popupMenu.show(myComponent, xPos, yPos);
```

Typically, you display a pop-up menu when the user clicks the right mouse button. Different look and feel options use a different key event to display the pop-up menu. For example, one look and feel scenario displays it when a right mouse button is released, whereas another displays it when a right mouse button is pressed. Swing makes this job easy for you to display the pop-up menu by providing a isPopupTrigger() method in the MouseEvent class. In a mouse pressed or released event, you need to call this method. If this method returns true, display the pop-up menu. The following snippet of code associates a mouse listener to a component and displays the pop-up menu:

```
// Create a mouse listener
MouseListener ml = new MouseAdapter() {
        @Override
        public void mousePressed(MouseEvent e) {
                if (e.isPopupTrigger()) {
                        popupMenu.show(e.getComponent(), e.getX(), e.getY());
                }
        }

        @Override
        public void mouseReleased(MouseEvent e) {
                if (e.isPopupTrigger()) {
                        popupMenu.show(e.getComponent(), e.getX(), e.getY());
                }
        }
};

// Add a mouse listener to myComponent
myComponent.addMouseListener(ml);
```

Whenever the user right clicks on myComponent, a pop-up menu will appear. Note that you need to add the same code in both mousePressed() and mouseReleased() methods. It is decided by the look and feel which event should display the popup menu.

Listing 2-7 contains a complete program showing how to use menus. The program is long. It does the repetitive work of creating and adding menu items and adding action listeners to them.

Listing 2-7. Working With Menus and Pop-up Menus

```java
// JMenuFrame.java
package com.jdojo.swing;

import javax.swing.JFrame;
import java.awt.Container;
import javax.swing.JMenuBar;
import javax.swing.JMenu;
import javax.swing.JMenuItem;
import javax.swing.JLabel;
import java.awt.event.ActionListener;
import javax.swing.JTextArea;
import java.awt.BorderLayout;
import java.awt.event.KeyEvent;
import javax.swing.KeyStroke;
import javax.swing.JPopupMenu;
import java.awt.event.MouseAdapter;
import java.awt.event.MouseEvent;
import java.awt.event.MouseListener;
import javax.swing.JScrollPane;

public class JMenuFrame extends JFrame {
    JLabel msgLabel = new JLabel("Right click to see popup menu");
    JTextArea msgText = new JTextArea(10, 60);
    JPopupMenu popupMenu = new JPopupMenu();

    public JMenuFrame(String title) {
        super(title);
        initFrame();
    }

    // Initialize the JFrame and add components to it
    private void initFrame() {
        this.setDefaultCloseOperation(JFrame.EXIT_ON_CLOSE);
        Container contentPane = this.getContentPane();

        // Add the message label and text area
        contentPane.add(new JScrollPane(msgText), BorderLayout.CENTER);
        contentPane.add(msgLabel, BorderLayout.SOUTH);

        // Set the menu bar for the frame
        JMenuBar menuBar = getCustomMenuBar();
        this.setJMenuBar(menuBar);

        // Create a popup menu and add a mouse listener to show it
        createPopupMenu();
    }
```

```java
private JMenuBar getCustomMenuBar() {
        JMenuBar menuBar = new JMenuBar();

        // Get the File and Help menus
        JMenu fileMenu = getFileMenu();
        JMenu helpMenu = getHelpMenu();

        // Add the File and Help menus to the menu bar
        menuBar.add(fileMenu);
        menuBar.add(helpMenu);

        return menuBar;
}

private JMenu getFileMenu() {
        JMenu fileMenu = new JMenu("File");

        // Set Alt-F as mnemonic for the File menu
        fileMenu.setMnemonic(KeyEvent.VK_F);

        // Prepare a New Menu item. It will have sub menus
        JMenu newMenu = getNewMenu();
        fileMenu.add(newMenu);

        JMenuItem openMenuItem = new JMenuItem("Open", KeyEvent.VK_O);
        JMenuItem exitMenuItem = new JMenuItem("Exit", KeyEvent.VK_F);

        fileMenu.add(openMenuItem);

        // You can add a JSeparator or just call the convenience method
        // addSeparator() on fileMenu. You can replace the following statement
        // with fileMenu.add(new JSeparator());
        fileMenu.addSeparator();
        fileMenu.add(exitMenuItem);

        // Add an ActionListener to the Exit menu item
        exitMenuItem.addActionListener(e -> System.exit(0));

        return fileMenu;
}

private JMenu getNewMenu() {
        // New menu will have two sub menus - Policy and Claim
        JMenu newMenu = new JMenu("New");

        // Add submenus to New menu
        JMenuItem policyMenuItem = new JMenuItem("Policy", KeyEvent.VK_P);
        JMenuItem claimMenuItem = new JMenuItem("Claim", KeyEvent.VK_L);
        newMenu.add(policyMenuItem);
        newMenu.add(claimMenuItem);

        return newMenu;
```

```java
    }

    private JMenu getHelpMenu() {
        JMenu helpMenu = new JMenu("Help");
        helpMenu.setMnemonic(KeyEvent.VK_H);

        JMenuItem indexMenuItem = new JMenuItem("Index", KeyEvent.VK_I);
        JMenuItem aboutMenuItem = new JMenuItem("About", KeyEvent.VK_A);

        // Set F1 as the accelerator key for the Index menu item
        KeyStroke f1Key = KeyStroke.getKeyStroke(KeyEvent.VK_F1, 0);
        indexMenuItem.setAccelerator(f1Key);

        helpMenu.add(indexMenuItem);
        helpMenu.addSeparator();
        helpMenu.add(aboutMenuItem);

        // Add an action listener to the index menu item
        indexMenuItem.addActionListener(e ->
                msgText.append("You have selected Help >>Index menu item.\n"));

        return helpMenu;
    }

    private void createPopupMenu() {
        // Create a popup menu and add a mouse listener to the frame,
        // so a popup menu is displayed when the user clicks a right mouse button
        JMenuItem popup1 = new JMenuItem("Popup1");
        JMenuItem popup2 = new JMenuItem("Popup2");
        JMenuItem popup3 = new JMenuItem("Popup3");

        // Create an action listener
        ActionListener al =  e -> {
                JMenuItem menuItem = (JMenuItem)e.getSource();
                String menuText = menuItem.getText();
                String msg = "You clicked " + menuText + " menu item.\n";
                msgText.append(msg);
        };

        // Add the same action listener to all popup menu items
        popup1.addActionListener(al);
        popup2.addActionListener(al);
        popup3.addActionListener(al);

        // Add menu items to popup menu
        popupMenu.add(popup1);
        popupMenu.add(popup2);
        popupMenu.add(popup3);
```

```
            // Create a mouse listener to show a popup menu
            MouseListener ml = new MouseAdapter() {
                    @Override
                    public void mousePressed(MouseEvent e) {
                            displayPopupMenu(e);
                    }

                    @Override
                    public void mouseReleased(MouseEvent e) {
                            displayPopupMenu(e);
                    }
            };

            // Add a mouse listener to the msg text and label
            msgText.addMouseListener(ml);
            msgLabel.addMouseListener(ml);
    }

    private void displayPopupMenu(MouseEvent e) {
            // Make sure this mouse event is supposed to show the popup menu.
            // Different platforms show the popup menu in different mouse events
            if (e.isPopupTrigger()) {
                    this.popupMenu.show(e.getComponent(), e.getX(), e.getY());
            }
    }

    // Display the CustomFrame
    public static void main(String[] args) {
            JMenuFrame frame = new JMenuFrame("JMenu and JPopupMenu Test");
            frame.pack();
            frame.setVisible(true);
    }
}
```

You can also use JRadioButtonMenuItem and JCheckBoxMenuItem as menu items in a menu. As the names suggest, they are displayed as radio buttons and checkboxes, and work the same as radio buttons and checkboxes. You can add any swing component to a JMenu. To use radio button-type menu items, you need to group multiple JRadioButtonMenuItem components into a button group so they represent exclusive choices. To handle the radio button selection change, you can add an ActionListener or ItemListener to the JRadioButtonMenuItem. To handle a change of state in JCheckBoxMenuItem, you need to use an ItemListener.

■ **Tip**   I'll finally reveal the secret of menus in Swing. A menu item in Swing is a button. Aha! You were working with buttons and calling them menus. Yes, that is correct. A JMenuBar and a JPopupMenu are simply containers with a BoxLayout. Go ahead and play with these containers by setting their properties and adding different Swing components to them. A JMenuItem is a simple button. A JMenu is a button and it has an associated container that is displayed when you select it.

JToolBar

A toolbar is a group of buttons that provides commonly used actions to the user in a JFrame. Typically, you provide a toolbar along with a menu. The toolbar contains small buttons with small icons. Typically, it only contains a subset of options available in the menu.

An object of the JToolBar class represents a toolbar. It acts as a container for the toolbar buttons. It is a little smarter container than other containers such as a JPanel. It can be moved around at runtime. It can be floatable. If it is floatable, it displays a handle that you can use to move it around. You can also use the handle to pop it out in a separate window. The following snippet of code creates some toolbar components:

```
// Create a horizontal JToolBar
JToolBar toolBar = new JToolBar();

// Create a horizontal JToolBar with a title. The title is
// displayed as a window title, when it floats in a separate window.
JToolBar toolBarWithTitle = new JToolBar("My ToolBar Title");

// Create a Vertical toolbar
JToolBar vToolBar = new JToolBar(JToolBar.VERTICAL);
```

Let's add some buttons to the toolbar. The buttons in a toolbar need to be smaller in size than usual buttons. You make a JButton smaller in size by setting its margin to zero. You should also add a tool tip to each toolbar button to give a quick hint to the user about its usage.

```
// Create a button for the toolbar
JButton newButton = new JButton("New");

// Set the margins to 0 to make the button smaller
newButton.setMargin(new Insets(0, 0, 0, 0));

// Set a tooltip for the button
newButton.setToolTipText("Add a new policy");

// Add the New button to the toolbar
toolBar.add(newButton);
```

Typically, you display only small icons in a toolbar button. You can use another constructor of the JButton that only accepts an Icon object as an argument. Finally, you need to add action listeners to the buttons, as you have been adding to other JButtons. When a user clicks a button in a toolbar, the action listener is notified, and the specified action is performed.

You can set the toolbar floatable/non-floatable using its setFloatable(boolean floatable) method. By default, a toolbar is floatable. Its setRollover(boolean rollOver) method lets you specify if you want to draw the border of the toolbar buttons only when the mouse hovers on them.

A toolbar should be added to the north, south, east, or west region in a BorderLayout to make it nicer to move the toolbar around in different regions. Listing 2-8 displays a JToolBar in a JFrame. Figure 2-23 shows a JFrame with a toolbar in its north region. Figure 2-24 shows the same JFrame with the toolbar floating in a separate window.

Listing 2-8. Using a JToolBar in a JFrame

```java
// JToolBarFrame.java
package com.jdojo.swing;

import java.awt.Container;
import javax.swing.JFrame;
import javax.swing.JToolBar;
import javax.swing.JButton;
import java.awt.Insets;
import java.awt.BorderLayout;
import javax.swing.JTextArea;
import javax.swing.JScrollPane;

public class JToolBarFrame extends JFrame {
    JToolBar toolBar = new JToolBar("My JToolBar");
    JTextArea msgText = new JTextArea(3, 45);

    public JToolBarFrame(String title) {
        super(title);
        initFrame();
    }

    // Initialize the JFrame and add components to it
    private void initFrame() {
        this.setDefaultCloseOperation(JFrame.EXIT_ON_CLOSE);
        Container contentPane = this.getContentPane();
        prepareToolBar();

        // Add the toolbar in the north and a JTextArea in the center
        contentPane.add(toolBar, BorderLayout.NORTH);
        contentPane.add(new JScrollPane(msgText), BorderLayout.CENTER);
        msgText.append("Move the toolbar around using its" +
                       " handle at the left end");
    }

    private void prepareToolBar() {
        Insets zeroInset = new Insets(0, 0, 0, 0);

        JButton newButton = new JButton("New");
        newButton.setMargin(zeroInset);
        newButton.setToolTipText("Add a new policy");

        JButton openButton = new JButton("Open");
        openButton.setMargin(zeroInset);
        openButton.setToolTipText("Open a policy");

        JButton exitButton = new JButton("Exit");
        exitButton.setMargin(zeroInset);
        exitButton.setToolTipText("Exit the application");
```

```
                // Add an action listener to the Exit toolbar button
                exitButton.addActionListener(e -> System.exit(0));

                toolBar.add(newButton);
                toolBar.add(openButton);
                toolBar.addSeparator();
                toolBar.add(exitButton);

                toolBar.setRollover(true);
        }

        // Display the frame
        public static void main(String[] args) {
                JToolBarFrame frame = new JToolBarFrame("JToolBar Test");
                frame.pack();
                frame.setVisible(true);
        }
}
```

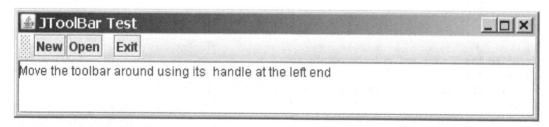

Figure 2-23. A JToolBar with three JButtons placed in the north region of a JFrame

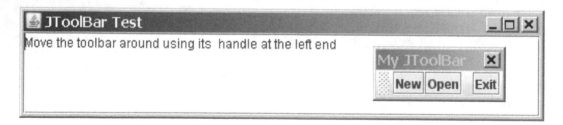

Figure 2-24. A JToolBar floating in a separate window

JToolBar Meets the Action Interface

What is common in all three components: JButton, JMenuItem, and an item in a JToolBar? All of them represent an action. Sometimes you give the user the same option as a menu item, as a toolbar item, and as a JButton. How would you disable an option that you had provided using three components? Don't you think that you need to disable them separately at least in three places because they are three different components representing the same option? You may be right. However, there is an easier way to handle this kind of situation in Swing. Whenever you have to provide an option for an action in different ways, you should work with the Action interface. You need to wrap your option's logic and properties in an Action object and use that object to construct the JButton, the JMenuItem, and the item in the toolbar. If you need to disable the option, you just need to call setEnabled(false) on the Action object only once and all options will be disabled. In such situations, the use of an Action object makes your programming life easier. Let's see it in action. Let's create an ExitAction class that is inherited from the AbstractAction class. Its actionPerformed() method simply exits the application. You set some properties in its constructor using its putValue() method, as shown:

```
public class ExitAction extends AbstractAction {
        public ExitAction(String action) {
                super(action);

                // Set tooltip text for the toolbar
                this.putValue(SHORT_DESCRIPTION, "Exit the application");

                // Set a mnemonic key
                this.putValue(MNEMONIC_KEY, KeyEvent.VK_E);
        }

        @Override
        public void actionPerformed(ActionEvent e) {
                System.exit(0);
        }
}
```

If you want to add an Exit menu item, a JButton, and a toolbar button, you can do so by first creating an object of the ExitAction class, and using it to create all your option items, as shown:

```
ExitAction exitAction = new ExitAction("Exit");
JButton exitButton = new JButton(ExitAction);
JMenuItem exitMenuItem = new JMenuItem(exitAction);

JButton exitToolBarButton = new JButton(exitAction);
exitToolBarButton.setMargin(new Insets(0,0,0,0));
```

Now you can add the exitButton to your JFrame, the exitMenuItem to your menu, and the exitToolBarButton to your toolbar. They all behave the same way because they are sharing the same exitAction object. If you want to disable the exit option in all three places, you can do so by calling exitAction.setEnabled(false) only once.

JTable

Swing lets you display and edit data in a tabular form using the JTable component. A JTable displays data using rows and columns. You can set the labels for column headers. You can also sort the table's data at runtime. Working with a JTable can be as simple as writing a few lines of code, or it can be as complex as writing a few hundred lines of code. A JTable is a complex and powerful Swing component that it deserves a chapter by itself. This section explains the basics of working with a JTable and provides you with some hints about its powerful features. A JTable uses many other classes and interfaces, which are in the javax.swing.table package. The JTable class itself is in the javax.swing package.

Let's start with the simplest JTable example. You can create a JTable by using its no-args constructor.

```
JTable table = new JTable();
```

Well, that was easy. However, what happens to its columns, rows, and data? All you got is an empty table with no visual components. You will fix these problems in a minute.

A JTable does not store data. It only displays data. It uses a model that stores the data, the number of columns, and the number of rows. An instance of the TableModel interface represents the model for a JTable. The DefaultTableModel class is an implementation of the TableModel interface. When you use the default constructor of the JTable class, Java sets an instance of the DefaultTableModel class as its model. If you want to add or remove columns/rows, you must work with its model. You can get the reference of the model of a JTable using its getModel() method. Let's add two rows and three columns to the table.

```
// Get the reference of the model of the table
DefaultTableModel tableModel = (DefaultTableModel)table.getModel();

// Set the number of rows to 2
tableModel.setRowCount(2);

// Set the number of columns to 3
tableModel.setColumnCount(3);
```

Let's set the value for a cell in the table. You can use the setValueAt(Object data, int row, int column) method of the table's model or the table to set a value in its cell. You will set "John Jacobs" as the value in the first row and the first column. Note that the first row and the column start at 0.

```
// Set the value at (0, 0) in the table's model
tableModel.setValueAt("John Jacobs", 0, 0);

// Set the value at (0, 0) in the table
// Works the same as setting the value using the table's model
table.setValueAt("John Jacobs", 0, 0);
```

If you add the table to a container, it will look as shown in Figure 2-25.

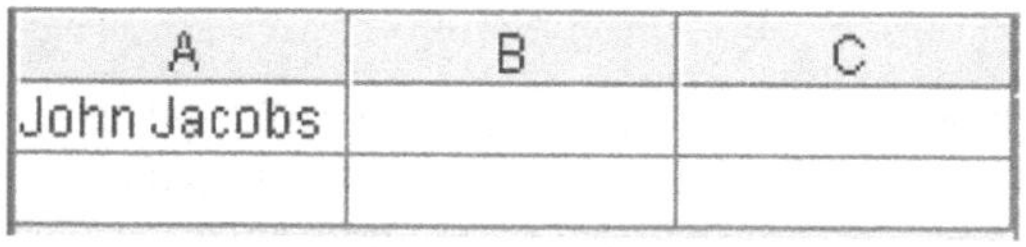

Figure 2-25. A JTable with two rows and three columns with default column header labels

Make sure that you add the table inside a JScrollPane. Note that you get two rows and three columns. The labels for the column headers are set as A, B, and C. You can double-click any cell to start editing the value in the cell. To get the value contained in a cell, you can use the getValueAt(int row, int column) method of the table's model or the JTable. It returns an Object. You can also add more columns or rows to the JTable by using the addColumn() and addRow() methods of the DefaultTableModel class. You can use the removeRow(int row) method of the its model class to remove a row from the model and thus from the JTable.

You can set custom labels for column headers using the model's setColumnIdentifiers() method as follows:

```
// Store the column headers in an array
Object[] columnHeaderLabels = new Object[]{"Name", "DOB", "Gender"};

// Set the column headers for the table using its model
tableModel.setColumnIdentifiers(columnHeaderLabels);
```

With the custom column headers, the table looks as shown in Figure 2-26.

Name	DOB	Gender
John Jacobs		

Figure 2-26. *A JTable with two rows, three columns, and custom column header labels*

You must add a JTable to a JScrollPane if you want the column headers to be visible all the times. If you do not add it to a JScrollPane, the column headers will not be visible when the number of rows exceeds the height available for the component. You can get the column headers component using JTable's getTableHeader() method and display it yourself (e.g. in the north region of a BorderLayout if the JTable is in the center region). You can select a row by clicking on the row. By default, a JTable lets you select multiple rows. You can use the getSelectedRow() method of a JTable to get the first selected row number, and the getselectedRows() method to get the row numbers of all selected rows. The getSelectedRowCount() method returns the selected row count.

You started with the simplest JTable. It was not, however, an easy experience working with the so-called simplest JTable, but now you know the basics of working with a JTable.

Let's repeat the example by creating the JTable using another constructor. The JTable class has another constructor that accepts the number of rows and columns as arguments. You can create a JTable with two rows and three columns as shown:

```
// Create a JTable with 2 rows and 3 columns
JTable table = new JTable(2, 3);
```

If you want to set the value for the first row and the first column to "John Jacobs", you do not need to use the table's model. You can use the setValueAt() method of the JTable to do the same.

```
table.setValueAt("John Jacobs", 0, 0);
```

This one was a little easier than the previous one. However, you will still get the default column header's labels set to A, B, and C. Two other constructors for the JTable let you set the number of rows and columns, and data in one go. They differ only in argument types: one lets you use an array of Object and another lets you use a Vector object. They are declared as follows:

- JTable(Object[][] rowData, Object[] columnNames)
- JTable(Vector rowData, Vector columnNames)

If you use a two-dimensional array of Object to set the row data, the number of the first dimension of the array decides the number of rows. If you use a Vector, the number of elements in the Vector decides the number of rows in the table. Each element in the Vector should be a Vector object that contains the data for a row. Here is how you construct a JTable using a two-dimensional array of Object. Figure 2-27 shows the table displaying all the data set in the code.

ID	Name	Gender
100	John Jacobs	Male
101	Barbara Gentry	Female

Figure 2-27. *A JTable with two rows, three columns, and data*

```
// Prepare the column headers
Object[] columnNames = {"ID", "Name", "Gender" } ;

// Create a two-dimensioanl array to contain the table's data
Object[][] rowData = new Object[][] {
  {new Integer(100), "John Jacobs", "Male" },
  {new Integer(101), "Barbara Gentry", "Female"}
};

// Create a JTable with the data and the column headers
JTable table = new JTable(rowData, columnNames);
```

So far, your table's data were hard-coded. The JTable treated all data as String and all cells in the table were editable. For example, you set the values for the ID column as integers and they were still displayed as left-justified text. A number should be right-justified in a cell. If you want to customize a JTable, you need to use your own model for the table. Recall that the TableModel interface defines the model for a JTable. Here is the declaration of the TableModel interface:

```
public interface TableModel
        public int getRowCount();
        public int getColumnCount();
        public String getColumnName(int columnIndex);
        public Class<?> getColumnClass(int columnIndex);
        public boolean isCellEditable(int rowIndex, int columnIndex);
        public Object getValueAt(int rowIndex, int columnIndex);
        public void setValueAt(Object aValue, int rowIndex, int columnIndex);
        public void addTableModelListener(TableModelListener l);
        public void removeTableModelListener(TableModelListener l);
}
```

The AbstractTableModel class implements the TableModel interface. It provides an empty implementation for the methods of the TableModel interface. It does not mention the way data should be stored. If you want to implement your own table model, you need to inherit your class from the AbstractTableModel class. If you implement at least the following three methods in your custom table model class, you will get a read-only table model:

- public int getRowCount();

- public int getColumnCount();

- public Object getValueAt(int row, int column);

The DefaultTableModel class inherits from the AbstractTableModel class. It provides a default implementation for all methods in the TableModel interface. It uses a Vector of Vectors to store the table's data.

You have greater control over workings of a JTable if you use your own table model. Listing 2-9 implements a simple table model using an array of arrays to store data.

Listing 2-9. Implementing a Simple Table Model

```java
// SimpleTableModel.java
package com.jdojo.swing;

import javax.swing.table.AbstractTableModel;

public class SimpleTableModel extends AbstractTableModel {
    private Object[][] data = {};
    private String[] columnNames = {"ID", "Name", "Gender"};
    private Class[] columnClass = {Integer.class, String.class, String.class};
    private Object[][] rowData = new Object[][]{
            {new Integer(100), "John Jacobs", "Male"},
            {new Integer(101), "Barbara Gentry", "Female"}
    };

    public SimpleTableModel() {
    }

    @Override
    public int getRowCount() {
        return rowData.length;
    }

    @Override
    public int getColumnCount() {
        return columnNames.length;
    }

    @Override
    public String getColumnName(int columnIndex) {
        return columnNames[columnIndex];
    }

    @Override
    public Class getColumnClass(int columnIndex) {
        return columnClass[columnIndex];
    }

    @Override
    public boolean isCellEditable(int rowIndex, int columnIndex) {
        boolean isEditable = true;
        if (columnIndex == 0) {
            isEditable = false; // Make the ID column non-editable
        }
        return isEditable;
    }

    @Override
    public Object getValueAt(int rowIndex, int columnIndex) {
        return rowData[rowIndex][columnIndex];
    }
```

```
        @Override
        public void setValueAt(Object aValue, int rowIndex, int columnIndex) {
                rowData[rowIndex][columnIndex] = aValue;
        }
}
```

In the getColumnClass() method, you specify the class of the column's data; the JTable will use this information to display the column's data appropriately. For example, it will display numbers in a column as right-justified. If you specify the type Boolean for a column, the JTable will use a JCheckBox in each cell of that column to display the Boolean value. Note that you have made the ID column non-editable by returning false from the isEditable() method for the columnIndex of 0. In the example, you have again hard-coded the table's data. However, you can read data from a database, a data file, network, or any other data source. The following snippet of code uses the custom model to create a JTable:

```
// Use the SimpleTableModel as the model for the table
JTable table = new JTable(new SimpleTableModel());
```

Note that your table model does not allow adding and deleting rows/columns. If you want these extended functionalities, you are better off inheriting the model class from the DefaultTableModel class and customizing the behavior you want to change.

You can have data sorting capability added to your JTable by calling its method setAutoCreateRowSorter(true). You can sort data in a column by clicking the column's header. After you call this method, a JTable will display an up/down arrow as part of a column header to indicate that a column is sorted in ascending or descending order. You can also use a row filter that will hide rows in a JTable based on some criteria, as shown:

```
// Set a row sorter for the table
TableRowSorter sorter = new TableRowSorter(table.getModel());
table.setRowSorter(sorter);

// Set an ID filter for the table
RowFilter<SimpleTableModel, Integer> IDFilter = new RowFilter<SimpleTableModel, Integer> () {

        @Override
        public boolean include(Entry<? extends SimpleTableModel,
                                    ? extends Integer> entry) {
                SimpleTableModel model = entry.getModel();
                int rowIndex = entry.getIdentifier().intValue();
                Integer ID = (Integer) model.getValueAt(rowIndex, 0);
                if (ID.intValue() <= 100) {
                        return false; // Do not show rows with an ID <= 100
                }
                return true;
        }
};

sorter.setRowFilter(IDFilter);
```

The above snippet of code sets a filter for a JTable, which is named table, so that rows with IDs less than or equal to 100 are not shown. The RowFilter is an abstract class; you must override its include() method to specify your filter criteria. It also has several static methods that return RowFilter objects of different kinds that you can use directly with a RowSorter object. The following are some examples of creating row filters:

```
// Create a filter that will show only rows that starts
// with "John" in the second column (column index = 1)
RowFilter nameFilter = RowFilter.regexFilter("^John*", 1);

// Create a filter that will show only rows that has a
// "Female" value in its third column (column index = 2)
RowFilter genderFilter = RowFilter.regexFilter("^Female$", 2);

// Create a filter that will show only rows that has 3rd,
// 5th and 7th columns values starting with "A"
RowFilter anyFilter1 = RowFilter.regexFilter("^A*", 3, 5, 7);

// Create a filter that will show only rows that has any
// column whose value starts with "A"
RowFilter anyFilter2 = RowFilter.regexFilter("^A*");
```

You can add a TableModelListener to a TableModel to listen for any changes that are made to the table's model.

■ **Tip** A JTable has many features that cannot be described in this section because of space limitation. It also lets you set a custom cell rendered to display a value in a cell. For example, you can display radio buttons in a cell that user can choose from instead of letting them edit plain text values.

JTree

A JTree is used to display hierarchical data in a tree-like structure as shown in Figure 2-28. You can think of a JTree as displaying a real tree upside down.

Figure 2-28. A JTree showing departments and a list of employees in the departments

Each item in a JTree is called a node. In the figure, Departments, Sales, John, etc. are nodes. A node is further categorized as a branch node or a leaf node. If a node can have other nodes underneath, which are called its children, it is called a branch node. If a node does not have children, it is called a leaf node. Departments, Sales, and Information Technology are examples of branch nodes, whereas John, Elaine, and Aarav are examples of leaf nodes. There is always a special branch in a real-world tree called the root. Similarly, a JTree always has a special branch node that is called the root node. Your JTree has a root node called Departments. In a JTree, you have the ability to make the root node visible or invisible by using its setRootVisible(boolean visibility) method.

A branch node is called a parent node for its children. Note that a child node can also be a branch node. Sales, Information Technology, and Advertising are child nodes of the Departments node. The Sales node has two children: John and Elaine. Both John and Elaine have the same parent node, which is the Sales node.

Nodes at the same level are called siblings. In other words, nodes that have the same parent node are called siblings. Sales, Information Technology, and Advertising are siblings; John and Elaine are siblings; Tejas and Aarav are siblings. Two terms, *ancestor* and *descendant*, are used frequently in the context of nodes. Nodes that are the parent of the parent of the parent and so on are all called ancestors. That is, nodes starting from grandpa and up are all ancestor nodes. Nodes starting from grandchild and down are all called descendants. For example, the Departments node is an ancestor of the Elaine node, and the Elaine node is a descendant of the Departments node.

You have learned enough terms related to a JTree. It's time to see a JTree in action. Classes related to JTree are the in javax.swing and javax.swing.tree packages. A JTree is composed of nodes. An instance of the TreeNode interface represents a node. The TreeNode interface declares methods that give you basic information about a node, such as its node type (branch or leaf), its parent node, its children nodes, etc.

MutableTreeNode is an interface that extends the TreeNode interface. It declares additional methods that allow you to change a node by inserting/removing child nodes or by changing the node object. The DefaultMutableTreeNode class is an implementation of the MutableTreeNode interface.

Before you start creating a node, you need to understand that a node is a visual representation (usually one line of text) of a Java object. In other words, a node wraps an object and usually displays a one-line text representation of that object. The object that a node represents is called the user object of that node. Therefore, before you build a node, you must have an object that your node will represent. Don't worry about creating a new class to build a node. You can just use a String to build your nodes. The following snippet of code creates some nodes that can be used in a JTree:

```
// Create a Departments node
DefaultMutableTreeNode root = new DefaultMutableTreeNode("Departments");

// Create a Sales node
DefaultMutableTreeNode sales = new DefaultMutableTreeNode("Sales");

// Create a John node
DefaultMutableTreeNode john = new DefaultMutableTreeNode("John");

// Create a customer node, assuming you have a Customer class.
// In this case, the node will wrap a Customer object
Customer cust101 = new Customer(101, "Joe");
DefaultMutableTreeNode c101Node = new DefaultMutableTreeNode(cust101);

// If you want to get the user object that a node wraps, you would
// use the getUserObject() method of the DefaultMutableTreeNode class
Customer c101Back = (Customer)c101Node.getUserObject();
```

Once you have a node, it is easy to add children to it using the add() or insert() method. The add() method appends the node to the end; the insert() method lets you specify the position of the new node. For example, to add a Sales node as a child node to the Departments root node you write

```
root.add(sales);
```

To add John as a child node to sales, you write

```
sales.add(john);
```

Once you have your nodes ready, it is easy to put them in a JTree. You need to create a JTree by specifying its root node.

```
JTree tree = new JTree(root);
```

Other constructors for the JTree class let you create a JTree in different ways. The no-args constructor is not very useful unless you are learning JTree. It creates a JTree with some nodes added to it, which are good in terms of saving you the hassle of adding nodes if you want to experiment with a JTree. You can also create a JTree by passing an array of Object or a Vector of Object to its constructors as the child nodes for the root of the JTree. A root will be added to the new JTree before adding the passed in objects as its child nodes. For example,

```
// Create a JTree. It will create a default root node called Root
// and it will add two, "One" and "Two", child nodes for Root.
// The Root node is not displayed by default.
JTree tree = new JTree(new Object[]{"One", "Two"});
```

Once you get your JTree component created, it is time to display it in a Swing container. Typically, you add a JTree to a JScrollPane, so it will have scrolling capability.

```
myContainer.add(new JScrollPane(tree));
```

How do you access or navigate through JTree nodes? There are two ways to access a node in a JTree: using a row number and using a tree path.

A JTree consists of nodes. How does a JTree display nodes? Recall that a node is an instance of the TreeNode class and it wraps an object of any type. Therefore, you may say that a node is a wrapper for an object. By default, a JTree calls the toString() method of the node object to get the text for the node to be displayed. If your node wraps an object whose toString() method does not return a meaningful string to be displayed in a JTree node, you can supply a custom string for that node by creating a custom JTree and overriding its convertValueToText() method. In the examples, you have wrapped a String object inside a node and the toString() method of a String object returns the string itself. Suppose you want to create a node for Customer objects. Make sure to override the toString() method of the Customer class and return a meaningful string to display in the Customer nodes such as customer name and id.

If you look at JTree nodes from top to bottom, each node is displayed in a separate horizontal row. The very first node (the root node, if the root node is visible) is row number zero. The second one is at row number 1, and so on. In Figure 2-28, the row numbers for Departments, Sales, John, Elaine, and Information Technology are 0, 1, 2, 3, and 4, respectively. Note that a row number is assigned to a node only if it is displayed. A node may not be displayed when its parent is collapsed. For example, the Advertising node has some child nodes that are not displayed and they do not have a row number assigned to them because Advertising node, which is their parent node, is collapsed. The getRowCount() method of a JTree returns the number of viewable nodes. Note that the number of viewable nodes changes as you expand and collapse nodes in a JTree.

An object of the TreePath class represents a node uniquely in a JTree. Its structure is similar to the path used to represent a file in a file-system. A file path represents a file uniquely by specifying its path starting from the root folder such as /Departments/Sales/John represents a file named John, which is under a Sales folder, which is under a Departments folder, which is under the root. A TreePath object encapsulates the same kind of information to represent a node in a JTree. It consists of an ordered array of nodes starting from the root. For example, if you need to construct a TreePath object for the node John in the example, you can do it as follows:

```
Object[] path = new Object[] {root, sales, john};
TreePath johnNodePath = new TreePath(path);
```

The getPath() method of the TreePath class returns the Object array and the getLastPathComponent() method returns the last element of the array, which is the reference to the node, which the TreePath object represents the path to. Typically, you will not construct a TreePath object when you work with a JTree. Rather, a TreePath object will be available to you in the JTree events. If you work with a JTree, each element of the array object that represents a TreePath object is an instance of TreeNode. If you are using the default tree model, the TreePath will consist of an array of DefaultMutableTreeNode objects. Having a TreePath to a node, you can get to the object that the node wraps as follows:

```
// Suppose path is an instance of the TreePath class and it represents a node
DefaultMutableTreeNode node = (DefaultMutableTreeNode)path.getLastPathComponent();
Object myObject = node.getUserObject();
```

A JTree provides two methods called getRowForPath() and getPathForRow() to convert a row number to a TreePath and vice versa. You will work with a TreePath when you learn about the JTree events shortly.

If you are not writing the code for an event of a JTree, you will not have a TreePath for a node (unless you stored the node reference itself, which is not required). In such cases, you can always start from the root node and keep navigating down the tree. A model for a JTree is an instance of the TreeModel class, which has a getRoot() method. Once you get the handle of the root node, you can use the children() method of the TreeNode class that returns an enumeration of all child nodes of a TreeNode. The following snippet of code defines a method navigateTree() that traverses all tree nodes, if you pass it the reference to the root node:

```
public void navigateTree(TreeNode node) {
    if (node.isLeaf()) {
        System.out.println("Got a leaf node: " + node);
        return;
    }
    else {
        System.out.println("Got a branch node: " + node);
        Enumeration e = node.children();

        while(e.hasMoreElements()) {
            TreeNode n = (TreeNode)e.nextElement();
            navigateTree(n); // Recursive method call
        }
    }
}
```

You can select a tree node by clicking it. A JTree uses a selection model to keep track of the selected nodes. You need to interact with its selection model to select nodes or get information about the selected nodes. The selection model is an instance of the TreeSelectionModel interface. A JTree allows the user to select nodes in three different modes. They are represented by three constants defined in the TreeSelectionModel interface:

- SINGLE_TREE_SELECTION: It allows users to select only one node at a time.
- CONTIGUOUS_TREE_SELECTION: It allows users to select any number of contiguous nodes.
- DISCONTIGUOUS_TREE_SELECTION: It allows users to select any number of nodes without any restrictions.

The following snippet of code demonstrates how to use some of the methods of the selection model of a JTree:

```
// Get selection model for JTree
TreeSelectionModel selectionModel = tree.getSelectionModel();

// Set the selection mode to discontinuous
selectionModel.setSelectionMode(TreeSelectionModel.DISCONTIGUOUS_TREE_SELECTION);

// Get the selected number of nodes
int selectedCount = selectionModel.getSelectionCount();

// Get the TreePath of all selected nodes
TreePath[] selectedPaths = selectionModel.getSelectionPaths();
```

You can add a TreeSelectionListener to a JTree, which will be notified when a node is selected or deselected. The following snippet of code demonstrates how to add a TreeSelectionListener to a JTree:

```
// Create a JTree. Java will add some nodes
JTree tree = new JTree();

// Add selection listener to the JTree
tree.addTreeSelectionListener((TreeSelectionEvent event) -> {
        TreeSelectionModel selectionModel = tree.getSelectionModel();
        TreePath[] paths = event.getPaths();
        for (TreePath path : paths) {
                Object node = path.getLastPathComponent();
                if (selectionModel.isPathSelected(path)) {
                        System.out.println("Selected: " + node);
                }
                else {
                        // Node is deselected
                        System.out.println("DeSelected: " + node);
                }
        }
});
```

You can expand a node by clicking the plus sign or by clicking the node itself. You can collapse a node by clicking its minus sign or by clicking the node itself. A JTree triggers two events when a node expands or collapses. It triggers a tree-will-expand event and a tree-expansion event in sequence. The tree-will-expand event is triggered just before a node is expanded or collapsed. If you throw an ExpandVetoException from this event, expansion (or collapse) is stopped. Otherwise, a tree-expansion event is triggered. The following snippet of code demonstrates how to write code for these events:

```
// Add a TreeWillExpandListener
tree.addTreeWillExpandListener(new TreeWillExpandListener() {
        @Override
        public void treeWillExpand(TreeExpansionEvent event)
                throws ExpandVetoException {
                System.out.println("Will Expand:" + event.getPath());
        }
```

```
        @Override
        public void treeWillCollapse(TreeExpansionEvent event) throws ExpandVetoException {
                System.out.println("Will Collapse: " + event.getPath());
        }
});

// Add TreeExpansionListener
tree.addTreeExpansionListener(new TreeExpansionListener() {
        @Override
        public void treeExpanded(TreeExpansionEvent event) {
                System.out.println("Exapanded: " + event.getPath());
        }

        @Override
        public void treeCollapsed(TreeExpansionEvent event) {
                System.out.println("Collapsed: " + event.getPath());
        }
});
```

■ **Tip** A JTree is a powerful and complex Swing component. It lets you customize almost everything in it. Each node is displayed in a JLabel. The icons that are displayed are different for branch and leaf nodes. The default icons depend on the look-and-feel. You can customize the default icons by creating your own tree cell renderer. You can also add a TreeModelListener to a JTree, which will notify you of any changes in its model. You can make a JTree editable by using its setEditable(true) method. You can edit a node's labels by double-clicking it.

JTabbedPane and JSplitPane

Sometimes, because of space limitation, it is not possible to display all pieces of information in a window. You can group and separate pieces of information in a window using a JTabbedPane. Figure 2-29 shows a JFrame that has a tabbed pane with two tabs titled General Information and Contacts to display the general and contact information of a person.

Figure 2-29. A JTabbedPane with two tabs

A JTabbedPane component acts like a container for other Swing components, arranging them in a tabbed fashion. It can display tabs using a title, an icon, or both. The user needs to click on a tab to view the tab's contents. The greatest advantage of using a JTabbedPane is space sharing. The contents of only one tab in a JTabbedPane are visible at a time. Users can switch between tabs to view the contents of another tab.

A JTabbedPane also lets you specify where to display the tabs. You can specify the tabs to be placed at the top, bottom, left, or right. Figure 2-29 displays the tabs at the top. If you have a JFrame named a frame, the following snippet of code produces the frame shown in Figure 2-29. The code adds a JLabel to the both tabs represented by two JPanels.

```
JPanel generalInfoPanel = new JPanel();
JPanel contactInfoPanel = new JPanel();
JTabbedPane tabbedPane = new JTabbedPane();
generalInfoPanel.add(new JLabel("General info components go here..."));
contactInfoPanel.add(new JLabel("Contact info components go here..."));

tabbedPane.addTab("General Information", generalInfoPanel);
tabbedPane.addTab("Contacts", contactInfoPanel);
frame.getContentPane().add(tabbedPane, BorderLayout.CENTER);
```

The getTabCount() method returns the number of tabs in a JTabbedPane. Every tab inside a JTabbedPane has an index. The first tab has an index of 0, the second tab has an index of 1, and so on. You can get the component that represents a tab using its index.

```
// Get the reference of the component for the Contact tabs
JPanel contactsPanel = tabbedPane.getTabComponentAt(1);
```

A JSplitPane is a splitter that can be used to split space between two components. The splitter bar can be displayed horizontally or vertically. When the available space is less than the space needed to display the two components, the user can move the splitter bar up/down or left/right, so one component gets more space than the other. If there is enough space, both components can be shown fully.

The JSplitPane class provides many constructors. You can create it using its default constructor and add two components using its setXxxComponent(Component c), where Xxx could be Top, Bottom, Left, or Right. It also lets you specify the way redrawing of components occurs when you change the position of the splitter bar. It could be continuous or non-continuous. If it is continuous, components are redrawn as you move the splitter bar. If it is non-continuous, the components are redrawn when you stop moving the splitter bar.

The following snippet of code shows two instances of the JPanel class added to a JSplitPane, which in turn is added to the content pane of a JFrame named frame. Figure 2-30 shows the resulting JFrame.

```
// Create two JPanels and a JSplitPane
JPanel generalInfoPanel = new JPanel();
JPanel contactInfoPanel = new JPanel();
JSplitPane splitPane = new JSplitPane();
generalInfoPanel.add(new JLabel("General info components go here..."));
contactInfoPanel.add(new JLabel("Contact info components go here..."));

// Add two JPanels to the JSplitPane and the JSplitPane
// to the content pane of the JFrame
splitPane.setLeftComponent(generalInfoPanel);
splitPane.setRightComponent(contactInfoPanel);
frame.getContentPane().add(splitPane, BorderLayout.CENTER);
```

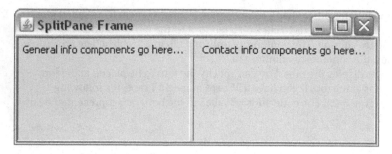

Figure 2-30. *Using a JSplitPane to split space between two components*

Custom Dialogs

A JDialog is a top-level Swing container. It is used as a temporary top-level container (or as a popup window) to aid in the working of the main window to get the user's attention. I am using the term *window* loosely to mean a Swing top-level container. Suppose you have a JFrame in which you have to display information about a person. You may not have enough room in the JFrame to display all details about a person. In this case, you can only display the basic personal minimum information on a JFrame and provide a button labeled "Person Details". When the user clicks this button, you can open a JDialog that displays detailed information about that person. This is an example of using a JDialog to display information to users. Another example of using a dialog window is to let the user choose a file from a file system. You can display a dialog to the user that would let him navigate through the file system and let him choose a file. You can also use a JDialog in other occasions as listed:

- *When you want to confirm an action from the user*: This is called a *confirmation dialog*. For example, when the user selects a person record in a window and tries to delete the person record, you display a confirmation message of "Are you sure you want to delete this person?" The dialog box displays two buttons labeled Yes and No' to indicate the user's choice.

- *When you want some input from the user*: This is referred to as an *input dialog*. For example, when focus moves to a date field, you may display a calendar in a JDialog and want the user to select a date. An input dialog can be as simple as entering/selecting one value or entering multiple values, such as a person's details.

- *When you want to display some message to the user*: This is called a *message dialog*. For example, when a user saves some information to a database, you want to inform the user with a message that indicates the status of the database transaction.

Creating a dialog window is very simple: just create a new class that inherits from the JDialog class. You can add any number of Swing components to your custom JDialog as you have been adding to a JFrame. A JDialog makes it a little easier to add components to it. You do not need to get the reference to its content pane to set its layout manager and add components. Rather, you can invoke the setLayout() and add() methods on the JDialog itself. These methods route the calls to its content pane. By default, a JDialog uses a BorderLayout as the layout manager.

Listing 2-10 lists a custom JDialog that displays current date and time in a JLabel and an OK JButton. When the user clicks the JButton, the JDialog is closed.

Listing 2-10. A Custom JDialog That Displays Current Date and Time

```java
// DateTimeDialog.java
package com.jdojo.swing;

import java.awt.BorderLayout;
import java.time.LocalDateTime;
import java.time.format.DateTimeFormatter;
import javax.swing.JButton;
import javax.swing.JDialog;
import javax.swing.JLabel;

public class DateTimeDialog extends JDialog {
        JLabel dateTimeLabel = new JLabel("Datetime placeholder");
        JButton okButton = new JButton("OK");

        public DateTimeDialog() {
                initFrame();
        }

        private void initFrame() {
                // Release all resources when JDialog is closed
                this.setDefaultCloseOperation(JDialog.DISPOSE_ON_CLOSE);

                this.setTitle("Current Date and Time");
                this.setModal(true);

                String currentDateTimeString = getCurrentDateTimeString();
                dateTimeLabel.setText(currentDateTimeString);

                // There is no need to add components to the content pane.
                // You can directly add them to the JDialog.
                this.add(dateTimeLabel, BorderLayout.NORTH);
                this.add(okButton, BorderLayout.SOUTH);

                // Add an action listeenr to the OK button
                okButton.addActionListener(e -> DateTimeDialog.this.dispose());
        }

        private String getCurrentDateTimeString() {
                LocalDateTime ldt = LocalDateTime.now();
                DateTimeFormatter formatter =
                        DateTimeFormatter.ofPattern("EEEE MMMM dd, yyyy hh:mm:ss a");
                String dateString = ldt.format(formatter);
                return dateString;
        }
}
```

The DateTimeDialog class is a simple example of a custom JDialog. To use it in your application, you need to create an instance of this JDialog, pack it, and make it visible, as shown:

```
DateTimeDialog dateTimeDialog = new DateTimeDialog();
dateTimeDialog.pack();
dateTimeDialog.setVisible(true);
```

If you are displaying a JDialog from another top-level container, say a JFrame or another JDialog, you may want to display it in the center of the top-level container. Sometimes you may want to display it in the center of the screen. You can place a JDialog in the center of a top-level container or a screen by using its setLocationRelativeTo(Component c) method. If you pass null as its argument, the JDialog is centered on the screen. Otherwise, it will be centered within the component that you pass as the argument.

```
// Center the JDialog within a frame, assuming that myFrame exists
dateTimeDialog.setLocationRelativeTo(myFrame);

// Place the JDialog in the center of screen
dateTimeDialog.setLocationRelativeTo(null);
```

You can create a JDialog with an owner, which could be another JDialog, a JFrame, or a JWindow. By specifying an owner for a JDialog, you are creating a parent-child relationship. When the owner (or the parent) of a JDialog is closed, the JDialog is also closed. When the owner is minimized or maximized, the JDialog is also minimized or maximized. A JDialog with an owner is always displayed on top of its owner. You can specify an owner of a JDialog in its constructors. When you create a JDialog using its no-args constructor, a hidden Frame is created as its owner. Note that it is a java.awt.Frame, not javax.swing.JFrame. The JFrame class inherits from the Frame class. You can also create a JDialog with null as its owner, and in that case, it does not have an owner.

By default, a JDialog is resizable. If you do not want users to resize your JDialog, you can do so by calling its setResizable(false) method.

Based on focus behavior of a JDialog, it can be categorized as

- Modal

- Modeless

When a modal JDialog is displayed, it blocks other displayed windows in the application. In other words, if a modal JDialog is displayed, you must close it before you can work with any other windows in that application. To make a JDialog modal, you can use its setModal(true) method. Some of the constructors of the JDialog class also let you specify whether the JDialog should be modal or modeless.

A modeless JDialog does not block any other displayed windows in the application. You can switch focus between other windows and the instances of modeless JDialog. By default, a JDialog is modeless.

You can also set the scope of modality for a modal JDialog. A JDialog can have one of the four types of modalities. They are defined by the four constants in java.awt.Dialog.ModalityType enum:

- MODELESS

- DOCUMENT_MODAL

- APPLICATION_MODAL

- TOOLKIT_MODAL

You can specify the modality type of a JDialog in its constructor or by using its setModalityType() method. The modality type of MODELESS means that the JDialog will not block any windows.

The modality type of DOCUMENT_MODAL means that the JDialog will block any windows in its parent hierarchy (its owner, owner of owner and so on). It will not block any window in its child hierarchy (its child, child of child, and so on). Suppose you have three windows displayed: frame is a JFrame; dialog1 is a JDialog whose owner is frame; dialog2 is another JDialog whose owner is dialog1. If you specify the modality type of DOCUMENT_MODAL for dialog1, you can work with dialog2, but not with frame. If dialog2 has a modality type of MODELESS, you can work with both dialog1 and dialog2, because dialog2 will not block any windows.

The modality type of APPLICATION_MODAL means that the JDialog will block any windows in that Java application, except those in its child hierarchy.

The modality type of TOOLKIT_MODAL means that the JDialog will block any windows run from the same toolkit, except those in its child hierarchy. In a Java application, it is the same as APPLICATION_MODAL. It is useful when you use it in applets or applications started using Java Web Start. You can think of a browser as an application, and multiple applets as top-level windows. All applets are loaded by the same toolkit. If you display a JDialog with its modality type as TOOLKIT_MODAL in one applet, it will block inputs to any other applets in the same browser. You must grant "toolkitModality" AWTPermission to for the applet to use a TOOLKIT_MODAL modality. The same behavior goes with multiple applications started with Java Web Start.

Listing 2-11 contains a program to experiment with modality types of JDialog. Use different values for the dialog1Modality and dialog2Modality variables and see how it affects blocking input in other windows.

Listing 2-11. Experimenting With Modality Types of JDialog

```java
// JDialogModalityTest.java
package com.jdojo.swing;

import javax.swing.JButton;
import javax.swing.JDialog;
import javax.swing.JFrame;
import java.awt.Dialog.ModalityType;

public class JDialogModalityTest {
    public static void main(String[] args) {
        JFrame frame = new JFrame("My JFrame");
        frame.setBounds(0, 0, 400, 400);
        frame.setVisible(true);

        final ModalityType dialog1Modality = ModalityType.DOCUMENT_MODAL;
        final ModalityType dialog2Modality = ModalityType.DOCUMENT_MODAL;
        final JDialog dailog1 = new JDialog(frame, "JDialog 1");

        JButton openBtn = new JButton("Open JDialog 2");
        openBtn.addActionListener(e -> {
            JDialog d2 = new JDialog(dailog1, "JDialog 2");
            d2.setBounds(200, 200, 200, 200);
            d2.setModalityType(dialog2Modality);
            d2.setVisible(true);
        });

        dailog1.add(openBtn);
        dailog1.setBounds(20, 20, 200, 200);
        dailog1.setModalityType(dialog1Modality);
        dailog1.setVisible(true);
    }
}
```

A `JDialog` is used frequently in a Swing application, for example, to display an error message to users. It is time consuming to create a custom `JDialog` every time you need a dialog window. The Swing designers realized this. They gave us the `JOptionPane` class that makes our life easier when using the frequently used `JDialog` types. I will discuss `JOptionPane` in the next section.

Standard Dialogs

The `JOptionPane` class makes it easy for you to create and show standard modal dialogs. It contains many static methods to create different kinds of `JDialog`, fill them with details, and show them as a modal `JDialog`. When a `JDialog` is closed, the method returns a value to indicate the user's action on the `JDialog`. Note that the `JOptionPane` class is inherited from the `JComponent` class. The `JOptionPane` class is not related to the `JDialog` class in any way, except that it is used as a factory to create standard dialogs. It also contains methods that return a `JDialog` object, which you can customize and use in your application. You can display the following four kinds of standard dialogs:

- Message Dialog
- Confirmation Dialog
- Input Dialog
- Option Dialog

The static methods of the `JOptionPane` class to display a standard `JDialog` has name like `showXxxDialog()`. The `Xxx` can be replaced with `Message`, `Confirm`, `Input`, and `Option`. You also have another version of the same method as `showInternalXxxDialog()`, which uses a `JInternalFrame` to display the dialog details instead of a `JDialog`. All four types of standard dialogs accept different types of arguments and return different types of values. Table 2-17 shows the list of arguments of these methods and their descriptions.

Table 2-17. *List of Standard Argument Types and Their Values Used With JOptionPane*

Argument Name	Argument Type	Description
parentComponent	Component	The `JDialog` is centered on the specified parent component. The top-level container that contains this component becomes the owner of the displayed `JDialog`. If it is `null`, the `JDialog` is centered on the screen.
message	Object	Typically, it is a string that needs to be displayed as a message in the dialog box. However, you can pass any object. If you pass a Swing component, it is simply displayed in the dialog box. If you pass an `Icon`, it is displayed in a `JLabel`. If you pass any other object, the `toString()` method is called on that object and the returned string is displayed. You can also pass an array of objects (typically an array of strings) and each element of the array will be displayed vertically one after another.
messageType	Int	It denotes the type of the message you want to display. Depending on the type of message, a suitable icon is displayed in the dialog box. The available message types are defined by the following constants in the `JOptionPane` class: `ERROR_MESSAGE`, `INFORMATION_MESSAGE`,`WARNING_MESSAGE`, `QUESTION_MESSAGE`,`PLAIN_MESSAGE`. The `PLAIN_MESSAGE` type does not display any icon. Another argument, which is of the `Icon` type, lets you specify your own icon to be displayed in the dialog box.

(continued)

Table 2-17. *(continued)*

Argument Name	Argument Type	Description
optionType	Int	It denotes the buttons that need to be displayed in the dialog box. The following is the list of constants defined in the JOptionPane class that you can use to get the standard buttons in a dialog box: DEFAULT_OPTION, YES_NO_OPTION, YES_NO_CANCEL_OPTION, OK_CANCEL_OPTION The DEFAULT_OPTION displays an OK button. Other options display a set of buttons, as their names suggest. You can customize the number of buttons and their text by supplying the options arguments to the showOptionDialog() method.
options	Object[]	This argument lets you customize the set of buttons that are displayed in a dialog box. If you pass a Component object in the array, that component is displayed in the row of buttons. If you specify an Icon object, the icon is displayed in a JButton. For any other types of objects that you pass, a JButton is displayed and the text of the JButton is the string returned from the toString() method of that object. Typically, you pass an array of strings as this argument to display a custom set of buttons in the dialog box.
title	String	It is the text that is displayed as the title of the dialog box. A default title is supplied if you do not pass this argument.
initialValue	Object	This argument is used in input dialogs. It denotes the initial value that is displayed in the input dialog.

Typically, when the user closes a dialog box, you want to check what button the user used to close the dialog box. There is an exception, though, when the dialog box has only one button, say an OK button. In such a case, either the method you use to display the dialog box does not return a value, or you simply ignore the returned value. Here is the list of constants that you can use to check for equality with the retuned value:

- OK_OPTION
- YES_OPTION
- NO_OPTION
- CANCEL_OPTION
- CLOSED_OPTION

The CLOSED_OPTION indicates that the user closed the dialog box using the close (X) menu button on the title bar or using other means such as by pressing Ctrl + F4 keys on the keyboard on the Windows platform. Other constants denote the normal button usage on the dialog box; for example, OK_OPTION denotes that the user clicked the OK button on the dialog box to close it.

JOptionPane also lets you customize the labels for the buttons that it shows. You are not limited to the standard set of buttons either. That is, you can display any number of buttons in the dialog box. In such cases, the JOptionPane's method used to display the dialog box will return 0 for the first button click, 1 for the second button click, 2 for the third button click, and so on. You will see an example of this type, when the showOptionDialog() method of the JOptionPane class is discussed shortly.

You can show a message dialog by using one of the showMessageDialog() static methods of the JOptionPane class. A message dialog always shows some kind of information to the user with one button, usually the OK button. The method does not return any value because all the user can do is click the OK button to close the dialog box. Signatures of the showMessageDialog() methods are as shown:

- showMessageDialog(Component parentComponent, Object message)

- showMessageDialog(Component parentComponent, Object message, String title, int messageType)

- showMessageDialog(Component parentComponent, Object message, String title, int messageType, Icon icon)

The following snippet of code shows a message dialog, as shown in Figure 2-31.

```
// Show an information message dialog
JOptionPane.showMessageDialog(null, "JOptionPane is cool!", "FYI",
        JOptionPane.INFORMATION_MESSAGE);
```

Figure 2-31. *An information message dialog using the JOptionPane .showMessageDialog() method*

You can display a confirmation dialog box by using the showConfirmDialog() method. When you use this method, you are interested in knowing the user's response, which is indicated by the return value of the method. The following snippet of code displays a confirmation dialog, as shown in Figure 2-32, and handles the user's response:

```
// Show a confirmation dialog box
int response = JOptionPane.showConfirmDialog(null,
                "Are you sure you want to save the changes?",
                "Confirm Save Changes",
                JOptionPane.YES_NO_CANCEL_OPTION,
                JOptionPane.QUESTION_MESSAGE);

    switch (response) {
            case JOptionPane.YES_OPTION:
                    System.out.println("You chose yes");
                    break;
            case JOptionPane.NO_OPTION:
                    System.out.println("You chose no");
                    break;
            case JOptionPane.CANCEL_OPTION:
                    System.out.println("You chose cancel");
                    break;
```

```
        case JOptionPane.CLOSED_OPTION:
                System.out.println("You closed the dialog box.");
                break;
        default:
                System.out.println("I do not know what you did ");
    }
```

Figure 2-32. *A confirmation dialog box using the JOptionPane.showConfirmDialog() method*

You can ask the user for an input using the showInputDialog() method. You can specify an initial value for the user's input. If you want the user to select a value from a list, you can pass an object array that contains the list. The UI will display the list in a suitable component such as a JComboBox or a JList. The following snippet of code displays an input dialog, as shown in Figure 2-33.

```
// Ask the user to enter some text about JOptionPane
String response = JOptionPane.showInputDialog("Please enter your opinion about input dialog.");

if (response == null) {
        System.out.println("You have cancelled the input dialog.");
}
else {
        System.out.println("You entered: " + response);
}
```

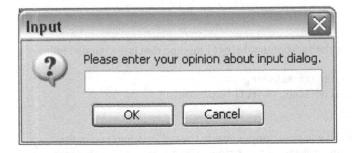

Figure 2-33. *A simple input dialog*

The version of the showInputDialog() method that you have used returns a String, which is the text the user enters in the input field. If the user cancels the input dialog, it returns null.

The following snippet of code displays an input dialog with a list of choices. The user may select one of the choices from the list. The dialog box is shown in Figure 2-34 This version of the showInputDialog() method returns an Object, not a String.

```
// Show an input dialog that shows the user three options: "Cool!", "Sucks", "Don't know".
// The default selected value is "Don't know".
JComponent parentComponent = null;
Object message = "Please select your opinion about JOptionPane";
String title = "JOptionPane Input Dialog";
int messageType = JOptionPane.INFORMATION_MESSAGE;
Icon icon = null;
Object[] selectionValues = new String[] {"Cool!", "Sucks", "Don't know"};
Object initialSelectionValue = selectionValues[2];
Object response = JOptionPane.showInputDialog(parentComponent, message,
title, messageType, icon, selectionValues, initialSelectionValue);

if (response == null) {
        System.out.println("You have cancelled the input dialog.");
}
else {
        System.out.println("You entered: " + response);
}
```

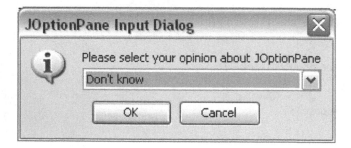

Figure 2-34. *An input dialog with a list of choices*

Finally, you can customize the option buttons using the showOptionDialog() method that is declared as follows:

```
int showOptionDialog(Component parentComponent, Object message,
String title, int optionType, int messageType, Icon icon, Object[] options,
Object initialValue)
```

The options parameter specifies the user's options. If you pass components in the options parameter, the components are displayed as options. If you pass any other objects such as strings, a button is displayed for each element in the options array.

The following snippet of code shows how to display custom buttons in a dialog box. It asks the user his opinion about a JOptionPane. The resulting dialog box is shown in Figure 2-35.

```
JComponent parentComponent = null;
Object message = "How is JOptionPane?";
String title = "JOptionPane Option Dialog";
int messageType = JOptionPane.INFORMATION_MESSAGE;
Icon icon = null;
Object[] options = new String[] {"Cool!", "Sucks", "Don't know" };
Object initialOption = options[2];
int response = JOptionPane.showOptionDialog(null, message, title,
                                    JOptionPane.DEFAULT_OPTION,
                                    JOptionPane.QUESTION_MESSAGE,
                                    icon, options, initialOption);
switch(response) {
        case 0:
        case 1:
        case 2:
                System.out.println("You selected:" + options[response]);
                break;
        case JOptionPane.CLOSED_OPTION:
                System.out.println("You closed the dialog box.");
                break;
        default:
                System.out.println("I don't know what you did.");
}
```

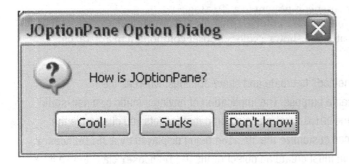

Figure 2-35. *Customizing the Option buttons using the JOptionPane.showOptionDialog() method*

By default, all dialog boxes, which you have displayed in this section, are not resizable. You want to customize them so that they are resizable. You can customize the dialog box displayed by the static methods of the JOptionPane by using the createDialog() methods of JOptionPane and performing a sequence of steps.

1. Create an object of JOptionPane.

2. Optionally, customize the properties of JOptionPane using its methods.

3. Use createDialog() method to get the reference of the dialog box.

4. Customize the dialog box.

5. Display the dialog box using its setVisible(true) method.

The following snippet of code displays the custom resizable dialog box shown in Figure 2-36.

```
// Show a custom resizable dialog box using
JOptionPane pane = new JOptionPane("JOptionPane is cool!", JOptionPane.INFORMATION_MESSAGE);
String dialogTitle = "Resizable Custom Dialog Using JOptionPane";
JDialog dialog = pane.createDialog(dialogTitle);
dialog.setResizable(true);
dialog.setVisible(true);
```

Figure 2-36. *A custom dialog box using the JOptionPane.createDialog() method*

File and Color Choosers

Swing has two built-in JDialogs that makes it easier to select a file/directory from the file system or a color graphically. A JFileChooser lets the user select a file from the file system. It provides non-static methods, unlike those you have seen in a JOptionPane, which create and show a file chooser component in a JDialog.

A JColorChooser is a Swing component that lets you choose a color graphically in a JDialog. It provides a static method, as you have seen in a JOptionPane, which creates and shows a color chooser component in a JDialog.

▪ **Tip** The JFileChooser class provides non-static methods to create and show JDialogs, whereas the JColorChooser class provides a static method for the same purpose. The implication of having a static or a non-static method is that a non-static method lets you customize the JDialog whereas a static method lets you customize the JDialog only through its arguments. It means that you can customize the JDialog being displayed by a JFileChooser, but not the JColorChooser. Another difference is that you must create an object of the JFileChooser class to use it. It is preferred to reuse the same JFileChooser object because it remembers the last visited directory, so when you reuse it, it navigates you to the last visited directory by default.

JFileChooser

Here are the steps you need to perform to display a file chooser in a JDialog.

1. Create an object of the JFileChooser class.

2. Optionally, customize its properties using its methods. You can customize properties such as should it let the user choose only files, only directories, or both; should it let the user select multiple files; apply a file filter criteria to show files based on your criteria, etc.

3. Use one of the three non-static methods, showOpenDialog(), showSaveDialog(), or showDialog(), to display it in a JDialog.

4. Check for the return value, which is an int, from the method call in the previous step. If it returns JFileChooser.APPROVE_OPTION, the user made a selection. The other two possible return values are JFileChooser.CANCEL_OPTION and JFileChooser.ERROR_OPTION, which indicate that either user cancelled the dialog box or some kind of error occurred. To get the selected file, call the getSelectedFile() or getSelectedFiles() method, which returns a File object and a File array, respectively. Note that a JFileChooser component only lets you select a file from a file system. It does not save or read a file. You can do whatever you like with the file reference returned from it.

5. You can reuse the file chooser object. It remembers the last visited folder.

By default, a JFileChooser starts displaying files from the user's default directory. You can specify the initial directory in its constructor or using its setCurrentDirectory() method.

```
// Create a file chooser with the default initial directory
JFileChooser fileChooser = new JFileChooser();

// Create a file chooser, with an initial directory of C:\myjava.
// You can specify a directory path according to your operating system syntax.
// C:\myjava is using Windows file path syntax.
JFileChooser fileChooser = new JFileChooser("C:\\myjava");
```

By default, a file chooser only allows files to be selected. Let's customize it so you can select a file or a directory. It should also allow multiple selections. The following snippet of code does this customization:

```
// Let the user select files and directories
fileChooser.setFileSelectionMode(JFileChooser.FILES_AND_DIRECTORIES);

// Aloow multiple selection
fileChooser.setMultiSelectionEnabled(true);
```

Let's display an open file chooser dialog box and check if the user selected a file. If the user makes a selection, print the file path on the standard output. The following snippet of code displays the dialog box shown in Figure 2-37.

```
// Display an open file chooser
int returnValue = fileChooser.showOpenDialog(null);

if(returnValue == JFileChooser.APPROVE_OPTION) {
        File selectedFile = fileChooser.getSelectedFile();
        System.out.println("You selected: " + selectedFile);
}
```

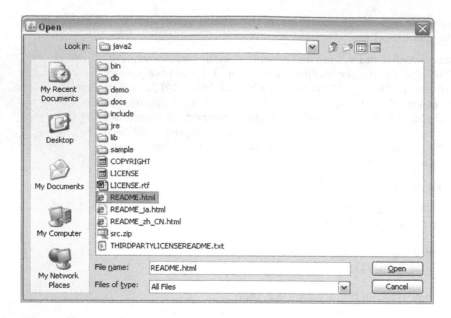

Figure 2-37. *An open file chooser dialog box using a JFileChooser*

All the three methods of the JFileChooser class accept a Component argument. It is used as the owner for the JDialog it displays and for centering the dialog box. Pass null as its parent component to center it on the screen.

Note that, in Figure 2-37, there are two buttons. One is labeled Open and another Cancel. The Open button is called the approve button. The title of the dialog box is Open. When you use the showSaveDialog() method of JFileChooser, you get the same dialog box, except that the text Open for the button and the title are replaced with the text Save. You can customize the dialog box title and the approve button text before displaying it as follows:

```
// Change the dialog's title
fileChooser.setDialogTitle("Open a picture file");

// Change the button's text
fileChooser.setApproveButtonText("Open File");
```

The third method, showDialog(), lets you specify the approve button text and dialog title as shown:

```
// Open a file chooser with Attach as its title and approve button's text
int returnValue = fileChooser.showDialog(null, "Attach");
if (returnValue == JFileChooser.APPROVE_OPTION) {
        File selectedFile = fileChooser.getSelectedFile();
        System.out.println("Attaching file: " + selectedFile);
}
```

Note that setting the approve button's text does not change the return value of the method. You still need to check if it returned a JFileChooser.APPROVE_OPTION so you can proceed with getting the selected file.

The default text for the approve button, when you use the showOpenDialog() and showSaveDialog() methods, depends on the look-and-feel. On Windows, they are Open and Save, respectively.

A JFileChooser lets you set a file filter. A file filter is a set of criteria that it applies before it shows a file in the dialog box. A file filter is an object of the FileFilter class, which is in the javax.swing.filechooser package. The FileFilter class is an abstract class. To create a file filter, you need to create a class inheriting it from the FileFilter class and override the accept() and getDescription() methods. The accept() method is called with a file reference when the file chooser wants to show a file. If the accept() method returns true, the file is shown. Otherwise, the file is not shown. The following snippet of code creates and sets a file filter to only show either a directory or a file with a doc extension. Keep in mind that user needs to navigate to the file system and you must show the directories.

```
// Create a file filter to show only a directory or .doc files
FileFilter filter = new FileFilter() {
        @Override
        public boolean accept(File f) {
                if (f.isDirectory()) {
                        return true;
                }

                String fileName = f.getName().toLowerCase();
                if (fileName.endsWith(".doc")) {
                        return true;
                }

                return false; // Reject any other files
        }

        @Override
        public String getDescription() {
                return "Word Document";
        }
};

// Set the file filter
fileChooser.setFileFilter(filter);

int returnValue = fileChooser.showDialog(null, "Attach");
if (returnValue == JFileChooser.APPROVE_OPTION) {
        // Process the file
}
```

Setting a file filter based on a file extension is so common that there is a direct support for it through the FileNameExtensionFilter class that inherits from the FileFilter class. Its constructor accepts the file extensions and its description. The second argument is a variable length argument. Note that a file extension is the part of the file name after the last dot. If a file name does not have a dot in its name, it does not have an extension. After you create an object of the FileNameExtensionFilter class, you need to call the addChoosableFileFilter() method of the file chooser to set a filter. The following snippet of code adds "java" and "jav" as file name extension filters.

```
FileNameExtensionFilter extFilter =
        new FileNameExtensionFilter("Java Source File", "java", "jav");
fileChooser.addChoosableFileFilter(extFilter);
```

You can add multiple file name extension filters to a file chooser. They are shown in a file chooser drop-down list as file types. If you want to restrict users to selecting only the files that you have set as the file filter, you need to remove the one file filter that lets the user select any files, which is called "accept all files filter". It is displayed as "All Files(*.*)" as file type on Windows.

```
// Disable "accept all files filter"
fileChooser.setAcceptAllFileFilterUsed(false);
```

You can check if "accept all files filter" is enabled by using the isAcceptAllFileFilterUsed() method, which returns true if a file chooser is using this filter. You can get the reference of "accept all files filter" using the getAcceptAllFileFilter() method. The following snippet of code sets the "accept all files filter" if it is not already set.

```
if (!fileChooser.isAcceptAllFileFilterUsed()) {
        fileChooser.setAcceptAllFileFilterUsed(true);
}
```

■ **Tip**   A JFileChooser has many features that you can use in your application. Sometimes you may want to get the associated icon for a file type. You can get the associated icon for a file type by using the file chooser's getIcon(java.io.File file) method, which returns an Icon object. Note that you can display an Icon object using a JLabel component. It also provides a mechanism to listen for selection changes and other actions performed by the user when it is shown in the dialog box.

JColorChooser

A JColorChooser lets you select a color using a dialog box. It is customizable. You can add more panels to the default color chooser. You can also embed the color chooser component in a container. It provides ways to listen to the user actions on the color chooser component. Its common use is very simple. You need to call its showDialog() static method, which will return a java.awt.Color object that represents the color that the user selects. Otherwise, it returns null. I will cover the Color class later in this chapter.

The showDialog() method's signature is as follows. It lets you specify the parent component and the title for the dialog box. You can also set the initial color, which will be displayed in the dialog box.

- static Color showDialog(Component parentComponent, String title, Color initialColor)

The following snippet of code lets the user select a color using a JColorChooser and prints a message on the standard output:

```
// Display a color chooser dialog
Color color = JColorChooser.showDialog(null, "Select a color", null);

// Check if user selected a color
if (color == null) {
        System.out.println("You cancelled or closed the color chooser");
}
else {
        System.out.println("You selected color: " + color);
}
```

JWindow

Like a JFrame, a JWindow is another top-level container. It is as an undecorated JFrame. It does not have features like a title bar, windows menu, etc. It is not a very commonly used top-level container. You can use it as a splash window that displays once when the application is launched and then automatically disappears after a few seconds. Please refer to the API documentation of the java.awt.SplashScreen class for more details on how to display a splash screen in a Java application. Like a JFrame, you can add Swing components to a JWindow.

Working with Colors

An object of the java.awt.Color class represents a color. You can create a Color object using its RGB (Red, Green, and Blue) components. RGB values can be specified as float or int values. As a float value, each component in RGB ranges from 0.0 to 1.0. As an int value, each component in RGB ranges from 0 to 255. There is another component called *alpha* that is associated with a color. The alpha value of a color defines the transparency of the color. As a float, its value ranges from 0.0 to 1.0, and as an int, its value ranges from 0 to 255. The value of 0.0 or 0 for alpha indicates that a color is fully transparent, whereas the value of 1.0 or 255 indicates that it is fully opaque.

You can create a Color object as follows. Note the value of the RGB components in the constructor Color(int red, int green, int blue).

```
// Create red color
Color red = new Color(255, 0, 0);

// Create green color
Color green = new Color(0, 255, 0);

// Create blue color
Color blue = new Color(0, 0, 255);

// Create white color
Color white = new Color(255, 255, 255);

// Create black color
Color black = new Color(0, 0, 0);
```

The alpha component is implicitly set to 1.0 or 255, which means that if you do not specify the alpha component for a color, the color is opaque. The following snippet of code creates a red transparent color by specifying the alpha component as 0:

```
// Create a transparent red color. The last argument of 0 is the alpha value.
Color transparentRed = new Color(255, 0, 0, 0);
```

The Color class defines many color constants for commonly used colors. For example, you do not need to create a red color. Rather, you can use Color.red or Color.RED constant. The Color.red constant exists since Java 1.0. The uppercase version of the same constants Color.RED has been added in Java 1.4 to follow the naming convention for constants (a constant's name should be in uppercase). Similarly, you have Color.black, Color.BLACK, Color.green, Color.GREEN, Color.darkGray, Color.DARK_GRAY, etc. If you have a Color object, you can obtain its red, green, blue, and alpha components using its getRed(), getGreen(), getBlue(), and getAlpha() methods, respectively.

There is another way to specify a color, and that is by using HSB (Hue, Saturation, and Brightness) components. The Color class has two methods called RGBtoHSB() and HSBtoRGB() that let you convert from the RBG model to the HSB model and vice versa.

A Color object is used with the setBackground(Color c) and setForeground(Color c) methods of the Swing components. All Swing components inherit these methods from JComponent. These method calls may be ignored by a look-and-feel. The background color is the color with which a component is painted, whereas the foreground color is usually the color of the text displayed in the component. There is one important thing, called transparency, to consider when you set the background color of a component. If a component is transparent, it does not paint pixels in its bounds. Rather, it lets the container's pixels show through. In order for the background color to take effect, you must make the component opaque by calling its setOpaque(true) method. The following code creates a JLabel and sets its background color to red and foreground (or text) color to black:

```
JLabel testLabel = new JLabel("Color Test");

// First make the JLabel opaque. By default, a JLabel is transparent.
testLabel.setOpaque(true);
testLabel.setBackground(Color.RED);
testLabel.setForeground(Color.BLACK);
```

■ **Tip**   The object of the Color class is immutable. It does not have any method that will let you set the color component values after you create a Color object. This makes it possible to share Color objects.

Working with Borders

Swing gives you the ability to draw a border around the edges of components. There are different kinds of borders:

- Bevel Border
- Soft Bevel Border
- Etched Border
- Line Border
- Titled Border
- Matte Border
- Empty Border
- Compound Border

Figure 2-38 shows how the different kinds of borders appear using the Windows look-and-feel.

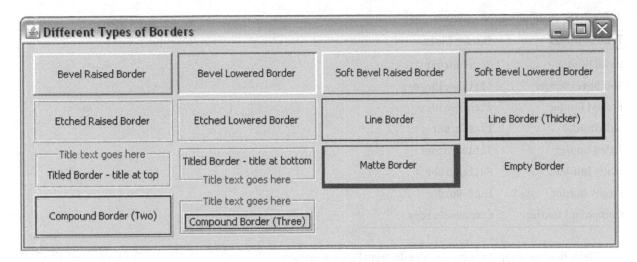

Figure 2-38. *Different types of borders*

Although you can set a border for any Swing component, the implementation of the Swing component may ignore it. It is very common to use a titled border with a JPanel to give a grouping effect. Many GUI tools have a group box GUI component to group the related components. Java does not have a group box component. If you need a grouping effect, you need to place your related components inside a JPanel, and set a titled border to it. Figure 2-39 shows a JPanel that has five address related fields, with a titled border with a title set to Address.

Figure 2-39. *Creating a group box effect using a JPanel with a titled border*

Setting a border for a Swing component is easy: you need to create a border object and use the setBorder(Border b) method of the component. Border is an interface that is implemented by all classes whose instances represent a specific kind of border. There is one class for each kind of border. You can also create a custom border by inheriting a class from the AbstractBorder class. All border-related classes and the Border interface are in the javax.swing.border package.

Border objects are designed to be shared. Although you can create a border object using the border class directly, it is advisable to use the javax.swing.BorderFactory class to create a border so that the border objects can be shared. The BorderFactory class takes care of caching and sharing of border objects. You just need to use its createXxxBorder() method to create a specific type of border, where Xxx is a border type. Table 2-18 lists the border classes for all border types.

Table 2-18. *Available Border Classes*

Type of Border	Border Class
Bevel Border	BevelBorder
Soft Bevel Border	SoftBevelBorder
Etched Border	EtchedBorder
Line Border	LineBorder
Titled Border	TitledBorder
Matte Border	MatteBorder
Empty Border	EmptyBorder
Compound Border	CompoundBorder

The following snippet of code creates different kinds of borders:

```
// Create bevel borders
Border bevelRaisedBorder = BorderFactory.createBevelBorder(BevelBorder.RAISED);
Border bevelLoweredBorder = BorderFactory.createBevelBorder(BevelBorder.LOWERED);

// Create soft bevel borders
Border softBevelRaisedBorder = BorderFactory.createSoftBevelBorder(BevelBorder.RAISED);
Border softBevelLoweredBorder = BorderFactory.createSoftBevelBorder(BevelBorder.LOWERED);

// Create etched borders
Border etchedRaisedBorder = BorderFactory.createEtchedBorder(EtchedBorder.RAISED);
Border etchedLoweredBorder = BorderFactory.createEtchedBorder(EtchedBorder.LOWERED);

// Create line borders
Border lineBorder = BorderFactory.createLineBorder(Color.BLACK);
Border lineThickerBorder = BorderFactory.createLineBorder(Color.BLACK, 3);

// Create titled borders
Border titledBorderAtTop =
        BorderFactory.createTitledBorder(etchedLoweredBorder,
                                "Title text goes here",
                                TitledBorder.CENTER,
                                TitledBorder.TOP);
Border titledBorderAtBottom =
        BorderFactory.createTitledBorder(etchedLoweredBorder,
                                "Title text goes here",
                                TitledBorder.CENTER,
                                TitledBorder.BOTTOM);

// Create a matte border
Border matteBorder = BorderFactory.createMatteBorder(1,3,5,7, Color.BLUE);

// Create an empty border
Border emptyBorder = BorderFactory.createEmptyBorder();
```

```
// Create compound borders
Border twoCompoundBorder = BorderFactory.createCompoundBorder(etchedRaisedBorder,
lineBorder);
Border threeCompoundBorder =
        BorderFactory.createCompoundBorder(titledBorderAtTop, twoCompoundBorder);
```

You can set a border to a component as follows:

```
myComponent.setBorder(matteBorder);
```

A bevel border gives you a three-dimensional effect by using shadows and highlights to the inside and outside edges of the border. You can have a raised or lowered effect. A soft bevel border is a bevel border with softer corners.

An etched border gives you a carved effect. It comes in two flavors: raised and lowered.

A line border simply draws a line. You can specify the color and thickness of the line.

You can supply a title to any border type. The title of a border is text that can be displayed at a specified position in the border, such as in the middle of the top/bottom border or above top/below bottom. You can also specify the justification of the title text, its color, and font. Note that you must have another border object to use a title border. A title border just lets you supply the title text to another kind of border.

A matte border lets you decorate a border with an icon. If you do not have an icon, you can specify the border's thickness.

An empty border, as the name implies, doesn't display anything. Can you guess why you need an empty border? A border adds spaces around a component. If you just want to add spaces around a component, you can use an empty border. An empty border lets you specify the spacing to be used for all four sides separately.

A compound border is a composite border that lets you combine any two kinds of borders into one border object. There are no restrictions on the number of levels of nesting. You can combine three borders by creating a compound border with the first two borders, and then combine the compound border with the third border to create the final compound border.

Working with Fonts

A font is used to represent text visually such as on a computer screen, printed paper, or any other device. An object of the java.awt.Font class represents a font in a Java program. You have been using the Font object in almost every program without referring to the Font class directly. Java took care of displaying the text in a specific font for you. For example, you have been using buttons, which display a label. To display the button's label, Java has been using a default font. You can specify a font for any text that you display in a Java program using a Font object. Using a Font object in code is easy: create an object of the Font class, and use the setFont(Font f) method of the component. Let's define the term "font" and related terms before using the Font class.

In the computer's memory, everything is a number represented in terms of 0s and 1s. So a character is also represented by 0s and 1s in memory. How do you represent a character on a computer screen or a piece of paper? A character is presented on a screen or a paper using a symbol. The shape of the symbol that represents a character is called a *glyph*. You can think of a glyph as a graphic representation (or image) of a character. The relationship between a character and a glyph is not always one-to-one.

A specific design of glyphs for a set of characters is called a *typeface*. Note that a typeface is the design aspect of the visual representation of characters (glyphs) and it does not refer to a specific implementation of glyphs. Table 2-19 lists some of the categories of typefaces with their descriptions and sample texts. The sample text in the table may not show in the same typeface if this is viewed on a device (e.g. a Kindle) that does not support all typefaces. Some names of typefaces are Times, Courier, Helvetica, Garamond, etc.

Table 2-19. Examples of Typefaces

Typeface	Description	Sample Text
Serif	Glyphs have finishing strokes at the end of the line. Note the difference in how the ending stroke of each character ends for serif and sans serif. On Windows, it is called Roman. Example: Times New Roman.	The quick brown fox...
Sans serif	Unlike serif, glyphs have no ending strokes. Compare the text sample for this category and for serif. You will find that glyphs for sans serif are made up of plain lines. On Windows, it is called Swiss. Example: Arial.	**The quick brown fox...**
Cursive	It looks like handwritten text where subsequent glyphs in a word are often joined. It is typically used in calligraphy. On Windows, it is called Script. Example: Mistral AV.	*The quick brown fox...*
Fantasy	It is a decorative typeface. On Windows, it is called Decorative. Example: Impact.	**The quick brown fox...**
Monospace	All glyphs that represent all characters are of the same width. On Windows, it is called Modern. Typically, it is used in computer programs.	`The quick brown fox...`

Apart from its shape design, the visual representation of a character has two other components: a style and a size. The style refers to its characteristics such as bold (blackness or lightness), italic, and regular (or roman). The size is measured in 10, 12, 14, etc. The height of a character is specified in *points*, where a point is 1/72 of an inch. The width of a character is specified in a *pitch*. A pitch determines how many characters can be shown in an inch. A typical value for a pitch ranges from 8 to 14.

Now let's define the term "font." A font is a set of glyphs in a specific typeface, style, and size to represent a set of characters. You can have fonts that use the same typeface, but they are of different styles and sizes. This collection of such fonts (the same typeface but different styles and sizes) is known as a font family. For example, Times is a font family name that contains fonts like Times Roman, Times Bold, Times Bold Italic, etc.

A font may be categorized as a bitmapped font or a vector font (also known as an object-oriented font or outline font) depending on the way it is stored and rendered. In a bitmapped font, each character is stored in a bitmap form (representing every bit) of a particular style and size. When you need to render a character on a screen or print it on a piece of paper, you need to locate the bitmap of the character of that style and size and render it. In a vector font, a geometrical algorithm defines each character's shape without referring to a specific size. When a character needs to be rendered in a vector font in a specific size, the algorithm is applied for that size. This is the reason a vector font is also known as a scalable font. TrueType and PostScript are the font technologies that use vector fonts. All Java implementation are required to support a TrueType font.

The number of fonts available on a computer may vary considerably. Your operating system may install some fonts, you may add some fonts, or you may delete some fonts. Since Java was designed to work on various operating systems, it lets you use a logical font family name of a font and it will figure out the best physical (the real one) font for you. This way, you do not have to worry about the actual font names, and if they will be available on all computers on which your programs will be executed. Java defines five logical font family names and maps them to physical font family names depending on the computer it is running on. The five logical font family names are as follows:

- Serif
- SansSerif
- Dialog
- DialogInput
- Monospace

You need to specify three elements when you create a font object: the logical family name, the style, and the size. The following snippet of code creates some Font objects:

```
// Create serif, plain font of size 10
Font f1 = new Font(Font.SERIF, Font.PLAIN, 10);

// Create SansSerif, bold font of size 10
Font f2 = new Font(Font.SANS_SERIF, Font.BOLD, 10);

// Create dialog, bold font of size 15
Font f3 = new Font(Font.DIALOG, Font.BOLD, 15);

// Create dialog input, bold and italic font of size 15
Font f4 = new Font(Font.DIALOG_INPUT, Font.BOLD|Font.ITALIC, 15);
```

The Font class contains constants for the logical font family names. If you want to apply more than one style to a font object, such as bold as well as italic, you need to use a bit mask union of Font.BOLD and Font.ITALIC as in Font.BOLD|Font.ITALIC.

To set the font for a Swing component, you need to use its setFont() method of the component, like so:

```
JButton closeButton = new JButton("Close");
closeButton.setFont(f4);
```

The Font class has several methods that let you work with a font object. For example, you can use the getFamily(), getStyle(), and getSize() methods to get the family name, style and size of a font object, respectively.

Validating Components

A component can be valid or invalid. The phrase "component" in this section also includes containers, unless specified otherwise. You can use the isValid() method to check if a component is valid. The method returns true if the component is valid. Otherwise, it returns false. A component is said to be valid if its size and position have been computed and its children are also valid. If a component is invalid, it means that its size and position need to be recomputed and it needs to be laid out again in its container.

When you add/remove a component to/from a container, the container is marked invalid. Before the container is made visible for the first time, the container is validated. The validation process of a container computes the size and location of all children in its containment hierarchy. Consider the following the snippet of code to show a frame:

```
MyFrame frame = new MyFrame("Test Frame");
frame.pack();
frame.setVisible(true);
```

The pack() method does two things:

- First, it computes the size and position of all children of the frame (that is, validates the frame).

- Second, it resizes the frame, so its children just fit into it.

The setVisible() method in the code is smart enough not to validate the frame again because the pack() method has already validated the frame. If you do not call the pack() method, before calling the setVisible() method, the setVisible() method will validate the frame.

So, a component is valid before it is displayed for the first time. How does a component become invalid? Adding/removing a component to/from a container makes a container invalid. Setting some properties such as the size of a component will also make that component invalid. When a component becomes invalid, its invalidity is propagated up the containment hierarchy. You can also invalidate a component or container by calling its invalidate() method. Note that calling the invalidate() method will make the component invalid, and it propagates the invalidity up the containment hierarchy. The reason it needs to mark all containers up the containment hierarchy as invalid is that if a component is laid out again (by recomputing its size/location), it will also affect the other component's size/position. So, if a component is invalidated, all components and containers up the containment hierarchy are also marked invalid.

What can you do to validate a component again? You need to use the validate() method of the component or the container. Unlike the invalidate() method, the validate() method propagates down the containment hierarchy and it validates all child components/containers of the component on which it is called. You may need to call the repaint() method after you call the validate() method so that the screen is repainted.

You can also revalidate a component. Note that the revalidation option is only available for a JComponent and it is not applicable to a container. You can revalidate a component by calling its revalidate() method. It schedules a validate() method call on the parent container. Which parent container of the component is validated? Is it the immediate parent, grandparent, or great-grandparent, etc.? A container can be a validation root. You can test if a container is a validation root by using the isValidateRoot() method. If this method returns true, the container is a validation root. When you call the revalidate() method on a component, it keeps going up in the containment hierarchy until it find a container that is a validation root. JRootPane and JScrollPane are validation roots. The call to the validate() method for the validation root is scheduled on the event dispatching thread. If there are multiple calls to revalidate(), they are all combined and a component is revalidated only once.

Painting Components and Drawing Shapes

The painting mechanism is central to any GUI. Do you know what it takes to show you a JFrame on the screen? It is a very complex process. It is done through painting an image, which you see on the screen as a JFrame. When you press a JButton inside a JFrame, the region occupied by that JButton is repainted using different shades and colors to give you an impression that the button has been pressed. Most of the time, Swing paints the appropriate region of the screen at the appropriate time. You may encounter situations where it is necessary for you to repaint a region of your Swing component. For example, when you add or remove a component from a Swing container after it is visible, you need to validate and repaint the container so that the modified area on the screen is repainted properly.

There is a manager for everything in Swing! You also have a repaint manager that is an instance of the RepaintManager class. It provides the painting service. You can request to repaint a component by calling the repaint() method on the component. The repaint() method is overloaded. You can also repaint only a part of the component instead of the entire component. The calls to the repaint() method are queued to the event dispatching thread. The repaint manager will repaint the component only once if many requests for repainting are pending when it starts repainting the component.

How would you perform custom painting on a Swing component? Swing lets you perform custom painting on a component using a callback mechanism. The JComponent class has a callback method called paintComponent(Graphics g). The Graphics class is in the java.awt package. It is used to draw on a component. Note that drawing can be realized on various devices such as on a computer screen, an off-screen image, or a printer. To implement a custom painting for a component, override its paintComponent() method. The paintComponent()

method in the JComponent class takes care of painting the background of the component. To make sure that the component's background is painted properly, you need to invoke the JComponent's paintComponent() method from the paintComponent() method of your component. Typical code for the paintComponent() method is as follows:

```java
import java.awt.Graphics;

public class YourCustomSwingComponent extends ASwingComponent {
        @Override
        public void paintComponent(Graphics g) {
                // Paint the background
                super.paintComponent(g);

                // Your custom painting code goes here
        }
}
```

The paintComponent() method of a component is called whenever repainting is needed or when the program calls the repaint() method.

When you call the repaint() method on a Swing component, the repaint manager may paint more than just the component that you requested to paint. There are many things to consider before a component is painted. When painting a component, the background of a component and its overlapping area with other components are the two most important things to consider. If a component is not opaque, the component's container must be painted before this component is painted. This is necessary so you do not see through the component's garbage background. If a component overlaps another component, at least the overlapping area must be painted with a consideration that shows the proper color and shape for the overlapping area. The painting of the overlapping area will include painting of all overlapped components.

A Graphics object has many methods that you can use to draw geometrical shapes and strings. You can draw different shapes such as rectangles, ovals, arcs, etc. A Graphics object has many drawing properties, such as a font, a color, a coordinate system (called translation), a clip (defines the area for drawing), a component on which to draw, etc. A Graphics object in the paintComponent() method argument has many properties already set. For example,

- The font is set to the font of the component.

- The color is set to the foreground color of the component.

- The translation is set to the upper-left corner of the component. The upper-left corner of the component represents the origin, that is, coordinate (0, 0).

- The clip is set to the area of the component that needs to be painted.

You can change these properties of the Graphics object inside the paintComponent() method. However, you need to be careful if you want to change the translation or clip. You should create a copy of the Graphics object and use the copy for drawing instead of changing the original Graphics object's properties. You can use the create() method of the Graphics class to create a copy of a Graphics object. Make sure that you call the dispose() method on the copy of the Graphics object to release the system resources that it used up. A typical logic to copy and use the Graphics objects is as shown:

```java
public void paintComponent(Graphics g) {
        // Create a copy of the passed in Graphics object
        Graphics gCopy = g.create();
```

```
        // Change the properties of gCopy and use it for drawing here

        // Dispose the copy of the Graphics object
        gCopy.dispose();
}
```

There are few things to note when you use a Graphics object for a component that is passed in to the paintComponent() method.

- It uses a Cartesian coordinate system with its origin at the upper-left corner of the component.

- The x-axis extends to the right and y-axis extends down, as shown in Figure 2-40.

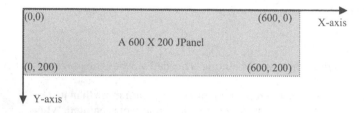

Figure 2-40. *The coordinate system used by a graphics object inside the paintComponent() method of a component. It shows the coordinates of four corners of a 600 X 200 JPanel*

- When you draw using a Graphics object, your drawings may extend outside the boundary of the component. However, any drawing that is outside of the clip area set in a Graphics object by the repaint manager will be ignored. In fact, the repaint manager will use only the clip area of the painted component to show it on the screen after the paintComponent() method returns. This is the reason why you should not change the clip property of the Graphics object inside a paintComponent() method. The clip property is set to the area of the component that needs to be painted.

- The translation property of a Graphics object is used to set up a coordinate system for drawing. The Graphics object that is passed in to the paintComponent() method already has the translation property set up, so the upper-left corner of the component represents the origin (0,0) of the coordinate system. If you change the translation property of the Graphics object inside the paintComponent() method, you better know what you are trying to do.

- The drawing is performed using the current color and font of the Graphics object.

There are numerous methods in the Graphics class to let you draw different kinds of shapes, such as a round rectangle, an arc, a polygon, etc. Table 2-20 lists a few of those methods. For the complete list of the methods, please refer to the API documentation of the Graphics class.

Table 2-20. *Methods of the Graphics Class*

Method	Description
void drawLine(int x1, int y1, int x2, int y2)	Draws a straight line from point (x1, y1) to point (x2, y2).
void drawRect(int x, int y, int width, int height)	Draws a rectangle whose upper-left corner's coordinate is (x, y). The specified width and height are the width and height of the rectangle, respectively.
void fillRect(int x, int y, int width, int height)	It is the same as drawRect() method with two differences. It fills the area with the current color of the Graphics object. Its width and height are one pixel less than the specified width and height.
void drawOval(int x, int y, int width, int height)	Draws an oval that fits into a rectangle defined with point (x, y) as its upper left corner and the specified width and height. If you specify the same width and height, it will draw a circle.
void fillOval(int x, int y, int width, int height)	It draws an oval and fills the area with the current color.
void drawstring(String str, int x, int y)	It draws the specified string str. The baseline of the leftmost character is at point (x, y).

Typically, you use a JPanel as a canvas for custom drawing. Listing 2-12 has the code that shows a class called DrawingCanvas, which is inherited from the JPanel class. In its constructor, it sets its preferred size. It overrides the paintComponent() method to draw some custom shapes and strings. Figure 2-41 shows the screen when a DrawingCanvas class is run.

Listing 2-12. A Custom JPanel Used as a Canvas for Drawing

```java
// DrawingCanvas.java
package com.jdojo.swing;

import javax.swing.JPanel;
import java.awt.Graphics;
import java.awt.Dimension;
import java.awt.Graphics2D;
import java.awt.BasicStroke;
import javax.swing.JFrame;

public class DrawingCanvas extends JPanel {
        public DrawingCanvas() {
                this.setPreferredSize(new Dimension(600, 75));
        }

        @Override
        public void paintComponent(Graphics g) {
                // Paint its background
                super.paintComponent(g);

                // Draw a line
                g.drawLine(10, 10, 50, 50);
```

```java
            // Draw a rectangle
            g.drawRect(80, 10, 40, 20);

            // Draw an oval
            g.drawOval(140, 10, 40, 20);

            // Fill an oval
            g.fillOval(200, 10, 40, 20);

            // Draw a circle
            g.drawOval(250, 10, 40, 40);

            // Draw an arc
            g.drawArc(300, 10, 50, 50, 60, 120);

            // Draw a string
            g.drawString("Hello Swing!", 350, 30);

            // Draw a thicker rectangle using Graphics2D
            Graphics2D g2d = (Graphics2D)g;
            g2d.setStroke(new BasicStroke(4));
            g2d.drawRect(450, 10, 50, 50);
    }

    public static void main(String[] args) {
        JFrame frame =
                new JFrame("Sample Drawings Using a Graphics Object");
        frame.getContentPane().add(new DrawingCanvas());
        frame.pack();
        frame.setVisible(true);
    }
}
```

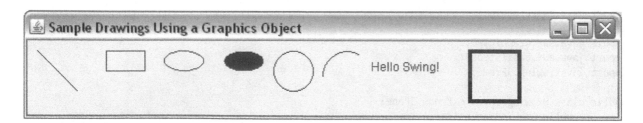

Figure 2-41. *Drawing shapes on a custom JPanel using a graphics object*

At runtime, you get an instance of Graphics2D class passed in to the paintComponent() method. The Graphics2D class inherits from the Graphics class and it has a very powerful API to draw geometrical shapes. For example, when you use a Graphics object, it draws shapes with a stroke (line width) of 1.0. If you use Graphics2D, you can use a custom stroke. The following snippet of code in the paintComponent() method of your DrawingCanvas class uses a stroke of 4.0 to draw a rectangle. To use the Graphics2D API inside the paintComponent() method, cast the passed in Graphics object to Graphics2D as shown:

```
Graphics2D g2d = (Graphics2D)g;
g2d.setStroke(new BasicStroke(4));
g2d.drawRect(450, 10, 50, 50);
```

The JComponent class has a getGraphics() method that returns a Graphics object for the component. If you need to draw on a component outside its paintComponent() method, you can use this method to get the Graphics object for the component to use it for drawing.

Immediate Painting

Swing takes care of repainting the regions of components that are visible at appropriate time. You can also request a repainting of a component by calling its repaint() method. The call to the repaint() method is asynchronous. That is, it is not carried out immediately. It is queued on the event dispatching thread and it will be carried out sometime in future. Sometimes a situation may warrant immediate painting. Use the paintImmediately() method of the component to carry out the painting immediately. The method is overloaded. The two versions are declared as follows:

- void paintImmediately(int x, int y, int w, int h)

- void paintImmediately(Rectangle r)

■ **Tip** It is more efficient to call the repaint() method if you need to paint more frequently or in a loop. Multiple calls to the repaint() method are coalesced into one call, whereas the calls to the paintImmediately() method are carried out individually.

Double Buffering

Different techniques can be used to paint a component on the screen. If a component is painted directly on the screen, it is known as an onscreen painting. If a component is painted using an off-screen buffer and that buffer is copied on to the screen in one step, it is called double buffering. There is another technique to paint a component that is called page flipping. Page flipping uses the computer's graphics card's capability to be used a video pointer, which is the address of the video contents, to display a video. Similar to double buffering, you draw the content to be displayed on an off-screen buffer. When you are done drawing onto an off-screen buffer, you change the video pointer of the graphics card to this off-screen buffer, and the graphics card will take care of displaying the images on the screen. Unlike double buffering, page flipping does not copy the contents from an off-screen buffer to an onscreen buffer. Rather, it redirects the graphics card to the new buffer. Double buffering and page flipping provide a better user experience by avoiding screen flickering when components are being painted.

Swing uses double buffering to paint all components. It lets you disable double buffering for a component. There is a catch when you disable the double buffering. Sometimes, disabling double buffering may not really do anything. If a container is being painted, Swing checks if the double buffering is enabled for the container. If the double buffering is enabled for the container, all its child components will use double buffering. Therefore, it does not help too simply disable double buffering on a component. If you want to disable double buffering, you may just want to disable it at the top-most level of the containment hierarchy that is the JRootPane. The repaint manager also lets you enable/disable double buffering globally for an application, as shown:

```
RepaintManager currentManager = RepaintManager.currentManager(component);
currentManager.setDoubleBufferingEnabled(false);
```

When double buffering is enabled, Swing will create an off-screen image and pass the graphics of that off-screen image to the paintComponent() method of the JComponent. When you draw anything using a Graphics object in the paintComponent() method, essentially you are drawing on the off-screen image. Finally, Swing will copy the off-screen image to the screen.

Double buffering also lets you create an off-screen image in your program. You can draw to that off-screen image and use that image wherever you want it in your application. You need to use the createImage() method of a component to create an off-screen image. The following code creates a custom JPanel called OffScreenImagePanel. In its paintComponent() method, it creates an off-screen image, fills the image with the color red, and uses that image to draw on to the JPanel. This is a trivial example. However, it demonstrates the steps that you need to perform to use an off-screen image in an application.

```
public class OffScreenImagePanel extends JPanel{
        public OffScreenImagePanel() {
                this.setPreferredSize(new Dimension(200, 200));
        }

        public void paintComponent(Graphics g) {
                super.paintComponent(g);

                // Create an offscreen image and fill a rectangle with red
                int w = this.getWidth();
                int h = this.getHeight();
                Image offScreenImage = this.createImage(w, h);
                Graphics imageGraphics = offScreenImage.getGraphics();
                imageGraphics.setColor(Color.RED);
                imageGraphics.fillRect(0, 0, w, h);

                // Draw the offscreen image on the JPanel
                g.drawImage(offScreenImage, 0, 0, null);
        }
}
```

JFrame Revisited

You have been using JFrames in this chapter in almost every program you have written. In this section, I will discuss some important events and properties of the JFrame.

You can set the state of a JFrame programmatically using the setExtendedState(int state) method. The state is specified using constants defined in the java.awt.Frame class from which the JFrame class is inherited.

```
// Display the JFrame maximized
frame.setExtendedState(JFrame.MAXIMIZED_BOTH);
```

Usually, you would change the state of a JFrame using the state buttons or state menu provided in its title bar's corners. Table 2-21 lists the constants that can be used to change the state of a JFrame.

Table 2-21. *The List of Constants That Define States of a JFrame*

JFrame State Constants	Description
NORMAL	JFrame is displayed in normal size.
ICONIFIED	JFrame is displayed in minimized state.
MAXIMIZED_HORIZ	JFrame is displayed maximized horizontally, but in normal size vertically.
MAXIMIZED_VERT	JFrame is displayed maximized vertically, but in normal size horizontally.
MAXIMIZED_BOTH	JFrame is displayed maximized horizontally as well as vertically.

Sometimes you may want to use a default button in your JFrame or JDialog. A default button is an instance of the JButton class, which is activated when the user presses a key on the keyboard. A key that activates the default button is defined by the look-and-feel. Typically, the key to activate the default button is the Enter key. You can set a default button for a JRootPane, which is present in a JFrame, JDialog, JWindow, JApplet, and JInternalFrame. Usually, you set the OK button as a default button on a JDialog. If a JRootPane has a default button set, pressing the Enter key will activate that button, and if you have an action-performed event handler added to that button, your code will be executed.

```
// Create a JButton
JButton okButton = new JButton("OK");

// Add an event handler to okButton here...

// Set okButton as the default button
frame.getRootPane().setDefaultButton(okButton);
```

You can add a window listener to a JFrame or any other top-level Swing window that will notify you of the seven kinds of changes in a window's state. The following snippet of code adds a window listener to a JFrame named frame. If you are interested in listening for only few window state changes, you can use the WindowAdapter class instead of the WindowListener interface. The WindowAdapter class provides an empty implementation of all the seven methods in the WindowListener interface.

```
frame.addWindowListener(new WindowListener() {
        @Override
        public void windowOpened(WindowEvent e) {
                System.out.println("JFrame has been made visible first time");
        }

        @Override
        public void windowClosing(WindowEvent e) {
                System.out.println("JFrame is closing.");
        }

        @Override
        public void windowClosed(WindowEvent e) {
                System.out.println("JFrame is closed.");
        }
```

```
        @Override
        public void windowIconified(WindowEvent e) {
                System.out.println("JFrame is minimized.");
        }

        @Override
        public void windowDeiconified(WindowEvent e) {
                System.out.println("JFrame is restored.");
        }

        @Override
        public void windowActivated(WindowEvent e) {
                System.out.println("JFrame is activated.");
        }

        @Override
        public void windowDeactivated(WindowEvent e) {
                System.out.println("JFrame is deactivated.");
        }
});

// Use the WindowAdapter class to intercept only the window closing event
frame.addWindowListener(new WindowAdapter() {
        @Override
        public void windowClosing(WindowEvent e) {
                System.out.println("JFrame is closing.");
        }
});
```

When you are done with a window (JFrame, JDialog or JWindow), you should call its dispose() method, which will make it invisible and release the resources to the operating system. Note that the dispose() method does not destroy or garbage collect the window object. As long as you hold the window's reference and it is reachable, Java would not destroy your window and you can again display it calling its setVisible(true) method.

Summary

Swing provides a huge set of components to develop GUI applications. Most of the Swing components are lightweight components that redraw using Java code without having using native peers. The JComponent class is the base class for all Swing components. A component that can contain other components is called a container. Swing provides two types of containers: top-level containers and non top-level containers. A top-level container is not contained within another container and it can be displayed directly on the desktop. An instance of the JFrame class represents a top-level container.

An object of the JButton class represents a button. A button is also known as a *push button* or a *command button*. The user presses or clicks a JButton to perform an action. A button can display text, an icon, or both.

An object of the JPanel class represents a container that can contain other components. Typically, a JPanel is is used to group related components together. A JPanel is a non top-level container.

An object of the JLabel class represents a label component that displays text, an icon, or both. Typically, the text in a JLabel is describes another component.

Swing provides several text components that let you display and edit different types of text. An object of the JTextField class is used to work with one line plain text. An object of the JTextArea is used to work with multiline plain text. An object of the JPasswordField is used to work with one line text in which the actual characters in the text are replaced with echo characters. An object of the JFormattedTextField lets you work with one line plain text where you can specify the format for the text such as displaying a date in mm/dd/yyyy format. An object of the JEditorPane lets you work with styled text such as in HTML and RTF formats. An object of the JTextPane lets you work with styled documents with embedded images and components. You can add an input verifier to a text component to validate the text entered by the user. An instance of the InputVerifier class acts as an input verifier. You can set an input verifier for a text component using the setInputVerifier() method of the JComponent class.

Swing provides many components that let you select one or more items from a list of items. Such components are objects of the JToggleButton, JCheckBox, JRadioButton, JComboBox, and JList classes. A ToggleButton can be in depressed or undepressed state and it represents a yes/no choice. A JCheckBox can be used to represent a yes/no choice. Sometimes a group of CheckBoxes is used to let the user select zero or more options. A group of JRadioButton is used to present users a set of mutually exclusive options. A ComboBox is used to provide the user with a mutualy exclusive set of choices where the user, optionally, can enter a new choice value. A ComboBox takes less space on the screen as compared to other choices, providing components because it folds all its choices and the user has to open the list of choices before he can make a selection. A JList lets the user select zero or multiple choices from a list of choices. All choices in a JList are visible to the user.

A JSpinner component combines the benefits of a JFormattedTextField and an editable JComboBox. It lets you set a list of choices as you set in a JComboBox, and at the same time, you can also apply a format to the displayed value. It shows only one value at a time from the list of choices. It lets you enter a new value.

A JScrollBar is used to provide scrolling capability for viewing a component that is bigger in size than the available space. A JScrollBar can be placed vertically or horizontally. The scolling is performed by dragging a knob along the track of the JScrollBar. You need to write the logic to provide the scolling capability using the JScrollBar component.

A ScollPane is a container that is used to wrap a component that is bigger in size than the available space. The ScrollPane provides automatic scolling capabilities in horizontal and vertical directions.

A JProgressBar is used to display the progress of a task. It can have a horizontal or vertical orientation. It has three values associated with it: the current value, the minimum value, and the maximum value. If the progress of a task is not known, the JProgressBar is said to be in indeterminate state.

A JSlider lets you select a value graphically from a set of values between two integers by sliding a knob along a track.

A JSeparator is a handy component when you want to add a separator between two components or two groups of components. Typically, a JSeparator is used in a menu to separate groups of related menu items. Typically, it appears as a horizontal or vertical solid line.

A menu component is used to provide a list of actions to the user in a compact form. An object the JMenuBar class represents a menu bar. An object of the JMenu, JMenuItem, JCheckBoxMenuItem, and JRadioButtonMenuItem class represent a menu item.

A toolbar is a group of small buttons that provides commonly used actions to the user in a JFrame. Typically, you provide a toolbar along with a menu.

A JTable is used to display and edit data in the tabular form. It presents the data in the form of rows and columns. Each column has a column header. Rows and columns are references using indexes starting at 0.

A JTree is used to display hierarchical data in a tree-like structure. Each item in a JTree is called a node. A node that has children is called a branch node. A node that has no children is called a leaf node. A branch node is called the parent node for its child nodes. The first node in the JTree that has no parent is called the root node.

A JTabbedPane component acts like a container for other Swing components, arranging them in a tabbed fashion. It can display tabs using a title, an icon, or both. Contents of only one tab are visible at a time. A JTabbedPane lets you share the space between multiple tabs.

A JSplitPane is a splitter that can be used to split space between two components. The splitter bar can be displayed horizontally or vertically. When the available space is less than the space needed to display the two components, the user can move the splitter bar up/down or left/right so one component gets more space than the other. If there is enough space, both components can be shown fully.

A JDialog is a top-level Swing container. It is used as a temporary top-level container (or as a pop-up window) to aid in the working with the main window to get the user's attention or user's input. The JOptionPane class provides many static methods to show different types of dialogs to the user using an instance of the JDialog class.

A JFileChooser lets the user select a file/directory from the file system using a built-in dialog. A JColorChooser is lets the user choose a color graphically using a built-in dialog.

A JWindow is an undecoarated top-level container. It is not a commonly used top-level container, except as a splash window that is displayed once when the application is launched and automatically disappears after a few seconds.

Swing lets you set the background and foreground colors of a component. An object of the java.awt.Color class represents a color. You can specify the color using the red, green, blue, and alpha components or using the hue, saturation, and brightness components. The Color class is immutable. It provides several constants that represent commonly used colors, for example, Color.RED and Color.BLUE constants represent the red and blue colors.

In Swing, you can draw a border around components. A border is represented by an instance of the Border interface. Different types of borders exist: bevel border, soft bevel border, etched border, line border, titled border, matte border, empty border, and compound border. The BorderFactory class provides factory methods to create all types of borders.

Swing lets you set the font for text displayed in components. An object of the java.awt.Font class represents a font in a Java program.

A component can be valid or invalid. The isValid() method of the component returns true if the component is invalid. An invalid component indicates that its position and size need to be recomputed and it needs to be laid out again. A component is valid before it is made visible the first time. Adding/removing components and changing properties that may change component's position, size, or both may make the component invalid. Calling the validate() method makes the component valid again.

Swing lets you draw many types of shapes (circles, rectangles, lines, polygons, etc.) using the Graphics object. Typically, you use a JPanel as a canvas for drawing shapes.

Swing provides two ways to repaint components: asynchronously and synchronously. Calling the repaint() method paints the componet asynchronously, Calling the paintImmediately() method paints the component immediately.

Painting of components can be perfomed onscreen or off-screen. The onscreen painting may result in flickers. The painting can be performed off-screen using a buffer and the buffer can be copied in one shot onscreen to avoid flickering. Such an off-screen painting is called double buffering and it provides better user experience by providing smooth painting on the screen.

CHAPTER 3

■ ■ ■

Advanced Swing

In this chapter, you will learn

- How to use labels in Swing components in HTML format
- About the threading model in Swing and how the event dispatch thread works
- How to execute a long-running task off the event dispatch thread
- How to use pluggable look and feel in Swing
- How to use skinnable look and feel using Synth
- How to perform drag and drop between Swing components
- How to create a multiple document interface (MDI) application
- How to use the `Toolkit` class to make a beep and know the screen details
- How to decorate Swing components using JLayer
- How to create translucent windows
- How to create shaped windows

Using HTML in Swing Components

Usually, you display the text on a component using one font and color, and in one line. If you want to display text on a component using different fonts and color or in multiple lines, you can do so using an HTML string as the text for the component. Swing components have built-in support for displaying HTML text as their labels. You can use an HTML-formatted string as a label for a `JButton`, `JMenuItem`, `JLabel`, `JToolTip`, `JTabbedPane`, `JTree`, etc. using an HTML string, which should start and end with the `<html>` and `</html>` tags, respectively. For example, if you want to display the text "**Close** Window" on a `JButton` as its label (**Close** in boldface font and Window in plain font), you can do so as follows:

```
JButton b1 = new JButton("<html><b>Close</b> Window</html>");
```

Most of the time, placing an HTML string inside `<html>` and `</html>` tags will work fine. However, if a line in an HTML string starts with a slash (/), it may not display correctly. For example, `<html>/Close Window</html>` will display nothing and `<html>/Close Window <b>Problem</b></html>` will display only Problem. To avoid this kind of problem, you can always place your HTML-formatted string inside the `<body>` HTML tag as in `<html><body>/Close Window</body></html>` and it will display as /Close Window. How can you display a string that contains HTML tags as a label? Swing lets you disable the default HTML interpretation using the html.disable component's client property. The following snippet of code disables the HTML property for a JButton and uses HTML tags in its label:

```
JButton b3 = new JButton();
b3.putClientProperty("html.disable", Boolean.TRUE);
b3.setText("<html><body>HTML is disabled</body></html>");
```

You must set the text for the component after you disable the html.disable client property. The following snippet of code shows some examples of using HTML formatted string as text for a JButton. The buttons are shown in Figure 3-1 when the code was run on Windows XP.

```
JButton b1 = new JButton();
JButton b2 = new JButton();
JButton b3 = new JButton();
b1.setText("<html><body><b>Close</b> Window</body></html>");
b2.setText("<html><body>Line 1 <br/>Line 2</body></html>");

// Disable HTML text display for b3
b3.putClientProperty("html.disable", Boolean.TRUE);
b3.setText("<html><body>HTML is disabled</body></html>");
```

Figure 3-1. Using an HTML-formatted string as text for Swing components' labels

Threading Model in Swing

Most classes in Swing are not thread safe. They were designed to work with only one thread. It does not mean that you cannot use multiple threads in a Swing application. All it means is that you must understand Swing's thread model to write a thread-safe Swing application.

Swing's thread safety rule is very simple. It states that once a Swing component has been realized, you must modify or access that component's state on the event dispatch thread. A component is considered to be realized if it has been painted or it is ready to be painted. A top-level container in Swing is realized when you call its pack(), setVisible(true), or show() method for the first time. When a top-level container is realized, all of its children are also realized.

What is the event dispatch thread? It is a thread automatically created by the JVM when it detects that it is working with a Swing application. The JVM uses this thread to execute the Swing component's event handlers. Suppose you have a JButton with an action listener. When you click the JButton, the code in the actionPerformed() method (which is the JButton's clicked event handler code) is executed by the event dispatch thread. You used a JButton in examples in previous chapters. You never paid attention to the thread that executed the actionPerformed() method of its action listener. Typically, you need not concern yourself about the threading issue in simple Swing applications like the ones you have been using. Now that you know an event dispatch thread exists in every Swing application, let's unravel the mystery of how it works. You will be using two classes throughout this discussion in this section. They are helper classes used in a Swing application to deal with its threading model. The classes are

- SwingUtilities
- SwingWorker

How do you know that your code is executing in the event dispatch thread? It is very simple to know whether your code is executing in the event dispatch thread or not, by using the static method isEventDispatchThread() of the SwingUtilities class. It returns true if your code is executing in the event dispatch thread. Otherwise, it returns false. For debugging purposes, you can write the following statement anywhere in your Java code. If it prints true, it means your code was executed in the event dispatch thread.

```
System.out.println(SwingUtilities.isEventDispatchThread());
```

Consider the program shown in Listing 3-1.

Listing 3-1. A Bad Swing Application

```java
// BadSwingApp.java
package com.jdojo.swing;

import javax.swing.SwingUtilities;
import java.awt.BorderLayout;
import java.awt.Container;
import javax.swing.JFrame;
import javax.swing.JComboBox;

public class BadSwingApp extends JFrame {
        JComboBox<String> combo = new JComboBox<>();

        public BadSwingApp(String title) {
                super(title);
                initFrame();
        }

        private void initFrame() {
                this.setDefaultCloseOperation(JFrame.EXIT_ON_CLOSE);
                Container contentPane = this.getContentPane();
                contentPane.add(combo, BorderLayout.NORTH);

                // Add an ItemEvent listener to the combobox
                combo.addItemListener(e ->
                        System.out.println("isEventDispatchThread(): " +
                                SwingUtilities.isEventDispatchThread()));

                combo.addItem("First");
                combo.addItem("Second");
                combo.addItem("Third");
        }
```

```
        public static void main(String[] args) {
                BadSwingApp badSwingApp = new BadSwingApp("A bad Swing App");
                badSwingApp.pack();
                badSwingApp.setVisible(true);
        }
}
```

The program is a simple Swing application, but it contains a potential bug. It displays a JComboBox in a JFrame. In the initFrame() method, it adds an item listener to the JComboBox. Then it adds three items to the JComboBox. The item listener simply prints a message showing whether it is executed by the event dispatch thread. As usual, you run the application by creating the frame, packing it, and making it visible. The application prints the following text on the standard output:

```
isEventDispatchThread(): false
```

Did I not say that it is the job of the event dispatch thread to execute events of all Swing components? Let's not lose hope, so select another item from the combo box such as "Second" or "Third" when the application is running. You would see the following message printed on the standard output:

```
isEventDispatchThread(): true
```

The first time, the item listener event for the combo box is executed on a non-event-dispatch thread, and from the second time onward, it is executed on the event dispatch thread. To know why this is happening in this small application, you need to know when the event dispatch thread is created, and when it starts handling events. The event dispatch thread waits for the events that are generated from the user's interaction with the GUI. Once the GUI is created, all the users' interactions with it are automatically handled by the event dispatch thread. In this case, the "main" thread created the BadSwingApp frame in the main() method. The item event was triggered when the code added the first item to the JComboBox even before GUI was created and shown. Since the "main" thread ran the creation of the BadSwingApp frame, the main thread also handled the item event. There are two problems with this program:

- It is not a good practice to add event handlers to a component first, and then do something that fires that event handler before the GUI is shown. Make it a rule of thumb to add all event handlers to a component at the end of the GUI-building code. You can fix this problem by just moving the addItem() calls before the addItemListener() call in the initFrame() method.

- You need to run all GUI code—from GUI building to making it visible—on the event dispatch thread. This is also a simple thing to do. You need to use the invokeLater(Runnable r) static method of the SwingUtilities class. The method takes a Runnable as its argument. It schedules the Runnable to run on the event dispatch thread. Here is the correct way to start a Swing application. You have not followed this way of starting your Swing application in any examples in the previous chapters. You always created and showed your frames in the main() method, which used the main thread to build and show the GUI. I did not follow the correct way of building and showing the GUI, because my focus was to demonstrate the topic that I was discussing. This is the right time for you to learn how to start your Swing applications correctly.

  ```
  // Correct way to start a Swing application
  SwingUtilities.invokeLater(() -> {
      BadSwingApp badSwingApp = new BadSwingApp("A bad Swing App");
      badSwingApp.pack();
      badSwingApp.setVisible(true);
  });
  ```

If you replace the existing code inside the main(String[] args) method of Listing 3-1 with this code, the application will print isEventDispatchThread(): true when it is run, because invokeLater() method of the SwingUtilities class will schedule the GUI-building code to run on the event dispatch thread. Once you start your application this way, it guarantees that all event handlers for your application will be executed on the event dispatch thread. The call to the SwingUtilities.invokeLater(Runnable r) method will start the event dispatch thread if it is not already started.

The SwingUtilities.invokeLater() method call returns immediately and the run() method of its Runnable argument is executed asynchronously. That is, its run() method's execution is queued to the event dispatch thread for later execution.

There is another important static method called invokeAndWait(Runnable r) in the SwingUtilities class. This method is executed synchronously and it does not return until the run() method of its Runnable argument has finished executing on the event dispatch thread. This method may throw an InterruptedException or InvocationTargetException.

■ **Tip** The SwingUtilities.invokeAndWait(Runnable r) method should not be called from the event dispatch thread because the thread that executes this method call waits until the run() method has finished. If you execute this method call from the event dispatch thread, it will be queued to the event dispatch thread and the same thread (the event dispatch thread) will be waiting. Executing this method call in the event dispatch thread generates a runtime error.

Sometimes you may want to use the invokeAndWait() method of the SwingUtilities class to start a Swing application instead of the invokeLater() method. For example, the following snippet of code starts a Swing application and prints a message on console that the application has started:

```
try {
        SwingUtilities.invokeAndWait(() -> {
                JFrame frame = new JFrame();
                frame.pack();
                frame.setVisible(true);
        });

        System.out.println("Swing application is running...");

        // You can perform some non-swing related work here
}
catch (Exception e) {
        e.printStackTrace();
}
```

Sometimes you may have to perform a time-consuming task in a Swing application. If you perform the time-consuming task on the event dispatch thread, your application will become unresponsive, which users are not going to like. You should perform long tasks in a separate thread other than the event dispatch thread. Note that it is likely that when the task is finished, you will want to update the GUI or display a result in a component, which is part of your GUI. This will require you to access Swing components from a non-event dispatch thread. You can use the invokeLater() and invokeAndWait() methods of the SwingUtilities class to update the Swing component from your separate thread. However, Swing provides a SwingWorker class, which makes it easy to work with multiple threads in a Swing application. It takes care of starting a new thread and executing some pieces of code in a new background thread and some pieces of code in the event dispatch thread. You need to know which methods in the SwingWorker class will be executed in the new thread and the event dispatch thread.

The SwingWorker<T,V> class is declared abstract. The type parameter T is the result type produced by this class and the type parameter V is the intermediate result type. You must create your custom class inheriting from it. It contains few methods of interest where you would write your custom code:

- doInBackground(): This is the method where you write the code to perform a time-consuming task. It is executed in a separate worker thread. If you want to publish intermediate results, you can call the publish() method of the SwingWorker class from this method, which in turn will call its process() method. Note that you are not supposed to access any Swing component in this method, as this method does not execute on the event dispatch thread.

- process(): This method is called as a result of a publish() method call. This method executes on the event dispatch thread, and you are free to access any Swing component in this method. A call to the process() method may be a result of many calls to the publish() method. Here are the method signatures for these two methods:

```
protected final void publish(V... chunks)
protected void process(List<V> chunks)
```

- The publish() method accepts a varargs argument. The process() method passes all arguments to the publish() method packed in a List. If more than one call to the publish() method are combined together, the process() method gets all those arguments in its List argument.

- done(): When the doInBackground() method finishes, normally or abnormally, the done() method is called on the event dispatch thread. You can access Swing components in this method. By default, this method does nothing.

- execute(): You call this method when you want to start executing your task in a separate thread. This method schedules the SwingWorker object to be executed on a worker thread.

- get(): This method returns the result of the task as returned from the doInBackground() method. If the SwingWorker object has not finished executing the doInBackground() method, the call to this method blocks until the result is ready. It is not suggested to call this method on the event dispatch thread, as it will block all events until it returns.

- cancel(boolean mayInterruptIfRunning): This method cancels the task if it is still running. If the task has not been started, the task never runs. Make sure to check for the cancelled state and for any interruptions in the doInBackground() method and exit the method accordingly. Otherwise, your process will not respond to the cancel() call.

- isCancelled(): It returns true if the process has been cancelled. Otherwise, it returns false.

- isDone(): It returns true if the task has completed. A task may complete normally or by throwing an exception or by cancellation. Otherwise, it returns false.

■ **Tip** It is important to note that a SwingWorker object is of a use-and-throw kind. That is, you cannot use it more than once. Calling its execute() method more than once does not do anything.

Let's start discussing a simple use of the SwingWorker class. Suppose you want to perform a time-consuming task that computes a number, say an integer, in a separate thread. You want to retrieve the result of the processing by polling. That is, you will periodically check if the process has finished processing. Here is a simple use of the SwingWorker class:

```
// First, create a custom SwingWorker class, say MySwingWorker.
public class MySwingWorker extends SwingWorker<Integer, Integer> {
        @Override
        protected Integer doInBackground() throws Exception {
                int result = -1;
                // Write code to perform the task

                return result;
        }
}


// Create an object of your SwingWorker class and execute the task
MySwingWorker mySW = new MySwingWorker();
mySW.execute();

// Keep checking for the result periodically. You need to wrap the get()
// call inside a try-catch to handle any exceptions.
if (mySW.isDone()) {
        int result = mySW.get();
}
```

Listing 3-2 and Listing 3-3 demonstrate how the SwingWorker class works. When you run the code in Listing 3-3, it displays a frame, shown in Figure 3-2. You can start the task by clicking the Start button. You can cancel the task anytime by clicking the Cancel button. The intermediate result is displayed in a JLabel. The SwingWorkerProcessor class is simple. It accepts a SwingWorkerFrame, a counter, and a time interval. It computes the sum of 1 to the number to the counter. It sleeps for the specified time interval after it adds a number to the result. It displays the intermediate iteration and the final result using the process() and done() methods.

Listing 3-2. A Custom SwingWorker Class

```
// SwingWorkerProcessor.java
package com.jdojo.swing;

import javax.swing.SwingWorker;
import java.util.List;

public class SwingWorkerProcessor extends SwingWorker<Integer, Integer> {
        private final SwingWorkerFrame frame;
        private int iteration;
        private int intervalInMillis;

        public SwingWorkerProcessor(SwingWorkerFrame frame, int iteration,
                int intervalInMillis) {
                this.frame = frame;
                this.iteration = iteration;
```

```java
        if (this.iteration <= 0) {
                this.iteration = 10;
        }

        this.intervalInMillis = intervalInMillis;

        if (this.intervalInMillis <= 0) {
                this.intervalInMillis = 1000;
        }
}

@Override
protected Integer doInBackground() throws Exception {
        int sum = 0;
        for (int counter = 1; counter <= iteration; counter++) {
                sum = sum + counter;

                // Publish the result to the GUI
                this.publish(counter);

                // Make sure it listens to an interruption and exits this
                // method by throwing an appropriate exception
                if (Thread.interrupted()) {
                        throw new InterruptedException();
                }

                // Make sure the loop exits, when the task is cancelled
                if (this.isCancelled()) {
                        break;
                }

                Thread.sleep(intervalInMillis);
        }

        return sum;
}

@Override
protected void process(List<Integer> data) {
        for (int counter : data) {
                frame.updateStatus(counter, iteration);
        }
}

@Override
public void done() {
        frame.doneProcessing();
}
}
```

Listing 3-3. A Swing Application to Demonstrate How a SwingWorker Class Works

```java
// SwingWorkerFrame.java
package com.jdojo.swing;

import javax.swing.JFrame;
import java.awt.Container;
import javax.swing.JLabel;
import javax.swing.JButton;
import java.awt.BorderLayout;
import java.util.concurrent.ExecutionException;

public class SwingWorkerFrame extends JFrame {
        String startMessage = "Please click the start button...";
        JLabel statusLabel = new JLabel(startMessage);
        JButton startButton = new JButton("Start");
        JButton cancelButton = new JButton("Cancel");
        SwingWorkerProcessor processor;

        public SwingWorkerFrame(String title) {
                super(title);
                initFrame();
        }

        private void initFrame() {
                this.setDefaultCloseOperation(EXIT_ON_CLOSE);
                Container contentPane = this.getContentPane();
                cancelButton.setEnabled(false);

                contentPane.add(statusLabel, BorderLayout.NORTH);
                contentPane.add(startButton, BorderLayout.WEST);
                contentPane.add(cancelButton, BorderLayout.EAST);

                startButton.addActionListener(e -> startProcessing());
                cancelButton.addActionListener(e -> cancelProcessing());
        }

        public void setButtonStatus(boolean canStart) {
                if (canStart) {
                        startButton.setEnabled(true);
                        cancelButton.setEnabled(false);
                }
                else {
                        startButton.setEnabled(false);
                        cancelButton.setEnabled(true);
                }
        }

        public void startProcessing() {
                setButtonStatus(false);
                processor = new SwingWorkerProcessor(this, 10, 1000);
                processor.execute();
        }
```

```java
    public void cancelProcessing() {
        // Cancel the processing
        processor.cancel(true);
        setButtonStatus(true);
    }

    public void updateStatus(int counter, int total) {
        String msg = "Processing " + counter + " of " + total;
        statusLabel.setText(msg);
    }

    public void doneProcessing() {
        if (processor.isCancelled()) {
            statusLabel.setText("Process cancelled ...");
        }
        else {
            try {
                // Get the result of processing
                int sum = processor.get();
                statusLabel.setText("Process completed. Sum is " + sum);
            }
            catch (InterruptedException | ExecutionException e) {
                e.printStackTrace();
            }
        }
        setButtonStatus(true);
    }

    public static void main(String[] args) {
        SwingUtilities.invokeLater(() -> {
            SwingWorkerFrame frame
                    = new SwingWorkerFrame("SwingWorker Frame");
            frame.pack();
            frame.setVisible(true);
        });
    }
}
```

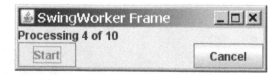

Figure 3-2. *Demonstrating the use of the SwingWorker class*

Pluggable Look and Feel

Swing supports pluggable look and feel (L&F). You can change the L&F for a Swing application using the setLookAndFeel(String lafClassName) static method of the UIManager class. The method throws checked exceptions that will require you to handle exceptions. The lafClassName argument of the method is the fully qualified name of the class providing the L&F. The following snippet of code sets the L&F for Windows using a generic catch block to handle all types of exceptions:

```
String windowsLAF= "com.sun.java.swing.plaf.windows.WindowsLookAndFeel";
try {
        UIManager.setLookAndFeel(windowsLAF);
}
catch (Exception e) {
        e.printStackTrace();
}
```

Typically, you set the L&F before you start a Swing application. If you change the L&F after the GUI has been shown, you will need to update the GUI using the updateComponentTreeUI(container) method of the SwingUtilities class. Changing the L&F may force changes in the component's size and you may want to pack your container using the pack() method again. You may end up writing the following three lines of code when you change the L&F of an application after the GUI has been shown:

```
// Assuming that frame is a reference to a JFrame object and windowsLAF contains the
// L&F class name for Windows L&F, set the new L&F, update the GUI, and pack the frame.
UIManager.setLookAndFeel(windowsLAF);
SwingUtilities.updateComponentTreeUI(frame);
frame.pack();
```

The following two methods of the UIManager class return the class names for the default Java L&F and the system L&F:

- String getCrossPlatformLookAndFeelClassName()
- String getSystemLookAndFeelClassName()

The system L&F gives the Swing components an L&F of the native system and it will differ from system to system. If you want your application to look the same as the native L&F, you can achieve that by using the following piece of code without worrying about the actual name of the class representing the system L&F on the machine your application will run:

```
// Set the system (or native) L&F
UIManager.setLookAndFeel(UIManager.getSystemLookAndFeelClassName());
```

It is not always necessary to set the L&F for your Swing application. Swing will use the default Java L&F on its own when you start the application. If the call to UIManager.setLookAndFeel() fails, your Swing application will use the current L&F, which is the default Java L&F if it is the first time you tried to set a new L&F. Although it is possible to create your own L&F, it is not easy to do so. However, Java 5.0 added the Synth L&F to facilitate the creation of a skinnable L&F. I will discuss Synth L&F in the next section.

You can use the UIManager class to list all installed L&F on your computer that you can use in your Swing application. The program in Listing 3-4 lists all available L&F on your machine. The output was obtained when the program was run on Windows; you may get a different output.

Listing 3-4. Knowing the Installed L&F on Your Machine

```java
// InstalledLookAndFeel.java
package com.jdojo.swing;

import javax.swing.UIManager;
import javax.swing.UIManager.LookAndFeelInfo;

public class InstalledLookAndFeel {
        public static void main(String[] args) {
                // Get the list of installed L&F
                LookAndFeelInfo[] lafList = UIManager.getInstalledLookAndFeels();

                // Print the names and class names of all installed L&F
                for (LookAndFeelInfo lafInfo : lafList) {
                        String name = lafInfo.getName();
                        String className = lafInfo.getClassName();
                        System.out.println("Name: " + name +
                                ", Class Name: " + className);
                }
        }
}
```

```
Name: Metal, Class Name: javax.swing.plaf.metal.MetalLookAndFeel
Name: Nimbus, Class Name: javax.swing.plaf.nimbus.NimbusLookAndFeel
Name: CDE/Motif, Class Name: com.sun.java.swing.plaf.motif.MotifLookAndFeel
Name: Windows, Class Name: com.sun.java.swing.plaf.windows.WindowsLookAndFeel
Name: Windows Classic, Class Name: com.sun.java.swing.plaf.windows.WindowsClassicLookAndFeel
```

Listing 3-5 builds a JFrame that lets you experiment with the installed L&F for the current platform. By default, the current L&F is selected. Select a different L&F from the list and the application's L&F is changed accordingly. You will get a different list of L&F on different platforms. Figure 3-3 and Figure 3-4 show the frame when the application was run on Windows and Linux, respectively.

Listing 3-5. Experimenting With Installed Look and Feels on the Current Platform

```java
// InstalledLAF.java
package com.jdojo.swing;

import java.awt.BorderLayout;
import java.awt.Container;
import java.awt.event.ItemEvent;
import java.util.Map;
import java.util.TreeMap;
import javax.swing.AbstractButton;
import javax.swing.BorderFactory;
import javax.swing.Box;
import javax.swing.ButtonGroup;
import javax.swing.JButton;
import javax.swing.JFrame;
import javax.swing.JLabel;
```

```java
import javax.swing.JPanel;
import javax.swing.JRadioButton;
import javax.swing.JTextField;
import javax.swing.LookAndFeel;
import javax.swing.SwingUtilities;
import javax.swing.UIManager;
import javax.swing.UIManager.LookAndFeelInfo;
import javax.swing.border.Border;
import javax.swing.border.EtchedBorder;

public class InstalledLAF extends JFrame {
    JLabel nameLbl = new JLabel("Name:");
    JTextField nameFld = new JTextField(20);
    JButton saveBtn = new JButton("Save");
    JTextField lafClassNameFld = new JTextField();
    ButtonGroup radioGroup = new ButtonGroup();
    static final Map<String, String> installedLAF = new TreeMap<>();

    static {
        for (LookAndFeelInfo lafInfo : UIManager.getInstalledLookAndFeels()) {
            installedLAF.put(lafInfo.getName(), lafInfo.getClassName());
        }
    }

    public InstalledLAF(String title) {
        super(title);
        initFrame();
    }

    private void initFrame() {
        this.setDefaultCloseOperation(JFrame.EXIT_ON_CLOSE);
        Container contentPane = this.getContentPane();

        // Get the current look and feel
        LookAndFeel currentLAF = UIManager.getLookAndFeel();
        String currentLafName = currentLAF.getName();
        String currentLafClassName = currentLAF.getClass().getName();

        lafClassNameFld.setText(currentLafClassName);
        lafClassNameFld.setEditable(false);

        // Build the panels
        JPanel topPanel = buildTopPanel();
        JPanel leftPanel = buildLeftPanel(currentLafName);
        JPanel rightPanel = buildRightPanel();
        contentPane.add(topPanel, BorderLayout.NORTH);
        contentPane.add(leftPanel, BorderLayout.WEST);
        contentPane.add(rightPanel, BorderLayout.CENTER);
    }
```

```java
        private void setLAF(String lafClassName) {
                try {
                        UIManager.setLookAndFeel(lafClassName);
                        SwingUtilities.updateComponentTreeUI(this);
                        this.pack();
                }
                catch (Exception e) {
                        e.printStackTrace();
                }
        }

        private JPanel buildTopPanel() {
                JPanel panel = new JPanel();
                panel.add(lafClassNameFld);
                panel.setBorder(getBorder("L&F Class Name"));
                return panel;
        }

        private JPanel buildLeftPanel(String currentLafName) {
                JPanel panel = new JPanel();
                panel.setBorder(getBorder("L&F Name"));
                Box vBox = Box.createVerticalBox();

                // Add a radio button for each installed L&F
                for (String lafName : installedLAF.keySet()) {
                        JRadioButton radioBtn = new JRadioButton(lafName);
                        if (lafName.equals(currentLafName)) {
                                radioBtn.setSelected(true);
                        }

                        radioBtn.addItemListener(this::changeLAF);
                        vBox.add(radioBtn);
                        radioGroup.add(radioBtn);
                }

                panel.add(vBox);
                return panel;
        }

        private JPanel buildRightPanel() {
                JPanel panel = new JPanel();
                panel.setBorder(getBorder("Swing Components"));

                Box hBox = Box.createHorizontalBox();
                hBox.add(nameLbl);
                hBox.add(nameFld);
                hBox.add(saveBtn);
                panel.add(hBox);

                return panel;
        }
```

```java
    private void changeLAF(ItemEvent e) {
        if (e.getSource() instanceof AbstractButton) {
            AbstractButton btn = (AbstractButton) e.getSource();
            String lafName = btn.getText();
            String lafClassName = installedLAF.get(lafName);
            this.lafClassNameFld.setText(lafClassName);
            try {
                UIManager.setLookAndFeel(lafClassName);
                SwingUtilities.updateComponentTreeUI(this);
                this.pack();
            }
            catch (Exception ex) {
                ex.printStackTrace();
            }
        }
    }

    private Border getBorder(String title) {
        Border etched = BorderFactory.createEtchedBorder(EtchedBorder.LOWERED);
        Border titledBorder = BorderFactory.createTitledBorder(etched, title);
        return titledBorder;
    }

    public static void main(String[] args) {
        SwingUtilities.invokeLater(() -> {
            InstalledLAF lafApp = new InstalledLAF("Swing L&F");
            lafApp.pack();
            lafApp.setVisible(true);
        });
    }
}
```

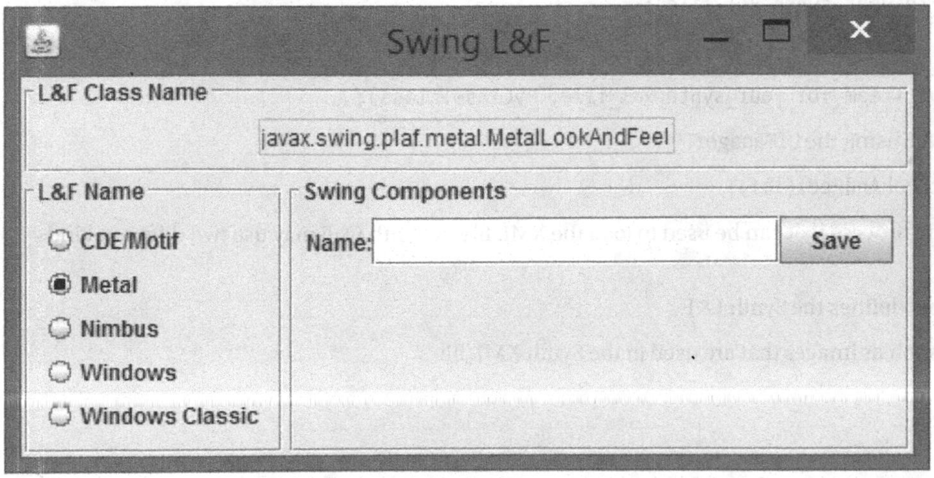

Figure 3-3. *The InstalledLAF frame on Windows*

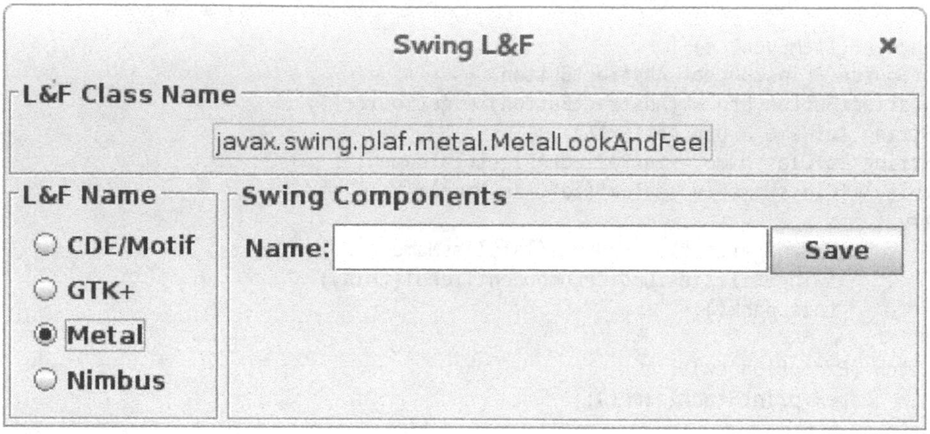

Figure 3-4. *The InstalledLAF frame on Linux*

Skinnable Look-and-Feel

Swing supports a skin-based L&F called *Synth*. What is a skin? A skin in a GUI is a set of attributes that defines the appearance of GUI components. Synth lets you define skins in an external XML file, and apply the skin at runtime to change the appearance of your Swing application. Before Synth was introduced, you needed to write a lot of Java code to have a custom L&F. With Synth, you do not need to write even one line of Java code to have a new custom L&F. Synth L&F is defined in an XML file. You need to perform the following steps to use the Synth L&F:

- Create an XML file and define the Synth L&F.

- Create an instance of the SynthLookAndFeel class.

  ```
  SynthLookAndFeel laf = new SynthLookAndFeel();
  ```

- Use the load() method of the SynthLookAndFeel object to load the Synth L&F from the XML file. The load() method is overloaded. You can use a URL or an input stream to the XML file.

  ```
  laf.load(url_to_your_synth_xml_file);
  ```

  or

  ```
  laf.load(input_steam_for_your_synth_xml_file, MyClass.class);
  ```

- Set the Synth L&F using the UIManager.

  ```
  UIManager.setLookAndFeel(laf);
  ```

Let's discuss the loading process that can be used to load the XML file. A Synth L&F may use two different kinds of external resources.

- The XML file that defines the Synth L&F

- The resources such as images that are used in the Synth XML file

When you use a URL to load a Synth XML file, the URL points to the XML file, and all paths for the resources referred to in that XML file will be resolved relative to the URL. The following snippet of code loads a Synth XML file using a URL:

```
URL url = new URL("file:///C:/synth/synth_look_and_feel.xml");
laf.load(url);
```

You can load a Synth XML file using a URL that may refer to a local file system or a network. You can use an `http` or `ftp` protocol to load a Synth XML file. You can also load a Synth XML file from a JAR file.

When you use the `load(InputStream input, Class resourceBase)` method to load the Synth XML file, the `input` parameter is the `InputStream` for the XML file to be loaded and the `resourceBase` class object is used to resolve the resources that are referred to inside that XML file. Suppose that you have the following folder structure on your computer on a Windows operating system:

```
C:\javabook
C:\javabook\images\myimage.png
C:\javabook\synth\synthlaf.xml
C:\javabook\book\chapter3\images\myimage.png
C:\javabook\book\chapter3\synth\synthlaf.xml
C:\javabook\book\chapter3\MyClass.class
```

Suppose `C:\javabook` is set in the CLASSPATH and `MyClass` is a Java class defined in the `com.jdojo.chapter3` package. The following snippet of code loads the `synthlaf.xml`:

```
// It will load C:\javabook\synth\synthlaf.xml because you are
// using a forward slash in the file path "/synth/synthlaf.xml"
Class cls = MyClass.class;
InputStream ins = cls.getResourceAsStream("/synth/synthlaf.xml");
laf.load(ins, cls);

// It will load C:\javabook\book\chapter3\synth\synthlaf.xml because you are
// not using a forward slash in the file path "synthlaf.xml"
Class cls = MyClass.class;
InputStream ins = cls.getResourceAsStream("synthlaf.xml");
laf.load(ins, cls);
```

In both cases, the class reference `cls` will be used to resolve the path to the resources referenced in the XML file. For example, if an image is referred as `images/myimage.png`, it will be loaded from `C:\javabook\book\chapter3\images\myimage.png`. If the image is referred to as `/images/myimage.png`", the `C:\javabook\images\myimage.png` file will be loaded.

Use the second version of the `load()` method, which is more flexible. You can package all your Synth L&F files and related resource files in a JAR file without worrying about their actual location at runtime. During development, you can place all your Synth files in a separate folder, which should be in your CLASSPATH. The only thing you need to pay attention to is that if the file name starts with a forward slash, the path is resolved using the CLASSPATH. If your file name does not start with a forward slash, the package path for that class is added in front of the file name and then the CLASSPATH is used to resolve the path to your file.

Let's start building your Synth L&F XML file. Set your goal before you start defining your Synth L&F. Figure 3-5 shows a sample `JFrame` that uses the Java default L&F.

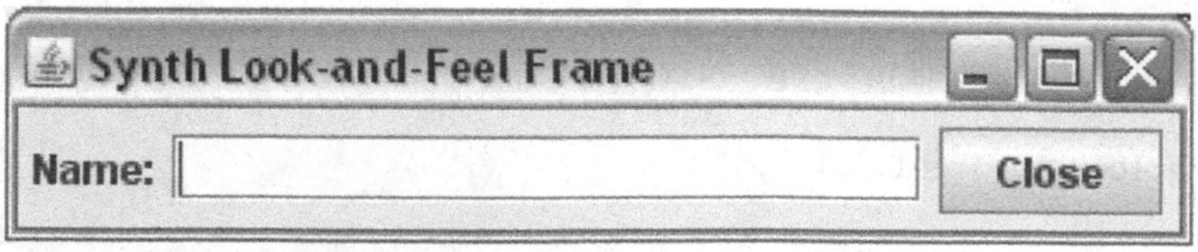

Figure 3-5. *A sample JFrame using the default Java L&F*

The JFrame contains three components: a JLabel, a JTextField, and a JButton. You will build an XML file to define a Synth L&F for these components. The Java code to create this screen is shown in Listing 3-6. The code that is of interest is in the main() method (shown below). For now, just create an empty XML file named synthlaf.xml and save it in the CLASSPATH.

```
try {
        SynthLookAndFeel laf = new SynthLookAndFeel();
        Class cls = SynthLookAndFeelFrame.class;
        InputStream ins = cls.getResourceAsStream("/synthlaf.xml");
        laf.load(ins, cls);
        UIManager.setLookAndFeel(laf);
}
catch (Exception e) {
        e.printStackTrace();
}
```

Listing 3-6. Using a Synth L&F for Swing Components

```
// SynthLookAndFeelFrame.java
package com.jdojo.swing;

import java.io.InputStream;
import java.awt.Container;
import java.awt.FlowLayout;
import javax.swing.JButton;
import javax.swing.JFrame;
import javax.swing.JLabel;
import javax.swing.JTextField;
import javax.swing.UIManager;
import javax.swing.plaf.synth.SynthLookAndFeel;

public class SynthLookAndFeelFrame extends JFrame {
        JLabel nameLabel = new JLabel("Name:");
        JTextField nameTextField = new JTextField(20);
        JButton closeButton = new JButton("Close");

        public SynthLookAndFeelFrame(String title) {
                super(title);
                initFrame();
        }

        private void initFrame() {
                this.setDefaultCloseOperation(EXIT_ON_CLOSE);
                Container contentPane = this.getContentPane();
```

```
            contentPane.setLayout(new FlowLayout());
            contentPane.add(nameLabel);
            contentPane.add(nameTextField);
            contentPane.add(closeButton);
        }

    public static void main(String[] args) {
        try {
                SynthLookAndFeel laf = new SynthLookAndFeel();
                Class c = SynthLookAndFeelFrame.class;
                InputStream ins = c.getResourceAsStream("/synthlaf.xml");
                laf.load(ins, c);
                UIManager.setLookAndFeel(laf);
        }
        catch (Exception e) {
                e.printStackTrace();
        }

        SynthLookAndFeelFrame frame =
                new SynthLookAndFeelFrame("Synth Look-and-Feel Frame");
        frame.pack();
        frame.setVisible(true);
        }
}
```

In its simplest form, a Synth XML file looks as shown:

```
<?xml version="1.0"?>
<synth version="1">
</synth>
```

The root element is <synth>, and optionally, you may specify a version number, which should be 1. You have not defined any L&F-related styles in the XML file. Let's run the SynthLookAndFeelFrame class with these contents in the synthlaf.xml file. If you encounter a problem in running the class because it does not find the synthlaf.xml file, change the load() method call in the main() method to use a URL instead of an InputStream. Figure 3-6 shows the JFrame that you get when you run the SynthLookAndFeelFrame class.

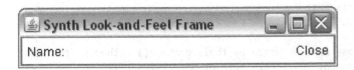

Figure 3-6. *A JFrame with a Synth L&F where the Synth XML file does not define any styles*

You did not expect a JFrame like this, did you? You will fix it in a minute. By default, a Synth L&F sets a white background with no border for all components. This is the reason why the JLabel, JTextField, and JButton run together on the screen. A JTextField is still there on the screen, but it has no border.

Let's define a style. A style is defined using a <style> element. It has a mandatory attribute named id that is a unique identifier for the style. The id attribute's value is used when you bind the style to a component.

```xml
<?xml version="1.0"?>
<synth version="1">
        <style id="buttonStyle">
                <!-- Style specific elements go here -->
        </style>
</synth>
```

Defining the style itself does not have any effect. You must bind a style to one or more components to see the style in action. Binding a style to a component is accomplished using a <bind> element, which has the three attributes:

- style
- type
- key

The style is the value of the id attribute of a style element that you are binding to this component.

The type attribute determines the type of binding. Its value is either region or name. Each Swing component has at least one region. Some components have more than one region. All regions of a component have a name. Regions are defined by constants in the Region class, which is in the javax.swing.plaf.synth package. For example, a JButton has one region called Button that is represented by the Region.BUTTON constant; a JTextField has one region called TextField that is represented by the Region.TEXT_FIELD constant; a JTabbedPane has four regions called TabbedPaneContent, TabbedPaneTabArea, TabbedPaneTab, and TabbedPane. Please refer to the documentation for the Region class for the complete list of regions. If you use the value name, it refers to the value returned by the getName() method of the component. You can set a name for a component using its setName() method.

The key attribute is a regular expression that is used to match the region or name depending on the value used for the type attribute. For example, the regular expression ".*" matches any region or name. Typically, you use ",*" as a key value to bind a default style to all components.

Here are some examples of using the <bind> element to bind a style to a component:

```xml
<!-- Bind a buttonStyle style to all JButtons -->
<bind style="buttonStyle" type="region" key="Button" />

<!-- Bind a defaultStyle to all Swing components -->
<bind style="defaultStyle" type="region" key=".*" />

<!-- Bind myDefaultStyle to all components whose name returned by their getName() method starts with
"com.jdojo". Here \. means one dot and .* means any characters zero or more times -->
<bind style="mydefaultStyle" type="name" key="com\.jdojo.*" />
```

Let's define some styles for a JButton. All styles must be defined inside a <style> element. You can set the opacity in a style using a <opaque> element. It has a value attribute that could be true or false, as shown:

```xml
<opaque value="true"/>
```

A component can be in one of the seven states: ENABLED, MOUSE_OVER, PRESSED, DISABLED, FOCUSED, SELECTED, or DEFAULT. Not all components support all seven states. You can define style properties that apply to a specific state or all states. You define state specific properties using a <state> element. You need to specify a value attribute with one of the seven state values if the style properties only apply to a specific state. If you want to define some style properties for more than one state, you can separate state names with an AND. The following <style> element will define styles for a component when a mouse is over it and it is also focused:

```
<state value="MOUSE_OVER AND FOCUSED">
...
</state>
```

If multiple styles exist for the same state, the style definition associated with the most specific state is used. Suppose you have defined styles for two states: MOUSE_OVER and FOCUSED and MOUSE_OVER. When the component has the mouse over its region and it is in focus, the first style is applied; if the component is not in focus, but it has a mouse over its region, the second style is applied.

Modify the synthlaf.xml file with the contents shown and rerun the application:

```xml
<?xml version="1.0"?>
<synth version="1">
  <style id="buttonStyle">
    <opaque value="true"/>
    <insets top="4" bottom="4" left="6" right="6"/>
    <imageIcon id="closeIconId" path="/images/close_icon.png"/>
    <property key="Button.textShiftOffset" type="Integer" value="2"/>
    <property key="Button.icon" type="idref" value="closeIconId"/>
    <state>
        <font name="Serif" size="14" style="BOLD"/>
        <color value="LIGHT_GRAY" type="BACKGROUND"/>
        <color value="BLACK" type="TEXT_FOREGROUND"/>
    </state>
    <state value="PRESSED">
            <color value="GRAY" type="BACKGROUND"/>
            <color value="BLACK" type="TEXT_FOREGROUND"/>
    </state>
  </style>
  <bind style="buttonStyle" type="region" key="Button"/>
</synth>
```

Press the Close button and you will find that it works much better than before. Its background color changes when you press it. Its text shifts right and down when it is in pressed.

Let's discuss all styles used in this XML file:

- The buttonStyle style defines styles for a JButton. The <opaque> element defines that the JButton will be opaque. The <insets> element sets the insets for the JButton.

- The `<imageIcon>` element defines an image resource. This element does not do anything by itself. You will need to refer to its id attribute's value in some other place when you need to use an image. Its path attribute refers to the path of the image file. It uses the getResource() method of the class object you pass to the load() method to locate the image file. You have used /images/close_icon.png as the path. It means that you need to have a folder named images under a folder, which is in the CLASSPATH, and you need to place a close_icon. png file under the images folder. If you used a URL to load a synth XML file, your path for the image will change accordingly. Suppose you loaded a Synth XML file using a URL string "file:///c:/mysynth/synthlaf.xml". This URL has file:///c:/mysynth/ as the base and all paths in your XML will be resolved relative to this base. For example, if you specify images/ close_icon.png as a path in a `<imageIcon>` element, file:///c:/mysynth/images/close_ icon.png will be the path used to load your image file. If you specify /images/close_icon. png as the path for in a `<imageIcon>` element, it will be treated as an absolute path, and Synth will attempt to load the image file using a file://images/close_icon.png path. It is very important that you understand how a resource lookup is affected by your choice of using different versions of the load() method of the SynthLookAndFeel class. It is better to use a URL and place all resources under the base folder of the URL. You can pack all resources including the Synth XML file in a JAR file and use a URL version of the load() method.

A `<property>` element is used to set a property for a component. You cannot set any property of a component using a `<property>` element. A `<property>` element has three attributes: key, type, and value. The key attribute specifies the property name. The type attribute is the type of property, and its value could be idref, boolean, dimension, insets, integer, or string. The type attribute is optional, and it defaults to idref, which means the value attribute's value is an id referring to another element. You have set two properties for the JButton. One is the Button.textShiftOffset property, which is used to shift the JButton's text when it is pressed. Another property is an image icon for the JButton called Button.icon. You have not specified the type attribute, which is defaulted to idref. The value attribute for the `<property>` element is closeIconId, which is the id of an `<imageIcon>` element that defines the close image.

You can define a color attribute using a `<color>` element. You set the value for the type and value attributes of a `<color>` element. The type attribute can have one of the four values: FOREGROUND, BACKGROUND, TEXT_FOREGROUND, TEXT_BACKGROUND, and FOCUS. You can specify the value for the value attribute using constant names from the java. awt.Color class or a hex value in #RRGGBB or #AARRGGBB form. In the hex form, AA, RR, GG, and BB are values for alpha, red, green, and blue components of the color.

You can define a font style using a `<font>` element. It has three attributes: name, size, and style. The style attribute is optional and it defaults to PLAIN. Other values for style attribute are BOLD and ITALIC.

Finally, you combine different styles and put them under a `<state>` element. You have set one set of styles for all states and one set for the PRESSED state in your buttonStyle. Note that your JButton will have a background color of LIGHT_GRAY by default. Its background color will change to GRAY when it is pressed. When you run the SynthLookAndFeel class with this XML file, the screen looks as shown in Figure 3-7. Note that you have set an icon for the Close button. The background color changes when you press the Close button.

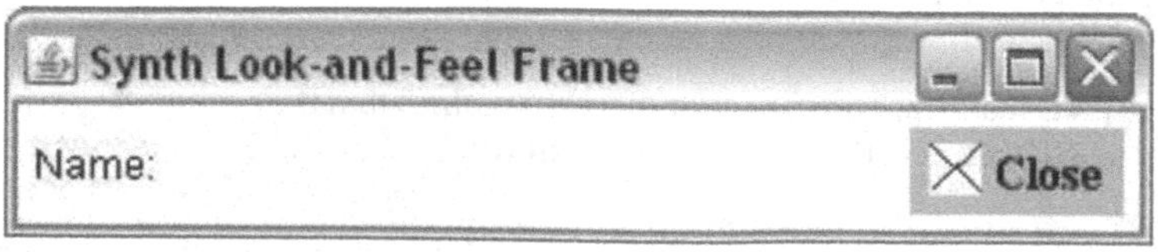

Figure 3-7. *Using an icon with the Synth look and feel*

You do not have a border for the JButton and JTextField. There are two ways to set a border in Synth: you can use an image or write Java code. I will discuss both ways to set a border. If you want a border to be painted by an image, you need to use an <imagePainter> element, as shown:

```
<imagePainter path="/images/line_border.png"
              sourceInsets="2 2 2 2"
              paintCenter="false"
              method="buttonBorder" />
```

The path attribute specifies the path of the image that is used to paint the border. The sourceInsets attribute specifies insets of the source image. The painterCenter attribute specifies if the center of the image should be drawn or just the border. If you want to draw a border, you should set this attribute to false. If you want to draw an image as a background, you should set this attribute to true. The method attribute is the name of the paint method in the javax.swing.plaf.synth.SynthPainter class. This class has a paint method to paint every component. The method name is of the form paintXxxYyy(), where Xxx is a component name and Yyy is an area to paint. The value of the method attribute is set to xxxYyy by leaving the "paint" word out and using a lowercase first character. For example, to paint a button's border, the paint method name is paintButtonBorder(). The method attribute value for this method is buttonBorder. You can also set an image as a background for a component using a <imagePainter> element. The following style will set button_background.png as the background for a JButton:

```
<imagePainter path="/images/button_background.png"
              sourceInsets="2 2 2 2"
              paintCenter="true"
              method="buttonBackground" />
```

■ **Tip**　By default, the image used in the <imagePainter> element is stretched to fit the size of the component. It means that if you want the same border around multiple components, you need to create only one image to represent that border. If you do not want the image stretched, you can set the stretch attribute of the <imagePainter> element to false.

If you want to write Java code to draw a border, you need to create a new class, which will inherit from the SynthPainter class as listed in Listing 3-7. You need to override a specific paint method. This class overrides the paintTextFieldBorder() and paintButtonBorder() methods. They simply draw a rectangle using a custom color and stroke value.

Listing 3-7. A Custom Synth Border Painter Class for a JTextField and a JButton

```java
// SynthRectBorderPainter.java
package com.jdojo.swing;

import javax.swing.plaf.synth.SynthPainter;
import javax.swing.plaf.synth.SynthContext;
import java.awt.Graphics;
import java.awt.Graphics2D;
import java.awt.BasicStroke;
import java.awt.Color;
```

```java
public class SynthRectBorderPainter extends SynthPainter {
        @Override
        public void paintTextFieldBorder(SynthContext context, Graphics g,
         int x, int y, int w, int h) {
                Graphics2D g2 = (Graphics2D)g;
                g2.setStroke(new BasicStroke(2));
                g2.setColor(Color.BLUE);
                g2.drawRect(x, y, w, h);
        }

        @Override
        public void paintButtonBorder(SynthContext context, Graphics g,
         int x, int y, int w, int h) {
                Graphics2D g2 = (Graphics2D)g;
                g2.setStroke(new BasicStroke(4));
                g2.setColor(Color.RED);
                g2.drawRect(x, y, w, h);
        }
}
```

Now, you need to specify in your Synth XML file that you want to use your custom painter class to paint your JButton's border. An <object> element represents a Java object in a Synth XML file. To specify a custom Java painter, you use a <painter> element, which needs an idref of an <object> element's id and a method name, as shown:

```xml
<object id="borderPainterId" class="com.jdojo.swing.SynthRectBorderPainter"/>
<painter idref="borderPainterId" method="buttonBorder"/>
```

You final version of the Synth XML file is shown below. You have used a custom Java code to paint the border for the Close button when it is pressed, and an image icon when it is not pressed. The border for the JTextField is drawn using your custom Java code. You can modify the XML content to set styles for the JLabel. Finally, the JFrame looks as shown in Figure 3-8.

```xml
<?xml version="1.0"?>
<synth version="1.0">
  <style id="buttonStyle">
    <opaque value="true"/>
    <insets top="4" bottom="4" left="6" right="6"/>
    <imageIcon id="closeIconId" path="/images/close_icon.png"/>
    <property key="Button.textShiftOffset" type="Integer" value="2"/>
    <property key="Button.icon" type="idref" value="closeIconId"/>
    <state>
      <imagePainter path="/images/line_border.png" sourceInsets="2 2 2 2"
                    paintCenter="false" method="buttonBorder"/>
      <font name="Serif" size="14" style="BOLD"/>
      <color value="LIGHT_GRAY" type="BACKGROUND"/>
      <color value="BLACK" type="TEXT_FOREGROUND"/>
    </state>
    <state value="PRESSED">
      <object id="borderPainterId"
              class="com.jdojo.swing.SynthRectBorderPainter"/>
```

```
      <painter idref="borderPainterId" method="buttonBorder"/>
      <color value="GRAY" type="BACKGROUND"/>
      <color value="BLACK" type="TEXT_FOREGROUND"/>
    </state>
  </style>
  <bind style="buttonStyle" type="region" key="Button"/>

  <style id="textFieldStyle">
    <insets top="4" bottom="4" left="4" right="4"/>
    <state>
      <color value="WHITE" type="BACKGROUND"/>
      <object id="textFieldPainterId" class="com.jdojo.swing.SynthRectBorderPainter"/>
      <painter idref="textFieldPainterId" method="textFieldBorder"/>
    </state>
  </style>
  <bind style="textFieldStyle" type="region" key="TextField"/>
</synth>
```

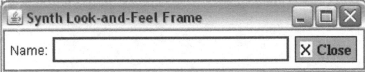

Figure 3-8. *Using borders in a Synth L&F*

Drag and Drop

Drag and drop (DnD) is a way to transfer data in an application. You can also transfer data using a clipboard with cut, copy, and paste actions.

DnD lets you transfer data by dragging a component and dropping it onto another component. The component that is dragged is called the *drag source*; it supplies the data to be transferred. The component onto which the drag source is dropped is called the *drop target*; it is the receiver of the data. It is the responsibility of the drop target to accept the drop action and import the data supplied by the drag source. The data transfer is accomplished using a Transferable object. Transferable is an interface in the java.awt.datatransfer package. The DnD mechanism is shown in Figure 3-9.

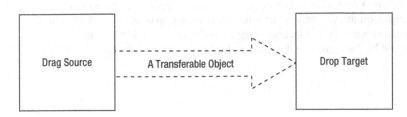

Figure 3-9. *The data transfer mechanism used in DnD*

The `Transferable` interface contains the following three methods:

- `DataFlavor[] getTransferDataFlavors()`

- `boolean isDataFlavorSupported(DataFlavor flavor)`

- `Object getTransferData(DataFlavor flavor) throws UnsupportedFlavorException, IOException`

Before you learn the three methods of the `Transferable` interface, you need to know why you need a `Transferable` object to transfer data using DnD. Why does the drag target not get the data directly from the drag source? You can transfer data using DnD within the same Java application, between two Java applications, from a native application to a Java application, and from a Java application to a native application. The scope of a data transfer is very wide, and it supports the transfer of a wide variety of data. The `Transferable` interface provides a mechanism to pack the data and its type in an object. The receiver can query this object about the data type it holds, and import the data if it fits the receiver's requirements. An object of the `DataFlavor` class represents the details about the data. I will not discuss the `DataFlavor` class in detail. It contains several constants to define the type of data; for example, `DataFlavor.stringFlavor` represents Java's Unicode string class. The first two methods of the `Transferable` interface give details about the data. The third one returns the data itself as an `Object`. The drop target will use the `getTransferData()` method to get the data supplied by the drag source.

Using DnD in Swing is easy. Most of the time, you need to write only one line of code to start using DnD. All you need is to enable the dragging on the component, like so:

```
// Enable DnD for myComponent
myComponent.setDragEnabled(true);
```

After that, you can start using DnD on `myComponent`. Using DnD is UI-dependent. On a Windows platform, you need to press the left mouse button on the drag source to start the drag action. To keep dragging the drag source, you need to move the mouse while holding the left mouse button down. Releasing the left mouse button while the mouse pointer is on a drop target performs the drop action. Throughout the DnD process, the user receives visual feedbacks.

All text components (`JFileChooser`, `JColorChooser`, `JList`, `JTree`, and `JTable`) have built-in drag support for DnD. All text components and `JColorChooser` have built-in drop support for DnD. For example, suppose you have a `JTextField` named `nameFld` and a `JTextArea` named `descTxtArea`. To start using DnD between them, you need to write the following two lines of code:

```
nameFld.setDragEnabled(true);
descTxtArea.setDragEnabled(true);
```

You can select text in the `JTextField`, drag it, and drop it onto the `JTextArea`. The selected text in the `JTextField` is transferred to the `JTextArea`. You can also drag text from the `JTextArea` to the `JTextField`.

How is the data transferred from one text component to another? Does it get copied or moved? The answer depends on the drag source and the user's action. A drag source declares the actions it supports. The user's action determines what action took place. For example, on the Windows platform, simple dragging indicates a `MOVE` action whereas dragging with the `Ctrl` key down indicates a Copy action, and dragging with `Ctrl` + `Shift` keys down indicates a `LINK` action. Actions are represented by the constants declared in the `TransferHandler` class:

- `TranferHandler.COPY`

- `TranferHandler.MOVE`

- `TranferHandler.COPY_OR_MOVE`

- `TranferHandler.LINK`

- `TranferHandler.NONE`

The drop action is not built-in for the JList, JTable, and JTree components. The reason is that the user's intention cannot be predicted when a drag source is dropped onto these components. You will need to write code to get the drop action in place for these components. Note that they have built-in support for the drag action. DnD provides you with appropriate information about the drop location on these components. These components let you specify the drop mode using their setDropMode(DropMode dm) method. A drop mode determines how the drop location is tracked during a DnD operation. Drop modes are represented by constants in the java.swing.DropMode enum as listed in Table 3-1.

Table 3-1. *The List of DropMode Enum Contants for JList, JTree, and JTable*

DropMode Enum Constant	Using Component	Description
ON	JList JTree JTable	The drop location is tracked using the index of existing items.
INSERT	JList JTree JTable	The drop location is tracked as the position where the data will be inserted.
INSERT_COLS	JTable	The drop location is tracked in terms of the column index where the new columns will be inserted.
INSERT_ROWS	JTable	The drop location is tracked in terms of the row index where the new rows will be inserted.
ON_OR_INSERT	JList JTree JTable	Tracks drop location as both ON and INSERT.
ON_OR_INSERT_ROWS ON_OR_INSERT_COLS	JTable	Tracks ON or INSERT with respect to row or column.
USE_SELECTION	JList JTree JTable	It works the same as ON. It is the default drop mode. If you drag onto a component that is already selected, this mode changes the selection to the item on which the mouse cursor is being dragged. However, the ON drop mode keeps the user's selection intact and selects the item temporarily on which a mouse cursor is dragged. ON is a better choice for the user's experience. This option is only provided for backward compatibility.

Let's write some code to use DnD with a JList. You need to do the following:

- Create a new class inheriting from the javax.swing.TransferHandler class.

- Override some of the methods in the new class to handle the data transfer.

- Use the JList's setTransferHandler() method to set an instance of your transfer handler class.

Listing 3-8 contains the code for a custom TransferHandler for a JList.

Listing 3-8. A Custom TransferHandler for a JList

```java
// ListTransferHandler.java
package com.jdojo.swing;

import java.awt.datatransfer.DataFlavor;
import java.awt.datatransfer.StringSelection;
import java.awt.datatransfer.Transferable;
import java.awt.datatransfer.UnsupportedFlavorException;
import java.io.IOException;
import javax.swing.DefaultListModel;
import javax.swing.JComponent;
import javax.swing.JList;
import javax.swing.TransferHandler;

public class ListTransferHandler extends TransferHandler {
    @Override
    public int getSourceActions(JComponent c) {
        return TransferHandler.COPY_OR_MOVE;
    }

    @Override
    protected Transferable createTransferable(JComponent source) {
        // Suppress the unchecked cast warning
        @SuppressWarnings("unchecked")
        JList<String> sourceList = (JList<String>)source;

        String data = sourceList.getSelectedValue();

        // Uses only the first selected item in the list
        Transferable t = new StringSelection(data);
        return t;
    }

    @Override
    protected void exportDone(JComponent source, Transferable data, int action) {
        // Suppress teh unchecked cast warning
        @SuppressWarnings("unchecked")
        JList<String> sourceList = (JList<String>)source;

        String movedItem = sourceList.getSelectedValue();

        if (action == TransferHandler.MOVE) {
            // Remove the moved item
            DefaultListModel<String> listModel
                = (DefaultListModel<String>) sourceList.getModel();
            listModel.removeElement(movedItem);
        }
    }
```

```java
@Override
public boolean canImport(TransferHandler.TransferSupport support) {
        // We only support drop, not copy-paste
        if (!support.isDrop()) {
                return false;
        }

        return support.isDataFlavorSupported(DataFlavor.stringFlavor);
}

@Override
public boolean importData(TransferHandler.TransferSupport support) {
        // This is necessary to handle paste
        if (!this.canImport(support)) {
                return false;
        }

        // Get the data
        Transferable t = support.getTransferable();
        String data = null;
        try {
                data = (String) t.getTransferData(DataFlavor.stringFlavor);
                if (data == null) {
                        return false;
                }
        }
        catch (UnsupportedFlavorException | IOException e) {
                e.printStackTrace();
                return false;
        }

        // Get the drop location for the JList
        JList.DropLocation dropLocation
                = (JList.DropLocation) support.getDropLocation();

        int dropIndex = dropLocation.getIndex();

        // Suppress the unchecked cast warning
        @SuppressWarnings("unchecked")
        JList<String> targetList = (JList<String>)support.getComponent();

        DefaultListModel<String> listModel
                = (DefaultListModel<String>)targetList.getModel();

        if (dropLocation.isInsert()) {
                listModel.add(dropIndex, data);
        }
```

```
            else {
                    listModel.set(dropIndex, data);
            }

            return true;
        }
}
```

If you want to support the drop action for only a JList, you only need to override two methods: canImport()
and importData() in your transfer handler class. The canImport() method returns true if the drop target wants to
transfer the data. Otherwise, it returns false. In your code, you are making sure that this operation is a drop operation
and that the drag source supplies a string data. Note that if you set a custom TransferHandler object to a component,
the same TransferHandler object will also be used for cut-copy-paste operations. You code supports only a drop
operation. The importData() method reads the data from a Transferable object and inserts or replaces the item in
the JList based on the user's action.

The default TransferHandler for the JList handles the drag action and supplies the data. However, once you
set your own TransferHandler, you lose the default feature, and you are responsible for adding that feature to your
TransferHandler. If you want to support a drag action, you need to write custom code for the createTransferable()
and getSourceActions() methods. The first method packs the data into a Transferable object and the second one
returns the kind of actions supported by the drag source. StringSelection is an implementation of the Transferable
interface to transfer Java strings.

If your drag source supports a MOVE action, you are supposed to provide code that will remove the item after the
move action. You get a placeholder to write cleanup code in the exportDone() method, as shown in Listing 3-9.

Listing 3-9 has the code that displays a JTextField and two JLists, which lets you demonstrate DnD for a
JList. Figure 3-10 shows the JFrame you get when you run the program in Listing 3-9. You can use DnD among any
of the three components: the JTextField and two JLists. There is one bug in the code. If you drag an item in the
JList and drop it in the same JList, nothing happens. It is left as an exercise for you to figure out this bug and fix it.
I will give you a hint: try removing the element before adding it to the same List in the importData() method of the
ListTransferHandler class. Also, this custom code supports only a single selection in the JList. You can customize
the code in the ListTransferHandler class to handle multiple selections in the JList.

Listing 3-9. Using DnD to Transfer Data Between Swing Components

```
// DragAndDropApp.java
package com.jdojo.swing;

import java.awt.BorderLayout;
import java.awt.Container;
import javax.swing.Box;
import javax.swing.DefaultListModel;
import javax.swing.DropMode;
import javax.swing.JFrame;
import javax.swing.JLabel;
import javax.swing.JList;
import javax.swing.JScrollPane;
import javax.swing.JTextField;
import javax.swing.ListSelectionModel;
import javax.swing.SwingUtilities;

public class DragAndDropApp extends JFrame {
        private JLabel newLabel = new JLabel("New:");
        private JTextField newTextField = new JTextField(10);
```

```java
private JLabel sourceLabel = new JLabel("Source");
private JLabel destLabel = new JLabel("Destination");
private JList<String> sourceList = new JList<>(new DefaultListModel<>());
private JList<String> destList = new JList<>(new DefaultListModel<>());

public DragAndDropApp(String title) {
        super(title);
        populateList();
        initFrame();
}

private void initFrame() {
        Container contentPane = this.getContentPane();

        Box nameBox = Box.createHorizontalBox();
        nameBox.add(newLabel);
        nameBox.add(newTextField);

        Box sourceBox = Box.createVerticalBox();
        sourceBox.add(sourceLabel);
        sourceBox.add(new JScrollPane(sourceList));

        Box destBox = Box.createVerticalBox();
        destBox.add(destLabel);
        destBox.add(new JScrollPane(destList));

        Box listBox = Box.createHorizontalBox();
        listBox.add(sourceBox);
        listBox.add(destBox);

        Box allBox = Box.createVerticalBox();
        allBox.add(nameBox);
        allBox.add(listBox);

        contentPane.add(allBox, BorderLayout.CENTER);

        // Our lists support only single selection
        sourceList.setSelectionMode(
                ListSelectionModel.SINGLE_SELECTION);
        destList.setSelectionMode(
                ListSelectionModel.SINGLE_SELECTION);

        // Enable Drag and Drop for components
        newTextField.setDragEnabled(true);
        sourceList.setDragEnabled(true);
        destList.setDragEnabled(true);

        // Set the drop mode to Insert
        sourceList.setDropMode(DropMode.INSERT);
        destList.setDropMode(DropMode.INSERT);
```

```java
            // Set the transfer handler
            sourceList.setTransferHandler(new ListTransferHandler());
            destList.setTransferHandler(new ListTransferHandler());
    }

    public void populateList() {
            DefaultListModel<String> sourceModel
                    = (DefaultListModel<String>) sourceList.getModel();

            DefaultListModel<String> destModel
                    = (DefaultListModel<String>) destList.getModel();
            for (int i = 0; i < 5; i++) {
                    sourceModel.add(i, "Source Item " + i);
                    destModel.add(i, "Destination Item " + i);
            }
    }

    public static void main(String[] args) {
            SwingUtilities.invokeLater(() -> {
                    DragAndDropApp frame = new DragAndDropApp("Drag and Drop Frame");
                    frame.pack();
                    frame.setVisible(true);
            });
    }
}
```

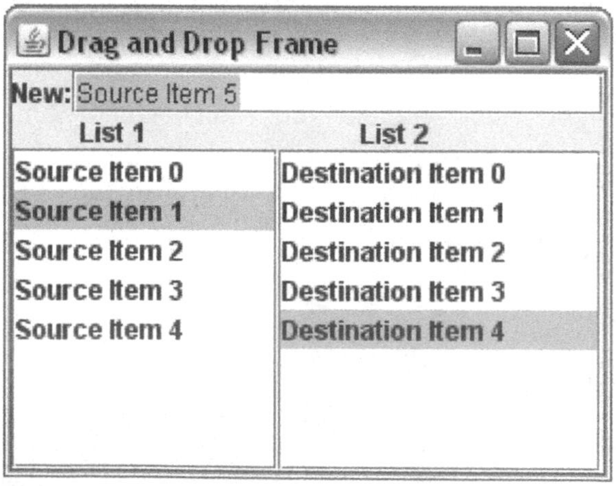

Figure 3-10. *A JFrame with a few Swing components supporting DnD*

Multiple Document Interface Application

Broadly speaking, there are three types of applications based on how windows are organized within an application to present information to users. They are

- Single Document Interface (SDI)
- Multiple Document Interface (MDI)
- Tabbed Document Interface (TDI)

In an SDI application, only one window is opened at any time. In an MDI application, one main window (also the called parent window) is opened, and multiple child windows are open within the main window. In a TDI application, one window is opened, which has multiple windows open as tabs. Microsoft Notepad is an example of an SDI application, Microsoft Word 97 is an example of an MDI application (newer versions of Microsoft Word are SDI), and Google Chrome browser is an example of a TDI application.

You can use Swing to develop SDI, MDI, and TDI applications. In an MDI application, you can open multiple frames that will be instances of the JInternalFrame class. You can organize multiple internal frames in many ways. For example, you can maximize and minimize them; you can view them side by side in a tiled fashion, or you can view them in a cascaded form. The following are four classes you will be working with in an MDI application:

- JInternalFrame
- JDesktopPane
- DesktopManager
- JFrame

An instance of the JInternalFrame class acts as a child window that is always displayed inside the area of its parent window. For the most part, working with it is the same as working with a JFrame. You add Swing components to its content pane, pack them using the pack() method, and make it visible using the setVisible(true) method. If you want to listen to window events such as activated, deactivated, etc., you need to add an InternalFrameListener to the JInternalFrame instead of a WindowListener, which is used for a JFrame. You can set various properties in its constructor or using setter methods. The following snippet of code shows how to use an instance of the JInternalFrame class:

```
String title = "A Child Window";
Boolean resizable = true;
Boolean closable = true;
Boolean maximizable = true;
Boolean iconifiable = true;
JInternalFrame iFrame =
        new JInternalFrame(title, resizable, closable, maximizable, iconifiable);

// Add components to the iFrame using iFrame.add(...)

// Pack eth frame and make it visible
iFrame.pack();
iFrame.setVisible(true);
```

An instance of the JDesktopPane class is used as a container (not as a top-level container) for all child windows that are instances of the JInternalFrame class. It uses a null layout manager. You add it to a JFrame. You would like to store the reference to the desktop pane as an instance variable to the JFrame, so that you can get to it to work with child windows later.

```
// Create a desktop pane
JDesktopPane desktopPane = new JDesktopPane();
```

```
// Add all JInternalFrames to the desktopPane
desktopPane.add(iFrame);
```

You can get all JInternalFrames that are added to a JDesktopPane using its getAllFrames() method.

```
// Get the list of child windows
JInternalFrame[] frames = desktopPane.getAllFrames();
```

A JDesktopPane uses an instance of the DesktopManager interface to manage all internal frames. The DefaultDesktopManager class is an implementation of the DesktopManager interface. If you want to customize the way a desktop manager manages the internal frames, you need to create your own class inheriting from DefaultDesktopManager. You can set your custom desktop manager using the setDesktopManager() method of JDesktopPane. The desktop manager has many useful methods. For example, if you want to close an internal frame programmatically, you can use its closeFrame() method. The user can also close an internal frame using the context menu that is provided if you make it closable. You can get the reference of the desktop manager using the desktop pane's getDesktopManager() method.

```
// Close the internal frame named frame1
desktopPane.getDesktopManager().closeFrame(frame1);
```

The JFrame class is used as a top-level container and it acts as the parent window of JInternalFrames. It contains an instance of JDesktopPane. Note that the pack() method of JFrame will not do any good in a MDI application because its only child, the desktop pane, uses a null layout manager. You must set its size explicitly. Typically, you display the JFrame maximized.

Listing 3-10 demonstrates how to develop an MDI application. Swing does not provide ways to organize your internal frames as tiled or cascaded windows, which is normal in any Windows-based MDI application. You can build the tiled and cascaded features into your Swing MDI application by applying simple logic to organize your internal frames and providing menu items to use them. Figure 3-11 shows the screen that is displayed when you run the program in Listing 3-10.

Listing 3-10. Developing an MDI Application Using Swing

```java
// MDIApp.java
package com.jdojo.swing;

import java.awt.BorderLayout;
import java.awt.Dimension;
import javax.swing.JDesktopPane;
import javax.swing.JFrame;
import javax.swing.JInternalFrame;
import javax.swing.JLabel;
import javax.swing.SwingUtilities;
import javax.swing.UIManager;

public class MDIApp extends JFrame {
        private final JDesktopPane desktopPane = new JDesktopPane();
```

```java
    public MDIApp(String title) {
        super(title);
        initFrame();
    }

    public void initFrame() {
        JInternalFrame frame1
                = new JInternalFrame("Frame 1", true, true, true, true);

        JInternalFrame frame2
                = new JInternalFrame("Frame 2", true, true, true, true);

        JLabel label1 = new JLabel("Frame 1 contents...");
        frame1.getContentPane().add(label1);
        frame1.pack();
        frame1.setVisible(true);

        JLabel label2 = new JLabel("Frame 2 contents...");
        frame2.getContentPane().add(label2);
        frame2.pack();
        frame2.setVisible(true);

        // Default location is (0,0) for a JInternalFrame.
        // Set the location of frame2, so that both frames are visible
        int x2 = frame1.getX() + frame1.getWidth() + 10;
        int y2 = frame1.getY();
        frame2.setLocation(x2, y2);

        // Add both internal frames to the desktop pane
        desktopPane.add(frame1);
        desktopPane.add(frame2);

        // Finally add the desktop pane to the JFrame
        this.add(desktopPane, BorderLayout.CENTER);

        // Need to set minimum size for the JFrame
        this.setMinimumSize(new Dimension(300, 300));
    }

    public static void main(String[] args) {
        try {
            // Set the system look and feel
            UIManager.setLookAndFeel(
                UIManager.getSystemLookAndFeelClassName());
        }
        catch (Exception e) {
            e.printStackTrace();
        }
```

```
            SwingUtilities.invokeLater(() -> {
                    MDIApp frame = new MDIApp("MDI Frame");
                    frame.pack();
                    frame.setVisible(true);
                    frame.setExtendedState(frame.MAXIMIZED_BOTH);
            });
        }
}
```

Figure 3-11. *An MDI application in Swing run on Windows*

When you work with an MDI application, you need to use the showInternalXxxDialog() methods of JOptionPane instead of the showXxxDialog() methods. For example, in an MDI application, you use the JOptionPane.showInternalMessageDialog() method instead of the JOptionPane.showMessageDialog(). The showInternalXxxDialog() version displays the dialog box, so they are always displayed within the top-level container, whereas the showXxxDialog() version displays a dialog box that can be dragged outside the boundary of the top-level container of the MDI application.

■ **Tip**   It is important to decide upfront whether you want to develop an SDI, MDI, or TDI application. Changing from one type to another is not an easy task.

The Toolkit Class

Java needs to communicate with the native system to provide most of the basic GUI functionalities. It uses a specific class on each platform to achieve that. The java.awt.Toolkit is an abstract class. Java uses a subclass of the Toolkit class on each platform to communicate with the native toolkit system. The Toolkit class provides a static getDefaultToolkit() factory method to get the toolkit object used on a particular platform. The Toolkit class contains useful methods to let you work with screen size and resolution, get access to the system clipboard, and to make a beeping sound, etc. Table 3-2 lists a few of the methods of the Toolkit class. The table contains methods that thorw a HeadlessExceotion. A HeadlessException is thrown when code that is dependent on a keyboard, display, or mouse is called in an environment that does not support a keyboard, display, or mouse.

Table 3-2. *The List of a Few Useful Methods of the java.awt.Toolkit Class*

Method of Toolkit Class	Description
abstract void beep()	Makes a beeping sound. It is useful in alerting the user when a severe error occurs in the application.
static Toolkit getDefaultToolkit()	Returns the current Toolkit instance used in the application.
abstract int getScreenResolution() throws HeadlessException	Returns the screen resolution in terms of dots per inch.
abstract Dimension getScreenSize() throws HeadlessException	Returns a Dimension object that contains the width and the height of the screen in pixels.
abstract Clipboard getSystemClipboard() throws HeadlessException	Returns an instance of the Clipboard class that represents a system clipboard.

The following snippet of code shows some examples of how to use the Toolkit class:

```
/* Copy the selected text from a JTextArea named dataTextArea to the system clipboard.
   If there is no text selection, beep and display a message.
*/
Toolkit toolkit = Toolkit.getDefaultToolkit();
String data = dataTextArea.getSelectedText();
if (data == null || data.equals("")) {
        toolkit.beep();
        JOptionPane.showMessageDialog(null, "Please select the text to copy.");
}
else {
        Clipboard clipboard = toolkit.getSystemClipboard();

        // Pack data as a string in a Transferable object
        Transferable transferableData = new StringSelection(data);
        clipboard.setContents(transferableData, null);
}

/* Paste text from the system clipboard to a TextArea, named dataTextArea.
   If there is no text in the system clipboard, beep and display a message.
*/
Toolkit toolkit = Toolkit.getDefaultToolkit();
Clipboard clipboard = toolkit.getSystemClipboard();
Transferable data = clipboard.getContents(null);
if (data != null && data.isDataFlavorSupported(DataFlavor.stringFlavor)) {
        try {
                String text = (String)data.getTransferData(DataFlavor.stringFlavor);
                dataTextArea.replaceSelection(text);
        }
        catch (Exception e) {
                e.printStackTrace();
        }
}
```

```
else {
        toolkit.beep();
        JOptionPane.showMessageDialog(null, "No text in the system clipboard to paste");
}

/* Set the size of a JFrame to the size of the screen. Note that you can also use the
   frame.setExtendedState(JFrame.MAXIMIZED_BOTH) method to use full screen area for a Jframe.
*/
JFrame frame = new JFrame("My Frame");
frame.setSize(Toolkit.getDefaultToolkit().getScreenSize());
```

Decorating Components Using JLayer

The JLayer class represents a Swing component. It is used to decorate another component, which is called the *target* component. It lets you perform custom painting over the component it decorates. It can also receive notifications of all events that are generated within its border. In other words, a JLayer lets you perform custom processing based on events occurring in the component it decorates.

When you work with the JLayer class, you also need to work with the LayerUI class. A JLayer delegates its work to a LayerUI for custom painting and event handling. To do anything meaningful with a JLayer, you need to create a subclass of the LayerUI class and override its appropriate methods to write your code.

The following steps are needed to use a JLayer in a Swing application.

1. Create a subclass of the LayerUI class. Override its various methods to implement the custom processing for the component. The LayerUI class takes a type parameter that is the type of the component it will work with.

2. Create an object of the LayerUI subclass.

3. Create a Swing component (target component) that you want to decorate with a JLayer such as a JTextField, a JPanel, etc.

4. Create an object of the JLayer class, passing the target component and the object of the LayerUI subclass to its constructor.

5. Add the JLayer object to your container, not the target component.

Let's see a JLayer in action. Suppose you want to use a JLayer to draw a blue rectangular border around a JTextField component. Your first step is to create a subclass of the LayerUI. Listing 3-11 contains the code for a BlueBorderUI class that inherits from the LayerUI class. It overrides the paint() method of the LayerUI class.

Listing 3-11. A Subclass of the LayerUI Class to Draw a Blue Border Around the Layer

```java
// BlueBorderUI.java
package com.jdojo.swing;

import java.awt.Color;
import java.awt.Graphics;
import java.awt.Graphics2D;
import javax.swing.JComponent;
import javax.swing.JTextField;
import javax.swing.plaf.LayerUI;
```

```java
public class BlueBorderUI extends LayerUI<JTextField> {
        @Override
        public void paint(Graphics g, JComponent layer) {
                // Let the superclass paint the component first
                super.paint(g, layer);

                // Create a copy of the Graphics object
                Graphics gTemp = (Graphics2D) g.create();

                // Get the dimension of the layer
                int width = layer.getWidth();
                int height = layer.getHeight();

                // Draw a blue rectangle that is custom your border
                gTemp.setColor(Color.BLUE);
                gTemp.drawRect(0, 0, width, height);

                // Destroy the copy of the Graphics object
                gTemp.dispose();
        }
}
```

The paint() method of the LayerUI is called whenever the target component needs to be painted. The method of the LayerUI class receives two arguments. The first argument is the reference of the Graphics object that you can use to draw on the component. The second argument is the reference of the JLayer object, not the target component. You can get the reference of the target component, the component the JLayer is decorating, using the second argument. You can cast the second argument to a JLayer type and use the getView() method of the JLayer class, which returns the reference of the target component. The logic inside the paint() method is simple. It creates a copy of its Graphics argument and draws a blue rectangle around the component. The passed-in Graphics object to this method is set up for painting this component. Copying the passed-in Graphics object is advised because making changes to the passed-in Graphics object may result in unexpected results.

Now you are ready to use the BlueBorderUI with a JLayer to draw a blue border around a JTextField. The following snippet of code shows the logic:

```java
// Create a JTextField as usual
JTextField firstName = new JTextField(10);

// Create an object of the BlueBorderUI
LayerUI<JTextField> ui = new BlueBorderUI();

// Create a JLayer object by wrapping the JTextField and BlueBorderUI
JLayer<JTextField> layer = new JLayer(firstName, ui);

// Add the layer object to a container, say the content pane of a frame.
// Note that you add the layer and not the component to a container.
contentPane.add(layer)
```

The target component and LayerUI may be passed to a JLayer when you create it. If you do not know the target component and/or the LayerUI for a JLayer, you may pass them later using the setView() and setUI() methods of the JLayer class. The getView() and getUI() methods of the JLayer class let you get the reference of the current target component and the LayerUI for a JLayer, respectively.

Listing 3-12 demonstrates how to use a JLayer to draw a border around two JTextField components. The code is simple and self-explanatory. When you run this program, it will display two JTextField components with blue borders in a JFrame.

Listing 3-12. Decorating JTextFeild Components Using JLayer

```java
// JLayerBlueBorderFrame.java
package com.jdojo.swing;

import java.awt.FlowLayout;
import javax.swing.JFrame;
import javax.swing.JLabel;
import javax.swing.JLayer;
import javax.swing.JTextField;
import javax.swing.SwingUtilities;
import javax.swing.plaf.LayerUI;

public class JLayerBlueBorderFrame extends JFrame {
        private JLabel firstNameLabel = new JLabel("First Name:");
        private JLabel lastNameLabel = new JLabel("Last Name:");
        private JTextField firstName = new JTextField(10);
        private JTextField lastName = new JTextField(10);

        public JLayerBlueBorderFrame(String title) {
                super(title);
                initFrame();
        }

        public void initFrame() {
                this.setLayout(new FlowLayout());
                this.setDefaultCloseOperation(JFrame.EXIT_ON_CLOSE);

                // Create an object of the LayerUI subclass - BlueBorderUI
                LayerUI<JTextField> ui = new BlueBorderUI();

                // Wrap the LayerUI and two JTextFields in two JLayers.
                // Note that a LayerUI object can be shared by multiple JLayers
                JLayer<JTextField> layer1 = new JLayer<>(firstName, ui);
                JLayer<JTextField> layer2 = new JLayer<>(lastName, ui);

                this.add(firstNameLabel);
                this.add(layer1); // Add layer1, not firstName to the frame

                this.add(lastNameLabel);
                this.add(layer2); // Add layer2, not lastName to the frame
        }
```

```
    public static void main(String[] args) {
        SwingUtilities.invokeLater(() -> {
            JLayerBlueBorderFrame frame
                    = new JLayerBlueBorderFrame("JLayer Test Frame");
            frame.pack();
            frame.setVisible(true);
        });
    }
}
```

Let's look at an example of how to handle events of a target component using a JLayer. A JLayer delegates the event processing task to the associated LayerUI. You need to perform the following steps to handle events in a LayerUI subclass.

1. Register for the events that a JLayer will process.

2. Write the event handler code in an appropriate method of the LayerUI subclass.

You need to call the setLayerEventMask(long layerEventMask) method of the JLayer class to register for all events that a JLayer is interested in. The layerEventMask parameter of this method must be a bitmask of the AWTEvent constants. For example, if a JLayer named layer is interested in key and focus events, you call this method as shown:

```
int layerEventMask = AWTEvent.KEY_EVENT_MASK | AWTEvent.FOCUS_EVENT_MASK;
layer.setLayerEventMask(layerEventMask);
```

Typically, a JLayer registers for events in the installUI() method of the LayerUI subclass. You need to override the installUI() method of the LayerUI class in your subclass. You need to set the event mask for the JLayer to zero when the UI is uninstalled. This is accomplished in the uninstallUI() method. The following snippet of code shows a JLayer registering for a focus event and resetting its event mask:

```
public class SmartBorderUI extends LayerUI<JTextField> {
    @Override
    public void installUI(JComponent c) {
        super.installUI(c);
        JLayer layer = (JLayer)c;

        // Register for the focus event
        layer.setLayerEventMask(AWTEvent.FOCUS_EVENT_MASK);
    }

    @Override
    public void uninstallUI(JComponent c) {
        super.uninstallUI(c);
        JLayer layer = (JLayer)c;

        // Reset the event mask
        layer.setLayerEventMask(0);
    }

    // Other code goes here
}
```

When a registered event is delivered to the JLayer, the eventDispatched(AWTEvent event, JLayer layer) method of the associated LayerUI is called. You may be tempted to override this method in your LayerUI subclass to handle all registered events. Technically, you are correct in overriding this method to handle events. However, there is a better way to provide the event handling code in a LayerUI subclass. The eventDispatched() method of the LayerUI class calls an appropriately named method when it receives an event. Those methods are declared as

```
protected void processXxxEvent(XxxEvent e, JLayer layer).
```

Here, Xxx is the name of the registered event. The following snippet of code shows examples of the event type and the declaration of the method that is called when the JLayer receives that kind of event:

```java
public class SmartBorderUI extends LayerUI<JTextField> {
        @Override
        protected void processFocusEvent(FocusEvent e, JLayer layer) {
                // Process the focus event here
        }

        @Override
        protected void processKeyEvent(KeyEvent e, JLayer layer) {
                // Process the key event here
        }

        @Override
        protected void processMouseEvent(MouseEvent e, JLayer layer) {
                // Process the mouse event here
        }

        // Other code goes here...
}
```

That is all you need to do to process events in a JLayer. Let's improve the previous example. This time, the JLayer will draw a border around a JTextField whose color will depend on whether the JTextField has focus. When it has focus, a red border is drawn. When it loses focus, a blue border is drawn.

Listing 3-13 contains the code for a SmartBorderUI class, which inherits from LayerUI. Its paint() method draws a red or blue border depending on whether the target component has focus. Its installUI() method registers for the focus event. The unInstallUI() method deregisters for the focus event by setting the event mask to zero. Its processFocusEvent() method handles the focus event. Note that this method is called when a focus event occurs on the target component. It calls the repaint() method, which in turn will call the paint() method, which paints the border according to the focus state of the component.

Listing 3-13. A Subclass of LayerUI for Decorating JTextField Based on Focus

```java
// SmartBorderUI.java
package com.jdojo.swing;

import java.awt.AWTEvent;
import java.awt.Color;
import java.awt.Graphics;
import java.awt.Graphics2D;
import java.awt.event.FocusEvent;
import javax.swing.JComponent;
import javax.swing.JLayer;
```

```java
import javax.swing.JTextField;
import javax.swing.plaf.LayerUI;

public class SmartBorderUI extends LayerUI<JTextField> {
        @Override
        public void paint(Graphics g, JComponent layer) {
                // Let the superclass paint the component first
                super.paint(g, layer);

                Graphics gTemp = (Graphics2D) g.create();
                int width = layer.getWidth();
                int height = layer.getHeight();

                // Suppress the unchecked warning
                @SuppressWarnings("unchecked")
                JLayer<JTextField> myLayer = (JLayer<JTextField>)layer;

                JTextField field = (JTextField)myLayer.getView();

                // When in focus, draw a red rectangle. Otherwise, draw a blue rectangle
                Color bColor;
                if (field.hasFocus()) {
                        bColor = Color.RED;
                }
                else {
                        bColor = Color.BLUE;
                }

                gTemp.setColor(bColor);
                gTemp.drawRect(0, 0, width, height);
                gTemp.dispose();
        }

        @Override
        public void installUI(JComponent c) {
                // Let the superclass do its job
                super.installUI(c);

                // Set the event mask for the layer stating that it is interested
                // in listening to the focus event for its target
                JLayer layer = (JLayer)c;
                layer.setLayerEventMask(AWTEvent.FOCUS_EVENT_MASK);
        }

        @Override
        public void uninstallUI(JComponent c) {
                // Let the superclass do its job
                super.uninstallUI(c);

                JLayer layer = (JLayer) c;
```

```
                    // Set the event mask back to zero
                    layer.setLayerEventMask(0);
        }

        @Override
        protected void processFocusEvent(FocusEvent e, JLayer layer) {
                    layer.repaint();
        }
}
```

Listing 3-14 contains the code that uses the SmartBorderUI class with a JLayer. When you run this program, it will display a JFrame with two JTextField components. Changing focus between the JTextField components will change their border colors.

Listing 3-14. Decorating JTextField Components Using Jlayer Based on Focus

```java
// JLayerSmartBorderFrame.java
package com.jdojo.swing;

import java.awt.FlowLayout;
import javax.swing.JFrame;
import javax.swing.JLabel;
import javax.swing.JLayer;
import javax.swing.JTextField;
import javax.swing.SwingUtilities;
import javax.swing.plaf.LayerUI;

public class JLayerSmartBorderFrame extends JFrame {
        private JLabel firstNameLabel = new JLabel("First Name:");
        private JLabel lastNameLabel = new JLabel("Last Name:");
        private JTextField firstName = new JTextField(10);
        private JTextField lastName = new JTextField(10);

        public JLayerSmartBorderFrame(String title) {
                super(title);
                initFrame();
        }

        public void initFrame() {
                this.setLayout(new FlowLayout());
                this.setDefaultCloseOperation(JFrame.EXIT_ON_CLOSE);

                // Create an object of LayerUI subclass - SmartBorderUI
                LayerUI<JTextField> ui = new SmartBorderUI();

                // Wrap the LayerUI and two JTextFields in two JLayers
                JLayer<JTextField> layer1 = new JLayer<>(firstName, ui);
                JLayer<JTextField> layer2 = new JLayer<>(lastName, ui);

                this.add(firstNameLabel);
                this.add(layer1); // Add layer1 and not firstName to the frame
```

```
        this.add(lastNameLabel);
        this.add(layer2); // Add layer2 and not lastName to the frame
    }

    public static void main(String[] args) {
        SwingUtilities.invokeLater(() -> {
            JLayerSmartBorderFrame frame
                    = new JLayerSmartBorderFrame("JLayer Test Frame");
            frame.pack();
            frame.setVisible(true);
        });
    }
}
```

Translucent Windows

Before discussing translucent windows in Swing, let's define three terms:

- Transparent

- Translucent

- Opaque

If something is transparent, you can see through it; clear water is transparent. If something is opaque, you cannot see through it; a concrete wall is opaque. If something is translucent, you can see through it, but not clearly. If something is translucent, it partially allows light to pass through; a plastic curtain is translucent. The terms "transparent" and "opaque" describe two opposite states, whereas the term "translucent" describes a state between transparent and opaque.

You can define the degree of translucency of a window such as a JFrame. A 90% translucent window is 10% opaque. The degree of translucency of a window can be defined using the alpha value of the color component for a pixel. You can define the alpha value of a color using the constructors of the Color class:

- `Color(int red, int green, int blue, int alpha)`

- `Color(float red, float green, float blue, float alpha)`

The value for the alpha argument is specified between 0 and 255, when the color components are specified in terms of int values. For the float type arguments, its value is between 0.0 and 1.0. The alpha value of 0 or 0.0 means transparent (100% translucent and 0% opaque). The alpha value of 255 or 1.0 means opaque (0% translucent and not transparent at all).

Three forms of translucency in a window are supported. They are represented by the following three constants of the WindowTranslucency enum:

- PERPIXEL_TRANSPARENT: In this form of translucency, a pixel in a window is either opaque or transparent. That is, the alpha value for a pixel is either 0.0 or 1.0.

- TRANSLUCENT: In this form of translucency, all pixels in a window have the same translucency, which can be defined by an alpha value between 0.0 and 1.0.

- PERPIXEL_TRANSLUCENT: In this form of translucency, each pixel in a window can have its own alpha value between 0.0 and 1.0. It lets you define the translucency in a window on a per pixel basis.

239

Not all platforms support all the three forms of translucency. You must check for the supported forms of translucency in your program before using them. Otherwise, your code may throw an UnsupportedOperationException. The isWindowTranslucencySupported() method of the GraphicsDevice class lets you check the forms of translucency that are supported on a platform. Listing 3-15 demonstrates how to check for translucency support on a platform. The code in this listing is short and self-explanatory. I have omitted checking in subsequent examples to keep the code shorter.

Listing 3-15. Checking for the Translucency support on a Platform

```java
// TranslucencySupport.java
package com.jdojo.swing;

import java.awt.GraphicsDevice;
import java.awt.GraphicsEnvironment;
import static java.awt.GraphicsDevice.WindowTranslucency.*;

public class TranslucencySupport {
        public static void main(String[] args) {
                GraphicsEnvironment graphicsEnv
                        = GraphicsEnvironment.getLocalGraphicsEnvironment();

                GraphicsDevice graphicsDevice
                        = graphicsEnv.getDefaultScreenDevice();

                // Print the translucency supported by the platform
                boolean isSupported
                        = graphicsDevice.isWindowTranslucencySupported(
                                PERPIXEL_TRANSPARENT);
                System.out.println("PERPIXEL_TRANSPARENT supported: "
                        + isSupported);

                isSupported
                        = graphicsDevice.isWindowTranslucencySupported(TRANSLUCENT);
                System.out.println("TRANSLUCENT supported: " + isSupported);

                isSupported = graphicsDevice.isWindowTranslucencySupported(
                        PERPIXEL_TRANSLUCENT);
                System.out.println("PERPIXEL_TRANSLUCENT supported: "
                        + isSupported);
        }
}
```

Let's see a uniform translucent JFrame in action. You can set the translucency of a JFrame using the setOpacity(float opacity) method. The value for the specified opacity must be between 0.0f and 1.0f. Before you call this method on a window, the following three conditions must be met:

- The platform must support the TRANSLUCENT translucency. You can use the logic from Listing 3-15 to check if the TRANSLUCENT translucency is supported by the platform.

- The window must be undecorated. You can make a JFrame or JDialog undecorated by calling the setUndecorated(false) method on them.

- The window must not be in full-screen mode. You can put a window in full-screen mode using the setFullScreenWindow(Window w) method of the GraphicsDevice class.

If all conditions are not met, setting the opacity of a window other than 1.0f throws an IllegalComponentStateException.

Listing 3-16 demonstrates how to use a uniform translucent JFrame. The following two statements in the initFrame() method in the listing is of interest to get a translucent JFrame. The first statement makes sure that the frame is undecorated, and the second one sets the translucency of the frame in terms of opacity.

Listing 3-16. Using a Uniform Translucent JFrame

```java
// UniformTranslucentFrame.java
package com.jdojo.swing;

import java.awt.BorderLayout;
import javax.swing.JButton;
import javax.swing.JFrame;
import javax.swing.SwingUtilities;

public class UniformTranslucentFrame extends JFrame {
    private JButton closeButton = new JButton("Close");

    public UniformTranslucentFrame(String title) {
        super(title);
        initFrame();
    }

    public void initFrame() {
        this.setDefaultCloseOperation(EXIT_ON_CLOSE);

        // Make sure the frame is undecorated
        this.setUndecorated(true);

        // Set 40% opacity. That is, 60% translucency.
        this.setOpacity(0.40f);

        // Set its size
        this.setSize(200, 200);

        // Center it on the screen
        this.setLocationRelativeTo(null);

        // Add a button to close the window
        this.add(closeButton, BorderLayout.SOUTH);

        // Exit the aplication when the close button is clicked
        closeButton.addActionListener(e -> System.exit(0));
    }

    public static void main(String[] args) {
        SwingUtilities.invokeLater(() -> {
            UniformTranslucentFrame frame
                    = new UniformTranslucentFrame("Translucent Frame");
            frame.setVisible(true);
        });
    }
}
```

```
// Make sure the frame is undecorated
this.setUndecorated(true);

// Set 40% opacity. That is, 60% translucency.
this.setOpacity(0.40f);
```

When you run this program, you can see the contents on your screen through the JFrame display area. A Close button is added to the frame to close it.

Let's see a per-pixel translucent JFrame in action. You will create a gradient effect (fading effect) inside a JPanel by setting the alpha value for its background color different for different pixels in its display area. You can get a per-pixel translucency in different ways. The easiest way to see it in action is to use a JPanel with a background color and setting the alpha component to a desired translucency. The following snippet of code illustrates this:

```
// Create a frame and set its properties
JFrame frame = new JFrame();
frame.setUndecorated(true);
frame.setBounds(0, 0, 200, 200);

// Set the background color of the frame to all zero, so that the per-pixel translucency works
frame.setBackground(new Color(0, 0, 0, 0));

// Create a blue JPanel with 128 alpha component
JPanel panel = new JPanel();
int alpha = 128;
Color bgColor = new Color(0, 0, 255, alpha);
panel.setBackground(bgColor);

// Add the JPanel to the frame and display it
frame.add(panel);
frame.setVisible(true);
```

Two things are different in the code. First, it sets the background color of the frame with all color components set to 0 to achieve the per-pixel translucency. Second, it sets the background color of the JPanel, which has an alpha component, to 128. You can add another JPanel with a different alpha component for its background color to the JFrame. This will give you two areas on the JFrame whose pixels use different translucency.

You can achieve a fancier result if you use an object of the GradientPaint class to paint your JPanel. A GradientPaint object fills a Shape with a linear gradient pattern. It requires you to specify two points, p1 and p2, and colors for each point, c1 and c2. The color on the connecting line between p1 and p2 will proportionally change from c1 to c2.

Listing 3-17 contains the code for a custom JPanel that uses a GradientPaint object to paint its area. The background color for the JPanel is specified in its constructor. It has overridden the paintComponent() to provide the custom painting effect. The gradient color pattern is provided by Graphics2D. The method checks if it have a Graphics2D object. The starting point, p1, is the upper left corner of the JPanel. The color for the starting point, c1, is the same as the one passed in the constructor. It uses 255 as its alpha component. The second point, p2, is the upper right corner of the JPanel, with the same color that uses a zero alpha component. This will give the JPanel a gradient effect from opaque at the left edge to gradually turning transparent at the right edge. You can experiment by changing the two points and the alpha component values for them to get a different gradient pattern. It sets the GradientPaint object as the Paint object for the Graphics2D object and calls the fillRect() method to paint the area of the JPanel.

Listing 3-17. A Custom JPanel With a Gradient Color Effect Using the Per-Pixel Translucency

```java
// TranslucentJPanel.java
package com.jdojo.swing;

import java.awt.Color;
import java.awt.GradientPaint;
import java.awt.Graphics;
import java.awt.Graphics2D;
import java.awt.Paint;
import javax.swing.JPanel;

public class TranslucentJPanel extends JPanel {
        private int red = 240;
        private int green = 240;
        private int blue = 240;

        public TranslucentJPanel(Color bgColor) {
                this.red = bgColor.getRed();
                this.green = bgColor.getGreen();
                this.blue = bgColor.getBlue();
        }

        @Override
        protected void paintComponent(Graphics g) {
                if (g instanceof Graphics2D) {
                        int width = this.getWidth();
                        int height = this.getHeight();
                        float startPointX = 0.0f;
                        float startPointY = 0.0f;
                        float endPointX = width;
                        float endPointY = 0.0f;
                        Color startColor = new Color(red, green, blue, 255);
                        Color endColor = new Color(red, green, blue, 0);

                        // Create a GradientPaint object
                        Paint paint = new GradientPaint(startPointX, startPointY,
                                                startColor,
                                                endPointX, endPointY,
                                                endColor);

                        Graphics2D g2D = (Graphics2D) g;
                        g2D.setPaint(paint);
                        g2D.fillRect(0, 0, width, height);
                }
        }
}
```

Listing 3-18 contains the code to see the per-pixel translucency in a JFrame in action. It adds three instances of the TranslucentJPanel class with the background color of red, green, and blue. A Close button is added to close the frame.

Listing 3-18. Using Per-Pixel Translucency in a JFrame

```java
// PerPixelTranslucentFrame.java
package com.jdojo.swing;

import java.awt.Color;
import java.awt.GridLayout;
import javax.swing.JButton;
import javax.swing.JFrame;
import javax.swing.SwingUtilities;

public class PerPixelTranslucentFrame extends JFrame {
        private JButton closeButton = new JButton("Close");

        public PerPixelTranslucentFrame(String title) {
                super(title);
                initFrame();
        }

        public void initFrame() {
                this.setDefaultCloseOperation(EXIT_ON_CLOSE);

                // Make sure the frame is undecorated
                this.setUndecorated(true);

                // Set the background color with all components as zero,
                // so per-pixel translucency is used
                this.setBackground(new Color(0, 0, 0, 0));

                // Set its size
                this.setSize(200, 200);

                // Center it on the screen
                this.setLocationRelativeTo(null);

                this.getContentPane().setLayout(new GridLayout(0, 1));

                // Create and add three JPanel with different color gradients
                this.add(new TranslucentJPanel(Color.RED));
                this.add(new TranslucentJPanel(Color.GREEN));
                this.add(new TranslucentJPanel(Color.BLUE));

                // Add a button to close the window
                this.add(closeButton);
                closeButton.addActionListener(e -> System.exit(0));
        }
```

```
    public static void main(String[] args) {
        SwingUtilities.invokeLater(() -> {
            PerPixelTranslucentFrame frame
                    = new PerPixelTranslucentFrame("Per-Pixel Translucent Frame");
            frame.setVisible(true);
        });
    }
}
```

Figure 3-12 shows the JFrame when the program is run. Notice the gradient effect in the frame. Each panel is more translucent as you move from left to right. The text shown the figure is not part of the JFrame. The text was displayed in the background when the JFrame was displayed. You can see through the translucent part of the JFrame.

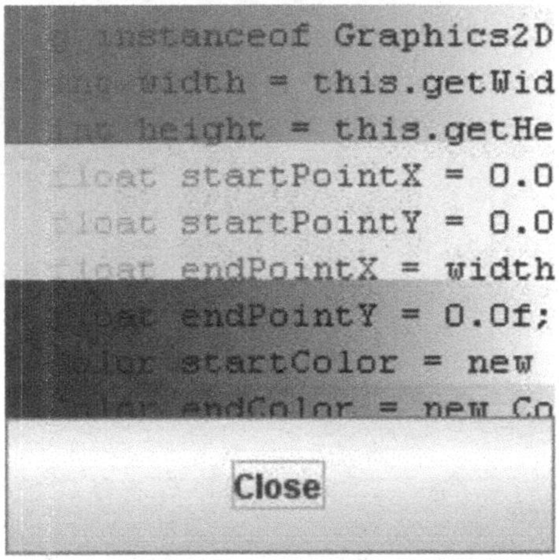

Figure 3-12. A JFrame using per-pixel translucency

Shaped Window

Swing lets you create a custom shaped window such as a round shaped JFrame, an oval shaped JDialog, etc. You can give a window a custom shape by using the setShape(Shape s) method of the Window class. The shape of the window is limited only by your imagination. You can create a shape by combining multiple shapes using the classes in the java.awt.geom package. The following snippet of code creates a shape that contains an ellipse placed above a rectangle. At the end, it sets the custom shape to a JFrame.

```
// Create a shape with an ellipse over a rectangle
Ellipse2D.Double ellipse = new Ellipse2D.Double(0, 0, 200, 100);
Rectangle2D.Double rect = new Rectangle2D.Double(0, 100, 200, 200);

// Combine an ellipse and a rectangle into a Path2D object to get a new shape
Path2D path = new Path2D.Double();
path.append(rect, true);
path.append(ellipse, true);
```

```
// Create a JFrame
JFrame frame = new JFrame("A Custom Shaped JFrame");

// Set the custom shape to the JFrame
Frame.setShape(path);
```

A Window owns a rectangular area on the screen. If you give a custom shape to a window, some of its parts may be cut off. The part of a shaped window that does not belong to the custom shape is not visible and not clickable. Figure 3-13 shows a custom shaped window with an ellipse placed above a rectangle. The window contains a Close button. The areas around the four corners of the ellipse are not visible and not clickable.

Figure 3-13. *A custom shaped window with an ellipse placed above a rectangle*

The following three criteria must be met to use a shaped window:

- The platform must support PERPIXEL_TRANSPARENT translucency. You can use the logic from Listing 3-15 to check whether the PERPIXEL_TRANSPARENT translucency is supported.

- The window must be undecorated. You can make a JFrame or JDialog undecorated by calling the setUndecorated(false) method on them.

- The window must not be in full-screen mode. You can put a window in full-screen mode using the setFullScreenWindow(Window w) method of the GraphicsDevice class.

Listing 3-19 contains the code that displays a shaped JFrame that was shown in Figure 3-13.

Listing 3-19. Using a Custom Shaped JFrame

```
// ShapedFrame.java
package com.jdojo.swing;

import java.awt.BorderLayout;
import java.awt.geom.Path2D;
import java.awt.geom.Ellipse2D;
import java.awt.geom.Rectangle2D;
import javax.swing.JButton;
import javax.swing.JFrame;
import javax.swing.SwingUtilities;
```

```java
public class ShapedFrame extends JFrame {
        private JButton closeButton = new JButton("Close");

        public ShapedFrame() {
                initFrame();
        }

        public void initFrame() {
                // Make sure the frame is undecorated
                this.setUndecorated(true);

                this.setDefaultCloseOperation(EXIT_ON_CLOSE);
                this.setSize(200, 200);

                // Create a shape with an ellipse placed over a rectangle
                Ellipse2D.Double ellipse = new Ellipse2D.Double(0, 0, 200, 100);
                Rectangle2D.Double rect = new Rectangle2D.Double(0, 100, 200, 200);

                // Combine the ellipse and rectangle into a Path2D object and
                // set it as the shape for the JFrame
                Path2D path = new Path2D.Double();
                path.append(rect, true);
                path.append(ellipse, true);
                this.setShape(path);

                // Add a Close button to close the frame
                this.add(closeButton, BorderLayout.SOUTH);
                closeButton.addActionListener(e -> System.exit(0));
        }

        public static void main(String[] args) {
                SwingUtilities.invokeLater(() -> {
                        // Display the custom shaped frame
                        ShapedFrame frame = new ShapedFrame();
                        frame.setLocationRelativeTo(null);
                        frame.setVisible(true);
                });
        }
}
```

The following part of the code inside the initFrame() method in this listing is of interest:

```java
// Make sure the frame is undecorated
this.setUndecorated(true);

// Create a shape with an ellipse placed over a rectangle
Ellipse2D.Double ellipse = new Ellipse2D.Double(0, 0, 200, 100);
Rectangle2D.Double rect = new Rectangle2D.Double(0, 100, 200, 200);

// Combine the ellipse and rectangle into a Path2D object and
// set it as the shape for the JFrame
```

```
Path2D path = new Path2D.Double();
path.append(rect, true);
path.append(ellipse, true);
this.setShape(path);
```

The first statement makes sure that the JFrame is undecorated. Two shapes, an ellipse and a rectangle, are created. Their coordinates and size are set to place the ellipse over the rectangle. A Path2D.Double object is used to connect the ellipse and rectangle together into a custom Shape object. Path2D is an abstract class in the java.awt.geom package. It declares two static inner classes, Path2D.Double and Path2D.Float, to store the coordinates of a shape in double precision and single precision floating-point numbers, respectively. Shape is an interface declared in the java.awt package. The Path2D class implements the Shape interface. Note that the setShape() method in the Window class takes an instance of the Shape interface as an argument. The append() method of the Path2D class appends the geometry of the specified Shape object to the path. The second argument to the append() method is an indicator whether you want to connect two shapes using a line segment. If it is true, a call to the moveTo() method is translated to the lineTo() method. In this case, the value of true for this argument is of no significance. Please explore the classes in the java.awt.geom package to learn more about the many interesting shapes that you can use in your Java application.

Summary

Swing components have built-in support for displaying HTML text as labels. You can use an HTML-formatted string as a label for a JButton, JMenuItem, JLabel, JToolTip, JTabbedPane, JTree, etc. using an HTML string, which should start and end with the <html> and </html> tags, respectively. If you do not want Swing to interpret text enclosed in HTML tags as HTML for a component, you can disable the feature by calling the putClientProperty("html.disable", Boolean.TRUE) method on the component.

Swing components are not thread-safe. You are supposed to update the component's states from a single thread called an event dispatch thread. All event handlers for components are executed in the event dispatch thread. Swing creates the event dispatch thread automatically. Swing provides a utility class called SwingUtilities to work with the event dispatch thread; its invokeLater(Runnable r) method schedules the specified Runnable to be executed on the event dispatch thread. It is safe to build the Swing GUI and show it on the event dispatch thread. The isEventDispatchThread() of the SwingUtilities class returns true if this method is executed by the event dispatch thread.

Running long-running tasks on the event dispatch thread will make your GUI unresponsive. Swing provides a SwingWorker class to execute long-running tasks on worker threads that are threads other than the event dispatch thread. The SwingWorker class provides features to publish the results of the task on the event dispatch thread that can update the Swing components safely.

Swing provides pluggable L&F. It ships with some predefined L&F. You can use the UIManager.setLookAndFeel() method to set a new L&F for your application.

Swing supports skinnable L&F called Synth that lets you define the L&F in an external XML file.

Drag and drop (DnD) is a way to transfer data between components in an application. Swing supports DnD between Swing component, and Swing components and native components. Using DnD, you can copy, move, and link data between two components.

Using Swing, you can develop a multiple document interface (MDI) application that consists of multiple frames managed by a desktop manager. Frames in an MPI application can be arranged in different ways; for example, they can be arranged in layers, they can be cascaded, they can be placed side by side, etc.

Swing provides an instance of the Toolkit class to communicate with the native system. The class contains many useful methods such as for making a beep sound, knowing the screen resolution and size, etc.

Swing lets you have translucent windows. Translucency can be defined to be the same for all pixels in the window or on a per-pixel basis.

In Swing, you are not limited to having only rectangular windows. It lets you create shaped windows. A shaped window can be of any shape, such as circular, oval, or any custom shape.

CHAPTER 4

■ ■ ■

Applets

In this chapter, you will learn

- What an applet is

- How to develop, deploy, and run applets

- How to use the `<applet>` tag to embed an applet in an HTML document

- How to install and configure Java Plug-in, which runs the applets

- How to use the `appletviewer` program to run applets

- The life cycle of applets

- How to pass parameters to applets

- How to publish an applet's parameters and applet's description

- How to use images and audio clips in applets

- How to customize the Java policy file to grant permissions to applets

- How to sign applets

What Is an Applet?

An *applet* is a Java program that is embedded in an HTML document and run in a web browser. The compiled Java code that makes up an applet is stored on a web server. The web browser downloads the applet code from the web server over the Internet, and runs the code locally in the browser's context. Typically, an applet has a graphical user interface (GUI). An applet has many security restrictions as far as what it can or cannot access on the client's computer. Restrictions on applets are necessary because applets may not be developed and used by the same person. An applet written with bad intentions may do harmful things to the client's machine if it is allowed full access to the client's machine. For example, security restrictions do not allow an applet to access the file system or start a program on the client machine. Suppose you open a web page with an applet that can read files on your machine. Without your knowledge, a rogue applet could send your private information stored on your machine to its server. To protect the applet users from this kind of mischief, it is necessary to have security restrictions in place when an applet is run. There are many security restrictions that can be configured using a policy file. I will discuss how to configure applet security policies later in this chapter.

Although a *servlet* is not related to an *applet*, I'll explain the difference between the two. Like an applet, a servlet is also a Java program that is deployed on a web server. Unlike an applet, a servlet runs on the web server itself and it does not include a GUI.

Developing an Applet

Developing an applet is a four-step process:

- Writing the Java code for the applet
- Packaging and deploying the applet files
- Installing and configuring Java Plug-in
- Viewing the applet

Writing Java code for an applet is not much different from writing code for a Swing application. You just need to learn a few standard classes and methods for applets that you will use in your code.

An applet is deployed on a web server and viewed in a web page using a web browser over the Internet/intranet. You can also view an applet using an applet viewer during development and testing. JDK ships an *appletviewer* program. The appletviewer program is installed in the JAVA_HOME\bin directory on your machine when you install the JDK. I will discuss using the appletviewer in detail later in this chapter.

To view an applet in a web page, you need to embed the reference to the applet in an HTML document. You can use any of the three HTML tags, <applet>, <object>, or <embed> to embed an applet in an HTML document. I will discuss using these tags in detail shortly.

The next two sections discuss how to write Java code for an applet, and how to view the applet.

Writing an Applet

Your applet class must be a subclass of the standard applet classes supplied by Java. There are two standard applet classes:

- java.applet.Applet
- javax.swing.JApplet

The Applet class supports AWT GUI components whereas the JApplet class supports Swing GUI components. The JApplet class inherits from the Applet class. I will discuss only JApplet in this chapter. Listing 4-1 shows the code for the simplest applet you can have.

Listing 4-1. The Simplest Applet

```
// SimplestApplet.java
package com.jdojo.applet;

import javax.swing.JApplet;

public class SimplestApplet extends JApplet {
        // No extra code is needed for your simplest applet
}
```

The SimplestApplet does not have any GUI parts or logic. Technically, it is a complete applet. If you test this applet in a browser, all you see is a blank area inside the web page.

Let's create another applet with a GUI, so you can see something in the browser. The new applet is called HelloApplet and it's shown in Listing 4-2.

Listing 4-2. A HelloApplet Applet That Displays a Message Using a JLabel

```java
// HelloApplet.java
package com.jdojo.applet;

import java.awt.Container;
import java.awt.FlowLayout;
import javax.swing.JApplet;
import javax.swing.JButton;
import javax.swing.JLabel;
import javax.swing.JOptionPane;
import javax.swing.JTextField;
import static javax.swing.JOptionPane.INFORMATION_MESSAGE;

public class HelloApplet extends JApplet {
    @Override
    public void init() {
        // Create Swing components
        JLabel nameLabel = new JLabel("Your Name:");
        JTextField nameFld = new JTextField(15);
        JButton sayHelloBtn = new JButton("Say Hello");

        // Add an action litener to the button to display the message
        sayHelloBtn.addActionListener(e -> sayHello(nameFld.getText()));

        // Add Swing components to the content pane of the applet
        Container contentPane = this.getContentPane();
        contentPane.setLayout(new FlowLayout());
        contentPane.add(nameLabel);
        contentPane.add(nameFld);
        contentPane.add(sayHelloBtn);
    }

    private void sayHello(String name) {
        String msg = "Hello there";
        if (name.length() > 0) {
            msg = "Hello " + name;
        }

        // Display the hello message
        JOptionPane.showMessageDialog(null,
                msg, "Hello", INFORMATION_MESSAGE);
    }
}
```

Does the code for the HelloApplet class look familiar? It is similar to working with a custom JFrame. The JApplet class contains an init() method. You need to override the method and add GUI parts to the applet. I will discuss writing code in the init() method of an applet in detail shortly. Like a JFrame, a JApplet has a content pane that holds the components for the applet. You added a JLabel, a JTextField, and a JButton to the content pane of the JApplet. The program logic is simple. The user may enter a name and click the Say Hello button that displays a message.

Unlike a Swing application, you should not add any GUI to your applet in its constructor even though it would work most of the time. The constructor for an applet is called to create an object of the applet class. The applet object does not get its "applet" status at the time it is created. It is still an ordinary Java object. If you use any features of an applet inside its constructor, these features will not work correctly because the applet object is just a simple Java object, not an "applet" in a real sense. After its creation, it gets the status of an applet, and its init() method is called by the environment (typically a browser) that displays it. This is the reason why you need to place all your GUI code (or any initialization code) in its init() method. The Applet class provides some other standard methods that you can override and write your logic to perform different kinds of work inside an applet.

You do not run an applet the same way you run a Swing application. Note that an applet class does not have a main() method. However, technically, it is possible to add a main() method to an applet, which does not help in running an applet in any way. To see an applet in action, you need to have an HTML file. You should have basic knowledge of HTML to work with an applet, but you do not need to be an expert in HTML. I will discuss how to view an applet in the next section. At this time, you should compile the HelloApplet class. You will have a class file named HelloApplet.class.

Deploying an Applet

Applets are Java programs. However, they are not run directly as any other Java programs. You need to do some plumbing before you can run an applet. An applet needs to be deployed before it can be used. There are two parts in the applet deployment:

- The Java Code that defines the applet GUI and logic
- An HTML document that contains applet's details such as its class name, archive file name containing the class file, width, height, etc.

You saw how to write the Java code for an applet in the previous section.

You embed the applet details in an HTML document using the <applet> tag. Both the applet code and the HTML document are deployed to the web server. The browser on the client machine requests the HTML document from the web server. When the browser finds the <applet> tag in the HTML document, it reads the applet's details, downloads the applet code from the web server, and runs the code as an applet in the browser. Does this mean that you need to have a web server to see your applets in action? The answer is no. You can test your applets without using a web server. You will need a web server to deploy your applets if you want to make your applets available for users. The following sections describe how to create an HTML document for an applet and how to deploy an applet to different environments.

Creating the HTML Document

An <applet> tag is used to embed an applet in an HTML document. The following is an example of an <applet> tag:

```
<applet code="com.jdojo.applet.HelloApplet" width="300" height="100" archive="myapplets.jar">
        This browser does not support Applets.
</applet>
```

You need specify the following mandatory attributes of the <applet> tag:

- code
- width
- height
- archive

The code attribute specifies the fully qualified class name of the applet. Optionally, you can append .class to the applet's fully qualified name. For example, both of the following <applet> tags work the same:

```
<!-- Use fully qualified name of the applet class as code -->
<applet code="com.jdojo.applet.HelloApplet">
...
</applet>

<!-- Use fully-qualified name of the applet class followed by .class -->
<applet code="com.jdojo.applet.HelloApplet.class">
...
</applet>
```

You can also use a forward slash instead of a dot to separate the sub-package names. For example, you can also specify the code attribute's value as "com/jdojo/applet/HelloApplet" and "com/jdojo/applet/HelloApplet.class".

The width and height attributes specify the initial width and height of the applet's area in the web page, respectively. You can specify the width and height attributes in pixel or in percentage. If the values are numbers, they are considered in pixels; for example, width="150" denotes a width of 150 pixels. If the values are followed by a percent sign (%), it denotes the percentage of the dimension of the container in which the applet is displayed; for example, width="50%" denotes that the width of the applet will be 50% of its container. Typically, the container is the browser window.

If you are using Java 7 Update 51 or later to view the applet, the archive attribute is mandatory. You need to bundle all files—class files and other resource files—for an applet in a JAR file. Bundling applet files in a JAR file makes the files smaller in size and results in a faster download for the applet's users. The value of the archive attribute is the name of the JAR file containing the files for the applet.

You may want to display a message in the web page if the browser does not support the <applet> tag. The message should be placed between the <applet> and </applet> tags as follows. The browser will ignore the message if it supports applets.

```
<applet>
        Inform the user that the browser does not support applets.
</applet>
```

Listing 4-3 shows the contents of the helloapplet.html file that you will use to test the applet. Note that the <applet> tag does not contain the archive attribute that will let you test the applet without having to create a JAR file.

Listing 4-3. Contents of the helloapplet.html File

```
<html>
        <head>
                <title>Hello Applet</title>
        </head>
        <body>
                <h3>Hello Applet in Action</h3>

                <applet code="com.jdojo.applet.HelloApplet" width="200" height="100">
                        This browser does not support Applets.
                </applet>
        </body>
</html>
```

Deploying Applets in Production

In a production environment, you must deploy your applet using a JAR file and sign the JAR file using a certificate issued by a trusted authority. A self-signing the JAR will not work. In a test environment, you can ignore this requirement, and you can use an unsigned JAR files or simply use class files. I will show you how to ignore this requirement to test the applets in this chapter. If you are learning applets for the first time, you may skip to the next section. You can revisit this section when you need to deploy your applet in the production environment.

Use the following steps to package and deploy applets. The steps refer to terms and commands related to created JAR files. Please refer to Chapter 8 in the book *Beginning Java Language Features* (ISBN: 978-1-4302-6658-7) for more details on creating JAR files.

1. Create a manifest file (say manifest.mf). It must contain a Permissions attribute. The following shows the contents of the manifest file:

    ```
    Manifest-Version: 1.0
    Permissions: sandbox
    ```

    The other value for the Permissions attribute is all-permissions. The value of sandbox indicates that the applet will run in the security sandbox and it does not require access to any additional resources on the client's machine. The value of all-permissions indicates that the applet needs access to the client's machine.

2. Create a JAR file that contains all class files for the applet and the manifest file created in the previous section. You can use the following command to create the JAR file named helloapplet.jar:

    ```
    jar cvfm helloapplet.jar manifest.mf com\jdojo\applet\*.class
    ```

3. Sign the helloapplet.jar file with the certificate you obtained from a trusted authority. Obtaining a certificate costs money (approximately $100). If you are just learning applets, you can skip this step. The "Signing Applets" section later in this chapter explains in detail how to sign an applet.

4. Deploy the signed helloapplet.jar file to the web server. You will need to consult the documentation of your web server on how to deploy applets. Some web servers provide deployment screens to let you deploy your JAR files and some let you drop the JAR file into a specific directory. The typical way of deploying files to a web server is to let the development IDE such as NetBeans and Eclipse package and deploy the necessary project files for you.

Deploying Applets for Testing

It will be too much trouble to package and deploy an applet for testing if you need to follow the steps described in the previous section. You can keep all class files and HTML files in the file system and test your applet. I assume that you have the applet files and that their full paths are similar to the following paths:

*   C:\myapplets\helloapplet.html

*   C:\myapplets\com\jdojo\applet\HelloApplet.class

The paths are shown using the file path syntax used on Windows. Please change them to the path syntax used by your operating system if you are not using Windows.

You are not required to store the applet files in a specific directory such as C:\myapplets. You can replace the directory C:\myapplets with a path to any directory. However, you must preserve the file paths after the C:\myapplets directory. You will be able to play with the directory structures for storing applet files after you read few more sections later.

If you have created the helloapplet.jar file to test the applet, I assume that you have added the archive attribute to the <applet> tag as archive="helloapplet.jar" in the helloapplet.html file and that the file paths will look as shown:

- C:\myapplets\helloapplet.html
- C:\myapplets\helloapplet.jar

Installing and Configuring Java Plug-in

Browsers use Java Plug-in to run applets. You must install and configure Java Plug-in before you can run your applet.

Installing the Java Plug-in

The Java Runtime Environment (JRE) is also known as Java Plug-in or Java add-on. The JRE (and hence Java Plug-in) is installed for you when you install JDK. The client machine running your applets does not need to install the JDK. It can just install the JRE. You can download the latest version of the JRE, which is 8.0 at the time of this writing, from www.oracle.com. The JRE is free to download, install, and use.

On Windows 8, using 64-bit JRE 8.0, I was able to run my applets only in Internet Explorer. I had to uninstall 64-bit JRE 8.0 and install 32-bit JRE 9.0 for my applets to work in all browsers, such as Google Chrome, Mozilla Firefox, and Internet Explorer.

On Linux, you need to do some manual setup to install Java Plug-in for the Firefox browser. Please follow the instructions at www.oracle.com/technetwork/java/javase/manual-plugin-install-linux-136395.html to set up the Java Plug-in on Linux.

Opening the Java Control Panel

You can configure Java Plug-in using the Java Control Panel program. The Java Control Panel program launches the window shown in Figure 4-1.

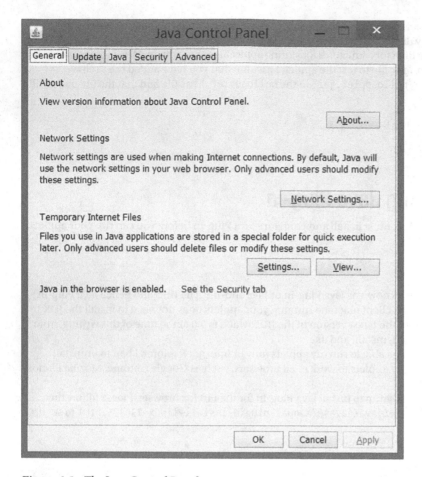

Figure 4-1. *The Java Control Panel*

On Windows 8, you can access the Java Control Panel via the following steps.

1. Open Search by pressing the Windows logo key + W. Make sure to select "Everywhere" for the search location. By default "Settings" is selected.

2. Enter "Java," "Java Control Panel," or "Configure Java" as the search term.

3. Click the Java icon to open the Java Control Panel.

4. If you could not find the Java Control Panel using Search, open the Control Panel by right-clicking the Start icon and selecting Control Panel from the menu. In the top-right corner in the Control Panel, you get a Search field. Enter "Java" in the Search field and you will see a program named Java. Click the program name to open the Java Control Panel.

On Windows 7, you can access Java Control Panel via the following steps.

1. Click the Start button, and then select the Control Panel option from the menu.

2. Enter Java Control Panel in the Search field in Control Panel.

3. Click the Java icon to open the Java Control Panel.

> ■ **Tip**   On Windows, you can directly launch the Java Control Panel by running the file `javacpl.exe` that is located under the `JRE_HOME\bin` directory. For JRE 8, the default path is `C:\Program Files\Java\jre8\bin\javacpl.exe`.

On Linux, you can access the Java Control Panel by running the `ControlPanel` program from the Terminal window. The `ControlPanel` program is installed in the `JRE_HOME\bin` directory where JRE_HOME is the directory in which you have installed the JRE. Suppose you have installed the JRE in /java8/jre directory. You need to run the following command from the Terminal window:

```
[/java8/jre/bin]$ ./ControlPanel
```

On Mac OS X (10.7.3 and above), you can access the Java Control Panel using the following steps:

- Go to the System Preferences by clicking the Apple icon in the upper left of screen.
- Click the Java icon to access the Java Control Panel.

Configuring Java Plug-in

You can configure a variety of settings for Java Plug-in using the Java Control Panel. In this section, I will describe how to bypass the signed JAR requirement for running applets. Open the Java Control Panel and select the Security tab, as shown in Figure 4-2.

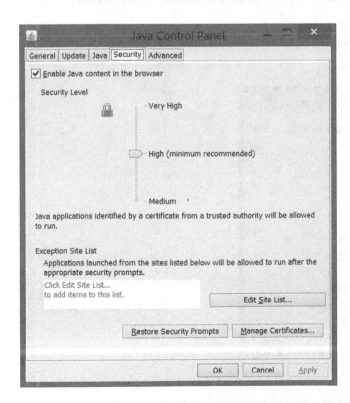

Figure 4-2. *Configuring the security settings in the Java Control Panel*

The checkbox labeled "Enable Java content in the browser" lets you enable/disable the support for running applets in the browser. By default, this checkbox is checked and applets can run in the browser. If this checkbox is unchecked, you cannot run applets in the browser.

The second setting is the security level, which you can set by sliding the knob of the vertical slider control. It can be set to the following three values:

- Very High: This is the most restrictive security level setting. Only signed applets with a valid certificate and that include the Permissions attribute in the manifest for the main JAR file are allowed to run with security prompts. All other applets are blocked.

- High: This is the minimum recommended and default security level setting. Applets that are signed with a valid or expired certificate and that include the Permissions attribute in the manifest for the main JAR file are allowed to run with security prompts. Applets are also allowed to run with security prompts when the revocation status of the certificate cannot be checked. All other applets are blocked.

- Medium: Only unsigned applets that request all permissions are blocked. All other applets are allowed to run with security prompts. Selecting this security level is not recommended. It will make your computer more vulnerable if you run a malicious applet.

For your testing purposes, you can set the security level to Medium. This will allow you to test applets packaged in an unsigned JAR file. You do not need to include the Permissions attribute in the manifest file either. It will also allow you to test your applets from the file system, avoiding the need for a web server to deploy your applets. You should change the security setting back to the recommended High or Very High as soon as you are done with testing. Note that using the Medium security level setting will show you warnings when you attempt to run any applets not meeting the security requirements. You will need to confirm when you get the warnings that you want to continue with running the applets despite the security risks.

The third setting on the Security tab is called Exception Site List. This lets you bypass the security requirements needed by the Security Level setting for the specified sites. Click the "Edit Site List" button to open the Exception Site List dialog box shown in Figure 4-3.

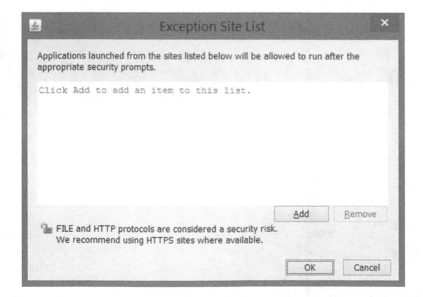

Figure 4-3. The Exception Site List Dialog Box

Click the Add button. You will see a blank row added for the location. Enter file:/// (Note the three ///) for the location. Click the Add button again. Clicking the Add button second time displays a Security Warning message stating that adding file:// (note two //) is a security risk. Click the Continue button on the warning dialog box. You get another blank row location. Enter http://localhost:8080. Repeat this step to add one more location, http://www.jdojo.com. The Exception Site List dialog box should look as shown in Figure 4-4. Now, click the OK button to return to the Security tab.

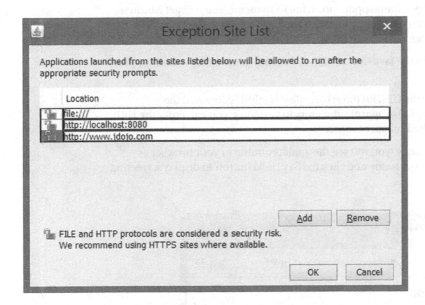

Figure 4-4. *The Exception Site List Dialog Box*

From now on, irrespective of the "Security Level" setting, you will be able to run all applets from the three sites:

- file:/// means applets from your file system using the file protocol.

- http://localhost:8080 means any web server running at port 8080 on your machine using the http protocol.

- http://www.jdojo.com means applets running from the website www.jdojo.com using the http protocol. I maintain jdojo.com. You can access the hello applets using the URL http://www.jdojo.com/myapplets/helloapplet.html.

Once you are done with the testing your applets, please remove these sites from the exception list so your computer is protected from running malicious applets.

Viewing an Applet

If you have been following the steps in the previous sections, viewing an applet is as simple as entering the URL of the hellapapplet.html file in the browser. Follow these steps to view the applet.

1. Open the browser of your choice, such as Google Chrome. Mozilla Firefox, or Internet Explorer.

2. Press Ctrl + O or select the Open menu option from the File menu. You will get a browse/open dialog box. Navigate to the directory in which you have stored the helloapplet.html file and open it in the browser.

3. Depending on the settings in the Java Control Panel, you may get security warnings, which you need to ignore.

4. Alternatively, you can enter the URL for the HTML file directly. If you saved the helloapplet.html file in the C:\myapplets directory in windows, you can enter the URL as file:///C:/myapplets/helloapplet.html.

5. If everything was set up correctly, you will see the applet running in your browser as shown in Figure 4-5. Enter your name and click the Say Hello button to display a greeting dialog box.

Figure 4-5. *The Hello Applet running from the file system in the Google Chrome browser*

If you are not able to view the applets using these steps, please read on the next section, which will describe how to view applets during testing using the appletviewer.

Using the appletviewer to Test Applets

You can use the appletviewer command to view an applet. It is available as appletviewer program in the JAVA_HOME\bin folder, where JAVA_HOME is the JDK installation folder on your machine. Here is the generic form of the command syntax:

```
appletviewer <options> <urls>
```

In <options>, you can specify various options for the command. You must specify one or more URLs separated by a space that contain the applet documents. You can use any of the following commands to view the applet described in the previous section. On Microsoft Windows, you can use the command prompt to enter the command. On Linux, use the Terminal window.

```
appletviewer http://www.jdojo.com/myapplets/helloapplet.html
```

or

```
appletviewer file:///C:/myapplets/helloapplet.html
```

You may get the following error when you run the above command:

```
'appletviewer' is not recognized as an internal or external command, operable program or batch file.
```

If you received the above error, you need to specify the full path for the appletviewer command, such as
C:\java8\bin\appletviewer, assuming you have installed the JDK in C:\java8 directory. You can try the following
command on the Windows command prompt:

```
C:\java8\appletviewer http://www.jdojo.com/myapplets/helloapplet.html
```

Figure 4-6 shows the applet running in the appletviewer window. Note that the appletviewer displays only the
applet from the document specified in the URL. All other HTML contents are ignored. For example, the applet does
not display the text from the helloapplet.html file that you had added inside the <h3> tag.

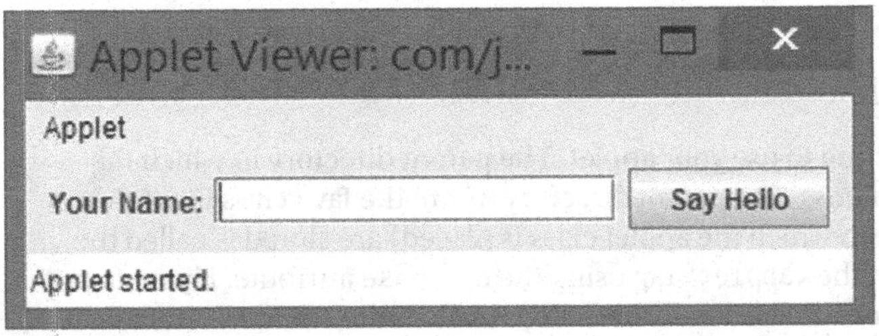

Figure 4-6. The Hello Applet running from the file system in the Google Chrome browser

If you want to view multiple applets using the appletviewer command, you can do so by specifying multiple
URLs on the command line. Each applet will be displayed in a separate applet viewer window. The following
command may be used to display two applets from two different web servers, where URL_PART1 could be
http://www.myserver1.com/myapplets1 and URL_PART2 could be http://www.myserver2.com/myapplets2:

```
appletviewer URL_PART1/applet1.html URL_PART2/applet2.html
```

The appletviewer command displays each applet found in the documents in a separate window. For example,
if applet1.html contains two applets and applet2.html contains three applets, the above command will open
five applet viewer windows. If the document referred to by the URL does not contain any applet, the appletviewer
command does not do anything. The content in the document referred to by the URL is ignored except for the part
that is related to an applet. The appletviewer window has a main menu called "Applet" that lets you reload an applet,
restart it, stop it, save it in serialized form, etc.

You can specify three options to the appletviewer command:

- -debug
- -encoding
- -Jjavaoptions

The -debug option lets you start the appletviewer in debug mode. You can specify the encoding of your document referred to by the URLs using the -encoding option. The -Jjavaoptions option lets you specify any Java options for the JVM. The -J part of the option is removed and the remaining part is passed to the JVM. The following are examples of using these options. Note that to specify the classpath environment variable for the appletviewer, you need to specify the -J options twice.

```
appletviewer -debug your_document_url_goes_here
appletviewer -encoding ISO-8859-1 your_document_url_goes_here
appletviewer -J-classpath -Jc:\myclasses your_document_url_goes_here
```

■ **Tip** If you are using the NetBeans IDE to develop your applets, right-clicking the applet's file, such as HelloApplet.java in the IDE, and selecting the Run File menu option runs your applet in the appletviewer.

Using the codebase Attribute

In the HelloApplet example, you placed the Java class file and the HTML file under the same parent directory. You files were placed as follows:

- ANY_DIR\html_file

- ANY_DIR\package_directories\class_file

You do not have to follow the above directory structure to use your applet. The parent directory in which the HTML file for the applet is stored is called the *document base*. The parent directory where the Java class files (always consider the directory structure needed for the package in which the applet class is placed) are stored is called the *code base*. You can specify a code base for your applet in the <applet> tag using the codebase attribute. If you do not specify the codebase attribute, the document base is used as codebase. The codebase attribute could be a relative URL or an absolute URL. Using an absolute URL for the code base opens up another possibility for storing applet class files. You can store an applet's HTML file on one web server and the Java classes on another. In such cases, you must specify an absolute codebase for the java classes.

A relative URL for the codebase attribute is resolved using the href attribute's value for the <base> tag in the HTML document. If a <base> tag is not specified in the HTML document, the URL from where the HTML document was downloaded is used to resolve the relative codebase URL. Let's look at some examples.

Example 1

The content of a helloapplet.html file is as follows. Note that you include a <base> tag and you do not specify the codebase attribute for the <applet> tag.

```
<html>
    <head>
        <title>Hello Applet</title>
        <base href="http://www.jdojo.com/myapplets/myclasses">
    </head>
    <body>
        <applet code="com.jdojo.applet.HelloApplet" width="150" height="100">
            This browser does not support Applets.
```

```
            </applet>
        </body>
</html>
```

The document is downloaded using the URL http://www.jdojo.com/myapplets/helloapplet.html. Since you have specified the <base> tag, the browser will look for the applet's class file at http://www.jdojo.com/myapplets/myclasses/com/jdojo/applet/HelloApplet.class.

Example 2

The content of a helloapplet.html file is as follows. Note that you include the <base> tag and you do not specify the codebase attribute for the <applet> tag as mydir.

```
<html>
        <head>
                <title>Hello Applet</title>
                <base href="http://www.jdojo.com/myapplets/myclasses">
        </head>
        <body>
                <applet code="com.jdojo.applet.HelloApplet" width="150" height="100"
                        codebase="mydir">
                        This browser does not support Applets.
                </applet>
        </body>
</html>
```

The document is downloaded using the URL http://www.jdojo.com/myapplets/helloapplet.html. Since you have specified the <base> tag, the browser will look for the applet's class file at http://www.jdojo.com/myapplets/myclasses/mydir/com/jdojo/applet/HelloApplet.class. Note that the codebase value of mydir is resolved using the <base> tag's href value. If you had specified the codebase value as ../xyzdir (two dots means one directory up), the browser will look for the class file at http://www.jdojo.com/myapplets/xyzdir/com/jdojo/applet/HelloApplet.class. Note that some browsers do not let you specify two dots to indicate one level up in a directory hierarchy as part of a codebase URL for security reasons.

Example 3

The content of a helloapplet.html file is as follows. Note that you have not included the <base> tag and you have specified the codebase attribute for the <applet> tag.

```
<html>
        <head>
                <title>Hello Applet</title>
        </head>
        <body>
                <applet code="com.jdojo.applet.HelloApplet"
                        width="150" height="100" codebase="abcdir">
                        This browser does not support Applets.
                </applet>
        </body>
</html>
```

The document is downloaded using the URL http://www.jdojo.com/myapplets/helloapplet.html. Since you have not specified the <base> tag, the relative URL for the codebase will be resolved using the URL used to download the HTML file and the browser will look for a class file at http://www.jdojo.com/myapplets/abcdir/com/jdojo/applet/HelloApplet.class.

If you use an absolute URL for the codebase, the browser will look for the applet's class files using that absolute URL, irrespective of the presence of a <base> tag in the HTML file and from where the HTML file is downloaded. Let's consider the following <applet> tag:

```
<applet code="com.jdojo.applet.HelloApplet" width="150" height="100"
        codebase="http://www.jdojo.com/myclasses">
        This browser does not support Applets.
</applet>
```

The browser will look for the applet's class files at http://www.jdojo.com/myclasses/com/jdojo/applet/HelloApplet.class. If you want to store the applet's class files and HTML files on different servers, you need to specify the codebase value as an absolute URL.

The Applet class provides two methods called getDocumentBase() and getCodeBase() to get the document base URL and the code base URL, respectively. The getDocumentBase() method returns the URL of the document that has an embedded <applet> tag. For example, if you enter the URL http://www.jdojo.com/myapplets/helloapplet.html in your browser to view the applet, http://www.jdojo.com/myapplets/helloapplet.html will be returned from the getDocumentBase() method. The getCodeBase() method returns the URL of the directory that is used to download the Java classes for the applet. The URL returned from this method depends on many factors, as you have just seen in the examples.

The Life Cycle of an Applet

An applet goes through different stages during its existence. It is created, initialized, started, stopped, and destroyed. An applet is first created by calling its constructor. At the time of its creation, it is a simple Java object and it does not get its "applet" status. After its creation, it gets its applet status and there are four methods in the Applet class that are called by the browser. You can place code in those methods to perform different kinds of logic. These methods are as follows:

- init()
- start()
- stop()
- destroy()

The init() Method

The init() method is called by the browser after an applet has been instantiated and loaded. You can override this method to place any code that performs initialization logic for your applet. Typically, you will place code to create a GUI for your applet in this method. This method is called only once during the lifetime of the applet.

The start() Method

The start() method is called just after the init() method. It may be called multiple times. Suppose you are viewing an applet in a web page, and you open another web page in the same browser window (or tab) by replacing the applet's web page. If you go back to the previous web page, and if the applet was cached, its start() method will be called again. If the applet was destroyed when you replaced the applet's web page by another web page, its life cycle will start over, and its init() and start() methods will be called in sequence. You can place any code in this method that starts a process, such as an animation when the applet is shown on a web page.

The stop() Method

The stop() method is the counterpart of the start() method. It may be called multiple times. Typically, it is called when the web page showing the applet is replaced by another web page. It is also called before the destroy() method is called. Typically, you place code in this method that stops any process such as an animation that was started in the start() method.

The destroy() Method

The destroy() method is called when the applet is destroyed. You can place code that performs logic to release any resources that were held during the lifetime of the applet. The stop() method is always called before the destroy() method is called. This method is called only once during the lifetime of an applet.

Listing 4-4 contains the code for an applet that displays a dialog box when the applet's init(), start(), stop(), and destroy() methods are called. It includes the number of times the start() and stop() methods are called in the messages.

Listing 4-4. An Applet to Demonstrate the Life Cycle of an Applet

```
// AppletLifeCycle.java
package com.jdojo.applet;

import javax.swing.JApplet;
import javax.swing.JLabel;
import javax.swing.JOptionPane;

public class AppletLifeCycle extends JApplet {
        private int startCount = 0;
        private int stopCount = 0;

        @Override
        public void init() {
                this.getContentPane().add(new JLabel("Applet Life Cycle!!!"));
                JOptionPane.showMessageDialog(null, "init()");
        }

        @Override
        public void start() {
                startCount++;
                JOptionPane.showMessageDialog(null, "start(): " + startCount);
        }

        @Override
        public void stop() {
                stopCount++;
                JOptionPane.showMessageDialog(null, "stop(): " + stopCount);
        }
```

```
        @Override
        public void destroy() {
                JOptionPane.showMessageDialog(null, "destroy()");
        }
}
```

Listing 4-5 contains the contents of the HTML file to view the `AppletLifeCycle` applet. It assumes that the HTML file and Java class file will be placed in a directory structure as shown:

```
ANY_DIR\appletlifecycle.html
ANY_DIR\com\jdojo\applet\AppletLifeCycle.class
```

If you have a different directory structure, you may need to include the `codebase` attribute in an `<applet>` tag. You can view applets using the steps described previously.

Listing 4-5. The Contents of the appletlifecycle.html File to View the AppletLifeCycle Applet

```html
<html>
        <head>
                <title>Lifecycle of an Applet</title>
        </head>
        <body>
                <applet code="com.jdojo.applet.AppletLifeCycle"
                        height="200" width="200">
                        This browser does not support Applets.
                </applet>
        </body>
</html>
```

Passing Parameters to Applets

You can let the users of your applets configure the applet by passing parameters to it in the HTML document. You can pass parameters to an applet using the `<param>` tag inside the `<applet>` tag. The `<param>` tag has two attributes called name and value. The `name` and `value` attributes of a `<param>` tag are used to specify a name and value of the parameter, respectively. You can pass multiple parameters to an applet using multiple `<param>` tags. The following HTML snippet passes two parameters to an applet:

```html
<applet code="MyApplet" width="100" height="100">
        <param name="buttonHeight" value="20" />
        <param name="buttonText" value="Hello" />
</applet>
```

The parameter names are `buttonHeight` and `buttonText` and their values are 20 and `Hello`, respectively. Make sure you have meaningful names for your applet parameter that make sense to the user who reads them. Technically, any string for a parameter name is fine. For example, technically, p1 and p2 are as good parameter names as `buttonHeight` and `buttonText`. However, the latter are more meaningful to the users.

The `Applet` class provides a `getParameter()` method that accepts the parameter name as its argument and returns the parameter value as a `String`. Note that it always returns a `String` irrespective of the value set for a parameter. For example, if you want to use the value 20 for the parameter `buttonHeight` as an integer, you need to convert the `String` into an integer in inside the applet's Java code. The name of the parameter that you pass to the `getParameter()` method is case-insensitive; both `getParameter("buttonHeight")` and getParameter("BUTTONHEIGHT") return the same value of 20 as a String. If the specified parameter has not been set in the HTML document, the getParameter() method returns null. The following snippet of code demonstrates how to use the getParameter() method in the code for an applet:

```
// buttonHeight and buttonText will get the values 20 and Hello
String buttonHeight = getParameter("buttonHeight");
String buttonText = getParameter("buttonText") ;

// bgColor will be null as there is no backgroundColor parameter set
String bgColor = getParameter("backgroundColor");
```

You can customize a few aspects of your applet using parameters. You do not have to change your code if the value of the parameter changes. If you pass parameters to your applet, make sure to assign a default value to each parameter, in case it is not set in the HTML document. For example, you can set the background color of your applet as an applet's parameter. If it is not set, you can default to a color such as gray or white.

Listing 4-6 shows the code for an AppletParameters applet. It uses two GUI components, a JTextArea to display a welcome message and a JButton. The welcome message and the button's text can be customized passing two parameters called welcomeText and helloButtonText. The applet code reads the two parameter values in its init() method. It sets the default values for parameters if they are not set in the HTML document. Listing 4-7 contains the HTML file's content and Figure 4-7 shows the applet in action. Figure 4-8 shows the message box that is displayed when you click the Say Hello button.

Listing 4-6. Passing Parameters to an Applet Using the <param> Tag

```
// AppletParameters.java
package com.jdojo.applet;

import java.awt.Container;
import java.awt.FlowLayout;
import javax.swing.JApplet;
import javax.swing.JButton;
import javax.swing.JOptionPane;
import javax.swing.JScrollPane;
import javax.swing.JTextArea;

public class AppletParameters extends JApplet {
        private JTextArea welcomeTextArea = new JTextArea(2, 20);
        private JButton helloButton = new JButton();

        @Override
        public void init() {
                Container contentPane = this.getContentPane();
                contentPane.setLayout(new FlowLayout());

                contentPane.add(new JScrollPane(welcomeTextArea));
                contentPane.add(helloButton);

                // Show parameters when the button is clicked
                helloButton.addActionListener(e -> showParameters());

                // Make the welcome JTextArea non-editable
                welcomeTextArea.setEditable(false);
```

```
            // Display the welcome message
            String welcomeMsg = this.getParameter("welcomeText");
            if (welcomeMsg == null || welcomeMsg.equals("")) {
                    welcomeMsg = "Welcome!";
            }
            welcomeTextArea.setText(welcomeMsg);

            // Set the hello button text
            String helloButtonText = this.getParameter("helloButtonText");
            if (helloButtonText == null || helloButtonText.equals("")) {
                    helloButtonText = "Hello";
            }

            helloButton.setText(helloButtonText);
    }

    private void showParameters() {
            String welcomeText = this.getParameter("welcomeText");
            String helloButtonText = this.getParameter("helloButtonText");

            String msg = "Parameters passed from HTML are\nwelcomeText="
                    + welcomeText + "\nhelloButtonText=" + helloButtonText;
            JOptionPane.showMessageDialog(null, msg);
    }
}
```

Listing 4-7. Contents of the appletparameters.html File Used to View the AppletParameters Applet

```
<html>
    <head>
            <title>Applet Parameters</title>
    </head>
    <body>
            <applet code="com.jdojo.applet.AppletParameters"
                    width="300" height="50">
                    <param name="welcomeText"
                            value="Welcome to the applet world!"/>
                    <param name="helloButtonText"
                             value="Say Hello"/>
                    This browser does not support Applets.
            </applet>
    </body>
</html>
```

Figure 4-7. *The AppletParameters applet running in a browser*

Figure 4-8. *The AppletParameters applet running in a browser*

■ **Tip** You can also use the getParameter() method of the Applet class to get the value of attributes of a <applet> tag. For example, you can use getParameter("code") to get the value of the code attribute of the <applet> tag.

Publishing the Applet's Parameter Information

An applet lets you publish information about the parameters it accepts. You may develop an applet that knows about its parameters. Your applet may be viewed using different applet viewers and by users other than you. Publishing the parameters that your applet accepts may be helpful for the program that is hosting the applet and to the user who is viewing it. For example, an applet viewer may let the user change the applet's parameters interactively and reload the applet. The Applet class provides a getParameterInfo() method, which you need to override in your applet class to publish information about your applet's parameters. It returns a two-dimensional (nX3) array of String. By default, it returns null. The array should have rows equal to the number of parameters it accepts. Each row should have three columns containing the parameter's name, type, and description. Implementing the getParameterInfo() method in your applet is not necessary for your applet to work. However, it is good practice to provide information about your applet's parameters through this method. Let's assume that the following <applet> tag is used to display your applet:

```
<applet code="MyApplet" width="100" height="100">
        <param name="buttonHeight" value="20" />
        <param name="buttonText" value="Hello" />
</applet>
```

One possible implementation for a getParameterInfo() method for the MyApplet class is as follows. Note that as a developer, you are just the publisher of the applet's parameter information. It is up to the applet viewer programs to use it in any way they choose.

```
public class MyApplet extends JApplet {
        // Other code for applet goes here...

        // Public applet's parameter info
        public String[][] getParameterInfo() {
                String[][] parametersInfo =
                                { {"buttonHeight",
                                   "integer",
                                   "Height for the Hello button in pixel"
                                },
                                {"buttonText",
                                 "String",
```

```
                              "Hello button's text"
                            }
                      };

            return parametersInfo;
      }
}
```

Publishing the Applet's Information

The Applet class provides a getAppletInfo() method that should return a text description of the applet. The default implementation of this method returns null. It is good practice to return a brief description of your applet from this method, so your applet users can know a little more about your applet. This description may be displayed in some manner by the tool that is used to view the applet. The following snippet of code illustrates using the getAppletInfo() method to provide information about your applet:

```
public class MyApplet extends JApplet {
      // Other applet's logic goes here...

      public String getAppletInfo() {
            return "My Demo Applet, Version 1.0, No Copyright";
      }
}
```

Other Attributes of the <applet> Tag

Table 4-1 lists all attributes for the <applet> tag and their usage. In addition to the attributes listed in this table, you can also use some other standard HTML attributes such as id, style, etc. with the <applet> tag.

Table 4-1. *The List of Attributes for the <applet> tag*

Name	Usage
Code	Specifies the fully qualified name of the applet's class or the applet's class file name.
codebase	Specifies the URL for the base directory that contains the applet's classes. If it is not specified, the document's base URL, specified in the <base> tag, or the URL from where the document is downloaded is used as its value. Its value could be a relative or absolute URL. A relative URL is resolved based on a document base URL in the <base> tag's value if present, or a URL from where the document is downloaded.
Width	Specifies the width of the applet in pixels or percentage of its container's width. For example, width="100" specifies the applet's width as 100 pixels whereas width="30%" specifies the applet's width as 30% of its container's width.
height	Specifies the height of the applet in pixel or percentage of its container's height. For example, height="200" specifies applet's height as 200 pixels whereas height="20%" specifies the applet's height as 20% of its container's height.

(*continued*)

Table 4-1. (*continued*)

Name	Usage
archive	Specifies a list of comma-separate archive files (JAR or ZIP files). The archive files may contain classes and other resources such as images, audios, etc., that are used by the applet. The archive file may use a relative or absolute URL. The relative URL is resolved using the codebase attribute's value. The download time is reduced significantly if your applet uses multiple classes and other resources that are packaged in archive files. If you do not use archives, each class and resource for your applet will be downloaded separately when they are needed. If you archive them, all files contained in the archives are downloaded using one connection to the server, thus reducing the download time. You can choose to place some files in archives and some in directories. If your applet needs a resource, it first looks for it in the archive, and then on the server in directories as specified by the codebase attribute value.
object	Specifies the name of the file that contains the serialized form of the applet. You can specify either a code attribute or an object attribute, but not both. When the applet is displayed, it will be deserialized, and its init() method will not be called. Its start() method will be called. This attribute is not used often.

Name	Specifies the name of the applet. You can use the name of the applet to find other applets running in the same web page. You can also specify the name of the applet by using a <param> tag with its name attribute value as "name". Both of the following will set the name of the applet to myapplet1:
	
	`<applet name="myapplet1" ...>`
	`...`
	`</applet>`
	
	or
	
	`<applet ...>`
	`<param name="name" value="myapplet1"/>`
	`</applet>`
	
	You can get the name of an applet by using the getParameter("name") method of the Applet class.

alt	Specifies alternate text to be displayed if the browser understands the <applet> tag but cannot run the applet. It is preferred to use text between the <applet> and </applet> tags to display the alternate text that can also include HTML formatting in your alternate text.

align	Specifies the position of the applet with respect to the surrounding contents. Its value could be bottom, middle, top, left, or right. Note that this attribute specifies the applet's position relative to its surrounding, not relative to its container. For example, using align="middle" will not make the applet appear in the middle of the browser window. If you want to place your applet in the middle of the browser window, you need to use another HTML technique such as placing the <applet> tag inside another container such as <p> and then setting the align attribute. For example, the following HTML piece of code will place an applet in the center of the browser window:
	
	`<p align="center">`
	`    <applet ...>...</applet>`
	`</p>`

hspace	Specifies the space in pixels that is left to the left and right of the applet.
vspace	Specifies the space in pixels that is left to the top and bottom of the applet.

Using Images in an Applet

Using images in an applet is simple. The `Applet` class has an overloaded `getImage()` method that returns a `java.awt.Image` object. Here are the two version of this method:

- `Image getImage(URL imageAbsoluteURL)`

- `Image getImage(URL baseURL, String imageURLPath)`

The first version takes an absolute URL of the image such as `http://www.jdojo.com/myapplets/images/welcome.jpg`. The second version takes a base URL and a URL path to the image. The URL for the image is resolved using the first argument, which is the base URL. Consider the following snippet of code in an applet:

```
URL baseURL = new URL("http://www.jdojo.com/myapplets/abc.html");
Image welcomeImage = getImage(baseURL, "images/welcome.jpg");
```

The contents of the `welcome.jpg` file will be fetched using the base URL and the relative image's URL from `http://www.jdojo.com/myapplets/images/welcome.jpg`. Consider the following snippet of code in an applet:

```
URL baseURL = new URL("http://www.jdojo.com/myapplets/abc.html");
Image welcomeImage = getImage(baseURL, "/images/welcome.jpg");
```

This time, the image URL path (`/images/welcome.jpg`) starts with a forward slash. This URL path will be resolved to `http://www.jdojo.com/images/welcome.jpg`. You can store all images under the directory where you store the HTML document, and always use the document base URL returned from `getDocumentBase()` method as the base URL to fetch the images.

The `getImage()` method returns immediately. The image is downloaded when the applet needs to paint it.

Listing 4-8 contains the code for an applet that uses an image. Listing 4-9 has the HTML content to view the applet.

Listing 4-8. Using Images in an Applet

```
// ImageApplet.java
package com.jdojo.applet;

import java.awt.Container;
import java.awt.Image;
import javax.swing.ImageIcon;
import javax.swing.JApplet;
import javax.swing.JLabel;

public class ImageApplet extends JApplet {
        JLabel imageLabel;

        @Override
        public void init() {
                Container contentPane = this.getContentPane();
                Image img = this.getWelcomeImage();
                if (img == null) {
                        imageLabel = new JLabel("Image parameter not set...");
                }
                else {
```

```
                        imageLabel = new JLabel(new ImageIcon(img));
                }
                contentPane.add(imageLabel);
        }

        private Image getWelcomeImage() {
                Image img = null;
                String imageURL = this.getParameter("welcomeImageURL");
                if (imageURL != null) {
                        img = this.getImage(this.getDocumentBase(), imageURL);
                }
                return img;
        }
}
```

Listing 4-9. Contents of the imageapplet.html File

```
<html>
        <head>
                <title>Using Images in Applet</title>
        </head>
        <body>
                <applet code="com.jdojo.applet.ImageApplet"
                        width="250" height="200">
                        <param name="welcomeImageURL"
                                value="images/welcome.jpg"/>
                        This browser does not support Applets.
                </applet>
        </body>
</html>
```

This example assumes the following directory structure, where ANY_DIR means a directory in your web server or local file system:

- ANY_DIR\myapplets\imageapplet.html

- ANY_DIR\myapplets\images\welcome.jpg

- ANY_DIR\myapplets\com\jdojo\applet\ImageApplet.class

The image URL path relative to the document base is specified as a parameter. If the image URL is not specified in the HTML code, the applet displays a string to that effect in a JLabel. If your directory structure is not the same as listed above, you will need to modify the applet's code or HTML contents before you can run this example successfully.

Playing Audio Clips in an Applet

It is easy to play an audio clip in an applet. The Applet class has an overloaded getAudioClip() method that returns an instance of the java.applet.AudioClip interface. Here are the two version of this method:

- AudioClip getAudioClip(URL audioAbsoluteURL)

- AudioClip getAudioClip(URL baseURL, String audioURLPath)

The getAudioClip() method works the same way as the getImage() method. It returns immediately. The audio clip is loaded when it is played. The AudioClip interface is declared as follows:

```
package java.applet;

public interface AudioClip {
        void play();
        void stop();
        void loop();
}
```

You can start playing an audio clip using the play() method. You can stop playing the audio clip using the stop() method. You can play an audio clip in a loop using its loop() method. The following code snippet demonstrates how to use an audio clip in an applet:

```
// Assuming that audios/myaudio.wav is stored under a directory
// where the HTML file for the applet is stored
AudioClip clip = getAudioClip(getDocumentBase(), "audios/myaudio.wav");
clip.play(); //* Play the clip

// Other logic goes here

clip.stop(); // Stop the clip
```

The Applet class contains some convenience methods that let you play an audio clip without dealing with the AudioClip interface. The applet will download the audio clip and play it for you. You just need to specify the URL of the audio clip and use the play() method of the Applet class as shown:

```
// Assuming that the following code is inside your applet class
this.play(this.getDocumentBase(), "audios/myfav.wav");
```

If you want to play an audio clip in a Java application, use the newAudioClip() static method of the Applet class to get the AudioClip object as shown:

```
URL myFavAudioURL = new URL("http://www.jdojo.com/myfav.wav");
AudioClip clip = Applet.newAudioClip(myFavAudioURL);
clip.play();
```

Interacting with the Applet's Environment

An applet context refers to the environment that runs the applet, such as a browser, an applet viewer, etc. An instance of the java.applet.AppletContext interface represents the applet's context. The Applet class provides a getAppletContext() method that returns the applet's context. Using an AppletContext object, you can open a new document, display a message in the applet's container status bar, and get reference to another applet running in the same document. The following snippet of code demonstrates some of the uses of the AppletContext object:

```
// Get the applet context object
AppletContext context = getAppletContext();

// Open the Yahoo's home page in a new window
URL yahooURL = null;
```

```
try {
        yahooURL = new URL("http://www.yahoo.com");
        context.showDocument(yahooURL, "_blank");
}
catch (MalformedURLException e) {
        e.printStackTrace();
}

// Show a brief message in the status bar
context.showStatus("Welcome to the applet world!");

// Get reference of another applet named "crazyApplet"
Applet crazyApplet = context.getApplet("crazyApplet");
if (crazyApplet != null) {
        context.showStatus("Found the crazy applet...");

        // Now you can invoke methods on crazyApplet
}
```

The showDocument() method opens another document specified by the first parameter. By using its second parameter, you can control the window in which it displays the new document. The valid values for the second parameter are: "_self", "_parent", "_top", "_blank", and "any existing/non-existing frame/window name". The same values are also used in standard HTML/JavaScript code.

The showStatus() method is used to display a short, but not very important, message in the status bar of a browser. The browser also uses the same status bar to display messages. You should not display an important message that needs the user's attention using this method. The user may not see your message, or it may be overwritten before the user has a chance to see it. If you need to display important messages, you should consider displaying it in the applet area.

The getApplet() and getApplets() methods are used to find other applets running in the same document. Refer to the next section for more details on how an applet may communicate with other applets.

■ **Tip** The applet context is not available when the applet object is created. Calling the getAppletContext() method in an applet's constructor returns null. The getImage() and getAudioClip() methods invoke a corresponding method in the AppletContext object. Since the AppletContext object for an applet is not available when the applet's constructor is executing, do not use the getImage() and getAudioClip() methods of Applet class in its constructor.

Communion of Applet, HTML, and JavaScript

An applet can open another HTML document using its showDocument() method. It can also display a brief message on the status bar of the browser by using its showStatus() method. There are many other possibilities when you work with applets. In fact, applets, HTML, and JavaScript coexist happily and they can comminute with each other. Here are some of the possibilities:

- An applet can communicate with another applet in the same HTML document.

- An applet can communicate with JavaScript by invoking JavaScript functions.

- JavaScript can communicate with an applet by accessing an applet's methods and fields.

Figure 4-9 shows a possible interaction among applets, HTML, and JavaScript.

275

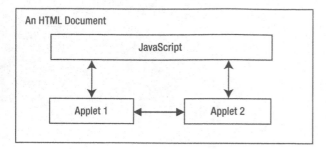

Figure 4-9. *Communication between applets, HTML, and JavaScript*

Before an applet can communicate with another applet, it must find the applet it wants to communicate with. The AppletContext class has two methods that let an applet find another applet in the same HTML document:

- Applet getApplet(String appletName)

- Enumeration<Applet> getApplets()

The getApplet() method requires you to pass the name of the applet you are looking for and it returns the reference of the applet if it is found. If it does not find the applet, it returns null. You must specify a name for your applet to be found for this method to work. You use this method as shown:

```
import java.applet.Applet;
...
Applet app = getAppletContext().getApplet("applet2");
if (app == null) {
        // applet2 is not found
}
else {
        // Work with applet2 object.
}
```

The getApplets() method returns the Enumeration of all applets on the page including the one that calls this method. You can use this method as shown:

```
import java.applet.Applet;
import java.util.Enumeration;
...
Enumeration<Applet> e = getAppletContext().getApplets();
while(e.hasMoreElements()) {
        Applet app = e.nextElement();
        // Work with app applet now
}
```

An applet can communicate with JavaScript using the netscape.javascript.JSObject class. The JSObject class is not part of the standard Java library. If you have installed JRE, it is packaged in the plugin.jar file, which is stored in a JRE_HOME\lib folder. If you use JSObject in your applet, you need to include the plugin.jar file in your

CLASSPATH in order for your applet's code to compile. You can get the reference of the browser window using the JSObject.getWindow() static method. You need to pass the reference of the applet to the JSObject.getWindow() method. The following snippet of code demonstrates how to call a JavaScript method from an applet:

```
// Need to import the JSObject class
import netscape.javascript.JSObject;

// Get the reference of the browser window
JSObject browserWindow = (JSObject)JSObject.getWindow(this);


/* You need to use the call() method of the browserWindow passing the
   JavaScript function name as a string and arguments as an Object array.
   Assume that helloJS(msgText) is a JavaScript function which accepts a
   string argument and returns some value.
*/
String methodName = "helloJS";
Object[] methodArgs = {"Hello from applet"};
Object returnValue = browserWindow.call(methodName, methodArgs);
```

To access JavaScript from inside an applet, you must include a MAYSCRIPT attribute in your <applet> tag. Your applet tag will look as follows:

```
<applet code="MyApplet" width="100" height="100" MAYSCRIPT>
...
</applet>
```

JavaScript provides references to all applets in the document as an applets property of the document object. The property is an array. You can access it using a zero-based index or an applet name. Suppose you have two applets in a document named applet1 and applet2. The following JavaScript functions have the code to call the pushMessage() method of all applets and applet1 on the page, assuming the all applets in the HTML document have a pushMessage(String msg) method:

```
// A JavaScript function.
// Call the pushMessage() method of all applets on the page
function pushMessageToAllApplets() {
        for(var i = 0; i < document.applets.length; i++) {
                document.applets[i].pushMessage("Hello");
        }
}

// A JavaScript function.
// Call the pushMessage() method of applet1 on the page
function pushMessageToApplet1() {
        document.applets["applet1"].pushMessage("Hello applet1");
}
```

You can access any public methods or fields of an applet from JavaScript code. Note that JavaScript is not a compiled language and it may throw runtime errors if the method or field name of the applet does not exist.

Packaging Applets in Archives

You can package all Java classes and resources such as images, audios, etc. for an applet in archives (JAR or ZIP files). You can use one or more archives to package your applet resources. All archive file names are specified in a comma-separated list as the value for `archive` attribute of the `<applet>` tag. The archive files names are resolved using the `codebase` attribute value.

```
<applet code="MyApplet"
        width="200"
        height="200"
        codebase="resources"
        archive="myclasses1.jar, myclasses2.jar, myimages.zip">
</applet>
```

If you package all your resources in archives, you do not have to maintain the specific directory structures on your web server to store your classes and other resources. Packaging all your resources for an applet in archives has a huge advantage with regards to applet loading time. It improves the applet loading time significantly, as it downloads the entire archive using one connection rather than connecting once for each file to download. However, if, for some reason, you cannot package all your applet classes and resources in archives, you may keep some in directories and package some in archives. If the applet needs a resource (class file, image, audio clips, etc.), it looks for it first in archives, and then on the server.

The Event Dispatching Thread and Applets

I covered a great deal about the role of the event-dispatching thread in a Swing application in Chapter 3. The discussion about the event-dispatching thread and Swing also applies to applets because applets also use Swing components. The four applet life cycle methods of `init()`, `start()`, `stop()`, and `destroy()` are called by applet viewers (typically a web browser) and they are not called on the event-dispatching thread. You are supposed to write your program so that all Swing-related code executes on the event-dispatching thread. You have been building your GUI in the `init()` method, and now you know that the `init()` method is not executed on the event-dispatching thread. So, you have not been following the correct way of working with Swing components. You have not come across any problems in your applets related to the event-dispatching thread because the examples so far have been trivial. If you are developing production-level applets, you need to follow the guidelines suggested.

You need to use the `invokeAndWait()` and `invokeLater()` methods of the `SwingUtilities` class to run your code on the event-dispatching thread. Usually, you use the `invokeLater()` method so your code is scheduled to run on the event-dispatching thread later. The `invokeLater()` method returns immediately. You should not use the `invokeLater()` method to build a GUI from the `init()` method of the applet. The reason is very obvious. An applet viewer (usually a web browser) calls the applet's `init()` and `start()` methods in sequence. When the `init()` method returns, it calls the `start()` method. If you use the `invokeLater()` method in the `init()` method to build the GUI, the `init()` method will return immediately (not necessarily after running the code to build the GUI, but just after scheduling the GUI building code to run later) and the applet viewer will call the `start()` method. That is, when the `start()` method executes, your GUI may not be ready. However, the assumption is that your applet must be initialized before the `init()` method returns, so that you can perform the next steps in its `start()` method. This is the reason why you need to use the `invokeAndWait()` method to build a GUI inside an applet's `init()` method, so you can be sure that when the `start()` method is called, your GUI is already in place. Here is the correct way to code the `init()` method of an applet. Listing 4-10 rewrites the `HelloApplet` class and calls it `BetterHelloApplet`. It uses the `initApplet()` method to build the GUI for the applet. The `initApplet()` method is called on the event-dispatching the thread from the `init()` method.

Listing 4-10. Using the Event-Dispatching Thread to Build a GUI in an Applet

```java
// BetterHelloApplet.java
package com.jdojo.applet;

import javax.swing.JApplet;
import javax.swing.SwingUtilities;
import java.awt.Container;
import java.awt.FlowLayout;
import java.lang.reflect.InvocationTargetException;
import javax.swing.JButton;
import javax.swing.JLabel;
import javax.swing.JOptionPane;
import javax.swing.JTextField;
import static javax.swing.JOptionPane.INFORMATION_MESSAGE;
import static javax.swing.JOptionPane.ERROR_MESSAGE;

public class BetterHelloApplet extends JApplet {
        @Override
        public void init() {
                try {
                        // Build the GUI on thw event-dispatching thread
                        SwingUtilities.invokeAndWait(() -> initApplet());
                }
                catch (InterruptedException | InvocationTargetException e) {
                        JOptionPane.showMessageDialog(null, e.getMessage(),
                                "Error", ERROR_MESSAGE);
                }
        }

        private void initApplet() {
                // This method is supposed to be executed on the
                // event-dispatching thread

                // Create Swing components
                JLabel nameLabel = new JLabel("Your Name:");
                JTextField nameFld = new JTextField(15);
                JButton sayHelloBtn = new JButton("Say Hello");

                // Add an action litener to the button to show the hello message
                sayHelloBtn.addActionListener(e -> sayHello(nameFld.getText()));

                // Add Swing components to the content pane of the applet
                Container contentPane = this.getContentPane();
                contentPane.setLayout(new FlowLayout());
                contentPane.add(nameLabel);
                contentPane.add(nameFld);
                contentPane.add(sayHelloBtn);
        }

        private void sayHello(String name) {
                String msg = "Hello there";
```

```
            if (name.length() > 0) {
                    msg = "Hello " + name;
            }

            // Display the hello message
            JOptionPane.showMessageDialog(null, msg, "Hello", INFORMATION_MESSAGE);
    }
}
```

The choice of using the invokeAndWait() and invokeLater() methods of the SwingUtilities class in other places depends on the situation at hand. As a rule of thumb, you need to execute the code for the init(), start(), stop(), and destroy() methods of your applet in the event-dispatching thread using one of the two methods of the SwingUtilities class. You can use the SwingWorker class to perform any task in a background thread and coordinate with Swing components using the event-dispatching thread. Please refer to the Chapter 3 for details on using threads in a Swing application.

Painting in Applets

The Applet class is inherited from the java.awt.Panel class. The JApplet class is inherited from the Applet class. If you want to draw graphics or strings on an applet surface directly, you need to override its paint(Graphics g) method and write your code. Note that if you add Swing components and draw onto their surface, you need to override the paintComponent(Graphics g) method of those Swing components. Alternatively, you can override the paint() method of the Applet class and perform the drawing as shown in Listing 4-11.

Listing 4-11. An Applet Using the paint() Method to Draw a String

```
// DrawingHelloApplet.java
package com.jdojo.applet;

import javax.swing.JApplet;
import java.awt.Graphics;

public class DrawingHelloApplet extends JApplet {
        @Override
        public void paint(Graphics g) {
                super.paint(g);
                g.drawString("Hello Applet!", 10, 20 );
        }
}
```

Is the Java Code Trusted?

There are two kinds of Java code that may run on your machine: trusted code and untrusted code. There are no hard and fast rules to designate which Java code is always trusted and which one is not. However, there are a few rules you can go by. By default, you should categorize all Java code that your web browser downloads over the Internet to run applets as untrusted because you do not know who wrote the code for the applets. You can categorize all local Java code that is run as applications on your machine as trusted code. The difference between trusted and untrusted code comes into picture when the code tries to access some privileged resources such as the local file system. By default, Java treats all locally stored code as trusted to give full access to the privileged resources. It treats the code downloaded over the network as untrusted. It does not grant access to the privileged resources to untrusted code.

Java lets you grant access to the privileged resources to some code and not to others using policy files. Let's consider an example to understand how you can customize security in Java using policy files. Listing 4-12 contains the code for the SecurityTest class. It writes a text message to a file called c:\sec_demo.txt. The file path is for the Windows platform. You can modify the file path when you run this program according to your choice.

Listing 4-12. A SecurityTest Class That Writes a Text Message to a File

```
// SecurityTest.java
package com.jdojo.applet;

import java.io.IOException;
import java.nio.file.Files;
import java.nio.file.Path;
import java.nio.file.Paths;

public class SecurityTest {
        public static void main(String[] args) throws IOException {
                // Message to be written to the file
                String msg = "Testing Java filee permission security...";

                // Change the path C:\sec_demo.txt to conform to the
                // syntax supported by your operating system
                Path filePath = Paths.get("C:\\sec_demo.txt");

                // Write message to the file
                Files.write(filePath, msg.getBytes());

                // Print a message
                System.out.println("Test message written to " + filePath);
        }
}
```

You can run this class using the following command:

```
java com.jdojo.applet.SecurityTest
```

The above command will print the following message on the standard output:

```
Test message written to c:\sec_demo.txt
```

Running the same SecurityTest class using the following command generates a runtime error. A partial error message is shown:

```
java -Djava.security.manager com.jdojo.applet.SecurityTest

Exception in thread "main" java.security.AccessControlException: access denied
("java.io.FilePermission" "C:\sec_demo.txt" "write")
...
```

You passed -Djava.security.manager as a JVM option when you ran the SecurityTest class the second time. This option tells the JVM to run the class using a security manager. When you ran this class the first time, it was run without a security manager, and the program was able to access the file system and write to a file. When a security manager is present, it checks for the permissions granted to the executing code, which needs to access some resources. Since you have not granted your code the permission to write to a file, you received the security exception when you ran the class the second time.

Policy files control Java security. Two default policy files grant permissions to Java code. JRE_HOME\jre\lib\security\java.policy is a system-wide policy file, where JRE_HOME is the directory where the Java Runtime environment is installed. Another policy file is user-specific and it is stored in USER_HOME\.java.policy, where USER_HOME is the user's home directory defined by a user.home system property. Note the dot in front of the user-specific default Java policy file name (.java.policy). You can also have custom policy files and specify their URLs at the command line when you run your application.

There is a configuration file stored in JRE_HOME\lib\security\java.security that contains detailed information about the default policy files locations and other security related details. The following is the partial content of the java.security file that is supplied with the JRE installation. It states the name of the two Java policy files—one in the Java home directory and one in the user's home directory. You can add some more default policy files to this by following the pattern for the key.

```
# The default is to have a single system-wide policy file,
# and a policy file in the user's home directory.
policy.url.1=file:${java.home}/lib/security/java.policy
policy.url.2=file:${user.home}/.java.policy
```

To make the example work and let it write to a C:\sec_demo.txt file, let's create a file named jsec.policy and add the following text to this file:

```
grant {
        permission java.io.FilePermission "c:\\sec_demo.txt", "read, write";  };
};
```

Save the custom security file as C:\jsec.policy. The grant statement in your custom policy file states the following: grant read and write permissions on C:\sec_demo.txt file to any code. The write permission is good enough to run the example. However, you have granted both read and write permissions in your policy file. Note the two backslashes in the file path (C:\\sec_demo.txt) in the grant statement. The policy file parser will translate the two backslashes into one and the file path will be treated as C:\sec_demo.txt. Run the SecurityTest class with the following command. The entire command is entered in one line.

```
java -Djava.security.manager -Djava.security.policy=file:/C:/jsec.policy com.jdojo.applet.SecurityTest
```

The following message will be printed on the standard output:

```
Test message written to c:\sec_demo.txt
```

This time you instructed the JVM to run the SecurityTest class using a security manager and a policy file at file:/C:/jsec.policy URL. Note that you use a URL to locate a policy file, not a file path. It means you can store your policy files at a web server and use a URL like http://www.jdojo.com/mysec.policy to locate the custom policy file. Note that, by default, the two policy files—one system-wide policy file and one user-specific policy file—are still used along with your custom policy file. If you did not want to create a custom policy file, you could have added the above permissions in any of the two default policy files and the application would have run the same.

I will not discuss Java security policy file formats in detail. JDK/JRE ships with a utility application called policytool that lets you work with a Java policy file graphically. It is installed in the JAVA_HOME\bin folder, where JAVA_HOME is the JDK or JRE installation folder on your machine.

To start the discussion on security restrictions and customization for applets, I will discuss a little more about the policy file format. Here are some more examples of granting permissions in a policy file. You can use Java comments in a policy file as well.

The simplified general syntax of granting permissions in policy files is

```
grant signedby "<signer names>", codebase "<code base URL>" {
        permission <permission class name> "<target name>", "<actions>";
};
```

The text in <...>is supplied by the writer of the policy file. Many of the options are optional. You can include multiple permission clauses in one grant block. You can have multiple grant blocks in one policy file. The signedby option indicates that the permissions are granted only to the code that is signed by the signers. For example, consider the following grant block:

```
grant signedby "John" {
        ...
};
```

The grant block indicates that the permissions are granted if the code is signed by John.
Consider the following grant block:

```
grant signedby "John, Robert, Cheryl" {
        ...
};
```

The grant block indicates that permissions are granted if the code is signed by John, Robert, and Cheryl. I will discuss more about code signing in the next section. If the signedby option is not present, the permissions are granted to the code based on other criteria, irrespective of whether the code is signed or not.

The codebase option is used to grant permissions to the code that is executed from a specific URL. Consider the following grant block:

```
grant codebase "file:/c:/classes" {
        ...
};
```

The grant block indicates that the code from file:/c:/classes URL will be granted the permissions. If the codebase option is not present, permissions are granted to the code that is downloaded and executed from any locations. Some examples of granting permissions in a Java policy file are as follows:

```
/* Grant read and write permission to the file c:\sec_demo.txt
   to code signed or unsigned and downloaded from any location.
*/
grant {
        permission java.io.FilePermission "c:\\sec_demo.txt", "read, write";
};

/* Grant write permission to the file c:\sec_demo.txt to code signed or
   unsigned and downloaded from file:/C:/classes/ URL.
*/
grant codebase "file:/C:/classes/" {
        permission java.io.FilePermission "c:\\sec_demo.txt", "write";
};

/* Grant two permissions to the code signed by John and downloaded
   from the file:/C:/classes/ URL.
```

1. Grant the execute permission on the file c:\crazy.exe
2. Grant the read permission for the system property user.home, so
   the code can execute the statement System.getProperty("user.home").
   If this permission is not granted, reading the property "user.home"
   will throw a security exception.
```
*/
grant signedby "John", codebase "file:/C:/classes/" {
        permission java.io.FilePermission "c:\\crazy.exe", "execute";
        permission java.util.PropertyPermission "user.home", "read";
};
```

You can grant java.io.FilePermission to a file or directory. You can use a file or directory path and a set of actions to grant the permissions on a file. You can grant any combinations of read, write, delete, and execute permissions on a file/directory. Multiple actions are separated by a comma. A policy file supports different formats to specify a file/directory path, such as those listed in Table 4-2.

Table 4-2. *The List of File/Directory Path Format Used in Granting the java.io.FilePermission*

File/Directory Path Format	Description
File path: C:\mydir\test.txt	Grants permissions only on this file.
Directory path: C:\mydir or C:\mydir\	Grants permissions only on this directory. (One trailing file separator is treated the same as no trailing separator for a directory. It is a forward slash on UNIX such as /usr/mydir or /usr/mydir/, and a backslash on Windows.
C:\mydir*	Grants permissions on all files under the C:\mydir directory. Note that it does not grant permissions on the C:\mydir directory itself.
*	Grants permissions on all files under the current directory.
C:\mydir\-	Grants permissions to all files and folders under C:\mydir and its subdirectories, recursively.
-	Grants permissions to all files and folders under the current directory and its subdirectories, recursively.

<<ALL FILES>>	Grants permissions on all files and folders under the file system. For example, the following grant clause grants read permission to all code on all files in the file system:
	
	`grant {`
	`    permission java.io.FilePermission "<<ALL FILES>>", "read";`
	`};`

Security Restrictions for Applets

By default, the code for an applet is treated as untrusted code and it is run under a security manager. If you run an applet from a local file system using a file protocol, the browser may relax some of these restrictions. These restrictions apply if the applet's code is downloaded using a network protocol such as http or https. The code for an applet that is downloaded over the network is considered untrusted by default, even if the web server from which the code is downloaded is running locally. The following is a partial list of restrictions that are applied to untrusted code and applets:

- It cannot access a local file system.

- It cannot connect to any machine, except the machine from which its code was downloaded.

- It cannot load a native library.

- It cannot start a program on the machine it is running on.

- It can read only a few system properties, which are considered harmless. It can read system properties, such as the OS.name, OS.version, java.version, etc. It cannot read potentially risky system properties, such as user.home, user.dir, java.class.path, etc.

- It cannot exit the JVM using the System.exit() method call.

- It displays pop-up windows with some visual hints to the users to indicate that the pop-up windows are being displayed from an applet and it is untrusted.

How can an applet perform some of the tasks that are restricted? There are two ways to let an applet perform the otherwise restricted tasks:

- You can customize the policy file and grant the specific permissions.

- You can use a signed applet.

Listing 4-13 contains the code for an applet that attempts to read the user.home system property. Listing 4-14 contains the HTML code to view the applet.

Listing 4-13. An Applet That Attempts to Read the user.home System Property

```
// ReadUserHomeApplet.java
package com.jdojo.applet;

import javax.swing.JApplet;
import javax.swing.JTextArea;
import java.io.StringWriter;
import java.io.PrintWriter;
import javax.swing.JScrollPane;
import java.awt.Container;

public class ReadUserHomeApplet extends JApplet {
        JTextArea msgTextArea = null;

        @Override
        public void init() {
                String msg = "";
                try {
                        String userHome = System.getProperty("user.home");
                        msg = "User's Home Directory is '" + userHome + "'";
                }
                catch (Throwable t) {
                        msg = this.getStackTrace(t);
                }
```

```
                this.msgTextArea = new JTextArea(msg, 10, 40);
                Container contentPane = this.getContentPane();
                contentPane.add(new JScrollPane(msgTextArea));
        }

        public String getStackTrace(Throwable t) {
                StringWriter sw = new StringWriter();
                PrintWriter pw = new PrintWriter(sw, true);
                t.printStackTrace(pw);
                pw.close();
                return sw.toString();
        }
}
```

Listing 4-14. Contents of the readuserhomeapplet.html File Used to View the ReadUserHomeApplet Applet

```
<html>
        <head>
                <title>Read User Home Directory</title>
        </head>
        <body>
                <applet code="com.jdojo.applet.ReadUserHomeApplet"
                        width="400"
                        height="300">
                        This browser does not support Applets.
                </applet>
        </body>
</html>
```

The applet code in Listing 4-13 is very simple. It uses the System.getProperty("user.home") method to read the user's home directory. By default, an applet is not allowed to read the user.home system property. When you view this applet, you get a security exception. The partial exception message is as follows:

```
java.security.AccessControlException: access denied ("java.util.PropertyPermission" "user.home"
"read")
...
```

The exception message is stating that the applet's code does not have a read permission of type java.util. PropertyPermission to read the user.home system property. The following grant block grants this permission to all code:

```
grant {
        permission java.util.PropertyPermission "user.home", "read";
};
```

Add this grant block to a .java.policy file in your home directory. If a .java.policy file does not exist in your home directory, you can create a new file with this name and add the above grant to it. On Windows XP, your home directory is C:\Documents and Settings\<your-user- name>. You can also get your user's home directory path by executing System.getProperty("user.home") statement in a standalone Java application that is not running under a security manager. After adding the above grant in a .java.policy file in the user's home directory, the ReadUserHomeApplet applet displays a message similar to the following:

```
User's Home Directory is 'C:\Documents and Settings\sharan'
```

Make sure that you remove the grant block from your .java.policy file after working on this example. Otherwise, any applet will be able to read your user's home directory on your machine without your knowledge. I will go through the same example in the next section using a signed applet.

Signing Applets

When an applet is run in a browser, it cannot access anything on the client's machine, except some information like OS name, version of the JVM, etc. When you want to give access to an applet the same as a Java application, you need to use a signed applet.

The concept behind a signed applet is the same as the concept behind a signed document. By signing a document, you approve it, and, by approving it, you take responsibility for what is contained in the document. It does not guarantee that someone else cannot tamper with the document after you have signed it. However, in case of any doubts about the document's authenticity, you can be contacted for verification. Whoever can verify your signature and trusts you can take your signed document to be authentic. The concept works the same for an applet. Recall that an applet's code is untrusted by default. If an applet is a signed applet, the user of the applet grants permissions to a signed applet in a Java policy file or he can trust the applet and grant permissions on the fly.

Before you can sign an applet, you must have a key pair called private/public key. You can generate a key pair using the keytool command that is installed in JAVA_HOME\bin folder, where JAVA_HOME is the folder in which you have installed the JDK or JRE. The generated keys are stored in a database known as a *keystore*. The keytool command also lets you create a keystore database. The private key is a secret key for you and the public key is for the public who wants to verify your signature. Once you have a key pair, you need to generate a certificate request (you can use the keytool command with a -certreq option to generate a certificate request) to send to a Certification Authority (CA) to get a certificate. A CA is an organization that issues a digital certificate. The digital certificate comprises the public key supplied by you and your identity. CA will charge you a moderate fee for issuing the certificate. DigiCert, Thawte, and VeriSign are some of the CAs available. You can also issue a certificate yourself and this is what you will do for the demonstration purpose in this section. However, if you are deploying your applet on the web for public use, you need to spend some money and get a certificate from a trusted CA to add more authenticity to your applet's signature. It is more likely that the public will trust a certificate issued by Thawte, rather than by you. Note starting from Java 7, your applet must be signed, packages in a JAR file with a manifest file having the attribute Permissions. Otherwise, your applet will not run by default.

You need to package your applet classes into a JAR file so that you can sign it. You can sign the JAR file with your secret private key using the jarsigner command that is available under the JAVA_HOME\bin folder, where JAVA_HOME is the installation folder for JDK or JRE. There are other tools available that you can use to sign a JAR file. The signing process will place the certificate and the public key in the JAR file for the users of the JAR file to verify the signature.

The following steps walk you through the process of signing and using an applet.

Step 1: Developing an Applet

You need to write the applet's source code and compile it to class files. Use the ReadUserHomeApplet class as listed in Listing 4-13. At the end of this step, you will have a ReadUserHomeApplet.class file.

Step 2: Packaging Class Files into a JAR File

Create a `manifest.mf` file with the following contents. Remember to add a blank line at the end of the file.

```
Manifest-Version: 1.0
Permissions: sandbox
```

Use the following command to create a `signedapplet.jar` file. The `jar` command is available in your `JDK_HOME\bin` folder.

```
jar cvfm signedapplet.jar manifest.mf com/jdojo/applet/ReadUserHomeApplet.class
```

Make sure that, in the JAR file, the path for the class file is set to `com/jdojo/applet`, which is the same as its package. To make sure that your JAR file contains the correct path for the class file, use the following command:

```
jar -tf signedapplet.jar
```

```
META-INF/
META-INF/MANIFEST.MF
com/jdojo/applet/ReadUserHomeApplet.class
```

At the end of this step, you will have a `signedapplet.jar` file.

Step 3: Generating Private/Public Key Pair

Use the `keytool` command to generate a private/public key pair as follows:

```
keytool -genkey -keystore mykeystore –alias Kishori
```

The above command will create a keystore file named `mykeystore`. It will generate a private/public key pair, which you can work with using an alias `Kishori`. Note that you need to specify an alias for your key pair. From now on, you will use the alias, `Kishori` in this case, to refer to your key in your keystore. The above command will ask for details that will identify you. You will need to enter those pieces of information. The keystore file is password protected. The private key is also password protected. You will need to use new passwords when you use the above command. Memorize those passwords because you will be asked for those passwords to access the keystore or the key pair referred to by alias `Kishori`.

You can certify the generated key yourself by using the following command:

```
keytool -keystore mykeystore -selfcert –alias Kishori
```

At the end of this step, you will have a file named `mykeystore` and you will have generated a key pair with an alias `Kishori`.

Step 4: Signing the JAR File

Use the following command to sign the JAR file:

```
jarsigner -keystore mykeystore signedapplet.jar Kishori
```

The above command will prompt you for a keystore password. At the end of this step, you will have a signed signedapplet.jar file. If you list the table of contents for the signedapplet.jar file, you will notice that the jarsigner command has added more files to it, as shown:

```
jar -tf signedapplet.jar

META-INF/MANIFEST.MF
META-INF/KISHORI.SF
META-INF/KISHORI.DSA
META-INF/
com/jdojo/applet/ReadUserHomeApplet.class
```

Step 5: Creating the HTML File

Create an HTML file to view the signed applet, as shown in Listing 4-15. Note the use of an archive attribute for the <applet> tag.

Listing 4-15. Contents of the signedreaduserhomeapplet.html File

```
<html>
        <head>
                <title>Read User Home Directory (signed Applet)</title>
        </head>
        <body>
                <applet code="com.jdojo.applet.ReadUserHomeApplet"
                        width="400" hcight="300"
                        archive="signedapplet.jar">
                        This browser does not support Applets.
                </applet>
        </body>
</html>
```

Step 6: Viewing the Signed Applet

A security-warning window is displayed by Java Plug-in when you attempt to view a signed applet. It lets you view the details of the signature that is used to sign the applet. You can click the Run button to run the applet. Checking "Always trust content from this publisher" checkbox and clicking Run will make Java Plug-in import the certificate as a trusted certificate, as shown in Figure 4-10.

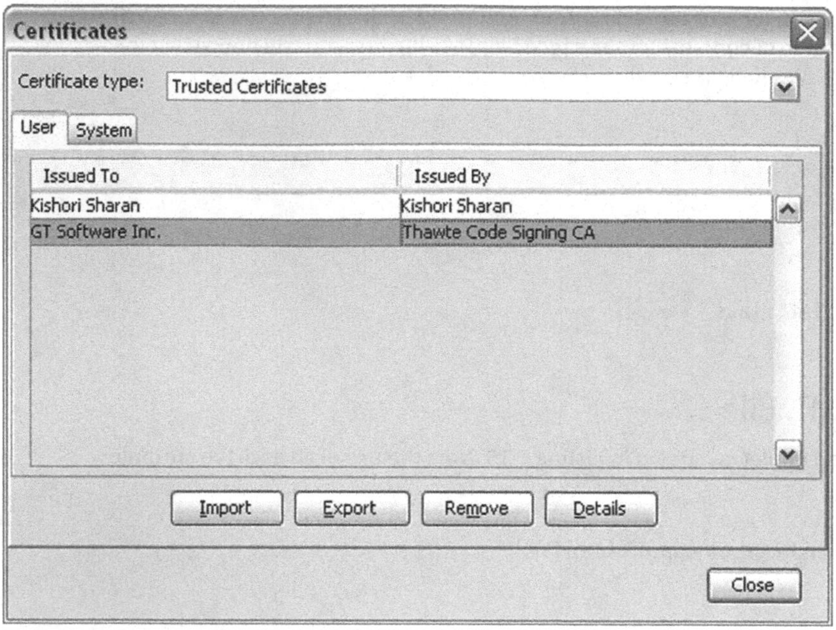

Figure 4-10. *The Certificates dialog in the Java Control Panel*

Once Java Plug-in stores the certificate in its trusted certificate repository, it will trust this certificate in the future without prompting you. You can delete a once-trusted certificate from the repository later by going to Java Control Panel ➤ Security Tab ➤ Manager Certificate.

By trusting a signed applet, you give all permissions to it. If you still want to apply permissions using a Java policy file to a signed and trusted applet, you need to use the usePolicy java.lang.RuntimePermission in the Java policy file, which will direct Java Plug-in not to prompt the user to accept the signed applet's certificate. Rather, it will apply the permissions granted to that applet from the policy file.

The following entry in the policy file (system-wide or user specific policy file) will direct Java Plug-in to use the policy file all the time:

```
grant {
        permission java.lang.RuntimePermission "usePolicy";
};
```

Your applet will be able to access resources as granted by you in the policy file. Java Plug-in will not prompt the user to trust an applet.

You can also direct Java Plug-in not to prompt users to grant access to a signed applet by switching off its "Allow user to grant permission to signed content" option by going to Java Control Panel ➤ Advanced Tab ➤ Secure User Environment. If this option is unchecked, users will get a security warning when they try to view the applet. By default, this option is enabled.

Summary

An applet is a Java program designed to be embedded in an HTML document and run in a web browser. Technically, an applet is a Java class that inherits from the `Applet` or `JApplet` class. If you inherit your applet's class from the `JApplet` class, writing code for applets is very similar to writing for Swing applications. Applets use Swing components to build the GUI.

An applet is embedded in an HTML document using the `<applet>` tag. The HTML document may be a static HTML file or generated dynamically such as in a JSP page. Typically, an applet's Java class files and resources such as images and audios are packaged in JAR files and stored on the web server. On the client machine, the browser requests the HTML document, parses the `<applet>` tag in the HTML document, downloads the applet's code, and runs the code inside the browser. By default, applets run in a security sandbox and they do not have access the client's machine resources such as the local file system. These restrictions may be relaxed using the Java policy files or signing the applet's JAR files.

The `<applet>` tag is used to embed an applet in an HTML document. The `<applet>` tag contains four mandatory attributes called `code`, `width`, `height`, and `archive`. The `code` attribute specifies the fully qualified name of the applet class. The `width` and `height` attributes specify the width and height of the applet's display area in the browser. The `archive` attribute specifies the archive files (JAR/ZIP) containing the applet's files. Note that the `archive` attribute is mandatory if you want to run your applet using the default Java Plug-in settings.

You need to install Java Plug-in (part of the JRE) to run the applets in the browser on your machine. You can configure Java Plug-in using the Java Control Panel program that is installed with Java Plug-in.

An applet has a life cycle. Its four methods called `init()`, `start()`, `stop()`, and `destroy()` are automatically called during its life cycle. The `init()` method is called by the browser after the applet has been instantiated and loaded. The `start()` method is called just after the `init()` method, and it may be called multiple times. The `stop()` method is the counterpart of the `start()` method, and it may be called multiple times. The `destroy()` method is called at the end of the life cycle of an applet when the applet is destroyed. These methods are not called on the event-dispatching thread. Use the `SwingUtilities` class, which was described in Chapter 3, to run any GUI-related code in the event-dispatching thread.

An instance of `AppletContext` object represents the context of the applet ruing it. You can use this object to interact with the applet's context such as the browser from the Java code.

In Java 7 and later, by default, applets are blocked if the following conditions are not met:

- The applet should be packaged in a signed JAR file.

- The manifest file in the applet's JAR file should contain a `Permissions` attribute whose value can be `sandbox` or `all-permissions`.

- The applet's JAR file should be signed with a certificate issues by a trusted authority.

You can relax these restrictions, though it's not recommended, by configuring Java Plug-in settings using the Java Control Panel.

CHAPTER 5

∎∎∎

Network Programming

In this chapter, you will learn

- What network programming is

- What the network protocol suite is

- What an IP address is and what the different IP addressing schemes are

- Special IP addresses and their uses

- What port numbers are and how they are used

- Using TCP and UDP client and server sockets for communication between remote computers

- The definitions of URI, URL, and URN and how to represent them in Java programs

- How to use non-blocking sockets

- How to use asynchronous socket channels

- Datagram-oriented socket channels and multicast datagram channels

The first few sections are intended to give a quick overview of basics related to network technologies for those readers who do not have a computer science background. If you understand terms like IP address, port number, network protocol suites, etc., you may skip these sections and start reading from the "Socket API and Client-Server Paradigm" section.

What Is Network Programming?

A network is a group of two or more computers or other types of electronic devices such as printers that are linked together with a goal to share information. Each device linked to a network is called a *node*. A computer that is linked to a network is called a *host*. Network programming in Java involves writing Java programs that facilitate the exchange of information between processes running on different computers on the network.

Java makes it easy to write network programs. Sending a message to a process running on another computer is as simple as writing data to a local file system. Similarly, receiving a message that was sent from a process running in another computer is as simple as reading data from a local file system. Most of the programs in this chapter will involve reading and writing data over the network, and they are similar to file I/O. Please refer to Chapters 7 through 10 in the book *Beginning Java Language Features* (ISBN: 978-1-4302-6658-7) for more details on file I/O. You will learn about a few new classes in this chapter that facilitate the communication between two computers on a network.

You do not need to have advanced level knowledge of networking technologies to understand or write Java programs in this chapter. This chapter covers high-level details of a few things that are involved in network communication.

A network can be categorized based on different criteria. Based on the geographical area that a network is spread over, it is categorized as

- *Local Area Network (LAN)*: It covers a small area such as a building or a block of buildings.

- *Campus Area Network (CAN)*: It covers a campus such as a university campus, interconnecting multiple LANs within that campus.

- *Metropolitan Area Network (MAN)*: It covers more geographical area than a LAN. Usually, it covers a city.

- *Wide Area Network (WAN)*: It covers a larger geographical area such as a region of a country or multiple regions in different countries in the world.

When two or more networks are connected using routers (also known as gateways), it is called *internetworking*, and the resulting combined network is called an *internetwork,* in short, *internet* (note the lowercase i). The global internetwork, which encompasses all networks in the world connected together, is referred to as the *Internet* (note the uppercase I).

Based on the topology (the arrangement of nodes in a network), a network may be categorized as *star*, *tree*, *ring*, *bus*, *hybrid*, etc.

Based on the technology a network uses to transmit the data, it can be categorized as *Ethernet, LocalTalk, Fiber Distributed Data Interface (FDDI), Token Ring, Asynchronous Transfer Mode (ATM)*, etc.

I will not cover any details about the different kinds of networks. Please refer to any standard textbook on networks to learn more about networks and network technologies in detail.

Communication between two processes on a computer is simple and it is achieved using interprocess communication as defined by the operating system. It is a very tedious task when two processes running on two different computers on an internet need to communicate. You need to consider many aspects of the communication before the two processes on two computers on an internet may start communicating. Some of the points that you need to consider are as follows:

- The two computers may be using different technologies such as different operating systems, different hardware, etc.

- They may be on two different networks that use different network technologies.

- They may be separated by many other networks, which may be using different technologies. That is, two computers are not on two networks that are interconnected directly. You need to consider not just two networks, but all networks that the data from one computer has to pass to reach another computer.

- They may be a few miles apart or on other sides of the globe. How do you transmit the information efficiently without worrying about the distance between the two computers?

- One computer may not understand the information sent by the other computer.

- The information sent over a network may be duplicated, delayed, or lost. How should the receiver and the sender handle these abnormal situations?

Simply put, two computers on a network communicate using messages (sequences of 0s and 1s). There must be well-defined rules to handle the above-mentioned issues (and many more). The set of rules to handle a specific task is known as a *protocol*. Many types of tasks are involved in handling network communication. There is a protocol defined to handle each specific task. There is a stack of protocols (also called *protocol suite*) that are used together to handle a network communication.

Network Protocol Suite

Modern networks are called *packet switching networks* because they transmit data in chunks called *packets*. Each packet is transmitted independent of other packets. This makes it easy to transmit the packets from the same computer to the same destination using different routes. However, it may become a problem if a computer sends two packets to a remote computer and the second packet arrives before the first one. For this reason, each packet also has a packet number along with its destination address. There are rules to rearrange the out-of-order arrival of the packets at the destination computer. The following discussion attempts to explain some of the mechanisms that are used to handle packets in a network communication.

Figure 5-1 shows a layered protocol suite called the *Internet Reference Model* or *TCP/IP Layering Model*. This is the most widely used protocol suite. Each layer in the model performs a well-defined task. The main advantage of having a layered protocol model is that any layer can be changed without affecting others. A new protocol can be added to any layer without changing other layers.

Application
Transport
Internet
Network Interface
Physical

Figure 5-1. *The Internet Protocol Suite showing its five protocol layers*

Each layer knows about only the layer immediately above and below it. Each layer in the protocol suite has two interfaces—one for the layer above it and one for the layer below it. For example, the transport layer has interfaces to the application layer and internet layer. That is, the transport layer knows how to communicate only with the application layer and the internet layer. It knows nothing about the network interface layer or the physical layer.

A user application such as a Java program uses the application layer to communicate to a remote application. The user application has to specify the protocol that it wants to use to communicate with the remote application. A protocol in an application layer defines the rules for formatting messages and associating the meaning to the information contained in the messages such as the message type, describing whether it is a request or a response, etc. After the application layer formats the message, it hands over the message to the transport layer. The examples of protocols in an application layer are Hypertext Transfer Protocol (HTTP), File Transfer Protocol (FTP), Gopher, Telecommunication Network (Telnet), Simple Mail Transfer Protocol (SMTP), and Network News Transfer Protocol (NNTP).

The transport layer protocol handles the ways messages are transported from one application on one computer to another application on the remote computer. It controls the data flow, error handling during data transmission, and connections between two applications. For example, a user application may hand over a very large chunk of data to the transport layer to transmit to a remote application. The remote computer may not be able to handle that large amount of data at once. It is the responsibility of the transport layer to pass a suitable amount of data at a time to the remote computer, so the remote application can handle the data according to its capacity. The data passed to the remote computer over a network may be lost on its way due to various reasons. It is the responsibility of the transport layer to retransmit the lost data. Note that the application layer passes data to be transmitted to the transport layer only once. It is the transport layer (not the application layer) that keeps track of the delivered and the lost data during a transmission. There may be multiple applications running, all of which use different protocols and exchange information with different remote applications. It is the responsibility of the transport layer to hand over messages sent to a remote application correctly. For example, you may be browsing the Internet using the HTTP protocol from one remote web server and downloading a file using the FTP protocol from another FTP server. Your computer is receiving messages from two remote computers and they are meant for two different applications running on your computer—one web browser to receive HTTP data and one FTP application to receive FTP data. It is the responsibility of the transport layer to pass the incoming data to the appropriate application. You can see how different layers of the protocol suite play different roles in data transmission over the network. Depending on the transport layer protocol being used, the transport layer adds relevant information to the message and passes it to the next layer, which is the internet layer. The examples of protocols used in the transport layer are Transmission Control Protocol (TCP), User Datagram Protocol (UDP), and Stream Control Transmission Protocol (SCTP).

The internet layer accepts the messages from the transport layer and prepares a packet suitable for sending over the internet. It includes the Internet Protocol (IP). The packet prepared by the IP is also known as an IP datagram. It consists of a header and a data area, apart from other pieces of information. The header contains the sender's IP address, destination IP address, time to live (TTL, which an integer), a header checksum, and many other pieces of information specified in the protocol. The IP prepares the message into datagrams, which are ready to be transmitted over the internet. The TTL in the IP datagram header specifies how long, in terms of the number of routers, an IP datagram can keep traveling before it needs to be discarded. Its size is one byte and its value could be between 1 and 255. When an IP datagram reaches a router in its route to the destination, the router decrements the TTL value by 1. If the decremented value is zero, the router discards the datagram and sends an error message back to the sender using Internet Control Message Protocol (ICMP). If the TTL value is still a positive number, the router forwards the datagram to the next router. The IP uses an address scheme, which assigns a unique address to each computer. The address is called an IP address. I will discuss the IP addressing scheme in detail in the next section. The internet layer hands over the IP datagram to the next layer, which is the network interface layer. The examples of protocols in an internet layer are Internet Protocol (IP), Internet Control Message Protocol (ICMP), Internet Group Management Protocol (IGMP), and Internet Protocol Security (IPsec).

The network interface layer prepares a packet to be transmitted on the network. The packet is called a *frame*. The network interface layer sits just on top of the physical layer, which involves the hardware. Note that the IP layer uses the IP address to identify the destination on a network. An IP address is a virtual address, which is completely maintained in software. The hardware is unaware of the IP address and it does not know how to transmit a frame using an IP address. The hardware must be given the hardware address, also called *Media Access Control* (MAC) address, of the destination that it needs to transmit the frame to. This layer resolves the destination hardware address from the IP address and places it in the frame header. It hands over the frame to the physical layer. The examples of protocols in a network interface layer are Open Shortest Path First (OSPF), Point-to-Point Protocol (PPP), Point-to-Point Tunneling Protocol (PPTP), and Layer 2 Tunneling Protocol (L2TP).

The physical layer consists of the hardware. It is responsible for converting the bits of information into signals and transmitting the signal over the wire.

■ **Tip** *Packet* is a generic term that is used to mean an independent chunk of data in network programming. Each layer of protocol also uses a specific term to mean the packet it deals with. For example, a packet is called a *segment* in the TCP layer; it is called a *datagram* in the IP layer; it is called a *frame* in the network interface and physical layers. Each layer adds a header (sometimes also a trailer) to the packet it receives from the layer before it, while preparing the packet to be transmitted over the network. Each layer performs the reverse action when it receives a packet from the layer below it. It removes the header from the packet; performs some actions, if needed; and hands over the packet to the layer above it.

When a packet sent by an application reaches the remote computer, it has to pass through the same layer of protocols in the reverse order. Each layer will remove its header, perform some actions, and pass the packet to the layer immediately above it. Finally, the packet reaches the remote application in the same format it started from the application on the sender's computer. Figure 5-2 shows the transmission of packets from the sender and the receiver computer. P1, P2, P3, and P4 are the packets in different formats of the same data. A protocol layer at a destination receives the same packet from the layer immediately below it, which the same protocol layer had passed to the layer immediately below it on the sender's computer.

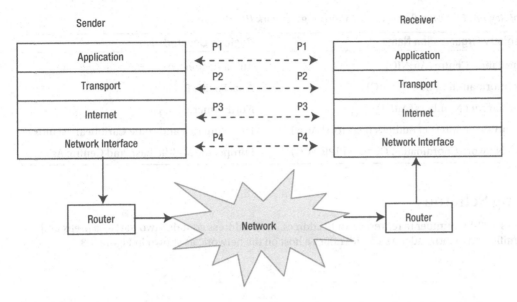

Figure 5-2. *Transmission of packets through the protocol layers on the sender's and receiver's computers*

IP Addressing Scheme

IP uses a unique address, called an IP address, to route an IP datagram to the destination. An IP address uniquely identifies a connection between a computer and a router. Normally, it is understood that an IP address identifies a computer. However, it should be emphasized that it identifies a connection between a computer and a router, not just a computer. A router is also assigned an IP address. A computer can be connected to multiple networks using multiple routers and each connection between the computer and the router will have a unique IP address. In such cases, the computer will be assigned multiple IP addresses and the computer is known as *multi-homed*. Multi-homing increases the availability of the network connection to a computer. If one network connection fails, the computer can use other available network connections.

An IP address contains two parts—a network identifier (I will call it a prefix) and a host identifier (I will call it a suffix). The prefix identifies a network on the Internet uniquely; the suffix identifies a host uniquely within that network. It is possible for two hosts to have IP addresses with the same suffix as long as they have a different prefix.

There are two versions of Internet Protocol—IPv4 (or simply IP) and IPv6, where v4 and v6 stand for version 4 and version 6. IPv6 is also known as Internet Protocol next generation (IPng). Note that there is no IPv5. When IP was in its full swing of popularity, it was at version 4. Before IPng was assigned a version number 6, version 5 was already assigned to another protocol called Internet Stream Protocol (ST).

Both IPv4 and IPv6 use an IP address to identify a host on a network. However, the addressing schemes in the two versions differ significantly. The next two sections will discuss the addressing schemes used by IPv4 and IPv6.

Since an IP address must be unique, its assignment is controlled by an organization called *Internet Assigned Numbers Authority* (IANA). IANA assigns a unique address to each network that belongs to an organization. The organization uses the network address and a unique number to form a unique IP address for each host on the network. IANA divides the IP address allocations to five Regional Internet Registry (RIR) organizations, which allocate IP addresses in specific regions as listed in Table 5-1. You can find more information on how to get a network address in your area from IANA at www.iana.com.

Table 5-1. The List of Regional Internet Registries for Allocating Network IP Addresses

Regional Internet Registry Organization Name	Regions Covered
African Network Information Centre (AfriNIC)	Africa Region
Asia-Pacific Network Information Centre (APNIC)	Asia/Pacific Region
American Registry for Internet Numbers (ARIN)	North America Region
Latin American and Caribbean Internet Address Registry (LACNIC)	Latin America and some Caribbean Islands
Réseaux IP Européens Network Coordination Centre (RIPE NCC)	Europe, the Middle East, and Central Asia

IPv4 Addressing Scheme

IPv4 (or simply IP) uses a 32-bit number to represent an IP address. An IP address contains two parts—a prefix and a suffix. The prefix identifies a network and the suffix identifies a host on the network, as shown in Figure 5-3.

```
0 1 2 3 4 5 6 7 8 9 10 ... 21 22 23 24 25 26 27 28 29 30 31
|              Prefix              |          Suffix          |
```

Figure 5-3. IPv4 addressing scheme

It is not easy for humans to remember a 32-bit number in binary format. IPv4 allows you to work with an alternate form using four decimal numbers. Each decimal number is in the range from 0 to 255. Programs take care of converting decimal numbers into a 32-bit binary number that will be used by the computer. The decimal number format of IPv4 is called dotted decimal format because a dot is used to separate two decimal numbers. Each decimal number represents the value contained in 8 bits of the 32-bit number. For example, an IPv4 address of 11000000101010000000000111100111 in the binary format can be represented as 192.168.1.231 in the dotted ·decimal format. The process of converting binary IPv4 to its decimal equivalent is shown in Figure 5-4. In 192.168.1.231, the part 192.168.1 identifies the network address (the prefix) and the part 231 (the suffix) identifies the host on that network.

32-bit Binary Representation	11000000	10101000	00000001	11100111
Decimal Value of Each Octet	192	168	1	231
Parts of IPv4 Address	Prefix			Suffix
Alternate Representation of IPv4	192.168.1.231			

Figure 5-4. Parts of an IPv4 address in binary and decimal formats

How do you know that 192.168.1 represents a prefix in an IPv4 address 192.168.1.231? A rule governs the value of a prefix and a suffix in an IPv4. I will discuss how to identify a prefix and suffix in an IPv4 later in this section, when I discuss the class type of a network.

How does an IPv4 address divide its 32 bits between a prefix and a suffix? IPv4 address space is divided in five categories called network classes, named A, B, C, D, and E. A class type defines how many bits of the 32 bits will be used to represent the network address part of an IP address. The leading bit (or bits) in the prefix defines the class of the IP address. This is also known as a *self-identifying* or *classful* IP address because you can tell which class it belongs to by looking at the IP address.

Table 5-2 lists the five network classes and their characteristics in IPv4. The leading bits in an IP address identify the class of the network. For example, if an IP address looks like 0XXX, where XXX is the last 31 bits of the 32 bits, it belongs to the class A network; if an IP address looks like 110XXX, where XXX is the last 29 bits of 32 bits, it belongs to the class C network. There can be only 128 networks of class A type and each network can have 16777214 hosts. The number of hosts that a class A network can have is very big and it is very unlikely that a network will have that many hosts. In a class C type of network, the maximum number of hosts that a network can have is limited to 254.

Table 5-2. *Five Classes of IPv4 in the Classful Addressing Scheme*

Network Class	Prefix	Suffix	Leading Bit(s) in Prefix	Number of Networks	Number of Hosts per Network
A	8 bits	24 bits	0	128	16777214
B	16 bits	16 bits	10	16384	65534
C	24 bits	8 bits	110	2097152	254
D	Not Defined	Not defined	1110	Not defined	Not defined
E	Not Defined	Not defined	1111	Not defined	Not defined

What happens if an organization is assigned a network address from class C and it has only 10 hosts to attach to the network? The remaining slots in the IP addresses in that network remain unused. Recall that the host (or suffix) part in an IP address must be unique within the network (the prefix part). On the other hand, if an organization needs to connect 300 computers to a network, it needs to get two class C network addresses because getting a class B network address, which can accommodate 65534 hosts, will again waste a great many IP addresses.

Note that if the number of bits allocated for a suffix is N, the number of hosts that can be used is $2^N - 2$. Two bits patterns—all 0s and all 1s—cannot be used for a host address. They are used for special purposes. This is the reason a class C network can have a maximum of 254 hosts and not 256. Class D addresses are used as multicast addresses. Class E addresses are reserved.

The fast growth of the Internet and the large number of IP addresses not being used prompted for a new addressing scheme. This scheme is simply based on one criterion—one should be able to use an arbitrary boundary between the prefix and suffix parts of an IP address, instead of predefined boundaries at 8, 16, and 24 bits. This will keep the unused addresses at a minimum. For example, if an organization needs a network number for a network with only 20 hosts, that organization can use only a 27-bit prefix and a 5-bit suffix.

Two terminologies called *subnetting* and *supernetting* are used to describe the situations when some bits from the suffix are used for the prefix and some bits from the prefix are used as the suffix. When bits from the suffix are used as the prefix, essentially, it creates more network addresses at the cost of host addresses. The extra network addresses are called *subnets*. Subnetting is achieved by using a number called a *subnet mask* or an *address mask*. A subnet mask is a 32-bit number that is used to compute the network address from an IP address. Using a subnet mask eliminates the restriction that the class of a network must predefine the network number part of the IP address. A logical AND is performed on the IP address and the subnet mask to compute the network number. In this scheme of addressing, an IP address is always specified with its subnet mask. A forward slash and subnet mask follows an IP address. For example, 140.10.11.9/255.255.0.0 denotes an IP address of 140.10.11.9 with a subnet mask 255.255.0.0. It is possible to use any subnet mask whose four decimal parts ranges from 0 to 255. In this example, 140.10.11.9 is a class B address. A class B address uses 16 bits for the prefix and 16 bits for the suffix. Let's take 6 bits off the suffix and add it to the prefix. Now, the prefix is 22 bits and the suffix is only 10 bits. By doing this, you have created additional network numbers at the cost of host numbers. To describe an IP address in this scheme of subnetting, you need to use a subnet mask of 255.255.252.0. If you write an IP address using this subnet mask as 140.10.11.9/255.255.252.0, the network address is computed as 140.10.8.0, like so:

```
IP Address:   10001100 00001010 00001011 00001001
Subnet Mask: 11111111 11111111 11111100 00000000
-------------------------------------------------
Logical AND: 10001100 00001010 00001000 00000000
                (140)    (10)     (8)      (0)
```

Classless Inter-Domain Routing (CIDR) is another IPv4 addressing scheme in which an IPv4 address is specified as four dotted decimal numbers along with another decimal number separated by a forward slash such as 192.168.1.231/24, where the last number 24 denotes the prefix-length (or number of bits used for a network number) in the 32-bit IPv4 address. Note that the CIDR addressing scheme lets you define the prefix/suffix boundary at any bits in 32-bit IPv4. By moving the bits from the prefix to the suffix, you can combine multiple networks and increase the number of hosts per network. This is called *supernetting*. You can create supernets as well as subnets using CIDR notation.

Some IP addresses in an IPv4 addressing scheme are reserved for broadcast and multicast IP addresses. I will discuss broadcasting and multicasting later in this chapter.

IPv6 Addressing Scheme

IPv6 is a new version of IP and it is the successor for IPv4. The address space in IPv4 was running out of addresses in the fast growing Internet world. IPv6 is aimed at providing enough address space, so that every computer in the world may get a unique IP address in the decades to come. Here are some of the main features of IPv6:

- IPv6 uses a 128-bit number for an IP address instead of a 32-bit number used in IPv4.

- It has different header formats for IP packets than IPv4. IPv4 has only one header per datagram, whereas IPv6 has one base header followed by multiple variable-length extension headers per datagram.

- IPv6 supports datagrams of a bigger size than IPv4.

- In IPv4, the routers performed an IP packet fragmentation. In IPv6, the sender host is supposed to perform a packet fragmentation rather than the routers. This means that the host that uses IPv6 must know in advance the path of the maximum transmission unit (MTU) that is the minimum of the maximum packet size allowed by all networks to the destination host. The IP datagram's fragmentation occurs when it has to enter a network that has a lower size transmission capacity than the network the datagram is leaving. In IPv4, the fragmentation is performed by the router, which detects a lower transmission capacity network in the route. Since IPv6 allows only the host to perform the fragmentation, the host must discover the minimum size datagram that can be routed through all possible routes from the source to the destination host.

- IPv6 supports specifying routing information for the datagrams in the headers so that routers can use it to route the datagrams through a specific route. This feature is helpful in delivering time-critical information.

- IPv6 is extensible. Any number of extension headers can be added to an IPv6 datagram, which can be interpreted in a new way.

IPv6 uses a 128-bit IP address. It uses an easy-to-understand notation to represent an IP address in a textual form. The 128 bits are divided into 8 fields of 16 bits each. Each field is written in hexadecimal form and separated by a colon. The following are some examples of IPv6 addresses:

- `F6DC:0:0:4015:0:BA98:C0A8:1E7`

- `F6DC:0:0:7678:0:0:0:A21D`

- `F6DC:0:0:0:0:0:0:A21D`

- `0:0:0:0:0:0:0:1`

It is common to have many fields in an IPv6 address with zero values, especially for all IPv4 addresses. The IPv6 address notation lets you compress contiguous fields of zero values by using two consecutive colons. You can use two colons to suppress contiguous zero value fields only once in an address. The above IPv6 address may be rewritten using the zero compression technique:

- `F6DC::4015:0:BA98:C0A8:1E7`

- `F6DC:0:0:7678::A21D`

- `F6DC::A21D`

- `::1`

Note that we could suppress only one of the two sets of contiguous zero fields in the second address, `F6DC:0:0:7678::A21D`. Rewriting it as `F6DC::7678::A21D` would be invalid as it uses two colons more than once. You can use two colons to suppress contiguous zero fields, which may occur in the beginning, middle, or end of the address string. If an address contains all zeros in it, you can represent it simply as `::`.

You can also mix hexadecimal and decimal formats in an IPv6 address. The notation is useful when you have an IPv4 address and want to write it in IPv6 format. You can write the first six 16-bit fields using a hexadecimal notation as described above and use dotted decimal notation for IPv4 for the last two 16-bit fields. The mixed notation takes the form `X:X:X:X:X:X:D.D.D.D`, where an `X` is a hexadecimal number and a `D` is a decimal number. You can rewrite the above IPv6 addresses using this notation as follows:

- `F6DC::4015:0:BA98:192.168.1.231`

- `F6DC:0:0:7678::0.0.162.29`

- `F6DC::0.0.162.29`

- `::0.0.0.1`

Unlike IPv4, IPv6 does not assign IP addresses based on network classes. Like IPv4, it uses CIDR addresses, so that the boundary between the prefix and suffix in an IP address can be specified at any arbitrary bit. For example, `::1` can be represented in CIDR notation as `::1/128`, where 128 is the prefix length.

■ **Tip**   IPv6 address should be enclosed in brackets ([ ]) when it is used inside a literal string as part of a URL. This rule does not apply to IPv4. For example, if you are accessing a web server on a loopback address using IPv4 address, you can use a URL like `http://127.0.0.1/index.html`. In an IPv6 address notation, you need to use a URL like `http://[::1]/index.html`. Make sure your browser supports IPv6 address notation in its URLs before using it.

Special IP Addresses

Some IP addresses are used for special purposes. Some of such IP addresses are as follows:

- Loopback IP Address
- Unicast IP Address
- Multicast IP Address
- Anycast IP Address
- Broadcast IP Address
- Unspecified IP Address

The following sections describe the use of these special IP addresses in detail.

Loopback IP Address

You need at least two computers connected via a network to test or run a network program. Sometimes it may not be feasible or desirable to set up a network when you want to test your network program during the development phase of your project. The designers of IP realized this need. There is a provision in the IP addressing scheme to treat an IP address as a loopback address to facilitate testing of network programs using only one computer. When the Internet layer in the protocol suite detects a loopback IP address as the destination for an IP datagram, it does not pass over the packet to the protocol layer below it (that is network interface layer). Rather, it turns around (or loops back, hence the name *loopback address*) and routes the packet back to the transport layer on the same computer. The transport layer will deliver the packet to the destination process on the same host as it would have done had the packet come from a remote host. A loopback IP address makes testing of a network program using one computer possible. Figure 5-5 depicts the way an Internet packet, which is addressed to a loopback IP address, is processed by the IP. The packet never leaves the source computer. It is intercepted by the internet layer and routed back to the same computer it started from.

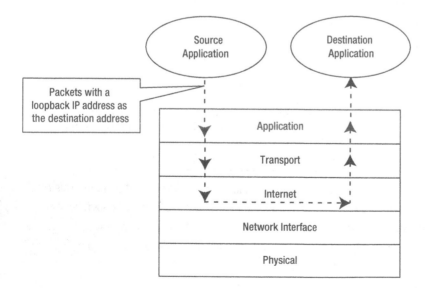

Figure 5-5. *An Internet packet that has a loopback IP address as its destination is routed back to the same computer from the Internet protocol in the internet layer*

Loopback IP addresses are reserved addresses and the IP is required not to forward a packet with a loopback IP address as its destination address to the network interface layer.

In an IPv4 addressing scheme, 127.X.X.X block is reserved for loopback addresses, where X is a decimal number between 0 and 255. Typically, 127.0.0.1 is used as a loopback address in IPv4. However, you are not limited to using only 127.0.0.1 as the only loopback address. If you wish, you can also use 127.0.0.2 or 127.3.5.11 as a valid loopback address. Typically, the name localhost is mapped to a loopback address of 127.0.0.1 on a computer.

In an IPv6 addressing scheme, there is only one loopback address, which is sufficient to perform any local testing for a network program. It is 0:0:0:0:0:0:0:1 or simply ::1.

Unicast IP Address

Unicast is one-to-one communication between two computers on a network in which an IP packet is delivered to a single remote host. A unicast IP address identifies a unique host on a network. IPv4 and IPv6 support unicast IP addresses.

Multicast IP Address

Multicast is a one-to-many communication where one computer sends an IP packet that is delivered to multiple remote computers. Multicasting lets you implement the concept of group interaction such as audio or video conferencing, where one computer sends information to all computers in the group. The benefit of using multicasting in place of multiple unicasts is that the sender sends only one copy of the packet. One copy of the packet travels along the network as long it can. If receivers of the packet are on multiple networks, a copy of the packet is made when needed, and each copy of the packet is routed independently. Finally, each receiver is delivered an individual copy of the packet. Multicasting is an efficient way of communication between group members as it reduces network traffic.

An IP packet has only one destination IP address. How is an IP packet delivered to multiple hosts using multicasting? IP contains some addresses in its address space as multicast addresses. If a packet is addressed to a multicast address, the packet will be delivered to multiple hosts. The concept of multicast packet delivery is the same as a group membership for an activity. When a group is formed, the group is given a group ID. Any information addressed to that group ID is delivered to all group members. In a multicast communication, a multicast IP address (similar to a group ID) is used. Multicast packets are addressed to that multicast address. Each interested host registers its IP address with the local router that it is interested in communication made on that multicast address. The registration process between a host and the local router is accomplished using an Internet Group Management Protocol (IGMP). When the router receives a packet with a multicast address, it delivers a copy of the packet to each host registered with it for that multicast address. A receiver may choose to leave the multicast group any time by informing the router.

A multicast packet may travel through many routers before it finds its way to the receiver hosts. All receivers of a multicast packet may not be on the same network. There are many protocols, such as Distance Vector Multicast Routing Protocol (DVMRP), that deal with routing of multicast packets.

Both IPv4 and IPv6 support multicast addressing. In IPv4, Class D network addresses are used for multicasting. That is, the four highest order bits are 1110 in a multicast address in IPv4. In IPv6, a multicast address has the first 8 bits set to 1. That is, a multicast address in IPv6 always starts with FF. For example, FF0X:0:0:0:0:0:2:0000 is a multicast address in IPv6.

Anycast IP Address

Anycast is a one-to-one_from_a_group communication where one computer sends a packet to a group of computers, but the packet is delivered to exactly one computer in the group. IPv4 does not support anycasting. IPv6 supports anycasting. In anycasting, the same address is assigned to multiple computers. When a router receives a packet, which is addressed to an anycast address, it delivers the packet to the nearest computer. Anycasting is useful when a service has been replicated at many hosts and you want to provide the service at the nearest host to the client. Sometimes, anycast addressing is also called *cluster addressing*. An anycast address is used from the unicast address space.

You cannot distinguish a unicast address from an anycast address by looking at their bit arrangements. When the same unicast address is assigned to multiple hosts, it is treated as an anycast address. Note that the router must know about the hosts that are assigned an anycast address, so that it can deliver the packets addressed to that anycast address to one of the nearest hosts.

Broadcast IP Address

Broadcast is a one-to-all communication where one computer sends a packet and that packet is delivered to all computers on the network. IPv4 assigns some addresses as broadcast addresses. When all 32 bits are set to 1, it forms a broadcast address and the packet is delivered to all hosts on the local subnet. When all bits in the host address are set to 1 and a network address is specified, it forms a broadcast address for the specified network number. For example, 255.255.255.255 is a broadcast address for a local subnet and 192.168.1.255 is a broadcast address for a network 192.168.1.0. IPv6 does not have a broadcast address. You need to use a multicast address as the broadcast address in IPv6.

Unspecified IP Address

0.0.0.0 in IPv4 and :: in IPv6 (note that :: denotes 128-bit IPv6 address with all bits set to zero) are known as unspecified addresses. A host uses this address as a source address to indicate that it does not have an IP address yet, such as during the boot up process when it is not assigned an IP address yet.

Port Numbers

A port number is a 16-bit unsigned integer ranging from 0 to 65535. Sometimes a port number is also referred to simply as a *port*. A computer runs many processes, which communicate with other processes running on remote computers. When the transport layer receives an incoming packet from the Internet layer, it needs to know which process (running in the application layer) on that computer should this packet be delivered to. A port number is a logical number that is used by the transport layer to recognize a destination process for a packet on a computer.

Each incoming packet to the transport layer has a protocol; for example, the TCP protocol handler in the transport layer handles a TCP packet and the UDP protocol handler in the transport layer handles a UDP packet.

In the application layer, a process uses a separate protocol of each communication channel it wants to communicate on with a remote process. A process uses a unique port number for each communication channel it opens for a specific protocol and registers that port number with the specific protocol module in the transport layer. Therefore, a port number must be unique for a specific protocol. For example, process P1 can use a port number 1988 for a TCP protocol and another called process P2 can use the same port number 1988 on the same computer for a UDP protocol. A process on a host uses the protocol and the port number of the remote process to send data to the remote process.

How does a process on a computer start communicating with a remote process? For example, when you visit Yahoo's web site, you simply enter http://www.yahoo.com as the web page address. In this web page address, http indicates the application layer protocol, which uses TCP as a transport layer protocol and www.yahoo.com is the machine name, which is resolved to an IP address using a Domain Name System (DNS). The machine identified by www.yahoo.com may be running many processes, which may use the http protocol. Which process on www.yahoo.com does your web browser connect to? Since many people use Yahoo's web site, it needs to run its http service at a well-known port, so that everyone can use that port to connect to it. Typically, the http web server runs at port 80. You can use http://www.yahoo.com:80, which is the same as using http://www.yahoo.com. It is not always necessary to run the http web server at port 80. If you do not run your http web server at port 80, people who want to use your http service must know the port you are using. IANA is responsible for recommending which port numbers to use for well-known services. IANA divides the port numbers into three ranges:

- Well-known Ports: 0 -1023

- Registered Ports: 1024 - 49151

- Dynamic and/or Private Ports: 49152 - 65535

Well-known port numbers are used by most commonly used services provided globally such as HTTP, FTP, etc. Table 5-3 lists some of the well-known ports that are used for well-known application layer protocols. Generally, you need administrative privileges to use a well-known port on a computer.

Table 5-3. *A Partial List of Well-Known Ports Used for Some Application Layer Protocols*

Application Layer Protocol	Port Number
echo	7
FTP	21
Telnet	23
SMTP	25
HTTP	80
POP3	110
NNTP	119

An organization (or a user) can register a port number with IANA in the registered ports range to be used by an application. For example, 1099 (TCP/UDP) port has been registered for the RMI Registry (RMI stands for Remote Method Invocation).

Any application can use a port number from dynamic/private port number range.

Socket API and Client-Server Paradigm

I have not yet started discussing Java classes that make network communication possible in a Java program. In this section, I will cover sockets and the client-server paradigm that is used in a network communication between two remote hosts.

I covered briefly the different lower layers of protocols and their responsibilities in the previous sections. It is time to move up in the protocol stack and discuss the interaction between the application layer and the transport layer. How does an application use these protocols to communicate with a remote application? Operating systems provide an application program interface (API) called a *socket*, which lets two remote applications communicate, taking advantage of lower level protocols in the protocol stack. A socket is not another layer of protocol. It is an interface between the transport layer and the application layer. It provides a standard way of communication between the two layers, which in turn provides a standard way of communication between two remote applications.

There are two kinds of sockets:

- A Connection-Oriented Socket

- A Connectionless Socket

A connection-oriented socket is also called a *stream socket*. A connectionless socket is also called a *datagram socket*. Note that the data is always sent one datagram at a time from one host to another on the Internet using IP datagrams.

Transmission Control Protocol (TCP), which is used in a transport layer, is one of the most widely used protocols to provide connection-oriented sockets. The application hands over data to a TCP socket and the TCP takes care of streaming the data to the destination host. The TCP takes care of all issues like ordering, fragmentation, assembly, lost data detection, duplicates data transmission, etc., on both sides of the communication, which gives the impression to the applications that data is flowing like a continuous stream of bytes from the source application to the destination application. No physical connection at the hardware level exists between two hosts that use TCP sockets. It is all implemented in software. Sometimes it is also called a *virtual connection*. The combination of two sockets uniquely defines a connection.

In a connection-oriented socket communication, the client and the server create a socket at their ends, establish a connection, and exchange information. TCP takes care of the errors that may occur during data transmission. TCP is also known as a reliable transport level protocol because it guarantees the delivery of the data. If it could not deliver the data for some reasons, it will inform the sender application about the error conditions. After it sends the data, it waits for an acknowledgment from the receiver to make sure that the data reached the destination. However, the reliability that TCP offers comes at a price. The overhead as compared to a connectionless protocol is much more significant, and it is slower. TCP makes sure that a sender sends the amount of data to the receiver, which can be handled by the receiver's buffer size. It also handles traffic congestion over the network. It slows down the data transmission when it detects traffic congestion. Java supports TCP sockets.

User Datagram Protocol (UDP), which is used in a transport layer, is the most widely used protocol that provides a connectionless socket. It is unreliable, but much faster. It lets you send limited sized data—one packet at a time, which is different from TCP, which lets you send data as a stream of any size, handling the details of segmenting them in appropriate size of packets. Data delivery is not guaranteed when you send data using UDP. However, it is still used in many applications and it works very well. The sender sends a UDP packet to a destination and forgets about it. If receiver gets it, it gets it. Otherwise, there is no way to know—for the receiver—that there was a UDP packet sent to it. You can compare the communication used in TCP and UDP to the communication used in a telephone and mailing a letter. A telephone conversation is reliable and it offers acknowledgment between two parties that are communicating. When you mail a letter, you do not know when the addressee receives it, or if he received it at all. There is another important difference between UDP and TCP. UDP does not guarantee the ordering of data. That is, if you send five packets to a destination using UDP, those five packets may arrive in any order. However, TCP guarantees that packets will be delivered in the order they were sent. Java supports UDP sockets.

Which protocol should you use: TCP or UDP? It depends on how the application will be used. If data integrity is of utmost significance, you should use TCP. If speed is prioritized over lower data integrity, you should use UDP. For example, a file transfer application should use TCP, whereas a video conferencing application should use UDP. If you lose video data of a few pixels, it does not matter much to the video conference. It can continue. However, if you lose a few bytes of data when a file is being transferred, that file may not be usable at all.

How do two remote applications start communicating? Which application initiates the communication? How does an application know that a remote application is interested in communicating with it? Have you ever dialed a customer service number of a company to talk to a customer service representative? If you have talked to a company's customer service representative, you already have experienced two remote applications communicate. I will refer to the mechanism of using a company's customer service to explain remote communication in this section. You and a company's representative are at two remote locations. You need a service and the company provides that service. In other words, you are the client and the company is a service provider (or a server). You do not know when you will need a service from the company. The company provides a customer service phone number, so you can contact the company. There is one more thing the company does. What is it that the company must do to provide you a service? Can you guess? It waits for your calls at the phone number that it gave you. The communication has to happen between you and the company, and the company has already taken one step forward in that communication by *passively* waiting for your call. As soon as you dial the company's number, a connection is established and you exchange information with the company's representative. Both of you hang up, at the end, to discontinue the communication. The network communication using sockets is similar to the communication that happens between you and the company's representative. If you understand this example of communication, understanding sockets is easy.

Two remote applications use a pair of sockets to communicate. You need two endpoints for any communication to occur. A socket is a communication endpoint on each side of the communication channel. Communication over a pair of sockets follows a typical client-server communication paradigm. One application creates a socket and passively waits to be contacted by another remote application. The application that waits for a remote application to contact it is called a *server application* or simply a *server*. Another application creates a socket and initiates the communication with the waiting server application. This is called a *client application* or simply a *client*. Many other steps must be performed before a client and a server can exchange information. For example, a server must advertise the location and other details about itself so a client may contact it.

A socket passes through different states. Each state marks an event. It is the state of the socket that tells us what a socket can do and what it cannot do. Generally, a socket's lifecycle is described by eight primitives listed in Table 5-4.

Table 5-4. *The List of Typical Socket Primitives and Their Descriptions*

Primitives	Description
Socket	Creates a socket, which is used by an application to serve as a communication endpoint.
Bind	Associates a local address to the socket. The local address includes an IP address and a port number. The port number must be a number between 0 and 65535. It should be unique for the protocol being used for the socket on the computer. For example, if a TCP socket uses port 12456, a UDP socket can also use the same port number 12456.
Listen	Defines the size of its wait queue for a client request. It is performed only by a connection-oriented server socket.
Accept	Waits for a client request to arrive. It is performed only by a connection-oriented server socket.
Connect	Attempts to establish a connection to a server socket, which is waiting on an accept primitive. It is performed by a connection-oriented client socket.
Send/Sendto	Sends data. Usually send indicates a send operation on a connection-oriented socket and Sendto indicates a send operation on a connectionless socket.
Receive/ReceiveFrom	Receives data. They are counterparts of Send and Sendto.
Close	Closes a connection.

The following sections elaborate each socket primitive.

The Socket Primitive

A server creates a socket by specifying what kind of socket it is: a stream socket or a datagram socket.

The Bind Primitive

The bind primitive associates the socket to a local IP address and a port number. Note that a host can have multiple IP addresses. A socket can be bound to one of the IP addresses of the host or all of them. Binding a socket to all available IP addresses for the host is also known as binding to a wildcard address. Binding reserves the port number for this socket. No other socket can use that port number for communication. The bound port will be used by the transport protocol (TCP as well as UDP) to route the data intended for this socket. I will explain more about transferring data between the transport layer and a socket little later in this section. For now, it is sufficient to understand that, in binding, the socket tells the transport layer that here is my IP address and port number, and if you get any data addressed to this address, please pass that data to me. The IP address and the port number to which a socket is bound are called the *local address* and the *local port* for the socket, respectively.

The Listen Primitive

A server informs the operating system to place the socket in a passive mode so it waits for the incoming client requests. At this point, the server is not yet ready to accept any client request. A server also specifies a wait queue size for the socket. When a client contacts the server at this socket, the client request is placed in that queue. Initially, the queue is empty. If a client contacts the server at this socket and the wait queue is full, the client's request is rejected.

The Accept Primitive

A server informs the operating system that this socket is ready to accept client requests. This step is not performed if the server is using a socket using a connectionless transport protocol such as UDP. This step is performed for TCP server sockets. When a socket sends an accept message to the operating system, it blocks until it receives a client request for a new connection.

The Connect Primitive

Only a connection-oriented client socket performs this step. This is the most important phase in a socket communication. The client socket sends a request to the server socket to establish a connection. The server socket has issued accept and has been waiting for a client request to arrive. The client socket sends the IP address and the port number of the server socket. Recall that a server socket binds an IP address and a port number before it starts listening and accepting connections from outside. Along with its request, a client socket also sends its own IP address and the port number to which it is already bound.

An important question arises at this point. How does the transport layer such as TCP know that the packet (in the form of a request for a connection) that came from a client has to be handed over to the server socket? During the binding phase, a socket specifies its local IP address and a local port number as well as a remote IP address and a remote port number. If the server socket wants to accept a connection only from a specific remote host IP address and port number, it can do so. Usually, the server socket will accept a connection from any client and it will specify an unspecified IP address and a zero port number as its remote address. A server socket passes five pieces of information—a local IP address, a local port number, a remote IP address, and a remote port number, and a buffer—to the transport layer. The transport layer stores them for future use in a special structure called a *Transmission Control Block* (TCB). When a packet from outside arrives at the transport layer, it looks up its TCB based on the four pieces of information contained in the incoming packet, <source IP address, source port number, destination IP address, destination port number>. Recall that the client sends the source and destination addresses in each TCP packet to the server. The transport layer attempts to find a buffer that is associated with the source and destination addresses. If it finds a buffer, it transfers the incoming data to the buffer and notifies the socket that there is some information for it in the buffer. If the server socket is accepting requests from any client (all zeroes in the remote address), the data from any client will be routed to its buffer.

Once a server socket detects a request from a client, it creates a new socket with the remote client's address information. The new socket is bound using a <local IP address, local port number (the same as server socket's port number), remote IP address, and remote port number> and a new buffer is created and bound to this combined addresses. In fact, two buffers are created for a socket: one for the incoming data and one for the outgoing data. At this point, a server socket lets the new socket communicate with the client socket that requested a connection. The server socket itself can close itself (accepting no more client requests for a connection) or it can start waiting again to accept another client request for a connection.

After a connection is established between two sockets (a client and a server), they can exchange information. A TCP connection supports full duplex connection. That is, data can be sent or received in both directions simultaneously.

A client socket knows its local IP address, local port number, remote IP address, and remote port number before it attempts to connect to a server. At the client end, the creation of a TCB follows similar rules.

Once the client and server sockets are in place, two sockets (the client socket and the server socket dedicated to the client) define a connection.

A server socket acts like a receptionist sitting at the front desk in an office (server). A client comes in and talks to the receptionist first. A connection request comes from a client to the server and contacts the server socket first. The receptionist hands over the client to another staff. At this point, the job of the receptionist is over with that client. She continues her work of waiting to welcome another client coming to the office. Meanwhile, the first client can continue talking to another staff as long as he needs. Similarly, the server socket creates a new socket and assigns that new socket to the client for any further communication. As soon as the server socket assigns a new socket to the client, its job is over with that client. It will wait for another incoming request for connection from another client. Note that apart from many other details, a socket has five important pieces of information associated with it: a protocol, a local IP address, a local port number, a remote IP address, and a remote port number.

The Send/Sendto Primitive

It is the stage when a socket sends data.

The Receive/ReceiveFrom Primitive

It is the stage when a socket receives data.

The Close Primitive

It is time to say goodbye. Finally, the server and client sockets close the connection.

Subsequent sections will discuss Java classes that support different kinds of sockets to facilitate network programming. Java classes that are related to network programming are in `java.net`, `javax.net`, and `javax.net.ssl` packages.

Representing a Machine Address

Internet protocol uses the IP addresses of machines to deliver packets. Using IP addresses in a program is not always easy because of its numeric format. You may be able to memorize and use IPv4 addresses because they are only four decimal numbers in length. Memorizing and using IPv6 addresses is a little more difficult because they are eight numbers in a hexadecimal format. Every computer also has a name such as www.yahoo.com. Using a computer name in your program makes your life much easier. Java provides classes that let you use a computer name or an IP address in a Java program. If you use a computer name, Java takes care of resolving the computer name to its IP address using a DNS.

An object of the InetAddress class represents an IP address. It has two subclasses, Inet4Address and Inet6Address, which represent IPv4 and IPv6 addresses, respectively. The InetAddress class does not have a public constructor. It provides six factory methods to create its object. They are as follows. All of them throw a checked UnknownHostException.

- `static InetAddress[] getAllByName(String host)`
- `static InetAddress getByAddress(byte[] addr)`
- `static InetAddress getByAddress(String host, byte[] addr)`
- `static InetAddress getByName(String host)`
- `static InetAddress getLocalHost()`
- `static InetAddress getLoopbackAddress()`

The host argument refers to a computer name or an IP address in the standard format. The addr argument refers to the parts of an IP address as a byte array. If you specify an IPv4 address, addr must be a 4-element byte array. For IPv6 addresses, it should be a 16-element byte array. The InetAddress class takes care of resolving the host name to an IP address using DNS.

Sometimes a host may have multiple IP addresses. The getAllByName() method returns all addresses as an array of InetAddress objects.

Typically, you create an object of the InetAddress class using one of the four factory methods and pass that object to other methods during a socket creation and connection. The following snippet of code demonstrates some of its uses. You will need to handle exceptions when you use the InetAddress class or its subclasses.

```
// Get the IP address of the yahoo web server
InetAddress yahooAddress = InetAddress.getByName("www.yahoo.com");

// Get the loopback IP address
InetAddress loopbackAddress = InetAddress.getByName(null);

/* Get the address of the local host. Typically, a name "localhost" is
   mapped to a loopback address. Here, we are trying to get the IP address
   of the local computer where this code executes and not the loopback address.
*/
InetAddress myComputerAddress = InetAddress.getLocalHost();
```

Listing 5-1 demonstrates the use of the InetAddress class and some of its methods. You may get a different output when you run the program.

Listing 5-1. Demonstrating the Use of the InetAddress Class

```java
// InetAddressTest.java
package com.jdojo.net;

import java.io.IOException;
import java.net.InetAddress;

public class InetAddressTest {
        public static void main(String[] args) {
                // Print www.yahoo.com address details
                printAddressDetails("www.yahoo.com");

                // Print the loopback address details
                printAddressDetails(null);

                // Print the loopback address details using IPv6 format
                printAddressDetails("::1");
        }

        public static void printAddressDetails(String host) {
                System.out.println("Host '" + host + "' details starts...");

                try {
                        InetAddress addr = InetAddress.getByName(host);
                        System.out.println("Host IP Address: " + addr.getHostAddress());
                        System.out.println("Canonical Host Name: " + addr.getCanonicalHostName());

                        int timeOutinMillis = 10000;
                        System.out.println("isReachable(): " + addr.isReachable(timeOutinMillis));
                        System.out.println("isLoopbackAddress(): " + addr.isLoopbackAddress());
                }
                catch (IOException e) {
                        e.printStackTrace();
                }
```

```
            finally {
                    System.out.println("Host '" + host + "' details ends...");
                    System.out.println("");
            }
        }
    }
}
```

```
Host 'www.yahoo.com' details starts...
Host IP Address: 98.139.183.24
Canonical Host Name: ir2.fp.vip.bf1.yahoo.com
isReachable(): false
isLoopbackAddress(): false
Host 'www.yahoo.com' details ends...

Host 'null' details starts...
Host IP Address: 127.0.0.1
Canonical Host Name: 127.0.0.1
isReachable(): true
isLoopbackAddress(): true
Host 'null' details ends...

Host '::1' details starts...
Host IP Address: 0:0:0:0:0:0:0:1
Canonical Host Name: BHMIS-JOOBXFL-D.corporate.local
isReachable(): true
isLoopbackAddress(): true
Host '::1' details ends...
```

Representing a Socket Address

A socket address contains two parts, an IP address and a port number. An object of the InetSocketAddress class represents a socket address. You can use the following constructors to create an object of the InetSocketAddress class:

- InetSocketAddress(InetAddress addr, int port)
- InetSocketAddress(int port)
- InetSocketAddress(String hostname, int port)

All constructors will attempt to resolve a host name to an IP address. If a host name could not be resolved, the socket address will be flagged as unresolved, which you can test using the isUnresolved() method. If you do not want this class to resolve the address when creating its object, you can use the following factory method to create the socket address:

```
static InetSocketAddress createUnresolved(String host, int port)
```

The getAddress() method returns an InetAddress object. If a host name is not resolved, the getAddress() method returns null. If you use an unresolved InetSocketAddress object with a socket, an attempt is made to resolve the host name during the bind process.

Listing 5-2 shows how to create resolved and unresolved InetSocketAddress objects. You may get a different output when you run the program.

Listing 5-2. Creating an InetSocketAddress Object

```java
// InetSocketAddressTest.java
package com.jdojo.net;

import java.net.InetSocketAddress;

public class InetSocketAddressTest {
        public static void main(String[] args) {
                InetSocketAddress addr1 = new InetSocketAddress("::1", 12889);
                printSocketAddress(addr1);

                InetSocketAddress addr2 =
                        InetSocketAddress.createUnresolved("::1", 12881);
                printSocketAddress(addr2);
        }

        public static void printSocketAddress(InetSocketAddress sAddr) {
                System.out.println("Socket Address: " + sAddr.getAddress());
                System.out.println("Socket Host Name: " + sAddr.getHostName());
                System.out.println("Socket Port: " + sAddr.getPort());
                System.out.println("isUnresolved(): " + sAddr.isUnresolved());
                System.out.println();
        }
}
```

```
Socket Address: /0:0:0:0:0:0:0:1
Socket Host Name: HYE6754
Socket Port: 12889
isUnresolved(): false

Socket Address: null
Socket Host Name: ::1
Socket Port: 12881
isUnresolved(): true
```

Creating a TCP Server Socket

An object of the ServerSocket class represents a TCP server socket in Java. A ServerSocket object is used to accept a connection request from a remote client. The ServerSocket class provides many constructors. You can use the no-args constructor to create an unbound server socket and use its bind() method to bind it to a local port and a local IP address. The following snippet of code shows how to create a server socket:

```java
// Create an unbound server socket
ServerSocket serverSocket = new ServerSocket();

// Create a socket address object
InetSocketAddress endPoint = new InetSocketAddress("localhost", 12900);
```

```
// Set the wait queue size to 100
int waitQueueSize = 100;

// Bind the server socket to localhost and at port 12900 with
// a wait queue size of 100
serverSocket.bind(endPoint, waitQueueSize);
```

There is no separate listen() method in the ServerSocket class that corresponds to the listen socket primitive. Its bind() method takes care of specifying the waiting queue size for the socket.

You can combine create, bind, and listen operations in one step by using any of the following constructors of the ServerSocket class. The default value for the wait queue size is 50. The default value for a local IP address is the wild-card address, which means all IP addresses of the server machine.

- ServerSocket(int port)

- ServerSocket(int port, int waitQueueSize)

- ServerSocket(int port, int waitQueueSize, InetAddress bindAddr)

You can combine the socket creation and bind steps into one statement as shown:

```
// Create a server socket at port 12900, with 100 as the wait
// queue size and at the localhost loopback address
ServerSocket serverSocket =
        new ServerSocket(12900, 100, InetAddress.getByName("localhost"));
```

Once a server socket is created and bound, it is ready to accept incoming connection requests from remote clients. To accept a remote connection request, you need to call the accept() method on the server socket. The accept() method call blocks until a request from a remote client arrives in its wait queue. When the server socket receives a request for a connection, it reads the remote IP address and the remote port number from the request and creates a new *active* socket. The reference of the newly created active socket is returned from the from the accept() method. An object of the Socket class represents the new active socket. The accept() method returns a new *active* socket because it is not a *passive* socket like a server socket, which waits for a remote request. It is an active socket because it is created for an active communication with the remote client. Sometimes this active socket is also called a *connection socket* because it handles the data transmission on a connection.

```
// Wait for a new remote connection request
Socket activeSocket = serverSocket.accept();
```

Once the server socket returns from the accept() method call, the number of sockets in the server application increases by one. You have one passive server socket and one more active socket. The new active socket is the endpoint at the server for the new client connection. At this point, you need to handle the communication with the client using the new active socket.

Now you are ready to read and write data on the connection represented by the new socket. A Java TCP socket provides a full duplex connection. It lets you read data from the connection as well as write data to the connection. The Socket class contains two methods called getInputStream() and getOutputStream() for this purpose. The getInputStream() method returns an InputStream object that you can use to read data from the connection. The getOutputStream() method returns an OutputStream object that you can use to write data to the connection. You use InputStream and OutputStream objects as if you are reading from and writing to a file on a local file system. I assume that you are familiar with Java I/O. If you are not familiar with Java I/O, please refer to Chapter 7 in the book *Beginning Java Language Features* (ISBN: 978-1-4302-6658-7) before you proceed in this section. However, you can still read about the UDP socket in the section later in this chapter. When you are done with reading/writing data on the connection, you close the InputStream/OutputStream, and finally close the socket. The following snippet of code reads a message from a client and echoes it to the client. Note that the server and the client must agree on the format of the message before they start communicating. The following snippet of code assumes that the client sends one line of text at a time:

```
// Create a buffered reader and a buffered writer from the socket's
// input and output streams, so that we can read/write one line at a time
BufferedReader br = new BufferedReader(
        new InputStreamReader(activeSocket.getInputStream()));

BufferedWriter bw = new BufferedWriter(
        new OutputStreamWriter(activeSocket.getOutputStream()));
```

You can use br and bw the same way you will use them to read from a file or write to a file. An attempt to read from an input stream blocks until data becomes available on the connection.

```
// Read one line of text from the connection
String inMsg = br.readLine();

// Write some text to the output buffer
bw.write('hello from server");
bw.flush();
```

At the end, close the connection using the socket's close() method. Closing the socket also closes its input and output streams. In fact, you can close one of the three (the input stream, the output stream, or the socket) and the other two will be closed automatically. An attempt to read/write on a closed socket throws a java.net.SocketException. You can check if a socket is closed by using its isClosed() method, which returns true if the socket is closed.

```
// Close the socket
activeSocket.close();
```

■ **Tip**   Once you close a socket, you cannot reuse it. You must create a new socket and bind it before using the new socket.

A server handles two kinds of work: accepting new connection requests and responding to already connected clients. If responding to a client takes a very small amount of time, you can use the strategy as shown:

```
ServerSocket serverSocket = create a server socket here;
while(true) {
        Socket activeSocket = serverSocket.accept();

        // Handle the client request on activeSocket here
}
```

The above strategy handles one client at a time. It is suitable only if the number of concurrent incoming connections is very low and a client's request takes a very small amount of time to respond. If a client request takes a significant amount of time to respond, all other clients will have to wait before they can be served.

Another strategy to work with multiple client requests is to handle each client's request in a separate thread so the server can serve multiple clients at the same time. The following pseudo code outlines this strategy:

```
ServerSocket serverSocket = create a server socket here;
while(true) {
        Socket activeSocket = serverSocket.accept();
        Runnable runnable = () -> {
                // Handle the client request on the activeSocket here
        };
        new Thread(runnable).start(); // start a new thread
}
```

The above strategy seems to work fine until you have too many threads that are created for concurrent client connections. Another strategy that works well in most of the situations is to have a thread pool to serve all client connections. If all threads in the pool are busy serving clients, the request should wait until a thread becomes free to serve it.

Listing 5-3 contains complete code for an echo server. It creates a new thread to handle each client request. You can run the echo server program now. However, it is not going to do much as you do not have a client program to connect to it. You will see it in action after you learn how to create the TCP client socket in the next section.

Listing 5-3. An Echo Server Based on TCP Sockets

```java
// TCPEchoServer.java
package com.jdojo.net;

import java.io.BufferedReader;
import java.io.BufferedWriter;
import java.io.IOException;
import java.io.InputStreamReader;
import java.io.OutputStreamWriter;
import java.net.InetAddress;
import java.net.ServerSocket;
import java.net.Socket;

public class TCPEchoServer {
        public static void main(String[] args) {
                try {
                        // Create a Server socket
                        ServerSocket serverSocket = new ServerSocket(12900, 100,
                                InetAddress.getByName("localhost"));
                        System.out.println("Server started at: " + serverSocket);

                        // Keep accepting client connections in an infinite loop
                        while (true) {
                                System.out.println("Waiting for a connection...");

                                // Accept a connection
                                final Socket activeSocket = serverSocket.accept();

                                System.out.println("Received a connection from " +
                                                activeSocket);
```

```
                                // Create a new thread to handle the new connection
                                Runnable runnable =
                                        () -> handleClientRequest(activeSocket);
                                new Thread(runnable).start(); // start a new thread
                        }
                }
                catch (IOException e) {
                        e.printStackTrace();
                }
        }

        public static void handleClientRequest(Socket socket) {
                BufferedReader socketReader = null;
                BufferedWriter socketWriter = null;

                try {
                        // Create a buffered reader and writer for teh socket
                        socketReader = new BufferedReader(
                                new InputStreamReader(socket.getInputStream()));
                        socketWriter = new BufferedWriter(
                                new OutputStreamWriter(socket.getOutputStream()));

                        String inMsg = null;
                        while ((inMsg = socketReader.readLine()) != null) {
                                System.out.println("Received from client: " + inMsg);

                                // Echo the received message to the client
                                String outMsg = inMsg;
                                socketWriter.write(outMsg);
                                socketWriter.write("\n");
                                socketWriter.flush();
                        }
                }
                catch (IOException e) {
                        e.printStackTrace();
                }
                finally {
                        try {
                                socket.close();
                        }
                        catch (IOException e) {
                                e.printStackTrace();
                        }
                }
        }
}
```

Creating a TCP Client Socket

An object of the Socket class represents a TCP client socket. You have already seen how an object of the Socket class works with a TCP server socket. For a server socket, you got an object of the Socket class as the return value from the server socket's accept() method. For a client socket, you will have to perform three additional steps: create, bind, and connect. The Socket class provides many constructors that let you specify the remote IP address and port number. These constructors bind the socket to a local host and an available port number. The following snippet of code shows how to create a TCP client socket:

```
// Create a client socket, which is bound to the localhost at any
// available port; connected to remote IP of 192.168.1.2 at port 3456
Socket socket = new Socket("192.168.1.2", 3456);

// Create an unbound client socket. bind it, and connect it.
Socket socket = new Socket();
socket.bind(new InetSocketAddress("localhost", 14101));
socket.connect(new InetSocketAddress("localhost", 12900));
```

Once you get a connected Socket object, you can use its input and output streams using the getInputStream() and getOutputStream() methods, respectively. You can read/write on the connection the same way you would read/write from/to a file using the input and output streams.

Listing 5-4 contains the complete code for an echo client application. It receives input from the user, sends the input to the echo server as listed in Listing 5-3, and prints the server's response on the standard output. Both applications, the echo server and the echo client, must agree on the format of the messages that they will be exchanging. They exchange one line of text at a time. It is important to note that you must append a new line with every message that is sent across the connection because you are using the readLine() method of the BufferedReader class, which returns only when it encounters a new line. The client application must use the same IP address and port number where the server socket is accepting the connection.

Listing 5-4. An Echo Client Based on TCP Sockets

```
// TCPEchoClient.java
package com.jdojo.net;

import java.io.BufferedReader;
import java.io.BufferedWriter;
import java.io.IOException;
import java.io.InputStreamReader;
import java.io.OutputStreamWriter;
import java.net.Socket;

public class TCPEchoClient {
        public static void main(String[] args) {
                Socket socket = null;
                BufferedReader socketReader = null;
                BufferedWriter socketWriter = null;
                try {
                        // Create a socket that will connect to localhost
                        // at port 12900. Note that the server must also be
                        // running at localhost and 12900.
                        socket = new Socket("localhost", 12900);
```

```java
            System.out.println("Started client socket at " +
                    socket.getLocalSocketAddress());

            // Create a buffered reader and writer using the socket's
            // input and output streams
            socketReader = new BufferedReader(
                    new InputStreamReader(socket.getInputStream()));
            socketWriter = new BufferedWriter(
                    new OutputStreamWriter(socket.getOutputStream()));

            // Create a buffered reader for user's input
            BufferedReader consoleReader =
                    new BufferedReader(new InputStreamReader(System.in));

            String promptMsg = "Please enter a message (Bye to quit):";
            String outMsg = null;

            System.out.print(promptMsg);
            while ((outMsg = consoleReader.readLine()) != null) {
                if (outMsg.equalsIgnoreCase("bye")) {
                    break;
                }

                // Add a new line to the message to the server,
                // because the server reads one line at a time.
                socketWriter.write(outMsg);
                socketWriter.write("\n");
                socketWriter.flush();

                // Read and display the message from the server
                String inMsg = socketReader.readLine();
                System.out.println("Server: " + inMsg);

                System.out.println(); // Print a blank line
                System.out.print(promptMsg);
            }
        }
        catch (IOException e) {
            e.printStackTrace();
        }
        finally {
            // Finally close the socket
            if (socket != null) {
                try {
                    socket.close();
                }
                catch (IOException e) {
                    e.printStackTrace();
                }
            }
        }
    }
}
```

Putting a TCP Server and Clients Together

Figure 5-6 shows the setup in which three clients are connected to a server. Two Socket objects, one at each end, represent a connection. The ServerSocket object in the server keeps waiting for incoming connection requests from a client.

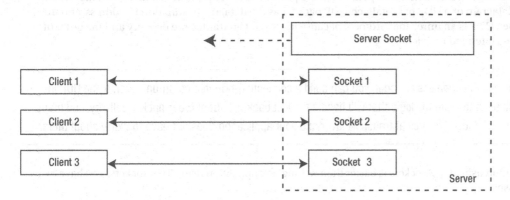

Figure 5-6. *A client-server setup using ServerSocket and socket objects*

Listing 5-3 and Listing 5-4 list the complete program for a TCP echo server and client application. You need to run the TCPEchoServer class first, and then the TCPEchoClient class. The server application waits for the client application to connect. The client application prompts the user to enter a text message on the console. Once the user enters a text message and presses the Enter key, the client application sends that text to the server. The server responds back with the same message. Both applications print the details about the conversation on the standard output. The following are the outputs for an echo server and an echo client. You can run multiple instances of the TCPEchoClient application. The server application handles each client connection in a separate thread.

The following is a sample output for the server application:

```
Server started at: ServerSocket[addr=localhost/127.0.0.1,port=0,localport=12900]
Waiting for a connection ...
Received a connection from Socket[addr=/127.0.0.1,port=1698,localport=12900]
Waiting for a connection ...
Received from client: Hello
```

The following is a sample output for the client application:

```
Started client socket at /127.0.0.1:1698
Please enter a message (Bye to quit):Hello
Server: Hello
Please enter a message (Bye to quit):Bye
```

Working with UDP Sockets

A socket based on UDP is connectionless and is based on datagrams, as opposed to a TCP socket, which is connection-oriented and is based on streams. The effect of being a connectionless socket is that the two sockets (client and server) do not establish a connection before they communicate. Recall that TCP has a server socket whose sole function was to listen for a connection request from remote clients. Since UDP is a connectionless protocol, there will not be a server socket when you work with UDP. In TCP sockets, the impression of having a stream-oriented data transmission between the client and server was produced by TCP in the transport layer because of its connection-oriented features. TCP maintained the state of the data being transmitted on each side of the connection. The implication of UDP being a connectionless protocol is that each side (client and server) sends or receives a chunk of data without any prior knowledge of communication between them. In a communication using UDP, each chunk of data that is sent to the same destination is independent of the previously sent data. The chunk of data that is sent using UDP is called a datagram or a UDP packet. Each UDP packet has the data, the destination IP address, and the destination port number. UDP is an unreliable protocol because it does not guarantee the delivery and the order of delivery of packets to the intended recipient.

■ **Tip**   Although UDP is a connectionless protocol, you can build a connection-oriented communication using UDP in your application. You will need to write the logic that will handle the lost packets, out of order packet delivery, and many more things. TCP provides all these features at transport layer and your application does not have to worry about them.

Writing an application using UDP sockets is easier than writing an application using TCP sockets. You have to deal with only two classes:

- DatagramPacket

- DatagramSocket

An object of the DatagramPacket class represents a UDP datagram that is the unit of data transmission over a UDP socket. An object of the DatagramSocket class represents a UDP socket that is used to send or receive a datagram packet. Here are the steps you need to perform to work with UDP sockets:

1. Create an object of the DatagramSocket class and bind it to a local IP address and a local port number.

2. Create an object of the DatagramPacket class to hold the destination address and the data to be transmitted.

3. Use the send() method to send the datagram packet to its destination. On the receiving end, use the receive() method to read the datagram packet.

You can use one of the constructors to create an object of the DatagramSocket class. All of them will create the socket and bind it to a local IP address and a local port number. Note that a UDP socket does not have a remote IP address and a remote port number because it is never connected to a remote socket. It can receive/send a datagram packet from/to any UDP socket.

```
// Create a UDP Socket bound to a port number 15900 at localhost
DatagramSocket udpSocket = new DatagramSocket(15900, "localhost");
```

The DatagramSocket class provides a bind() method, which lets you bind the socket to a local IP address and a local port number. Typically, you do not need to use this method as you specify the socket address to which it needs to be bound in its constructor, as you just did.

A DatagramPacket contains three things: a destination IP address, a destination port number, and the data. The constructors for the DatagramPacket class fall into two categories. Constructors in one of the categories let you create a DatagramPacket object to receive a packet. They require only the buffer size, offset, and length of data in that buffer. Constructors in the other category let you create a DatagramPacket object to send a packet. They require you to specify the destination address along with the data. If you have created a DatagramPacket without specifying the destination address, you can set the destination address afterwards using the setAddress() and setPort() methods.

Constructors of the DatagramPacket class to create a packet to receive data are as follows:

- `DatagramPacket(byte[] buf, int length)`

- `DatagramPacket(byte[] buf, int offset, int length)`

Constructors of the DatagramPacket class to create a packet to send data are as follows:

- `DatagramPacket(byte[] buf, int length, InetAddress address, int port)`

- `DatagramPacket(byte[] buf, int offset, int length, InetAddress address, int port)`

- `DatagramPacket(byte[] buf, int length, SocketAddress address)`

- `DatagramPacket(byte[] buf, int offset, int length, SocketAddress address)`

The following snippet of code demonstrates some of the ways to create a datagram packet:

```
// Create a packet to receive 1024 bytes of data
byte[] data = new byte[1024];
DatagramPacket packet = new DatagramPacket(data, data.length);

// Create a packet that a has buffer size of 1024, but it will receive
// data starting at offset 8 (offset zero means the first element in
// the array) and it will receive only 32 bytes of data.
byte[] data2 = new byte[1024];
DatagramPacket packet2 = new DatagramPacket(data2, 8, 32);

// Create a packet to send 1024 bytes of data that has a destination
// address of "localhost" and port 15900. Will need to populate data3
// array before sending the packet.
byte[] data3 = new byte[1024];
DatagramPacket packet3 = new DatagramPacket(data3, 1024,
                            InetAddress.getByName("localhost"), 15900);

// Create a packet to send 1024 bytes of data that has a destination
// address of "localhost" and port 15900. Will need to populate data4
// array before sending the packet. The code sets the destination
// address by calling methods on the packet instead of specifying it
// in its constructor.
byte[] data4 = new byte[1024];
DatagramPacket packet4 = new DatagramPacket(data4, 1024);
packet4.setAddress(InetAddress.getByName("localhost"));
packet4.setPort(15900);
```

It is very important to understand that data in the packet always has offset and length specified. You need to use those two pieces of information while reading the data from a packet. Suppose that a receivedPacket object reference represents a DatagramPacket that you have received from a remote UDP socket. The getData() method of the DatagramPacket class returns the buffer (a byte array) of the packet. A packet can have a bigger buffer than the size of the received data from a remote client. In such cases, you must use the offset and the length to read the data from the buffer that was received without touching the garbage data in the buffer. If a packet's buffer size is smaller than the size of the data received, the extra bytes are silently ignored. You should use the code similar to the one shown below to read data that a socket receives. The point is that you should use data in the receiving buffer starting from its specified offset and as many bytes as indicated by its length property.

```
// Get the packet's buffer, offset, and length
byte[] dataBuffer = receivedPacket.getData();
int offset = receivedPacket.getOffset();
int length = receivedPacket.getLength();

// Copy the received data using offset and length to receivedData array,
// which will hold all good data
byte[] receivedData = new byte[length];
System.arraycopy(dataBuffer, offset, receivedData, 0, length);
```

Creating a UDP socket (client as well as server) is as simple as creating an object of the DatagramSocket class. You can use its send() method to send a packet. You can use the receive() method to receive a packet from a remote socket. The receive() method blocks until a packet arrives. You supply an empty datagram packet to the receive() method. The socket populates it with information that it receives from the remote socket. If the supplied datagram packet has a smaller data buffer size than that of the received datagram packet, the received data is truncated silently to fit into the supplied datagram packet. If the supplied datagram packet has a bigger data buffer size than that of the received one, the socket will copy the received data to the supplied data buffer in its segment indicated by its offset and length properties and would not touch the other parts of the buffer. Note that the available data buffer size is not the size of the byte array. Rather, it is defined by the length. For example, suppose you have a datagram packet with a byte array of 32 elements with an offset of 2 and a data buffer length of 8. If you pass this datagram packet to the receive() method, the maximum of 8 bytes of received data will be copied. The data will be copied from the third element in the buffer to the eleventh element as indicated by the offset 2 and the length 8, respectively.

```
// Create a UDP socket bound to a port number 15900 at localhost
DatagramSocket socket = new DatagramSocket(15900,
                             InetAddress.getByName("localhost"));

// Send a packet assuming that you have a datagram packet in p
socket.send(p);

// Receive a packet
DatagramPacket p2 = new DatagramPacket(new byte[1024], 1024);
socket.receive(p2);
```

Creating a UDP Echo Server

Creating an echo server using UDP is very easy. It takes only four lines of real code. Use the following steps to create an UDP echo server:

1. Create a DatagramSocket object to represent a UDP socket.

2. Create a DatagramPacket object to receive the packet from a remote client.

3. Call the receive() method of the socket to wait for a packet to arrive.

4. Call the send() method of the socket passing the same packet that you received. When a UDP packet is received by a server, it contains the sender's address. You do not need to change anything in the packet to echo back the same message to the sender of the packet. When you prepare a datagram packet for sending, you need to set a destination address. When the packet arrives at its destination, it contains its sender's address. This is useful in case the receiver wants to respond to the sender of the datagram packet.

The following snippet of code shows how to write a UDP echo server:

```
DatagramSocket socket = new DatagramSocket(15900);
DatagramPacket packet = new DatagramPacket(new byte[1024], 1024);
while(true) {
        // Receive the packet
        socket.receive(packet);

        //Send back the same packet to the sender
        socket.send(packet);
}
```

Listing 5-5 has the expanded version of the same code for a UDP echo server. It contains the same basic logic as shown above. Additionally, it has code to handle errors and print the packet's details on the standard output.

Listing 5-5. An Echo Server Based on UDP Sockets

```
// UDPEchoServer.java
package com.jdojo.net;

import java.io.IOException;
import java.net.DatagramPacket;
import java.net.DatagramSocket;
import java.net.InetAddress;

public class UDPEchoServer {
        public static void main(String[] args) {
                final int LOCAL_PORT = 15900;
                final String SERVER_NAME = "localhost";

                try {
                        DatagramSocket udpSocket =
                                new DatagramSocket(LOCAL_PORT,
                                        InetAddress.getByName(SERVER_NAME));

                        System.out.println("Created UDP server socket at " +
                                udpSocket.getLocalSocketAddress() + "...");

                        // Wait for a message in a loop and echo the same
                        // message to the sender
                        while (true) {
                                System.out.println("Waiting for a UDP packet" +
                                                " to arrive...");

                                // Prepare a packet to hold the received data
                                DatagramPacket packet =
                                        new DatagramPacket(new byte[1024], 1024);

                                // Receive a packet
                                udpSocket.receive(packet);
```

```
                            // Print the packet details
                            displayPacketDetails(packet);

                            // Echo the same packet to the sender
                            udpSocket.send(packet);
                    }
            }
            catch (IOException e) {
                    e.printStackTrace();
            }
    }

    public static void displayPacketDetails(DatagramPacket packet) {
            // Get the message
            byte[] msgBuffer = packet.getData();
            int length = packet.getLength();
            int offset = packet.getOffset();

            int remotePort = packet.getPort();
            InetAddress remoteAddr = packet.getAddress();
            String msg = new String(msgBuffer, offset, length);

            System.out.println("Received a packet:[IP Address=" +
                            remoteAddr + ", port=" + remotePort +
                            ", message=" + msg + "]");
    }
}
```

Listing 5-6 contains the program for the client application that uses a UDP socket to send/receive messages to/from the UDP echo server. Note that the client and server exchange one line of text at a time.

Listing 5-6. An Echo Client Based on UDP Sockets

```
// UDPEchoClient.java
package com.jdojo.net;

import java.io.BufferedReader;
import java.io.InputStreamReader;
import java.net.DatagramPacket;
import java.net.DatagramSocket;
import java.net.InetAddress;
import java.net.UnknownHostException;

public class UDPEchoClient {
    public static void main(String[] args) {
            DatagramSocket udpSocket = null;
            BufferedReader br = null;
            try {
                    // Create a UDP socket at localhost using an available port
                    udpSocket = new DatagramSocket();
```

```java
        String msg = null;

        // Create a buffered reader to get an input from a user
        br = new BufferedReader(new InputStreamReader(System.in));

        String promptMsg = "Please enter a message (Bye to quit):";
        System.out.print(promptMsg);

        while ((msg = br.readLine()) != null) {
            if (msg.equalsIgnoreCase("bye")) {
                break;
            }

            // Prepare a packet to send to the server
            DatagramPacket packet = UDPEchoClient.getPacket(msg);

            // Send the packet to the server
            udpSocket.send(packet);

            // Wait for a packet from the server
            udpSocket.receive(packet);

            // Display the packet details received from
            // the server
            displayPacketDetails(packet);

            System.out.print(promptMsg);
        }
    }
    catch (Exception e) {
        e.printStackTrace();
    }
    finally {
        // Close the socket
        if (udpSocket != null) {
            udpSocket.close();
        }
    }
}

public static void displayPacketDetails(DatagramPacket packet) {
    byte[] msgBuffer = packet.getData();
    int length = packet.getLength();
    int offset = packet.getOffset();
    int remotePort = packet.getPort();
    InetAddress remoteAddr = packet.getAddress();
    String msg = new String(msgBuffer, offset, length);
    System.out.println("[Server at IP Address=" + remoteAddr +
                    ", port=" + remotePort + "]: " + msg);

    // Add a line break
    System.out.println();
}
```

```java
public static DatagramPacket getPacket(String msg)
                              throws UnknownHostException {
        // We will send and accept a message of 1024 bytes in length.
        // longer messages will be truncated
        final int PACKET_MAX_LENGTH = 1024;
        byte[] msgBuffer = msg.getBytes();

        int length = msgBuffer.length;
        if (length > PACKET_MAX_LENGTH) {
                length = PACKET_MAX_LENGTH;
        }

        DatagramPacket packet = new DatagramPacket(msgBuffer, length);

        // Set the destination address and the port number
        int serverPort = 15900;
        final String SERVER_NAME = "localhost";
        InetAddress serverIPAddress =
                        InetAddress.getByName(SERVER_NAME);
        packet.setAddress(serverIPAddress);
        packet.setPort(serverPort);

        return packet;
    }
}
```

To test the UDP echo application, you need to run the UDPEchoServer and UDPEchoClient classes. You need to run the server first. The client application will prompt you to enter a message. Enter a text message and press the Enter key to send that message to the server. The server will echo the same message. Both applications display the messages being exchanged on the standard output. They also display the packet details, such as the sender's IP address and port number. The server application uses port number 15900 and the client application uses any available UDP port on the computer. If you get an error, it means that port number 15900 is in use, so you need to change the port number in the server program and use the new port number in the client program to address the packet. The server is designed to handle multiple clients at a time. You can run multiple instances of the UDPEchoClient class. Note that the server runs in an infinite loop and you must stop the server application manually.

The following is a sample log on the server console:

```
Created UDP server socket at /127.0.0.1:15900...
Waiting for a UDP packet to arrive...
Received a packet:[IP Address=/127.0.0.1, port=1522, message=Hello]
Waiting for a UDP packet to arrive...
Received a packet:[IP Address=/127.0.0.1, port=1522, message=Nice talking to you]
Waiting for a UDP packet to arrive...
```

The following is a sample log on the client console:

```
Please enter a message (Bye to quit):Hello
[Server at IP Address=localhost/127.0.0.1, port=15900]: Hello

Please enter a message (Bye to quit):Nice talking to you
[Server at IP Address=localhost/127.0.0.1, port=15900]: Nice talking to You

Please enter a message (Bye to quit):bye
```

A Connected UDP Socket

UDP sockets do not support an end-to-end connection like the TCP sockets. The DatagramSocket class contains a connect() method. This method allows an application to restrict sending and receiving of UDP packets to a specific IP address at a specific port number. Consider the following snippet of code:

```
InetAddress localIPAddress = InetAddress.getByName("192.168.11.101");
int localPort = 15900;
DatagramSocket socket = new DatagramSocket(localPort, localIPAddress);

// Connect the socket to a remote address
InetAddress remoteIPAddress = InetAddress.getByName("192.168.12.115");
int remotePort = 17901;
socket.connect(remoteIPAddress, remotePort);
```

The socket is bound to the local IP address 192.168.11.101 and local UDP port number 15900. It is connected to a remote IP address of 192.168.12.115 and a remote UDP port number 17901. It means that the socket object can be used to send/receive a datagram packet only to/from another UDP socket running at an IP address of 192.168.12.115 at the port number 17901. After you have called the connect() method on a UDP socket, you do not need to set the destination IP address and the port number for the outgoing datagram packets. The socket will add the destination IP address and port number that were used in the connect() method's call to all outgoing packets. If you do supply a destination address with a packet before you send it, the socket will make sure the destination address supplied in the packet is the same as the remote address used in the connect() method call. Otherwise, the send() method will throw an IllegalArgumentException.

Using the connect() method of a UDP socket has two advantages:

- It sets the destination address for the outgoing packets every time you send a packet.

- It restricts the socket to communicate only to the remote host whose IP address was used in the connect() method's call.

Now you understand that UDP sockets are connectionless and you do not have a real connection using a UDP socket. The connect() method in the DatagramSocket class does not provide any kind of connection for UDP sockets. Rather, it is useful for restricting the communication to a specific remote UDP socket.

UDP Multicast Sockets

Java supports UDP multicast sockets that can receive datagram packets sent to a multicast IP address. An object of the MulticastSocket class represents a multicast socket. Working with a MulticastSocket socket is similar to working with a DatagramSocket with one difference: a multicast socket is based on a group membership. After you have created and bound a multicast socket, you need to call its joinGroup(InetAddress multiCastIPAddress) method to make this socket a member of the multicast group defined by the specified multicast IP address, multiCastIpAddress. Once it becomes a member of a multicast group, any datagram packet sent to that group will be delivered to this socket. There can be multiple members in a multicast group. A multicast socket can be a member of multiple multicast groups. If a member decides not to receive a multicast packet from a group, it can leave the group by calling the leaveGroup(InetAddress multiCastIPAddress) method.

In IPv4, any IP address in the range 224.0.0.0 to 239.255.255.255 can be used as a multicast address to send a datagram packet. The IP address 224.0.0.0 is reserved and you should not use it in your application. A multicast IP address cannot be used as a source address for a datagram packet, which implies that you cannot bind a socket to a multicast address.

A socket itself does not have to be a member of a multicast group to send a datagram packet to a multicast address.

Java 7 added the IP multicast capability to the DatagramChannel class. Please refer to the "Multicasting Using Datagram Channels" section later in this chapter on how to use a datagram channel for IP multicasting. Note that the DatagramChannel class was added in Java 1.4, which did not have the IP multicast capability.

Listing 5-7 contains a program that creates a multicast socket that receives datagram packets addressed to the 230.1.1.1 multicast IP address.

Listing 5-7. A UDP Multicast Socket That Receives UDP Multicast Messages

```java
// UDPMultiCastReceiver.java
package com.jdojo.net;

import java.io.IOException;
import java.net.DatagramPacket;
import java.net.InetAddress;
import java.net.MulticastSocket;

public class UDPMultiCastReceiver {
    public static void main(String[] args) {
        int mcPort = 18777;
        String mcIPStr = "230.1.1.1";
        MulticastSocket mcSocket = null;
        InetAddress mcIPAddress = null;
        try {
            mcIPAddress = InetAddress.getByName(mcIPStr);
            mcSocket = new MulticastSocket(mcPort);
            System.out.println("Multicast Receiver running at:" +
                            mcSocket.getLocalSocketAddress());

            // Join the group
            mcSocket.joinGroup(mcIPAddress);

            DatagramPacket packet =
                    new DatagramPacket(new byte[1024], 1024);

            while (true) {
                System.out.println("Waiting for a multicast message...");
                mcSocket.receive(packet);
                String msg = new String(packet.getData(),
                                    packet.getOffset(),
                                    packet.getLength());
                System.out.println("[Multicast Receiver] Received:" + msg);
            }
        }
        catch (Exception e) {
            e.printStackTrace();
        }
        finally {
            if (mcSocket != null) {
                try {
                    mcSocket.leaveGroup(mcIPAddress);
                    mcSocket.close();
                }
```

```
                                    catch (IOException e) {
                                        e.printStackTrace();
                                    }
                            }
                    }
            }
}
```

Listing 5-8 contains a program that sends a message to the same multicast address. Note that you can run multiple instances of the UDPMulticastReceiver class and all of them will become a member of the same multicast group. When you run the UDPMulticastSender class, it will send a message to the group, and all members in the group will receive a copy of the same message. The UDPMulticastSender class uses a DatagramSocket, not a MulticastSocket to send a multicast message.

Listing 5-8. A UDP Datagram Socket, a Multicast Sender Application

```java
// UDPMultiCastSender.java
package com.jdojo.net;

import java.net.DatagramPacket;
import java.net.DatagramSocket;
import java.net.InetAddress;

public class UDPMultiCastSender {
    public static void main(String[] args) {
        int mcPort = 18777;
        String mcIPStr = "230.1.1.1";
        DatagramSocket udpSocket = null;

        try {
            // Create a datagram socket
            udpSocket = new DatagramSocket();

            // Prepare a message
            InetAddress mcIPAddress = InetAddress.getByName(mcIPStr);

            byte[] msg = "Hello multicast socket".getBytes();
            DatagramPacket packet =
                    new DatagramPacket(msg, msg.length);
            packet.setAddress(mcIPAddress);
            packet.setPort(mcPort);
            udpSocket.send(packet);

            System.out.println("Sent a multicast message.");
            System.out.println("Exiting application");
        }
        catch (Exception e) {
            e.printStackTrace();
        }
```

```
        finally {
                if (udpSocket != null) {
                        try {
                                udpSocket.close();
                        }
                        catch (Exception e) {
                                e.printStackTrace();
                        }
                }
        }
    }
}
```

URI, URL, and URN

A Uniform Resource Identifier (URI) is a sequence of characters that identifies a resource. The Request for Comments (RFC) 3986 defines the generic syntax for a URI. The full text of this RFC is available at `http://www.ietf.org/rfc/rfc3986.txt`. A resource identifier can identify a resource by a location, a name, or both. This section gives an overview of the URI. If you are interested in details about the URI, you are advised to read RFC3986.

A URI that uses a location to identify a resource is called Uniform Resource Locator (URL). For example, `http://www.yahoo.com/index.html` represents a URL that identifies a document named `index.html` at the host `www.yahoo.com`. Another example of a URL is `mailto:ksharan@jdojo.com` in which the `mailto` protocol instructs the application that interprets it to open up an email application to send an email to the email address specified in the URL. In this case, the URL is not locating any resources. Rather, it is identifying the details of an email. You can also set the subject and the body parts of an email using the `mailto` protocol. Therefore, a URL does not always imply a location of a resource. Sometimes the resource may be abstract, as in the case of the `mailto` protocol. Once you locate a resource using a URL, you can perform some operations, such as retrieve, update, or delete, on the resource. The details of how the operations are performed depend on the scheme being used in the URL. A URL just identifies the parts of a resource location and scheme to locate it, not the details of any operations that can be performed on the resource.

A URI that uses a name to identify a resource is called a Uniform Resource Name (URN). For example, `URN:ISBN:978-1-4302-6661-7` represents a URN, which identifies a book using International Standard Book Numbers (ISBN) namespace.

URL and URN are subsets of URI. Therefore, the discussion about URI applies to both URL and URN. The detailed syntax of a URI depends on the scheme it uses. In this section, I will cover a generic syntax of the URI, which is typically a URL. The next section will explore Java classes that are used to represent URIs and URLs in Java programs.

A URI can be absolute or relative. A relative URI is always interpreted in the context of another absolute URI, which is called the base URI. In other words, you must have an absolute URI to make a relative URI meaningful.

An absolute URI has the following generic format:

`<scheme>:<scheme-specific-part>`

The `<scheme-specific-part>` depends on the `<scheme>`. For example, an `http` scheme uses one format, and a `mailto` scheme uses another format. Another generic form of a URI is as follows. Typically, but not necessarily, it represents a URL.

`<scheme>://<authority><path>?<query>#<fragment>`

Here, `<scheme>` indicates a method to access a resource. It is the protocol name such as `http`, `ftp`, etc. We all use the term "protocol" for what is termed a "scheme" in the URI specification. If the term "scheme" throws you off, you can read it as "protocol" whenever it appears in this section. The `<scheme>` and `<path>` parts are required in a URI. All other parts are optional. The `<path>` part may be an empty string.

The `<authority>` part indicates the server name (or IP address) or a scheme-specific registry. If the `<authority>` part represents a server name, it may be written in the form of `<userinfo>@host:port`. If a `<authority>` is present in a URI, it begins with two forward slashes; it is an optional part. For example, a URL that identifies a file in a local file system on a machine uses the `file` scheme as `file:///c:/documents/welcome.doc`.

The URI syntax uses a hierarchical syntax in its `<path>` part, which locates the resource on the server. Multiple parts of the `<path>` are separated by a forward slash (/).

The `<query>` part indicates that the resource is obtained by executing the specified query. It consists of name-value pairs separated by an ampersand (&). The name and value are separated by an equal sign (=). For example, `id=123&rate=5.5` is a query, which has two parts, `id` and `rate`. The value for `id` is `123` and the value for `rate` is `5.5`.

The `<fragment>` part identifies a secondary resource, typically a subset of the primary resource identified by another part of the URI.

The following is an example of a URI, which is also broken into parts:

```
URI:       http://www.jdojo.com/java/intro.html?id=123#conclusion
Scheme:    http
Authority: www.jdojo.com
Path:      /java/intro.html
Query:     id=123
Fragment:  conclusion
```

The URI represents a URL that refers to a document named `intro.html` on the `www.jdojo.com` server. The scheme `http` indicates that the document can be retrieved using the `http` protocol. The query `id=123` indicates that the document is obtained by executing this query. The fragment part `conclusion` can be interpreted differently by different applications that use the document. In case of an HTML document, the fragment part is interpreted by the web browser as the part of the main document.

Not all parts of a URI are mandatory. Which parts are mandatory and which parts are optional depend on the scheme that is used. One of the goals of using a URI to identify a resource was to make it universally readable. For this reason, there is a well-defined set of characters that can be used to represent a URI. URI syntax uses some reserved characters that have special meaning and they can only be used in specific parts of a URI. In other parts, the reserved characters need to be escaped. A character is escaped by using a percent character followed by its ASCII value in a hexadecimal format. For example, ASCII value of space is 32 in decimal format, and it is 20 in hexadecimal format. If you want to use a space character in a URI, you must use %20, which is the escaped form for a space. Since the percent sign is used as part of an escape character, you must use %25 to represent a % character in a URI (25 is the hexadecimal value for number 37 in decimal. The ASCII value for % is 37 in decimal). For example, if you want to use a value of 5.2% in a query, the following is an invalid URI:

```
http://www.jdojo.com/details?rate=5.2%
```

To make it a valid URI, you need to escape the percent sign character as %25 as shown:

```
http://www.jdojo.com/details?rate=5.2%25
```

It is important to understand the usage of a relative URI. A relative URI is always interpreted in the context of an absolute URI, which is called the base URI. An absolute URI starts with a scheme. A relative URI inherits some parts of its base URI. Let's consider a URI that refers to an HTML document as shown:

```
http://www.jdojo.com/java/intro.html
```

The document referred to in the URI is `intro.html`. Its path is `/java/intro.html`. Suppose two documents named `brief_intro.html` and `detailed_intro.html` reside (physically or logically) in the same path hierarchy as `intro.html`. The following are the absolute URIs for all three documents:

- `http://www.jdojo.com/java/intro.html`

- `http://www.jdojo.com/java/brief_intro.html`

- `http://www.jdojo.com/java/detailed_intro.html`

If you are already in the `intro.html` context, it will be easier to refer to the other two documents using their names instead of their absolute URI. What does it mean by being in the `intro.html` context? When you use the `http://www.jdojo.com/java/intro.html` URI to identify a resource, it has three parts: a scheme (`http`), a server name (`www.jdojo.com`), and a document path (`/java/intro.html`). The path indicates that the document is under the java path hierarchy, which in turn is at the root of the path hierarchy. All details—scheme, server name, path details, excluding the document name itself (`intro.html`)—make up the context for the `intro.html` document. If you look at the URI for the other two documents listed above, you will notice that all details about them are the same as for `intro.html`. In other words, you can state that the context for the other two documents is the same as for `intro.html`. In this case, with an absolute URI of the `intro.html` document as base URI, the relative URIs for the other two documents are their names: `brief_intro.html` and `detailed_intro.html`. It can be listed as follows:

- `Base URI: http://www.jdojo.com/java/intro.html`

- `Relative URI: brief_intro.html`

- `Relative URI: detailed_intro.html`

In the list, the two relative URIs inherit the scheme, server name, and path hierarchy from the base URI. It is to be emphasized that a relative URI never makes sense without specifying its base URI.

When a relative URI has to be used, it must be resolved to its equivalent absolute URI. The URI specification lays down rules to resolve a relative URI. I will discuss some of the most commonly used forms of relative URIs and their resolutions. There are two special characters used to define the `<path>` part of a URI. They are a dot and two dots. A dot means the current path hierarchy. Two dots mean one up in the path hierarchy. You must have seen these two sets of characters being used in a file system to mean the current directory and parent directory. You can think of their meanings in a URI the same way, but a URI does not assume any directory hierarchy. In a URI, a path is considered as hierarchical, and it is not tied to a file system hierarchical structure at all. However, in practice, when you work with web-based applications, URLs are usually mapped to a file system hierarchical structure. In the normalized form of a URI, dots are replaced appropriately. For example, `s://sn/a/./b` is normalized to `s://sn/a/b`, and `s://sn/a/../b` is normalized to `s://sn/b`. The non-normalized and normalized forms refer to the same URL. The normalized form has extra characters removed. By just looking at two URIs, you cannot say that they are referring to the same resource or not. You must normalize them before you compare them for equality. During the comparison process, scheme, server name, and hexadecimal digits are considered case-insensitive. Here are some rules to resolve a relative URI:

- If a URI starts with a scheme, it is considered an absolute URI.

- If a relative URI starts with an authority, it inherits scheme from its base URI.

- If a relative URI is an empty string, it is the same as the base URI.

- If a relative URI has a fragment part only, the resolved URI uses the new fragment. If a base URI had a fragment, it is replaced with the fragment of the relative URI. Otherwise, the fragment of the relative URI is added to the base URI.

- A relative URI's path does not start with a forward slash (`/`). If the base URI has a path, remove the last component of the path in the base URI and append the relative URI. Note that the last component of the path may be an empty string as in *http://www.abc.com/*.

- If a relative URL starts with a path, which in turn starts with a forward slash (`/`), the base URI's path is replaced with the relative URI's path.

Table 5-5 contains examples of using these rules. The examples in the table conform to the rules followed in Java URI and URL classes. Java rules deviate slightly in a few cases from the rules set in the URI specification.

Table 5-5. *Examples of How a Relative URI is Resolved to an Absolute URI Using a Base URI*

Base URI	Relative URI	Resolved Relative URI	Description of the Relative URI
h://sn/a/b/c	http://sn2/foo	h://sn2/foo	It is an absolute URI.
h://sn/a/b/c	//sn2/h/k	h://sn2/h/k	It starts with an authority
h://sn/a/b/c		h://sn/a/b/c	It is an empty string.
h://sn/a/b/c	#k	h://sn/a/b/c#k	It contains a fragment only.
h://sn/a/b/c#a	#k	h://sn/a/b/c#k	It contains a fragment only.
h://sn/a/b/	foo	h://sn/a/b/foo	The path does not start with a /.
h://sn/a/b/c	foo	h://sn/a/b/foo	The path does not start with a /.
h://sn/a/b/c?d=3	foo	h://sn/a/b/foo	The path does not start with a /.
h://sn/	foo	h://sn/foo	The path does not start with a /.
h://sn	foo	h://sn/foo	The path does not start with a /.
h://sn/a/b/	/foo	h://sn/foo	The path starts with a /.
h://sn/a/b/c	/foo	h://sn/foo	The path starts with a /.
h://sn/a/b/c?d=3	/foo	h://sn/foo	The path starts with a /.
h://sn/	/foo	h://sn/foo	The path starts with a /.
h://sn	/foo	h://sn/foo	The path starts with a /.

■ **Tip** You can also use a host name or IP address as an authority in a URI. IPv4 can be used in its dotted decimal format such as http://192.168.10.178/docs/toc.html. IPv6 must be enclosed in brackets such as http://[1283::8:800:200C:A43A]/docs/toc.html.

URI and URL as Java Objects

Java represents a URI and a URL as objects. It provides the following four classes that you can use to work with a URI and a URL as objects in a Java program:

- java.net.URI
- java.net.URL
- java.net.URLEncoder
- java.net.URLDecoder

An object of the URI class represents a URI. An object of the URL class represents a URL. URLEncoder and URLDecoder are utility classes that help encode and decode URI strings. I will discuss other Java classes in the next sections that are used to retrieve the resource identified by a URL.

The URI class has many constructors. They let you pass variable combinations of parts (scheme, authority, path, query, and fragment) of a URI. All constructors throw a checked exception called URISyntaxException. They throw an exception because strings, which you use to construct a URI object, may not be in conformity with the URI specification.

```
// Create a URI object
URI baseURI = new URI("http://www.yahoo.com");

// Create a URI with relative URI string and resolve it using baseURI
URI relativeURI = new URI("welcome.html");
URI resolvedRelativeURI = baseURI.resolve(relativeURI);
```

Listing 5-9 demonstrates how to use the URI class in a Java program.

Listing 5-9. A Sample Class That Demonstrates the Use of the java.net.URI Class

```
// URITest.java
package com.jdojo.net;

import java.net.URI;
import java.net.URISyntaxException;

public class URITest {
    public static void main(String[] args) {
        String baseURIStr = "http://www.jdojo.com/javaintro.html?" +
                            "id=25&rate=5.5%25#foo";
        String relativeURIStr = "../sports/welcome.html";

        try {
            URI baseURI = new URI(baseURIStr);
            URI relativeURI = new URI(relativeURIStr);

            // Resolve the relative URI with respect to the base URI
            URI resolvedURI = baseURI.resolve(relativeURI);

            printURIDetails(baseURI);
            printURIDetails(relativeURI);
            printURIDetails(resolvedURI);
        }
        catch (URISyntaxException e) {
            e.printStackTrace();
        }
    }

    public static void printURIDetails(URI uri) {
        System.out.println("URI:" + uri);
        System.out.println("Normalized:" + uri.normalize());
```

```
        String parts = "[Scheme=" + uri.getScheme() +
                        ", Authority=" + uri.getAuthority() +
                        ", Path=" + uri.getPath() +
                        ", Query:" + uri.getQuery() +
                        ", Fragment:" + uri.getFragment() + "]";

        System.out.println(parts);
        System.out.println();
    }
}
```

```
URI:http://www.jdojo.com/javaintro.html?id=25&rate=5.5%25#foo
Normalized:http://www.jdojo.com/javaintro.html?id=25&rate=5.5%25#foo
[Scheme=http, Authority=www.jdojo.com, Path=/javaintro.html, Query:id=25&rate=5.5%, Fragment:foo]

URI:../sports/welcome.html
Normalized:../sports/welcome.html
[Scheme=null, Authority=null, Path=../sports/welcome.html, Query:null, Fragment:null]

URI:http://www.jdojo.com/../sports/welcome.html
Normalized:http://www.jdojo.com/../sports/welcome.html
[Scheme=http, Authority=www.jdojo.com, Path=/../sports/welcome.html, Query:null, Fragment:null]
```

You can also get a URL object from a URI object using its toURL() method as shown:

```
URL baseURL = baseURT.toURI();
```

You can also create a URI object using the create(String str) static method of the URI class. The create() method does not throw a checked exception. It throws a runtime exception. Therefore, its use will not force you to handle the exception. You should use this method only when you know that a URI string is well-formed.

```
URI uri2 = URI.create("http://www.yahoo.com");
```

An instance of the java.net.URL class represents a URL in a Java program. Although every URL is also a URI, Java does not inherit the URL class from the URI class. Java uses the term protocol to refer to the scheme part in the URI specification. You can create a URL object by providing a string that has all URL's parts concatenated, or by providing parts of a URL separately. If strings that you supply to create a URL object are not valid, the constructors of the URL class will throw a MalformedURLException checked exception. You must handle this exception when you create a URL object.

Listing 5-10 demonstrates how to create a URL object. The URL class lets you create an absolute URL from a relative URL and a base URL using one of its constructors.

Listing 5-10. A Sample Class That Demonstrates the Use of the java.net.URL Class

```
// URLTest.java
package com.jdojo.net;

import java.net.URL;

public class URLTest {
    public static void main(String[] args) {
        String baseURLStr = "http://www.ietf.org/rfc/rfc3986.txt";
        String relativeURLStr = "rfc2732.txt";
```

```
            try {
                    URL baseURL = new URL (baseURLStr);
                    URL resolvedRelativeURL = new URL(baseURL, relativeURLStr);
                    System.out.println("Base URL:" + baseURL);
                    System.out.println("Relative URL String:" + relativeURLStr);
                    System.out.println("Resolved Relative URL:" + resolvedRelativeURL);
            }
            catch (Exception e) {
                    e.printStackTrace();
            }
        }
    }
}
```

```
Base URL:http://www.ietf.org/rfc/rfc3986.txt
Relative URL String:rfc2732.txt
Resolved Relative URL:http://www.ietf.org/rfc/rfc2732.txt
```

Typically, you create a URL object to retrieve the resource identified by the URL. Note that you can create an object of the URL class as long as the URL is well formed textually and the protocol to handle the URL is available. The successful creation of a URL object in a Java program does not guarantee the existence of the resource at the server specified in the URL. The URL class provides methods that you can use in conjunction with other classes to retrieve the resource identified by the URL.

The URL class makes sure that it can handle the protocol specified in the URL string. For example, it will not let you create a URL object with a string as ppp://www.sss.com/ unless you develop and supply it a protocol handler for a ppp protocol. I will discuss in detail how to retrieve the resource identified by a URL in the next section.

Sometimes you do not know the parts of the URL string in advance. You get the parts of the URL at runtime as input from other parts of the program or from the user. In such cases, you will need to encode the parts of the URL before you can use them to create a URL object. Sometimes you get a string in encoded form and you want it to be decoded. An encoded string will have all the restricted characters properly escaped.

The URLEncoder and URLDecoder classes are used to encode and decode strings, respectively. The URLEncoder.encode(String source, String encoding) static method is used to encode a source string using the specified encoding. The URLDecoder.decode(String source, String encoding) static method is used to decode a source string using a specified encoding. The following snippet of code shows how to encode/decode strings. Typically, you encode/decode the value part of name-value pairs in the query part of a URL. Note that you should never attempt to encode the entire URL string. Otherwise, it will encode some of the reserved characters such a forward slash and the resulting URL string will be invalid.

```
String source = "this is a test for 2.5% and &" ;
String encoded = URLEncoder.encode(source, "utf-8");
String decoded = URLDecoder.decode(encoded, "utf-8");
System.out.println("Source: " + source);
System.out.println("Encoded: " + encoded);
System.out.println("Decoded: " + decoded);
```

```
Source: this is a test for 2.5% and &
Encoded: this+is+a+test+for+2.5%25+and+%26
Decoded: this is a test for 2.5% and &
```

Accessing the Contents of a URL

A URL has a protocol that is used to communicate with the remote application that hosts the URL's contents. For example, the URL http://www.yahoo.com/index.html uses the http protocol. In a URL, you specify a protocol that is used by the application layer in the protocol suite. When you need to access the URL's contents, the computer will use some kind of protocols from lower layers in the protocol suite (transport, Internet layers, etc.) to communicate with the remote host. The http application layer protocol uses TCP/IP protocols in lower layers. In a distributed application, it is very frequent that you need to retrieve (or read) the resource (could be text, html content, image files, audio/video files or any other kind of information) identified by a URL. Although it is possible to open a socket every time you need to read the contents of URL, it is time consuming and cumbersome for programmers. After all, programmers need some way to be more productive than writing repetitive code for what seems to be a routine job. Java designers realized this need and they have provided a very easy (yes, it is very easy) way to read/write data from/to a URL. This section will explore some of the ways, from very simple to quite complex, to read/write data from/to a URL.

As the data passes from one layer to another in the protocol suite, each layer adds a header to the data. Since a URL uses a protocol in the application layer, it also contains its own header. The format of the header depends on the protocol being used. When the http request is send to a remote host, the application layer in the source host adds the http header to the data. The remote host has an application layer that handles the http protocol and it uses the header information to interpret the contents. In summary, a URL data will have two parts: a header part and a contents part. The URL class along with some other classes let you read/write both header and content parts of a URL. I will start with the simplest case of reading the contents of a URL.

Before you read/write from/to a URL, you need to have a working URL that you can access. You can read content of any URL that is publicly available on the Internet. For this discussion, I will assume that you are familiar with Java Server Pages (JSP) and you have access to a web server where you can deploy a JSP page. If you do not know JSP, you can just replace the URL used in examples of this section with any publicly available URL; for example, the URL http://www.yahoo.com will work fine, and you should be able to run all examples. Writing data to a URL is a little different. It will be easier if you can run your JSP to see how writing to a URL works. I assume that you have deployed a web application on a web server and it has a web page called echo_params.jsp.

Listing 5-11 shows the content of this JSP page. It performs two things. It reads the HTTP request method, which can be GET or POST, and prints it. It reads all the parameters passed in with the HTTP request and prints the list of parameter names and values.

Listing 5-11. The Contents of the echo_params.jsp File

```
<%@ page contentType="text/html;charset=windows-1252"%>
<html>
    <head>
        <meta http-equiv="Content-Type" content="text/html;
                charset=windows-1252"/>
        <title>Echo Request Method and Parameters</title>
    </head>
    <body>
        <h1>URL Connection Test</h1>
        <%
        out.println("Request Method: " + request.getMethod());
        out.println("<br/><br/>");

        out.println("<u>List of Parameter Names and Values</u><br/>");
        java.util.Enumeration paramNames =
                request.getParameterNames();
```

```
                    while(paramNames.hasMoreElements()) {
                        String paramName  = (String)paramNames.nextElement();
                        String paramValue = request.getParameter(paramName);
                        out.println("Name: " + paramName + ", Value: " + paramValue);
                        out.println("<br/>");
                    }
                %>
            </body>
</html>
```

The URL class lets you read the contents (not header) of a URL by just writing two lines of code as shown:

```
URL url = new URL("your URL string goes here");
InputStream ins = url.openStream();
```

Listing 5-12 has the complete program that reads a URL's contents. You will need to change the URL in this program according to your web server setup. The output shows that you do access the JSP, and the JSP gets the query (id=123) passed to it and transmits back the generated HTML contents. The HTML request was sent using the GET method. If you want to use the POST method to send a request to a URL, you will need to use the URLConnection class, which I will discuss next. I have formatted the output for better readability.

Listing 5-12. A Simple URL Contents Reader Program

```java
// SimpleURLContentReader.java
package com.jdojo.net;

import java.io.BufferedReader;
import java.io.IOException;
import java.io.InputStream;
import java.io.InputStreamReader;
import java.net.URL;

public class SimpleURLContentReader {
    public static String getURLContent(String urlStr) {
        BufferedReader br = null;
        try {
            URL url = new URL(urlStr);

            // Get the input stream
            InputStream ins = url.openStream();

            // Wrap input stream into a reader
            br = new BufferedReader(new InputStreamReader(ins));

            StringBuilder sb = new StringBuilder();
            String msg = null;
            while ((msg = br.readLine()) != null) {
                sb.append(msg);
                sb.append("\n"); // Append a new line
            }

            return sb.toString();
        }
```

```java
                catch (IOException e) {
                        e.printStackTrace();
                }
                finally {
                        if (br != null) {
                                try {
                                        br.close();
                                }
                                catch (IOException e) {
                                        e.printStackTrace();
                                }
                        }
                }

                // If we get here it means there was an error
                return null;
        }

        public static void main(String[] args) {
                String urlStr = "http://localhost:8080/docsapp/" +
                                "echo_params.jsp?id=123";
                String content = getURLContent(urlStr);
                System.out.println(content);
        }
}
```

```html
<html>
  <head>
    <meta http-equiv="Content-Type" content="text/html;
        charset=windows-1252"/>
    <title>Echo Request Method and Parameters</title>
  </head>
  <body>
    <h1>URL Connection Test</h1>
    Request Method: GET
    <br/><br/>
    <u>List of Parameter Names and Values</u><br/>
    Name: id, Value: 123
    <br/>
  </body>
</html>
```

Once you get the input stream, you can use it for reading the content of the URL. Another way of reading the content of a URL is by using the getContent() method of the URL class. Since getContent() can return any kind of content, its return type is the Object type. You will need to check what kind of object it returns before you use the contents of the object. For example, it may return an InputStream object, and in that case, you will need to read data from the input stream. The following are the two versions of the getContent() method:

- final Object getContent() throws IOException
- final Object getContent(Class[] classes) throws IOException

The second version of the method lets you pass an array of class type. It will attempt to convert the content object to one of the classes you pass to it in the specified order. If the content object does not match any of the types, it will return null. You will still need to write if statements to know what type of object was returned from the getContent() method, as shown:

```
URL baseURL = new URL ("your url string goes here");
Class[] c = new Class[] {String.class, BufferedReader.class, InputStream.class};

Object content = baseURL.getContent(c);
if (content == null) {
        // Contents are not of any of the three kinds
}
else if (content instanceof String) {
        // You got a string
}
else if (content instanceof BufferedReader) {
        // You got a reader
}
else if (content instanceof InputStream) {
        // You got an input stream
}
```

If you read the contents of a URL using the openStream() or getContent() method, the URL class handles many of the complexities of using sockets internally. The downside of this approach is that you do not have any control over the connection settings. You cannot write data to the URL using this approach. Also, you do not have access to the header information for the protocol used in a URL. Don't despair; Java provides another class named URLConnection that lets you do all of these in a simple and concise manner. URLConnection is an abstract class and you cannot create its object directly. You need to use the openConnection() method of the URL object to get a URLConnection object. The URL class will handle the creation of an URLConnection object, which will be appropriate to handle the data for the protocol used in the URL. The following snippet of code shows how to use an URLConnection object to read and write data to a URL:

```
URL url = new URL("your URL string goes here");

// Get a connection object
URLConnection connection = url.openConnection();

// Indicate that you will be writing to the connection
connection.setDoOutput(true);

// Get output/input streams to write/read data
OutputStream ous = connection.getOutputStream();
InputStream ins = connection.getInputStream(); // Caution. Read below
```

The openConnection() method of the URL class returns a URLConnection object, which is not connected to the URL source yet. You must set all connection-related parameters to this object before it is connected. For example, if you want to write data to the URL, you must call the setDoOutput(true) method on the connection object before it is connected. A URLConnection object gets connected when you call its connect() method. However, it is connected implicitly when you call its methods that require a connection. For example, writing data to a URL and reading the URL's data or header fields will connect the URLConnection object automatically, if it is not already connected.

Here are few things you must follow if you want to avoid problems when you work with an URLConnection to read and write data to a URL:

- When you are only reading data from a URL, you can get the input stream using its getInputStream() method. Use the input stream to read data. It will use a GET method for the request to the remote host. That is, if you are passing some parameters to the URL, you must do so by adding the query part to the URL.

- If you are writing as well as reading data from a URL, you must call the setDoOutput(true) before you connect. You must finish writing the data to the URL before you start reading the data. Writing data to a URL will change the request method to POST. You cannot even get the input stream before you finish writing data to the URL. In fact, the getInputStream() method sends a request to the remote host. Your intention is to send the data to the remote host and read the response from the remote host. This one gets as tricky as it can. Here is a little more explanation, using a snippet of code, assuming that connection is an URLConnection object:

```
// Incorrect - 1. Get input and output streams
// you must get the output stream first
InputStream ins = connection.getInputStream();
OutputStream ous = connection.getOutputStream();

// Incorrect - 2. Get output and input streams
// you must get the output stream and finish writing
// before you should get the input stream
OutputStream ous = connection.getOutputStream();
InputStream ins = connection.getInputStream();

// Correct. Get output stream and get done with it.
// And, then get the input stream and read data.
OutputStream ous = connection.getOutputStream();

// Write logic to write data using ous object here. Make sure
// you are done writing data before you call the
// getInputStream() method as shown below
InputStream ins = connection.getInputStream();

// Write logic to read data
```

- Using the getInputStream() method and reading header fields, using any method such as getHeaderField(String headerName), have the same effect. The URL's server supplies both header and content. An URLConnection must send the request to get them.

Listing 5-13 contains the complete code that writes/reads data to/from the echo_params.jsp page as listed in Listing 5-11. Note that you will need the echo_params.jsp page deployed to a web server for this example to work. I have formatted the output for better readability.

Listing 5-13. A URL Reader/Writer Class That Writes/Reads Data to/from a URL

```java
// URLConnectionReaderWriter.java
package com.jdojo.net;

import java.io.BufferedReader;
import java.io.BufferedWriter;
import java.io.IOException;
import java.io.InputStream;
import java.io.InputStreamReader;
import java.io.OutputStream;
import java.io.OutputStreamWriter;
import java.io.UnsupportedEncodingException;
import java.net.URL;
import java.net.URLConnection;
import java.net.URLEncoder;
import java.util.Map;

public class URLConnectionReaderWriter {
        public static String getURLContent(String urlStr, String input) {
                BufferedReader br = null;
                BufferedWriter bw = null;

                try {
                        URL url = new URL(urlStr);
                        URLConnection connection = url.openConnection();

                        // Must call setDoOutput(true) to indicate that we
                        // will write to the connection. By default, it is fals
                        // By default, setDoInput() is set to true.
                        connection.setDoOutput(true);

                        // Now, connect to the remote object
                        connection.connect();

                        // Write data to the URL first before reading the response
                        OutputStream ous = connection.getOutputStream();
                        bw = new BufferedWriter(new OutputStreamWriter(ous));
                        bw.write(input);
                        bw.flush();
                        bw.close();

                        // Must be placed after writing the data. Otherwise,
                        // it will result in error, because if write is performed,
                        // read must be performed after the write
                        printRequestHeaders(connection);

                        InputStream ins = connection.getInputStream();

                        // Wrap the input stream into a reader
                        br = new BufferedReader(new InputStreamReader(ins));
```

```java
                    StringBuffer sb = new StringBuffer();
                    String msg = null;
                    while ((msg = br.readLine()) != null) {
                            sb.append(msg);
                            sb.append("\n"); // Append a new line
                    }

                    return sb.toString();
            }
            catch (IOException e) {
                    e.printStackTrace();
            }
            finally {
                    if (br != null) {
                            try {
                                    br.close();
                            }
                            catch (IOException e) {
                                    e.printStackTrace();
                            }
                    }
            }

            // If we arrive here it means there was an error
            return null;
    }

    public static void printRequestHeaders(URLConnection connection) {
            Map headers = connection.getHeaderFields();
            System.out.println("Request Headers are:");
            System.out.println(headers);
            System.out.println();
    }

    public static void main(String[] args) {
            // Change the URL to point to the echo_params.jsp page
            // on your web server
            String urlStr = "http://www.jdojo.com/docsapp/echo_params.jsp";
            String query = null;
            try {
                    // Encode the query. We need to encode only the value
                    // of the name parameter. Other names and values are fine
                    query = "id=789&name=" +
                            URLEncoder.encode("John & Co.", "utf-8");

                    // Get the content and display it on the console
                    String content = getURLContent(urlStr, query);
                    System.out.println(content);
            }
```

```
            catch (UnsupportedEncodingException e) {
                e.printStackTrace();
            }
        }
}
```

```
Request Headers are:
{null=[HTTP/1.1 200 OK], Date=[Fri, 19 Dec 2008 02:15:14 GMT], Content-Length=[402],
Set-Cookie=[JSESSIONID=567B1B9F853DD22DD73AB8452E220E0A; Path=/examples],
Content-Type=[text/html;charset=windows-1252], Server=[Apache-Coyote/1.1]}
<html>
  <head>
    <meta http-equiv="Content-Type" content="text/html;
        charset=windows-1252"/>
    <title>Echo Request Method and Parameters</title>
  </head>
  <body>
  <h1>URL Connection Test</h1>
  Request Method: POST
<br/><br/>
<u>List of Parameter Names and Values</u><br/>Name: name, Value: John & Co.
<br/>Name: id, Value: 789
<br/>
  </body>
</html>
```

This time, you are using the POST method to send data to the URL. Note that the data that you send has been encoded using the URLEncoder class. You needed to encode only the value of the name field, which is "John & Co." because the ampersand in the value will conflict with the name-value pair separator in the query string. The program has plenty of comments to warn you of any dangers if you change the sequence of any statements.

The program prints information about all headers that are returned in a java.util.Map object. The URLConnection class provides several ways to get the header field's values. For commonly used headers, it provides a direct method. For example, the methods called getContentLength(), getContentType(), and getContentEncoding() return the value of the header fields that indicate length, type, and encoding of the URL's contents, respectively. If you know the header field name or its index, you can use the getHeaderField(String headerName) or getHeaderField(int headerIndex) method to get its value. The getHeaderFields() method returns a Map object whose keys represent the header field names and the values represent the header field values. Use caution when reading a header field because it has the same effect on the URLConnection object as reading the contents. If you wish to write data to a URL, you must first write the data before you can read the header fields.

Java lets you read the contents of a JAR file using the jar protocol. Suppose you have a JAR file called myclasses.jar, which has a class file whose path is myfolder/Abc.class. You can get a JarURLConnection from a URL and use its methods to access the JAR file data. Note that you can only read JAR file contents from a URL. You cannot write to a JAR file URL. The following snippet of code shows how to get a JarURLConnection object. You will need to use its methods to get the JAR specific data.

```
String str = "jar:http://www.abc.com/myclasses.jar!/myfolder/Abc.class";
URL url = new URL(str);
JarURLConnection connection = (JarURLConnection)url.openConnection();

// Use the connection object to access any jar related data.
```

■ **Tip** You have read many words of caution in this section about using a URLConnection object. Here is one more: a URLConnection object must be used for only one request. It works on the concept of obtain-use-and-throw. If you wish to write or read data from a URL multiple times, you must call the URL's openConnection() each time separately.

Non-Blocking Socket Programming

In previous sections, I discussed TCP and UDP sockets. The connect(), accept(), read(), and write() methods of the Socket and ServerSocket classes block until the operation is complete. For example, a client socket's thread is blocked if it calls the read() method to read data from a server until the data is available. Would it not be nice if you could call the read() method on a client socket and start doing something else until the data from the server arrives? When data is available from the server, the client socket will be notified, which will read the data at an appropriate time. Another big issue that you face with socket programming is the scalability of a server application. In previous sections, I suggested that you would need to create a new thread to handle each client connection or you would have a pool of threads to handle all client connections. Both ways, you will be creating and maintaining a bunch of threads in your program. Wouldn't it be nice if you didn't have to deal with threads in a server program to handle multiple clients? Non-blocking socket channels offer all of these nice features. As always, a good feature has a price tag associated with it; so too with the non-blocking socket channel. It has a bit of a learning curve. You are used to programming where things happen sequentially. With non-blocking socket channels, you will need to change your mindset about the way you think about performing things in a program. Changing your mindset takes time. Your program will be performing multiple things that will not be performed sequentially. If you are learning Java for the first time, you can skip this section and revisit it later when you gain some more experience in writing complex Java programs.

It is assumed that you have a good understanding of socket programming using ServerSocket and Socket classes. It is further assumed that you have a basic understanding of *New Input/Output* in Java using buffers and channels. This section uses some classes that are contained in java.nio, java.nio.channels, and java.nio.charset packages.

Let's start by comparing classes that are involved in blocking and non-blocking socket communications. Table 5-6 lists the main classes that are used in blocking and non-blocking socket applications.

Table 5-6. Comparison of Classes Involved in Blocking and Non-Blocking Socket Programming

Classes Used in Blocking Socket-Based Communication	Classes Used in Non-Blocking Socket-Based Communication
ServerSocket	ServerSocketChannel
	The ServerSocket class still exists behind the scenes.
Socket	SocketChannel
	The Socket class still exists behind the scenes.
InputStream OutputStream	No corresponding classes exist. A SocketChannel is used to read/write data
No corresponding class exists.	Selector
No corresponding class exists.	SelectionKey

You will work with a ServerSocketChannel object primarily to accept a new connection request in a server instead of using a ServerSocket. The ServerSocket has not disappeared. It is still at play behind the scenes. If you need the reference of the ServerSocket object being used internally, you can get it by using the socket() method of the ServerSocketChannel object. You can think of a ServerSocketChannel object as a wrapper for a ServerSocket object.

You will work with a SocketChannel to communicate between a client and a server instead of a Socket. A Socket object is still at play behind the scenes. You can get the reference of the Socket object using the socket() method of the SocketChannel class. You can think of a SocketChannel object as a wrapper for a Socket object.

Before I start discussing the mechanism that is used by the non-blocking sockets to give you a more efficient and scalable application interface, it would be helpful to look at a real-world example. Let's discuss the way orders are placed and served in a fast food restaurant. Suppose the restaurant expects the maximum ten customers and the minimum of zero customers at any time. A customer comes to the restaurant, places his order, and is served the food. How many servers should that restaurant employ? In the best case, it may employ only one server that can handle receiving orders from all customers and serving their food. In the worst case, it can have ten servers—one server reserved for one customer. In the latter case, if there are only three customers in the restaurant, seven servers will be idle.

Let's take the middle path in the restaurant management. Let's have a few servers in the kitchen to cook and one server at the counter to receive orders. A customer comes, places an order with the server at the counter, the customer gets an order id, the customer leaves the counter, the server at the counter passes on the order to one of the servers in the kitchen, and the server starts taking an order from the next customer. At this point, the customer is free to do something else while his order is being prepared. The server at the counter is dealing with other customers. Servers in the kitchen are busy preparing the food according to the orders placed. No one is waiting for anyone. As soon as the food item in an order is ready, the server at the counter receives it from the server in the kitchen and calls the order number so the customer who placed that order will pick up his food. A customer may get his food in multiple installments. He can eat the food that he has been served while the remaining items in his order are being prepared in the kitchen. This architecture is the most efficient architecture you can have in a restaurant. It keeps everyone busy most of the time and makes efficient use of the resources. This is the approach that non-blocking socket channels follow.

Another approach would be that the customer comes in, places his order, waits until his order is complete and he is served, and then the next customer places his order and so on. This is the approach that blocking sockets follow. If you understand the approach taken by the fast food restaurant for the efficient use of resources, you can understand the non-blocking socket channels easily. I will compare the people used in the restaurant example with objects used in non-blocking sockets in the following discussion.

Let's first discuss the situation on the server side. The server side is your restaurant. The person at the counter, who interfaces with all customers, is called a *selector*. A selector is an object of the Selector class. Its sole job is to interact with the outside world. It sits between remote clients interacting with the server and the things inside the server. A remote client never interacts with objects working inside the server, as a customer in the restaurant never interacts directly with servers in the kitchen. Figure 5-7 shows the architecture of non-blocking socket channels communication. It shows where the selector fits into the architecture.

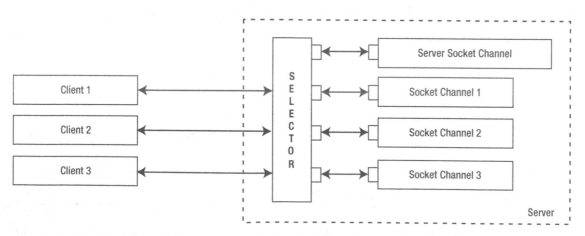

Figure 5-7. Architecture of Non-Blocking Client-Server Sockets

You cannot create a selector object directly using its constructor. You need to call its open() static method to get a selector object as shown:

```
// Get a selector object
Selector selector = Selector.open();
```

A ServerSocketChannel is used to listen for a new connection request from clients. Again, you cannot create a new ServerSocketChannel object using its constructor. You need to call its open() static method as shown:

```
// Get a server socket channel
ServerSocketChannel ssChannel = ServerSocketChannel.open();
```

By default, a server socket channel or a socket channel is a blocking channel. You need to configure it to make it a non-blocking channel as shown:

```
// Configure the server socket channel to be non-blocking
ssChannel.configureBlocking(false);
```

Your server socket channel needs to be bound to a local IP address and a local port number, so a remote client may contact it for new connections. You bind a server socket channel using its bind() method. The bind() method has been added to the ServerSocketChannel and the SocketChannel in Java 7. Prior to Java 7, you need to call the bind() method on the socket that is associated with the channels.

```
InetAddress hostIPAddress = InetAddress.getByName("localhost");
int port = 19000;

// Prior to Java 7
ssChannel.socket().bind(new InetSocketAddress(hostIPAddress, port));

// Java 7 and later
ssChannel.bind(new InetSocketAddress(hostIPAddress, port));
```

The most important step is taken now. The server socket has to register itself with the selector showing interest in some kind of operation. It is like a pizza maker in a restaurant letting the server at the counter know that he is ready to make pizza for customers and he needs to be notified when an order for pizza is placed. There are four kinds of operations for which you can register a channel with the selector. They are defined as integer constants in the SelectionKey class listed in Table 5-7.

Table 5-7. The List of Operations Recognized by the Selector

Operation Type	Value (Constants in SelectionKey class)	Who Can Register for This Operation	Description
Connect	OP_CONNECT	SocketChannel at client	Selector will notify about the connect operation progress.
Accept	OP_ACCEPT	ServerSocketChannel at server	Selector will notify when a client request for a new connection arrives
Read	OP_READ	SocketChannel at client and server	Selector will notify when the channel is ready to read some data.
Write	OP_WRITE	SocketChannel at client and server	Selector will notify when channel is ready to write some data.

A ServerSocketChannel only listens for accepting a new client connection request, and therefore, it can register for only one operation as shown:

```
// Register the server socket channel with the selector for accept operation
ssChannel.register(selector, SelectionKey.OP_ACCEPT);
```

The register() method of ServerSocketChannel returns an object of type SelectionKey. You can think of this object as a registration certificate with the selector. You can store this key object in a variable if you need to use it later. The example ignores it. The selector has a copy of your key (registration details) and it will use it in the future to notify you of any operation for which your channel is ready.

At this point, your selector is ready to intercept an incoming request for a client connection and pass it on to the server socket channel. Suppose a client attempts to connect to the server socket channel at this time. How does interaction between the selector and the server socket channel take place? When the selector detects that there is a registered key with it, which is ready for an operation, it places that key (an object of the SelectionKey class) in a separate group called the *ready set*. A java.util.Set object represents a ready set. You can determine the number of keys in a ready state by calling the select() method of a Selector object.

```
// Get the key count in the ready set
int readyCount = selector.select();
```

Once you get at least one ready key in the ready set, you need to get the key and look at the details, You can get all ready keys from the ready set as shown:

```
// Get the set of ready keys
Set readySet = selector.selectedKeys();
```

Note that you register a key for one or more operations. You need to look at the key details for its readiness for a particular operation. If a key is ready for accepting a new connection request, its isAcceptable() method will return true. If a key is ready for a connection operation, its isConnectable() method will return true. If a key is ready for read and write operations, its isReadable() and isWritable() methods will return true. You may observe that there is a method to check for the readiness for each operation type. When you are processing a ready set, you will also need to remove the key from the ready set. Here is some typical code that processes the ready set in a server application. An infinite loop is typical on a server application because you need to keep looking for the next ready set once you are done with the current ready set.

```
while(true) {
        // Get count of keys in the ready set. If ready key count is
        // greater than zero, process each key in the ready set.
}
```

The following snippet of code shows the typical logic that you can use to process all keys in a ready set:

```
SelectionKey key = null;
Iterator iterator = readySet.iterator();

while (iterator.hasNext()) {
        // Get the next ready selection key object
        key = (SelectionKey)iterator.next();

        // Remove the key from ready set
        iterator.remove();
```

```
        // Process the key according to the operation
        if (key.isAcceptable()) {
                // Process new connection
        }

        if (key.isReadable()) {
                // Read from the channel
        }

        if (key.isWritable()) {
                // Write to the channel
        }
}
```

How do you accept a connection request from a remote client on a server socket channel? The logic is similar to accepting a remote connection request using a ServerSocket object. A SelectionKey object has a reference to the ServerSocketChannel that registered it. You can get to the ServerSocketChannel object of a SelectionKey object using its channel() method. You need to call the accept() method on the ServerSocketChannel object to accept a new connection request. The accept() method returns an object of the SocketChannel class that is used to communicate (read and write) with a remote client. You need to configure the new SocketChannel object to be a non-blocking socket channel. The most important point that you need to understand is that the new SocketChannel object must register itself for read, write, or both operations with the selector to start reading/writing data on the connection channel. The following snippet of code shows the logic to accept a remote connection request:

```
ServerSocketChannel ssChannel = (ServerSocketChannel)key.channel();
SocketChannel sChannel = (SocketChannel)ssChannel.accept();
sChannel.configureBlocking(false);

// Register only for read. Your message is small and you write it back
// to the client as soon as you read it.
sChannel.register(key.selector(), SelectionKey.OP_READ);
```

If you wish to register the socket channel with a selector for a read and a write, you can do so as shown:

```
// Register for read and write
sChannel.register(key.selector(), SelectionKey.OP_READ | SelectionKey.OP_WRITE);
```

Once your socket channel is registered with the selector, it will be notified through the selector's ready set when it receives any data from the remote client or when you can write data to the remote client on its channel.

If data becomes available on a socket channel, the key.isReadable() will return true for this socket channel. A typical read operation looks as follows. You must have a basic understanding of Java NIO (New Input/Output) to read data using channels and buffers.

```
SocketChannel sChannel = (SocketChannel) key.channel();
ByteBuffer buffer = ByteBuffer.allocate(1024);
int bytesCount = sChannel.read(buffer);
String msg = "";
```

```
if (bytesCount > 0) {
        buffer.flip();
        Charset charset = Charset.forName("UTF-8");
        CharsetDecoder decoder = charset.newDecoder();
        CharBuffer charBuffer = decoder.decode(buffer);
        msg = charBuffer.toString();
        System.out.println("Received Message: " + msg);
}
```

If you can write to a channel, the selector will place the associated key in its ready set whose isWritable() method will return true. Again, you need to understand Java NIO to use the ByteBuffer object to write data on a channel.

```
SocketChannel sChannel = (SocketChannel)key.channel();
String msg = "message to be sent to remote client goes here";
ByteBuffer buffer = ByteBuffer.wrap(msg.getBytes());
sChannel.write(buffer);
```

What happens on a client side is easy to understand. You start with getting a selector object, and you get a SocketChannel object by calling the SocketChannel.open() method. At this point, you need to configure the socket channel to be non-blocking before you connect to the server. Now you are ready to register your socket channel with the selector. Typically, you register with the selector for connect, read, and write operations. Processing the ready set of the selector is done the same way you processed the ready set of the selector in the server application. The code for reading and writing to the channel is similar to the server side code. The following snippet of code shows the typical logic used in a client application:

```
InetAddress serverIPAddress = InetAddress.getByName("localhost");
int port = 19000;
InetSocketAddress serverAddress = new InetSocketAddress(serverIPAddress, port);

// Get a selector
Selector selector = Selector.open();

// Create and configure a client socket channel
SocketChannel channel = SocketChannel.open();
channel.configureBlocking(false);

// Connect to the server
channel.connect(serverAddress);

// Register the channel for connect, read and write operations
int operations = SelectionKey.OP_CONNECT | SelectionKey.OP_READ | SelectionKey.OP_WRITE;
channel.register(selector, operations);

// Process the ready set of the selector here
```

When you get a connect operation on a client side SocketChannel, it may mean either a successful or failed connection. You can call the finishConnect() method on the SocketChannel object to finish the connection process. If the connection has failed, the finishConnect() call will throw an IOException. Typically, you handle a connect operation as follows:

```
if (key.isConnectable()) {
        try {
                // Call to finishConnect() is in a loop as it is non-blocking
                // for your channel
                while(channel.isConnectionPending()) {
                        channel.finishConnect();
                }
        }
        catch (IOException e) {
                // Cancel the channel's registration with the selector
                key.cancel();
                e.printStackTrace();
        }
}
```

It is time to build an echo client application and an echo server application using these channels. Listing 5-14 and Listing 5-15 contain the complete code for a non-blocking socket channel for an echo server and an echo client, respectively.

Listing 5-14. A Non-Blocking Socket Channel Echo Server Program

```
// NonBlockingEchoServer.java
package com.jdojo.net;

import java.io.IOException;
import java.net.InetAddress;
import java.net.InetSocketAddress;
import java.nio.ByteBuffer;
import java.nio.CharBuffer;
import java.nio.channels.SelectionKey;
import java.nio.channels.Selector;
import java.nio.channels.ServerSocketChannel;
import java.nio.channels.SocketChannel;
import java.nio.charset.Charset;
import java.nio.charset.CharsetDecoder;
import java.util.Iterator;
import java.util.Set;

public class NonBlockingEchoServer {
        public static void main(String[] args) throws Exception {
                InetAddress hostIPAddress = InetAddress.getByName("localhost");
                int port = 19000;

                // Get a selector
                Selector selector = Selector.open();
```

```java
        // Get a server socket channel
        ServerSocketChannel ssChannel = ServerSocketChannel.open();

        // Make the server socket channel non-blocking and bind it to an address
        ssChannel.configureBlocking(false);
        ssChannel.socket().bind(new InetSocketAddress(hostIPAddress, port));

        // Register a socket server channel with the selector for accept operation,
        // so that it can be notified when a new connection request arrives
        ssChannel.register(selector, SelectionKey.OP_ACCEPT);

        // Now we will keep waiting in a loop for any kind of request
        // that arrives to the server - connection, read, or write
        // request. If a connection request comes in, we will accept
        // the request and register a new socket channel with the selector
        // for read and write operations. If read or write requests come
        // in, we will forward that request to the registered channel.
        while (true) {
            if (selector.select() <= 0) {
                continue;
            }
            processReadySet(selector.selectedKeys());
        }
    }

    public static void processReadySet(Set readySet) throws Exception {
        SelectionKey key = null;
        Iterator iterator = null;
        iterator = readySet.iterator();
        while (iterator.hasNext()) {
            // Get the next ready selection key object
            key = (SelectionKey) iterator.next();

            // Remove the key from the ready key set
            iterator.remove();

            // Process the key according to the operation it is ready for
            if (key.isAcceptable()) {
                processAccept(key);
            }

            if (key.isReadable()) {
                String msg = processRead(key);
                if (msg.length() > 0) {
                    echoMsg(key, msg);
                }
            }
        }
    }
```

```java
        public static void processAccept(SelectionKey key) throws IOException {
                // This method call indicates that we got a new connection
                // request. Accept the connection request and register the new
                // socket channel with the selector, so that client can
                // communicate on a new channel
                ServerSocketChannel ssChannel = (ServerSocketChannel)key.channel();
                SocketChannel sChannel = (SocketChannel) ssChannel.accept();
                sChannel.configureBlocking(false);

                // Register only for read. Our message is small and we write it
                // back to the client as soon as we read it
                sChannel.register(key.selector(), SelectionKey.OP_READ);
        }

        public static String processRead(SelectionKey key) throws Exception {
                SocketChannel sChannel = (SocketChannel) key.channel();
                ByteBuffer buffer = ByteBuffer.allocate(1024);
                int bytesCount = sChannel.read(buffer);
                String msg = "";

                if (bytesCount > 0) {
                        buffer.flip();
                        Charset charset = Charset.forName("UTF-8");
                        CharsetDecoder decoder = charset.newDecoder();
                        CharBuffer charBuffer = decoder.decode(buffer);
                        msg = charBuffer.toString();
                        System.out.println("Received Message: " + msg);
                }

                return msg;
        }

        public static void echoMsg(SelectionKey key, String msg) throws IOException {
                SocketChannel sChannel = (SocketChannel) key.channel();
                ByteBuffer buffer = ByteBuffer.wrap(msg.getBytes());
                sChannel.write(buffer);
        }
}
```

Listing 5-15. A Non-Blocking Socket Channel Echo Client Program

```java
// NonBlockingEchoClient.java
package com.jdojo.net;

import java.io.BufferedReader;
import java.io.IOException;
import java.io.InputStreamReader;
import java.net.InetAddress;
import java.net.InetSocketAddress;
import java.nio.ByteBuffer;
import java.nio.CharBuffer;
import java.nio.channels.SelectionKey;
```

```java
import java.nio.channels.Selector;
import java.nio.channels.SocketChannel;
import java.nio.charset.Charset;
import java.nio.charset.CharsetDecoder;
import java.util.Iterator;
import java.util.Set;

public class NonBlockingEchoClient {
        private static BufferedReader userInputReader = null;

        public static void main(String[] args) throws Exception {
                InetAddress serverIPAddress = InetAddress.getByName("localhost");
                int port = 19000;
                InetSocketAddress serverAddress = new InetSocketAddress(serverIPAddress, port);

                // Get a selector
                Selector selector = Selector.open();

                // Create and configure a client socket channel
                SocketChannel channel = SocketChannel.open();
                channel.configureBlocking(false);
                channel.connect(serverAddress);

                // Register the channel for connect, read and write operations
                int operations =
                        SelectionKey.OP_CONNECT | SelectionKey.OP_READ | SelectionKey.OP_WRITE;
                channel.register(selector, operations);

                userInputReader = new BufferedReader(new InputStreamReader(System.in));
                while (true) {
                        if (selector.select() > 0) {
                                boolean doneStatus = processReadySet(selector.selectedKeys());
                                if (doneStatus) {
                                        break;
                                }
                        }
                }

                channel.close();
        }

        public static boolean processReadySet(Set readySet) throws Exception {
                SelectionKey key = null;
                Iterator iterator = null;
                iterator = readySet.iterator();
                while (iterator.hasNext()) {
                        // Get the next ready selection key object
                        key = (SelectionKey) iterator.next();

                        // Remove the key from the ready key set
                        iterator.remove();
```

```java
                    if (key.isConnectable()) {
                            boolean connected = processConnect(key);
                            if (!connected) {
                                    return true; // Exit
                            }
                    }

                    if (key.isReadable()) {
                            String msg = processRead(key);
                            System.out.println("[Server]: " + msg);
                    }

                    if (key.isWritable()) {
                            String msg = getUserInput();
                            if (msg.equalsIgnoreCase("bye")) {
                                    return true; // Exit
                            }
                            processWrite(key, msg);
                    }

            }

            return false; // Not done yet
    }

    public static boolean processConnect(SelectionKey key) {
            SocketChannel channel = (SocketChannel) key.channel();

            try {
                    // Call the finishConnect() in a loop as it is non-blocking
                    // for your channel
                    while (channel.isConnectionPending()) {
                            channel.finishConnect();
                    }
            }
            catch (IOException e) {
                    // Cancel the channel's registration with the selector
                    key.cancel();
                    e.printStackTrace();
                    return false;
            }

            return true;
    }

    public static String processRead(SelectionKey key) throws Exception {
            SocketChannel sChannel = (SocketChannel) key.channel();
            ByteBuffer buffer = ByteBuffer.allocate(1024);
            sChannel.read(buffer);
            buffer.flip();
```

```
            Charset charset = Charset.forName("UTF-8");
            CharsetDecoder decoder = charset.newDecoder();
            CharBuffer charBuffer = decoder.decode(buffer);
            String msg = charBuffer.toString();
            return msg;
        }

        public static void processWrite(SelectionKey key, String msg) throws IOException {
            SocketChannel sChannel = (SocketChannel) key.channel();
            ByteBuffer buffer = ByteBuffer.wrap(msg.getBytes());
            sChannel.write(buffer);
        }

        public static String getUserInput() throws IOException {
            String promptMsg = "Please enter a message(Bye to quit): ";
            System.out.print(promptMsg);
            String userMsg = userInputReader.readLine();
            return userMsg;
        }
}
```

You need to run the NonBlockingEchoServer class first, and then one or more instances of the NonBlockingEchoClient class. They work similar to your other two echo client-server programs. Note that, this time, you may not see the messages from the server just after you enter a message in the client application. The client application sends a message to the server and it does not wait for the message to be echoed back. Rather, it processes the server message when the socket channel receives the notification from the selector. Therefore, it is possible to get the two messages echoed back from the server at one time. Exception handling has been left out in these examples to keep the code simple and readable.

Socket Security Permissions

You can control the access for a Java program to use sockets using an instance of the java.net.SocketPermission class. The generic format used to grant a socket permission in a Java policy file is as follows:

```
grant {
        permission java.net.SocketPermission "target", "actions";
};
```

The target is of the form <host name>:<port range>. The possible values of actions are accept, connect, listen, and resolve.

The listen action is meaningful only when "localhost" is used as the host name. The resolve action refers to DNS lookup and it is implied if any of the other three actions is present.

A host name could be either a DNS name or an IP address. You can use an asterisk (*) as a wildcard character in the DNS host name. If an asterisk is used, it must be used as the leftmost character in the DNS name. If the host name consists only of an asterisk, it refers to any host. The "localhost" for the host name refers to the local machine. You can indicate the port range for the host name in different formats as described below. Here N1 and N2 indicate port numbers (0 to 65535) and it is assumed that N1 is less than N2. Table 5-8 lists the format used for indicating the port range.

Table 5-8. *The <port range> Format for java.net.SocketPermission Security Settings*

Port Range Value	Description
N1	Only one port number—N1
N1-N2	Port numbers from N1 to N2
N1-	Port numbers from N1 and greater
-N1	Port numbers from N1 and less

The following are examples of using a `java.net.SocketPermission` in a Java policy file:

```
// Grant to all codebase
grant {
        // Permission to connect with 192.168.10.123 at port 5000
        permission java.net.SocketPermission "192.168.10.123:5000", "connect";

        // Connect permission to any host at port 80
        permission java.net.SocketPermission "*:80", "connect";

        // All socket permissions to on port >=1024 on the localhost
        permission java.net.SocketPermission "localhost:1024-", "listen, accept, connect";
};
```

Asynchronous Socket Channels

Java 7 added support for asynchronous socket operations such as connect, read, and write. The asynchronous socket operations are performed using the following two socket channel classes:

- `java.nio.channels.AsynchronousServerSocketChannel`
- `java.nio.channels.AsynchronousSocketChannel`

An `AsynchronousServerSocketChannel` serves as a server socket that listens for new incoming client connections. Once it accepts a new client connection, the interaction between the client and the server is handled by an `AsynchronousSocketChannel` at both ends. Asynchronous socket channels are set up very similar to the synchronous sockets. The main difference between the two setups is that the request for an asynchronous socket operation returns immediately and the requestor is notified when the operation is completed, whereas in a synchronous socket operation the request for a socket operation blocks until it is complete. Because of the asynchronous nature of the operations with the asynchronous socket channels, the code to handle the completion or failure of a socket operation is a bit complex.

In an asynchronous socket channel, you request an operation using one of the methods of the asynchronous socket channel classes. The method returns immediately. You receive a notification about the completion or failure of the operation later. The methods that allow you to request asynchronous operations are overloaded. One version returns a `Future` object that lets you check the status of the requested operation. For details on using a `Future` object, please refer to Chapter 6 in the book *Beginning Java Language Features* (ISBN: 978-1-4302-6658-7). Another version of those methods lets you pass a `CompletionHandler`. When the requested operation completes successfully, the `completed()` method of the `CompletionHandler` is called. When the requested operation fails, the `failed()` method of the `CompletionHandler` is called. The following snippet of code demonstrates both approaches of handling the completion/failure of a requested asynchronous socket operation. It shows how a server socket channel accepts a client connection asynchronously.

```
/* Using a Future Object */
// Get a server socket channel instance
AsynchronousServerSocketChannel server = get a server instance...;

// Bind the socket to a host and a port
server.bind(your_host, your_port);

// Start accepting a new client connection. Note that the accept()
// method returns immediately by returning a Future object
Future<AsynchronousSocketChannel> result = server.accept();

// Wait for the new client connection by calling the get() method of
// the Future object. Alternatively, you can poll the Future object
// periodically using its isDone() method
AsynchronousSocketChannel newClient = result.get();

// Handle the newClient here and call the server.accept() again to accept
// another client connection

/* Using a CompletionHandler Object */
// Get a server socket channel instance
AsynchronousServerSocketChannel server = get a server instance...;

// Bind the socket to a host and a port
server.bind(your_host, your_port);

// Start accepting a new client connection. The accept() method returns
// immediately. The completed() or failed() method of the ConnectionHandler
// will be called upon completion or failure of the requested operation
YourAnyClass attach = ...; // Get an attachment
server.accept(attach, new ConnectionHandler());
```

The above version of the accept() method accepts an object of any class as an attachment. It could be a null reference. The attachment is passed to the completed() and failed() methods of the completion handler, which is an object of ConnectionHandler in this case. The ConnectionHandler class may look as follows.

```
private static class ConnectionHandler implements CompletionHandler<AsynchronousSocketChannel,
YourAnyClass> {
        @Override
        public void completed(AsynchronousSocketChannel client, YourAnyClass attach) {
                // Handle the new client connection here and again start
                // accepting a new client connection
        }

        @Override
        public void failed(Throwable e, YourAnyClass attach) {
                // Handle the failure here
        }
}
```

In this section, I will cover the following three steps in detail. During the discussion, I will build an application that consists of an echo server and a client. Clients will send messages to the server asynchronously and the server will echo back the message to the client asynchronously. It is assumed that you are familiar working with buffers and channels.

- Setting up an asynchronous server socket channel
- Setting up an asynchronous client socket channel
- Putting the asynchronous server and client socket channels in action

Setting Up an Asynchronous Server Socket Channel

An instance of the AsynchronousServerSocketChannel class is used as an asynchronous server socket channel to listen to the new incoming client connections. Once a connection to a client is established, an instance of the AsynchronousSocketChannel class is used to communicate with the client. The static open() method of the AsynchronousServerSocketChannel class returns an object of the AsynchronousServerSocketChannel class, which is not yet bound.

```
// Create an asynchronous server socket channel object
AsynchronousServerSocketChannel server = AsynchronousServerSocketChannel.open();

// Bind the server to the localhost and the port 8989
String host = "localhost";
int port = 8989;
InetSocketAddress sAddr = new InetSocketAddress(host, port);
server.bind(sAddr);
```

At this point, your server socket channel can be used to accept a new client connection by calling its accept() method as follows. The code uses two classes, Attachment and ConnectionHandler, which are described later.

```
// Prepare the attachment
Attachment attach = new Attachment();
attach.server = server;

// Accept new connections
server.accept(attach, new ConnectionHandler());
```

Typically, a server application runs indefinitely. You can make the server application run forever by waiting on the main thread in the main() method as follows:

```
try {
        // Wait indefinitely until someone interrups the main thread
        Thread.currentThread().join();
}
catch (InterruptedException e) {
        e.printStackTrace();
}
```

You will use the completion handler mechanism to handle the completion/failure notification for the server socket channel. An object of the following Attachment class will be used to serve as an attachment to the completion handler. An attachment object is used to pass the context for the server socket that may be used inside the completed() and failed() methods of the completion handler.

```
class Attachment {
        AsynchronousServerSocketChannel server;
        AsynchronousSocketChannel client;
        ByteBuffer buffer;
        SocketAddress clientAddr;
        boolean isRead;
}
```

You need a CompletionHandler implementation to handle the completion of an accept() call. Let's call your class as ConnectionHandler as shown:

```
private static class ConnectionHandler implements CompletionHandler<AsynchronousSocketChannel,
Attachment> {
        @Override
        public void completed(AsynchronousSocketChannel client, Attachment attach) {
                try {
                        // Get the client address
                        SocketAddress clientAddr = client.getRemoteAddress();

                        System.out.format("Accepted a connection from %s%n", clientAddr);

                        // Accept another connection
                        attach.server.accept(attach, this);

                        // Handle the client connection by invoking an asyn read
                        Attachment newAttach = new Attachment();
                        newAttach.server = attach.server;
                        newAttach.client = client;
                        newAttach.buffer = ByteBuffer.allocate(2048);
                        newAttach.isRead = true;
                        newAttach.clientAddr = clientAddr;

                        // Create a new completion handler for reading to and writing
                        // from the new client
                        ReadWriteHandler readWriteHandler = new ReadWriteHandler();

                        // Read from the client
                        client.read(newAttach.buffer, newAttach, readWriteHandler);
                }
                catch (IOException e) {
                        e.printStackTrace();
                }

        }
```

```
        @Override
        public void failed(Throwable e, Attachment attach) {
                System.out.println("Failed to accept a connection.");
                e.printStackTrace();
        }
}
```

The ConnectionHandler class is simple. In its failed() method, it prints the exception stack trace. In its completed() method, it prints a message that a new client connection has been established and starts listening for another new client connection by calling the accept() method on the server socket again. Note the reuse of the attachment in another accept() method call inside the completed() method. It uses the same CompletionHandler object again. Note that the attach.server.accept(attach, this) method call uses the keyword this to refer to the same instance of the completion handler. At the end, it prepares a new instance of the Attachment class, which wraps the details of handling (reading and writing) the new client connection, and calls the read() method on the client socket to read from the client. Note that the read() method uses another completion handler, which is an instance of the ReadWriteHandler class. The code for the ReadWriteHandler is as follows:

```
private static class ReadWriteHandler implements CompletionHandler<Integer, Attachment> {
        @Override
        public void completed(Integer result, Attachment attach) {
                if (result == -1) {
                        try {
                                attach.client.close();
                                System.out.format("Stopped listening to the client %s%n",
                                                attach.clientAddr);
                        }
                        catch (IOException ex) {
                                ex.printStackTrace();
                        }
                        return;
                }

                if (attach.isRead) {
                        // A read to the client was completed

                        // Get the buffer ready to read from it
                        attach.buffer.flip();

                        int limits = attach.buffer.limit();
                        byte bytes[] = new byte[limits];
                        attach.buffer.get(bytes, 0, limits);
                        Charset cs = Charset.forName("UTF-8");
                        String msg = new String(bytes, cs);

                        // Print the message from the client
                        System.out.format("Client at %s says: %s%n", attach.clientAddr, msg);

                        // Let us echo back the same message to the client
                        attach.isRead = false; // It is a write
```

```
                        // Prepare the buffer to be read again
                        attach.buffer.rewind();

                        // Write to the client again
                        attach.client.write(attach.buffer, attach, this);
                }
                else {
                        // A write to the client was completed.
                        // Perform another read from the client
                        attach.isRead = true;

                        // Prepare the buffer to be filled in
                        attach.buffer.clear();

                        // Perform a read from the client
                        attach.client.read(attach.buffer, attach, this);
                }
        }

        @Override
        public void failed(Throwable e, Attachment attach) {
                e.printStackTrace();
        }
}
```

The first argument called result of the completed() method is the number of bytes that is read from or written to the client. Its value of -1 indicates the end-of-stream, and in that case, the client socket is closed. If a read operation was completed, it displays the read text on the standard output and writes back the same text to the client. If a write operation to a client was completed, it performs a read on the same client.

Listing 5-16 contains the complete code for your asynchronous server socket channel. It uses three inner classes: one for the attachment, one for the connection completion handler, and one for the read/write completion handler. The AsyncEchoServerSocket class can be run now. However, it will not do any work as it needs a client to connect to it to echo back messages that are sent from the client. You will develop your asynchronous client socket channel in the next section, and then, in the subsequent section, you will test both server and client socket channels together.

Listing 5-16. A Server Application That Uses Asynchronous Server Socket Channel

```
// AsyncEchoServerSocket.java
package com.jdojo.net;

import java.io.IOException;
import java.net.SocketAddress;
import java.nio.ByteBuffer;
import java.nio.charset.Charset;
import java.net.InetSocketAddress;
import java.nio.channels.CompletionHandler;
import java.nio.channels.AsynchronousSocketChannel;
import java.nio.channels.AsynchronousServerSocketChannel;

public class AsyncEchoServerSocket {
        private static class Attachment {
                AsynchronousServerSocketChannel server;
                AsynchronousSocketChannel client;
```

```
        ByteBuffer buffer;
        SocketAddress clientAddr;
        boolean isRead;
    }

    private static class ConnectionHandler implements
                CompletionHandler<AsynchronousSocketChannel, Attachment> {
        @Override
        public void completed(AsynchronousSocketChannel client, Attachment attach) {
            try {
                    // Get the client address
                    SocketAddress clientAddr = client.getRemoteAddress();
                    System.out.format("Accepted a connection from %s%n",
                            clientAddr);

                    // Accept another connection
                    attach.server.accept(attach, this);

                    // Handle the client connection by using an asyn read
                    ReadWriteHandler rwHandler = new ReadWriteHandler();
                    Attachment newAttach = new Attachment();
                    newAttach.server = attach.server;
                    newAttach.client = client;
                    newAttach.buffer = ByteBuffer.allocate(2048);
                    newAttach.isRead = true;
                    newAttach.clientAddr = clientAddr;
                    client.read(newAttach.buffer, newAttach, rwHandler);
            }
            catch (IOException e) {
                    e.printStackTrace();
            }

        }

        @Override
        public void failed(Throwable e, Attachment attach) {
            System.out.println("Failed to accept a connection.");
            e.printStackTrace();
        }
    }

    private static class ReadWriteHandler
        implements CompletionHandler<Integer, Attachment> {
        @Override
        public void completed(Integer result, Attachment attach) {
            if (result == -1) {
                    try {
                            attach.client.close();
                            System.out.format(
                                    "Stopped listening to the client %s%n",
                                    attach.clientAddr);
                    }
```

```
                            catch (IOException ex) {
                                    ex.printStackTrace();
                            }
                            return;
                    }

            if (attach.isRead) {
                            // A read to the client was completed

                            // Get the buffer ready to read from it
                            attach.buffer.flip();

                            int limits = attach.buffer.limit();
                            byte bytes[] = new byte[limits];
                            attach.buffer.get(bytes, 0, limits);
                            Charset cs = Charset.forName("UTF-8");
                            String msg = new String(bytes, cs);

                            // Print the message from the client
                            System.out.format("Client at %s says: %s%n",
                                            attach.clientAddr, msg);

                            // Let us echo back the same message to the client
                            attach.isRead = false; // It is a write

                            // Prepare the buffer to be read again
                            attach.buffer.rewind();

                            // Write to the client
                            attach.client.write(attach.buffer, attach, this);
                    }
                    else {
                            // A write to the client was completed. Perform
                            // another read from the client
                            attach.isRead = true;

                            // Prepare the buffer to be filled in
                            attach.buffer.clear();

                            // Perform a read from the client
                            attach.client.read(attach.buffer, attach, this);
                    }
            }

            @Override
            public void failed(Throwable e, Attachment attach) {
                    e.printStackTrace();
            }
    }
```

```java
    public static void main(String[] args) {
        try (AsynchronousServerSocketChannel server =
                AsynchronousServerSocketChannel.open()) {
            // Bind the server to the localhost and the port 8989
            String host = "localhost";
            int port = 8989;
            InetSocketAddress sAddr =
              new InetSocketAddress(host, port);
            server.bind(sAddr);

            // Display a message that server is ready
            System.out.format("Server is listening at %s%n", sAddr);

            // Prepare the attachment
            Attachment attach = new Attachment();
            attach.server = server;

            // Accept new connections
            server.accept(attach, new ConnectionHandler());

            try {
                // Wait until the main thread is interrupted
                Thread.currentThread().join();
            }
            catch (InterruptedException e) {
                e.printStackTrace();
            }
        }
        catch (IOException e) {
            e.printStackTrace();
        }
    }
}
```

Setting up an Asynchronous Client Socket Channel

An instance of the AsynchronousSocketChannel class is used as an asynchronous client socket channel in a client application. The static open() method of the AsynchronousSocketChannel class returns an open channel of the AsynchronousSocketChannel type that is not yet connected to a server socket channel. The channel's connect() method is used to connect to a server socket channel. The following snippet of code shows how to create an asynchronous client socket channel and connect it to a server socket channel. It uses a Future object to handle the completion of the connection to the server.

```java
// Create an asynchronous socket channel
AsynchronousSocketChannel channel = AsynchronousSocketChannel.open();

// Connect the channel to the server
String serverName = "localhost";
int serverPort = 8989;
SocketAddress serverAddr = new InetSocketAddress(serverName, serverPort);
```

```
Future<Void> result = channel.connect(serverAddr);
System.out.println("Connecting to the server...");

// Wait for the connection to complete
result.get();

// Connection to the server is complete now
System.out.println("Connected to the server...");
```

Once the client socket channel is connected to a server, you can start reading from the server and writing to the server using the channel's read() and write() methods asynchronously. Both methods let you handle the completion of the operation using a Future object or a CompletionHandler object. You will use an Attachment class as shown to pass the context to the completion handler:

```
class Attachment {
        AsynchronousSocketChannel channel;
        ByteBuffer buffer;
        Thread mainThread;
        boolean isRead;
}
```

In the Attachment class, the channel instance variable holds the reference to the client channel. The buffer instance variable holds the reference to the data buffer. You will use the same data buffer for reading and writing. The mainThread instance variable holds the reference to the main thread of the application. When the client channel is done, you can interrupt the waiting main thread, so the client application terminates. The isRead instance variable indicates if the operation is a read or a write. If it is true, it means it is a read operation. Otherwise, it is a write operation.

Listing 5-17 contains the complete code for an asynchronous client socket channel. It uses two inner classes called Attachment and ReadWriteHandler. An instance of the Attachment class is used as an attachment to the read() and write() asynchronous operations. An instance of the ReadWriteHandler class is used as a completion handler for the read() and write() operations. Its getTextFromUser() method prompts the user to enter a message on the standard input and returns the user-entered message. The completed() method of the completion handler checks if it is a read or a write operation. If it is a read operation, it prints the text that was read from the server on the standard output. It prompts the user for another message. If the user enters Bye, it terminates the application by interrupting the waiting main thread. Note that the channel is closed automatically when the program exits the try block because it is opened inside a try-with-resources block in the main() method.

Listing 5-17. An Asynchronous Client Socket Channel

```
// AsyncEchoClientSocket.java
package com.jdojo.net;

import java.io.BufferedReader;
import java.io.IOException;
import java.io.InputStreamReader;
import java.net.InetSocketAddress;
import java.net.SocketAddress;
import java.nio.ByteBuffer;
import java.nio.charset.Charset;
import java.util.concurrent.Future;
import java.nio.channels.CompletionHandler;
import java.util.concurrent.ExecutionException;
import java.nio.channels.AsynchronousSocketChannel;
```

```java
public class AsyncEchoClientSocket {
        private static class Attachment {
                AsynchronousSocketChannel channel;
                ByteBuffer buffer;
                Thread mainThread;
                boolean isRead;
        }

        private static class ReadWriteHandler
                implements CompletionHandler<Integer, Attachment> {

                @Override
                public void completed(Integer result, Attachment attach) {
                        if (attach.isRead) {
                                attach.buffer.flip();

                                // Get the text read from the server
                                Charset cs = Charset.forName("UTF-8");

                                int limits = attach.buffer.limit();
                                byte bytes[] = new byte[limits];
                                attach.buffer.get(bytes, 0, limits);
                                String msg = new String(bytes, cs);

                                // A read from the server was completed
                                System.out.format("Server Responded: %s%n", msg);

                                // Prompt the user for another message
                                msg = this.getTextFromUser();
                                if (msg.equalsIgnoreCase("bye")) {
                                        // Interrupt the main thread, so the program terminates
                                        attach.mainThread.interrupt();
                                        return;
                                }

                                // Prepare buffer to be filled in again
                                attach.buffer.clear();
                                byte[] data = msg.getBytes(cs);
                                attach.buffer.put(data);

                                // Prepared buffer to be read
                                attach.buffer.flip();

                                attach.isRead = false; // It is a write

                                // Write to the server
                                attach.channel.write(attach.buffer, attach, this);
                        }
```

```java
                else {
                        // A write to the server was completed. Perform another
                        // read from the server
                        attach.isRead = true;

                        // Prepare the buffer to be filled in
                        attach.buffer.clear();

                        // Read from the server
                        attach.channel.read(attach.buffer, attach, this);
                }
        }

        @Override
        public void failed(Throwable e, Attachment attach) {
                e.printStackTrace();
        }

        private String getTextFromUser() {
                System.out.print("Please enter a message (Bye to quit):");
                String msg = null;

                BufferedReader consoleReader =
                        new BufferedReader(new InputStreamReader(System.in));
                try {
                        msg = consoleReader.readLine();
                }
                catch (IOException e) {
                        e.printStackTrace();
                }

                return msg;
        }
}

public static void main(String[] args) {
        // Use a try-with-resources to open a channel
        try (AsynchronousSocketChannel channel
                = AsynchronousSocketChannel.open()) {
                // Connect the client to the server
                String serverName = "localhost";
                int serverPort = 8989;
                SocketAddress serverAddr =
                        new InetSocketAddress(serverName, serverPort);

                Future<Void> result = channel.connect(serverAddr);
                System.out.println("Connecting to the server...");

                // Wait for the connection to complete
                result.get();
```

```
                       // Connection to the server is complete now
                       System.out.println("Connected to the server...");

                       // Start reading from and writing to the server
                       Attachment attach = new Attachment();
                       attach.channel = channel;
                       attach.buffer = ByteBuffer.allocate(2048);
                       attach.isRead = false;
                       attach.mainThread = Thread.currentThread();

                       // Place the "Hello" message in the buffer
                       Charset cs = Charset.forName("UTF-8");
                       String msg = "Hello";
                       byte[] data = msg.getBytes(cs);
                       attach.buffer.put(data);
                       attach.buffer.flip();

                       // Write to the server
                       ReadWriteHandler readWriteHandler = new ReadWriteHandler();
                       channel.write(attach.buffer, attach, readWriteHandler) ;

                       // Let this thread wait for ever on its own death until interrupted
                       attach.mainThread.join();
                  }
             catch (ExecutionException | IOException e) {
                       e.printStackTrace();
                  }
             catch(InterruptedException e) {
                       System.out.println("Disconnected from the server.");
                  }
             }
        }
}
```

Putting the Server and the Client Together

At this point, your asynchronous server and client programs are ready. You need to use the following steps to run the server and the client.

Running the Server Application

Run the AsyncEchoServerSocket class as listed in Listing 5-16. You should get a message on the standard output as follows:

```
Server is listening at localhost/127.0.0.1:8989
```

If you get the above message, you need to proceed to the next step. If you do not get the above message, it is most likely that the port 8989 is being used by another process. In such a case, you should get the following error message:

```
java.net.BindException: Address already in use: bind
```

If you get "Address already in use" error message, you need to change the port value in the AsyncEchoServerSocket class from 8989 to some other value and retry running the AsyncEchoServerSocket class. If you change the port number in the server program, you must also change the port number in the client program to match the server port number. The server socket channel listens at a port and the client must connect to the same port on which the server is listening.

Running the Client Applications

Before proceeding with this step, make sure that you were able to perform the previous step successfully. Run one or more instances of the AsyncEchoClientSocket class that is listed in Listing 5-17. You should get the following message on the standard output if the client application was able to connect to the server successfully:

```
Connecting to the server...
Connected to the server...
Server Responded: Hello
Please enter a message (Bye to quit):
```

You might receive the following error message when you attempt to run the AsyncEchoClientSocket class:

```
Connecting to the server...
java.util.concurrent.ExecutionException: java.io.IOException: The remote system refused the
network connection.
```

Typically, this error message indicates one of the following problems:

- The server is not running. If this is the case, make sure that server is running.

- The client is attempting to connect to the server on a different host and port than the host and the port on which the server is listening. If this is the case, make sure that the server and the client are using the same host names (or IP addresses) and the port numbers.

You will need to stop the server program manually such as by pressing Ctrl + C keys on the command prompt on Windows.

Datagram-Oriented Socket Channels

An instance of the java.nio.channels.DatagramChannel class represents a datagram channel. By default, it is blocking. You can configure it to be non-blocking by using the configureBlocking(false) method.

To create a DatagramChannel, you need to invoke one of its open() static methods. If you want to use it for IP multicasting, you need to specify the address type (or protocol family) of the multicast group as an argument to its open() method. The open() method creates a DatagramChannel object, which is not connected. If you want your datagram channel to send and receive datagrams only to a specific remote host, you need to use its connect() method to connect the channel to that specific host. A datagram channel that is not connected may send datagrams to and receive datagrams from any remote host. The following sections outline the steps that are typically needed to send/receive datagrams using a datagram channel.

Creating the Datagram Channel

You can create a datagram channel using the open() method of the DatagramChannel class. The following snippet of code shows three different ways to create a datagram channel:

```
// Create a new datagram channel to send/receive datagram
DatagramChannel channel = DatagramChannel.open();

// Create a datagram channel to receive datagrams from a multicast group
// that uses IPv4 address type
DatagramChannel ipv4MulticastChannel = DatagramChannel.open(StandardProtocolFamily.INET);

// Create a datagram channel to receive datagrams from a multicast group
// that uses IPv6 address type
DatagramChannel iPv6MulticastChannel = DatagramChannel.open(StandardProtocolFamily.INET6);
```

Setting the Channel Options

You can set the channel options using the setOption() method of the DatagramChannel class. Some options must be set before binding the channel to a specific address, whereas some can be set after the binding. The setOption() method was added to the DatagramChannel class in Java 7. If you are using a prior Java version, you will need to use the socket() method to get the DatagramSocket reference and use one of the methods of the DatagramSocket class to set the channel options. The following snippet of code shows how to set the channel options. Table 5-9 contains the list of socket options and their descriptions. The socket options are defined as constants in the StandardSocketOptions class.

```
// To bind multiple sockets to the same socket address,
// you need to set the SO_REUSEADDR option for the socket

// In Java 7 and later
channel.setOption(StandardSocketOptions.SO_REUSEADDR, true)

// Prior to Java 7
DatagramSocket socket = channel.socket();
socket.setReuseAddress(true);
```

Table 5-9. *The List of Standard Socket Options*

Socket Option Name	Description
SO_SNDBUF	The size of the socket send buffer in bytes. Its value is of Integer type.
SO_RCVBUF	The size of the socket receive buffer in bytes. Its value is of Integer type.
SO_REUSEADDR	For datagram sockets, it allows multiple programs to bind to the same address. Its value is of Boolean type. This option should be enabled for IP multicasting using the datagram channels.
SO_BROADCAST	Allows transmission of broadcast datagrams. Its value is of type Boolean.
IP_TOS	The Type of Service (ToS) octet in the Internet Protocol (IP) header. Its value is of the Integer type.

(continued)

Table 5-9. (*continued*)

Socket Option Name	Description
IP_MULTICAST_IF	The network interface for Internet Protocol (IP) multicast datagrams. Its value is a reference of NetworkInterface type.
IP_MULTICAST_TTL	The time-to-live for Internet Protocol (IP) multicast datagrams. Its value is of type Integer in the range of 0 to 255.
IP_MULTICAST_LOOP	Loopback for Internet Protocol (IP) multicast datagrams. Its value is of type Boolean.

Binding the Datagram Channel

Bind the datagram channel to a specific local address and port using the bind() method of the DatagramChannel class. If you use null as the bind address, this method will bind the socket to an available address automatically. The bind() method was added to the DatagramChannel class in Java 7. If you are using a prior Java version, you can bind a datagram channel using its underlying socket. The following snippet of code shows how to bind a datagram channel:

```
/* In Java 7 and later */
// Bind the channel to any available address automatically
channel.bind(null);

// Bind the channel to "localhost" and port 8989
InetSocketAddress sAddr = new InetSocketAddress("localhost", 8989);
channel.bind(sAddr);

/* Prior to Java 7 */
// Get the socket reference
DatagramSocket socket = channel.socket();

// Bind the channel to any available address automatically
socket.bind(null);

// Bind the channel to "localhost" and port 8989
InetSocketAddress sAddr = new InetSocketAddress("localhost", 8989);
socket.bind(sAddr);
```

Sending Datagrams

To send a datagram to a remote host, use the send() method of the DatagramChannel class. The method accepts a ByteBuffer and a remote SocketAddress. If you call the send() method on an unbound datagram channel, the send() method binds the channel automatically to an available address.

```
// Prepare a message to send
String msg = "Hello";
ByteBuffer buffer = ByteBuffer.wrap(msg.getBytes());
```

```
// Pack the remote address and port into an object
InetSocketAddress serverAddress = new InetSocketAddress("localhost", 8989);

// Send the message to the remote host
channel.send(buffer, serverAddress);
```

The receive() method of the DatagramChannel class lets a datagram channel receive a datagram from a remote host. This method requires you to provide a ByteBuffer to receive the data. The received data is copied to the specified ByteBuffer at its current position. If the ByteBuffer has less space available than the received data, the extra data is discarded silently. The receive() method returns the address of the remote host. If the datagram channel is in a non-blocking mode, the receive() method returns immediately by returning null. Otherwise, it waits until it receives a datagram.

```
// Prepare a ByteBufer to receive data
ByteBuffer buffer = ByteBuffer.allocate(1024);

// Wait to receive data from a remote host
SocketAddress remoteAddress = channel.receive(buffer);
```

Close the Channel

Finally, close the datagram channel using its close() method.

```
// Close the channel
channel.close();
```

Listing 5-18 contains a program that acts as an echo server. Listing 5-19 has a program that acts as a client. The echo server waits for a message from a remote client. It echoes the message that it receives from the remote client. You need to start the echo server program before starting the client program. You can run multiple client programs simultaneously.

Listing 5-18. An Echo Server Based on the Datagram Channel

```java
// DGCEchoServer.java
package com.jdojo.net;

import java.io.IOException;
import java.net.InetSocketAddress;
import java.net.SocketAddress;
import java.nio.ByteBuffer;
import java.nio.channels.DatagramChannel;

public class DGCEchoServer {
        public static void main(String[] args) {
                DatagramChannel server = null;

                try {
                        // Create a datagram channel and bind it to localhost at port 8989
                        server = DatagramChannel.open();
                        InetSocketAddress sAddr = new InetSocketAddress("localhost", 8989);
                        server.bind(sAddr);
```

```java
            ByteBuffer buffer = ByteBuffer.allocate(1024);

            // Wait in an infinite loop for a client to send data
            while (true) {
                System.out.println("Waiting for a message from" +
                                   " a remote host at " + sAddr);

                // Wait for a client to send a message
                SocketAddress remoteAddr = server.receive(buffer);

                // Prepare the buffer to read the message
                buffer.flip();

                // Convert the buffer data into a String
                int limits = buffer.limit();
                byte bytes[] = new byte[limits];
                buffer.get(bytes, 0, limits);
                String msg = new String(bytes);

                System.out.println("Client at " + remoteAddr +
                                   " says: " + msg);

                // Reuse the buffer to echo the message to the client
                buffer.rewind();

                // Send the message back to the client
                server.send(buffer, remoteAddr);

                // Prepare the buffer to receive the next message
                buffer.clear();
            }
        }
        catch (IOException e) {
            e.printStackTrace();
        }
        finally {
            // Close the channel
            if (server != null) {
                try {
                    server.close();
                }
                catch (IOException e) {
                    e.printStackTrace();
                }
            }
        }
    }
}
```

Listing 5-19. A Client Program Based on the Datagram Channel

```java
// DGCEchoClient.java
package com.jdojo.net;

import java.io.IOException;
import java.net.InetSocketAddress;
import java.nio.ByteBuffer;
import java.nio.channels.DatagramChannel;

public class DGCEchoClient {
    public static void main(String[] args) {
        DatagramChannel client = null;
        try {
            // Create a new datagram channel
            client = DatagramChannel.open();

            // Bind the client to any available local address and port
            client.bind(null);

            // Prepare a message for the server
            String msg = "Hello";
            ByteBuffer buffer = ByteBuffer.wrap(msg.getBytes());
            InetSocketAddress serverAddress =
                    new InetSocketAddress("localhost", 8989);

            // Send the message to the server
            client.send(buffer, serverAddress);

            // Reuse the buffer to receive a response from the server
            buffer.clear();

            // Wait for the server to respond
            client.receive(buffer);

            // Prepare the buffer to read the message
            buffer.flip();

            // Convert the buffer into a string
            int limits = buffer.limit();
            byte bytes[] = new byte[limits];
            buffer.get(bytes, 0, limits);
            String response = new String(bytes);

            // Print the server message on the standard output
            System.out.println("Server responded: " + response);
        }
        catch (IOException e) {
            e.printStackTrace();
        }
```

```
            finally {
                // Close the channel
                if (client != null) {
                    try {
                        client.close();
                    }
                    catch (IOException e) {
                        e.printStackTrace();
                    }
                }
            }
        }
    }
}
```

Multicasting Using Datagram Channels

Java 7 added support for IP multicasting to a datagram channel. A datagram channel that is interested in receiving multicast datagrams joins a multicast group. The datagrams that are sent to a multicast group are delivered to all its members. The following sections outline the steps that are typically needed to set up a client application that is interested in receiving a multicast datagram.

Creating the Datagram Channel

Create a datagram channel to use a specific multicast address type as follows. In your application, you will be using IPv4 or IPv6, not both.

```
// Need to use INET protocol family for an IPv4 addressing scheme
DatagramChannel client = DatagramChannel.open(StandardProtocolFamily.INET);

// Need to use INET6 protocol family for an IPv6 addressing scheme
DatagramChannel client = DatagramChannel.open(StandardProtocolFamily.INET6);
```

Setting the Channel Options

Set the options for the client channel using the setOption() method as shown:

```
// Let other sockets reuse the same address
client.setOption(StandardSocketOptions.SO_REUSEADDR, true);
```

Binding the Channel

Bind the client channel to a local address and a port as shown:

```
int MULTICAST_PORT = 8989;
client.bind(new InetSocketAddress(MULTICAST_PORT));
```

Setting the Multicast Network Interface

Set the socket option IP_MULTICAST_IF that specifies the network interface on which the client channel will join the multicast group.

```
// Get the reference of a network interface named "eth1"
NetworkInterface interf = NetworkInterface.getByName("eth1");

// Set the IP_MULTICAST_IF option
client.setOption(StandardSocketOptions.IP_MULTICAST_IF, interf);
```

Listing 5-20 contains the complete program that prints the names of all network interfaces available on your machine. It also prints whether a network interface supports multicast and whether it is up. You may get a different output when you run the code on your machine. You will need to use the name of one of the available network interfaces that supports multicast and that network interface should be up. For example, as shown in the output, the network interface named eth1 is up and support multicast on my machine, so I used eth1 as the network interface for working with multicast messages.

Listing 5-20. Listing the Available Network Interface on a Machine

```java
// ListNetworkInterfaces.java
package com.jdojo.net;

import java.net.NetworkInterface;
import java.net.SocketException;
import java.util.Enumeration;

public class ListNetworkInterfaces {
    public static void main(String[] args) {
        try {
            Enumeration<NetworkInterface> e =
                NetworkInterface.getNetworkInterfaces();
            while (e.hasMoreElements()) {
                NetworkInterface nif = e.nextElement();
                System.out.println("Name: " + nif.getName() +
                    ", Supports Multicast: " + nif.supportsMulticast() +
                    ", isUp(): " + nif.isUp()) ;
            }
        }
        catch (SocketException ex) {
            ex.printStackTrace();
        }

    }
}
```

```
Name: lo,      Supports  Multicast:  true,   isUp(): true
Name: eth0,    Supports  Multicast:  true,   isUp(): false
Name: wlan0,   Supports  Multicast:  true,   isUp(): false
Name: eth1,    Supports  Multicast:  true,   isUp(): true
Name: net0,    Supports  Multicast:  false,  isUp(): false
Name: net1,    Supports  Multicast:  false,  isUp(): true
Name: wlan1,   Supports  Multicast:  true,   isUp(): false
Name: eth2,    Supports  Multicast:  true,   isUp(): false
Name: eth3,    Supports  Multicast:  true,   isUp(): false
Name: eth4,    Supports  Multicast:  true,   isUp(): false
Name: wlan2,   Supports  Multicast:  true,   isUp(): false
Name: wlan3,   Supports  Multicast:  true,   isUp(): false
Name: wlan4,   Supports  Multicast:  true,   isUp(): false
Name: wlan5,   Supports  Multicast:  true,   isUp(): false
Name: wlan6,   Supports  Multicast:  true,   isUp(): false
Name: wlan7,   Supports  Multicast:  true,   isUp(): false
Name: wlan8,   Supports  Multicast:  true,   isUp(): false
Name: wlan9,   Supports  Multicast:  true,   isUp(): false
Name: wlan10,  Supports  Multicast:  true,   isUp(): false
```

Joining the Multicast Group

Now it is time to join the multicast group using the join() method as follows. Note that you must use a multicast IP address for the group.

```
String MULTICAST_IP = "239.1.1.1";
// Join the multicast group on interf interface
InetAddress group = InetAddress.getByName(MULTICAST_IP);
MembershipKey key = client.join(group, interf);
```

The join() method returns an object of the MembershipKey class that represents the membership of the datagram channel with the multicast group. If a datagram channel is not interested in receiving multicast datagrams anymore, it can use the drop() method of the key to drop its membership from the multicast group.

■ **Tip** A datagram channel may decide to receive multicast datagrams only from selective sources. You can use the block(InetAddress source) method of the MembershipKey class to block a multicast datagram from the specified source address. Its unblock(InetAddress source) lets you unblock a previously blocked source address.

Receiving a Message

At this point, receiving datagrams that are addressed to the multicast group is just a matter of calling the receive() method on the channel as shown:

```
// Prepare a buffer to receive the message from the multicast group
ByteBuffer buffer = ByteBuffer.allocate(1048);

// Wait to receive a message from the multicast group
client.receive(buffer);
```

After you are done with the channel, you can drop its membership from the group as shown:

```
// We are no longer interested in receiving multicast message from the group.
// So, we need to drop the channel's membership from the group
key.drop();
```

Closing the Channel

Finally, you need to close the channel using its close() method as shown:

```
// Close the channel
client.close();
```

To send a message to a multicast group, you do not need to be a member of that multicast group. You can send a datagram to a multicast group using the send() method of the DatagramChannel class.

Listing 5-21 contains a class with three constants that are used in the subsequent two classes to build the multicast application. The constants contain the multicast IP address, multicast port number, and multicast network interface name that will be used in the subsequent example. Please make sure that the value eth1 for the MULTICAST_INTERFACE_NAME constant is the network interface name on your machine that supports multicast and it is up. You can get the list of all network interfaces on your machine by running the program in Listing 5-20.

Listing 5-21. A DatagramChannel-Based Multicast Client Program

```java
// DGCMulticastUtil.java
package com.jdojo.net;

public class DGCMulticastUtil {
        public static final String MULTICAST_IP = "239.1.1.1";
        public static final int MULTICAST_PORT = 8989;

        /* You need to change the following network interface name "eth1"
           to the network interface name that supports multicast and is up
           on your machine. Please run class ListNetworkInterfaces to get
           the list of all available network interface on your machine.
         */
        public static final String MULTICAST_INTERFACE_NAME = "eth1";
}
```

Listing 5-22 contains a program that joins a multicast group as a member. It waits for a message from a multicast group to arrive, prints the message, and quits. Listing 5-23 contains a program that sends a message to the multicast group. You can run multiple instances of the DGCMulticastClient class and then run the DGCMulticastServer class. All client instances should receive and print the same message on the standard output.

Listing 5-22. A DatagramChannel-Based Multicast Client Program

```java
// DGCMulticastClient.java
package com.jdojo.net;

import java.io.IOException;
import java.net.InetAddress;
import java.net.InetSocketAddress;
import java.net.NetworkInterface;
import java.net.StandardProtocolFamily;
import java.net.StandardSocketOptions;
import java.nio.ByteBuffer;
import java.nio.channels.DatagramChannel;
import java.nio.channels.MembershipKey;

public class DGCMulticastClient {
        public static void main(String[] args) {
                MembershipKey key = null;

                // Create, configure and bind the client datagram channel
                try (DatagramChannel client =
                                DatagramChannel.open(StandardProtocolFamily.INET)) {
                        // Get the reference of a network interface
                        NetworkInterface interf = NetworkInterface.getByName(
                                DGCMulticastUtil.MULTICAST_INTERFACE_NAME);

                        client.setOption(StandardSocketOptions.SO_REUSEADDR, true);
                        client.bind(new InetSocketAddress(DGCMulticastUtil.MULTICAST_PORT));
                        client.setOption(StandardSocketOptions.IP_MULTICAST_IF, interf);

                        // Join the multicast group on the interf interface
                        InetAddress group =
                                InetAddress.getByName(DGCMulticastUtil.MULTICAST_IP);
                        key = client.join(group, interf);

                        // Print some useful messages for the user
                        System.out.println("Joined the multicast group:" + key);
                        System.out.println("Waiting for a message from the" +
                                                " multicast group....");

                        // Prepare a data buffer to receive a message from the multicast group
                        ByteBuffer buffer = ByteBuffer.allocate(1048);

                        // Wait to receive a message from the multicast group
                        client.receive(buffer);
```

```
                    // Convert the message in the ByteBuffer into a string
                    buffer.flip();
                    int limits = buffer.limit();
                    byte bytes[] = new byte[limits];
                    buffer.get(bytes, 0, limits);
                    String msg = new String(bytes);

                    System.out.format("Multicast Message:%s%n", msg);
            }
            catch (IOException e) {
                    e.printStackTrace();
            }
            finally {
                    // Drop the membership from the multicast group
                    if (key != null) {
                            key.drop();
                    }
            }
        }
    }
}
```

Listing 5-23. A DatagramChannel-Based Multicast Program That Sends a Message to a Multicast Group

```
// DGCMulticastServer.java
package com.jdojo.net;

import java.io.IOException;
import java.net.InetSocketAddress;
import java.net.NetworkInterface;
import java.net.StandardSocketOptions;
import java.nio.ByteBuffer;
import java.nio.channels.DatagramChannel;

public class DGCMulticastServer {
        public static void main(String[] args) {
                // Get a datagram channel object to act as a server
                try (DatagramChannel server = DatagramChannel.open()) {
                        // Bind the server to any available local address
                        server.bind(null);

                        // Set the network interface for outgoing multicast data
                        NetworkInterface interf = NetworkInterface.getByName(
                                DGCMulticastUtil.MULTICAST_INTERFACE_NAME);

                        server.setOption(StandardSocketOptions.IP_MULTICAST_IF, interf);

                        // Prepare a message to send to the multicast group
                        String msg = "Hello from multicast!";
                        ByteBuffer buffer = ByteBuffer.wrap(msg.getBytes());
```

```
                    // Get the multicast group reference to send data to
                    InetSocketAddress group
                            = new InetSocketAddress(DGCMulticastUtil.MULTICAST_IP,
                                    DGCMulticastUtil.MULTICAST_PORT);

                    // Send the message to the multicast group
                    server.send(buffer, group);

                    System.out.println("Sent the multicast message: " + msg);
                }
                catch (IOException e) {
                    e.printStackTrace();
                }
            }
        }
    }
```

Further Reading

Network programming in Java is a vast topic. There are a few books written especially on this topic. This chapter covers only the basics of the network programming support that is available in Java. Java also supports secured socket communications using a Secured Socket Layer (SSL) protocol. The classes for secured socket communication programming are in the javax.net.ssl package. This chapter does not cover SSL sockets. I have not covered many of the options for sockets that you can use in your Java programs. If you want to do advanced level network programming in Java, it is recommended that you read a book that devotes itself solely to network programming in Java after you finish this chapter.

Summary

A network is a group of two or more computers or other types of electronic devices such as printers, linked together with a goal to share information. Each device linked to a network is called a node. A computer that is linked to a network is called a host. Network programming in Java involves writing Java programs that facilitate exchange of information between processes running on different computers on the network.

The communication between two remote hosts is performed by a layered protocol suite called the Internet Reference Model or TCP/IP Layering Model. The protocol suite consists of five layers named application, transport, internet, network interface, and physical. A user application such as a Java program uses the application layer to communicate to a remote application. The transport layer protocol handles the ways messages are transported from one application on one computer to another application on a remote computer. The internet layer accepts the messages from the transport layer and prepares a packet suitable for sending over the internet. It includes the Internet Protocol (IP). The packet prepared by IP is also known as an IP datagram and it consists of a header and a data area, apart from other pieces of information. The network interface layer prepares a packet to be transmitted on the network. The packet is called a frame. The network interface layer sits on top of the physical layer, which involves the hardware. The physical layer consists of the hardware. It is responsible for converting the bits of information into signals and transmitting the signal over the wire.

An IP address uniquely identifies a connection between a computer and a router. There are two versions of Internet Protocol—IPv4 (or simply IP) and IPv6, where v4 and v6 stand for version 4 and version 6. IPv6 is also known as Internet Protocol next generation (IPng). An object of the InetAddress class represents an IP address in Java programs. The InetAddress class has two subclasses, Inet4Address and Inet6Address, which represent IPv4 and IPv6 addresses, respectively.

A port number is a 16-bit unsigned integer ranging from 0 to 65535 that is used to uniquely identify a process for a specific protocol.

An object of the InetSocketAddress class represents a socket address that combines an IP address and a port number.

An object of the ServerSocket class represents a TCP server socket for accepting connections from remote hosts. An object of the Socket class represents a server/client socket. The client and server applications exchange information using objects of the Socket class. The Socket class provides the getInputStream() and getOutputStream() methods to obtain the input and output streams of the socket, respectively. The input stream of the socket is used to read the data from the socket and the output stream of the socket is used to write data to the socket.

An object of the DatagramPacket class represents a UDP datagram that is the unit of data transmission over a UDP socket. An object of the DatagramSocket class represents a UDP server/client socket.

A Uniform Resource Identifier (URI) is a sequence of characters that identifies a resource. A URI that uses a location to identify a resource is called Uniform Resource Locator (URL). A URI that uses a name to identify a resource is called a Uniform Resource Name (URN). URL and URN are subsets of URI. An object of the java.net.URI class represents a URI in Java. An object of the java.net.URL class represents a URL in Java. Java provides classes to access the contents identified by a URL.

Java supports non-blocking socket channels using the ServerSocketChannel, SocketChannel, Selector, and SelectionKey classes in the java.nio.channels package.

Java also supports asynchronous socket channels through the AsynchronousServerSocketChannel and AsynchronousSocketChannel classes in the java.nio.channels package.

Java supports datagram-oriented socket channel through the DatagramChannel class. IP multicasting is also supported on datagram channels.

CHAPTER 6

■ ■ ■

JDBC API

In this chapter, you will learn

- What JDBC API is

- Types of JDBC drivers

- A brief overview of Java DB

- How to connect to a database using a JDBC driver

- What transaction isolation levels are

- JDBC-data-types-to-Java-data-types mapping

- How to execute SQL statements in Java programs and processing the results

- Using rowsets, batch updates, and large objects (LOBs)

- How to retrieve SQL warning and enable JDBC tracing

What Is the JDBC API?

The JDBC API provides a standard database-independent interface to interact with any tabular data source. Most of the time, it is used to interact with a relational database management system (RDBMs). However, using the JDBC API, it is possible to interact with any tabular data source, such as an Excel Spreadsheet, a flat file, etc. Typically, you use the JDBC API to connect to a database, query the data, and update the data. It also lets you execute SQL stored procedures in a database using a database-independent syntax.

The main purpose of using a database is to manage business data. Every database provides developers with the following three things to manage data:

- A standard SQL syntax

- An extension to the standard SQL syntax called a proprietary SQL syntax

- A proprietary programming language

For example, Oracle databases use PL/SQL as a programming language that you can use to write stored procedures, functions, and triggers. Microsoft SQL Server uses Transact-SQL (T-SQL) as the programming language to write stored procedures, functions, and triggers. If you want to process a set of rows in a database, you need to know the syntax and logic to process cursors in a specific database-dependent language. Using the JDBC API relieves you of the pain of learning a different syntax to process a cursor in different databases. It requires you to write a query (a SELECT statement) using a standard SQL syntax. It provides Java APIs to process the result set of that query in a database-independent manner.

Using the JDBC API to access data in a database hides the implementation differences that exist in different types of databases. It achieves database transparency by defining most of its API using interfaces and letting the database vendors (or any third-party vendors) provide the implementations for those interfaces. The collection of the implementation classes that is supplied by a vendor to interact with a specific database is called a *JDBC driver*. There are different kinds of JDBC drivers that exist for different databases (or for the same database). They differ in the way they are implemented. Some JDBC drivers are written in pure Java. For purely Java-implemented JDBC drivers, you just need to include the vendor-supplied classes in your application CLASSPATH. Some JDBC drivers need a proprietary software installation on the client machine to interact with a database. The next section discusses the JDBC driver types.

System Requirements

This chapter is all about interacting with databases using Java programs. You must have access to a database such as an Oracle database, Microsoft SQL Server, Sybase database, DB2, MySQL, Java DB, etc. You will also need to have a JDBC driver for your database. Some JDBC drivers do not need special installation. Rather, you can use them by placing the supplied JDBC driver files (usually a JAR file) in the CLASSPATH on your machine. If you do not have access to a database and the required JDBC driver, you will not be able to run the examples listed in this chapter. All major database vendors make the JDBC driver available for download from their official web sites for free. Whenever necessary, this chapter provides the syntax and the script to create database objects and routines in the few DBMSs—MySQL, Java DB (Apache Derby), Oracle Database, DB2, Microsoft SQL Server, and Sybase Adaptive Server Anywhere. If you are using a DBMS to run the JDBC programs in this chapter, other than the ones listed here, you will need to refer to your DBMS documentation for the syntax to create database objects.

Types of JDBC Drivers

You can use three types of JDBC drivers in your Java programs to connect to a DBMS. Figure 6-1 shows the architecture of those JDBC drivers. This section describes those types of JDBC drivers in brief.

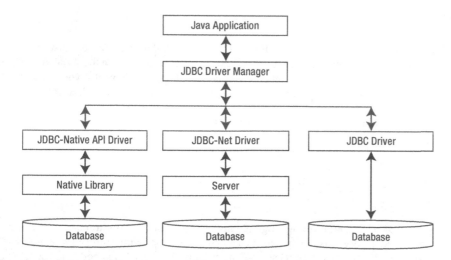

Figure 6-1. *The architecture of JDBC drivers*

■ **Note** Prior to Java 8, the JDBC API provided one more type of JDBC driver called the JDBC-ODBC bridge. This driver has been removed in Java 8.

JDBC Native API Driver

The JDBC-Native API driver uses a DBMS-specific native library to perform all database activities. It translates JDBC calls into DBMS-specific calls, and the DBMS native library communicates with the database. You must install DBMS-specific client software to use this type of driver. It is platform-dependent.

JDBC-Net Driver

The JDBC-Net driver is written in pure Java. It needs a server to work with a database. The driver translates the JDBC calls into a network protocol and passes the calls to the server. The server translates the network calls to DBMS-specific calls. The JDBC driver running at the client machine is unaware of the technology (or DBMS driver types) that the server will use to perform the database activities. The server can use different types of database drivers to connect to different databases and it will be transparent to the client. It is a platform-independent driver. The client machine needs to include only the Java classes required to use the driver. There is no additional installation needed on the client machine.

JDBC Driver

The JDBC driver is also known as a direct-to-database pure Java driver. It is written in pure Java. It converts the JDBC calls into DBMS-specific calls and sends the calls directly to the database. It is the best suitable driver type to be used in applets. All you need to do is to include the driver JAR/ZIP files with your application or applet. All major DBMS vendors supply this type of JDBC driver.

A Brief Overview of Java DB

You will need access to a relational database to run the example in this chapter. If you do not have access to a database, you can use the Java DB database that is installed on your machine when you install the JDK. The Java DB is a relational database management system that is based on the Java programming language and SQL. It is the Oracle release of the Apache Derby project. Technical documentation on the Java DB can be found at http://docs.oracle.com/javadb/.

In the following sections, I will discuss the minimum required information to get you started with Java DB, such as how to start, stop, and run SQL commands in Java DB.

Java DB Installation Files

Suppose JDK_HOME is the directory where you have installed the JDK. For example, if you have installed the JDK in C:\java8 on Windows, the value for JDK_HOME will be C:\java8; if you have installed the JDK in /home/ksharan/java8 on UNIX-like operating system, the value for JDK_HOME will be /home/ksharan/java8. The Java DB files are installed in the db subdirectory of the JDK_HOME. The db directory contains two subdirectories called bin and lib. The bin subdirectory contains many command files to work with the database. For example, the startNetworkServer.bat file is used to start the network Java DB server on Windows and startNetworkServer is used to start the network Java DB server on UNIX; you can use the ij.bat command on Windows and the ij command on UNIX to connect to the Java DB and run SQL commands (ij stands for interactive Java DB). The lib subdirectory contains all JAR files that are used to work with Java DB.

Configuring Java DB

Typically, you do not need to configure Java DB when you have installed JDK8. If you come across any errors in starting up the database or running SQL commands from the command line, you need to set the following environment variables:

- Set the DERBY_HOME environment variable to the JDK_HOME\db directory.
- Set the JAVA_HOME environment variable to the JDK_HOME directory.
- Include the JDK_HOME\bin directory in the PATH environment variable.

When you work with Java DB server and client applications, you need to include some Java DB libraries in CLASSPATH. All libraries are JAR files located in JDK_HOME\db\lib directory. Table 6-1 contains the list of Java DB libraries.

Table 6-1. *Libraries Used in Java DB Server and Client Applications*

Library Name	Description
derby.jar	Contains the Java DB database engine code. Used for Java DB running in embedded mode. For Java DB running in server mode, it is needed on the server.
derbytools.jar	Required for running all Java DB tools such as ij, dblook, etc.
derbyrun.jar	An executable JAR file used to start Java DB tools. Including this file in the CLASSPATH also includes derby.jar, derbyclient.jar, derbytools.jar, derbynet.jar files in the CLASSPATH.
derbynet.jar	Contains the Java DB Network Server code. It is required to start the Java DB Network Server.
derbyclient.jar	Contains the Java DB Network Client JDBC driver. It is required for a Java application to connect to a Java DB server over a network.

Running the Java DB Server

Java DB can run in two modes:

- Embedded Mode
- Server Mode

In embedded mode, Java DB is started for a single user Java application inside the same JVM as the Java application. The Java application starts and stops the Java DB. This is the most suitable mode for learning the database programming using JDBC API. You will not need to perform any setup to use Java DB in this mode. I will explain how to use this mode in detail later. All examples in this chapter use Java DB running in this mode unless specified otherwise.

In server mode, Java DB can be used by multiple users concurrently over the network. The Java DB runs in a separate JVM. Applications running in separate JVMs may connect to Java DB running in this mode.

You can use command prompts or NetBeans IDE for Java DB administration. The following sections explain both.

Using Command Prompts

Use the following command to start Java DB in server mode:

```
c:\java8\db\bin> startNetworkServer

Tue Jun 17 23:25:27 CDT 2014 : Security manager installed using the Basic server security policy.
Tue Jun 17 23:25:27 CDT 2014 : Apache Derby Network Server - 10.10.1.3 - (1557168) started and ready
to accept connections on port 1527
```

You may get an `AccessControlException` in starting the server. The error message may read as follows:

```
java.security.AccessControlException: access denied ("java.net.SocketPermission" "localhost:1527"
"listen,resolve")
```

To resolve the `AccessControlException`, you can start the server with no security manager installed as follows:

```
c:\java8\db\bin> startNetworkServer -noSecurityManager
```

You can also resolve the `AccessControlException` by granting the `listen` and `resolve` access to the host and port on which the server is starting in the `JRE_HOME\lib\security\java.policy` file. The following entry in the `java.policy` file grants the required access:

```
grant {
    permission java.net.SocketPermission "localhost:1527", "listen";
};
```

By default, in server mode, Java DB starts at localhost (or the loopback IP address) and at port 1527. If you want to access Java DB from other computers, you need to configure some properties on the command line or in the properties file.

The easiest way to configure the Java DB properties is to set them on the command line. The following command starts the Java DB server that listens at myhost at port number 1537:

```
c:\java8\db\bin>startNetworkServer -h myhost -p 1537
```

You can also use the `java` command to start the Java DB server. The following command starts the Java DB server, additionally setting the `CLASSPATH` and the `derby.system.home` property:

```
C:\java8\db\bin>java -classpath C:\java8\db\lib\derbynet.jar -Dderby.system.home=C:\myderbyhome
org.apache.derby.drda.NetworkServerControl start -h localhost
```

You can set the Java DB properties in the text file named `derby.properties` located in a directory specified by the `derby.system.home` property. You can specify the `derby.system.home` property when you start the Java DB server. If the `derby.system.home` property is not specified, it defaults to the current working directory.

I used NetBeans to run Java DB on Windows and Linux for the user ksharan. By default, the NetBeans IDE sets the `derby.system.home` property to a `.netbeans-derby` subdirectory under the user's home directory. Using the NetBeans IDE, the `derby.properties` file was placed on my machines as follows:

- On Windows: `C:\Users\ksharan\.netbeans-derby\derby.properties`

- On Linux: `/home/ksharan/.netbeans-derby/derby.properties`

Set the `derby.drda.host` property to the host name or the IP address on which you want to start the Java DB in sever mode. If you set this property to 0.0.0.0, Java DB listens on all network interfaces. Set the `derby.drda.portNumber` property to listen to a port different from the default port 1527. The following are the contents of the `derby.properties` file that sets a custom host and port number:

```
# Contents of the derby.properties file
# Set the IP address 192.168.1.1 as the host
derby.drda.host=192.168.1.1

# Set 1528 as the port number
derby.drda.portNumber=1528
```

Use the following command to stop the Java DB running in server mode. Note that you will need to run this command using a separate command prompt.

```
c:\java8\db\bin>stopNetworkServer
Tue Jun 17 23:26:49 CDT 2014 : Apache Derby Network Server - 10.10.1.3 - (1557168) shutdown
```

■ **Tip** The Java DB database server can have several databases. A database in Java DB is portable. Files for each database are stored in a separate directory. Moving a Java DB database is as simple as moving the directory for that database. The directory is named the same as the database name. By default, all database directories are stored in the directory specified in the derby.system.home property.

After you start the Java DB server, you can connect to it and execute SQL commands, using the ij command-line tool. The ij tool is located in the JDK\db\bin directory. Assuming that the Java DB server is running at localhost at port 1527, the following commands start the ij tool, connect to a Java DB database named beginningJavaDB, execute a SELECT SQL statement, and exit the tool using the exit command. If you do not have a person table in the database, you may get an error when you execute the SELECT statement.

```
c:\java8\db\bin>ij
ij version 10.10
ij> connect 'jdbc:derby://localhost:1527/beginningJavaDB';
ij> select * from person;
PERSON_ID  |FIRST_NAME           |LAST_NAME            |&|DOB      |INCOME
------------------------------------------------------------------------

0 rows selected
ij> exit;
c:\java8\db\bin>
```

You do not need to start the Java DB server if you want to work with a Java DB database in embedded mode. The following command sets the classpath, sets the derby.system.home property, and starts the ij tool. Note that the command was entered on one line. After starting the ij tool, I connected to the beginningJavaDB database in embedded mode and executed SQL commands, as shown. If you do not have a person table in the database, you may get an error when you execute the SELECT statement.

```
c:\java8\db\bin>java -classpath C:\java8\db\lib\derbyrun.jar;
-Dderby.system.home=C:\Users\ksharan\.netbeans-derby org.apache
.derby.tools.ij
ij version 10.10
ij>connect 'jdbc:derby:beginningJavaDB';
ij> select * from person;
PERSON_ID  |FIRST_NAME           |LAST_NAME            |&|DOB      |INCOME
------------------------------------------------------------------------

0 rows selected
ij> exit;
c:\java8\db\bin>
```

Using the NetBeans IDE

Working with Java DB is easy when you use the NetBeans IDE. You can use the Services tab in Navigator in the NetBeans IDE to start, stop, and run SQL commands in Java DB. Figure 6-2 shows the Java DB under the Databases node on the Services tab in the NetBeans IDE. If you do not see the Services tab, you can show it by choosing the menu option Windows > Services or by pressing Ctrl + 5.

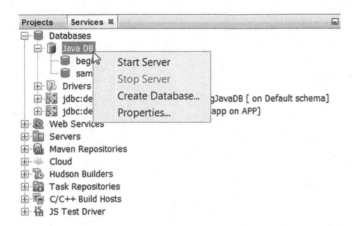

Figure 6-2. *Using Java DB on the Services tab from inside the NetBeans IDE*

To start and stop the Java DB, select the Java DB node on the Services tab, right-click, and choose the appropriate option.

All databases in Java DB are listed under the Java DB node. Java DB is installed with a pre-built database named sample. You can create your own databases by choosing the Create Database option as shown in Figure 6-2.

To connect to a specific database, select the database name under the Java DB node, right-click it, and select the Connect menu option as shown in Figure 6-3.

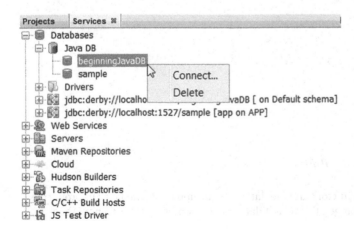

Figure 6-3. *Connecting to a Java DB database from inside the NetBeans IDE*

After you are connected to a database, you can execute SQL commands in that database using the NetBeans IDE. The Databases node in the Services tab contains one Database Connection node for each Java DB database. Select the Database Connection node for your database, right-click, and select the Execute Command menu option as shown in Figure 6-4. It will open a SQL editor. You can enter SQL commands in the SQL editor. To execute the SQL command, use the Run SQL toolbar button or press Ctrl + Shift + E.

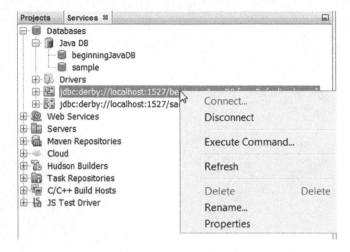

Figure 6-4. *Executing SQL commands in Java DB from inside the NetBeans IDE*

By default, the NetBeans IDE stores all Java DB databases in the subdirectory named .netbeans-derby in the user's home directory. You can change the default location by using the Java DB properties dialog. You can open the Java DB properties dialog by choosing the Databases > Data DB > Right-click > Properties menu shown in Figure 6-5.

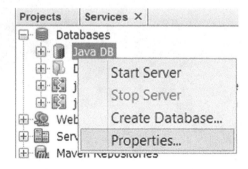

Figure 6-5. *Setting properties for Java DB in the NetBeans IDE*

You can change the default Java DB installation directory and the database location using the Java DB properties dialog shown in Figure 6-6. The figure shows that I changed the default database location to the C:\kishori\books\java_8\projects\Test directory on Windows.

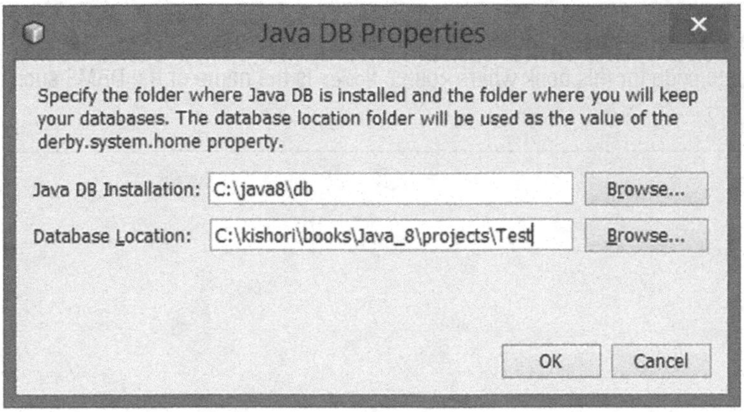

Figure 6-6. *The Java Db Properties dialog*

Creating a Database Table

The primary goal of using the JDBC API is to manipulate data contained in tables in a database. You may manipulate data in tables using the SQL statements SELECT, INSERT, UPDATE, and DELETE, which use table names directly. Sometimes you may not refer to the table names in your JDBC calls directly. Rather, you may execute a stored procedure using the JDBC API, and the stored procedure uses table names. One way or the other, you end up using tables when you work with JDBC. Most of the time in this chapter, you will work with one table. You will name your table person. You may create more tables along the way when you need to work on specific types of database processing using JDBC. It is assumed that you have created a table named person in the database of your choice. The table description is shown in Table 6-2.

Table 6-2. *Generic Description of a Database Table Named Person*

Column Name	Data Type	Length	Null Value Allowed	Comments
person_id	integer		No	Primary Key
first_name	string	20	No	
last_name	string	20	No	
gender	string	1	No	
Dob	date		Yes	
income	double		Yes	

The data types of columns shown in this table are generic. You will need to use data types specific to your DBMS. For example, for the first_name column, you can use the data type of varchar2(20) in the Oracle database and varchar(20) in the SQL Server database. Similarly, for the person_id column, you can use a data type of number(8, 0) in the Oracle database and int in the SQL Server database.

Every DBMS provides a tool, either character-based, graphical, or both, that lets you work with database objects such as tables, stored procedures, functions, etc. For example, you can use the Oracle SQL*PLUS tool for Oracle DBMS from Oracle, the SQL Server Management Studio tool for SQL Server DBMS from Microsoft, the Interactive SQL tool for Adaptive Server Anywhere (ASA) from Sybase, etc.

The following sections show the database scripts to create the person table in different databases. You will need to consult the documentation for your database on how to run the script to create the person table.

■ **Note**   All database scripts such as to create tables and stored procedures are available under the
dbscripts\<DBMS-Name> directory with the source code for this book where <DBMS-Name> is the name of the DBMS such
as Oracle, DB2 etc.

Oracle Database

```
create table person (
        person_id number(8,0) not null,
        first_name varchar2(20) not null,
        last_name varchar2(20) not null,
        gender char(1) not null,
        dob date,
        income number(10,2),
        constraint pk_person primary key(person_id)
);
```

Adaptive Server Anywhere Database

```
create table person (
        person_id integer not null default null,
        first_name varchar(20) not null default null,
        last_name varchar(20) not null default null,
        gender char(1) not null default null,
        dob date null default null,
        income double null default null,
        primary key (person_id)
);
```

SQL Server Database

```
create table person (
        person_id int NOT NULL,
        first_name varchar(20) NOT NULL,
        last_name varchar(20) NOT NULL,
        gender char(1) NOT NULL,
        dob datetime NULL,
        income decimal(10,2) NULL,
        constraint pk_person primary key (person_id)
);
```

DB2 Database

```
create table person (
        person_id integer not null,
        first_name varchar(20) not null,
```

```
        last_name varchar(20) not null,
        gender character (1)  not null,
        dob date,
        income double,
        constraint pk_person_id primary key (person_id)
);
```

MySQL Database

```
create table person (
        person_id integer not null primary key,
        first_name varchar(20) not null,
        last_name varchar(20) not null,
        gender char(1) not null,
        dob datetime null,
        income double null
);
```

Java DB Database

```
create table person (
        person_id integer not null,
        first_name varchar(20) not null,
        last_name varchar(20) not null,
        gender char(1) not null,
        dob date,
        income double,
        primary key(person_id)
);
```

You can run the program shown later in Listing 6-3 to create the person table in Java DB. To create the person table in another database, you may have to change the CREATE TABLE syntax in the program.

Connecting to a Database

Here are the steps that you need to follow to connect to a database.

- Obtain the JDBC driver and add it to the CLASSPATH environment variable on your machine.
- Register the JDBC driver with the DriverManager.
- Construct a connection URL.
- Use the getConnection() static method of DriverManager to establish a connection.

The following sections describe these steps in detail.

Obtaining the JDBC Driver

You need to have the JDBC driver for your database before you can connect to the database using JDBC. You can get a JDBC driver from the vendor of your database. For example, if you are using the Oracle DBMS, you can download the JDBC driver from its official web site at www.oracle.com. All database vendors that support JDBC will let you download the JDBC driver for their DBMS from their official web sites for free. Typically, a JDBC driver is bundled in one or more JAR/ZIP files.

If you are using Java DB, the JDBC drivers were copied on your machine when you installed the JDK. You do not need to download any additional JDBC drivers.

Setting up the CLASSPATH

If you are using a JDBC driver, you need to place the JAR/ZIP files for your JDBC driver in the CLASSPATH on your machine, so that your Java programs can use the Java classes that implement the JDBC driver for your database.

If you are using Java DB, please refer to Table 6-1 for the JAR file that you will need to use in your case. To run all examples in this chapter that use Java DB in embedded mode, you will need the derby.jar file in the CLASSPATH. The derby.jar file is the JDBC driver needed to use the Java DB in embedded mode. If you are connecting to Java DB over a network, you will need to include the derbyclient.jar file in the CLASSPATH.

Registering a JDBC Driver

You need to register a JDBC driver, which you want to use to connect to a database. A JDBC driver is registered with the java.sql.DriverManager class.

What is a JDBC driver? Technically, a JDBC driver is a class that implements the java.sql.Driver interface. DBMS vendors supply the JDBC driver class along with any other classes it uses. You must know the name of the JDBC driver class before you can register it with the DriverManager class. If you do not know the name of the driver class, please refer to the documentation of the JDBC driver for your DBMS.

In the next section, I will list the driver class names for some DBMSs. The name may vary depending on the version of DBMS or the supplier of the driver class. Sometimes different vendors supply the drivers for the same DBMS. Different vendors will use different driver class names and different connection URL formats to connect to the same DBMS.

Why do you need to register a JDBC driver with the DriverManager? Java does not know how to connect to a database. It depends on the JDBC driver to connect to a database. Think of a JDBC driver as a Java class whose object will be used by the DriverManager to connect to a database. The question is, "How does the DriverManager know about the JDBC driver you want to use to connect to a database?" Of course, it has no way to know about the JDBC driver by itself. Therefore, registering a driver with the DriverManager is simply telling the DriverManager about your JDBC driver class name. By registering a JDBC driver, you are telling the DriverManager that if you ask the DriverManager to establish a connection to a database, it needs to try using this driver. Can you register multiple JDBC drivers with the DriverManager? Yes. You can register multiple JDBC drivers. When you need to establish a connection to a database, you must pass a connection URL to the DriverManager. The DriverManager passes the connection URL to all registered drivers one by one, and asks them to connect to the database using information that you supply in the connection URL. If a driver recognizes the connection URL, it connects to the database and returns the connection to the DriverManager. An object of the java.sql.Connection interface represents a database connection in a Java program. If none of the registered drivers recognize a connection URL, the DriverManager will throw a SQLException stating that it could not find a suitable driver.

There are three ways to register a JDBC driver with the DriverManager:

- By setting the jdbc.drivers system property

- By loading the driver class into the JVM

- By using the registerDriver() method of the DriverManager class

Setting the jdbc.drivers System Property

You can register a JDBC driver class name using the jdbc.drivers system property. You can set this property in your computer globally; you can pass this property on the command line when you run your application, or you can set this property in your application using the System.setProperty() method. A colon separates each driver to be registered. Here are some examples:

```
// Register Sybase and Oracle drivers in the Java code
String drivers = "com.sybase.jdbc2.jdbc.SybDriver:oracle.jdbc.driver.OracleDriver";
System.setProperty("jdbc.drivers", drivers);

// Pass driver names to be registered as command-line arguments.
// The following command is entered in one line.
java -Djdbc.drivers=com.sybase.jdbc2.jdbc.SybDriver:oracle.jdbc.driver.OracleDriver
com.jdojo.jdbc.Test
```

Loading the Driver Class

You can create an object of the driver class. When the driver class is loaded in the JVM, it registers itself with the DriverManager. For a class to be loaded, you can use a Class.forName("driver class name") method or create an object of the class as follows:

```
// Register the Oracle JDBC driver
new oracle.jdbc.driver.OracleDriver();

// Register the Oracle JDBC driver using the Class.forName() method.
// Exception handling has been omitted.
Class.forName("oracle.jdbc.driver.OracleDriver")

// Register the Java DB embedded driver
new org.apache.derby.jdbc.EmbeddedDriver();

// Register the Java DB network client driver
new org.apache.derby.jdbc.ClientDriver();
```

You do not need to keep the reference of the driver object because the goal is to load the driver class in the JVM. When the driver's class is loaded into the JVM, the static initializer of the driver's class is executed in which the driver class registers itself with the DriverManager.

Using the registerDriver() Method

You can call the registerDriver(java.sql.Driver driver) static method of the DriverManager class with an object of a JDBC driver class to register the JDBC driver.

```
// Register the Oracle JDBC driver with DriverManager
DriverManager.registerDriver(new oracle.jdbc.driver.OracleDriver());

// Register the Java DB embedded driver
DriverManager.registerDriver(new org.apache.derby.jdbc.EmbeddedDriver());

// Register the Java DB network client driver
DriverManager.registerDriver(new org.apache.derby.jdbc.ClientDriver());
```

You can follow one of the above three methods to register a JDBC driver. The first way offers more flexibility. It lets you change the JDBC driver without changing your Java code. You can also specify a connection URL (discussed next) using a system property or as a command-line argument. This way, not only can you use a different JDBC driver, but also a different DBMS without modifying the Java code.

Constructing a Connection URL

A database connection is established using a connection URL. The format of a connection URL is dependent upon the DMBS and a JDBC driver. There are three parts of a connection URL. A colon separates two parts of the connection URL. The syntax to define the connection URL is

```
<protocol>:<sub-protocol>:<data-source-details>
```

The `<protocol>` part is always set to `jdbc`. The `<sub-protocol>` part is vendor-specific. The `<data-source-details>` part is DBMS specific that is used to locate the database. In some cases, you can also specify some connection properties in this last part of the URL. The following is an example of a connection URL that uses Oracle's thin JDBC driver to connect to an Oracle DBMS:

```
jdbc:oracle:thin:@localhost:1521:chanda
```

As always, the protocol part is `jdbc`. The sub-protocol part is `oracle:thin`, which identifies the Oracle Corporation as the vendor, and the type of the driver it will use, which is `thin`. The data source details part is `@localhost:1521:chanda`. It has three subparts. The `@localhost` identifies the server name. You could use an IP address or a machine name of your Oracle database server instead. Then, it contains the port number at which Oracle's Transport Network Substrate (TNS) listener is running. The last part is an Oracle's instance name, which is chanda in this example. The following is another example of a connection URL that identifies a database in a Java DB server:

```
jdbc:derby://192.168.1.3:1527/beginningJavaDB;create=true
```

As always, the protocol part is `jdbc`. The subprotocol part is `derby`, which identifies the Apache Derby DBMS. Recall that Java DB is an Oracle's release of the Apache Derby project. The `192.168.1.3:1527` part the machine's IP address and the port number where Java DB server is running. The database name is `beginningJavaDB`. The last part, `create=true`, is the connection property that indicates that if a database named `beginningJavaDB` does not exist, create a new database with this name.

The following sections describe the formats for a connection URL for some DBMSs. You need to visit the official web site of a vendor to download a specific JDBC driver. You can also get the detailed information about using the JDBC drivers at the vendor's web site.

Oracle Database

```
DBMS: Oracle 10g
Vendor: Oracle Corporation
Web Site: http://www.oracle.com
Driver Type: JDBC Driver (thin - Pure Java)
URL Format: jdbc:oracle:thin:@<server>:<port>:<instance>
URL Example: jdbc:oracle:thin:@localhost:1521:chanda
Driver Class: oracle.jdbc.driver.OracleDriver
```

It is implemented 100% in Java. If you are using a thin Oracle driver, you do not need to install any Oracle-specific configuration software. If you are using JDBC to connect to an Oracle database in an applet, this is the driver you should use:

```
DBMS: Oracle 10g
Vendor: Oracle Corporation
Web Site: http://www.oracle.com
Driver Type: JDBC-Native Driver (OCI - Oracle Call Interface)
URL Format: jdbc:oracle:oci:@<tns-alias>
URL Example: jdbc:oracle:oci:@orcl
Driver Class: oracle.jdbc.driver.OracleDriver
```

You need to install the Oracle client software to use the OCI driver. The JDBC driver converts the standard JDBC calls to OCI calls, which are sent to the database. The `<tns-alias>` part of the URL comes from an entry in the `tnsnames.ora` file. A typical TNS alias entry in a `tnsnames.ora` file looks as follows:

```
ORCL =
  (DESCRIPTION =
    (ADDRESS = (PROTOCOL = TCP)(HOST = HYE6754)(PORT = 1521))
   .(CONNECT_DATA =
      (SERVER = DEDICATED)
      (SERVICE_NAME = orcl)
    )
  )
```

The Oracle JDBC driver also lets you specify the entire text for a TNS alias as the part of the JDBC connection URL as shown:

```
String dbURL="jdbc:oracle:oci:@(DESCRIPTION =" +
    "(ADDRESS = (PROTOCOL = TCP)(HOST = HYE6754)(PORT = 1521))" +
    "(CONNECT_DATA =(SERVER = DEDICATED)(SERVICE_NAME = orcl)))";
```

Adaptive Server Anywhere Database

```
DBMS: Adaptive Server Anywhere 9.0
Driver Type: JDBC Driver (Pure Java)
Vendor: Sybase Inc.
Web Site: http://www.sybase.com
URL Format: jdbc:sybase:Tds:<server>:<port>
URL Example: jdbc:sybase:Tds:localhost:2638
Driver Class: com.sybase.jdbc2.jdbc.SybDriver
```

SQL Server Database

You can use either of the following two JDBC drivers to connect to a SQL Server database:

```
// Driver #1
DBMS: SQL Server
Vendor: Microsoft Corporation
Web Site: http://www.microsoft.com
Driver Type: JDBC Driver (Pure Java)
```

```
URL Format: jdbc:SQLserver://<server>:<port>
URL Example: jdbc:SQLserver://HYE6754:1433;Database=chanda
Driver Class: com.microsoft.SQLserver.jdbc.SQLServerDriver


// Driver #2
DBMS: SQL Server
Vendor: SourceForge Inc.
Web Site: http://www.sourceforge.net
Driver Type: JDBC Driver (Pure Java)
URL Format: jdbc:jtds:<server_type>://<server>:<port>/<database>;<props>
URL Example: jdbc:jtds:sqlserver://HYE6754:1433/chanda
Driver Class: net.sourceforge.jtds.jdbc.Driver
```

When you use the driver #2, you can specify sqlserver or sybase as <server_type> to connect to SQL Server or Sybase DBMS, respectively. <props> is a comma-separated list of property=value pairs, where property is the name of the database property and value is its value. For example, if you want to specify the user and password as part of the URL, you can use <props> as user=myuserid;password=mysecretpassword.

The parts of the URL, <port>, <database>, and <props>, are optional. If you do not specify them, their default values will be used. The default value for <port> is 1433 for SQL Server and 7100 for Sybase.

MySQL Database

```
DBMS: MySQL Server 5.0
Vendor: Oracle Corporation
Web Site: http://www.oracle.com
Driver Type: JDBC Driver (Pure Java)
URL Format: jdbc:mySQL://<server>:<port>/<database>?<props>
URL Example: jdbc:mySQL://HYE6754:3306/chanda
Driver Class: com.mySQL.jdbc.Driver
```

Most parts in the connection URL are optional for MySQL databases. For example, you can use the shortest connection URL for MySQL as jdbc:mySQL://, and all other parts will be assumed as their default values. The default value for <server> and <port> are localhost and 3306. You can supply a comma-separated list of <server>:<port> values to be used as fail-over servers. If you do not supply the value for <database>, you can either call the setCatalog("catalog name") method on the Connection object after establishing the connection, or supply the catalog name as part of all your queries. You have specified chanda as your database in the example URL. The <props> is an ampersand(&)-separated list of name=value pairs. For example, you can pass the user id and password with the connection URL as follows. It uses root as the user id and chanda as the password.

```
jdbc:mySQL://localhost:3306/chanda?user=root&password=chanda.
```

DB2 Database

```
DBMS: DB2
Vendor: IBM
Web Site: http://www.ibm.com
Driver Type: JDBC Driver (Pure Java)
URL Format: jdbc:db2://<server>:<port>/<database>?<props>
URL Example: jdbc:db2://localhost:50000/chandaDB
Driver Class: com.ibm.db2.jcc.DB2Driver
```

You can use `jdbc:db2:` or `jdbc:db2j:net:` as the initial part of the URL. If the URL starts with `jdbc:db2:`, it indicates that the connection is to a server in the DB2 UDB family. If the URL starts with `jdbc:db2j:net:`, it indicates that that the connection is to a remote IBM[R] Cloudscape[TM] server. The `<props>` part in the URL is a comma-separated list of `name=value` pairs of properties for the database connection. For example, the following URL specifies the `user` and `password` properties as `admin` and `secret`, respectively:

```
jdbc:db2://localhost:5021/chandaDB:user=admin;password=secret;
```

Please visit IBM's official web site for more details about the properties that you can set in the JDBC connection URL.

Java DB Database

```
DBMS: Java DB (Apache Derby)
Web Site: http://www.oracle.com
Driver Type: JDBC Driver (Pure Java)
URL Format: jdbc:derby://<server>:<port>/<database>;<props>
URL Example: jdbc:derby://localhost:1527/beginningJavaDB;create=true
Driver Class: org.apache.derby.jdbc.ClientDriver
```

The default user name and password are app and app, respectively. The property `create=true` is specified to create an empty database, if it does not exist. There are other types of JDBC drivers for Java DB. The client driver lets you connect to it when the Java DB is running as a server and your application accesses it as a client. You can also start the Java DB in the same JVM your application is running, and your application and Java DB will run in the same process. When Java DB runs in the same process as your application, you can use the embedded JDBC driver to access the database.

Loading the JDBC driver for the embedded Java DB starts the Java DB database. The following is an example of the connection URL to start the Java DB in embedded mode and connect to a database named beginningJavaDB:

```
jdbc:derby:beginningJavaDB
```

Recall that a Java DB database has a directory with the same name as the database name. How will the JDBC driver find the beginningJavaDB directory using this connection URL? It will use the directory specified by the `derby.system.home` property. If the property is not specified, it will use the current directory. The following java command starts a Java application by specifying the `derby.system.home` property:

```
java -Dderby.system.home=C:\myDatabases com.jdojo.jdbc.MyApp
```

If you use the database name inside the MyApp class, it will be searched in the C:\myDatabases directory.

You can also specify the full path of the database directory in the connection URL. The following connection URL specifies the full path of the database on Windows:

```
jdbc:derby:C:/myDatabases/beginningJavaDB
```

In the database full path, you can use a forward slash as the path separator on Windows as well as UNIX.

If your database directory is in the CLASSPATH, you can construct a connection URL using the `classpath` sub-protocol as follows:

```
jdbc:derby:classpath:beginningJavaDB
```

The connection URL will look for a beginningJavaDB directory in the CLASSPATH. If your database in the test directory under a directory in the CLASSPATH, you can construct the connection URL as follows:

```
jdbc:derby:classpath:test/beginningJavaDB
```

Java DB is very flexible in letting you specify the connection URL. It also lets you access a read-only database from a JAR/ZIP file. The following connection URL looks for the beginningJavaDB database under the test directory in the C:\myDatabases.jar file:

```
jdbc:derby:jar:(C:/myDatabases.jar)test/beginningJavaDB
```

Establishing the Database Connection

It is time to connect to the database. You need to use the getConnection() static method of the DriverManager class to establish a connection to a database. It returns an object of the java.sql.Connection interface, which represents the database connection. The getConnection() method takes a connection URL, a user id, a password, and any number of name-value pairs using a java.util.Properties object. The getConnection() method is overloaded:

- static Connection getConnection(String url) throws SQLException

- static Connection getConnection(String url, Properties info) throws SQLException

- static Connection getConnection(String url, String user, String password) throws SQLException

You will find it annoying that you need to handle the java.sql.SQLException exception for almost every operation with a database using a JDBC driver. It is a checked exception and the compiler will force you to handle it either by placing your code in a try-catch block or by using a throws clause. Even though you write only one line of code, you will end up using a try-catch block. You will create a utility class with some static methods for a one-liner code that will handle the exceptions for you. Whenever you need to use that one-liner code functionality, you will use the utility class methods instead of using the JDBC methods directly. This approach will avoid bloated code in the examples in this chapter.

The following snippet of code establishes a connection to a database named beginningJavaDB in Java DB running in embedded mode:

```
// Register the JDBC driver
Driver derbyEmbeddedDriver = new org.apache.derby.jdbc.EmbeddedDriver();
DriverManager.registerDriver(derbyEmbeddedDriver);

// Prepare the connection URL
String dbURL = "jdbc:derby:beginningJavaDB;create=true";

Connection conn = null;

try {
        conn = DriverManager.getConnection(dbURL, "root", "chanda");
        System.out.println("Connected to database successfully");

        // Perform database activities here...
}
```

```
catch(SQLException e) {
        e.printStackTrace();
}
finally {
        if (conn != null) {
                try {
                        // Close the connection
                        conn.close();
                }
                catch (SQLException e) {
                        e.printStackTrace();
                }
        }
}
```

The Connection interface inherits from the java.lang.AutoCloseable interface. That means you can also use a try-with-resources block to obtain a Connection that will be automatically closed when the control exits the try block. You can rewrite the above code using a try-with-resources block as follows:

```
// Register the JDBC driver
Driver derbyEmbeddedDriver = new org.apache.derby.jdbc.EmbeddedDriver();
DriverManager.registerDriver(derbyEmbeddedDriver);

// Prepare the connection URL
String dbURL = "jdbc:derby:beginningJavaDB;create=true";

try (Connection conn = DriverManager.getConnection(dbURL, "root", "chanda")) {

        System.out.println("Connected to database successfully");

        // Perform database activities here...
}
catch (SQLException e) {
        e.printStackTrace();
}
```

If you need to connect to any other database, you will need to change two things: the JDBC driver that you register and the connection URL. Both the driver and the connection URL are DBMS-specific. Note the use of a try-catch-finally block in the code. When you are done with a database connection, you need to close it by using the close() method of the Connection object. The close() method of the Connection object throws a SQLException, which forces you to use another try-catch block. In a typical Java program, you will not close a connection just after connecting to a database. You will use the Connection object to perform some database activities, and then, you close the connection.

Listing 6-1 contains the code for a JDBCUtil class, which you will use throughout this chapter to work with database connections. All of its methods are static and they are used to establish and close a database connection, close a Statement, close a ResultSet, commit a transaction, rollback a transaction, etc. I will discuss the Statement and ResultSet objects later in this chapter.

Listing 6-1. A Utility Class That Will be Used to Work With a Database

```java
// JDBCUtil.java
package com.jdojo.jdbc;

import java.sql.Connection;
import java.sql.Driver;
import java.sql.DriverManager;
import java.sql.ResultSet;
import java.sql.SQLException;
import java.sql.Statement;

public class JDBCUtil {
    public static Connection getConnection() throws SQLException {
        // Register the Java DB embedded JDBC driver
        Driver derbyEmbeddedDriver = new org.apache.derby.jdbc.EmbeddedDriver();
        DriverManager.registerDriver(derbyEmbeddedDriver);

        // Construct the connection URL
        String dbURL = "jdbc:derby:beginningJavaDB;create=true;";
        String userId = "root";
        String password = "chanda";

        // Get a connection
        Connection conn = DriverManager.getConnection(dbURL, userId, password);

        // Set the auto-commit off
        conn.setAutoCommit(false);

        return conn;
    }

    public static void closeConnection(Connection conn) {
        try {
            if (conn != null) {
                conn.close();
            }
        }
        catch (SQLException e) {
            e.printStackTrace();
        }
    }

    public static void closeStatement(Statement stmt) {
        try {
            if (stmt != null) {
                stmt.close();
            }
        }
        catch (SQLException e) {
            e.printStackTrace();
        }
    }
```

```java
        public static void closeResultSet(ResultSet rs) {
                try {
                        if (rs != null) {
                                rs.close();
                        }
                }
                catch (SQLException e) {
                        e.printStackTrace();
                }
        }

        public static void commit(Connection conn) {
                try {
                        if (conn != null) {
                                conn.commit();
                        }
                }
                catch (SQLException e) {
                        e.printStackTrace();
                }
        }

        public static void rollback(Connection conn) {
                try {
                        if (conn != null) {
                                conn.rollback();
                        }
                }
                catch (SQLException e) {
                        e.printStackTrace();
                }
        }

        public static void main(String[] args) {
                Connection conn = null;
                try {
                        conn = JDBCUtil.getConnection();
                        System.out.println("Connetced to the database.");
                }
                catch (SQLException e) {
                        e.printStackTrace();
                }
                finally {
                        JDBCUtil.closeConnection(conn);
                }
        }
}
```

To connect to a database, you will use the JDBCUtil.getConnection() method. To close a connection, you will use the JDBCUtil.closeConnection() method. The getConnection() method uses Java DB-specific JDBC driver class and connection URL format. You must change the code in the getConnection() method, which will be specific to the DBMS that you want to connect to. It is important to note that you must be able to run the JDBCUtil class and make sure that you are able to connect to a DBMS successfully, before you can run other examples in this chapter.

> ■ **Tip** One of the most common mistakes that beginners make is not including the JDBC driver's Java classes (usually a JAR/ZIP file) in the CLASSPATH. Make sure that you have your JDBC driver-related classes included in the CLASSPATH. For example, include the derby.jar file in the CLASSPATH to use the Java DB embedded JDBC driver.

Setting the Auto-Commit Mode

When you connect to a database, the auto-commit property for the Connection object is set to true by default. If a connection is in an auto-commit mode, a SQL statement is committed automatically after its successful execution. If a connection is not in an auto-commit mode, you must call the commit() or rollback() method of the Connection object to commit or rollback a transaction. Typically, you disable the auto-commit mode for a connection in a JDBC application, so your application logic controls the final outcome of the transaction. To disable the auto-commit mode, you need to call the setAutoCommit(false) on the Connection object after connection has been established. If a connection URL allows you to set the auto-commit mode, you can also specify it as part of the connection URL. You set the auto-commit mode of your connection in the JDBCUtil.getConnection() method to false after you get a Connection object.

```
// Get a connection
Connection conn = DriverManager.getConnection(dbURL, userId, password);

// Set the auto-commit off
conn.setAutoCommit(false);
```

If you have enabled the auto-commit mode for your connection, you cannot use its commit() and rollback() methods. Calling the commit() and rollback() methods on a Connection object, which has enabled the auto-commit mode, throws an exception. JDBC also lets you use save points in a transaction, so that you can apply a partial rollback to a transaction. I will have an example of using save points later in this chapter.

If the setAutoCommit() method is called to change the auto-commit mode of a connection in the middle of a transaction, the transaction is committed at that time. Typically, you would set the auto-commit mode of a connection just after connecting to the database.

Committing and Rolling Back Transactions

If the auto-commit mode is disabled for a connection, you can use the commit() or rollback() method to commit or rollback a transaction. A typical pseudo code in a JDBC application that performs a database transaction is as shown:

```
Connection conn = get a connection;

// Disable auto-commit mode
conn.setAutoCommit(false);

// Perform database transaction activities here
```

```
IF transaction is successful THEN
        conn.commit(); // Commit the transaction
ELSE
        conn.rollback(); // Rollback the transaction
END IF

conn.close();              // Close the connection
```

The error handling code is not shown. Typically, a try-catch or try-catch-finally block replaces the IF statement shown above.

Transaction Isolation Level

In a multi-user database, you will often come across the following two terms:

- Data concurrency
- Data consistency

Data concurrency refers to the ability of multiple users to use the same data concurrently. Data consistency refers to the accuracy of the data that is maintained when multiple users are manipulating the data concurrently. As the data concurrency increases (i.e. more users work on the same data), care must be taken to maintain a desired level of data consistency. A database maintains data consistency using locks and by isolating one transaction from another. How much a transaction is isolated from another transaction depends on the desired level of data consistency. Let's look at three phenomena where data consistency may be compromised in a multi-user environment where multiple concurrent transactions are supported.

Dirty Read

In a dirty read, a transaction reads uncommitted data from another transaction. Consider the following sequence of steps, which results in inconsistent data because of a dirty read:

- Transaction A inserts a new row in a table and it has not committed it yet.
- Transaction B reads the uncommitted row inserted by the transaction A.
- Transaction A rollbacks the changes.
- At this point, transaction B is left with data for a row that does not exist.

Non-Repeatable Read

In a non-repeatable read, when a transaction re-reads the data, it finds that the data has been modified by another transaction that has been already committed. Consider the following sequence of steps, which results in inconsistent data because of a non-repeatable read:

- Transaction A reads a row.
- Transaction B modifies or deletes the same row and commits the changes.
- Transaction A re-reads the same row and finds that the row has been modified or deleted.

Phantom Read

In a phantom read, when a transaction re-executes the same query, it finds more data that satisfies the query. Consider the following sequence of steps, which results in inconsistent data, because of a phantom read:

- Transaction A executes a query (say Q) and finds X number of rows matching the query.

- Transaction B inserts some rows that satisfy the query Q criteria and commits.

- Transaction A re-executes the same query (Q) and finds Y number of rows (Y > X) matching the query.

Note that the difference between a non-repeatable read and a phantom read is that the former finds that the rows have changed between reads and the latter finds that there are more rows matching the same query.

The ANSI SQL-92 standard defines four transaction isolation levels in terms of the above-described three situations for data consistency. Each isolation level defines what kinds of data inconsistencies are allowed, or not allowed. The four transaction isolation levels are as follows:

- Read Uncommitted

- Read Committed

- Repeatable Read

- Serializable

Table 6-3 shows the four isolation levels and the three permitted situations. It is up to a DBMS to decide how they implement these isolation levels. A DBMS may offer additional isolation levels. A DBMS may implement the same isolation level a little differently. Please consult your DBMS documentation for more details about the isolation levels that your DBMS supports.

Table 6-3. *Four Isolation Levels Defined by ANSI SQL-92*

Isolation Level	Dirty Read	Non-Repeatable Read	Phantom Read
Read Uncommitted	Permitted	Permitted	Permitted
Read Committed	Not Permitted	Permitted	Permitted
Repeatable Read	Not Permitted	Not Permitted	Permitted
Serializable	Not Permitted	Not Permitted	Not Permitted

Java defines the following four constants in the Connection interface that correspond to the four isolation levels defined by the ANSI SQL-92 standard:

- TRANSACTION_READ_UNCOMMITTED

- TRANSACTION_READ_COMMITTED

- TRANSACTION_REPEATABLE_READ

- TRANSACTION_SERIALIZABLE

You can set the isolation level of a transaction for a database connection using the setTransactionIsolation(int level) method of the Connection interface.

```
// Get a Connection object
Connection conn = get a connection object...;

// Set the transaction isolation level to read committed
conn.setTransactionIsolation(Connection.TRANSACTION_READ_COMMITTED);
```

You can use the getTransactionIsolation() method of the Connection interface to get the current setting for the transaction isolation level for the connection. The default transaction isolation level is JDBC driver-dependent. You can also use the following three methods of the DatabaseMetaData interface to get more insight about the transaction isolation levels supported by a DBMS. The method names are self-explanatory.

- int getDefaultTransactionIsolation() throws SQLException

- boolean supportsTransactions() throws SQLException

- boolean supportsTransactionIsolationLevel(int level) throws SQLException

The Connection interface defines a TRANSACTION_NONE constant to indicate that a JDBC driver does not support transactions and it is not a JDBC-compliant driver. This constant is not used with the setTransactionIsolation() method. The getTransactionIsolation() method may return this constant. You can change the transaction isolation for a Connection object any time. However, the effect of changing the transaction isolation of a connection is JDBC driver-dependent if it is changed when a transaction is in progress.

JDBC-Types-to-Java-Types Mapping

The JDBC API allows you to access and manipulate data stored in a database in a Java environment. The database uses its own data types, whereas Java uses its own. Table 6-4 lists the mappings between JDBC data types and Java data types.

Table 6-4. *Data Types Mapping Between JDBC and Java*

JDBC Type	Java Type
ARRAY	java.sql.Array
BIGINT	long
BINARY	byte[]
BIT	boolean
BLOB	java.sql.Blob
BOOLEAN	boolean
CHAR	String
CLOB	java.sql.Clob
DATALINK	java.net.URL
DATE	java.sql.Date
DATE	java.time.LocalDate
DECIMAL	java.math.BigDecimal
DISTINCT	Mapping of underlying type

(*continued*)

Table 6-4. (*continued*)

JDBC Type	Java Type
DOUBLE	double
FLOAT	double
INTEGER	int
JAVA_OBJECT	underlying Java class
LONGNVARCHAR	String
LONGVARBINARY	byte[]
LONGVARCHAR	String
NCHAR	String
NCLOB	java.sql.NClob
NUMERIC	java.math.BigDecimal
NVARCHAR	String
REAL	float
REF	java.sql.Ref
REF_CURSOR	Java.sql.ResultSet
ROWID	java.sql.RowId
SMALLINT	short
SQLXML	java.sql.SQLXML
STRUCT	java.sql.Struct
TIME	java.sql.Time
TIME	java.time.LocalTime
TIME_WITH_TIMEZONE	java.time.OffsetTime
TIMESTAMP	java.sql.Timestamp
TIMESTAMP_WITH_TIMEZONE	java.time.OffsetDateTime
TINYINT	byte
VARBINARY	byte[]
VARCHAR	String

Java 8 added the JDBC types named REF_CURSOR, TIME_WITH_TIMEZONE, and TIMESTAMP_WITH_TIMEZONE. Prior to Java 8, you could work with date, time, and timestamp JDBC types using the Date, Time, and Timestamp classes in the java.sql package. In Java 8, the date- and time-related JDBC types have also been mapped to the new date and time classes in the java.time package. For example, you can use a java.sql.Date or a java.time.LocalDate object for the DATE JDBC type. If you are using the date- and time-related objects from the java.time package for a JDBC DATE type, you will need to use them as objects and use methods like getObject() and setObject() to get and set their values. Several methods have been added in the Date, Time, and Timestamp classes in the java.sql package to facilitate conversion between SQL dates/times and new dates/times in the java.time package.

All values listed in the JDBC Type column are defined as constants in the Types class. Java 8 added a new enum type called JDBCType that contains constants with the same name as the constants in the Types class. The JDBCType enum inherits from the SQLType interface that was also added in Java 8. When a data types expected in a method's argument, you will see the argument's type as int in old methods and you will need to pass one of the constants in the Type class. Java 8 has overloaded some these methods to use the JDBCType enum instead. Whenever possible, use the constants in the JDBCType enum for the data types for type safety.

If you have to refer to a JDBC type in your Java code, you need to use the corresponding constant from the Types class. For example, suppose you need to set a null value for a parameter in a PreparedStatement object. The parameter type is of int type. The PreparedStatement interface provides a setNull() method as follows:

- void setNull(int parameterIndex, int sqlType) throws SQLException

The second parameter to the setNull() method accepts sqlType, which is the JDBC data type and is defined by the constants in the java.sql.Types class. Suppose the index of the parameter in PreparedStatement is 2. You will call the setNull() method as shown:

```
myPreparedStmt.setNull(2, java.sql.Types.INTEGER);
```

This table also tells you about the type of the Java variables you need to use to read data from a database. Suppose a column is declared varchar(20) in a database table. Table 6-4 maps the JDBC VARCHAR data type to the Java String type. It means that you need to use a String reference type variable in your Java program to hold the value of a VARCHAR type in the database. Suppose you are reading the value of a first_name column from a database table using a ResultSet object, which is declared as varchar(20). Your code would be similar to the following code:

```
String firstName = myResultSet.getString("first_name");
```

The mapping shown in this table is used throughout this chapter when you get, set, or update values that cross a JDBC-JAVA boundary. You will be using three sets of methods while working with data in JDBC programs: getXxx(), setXxx(), and updateXxx(), where Xxx indicates a data type such as int, String, Date, etc. These methods are found in many interfaces that are used in this chapter such as PreparedStatement, ResultSet, etc.

A getXxx() method is used to read data from a JDBC environment to a Java program. A setXxx() method is used to set a value in a Java program that will finally be passed to a JDBC environment. An updateXxx() method is used to update a data element that was retrieved from a JDBC environment and the updated value will be passed again to a JDBC environment. For example, you use getInt(), setInt(), and updateInt() to read, set, and update a value that is of type INTEGER in a database and is represented as int data type in Java code. You can use the getObject(), setObject(), and updateObject() methods to work with all data types provided the supplied arguments to the method are assignment compatible with the actual data types. Wherever possible, an implicit data type conversion is performed internally by the JDBC API. For example, if a JDBC type maps to a short type in Java, you can use the getShort() method to read its value. If you use the getInt() method to read a short value, the short value is implicitly converted to int. Another example of this is to read a JDBC INTEGER value using a getString() method. Suppose you want to read the value of an INTEGER type column, person_id, from a result set. You can use either of the following two statements. The JDBC driver will perform implicit conversion from int to String in the second statement.

```
int personIdInt = myResultSet.getInt("person_id");
String personIdStr = myResultSet.getString("person_id");
```

Knowing About the Database

The same database feature may be supported differently, or not supported at all, by different DBMSs. Sometimes a JDBC driver may implement a wrapper around the feature supported by the underlying DBMS. An instance of the DatabaseMetaData interface gives you detailed information about the features supported by a DBMS through the JDBC driver. The JDBC driver vendor supplies the implementation class for the DatabaseMetaData interface. You can get a DatabaseMetaData object using the getMetaData() method of the Connection object as shown:

```
Connection conn = JDBCUtil.getConnection();

// Get DatabaseMetaData object
DatabaseMetaData dbmd = conn.getMetaData();
```

Listing 6-2 contains the complete code that prints some pieces of information about the database you are connected to. The output shows the database information about the Java DB, supported features, and JDBC driver. You may get a different output.

Listing 6-2. Using a DatabaseMetaData Object to Know About a DBMS

```java
// DatabaseMetaDataTest.java
package   com.jdojo.jdbc;

import java.sql.Connection;
import java.sql.SQLException;
import java.sql.DatabaseMetaData;

public class DatabaseMetaDataTest {
        public static void main(String[] args) {
                Connection conn = null;
                try {
                        conn = JDBCUtil.getConnection();

                        // Get DatabaseMetaData object
                        DatabaseMetaData dbmd = conn.getMetaData();

                        System.out.println("About the database...");

                        String dbName = dbmd.getDatabaseProductName();
                        String dbVersion = dbmd.getDatabaseProductVersion();
                        String dbURL = dbmd.getURL();
                        System.out.println("Database Name:" + dbName);
                        System.out.println("Database Version:" + dbVersion);
                        System.out.println("Database URL:" + dbURL);

                        System.out.printf("%nAbout JDBC driver...%n");
                        String driverName = dbmd.getDriverName();
                        String driverVersion = dbmd.getDriverVersion();
                        System.out.println("Driver Name:" + driverName);
                        System.out.println("Driver Version:" + driverVersion);
```

```
                System.out.printf("%nAbout supported features...%n");
                boolean ansi92BiEntry = dbmd.supportsANSI92EntryLevelSQL();
                boolean ansi92Intermediate =
                        dbmd.supportsANSI92IntermediateSQL();
                boolean ansi92Full = dbmd.supportsANSI92FullSQL();
                boolean supportsBatchUpdates = dbmd.supportsBatchUpdates();
                System.out.println("Supports Entry Level ANSI92 SQL:" +
                                ansi92BiEntry);
                System.out.println("Supports Intermediate Level ANSI92 SQL:" +
                            ansi92Intermediate);
                System.out.println("Supports Full Level ANSI92 SQL:" +
                                ansi92Full);
                System.out.println("Supports batch updates:" +
                                supportsBatchUpdates);
        }
        catch (SQLException e) {
                e.printStackTrace();
        }
        finally {
                JDBCUtil.closeConnection(conn);
        }
    }
}
```

```
About the database...
Database Name:Apache Derby
Database Version:10.10.1.3 - (1557168)
Database URL:jdbc:derby:beginningJavaDB

About JDBC driver...
Driver Name:Apache Derby Embedded JDBC Driver
Driver Version:10.10.1.3 - (1557168)

About supported features...
Supports Entry Level ANSI92 SQL:true
Supports Intermediate Level ANSI92 SQL:false
Supports Full Level ANSI92 SQL:false
Supports batch updates:true
```

The DatabaseMetaData interface has many methods. Please refer to the API documentation on this interface for more details. Typically, a tool uses this interface to present the user with features supported by a DBMS. If you are working on a JDBC project that may use different DBMS and JDBC drivers, you will need to use a DatabaseMetaData object, so you can inform the user at runtime what features your application will support based on the JDBC driver and the DBMS they use.

Executing SQL Statements

You can execute different types of SQL statements using a JDBC driver. Based on the type of work that a SQL statement performs in a DBMS, it can be categorized as follows:

- **A Data Definition Language (DDL) Statement:** Examples of DDL statements are CREATE TABLE, ALTER TABLE, etc.

- **A Data Manipulation Language (DML) Statement:** Examples of DML statements are SELECT, INSERT, UPDATE, DELETE, etc.

- **A Data Control Language (DCL) Statement:** Examples of DCL statements are GRANT and REVOKE.

- **A Transaction Control Language (TCL) Statement:** Example of TCL statements are COMMIT, ROLLBACK, SAVEPOINT, etc.

You can execute DDL, DML, and DCL statements using different types of JDBC statement objects. An instance of the Statement interface represents a SQL statement in a Java program. You can execute TCL statements using the methods of a Connection object.

Java uses three different interfaces to represent SQL statements in different formats:

- Statement

- PreparedStatement

- CallableStatement

The PreparedStatement interface inherits from the Statement interface and the CallableStatement interface inherits from the PreparedStatement interface. You need not worry about the implementation details of these interfaces at all. The vendor of the JDBC driver will supply the implementation classes for these interfaces. You just need to know which method to call on a Connection object to get a specific type of the Statement object.

If you have a SQL statement in the form of a string, you can use a Statement object to execute it. The SQL statement may or may not return a result set. Typically, a SELECT statement returns a result set with zero or more records. The SQL statements in the string format are compiled each time they are executed.

You can use a PreparedStatement, if you want to precompile a SQL statement once and execute it multiple times. It lets you specify a SQL statement in the form of a string that uses placeholders. You need to supply the values of the placeholders before you execute the statement. Using a PreparedStatement object is preferred over using a Statement object for the following three reasons:

- The SQL statement in a string form may be subject to hackers attack using a SQL injection technique. Consider a trivial example of a SQL injection as shown in the following code for a getSQL() method:

```
public String getSQL(String personID) {
        String SQL = "select * from person " +
                        "where person_id = " + personId;
        return SQL;
}
```

- The method accepts a personId and returns a SELECT statement. If this method is called as getSQL("101"), you do not have any problems. You will get a SQL statement as shown:

```
select * from person where person_id = 101
```

- This query will return a maximum of one record from the database assuming that person_id is the primary key for the person table.

- However, if this method is called as getSQL("101 or 1 = 1"), it will return a SELECT statement as follows:

```
select * from person where person_id = 101 or 1 = 1
```

- The above statement is dangerous to execute in a production database. It will return all records from the person table to the client, which may pose a security risk. It may also degrade the performance of the database server and/or application server, which may result in a denial of service for other users.

- A PreparedStatement constructs a SQL in a string format using placeholders. The above SELECT statement will be written as follows:

```
String pSQL = "select * from person where person_id = ?";
```

- Note the use of the question mark in the statement. A question mark is used as a placeholder. Its value is supplied later using a method of the PreparedStatement object. Using a PreparedStatement eliminates the threat of a SQL injection.

- The PreparedStatement improves the performance of your JDBC application by compiling a statement once and executing it multiple times.

- A PreparedStatement lets you use Java data types to supply values in a SQL statement instead of using strings. For example, say you want to write a query to get person records whose birth date is later than January 1, 1970. You may write a query as follows:

```
select * from person where dob > '1970-01-01'
```

- However, this query will not execute properly in all databases. It assumes that a date literal can be specified in the yyyy-mm-dd format. Different databases use different formats for a date string literal. If you use a PreparedStatement, you can rewrite this query as shown:

```
select * from person where dob > ?
```

- You can use a java.sql.Date object to specify the value for the dob criterion and the JDBC driver will take care of converting it into a DBMS-specific value of the date data type.

You can use a CallableStatement object to execute a database-stored procedure or function in a database. The stored procedure may return result sets.

Let's look at the three types of Statement objects one at a time in subsequent sections.

Results of Executing a SQL Statement

When you execute a SQL statement, the DBMS may return zero or more results. The results may include update counts (number of records affected in the database) or result sets (a group of records).

When you execute a SELECT statement, it returns a result set. When you execute an UPDATE or DELETE statement, it returns an update count, which is the number of records affected in the database by the SQL.

When you execute a stored procedure, it may return multiple update counts as well as multiple result sets. When there is a possibility of mixed results of update counts and result sets being returned from a SQL execution, it becomes trickier to process the results. A JDBC driver will let you get to the results in the order they were returned from the database. Please refer to the "Handling Multiple Results from a Statement" section later in this chapter for a complete discussion and examples of how to process multiple result sets and update counts.

415

Using the Statement Interface

You can use a Statement to execute any kind of SQL statement, provided the SQL statement is supported by the JDBC driver and the DBMS. Typically, you use one of its three methods called execute(), executeUpdate(), and executeQuery() to execute a SQL statement. These methods are overloaded. The following is a list of one of their versions that accept a SQL statement as a string:

- boolean execute(String SQL) throws SQLException

- int executeUpdate(String SQL) throws SQLException

- ResultSet executeQuery(String SQL) throws SQLException

Before I discuss which one the three methods of a Statement object to use in the code, here are the steps to execute a SQL statement using a Statement object:

1. Get a connection object.

    ```
    Connection conn = JDBCUtil.getConnection();
    ```

2. Create a Statement object using the createStatement() method of the Connection object.

    ```
    Statement stmt = conn.createStatement();
    ```

3. Execute one or more SQL statements by calling one of the three methods of the Statement object.

    ```
    // Increase everyone's income by 10%
    String sql = "update person set income = income * 1.1";
    int rowsUpdated = stmt.executeUpdate(sql);

    // Execute other SQL statements using stmt
    ```

4. Close the Statement object to release the resources.

    ```
    stmt.close();
    ```

5. Commit the transaction.

    ```
    conn.commit();
    ```

The execute() method in the Statement interface is a general-purpose method that you can use to execute any types of SQL statements. Typically, it is used to execute a SQL statement that does not return a result set, such as a DDL statement like CREATE TABLE. The returned value from the execute() method indicates the status of the returned result set. If the first result is a ResultSet object, it returns true. It returns false if the first result is an update count or no result is returned from the DBMS.

The executeUpdate() method is used to execute a SQL statement that updates the data in the database such as INSERT, UPDATE and DELETE statements. It returns the number of rows affected in the database by the execution of the statement. You may use this method to execute other kinds of SQL statements, such as a CREATE TABLE statement, which do not return anything. The method returns zero when the SQL statement does not return anything. You should not use this method to execute a SELECT statement.

■ **Tip** Java 8 has added a `executeLargeUpdate()` method that works the same as the `executeUpdate()` method, except that it returns a `long` instead of an `int`. Use this method when you expect the update count to exceed `Integer.MAX_VALUE`.

The executeQuery() method is especially designed to execute a SQL statement that produces one and only one result set. It is best suited for executing a SELECT statement. Although you can execute a stored procedure, which produces a result set, using this method of the Statement interface, you should instead use the specially designed CallableStatement interface's execute() method to execute a stored procedure.

A Statement object executes a SQL statement stored in a string. Databases have their own data types. How do you pass everything in a string format? Sometimes you may need to use some objects in a SQL statement that may not be expressed in a string format such as a binary large object. You can use a PreparedStatement to have more control over preparing a SQL statement, which cannot be expressed in a string format.

Most commonly, you will encounter problems in expressing date, time, and timestamp values in a string format. Suppose you want to increase the income of all persons by 20% whose date of birth is greater than January 25, 1970. Your update statement may look like the one shown:

```
String sql = "update person " +
             "set income = income * 1.2 " +
             "where dob > '1970-01-25'";
```

Not all DBMSs will recognize '1970-01-25' as a date. JDBC defines escape sequences for the date, time, and timestamp data types. It is of the form

```
{<type> '<value>'}
```

Table 6-5 lists the format and examples for date, time and timestamp escape sequences that you need to use in your SQL strings. A JDBC driver will convert the escape sequences in a format, which is appropriate for the database. You can rewrite the above update statement using a date escape sequence as follows:

```
String sql = "update person " +
             "set income = income * 1.2 " +
             "where dob > {d '1970-01-25'}";
```

Table 6-5. *JDBC Escape Sequences for Date, Time, and Timestamp Data Types*

Data Type	\<type>	\<value> format	Example
Date	d	yyyy-mm-dd	{d '1970-01-25'}
Time	t	hh:mm:ss	{t '01:09:50'}
Timestamp	ts	yyyy-mm-dd hh:mm:ss.f...	{ts '1970-01-25 01:09:50'}

The (.f...) part in a timestamp format is the fractional part of a second, which is optional.
yyyy – Four digits year
mm - Two digits month
dd – Two digits date
hh – Hour
mm – Minute
ss – Second
f – Fractional part of second

Most of the examples in this chapter use the person table in the database. It is assumes that you have created the person table in the database you are using. The generic definition of the person table is shown in Table 6-2. If you have not created the table yet, you can run the program in Listing 6-3. The program uses the CREATE TABLE syntax for Java DB. If you are using a DBMS other than Java DB, please change the syntax before running the program. It prints the following message when the person table is created successfully:

```
Person table created.
```

If the person table already exists, the program prints the following error message for Java DB:

```
Table/View 'PERSON' already exists in Schema 'ROOT'.
```

The error message may be different for the DBMS other than Java DB, but it will convey the same meaning that the person table already exists in the database.

Listing 6-3. Creating the person Table in the Database

```java
// CreatePersonTable.java
package com.jdojo.jdbc;

import java.sql.Connection;
import java.sql.SQLException;
import java.sql.Statement;

public class CreatePersonTable {
        public static void main(String[] args) {
                Connection conn = null;
                try {
                        conn = JDBCUtil.getConnection();

                        // Create a SQL string
                        String SQL = "create table person ( " +
                                        "person_id integer not null, " +
                                        "first_name varchar(20) not null, " +
                                        "last_name varchar(20) not null, " +
                                        "gender char(1) not null, " +
                                        "dob date, " +
                                        "income double," +
                                        "primary key(person_id))";

                        Statement stmt = null;
                        try {
                                stmt = conn.createStatement();
                                stmt.executeUpdate(SQL);
                        }
                        finally {
                                JDBCUtil.closeStatement(stmt);
                        }
```

```
                    // Commit the transaction
                    JDBCUtil.commit(conn);

                    System.out.println("Person table created.");
            }
            catch (SQLException e) {
                    System.out.println(e.getMessage());
                    JDBCUtil.rollback(conn);
            }
            finally {
                    JDBCUtil.closeConnection(conn);
            }
        }
}
```

Listing 6-4 contains the complete code that inserts three records in the person table. Note that it uses utility methods of the JDBCUtil class (see Listing 6-1) to perform some of the activities such as getting a Connection object, closing Statement object, committing/rolling back a transaction, etc. If you run the program in Listing 6-4 more than once, it will print an error message stating that you are trying to insert duplicate key in the person table because you have defined the person_id as the primary key in the table, and every time you run the program, it inserts the same set of person_id values.

Listing 6-4. Executing a SQL INSERT Statement Using a Statement Object

```
// InsertPersonTest.java
package  com.jdojo.jdbc;

import java.sql.Connection;
import java.sql.SQLException;
import java.sql.Statement;

public class InsertPersonTest {
        public static void main(String[] args) {
                Connection conn = null;
                try {
                        conn = JDBCUtil.getConnection();

                        // Insert 3 person records
                        insertPerson(conn, 101, "John", "Jacobs",
                                        "M", "{d '1970-01-01'}", 60000);
                        insertPerson(conn, 102, "Donna", "Duncan",
                                        "F", "{d '1960-01-01'}", 70000);
                        insertPerson(conn, 103, "Buddy", "Rice",
                                        "M", "{d '1975-01-01'}", 45000);

                        // Commit the transaction
                        JDBCUtil.commit(conn);

                        System.out.println("Inserted persons successfully.");
                }
                catch (SQLException e) {
                        System.out.println(e.getMessage());
                        JDBCUtil.rollback(conn);
                }
```

```
                    finally {
                            JDBCUtil.closeConnection(conn);
                    }
            }

        public static void insertPerson(Connection conn, int personId,
                String firstName, String lastName, String gender, String dob,
                double income) throws SQLException {

                // Create a SQL string
                String SQL = "insert into person " +
                                "(person_id, first_name, last_name," +
                                " gender, dob, income) " +
                                "values " +
                                "(" + personId + ", " +
                                "'" + firstName + "'" + ", " +
                                "'" + lastName + "'" + ", " +
                                "'" + gender + "'" + ", " +
                                dob + ", " +
                                income + ")";

                Statement stmt = null;
                try {
                        stmt = conn.createStatement();
                        stmt.executeUpdate(SQL);
                }
                finally {
                        JDBCUtil.closeStatement(stmt);
                }
        }
}
```

You can execute any other SQL statements such as an UPDATE or DELETE statement using a Statement object. Listing 6-5 and Listing 6-6 demonstrate how to execute UPDATE and DELETE statements using a Statement object.

Listing 6-5. Executing a SQL UPDATE Statement Using a Statement Object

```
// UpdatePersonTest.java
package  com.jdojo.jdbc;

import java.sql.Connection;
import java.sql.SQLException;
import java.sql.Statement;

public class UpdatePersonTest {
        public static void main(String[] args) {
                Connection conn = null;
                try {
                        conn = JDBCUtil.getConnection();

                        // Give everyone a 5% raise
                        giveRaise(conn, 5.0);
```

```
                // Commit the transaction
                JDBCUtil.commit(conn);

                System.out.println("Updated person records successfully.");
            }
        catch (SQLException e) {
                System.out.println(e.getMessage());
                JDBCUtil.rollback(conn);
            }
        finally {
                JDBCUtil.closeConnection(conn);
            }
    }

    public static void giveRaise(Connection conn, double percentRaise)
                        throws SQLException {
        String SQL = "update person " +
            "set income = income + income * " + (percentRaise/100);
        Statement stmt = null;
        try {
                stmt = conn.createStatement();
                int updatedCount = stmt.executeUpdate(SQL);

                // Print how many records were updated
                System.out.println("Gave raise to " +
                        updatedCount + " person(s).");
            }
        finally {
                JDBCUtil.closeStatement(stmt);
            }
        }
    }
}
```

Listing 6-6. Executing a SQL DELETE Statement Using a Statement Object

```
// DeletePersonTest.java
package  com.jdojo.jdbc;

import java.sql.Connection;
import java.sql.SQLException;
import java.sql.Statement;

public class DeletePersonTest {
    public static void main(String[] args) {
        Connection conn = null;
        try {
                conn = JDBCUtil.getConnection();

                // Delete the person with person_id = 101
                deletePerson(conn, 101);
```

```
                        // Commit the transaction
                        JDBCUtil.commit(conn);
                }
                catch (SQLException e) {
                        System.out.println(e.getMessage());
                        JDBCUtil.rollback(conn);
                }
                finally {
                        JDBCUtil.closeConnection(conn);
                }
        }

        public static void deletePerson(Connection conn, int personId)
                        throws SQLException {
                String SQL = "delete from person " +
                                "where person_id = " + personId;
                Statement stmt = null;
                try {
                        stmt = conn.createStatement();
                        int deletedCount = stmt.executeUpdate(SQL);

                        // Print how many persons were deleted
                        System.out.println("Deleted " +
                                                deletedCount + " person(s).");
                }
                finally {
                        JDBCUtil.closeStatement(stmt);
                }
        }
}
```

Using the PreparedStatement Interface

The PreparedStatement interface inherits from the Statement interface. It is preferred over the Statement interface to execute a SQL statement. It precompiles the SQL statement provided DBMS supports a SQL statement precompilation. It reuses the precompiled SQL statement if the statement is executed multiple times. It lets you prepare a SQL statement, which is in a string format, using placeholders for input parameters.

A question mark in a SQL string is a placeholder for an input parameter whose value will be supplied before the statement is executed. Suppose you want to use a PreparedStatement to insert a record in the person table. Your SQL statement in a string format would be as follows:

```
String sql = "insert into person " +
            "(person_id, first_name, last_name, gender, dob, income) " +
            "values " +
            "(?, ?, ?, ?, ?, ?)";
```

In this example, each of the six question marks is a placeholder for a value. The first question mark is a placeholder for person_id, the second one for first_name, and so on. Each placeholder has an index. The first placeholder in a SQL string is given an index of 1, the second placeholder an index of 2, and so on. Note that the index of the placeholder starts at 1, not 0.

You can create a PreparedStatement using the prepareStatement() method of the Connection object. The prepareStatement() method is overloaded. In its simplest form, it accepts a SQL string as follows:

```
String sql = "your sql statement goes here";
Connection conn = JDBCUtil.getConnection();

// Obtain a PreparedStatement for the sql
PreparedStatement pstmt = conn.prepareStatement(sql);
```

The next step is to supply the values for the placeholders one-by-one using a setXxx() method of the PreparedStatement interface, where Xxx is the data type of the placeholder. The setXxx() method accepts two parameters: the first one is the index of the placeholder and the second one is the value for the placeholder. The second argument for the setXxx() method must be compatible with Xxx, which is the data type of the placeholder. If you want to set the values for the six placeholders for the INSERT statement to insert a record in the person table, you do it as follows:

```
pstmt.setInt(1, 301);        // person_id
pstmt.setString(2, "Tom");   // first name
pstmt.setString(3, "Baker"); // last name
pstmt.setString(4, "M");     // gender

/* Set dob as January 25, 1970. This time, you have a lot more control
   on the data type. You need to use the java.sql.Date data type to set
   the dob. You can use the valueOf() static method to get a java.sql.Date
   object from a date in a string format
 */
java.sql.Date dob = java.sql.Date.valueOf("1970-01-25");

pstmt.setDate(5, dob);       // dob
pstmt.setDouble(6, 45900);   // income
```

Now it is time to send the SQL statement with the values for the placeholders to the database. You execute a SQL statement in a PreparedStatement using one of its execute(), executeUpdate(), and executeQuery() methods. These methods take no arguments. Recall that the Statement interface has the same methods, which take SQL strings as their arguments. The PreparedStatement interface has added three methods with the same name, which take no arguments, because it gets its SQL string when it is created.

```
// Execute the INSERT statement in pstmt
pstmt.executeUpdate();
```

How do you reuse a PreparedStatement? Simply repopulate the placeholder values and call one of its execute() methods again. When you invoke the setXxx() method on a PreparedStatement object again, its previously set value for the specified placeholder is overwritten with the new value. A PreparedStatement keeps holding the set values for its placeholder even after it is executed. Therefore, if you want to set the same value for a placeholder for multiple executions, you need to set the value for that placeholder only once. If you want to clear the values of all placeholders, you can use the clearParameters() method of the PreparedStatement interface. The following snippet of code sets the values for all six placeholders again, and executes the statement:

```
// Set new values for placeholder
pstmt.setInt(1, 401);        // person_id
pstmt.setString(2, "Pam");   // first name
pstmt.setString(3, "Baker"); // last name
```

```
pstmt.setString(4, "F");        // gender
pstmt.setDate(5, java.sql.Date.valueOf("1970-01-25")); // dob
pstmt.setDouble(6, 25900);      // income

// Execute the INSERT statement in pstmt to insert another row
pstmt.executeUpdate();
```

When you are done with executing the statement in a PreparedStatement object, you need to close it using its close() method.

```
// Close the PreparedStatement
pstmt.close();
```

Listing 6-7 demonstrates how to use a PreparedStatement object to execute an INSERT SQL statement. Note that this example reuses the PreparedStatement to insert two records in the person table.

Listing 6-7. Using a PreparedStatement Object to Execute an INSERT Statement

```java
// PreparedStatementTest.java
package  com.jdojo.jdbc;

import java.sql.Connection;
import java.sql.Date;
import java.sql.PreparedStatement;
import java.sql.SQLException;
import java.sql.Types;

public class PreparedStatementTest {
        public static void main(String[] args) {
                Connection conn = null;
                PreparedStatement pstmt = null;
                try {
                        conn = JDBCUtil.getConnection();
                        pstmt = getInsertSQL(conn);

                        // Need to get dob in java.sql.Date object
                        Date dob = Date.valueOf("1970-01-01");

                        // Insert two person records
                        insertPerson(pstmt, 401, "Sara", "Jain", "F", dob, 0.0);
                        insertPerson(pstmt, 501, "Su", "Chi", "F", null, 10000.0);

                        // Commit the transaction
                        JDBCUtil.commit(conn);

                        System.out.println("Updated person records successfully.");
                }
                catch (SQLException e) {
                        System.out.println(e.getMessage());
                        JDBCUtil.rollback(conn);
                }
```

```
                finally {
                        JDBCUtil.closeStatement(pstmt);
                        JDBCUtil.closeConnection(conn);
                }
        }

        public static void insertPerson(PreparedStatement pstmt,
                int personId, String firstName, String lastName,
                String gender, Date dob, double income) throws SQLException {
                // Set all the input parameters
                pstmt.setInt(1, personId);
                pstmt.setString(2, firstName);
                pstmt.setString(3, lastName);
                pstmt.setString(4, gender);

                // Set the dob value properly if it is null
                if (dob == null) {
                        pstmt.setNull(5, Types.DATE);
                }
                else {
                        pstmt.setDate(5, dob);
                }

                pstmt.setDouble(6, income);

                // Execute the statement
                pstmt.executeUpdate();
        }

        public static PreparedStatement getInsertSQL(Connection conn)
                        throws SQLException {
                String SQL = "insert into person " +
                  "(person_id, first_name, last_name, gender, dob, income) " +
                  "values " +
                  "(?, ?, ?, ?, ?, ?)";
                PreparedStatement pstmt = conn.prepareStatement(SQL);
                return pstmt;
        }
}
```

CallableStatement Interface

The CallableStatement interface inherits from the PreparedStatement interface. It is used to call a SQL stored procedure or a function in a database. You can also call a stored procedure or a function using the Statement object. However, using a CallableStatement is the preferred way.

The JDBC API makes it possible to call SQL stored procedures and functions using a standard syntax. To execute a stored procedure, a different DBMS may use a different syntax. If you are using the JDBC API to call a stored procedure, you need to learn only one standard way to execute stored procedures in all DBMSs. The JDBC specification defines an escape sequence for stored procedures/functions to execute them in a database.

To find out if your DBMS supports stored procedures, you can call the supportsStoredProcedures() method of a DatabaseMetaData object. It returns true if the DBMS supports stored procedures. A JDBC driver may let you call a DBMS function using the same syntax. To know if you can call a DBMS function using the same syntax, use the supportsStoredFunctionsUsingCallSyntax() method of a DatabaseMetaData object. If it returns true, you can use the same syntax to call a database function. From here on, I will use the phrase "stored procedure" to mean both database stored procedures and functions.

The general syntax for calling a stored procedure is as follows:

```
{? = call <procedure_name>(param1, param2, param3, ...)}
```

The call to a stored procedure is placed within braces ({}). The first question mark is a placeholder for the return value from the stored procedure. The placeholder for the return value is followed by = call. If the stored procedure does not return a value, the ? = part is omitted. <procedure_name> is the name of a stored procedure. If the stored procedure accepts any parameters, the list of parameters is enclosed in parentheses after the procedure name. If a stored procedure does not accept any parameters, the opening parenthesis, parameter lists, and closing parenthesis after <procedure_name> are omitted. Table 6-6 lists some examples using the general syntax for calling stored procedures.

Table 6-6. *Examples of Using Stored Procedure Escape Syntax for Calling Database Stored Procedures*

Stored Procedure Description	The Syntax to Call the Stored Procedure
Accepts no parameters Returns no value	{call <procedure_name>}
Accepts two IN parameters Returns no value	{call <procedure_name>(?, ?)}
Accepts two IN and one OUT parameters Returns no value	{call <procedure_name>(?, ?, ?)}
Accepts no parameters Returns a value	{? = call <procedure_name>}
Accepts two IN parameters Returns a value	{? = call <procedure_name>(?, ?)}
Accepts two IN and one OUT parameters Returns a value	{? = call <procedure_name>(?, ?, ?)}

A stored procedure may accept different type of parameters: IN, OUT, and INOUT. You can use placeholders (question marks) for all types of parameters. You cannot distinguish the type of parameters by just looking at a SQL string that uses placeholders. It is up to you to know which placeholder is of type IN, OUT, or INOUT parameter, and treat them accordingly. The next three sections will describe how to treat IN, OUT and INOUT parameter types in a CallableStatement.

Using IN Parameters

An IN parameter type means that caller has to pass a value for that parameter when it calls the stored procedure. Before executing a CallableStatement, you must call one of the setXxx() methods to set the value for all IN type parameters. Otherwise, you will get an error when you try to execute a CallableStatement with some IN parameters not set.

Suppose there are two IN parameters in a SQL statement and their placeholders are at index 1 and index 2. The IN parameter at index 1 is of int type and at index 2 is of double type. Your code logic would resemble the code shown:

```
CallableStatement cstmt = prepare the call...;

// Set the value of the IN parameter at index 1
cstmt.setInt(1, 101);

// Set the value of the IN parameter at index 2
cstmt.setDouble(2, 22.56);

// Execute the statement here
```

Using OUT Parameters

An OUT parameter type means that the caller has to pass a placeholder to the stored procedure for that parameter and the stored procedure will set the value, which the caller can read after the stored procedure has finished executing. Before executing a CallableStatement, you must register an OUT parameter by calling the registerOutParameter (int placeholderIndex, int sqlType) or the registerOutParameter(int parameterIndex, java.sql.SQLType sqlType) method of the CallableStatement interface. After executing the stored procedure, you need to use one of the getXxx() methods to read the value of the OUT parameter.

Suppose there is an OUT parameter in a SQL statement that is at index 2 and it is of type double. Here is how you would register it and read its value:

```
CallableStatement cstmt = prepare the call...;

// Register the OUT parameter at index 2
cstmt.registerOutParameter(2, java.sql.Types.DOUBLE);

// Execute the statement here

// Read the value of the OUT parameter
double outParamValue = cstmt.getDouble(2);
```

Using INOUT Parameters

An INOUT parameter works as a combination of IN and OUT parameter types. The caller can pass a value to the stored procedure using an INOUT parameter type. The stored procedure changes the value of the INOUT parameter during its execution and the caller can read the value set by the stored procedure after the stored procedure has finished executing. You must register the INOUT parameter using the registerOutParameter(int placeholderIndex, int sqlType) or the registerOutParameter(int parameterIndex, java.sql.SQLType sqlType) method of the CallableStatement interface before executing the stored procedure. You need to use one of the setXxx() methods of the CallableStatement interface to set the value for an INOUT parameter. After a stored procedure has been executed, you need to use one of the getXxx() methods of the CallableStatement interface to read the value passed back from the stored procedure.

Suppose there is an INOUT parameter in a SQL statement that is at index 1 and it is of type double. Here is how you would register it, pass a value in it, and read its value:

```
CallableStatement cstmt = prepare the call...;

// Register the INOUT parameter at index 1
cstmt.registerOutParameter(1, java.sql.Types.DOUBLE);

// Set a value of 55.78 for the INOUT parameter
cstmt.setDouble(1, 55.78);

// Execute the statement here

// Read the value of the INOUT parameter
double inOutParamValue = cstmt.getDouble(1);
```

Return Parameter is OUT Parameter Type

If a stored procedure returns a value and you want to capture the returned value, its placeholder (the first question mark) must be registered as an OUT parameter using the registerOutParameter() method of the CallableStatement interface. If a return value placeholder is present in the call syntax, it is always the first OUT parameter and you need to use 1 as its index in the registerOutParameter() and getXxx() methods

Executing a CallableStatement

Before you execute a stored procedure, you need to prepare a CallableStatement by calling the prepareCall() method of the Connection object. The prepareCall() method accepts a SQL string as a parameter. The following snippet of code shows how to prepare a CallableStatement:

```
Connection conn = JDBCUtil.getConnection();
String SQL = "{call myProcedure}";
CallableStatement cstmt = conn.prepareCall(SQL);
```

The CallableStatement interface does not add any new methods to execute a SQL statement. To execute the SQL statement, you need to call one of the following three methods with no parameters. All three methods are inherited from the PreparedStatement interface.

- execute()

- executeUpdate()

- executeQuery()

The method you need to use to execute a SQL statement in a CallableStatement object depends on what is returned from the execution of the stored procedure.

- If it returns mixed results (result sets and update counts), use the execute() method.

- If it returns an update count, use the executeUpdate() method.

- If it returns a ResultSet, use the executeQuery() method.

Let's look at some examples of calling a stored procedure with different types of parameters and with/without a return value.

Example #1

Stored Procedure: `process_salary`
Comments: It accepts no parameters and returns no value

```
Connection conn = JDBCUtil.getConnection();
String sql = "{call process_salary}";
CallableStatement cstmt = conn.prepareCall(sql);
cstmt.execute();
```

Example #2

Stored Procedure: `give_raise(integer person_id IN, double raise IN)`
Comments: It accepts two IN parameters and does not return any value.

```
Connection conn = JDBCUtil.getConnection();
String sql = "{call give_raise(?, ?)}";
CallableStatement cstmt = conn.prepareCall(sql);

// Set the value for person_id parameter at index 1
cstmt.setInt(1, 101);

// Set the value for raise parameter at index 2
cstmt.setDouble(2, 4.5);

// Execute the stored procedure
cstmt.execute();
```

Example #3

Stored Procedure: `get_employee_count(integer dept_id IN) RETURNS integer`
Comments: It accepts an IN parameter and returns an integer value.

```
Connection conn = JDBCUtil.getConnection();
String sql = "{? = call get_employee_count(?)}";
CallableStatement cstmt = conn.prepareCall(sql);

// Register the first placeholder - the return value as an OUT parameter
cstmt.registerOutParameter(1, java.sql.Types.INTEGER);

// Set the value for dept_id parameter at index 2
cstmt.setInt(2, 1001);

// Execute the stored procedure
cstmt.execute();

// Read the returned value - our first OUT parameter has an index of 1
int employeeCount = cstmt.getInt(1);

System.out.println("Employee Count is " + employeeCount);
```

Example #4

Stored Procedure: `give_raise(person_id int IN, raise double IN, old_income double OUT, new_income double OUT)`
Comments: It accepts two IN parameters and two OUT parameters.

```
Connection conn = JDBCUtil.getConnection();
String sql = "{call give_raise(?, ?, ?, ?)}";

CallableStatement cstmt = conn.prepareCall(sql);

// Register the OUT parameters: old_income(index 3), new_income(index 4)
cstmt.registerOutParameter(3, Types.DOUBLE);
cstmt.registerOutParameter(4, Types.DOUBLE);

// Set values for person_id at index 1 and for raise at index 2
cstmt.setInt(1, 1001);
cstmt.setDouble(2, 4.5);

// Execute the stored procedure
cstmt.execute();

// Read the values of the OUT parameters old_income(index 3)
// and new_income (index 4)
double oldIncome = cstmt.getDouble(3);
double newIncome = cstmt.getDouble(4);
System.out.println("Old Income:" + oldIncome);
System.out.println("New Income:" + newIncome);
```

■ **Tip** You can pass the value for an IN parameter using a literal value or a placeholder. If you use a placeholder for an IN parameter, you will need to use the `setXxx()` method to set its value before executing the stored procedure. It is preferred to use a placeholder for an IN parameter and use a `setXxx()` to set its value. For example, suppose a stored procedure, `process_person(integer person_id IN)`, accepts an IN type parameter. You can prepare the call syntax as `"{call process_person(1001)}"` or `"{call process_person(?)}"`. In the latter case, you will need to use the `setInt(1, 1001)` method to set the value for the `person_id` parameter.

Let's discuss an example in which you create a stored procedure in a database and call it using a `CallableStatement` in a Java program. You create a stored procedure named `give_raise`. It accepts two IN parameters called `person_id` and `raise`. It accepts two OUT parameters to pass back the old and new values of the income for a `person_id`. If the person's income is `null`, it sets the income to 20000. If a person is not found, it passes back `null` in both OUT parameters.

The following are the SQL scripts for `give_raise` procedure for some DBMSs. You need to run the script for your DBMS before you can run the program in Listing 6-9. If you do not find a script for the DBMS you are using, you can easily write the code for your DBMS by looking at the code in this table for any DBMS whose syntax looks familiar to you. You will see an example of a stored procedure that generates a result set later in this chapter.

Adaptive Server Anywhere Database

```
create procedure give_raise(IN @person_id integer, IN @raise double,
                            OUT @old_income double, OUT @new_income double)
begin
 select @old_income = null, @new_income = null;

 if exists(select null from person where person_id = @person_id) then
   select income into @old_income
    from person
   where person_id = @person_id;

   if @old_income is null then
     select 20000.00 into @new_income;
   else
     select @old_income * (1 + @raise/100) into @new_income;
   end if;

   update person
      set income = @new_income
    where person_id = @person_id;
 end if;
end;
```

MySQL Database

```
DELIMITER $$

DROP PROCEDURE IF EXISTS give_raise $$

CREATE PROCEDURE give_raise(in person_id_param int, in raise double,
                            out old_income double, out new_income double)
BEGIN

set old_income = null, new_income = null;

if exists(select null from person where person_id=person_id_param) then
    select income into old_income
      from person
     where person_id = person_id_param;

    if old_income is null then
        select 20000.00 into new_income;
    else
        select old_income * (1 + raise/100) into new_income;
    end if;

    update person
       set income = new_income
     where person_id = person_id_param;
```

```
end if;

END $$

DELIMITER ;
```

Oracle Database

```
create or replace procedure give_raise(person_id_param number,
                                        raise_param number,
                                        old_income out number,
                                        new_income out number)
is
 person_count number;
begin
 old_income := null;
 new_income := null;

 select count(*)
   into person_count
   from person
  where person_id = person_id_param;

 if person_count = 1 then
    select income into old_income
      from person
     where person_id = person_id_param;

    if old_income is null then
       new_income := 20000.00;
    else
       new_income := old_income * (1 + raise_param/100) ;
    end if;
    update person
       set income = new_income
     where person_id = person_id_param;
 end if;

end give_raise;
```

SQL Server Database

```
-- Drop stored procedure if it already exists
IF EXISTS (
  SELECT *
    FROM INFORMATION_SCHEMA.ROUTINES
   WHERE SPECIFIC_SCHEMA = N'dbo'
     AND SPECIFIC_NAME = N'give_raise'
)
```

```
    DROP PROCEDURE dbo.give_raise
GO

CREATE PROCEDURE dbo.give_raise
        @person_id int,
        @raise decimal(5, 2),
    @old_income decimal(10, 2) OUTPUT,
    @new_income decimal(10, 2) OUTPUT
AS
BEGIN
        SET NOCOUNT OFF

        SELECT @old_income = null, @new_income = null;

        IF EXISTS (SELECT null FROM person WHERE person_id = @person_id)
        BEGIN
                SELECT @old_income = income
         FROM person
        WHERE person_id = @person_id;

                IF @old_income is null
                        SELECT @new_income = 20000.00;
                ELSE
                        SELECT @new_income = @old_income * (1 + @raise/100);

            update person
          set income = @new_income
        WHERE person_id = @person_id;
    END;
END;
GO
```

DB2 Database

```
create procedure give_raise(IN person_id_param int,
                            IN raise_param double,
                            OUT old_income double,
                            OUT new_income double)
language sql
begin

 declare person_count int;

 set old_income = null;
 set new_income = null;

 select count(*) into person_count
   from person
 where person_id = person_id_param;
```

```
if person_count = 1 then
     select income into old_income
      from person
     where person_id = person_id_param;

    if old_income is null then
       set new_income = 20000.00;
    else
       set new_income = old_income * (1 + raise_param/100) ;
    end if;

    update person
       set income = new_income
     where person_id = person_id_param;
 end if;
end
@
```

Note: @ is used as statement terminator in the above syntax to create the stored procedure.

Java DB Database

Java DB lets you write stored procedure using the Java programing language. You can use a static method of a class as a stored procedure in Java DB. To get the reference of the database connection that executes the stored procedure, you pass jdbc:default:connection as the connection URL to the DriverManager. Listing 6-8 contains the code for the JavaDBGiveRaiseSp class whose giveRaise() static method will be used as a stored procedure. You will need to do some setup work, which is described next, before you can use this method as a stored procedure. For now, just compile the class and include it in CLASSPATH.

Listing 6-8. The Java Code for the give_raise Stored Procedure in Java DB

```java
// JavaDBGiveRaiseSp.java
package com.jdojo.jdbc;

import java.sql.SQLException;
import java.sql.PreparedStatement;
import java.sql.Connection;
import java.sql.DriverManager;
import java.sql.ResultSet;

public class JavaDBGiveRaiseSp {
        public static void giveRaise(int personId, double raise,
                        double[] oldIncomeOut, double[] newIncomeOut) throws SQLException {
                double oldIncome = 0.0;
                double newIncome = 0.0;

                // Must use the following URL to get the reference of the Conenction
                // object in whose context this method is called.
                String dbURL = "jdbc:default:connection";
                Connection conn = DriverManager.getConnection(dbURL);
```

```
String sql = "select income from person where person_id = ?";
PreparedStatement pstmt = conn.prepareStatement(sql);
pstmt.setInt(1, personId);

ResultSet rs = pstmt.executeQuery();
if (!rs.next()) {
        return;
}

oldIncome = rs.getDouble("income");
if (rs.wasNull()) {
        newIncome = 20000.00;
}
else {
        newIncome = oldIncome * (1 + raise / 100);
}

String updateSql = "update person " +
                   "set income = ? " +
                   "where person_id = ?";
PreparedStatement updateStmt =
        conn.prepareStatement(updateSql);
updateStmt.setDouble(1, newIncome);
updateStmt.setInt(2, personId);
updateStmt.executeUpdate();

// Close the statement
updateStmt.close();

oldIncomeOut[0] = oldIncome;
newIncomeOut[0] = newIncome;
    }
}
```

After you have written the Java code for the stored procedure, you need to create the stored procedure in your Java DB database. Use the following command to create the give_raise stored procedure:

```
--Command to create a stored procedure
CREATE PROCEDURE give_raise(IN person_id integer, IN raise double, OUT old_income Double, OUT
new_income Double)
PARAMETER STYLE JAVA
LANGUAGE JAVA
MODIFIES SQL DATA
EXTERNAL NAME 'com.jdojo.jdbc.JavaDBGiveRaiseSp.giveRaise';
```

You can execute the command using the ij command-line tool or NetBeans IDE. Please refer to the "A Brief Overview of Java DB" section earlier in this chapter for more details on how to execute SQL commands in Java DB.

To get the give_raise stored procedure working in Java DB, you need to install the JavaDBGiveRaiseSp class into the database after bundling it into a JAR file. Please refer to the Java DB documentation on how to install a Java JAR into the database. Another way (and the easier way) of making the Java stored procedure code available to the Java DB is to include the class in the user's CLASSPATH. You do not need to perform this step if you are running the examples in this chapter using the NetBeans IDE. The JavaDBGiveRaiseSp class is included in the NetBeans project, and therefore, the class is already in the CLASSPATH when the examples are run from inside the NetBeans IDE.

Listing 6-9 shows the complete code to execute the stored procedure give_raise. You can run the CallableStatementTest class by using different values for person_id and raise in its main() method.

Listing 6-9. Using a CallableStatement Statement to Call a Stored Procedure

```java
// CallableStatementTest.java
package  com.jdojo.jdbc;

import java.sql.CallableStatement;
import java.sql.Connection;
import java.sql.SQLException;
import java.sql.Types;

public class CallableStatementTest {
        public static void main(String[] args) {
                Connection conn = null;
                try {
                        conn = JDBCUtil.getConnection();

                        // Give a 5% raise to person_id 101
                        giveRaise(conn, 102, 5.0);

                        // Give a 5% raise to dummy person_id
                        giveRaise(conn, -100, 5.0);

                        // Commit the transaction
                        JDBCUtil.commit(conn);
                }
                catch (SQLException e) {
                        System.out.println(e.getMessage());
                        JDBCUtil.rollback(conn);
                }
                finally {
                        JDBCUtil.closeConnection(conn);
                }
        }

        public static void giveRaise(Connection conn, int personId,
                                        double raise) throws SQLException {
                String SQL = "{call app.give_raise(?, ?, ?, ?)}";
                CallableStatement cstmt = null;
                try {
                        // Prepare the call
                        cstmt = conn.prepareCall(SQL);

                        // Set the IN parameters
                        cstmt.setInt(1, personId);
                        cstmt.setDouble(2, raise);

                        // Register the OUT parameters
                        cstmt.registerOutParameter(3, Types.DOUBLE);
                        cstmt.registerOutParameter(4, Types.DOUBLE);
```

```
            // Execute the stored procedure
            int updatedCount = cstmt.executeUpdate();

            // Read the OUT parameters values
            double oldIncome = cstmt.getDouble(3);
            boolean oldIncomeisNull = cstmt.wasNull();

            double newIncome = cstmt.getDouble(4);
            boolean newIncomeisNull = cstmt.wasNull();

            // Display the results
            System.out.println("Updated Record: " + updatedCount);

            System.out.println("Old Income: " + oldIncome +
                                ", New Income: " + newIncome);

            System.out.println("Old Income was null: " +
                                oldIncomeisNull +
                                ", New Income is null: " +
                                newIncomeisNull);
        }
        finally {
            JDBCUtil.closeStatement(cstmt);
        }
    }
}
```

Processing Result Sets

A set of rows obtained by executing a SQL SELECT statement in a database is known as a result set. JDBC lets you execute a SELECT statement in the database and process the returned result set in the Java program using an instance of the ResultSet interface. The following sections discuss different ways of processing result sets using the JDBC API.

What Is a ResultSet?

When you execute a query (a SELECT statement) in a database, it returns the matching records in the form of a result set. You can consider a result set as a data arranged in rows and columns. The SELECT statement determines the number of rows and columns that is contained in the result set. The Statement (or PreparedStatement or CallableStatement) object returns the result of a query as a ResultSet object. I am using two phrases here: "result set" and "ResultSet." By "result set," I mean the data in the form of rows and columns, and by "ResultSet," I mean an instance of a class that implements the ResultSet interface that lets you access and manipulate that data. A ResultSet object also contains information about the properties of the columns in the result set such as the data types of the columns, names of the columns, etc.

A ResultSet object maintains a cursor, which points to a row in the result set. It works similar to a cursor object in database programs. You can scroll the cursor to a specific row in the result set to access or manipulate the column values for that row. The cursor can point to only one row at a time. The row to which it points at a particular point in time is called the *current row*. There are different ways to move the cursor of a ResultSet object to a row in the result set. I will discuss all different ways to move the cursor shortly.

The following three properties of a ResultSet object need to be discussed before you can look at an example:

- Scrollability
- Concurrency
- Holdability

Scrollability determines the ability of the ResultSet to scroll through the rows. By default, a ResultSet is scrollable only in the forward direction. When you have a forward-only scrollable ResultSet, you can move the cursor starting from the first row to the last row. Once you move to the last row, you cannot reuse the ResultSet object because you cannot scroll back in a forward-only scrollable ResultSet. You can also create a ResultSet that can scroll in the forward as well as the backward direction. I will call this ResultSet a *bidirectional scrollable* ResultSet. A bidirectional scrollable ResultSet has another property called *update sensitivity*. It determines whether the changes in the underlying database will be reflected in the result set while you are scrolling through its rows. A scroll *sensitive* ResultSet shows you changes made in the database, whereas a scroll *insensitive* one would not show you the changes made in the database after you have opened the ResultSet. The following three constants in the ResultSet interface are used to specify the scrollability of a ResultSet:

- TYPE_FORWARD_ONLY: Allows a ResultSet object to move only in the forward direction.
- TYPE_SCROLL_SENSITIVE: Allows a ResultSet object to move in the forward and backward directions. It makes the changes in the underlying database made by other transactions or statements in the same transaction visible to the ResultSet object. This type of ResultSet is aware of the changes made to its data by other means.
- TYPE_SCROLL_INSENSITIVE: Allows a ResultSet object to move in the forward and backward directions. It does not make the changes in the underlying database made by other transactions or statements in the same transaction visible to the ResultSet object while scrolling. This type of ResultSet determines its data set when it is open and the data set does not change if it is updated through any other means except through this ResultSet object itself. If you want to get up-to-date data, you must re-execute the query.

Concurrency refers to its ability of the ResultSet to update data. By default, a ResultSet is read-only and it does not let you update its data. If you want to update data in a database through a ResultSet, you need to request an updatable result set from the JDBC driver. The following two constants in the ResultSet interface are used to specify the concurrency of a ResultSet:

- CONCUR_READ_ONLY: Makes a result set read-only.
- CONCUR_UPDATABLE: Makes a result set updatable.

Holdability refers to the state of the ResultSet after a transaction that it is associated with has been committed. A ResultSet may be closed or kept open when the transaction is committed. The default value of the holdability of a ResultSet is dependent on the JDBC driver. The holdability of a ResultSet is specified using one of the following two constants defined in the ResultSet interface:

- HOLD_CURSORS_OVER_COMMIT: Keeps the ResultSet open after the transaction is committed.
- CLOSE_CURSORS_AT_COMMIT: Closes the ResultSet after the transaction is committed.

You need to verify your JDBC driver's documentation for support for these properties before using them. You can get information about the supported properties by a JDBC driver of a ResultSet object using the following three methods of the DatabaseMetaData interface. Recall that you can get a DatabaseMetaData object using the getMetaData() method of a Connection object.

- supportsResultSetType()

- supportsResultSetConcurrency()

- supportsResultSetHoldability()

Listing 6-10 demonstrates how to use these methods to check for these ResultSet properties. The calls to these methods are placed inside a try-catch block to catch a Throwable, because some JDBC drivers throw a runtime exception when they do not support a feature. The output is for the Java DB DBMS. You may get a different output when you are connected to a different DBMS.

Listing 6-10. Checking for Properties of a ResultSet Supported by a JDBC Driver

```java
// SupportedResultSetProperties.java
package com.jdojo.jdbc;

import java.sql.Connection;
import java.sql.DatabaseMetaData;
import static java.sql.ResultSet.CLOSE_CURSORS_AT_COMMIT;
import static java.sql.ResultSet.CONCUR_READ_ONLY;
import static java.sql.ResultSet.CONCUR_UPDATABLE;
import static java.sql.ResultSet.HOLD_CURSORS_OVER_COMMIT;
import static java.sql.ResultSet.TYPE_FORWARD_ONLY;
import static java.sql.ResultSet.TYPE_SCROLL_INSENSITIVE;
import static java.sql.ResultSet.TYPE_SCROLL_SENSITIVE;
import java.sql.SQLException;

public class SupportedResultSetProperties {
    public static void main(String[] args) {
        Connection conn = null;
        try {
            conn = JDBCUtil.getConnection();
            DatabaseMetaData dbmd = conn.getMetaData();

            System.out.println("Supported result set scrollability.");
            printScrollabilityInfo(dbmd);

            System.out.println();
            System.out.println("Supported result set concurrency.");
            printConcurrencyInfo(dbmd);

            System.out.println();
            System.out.println("Supported result set holdability.");
            printHoldabilityInfo(dbmd);
        }
        catch (SQLException e) {
            e.printStackTrace();
        }
        finally {
            JDBCUtil.closeConnection(conn);
        }
    }
```

```java
    public static void printScrollabilityInfo(DatabaseMetaData dbmd) {
        try {
            boolean forwardOnly
                = dbmd.supportsResultSetType(TYPE_FORWARD_ONLY);

            boolean scrollSensitive
                = dbmd.supportsResultSetType(TYPE_SCROLL_SENSITIVE);

            boolean scrollInsensitive
                = dbmd.supportsResultSetType(TYPE_SCROLL_INSENSITIVE);

            System.out.println("Forward-Only: " + forwardOnly);
            System.out.println("Scroll-Sensitive: " + scrollSensitive);
            System.out.println("Scroll-Insensitive: " + scrollInsensitive);
        }
        catch (SQLException e) {
            System.out.println("Could not get scrollability information.");
            System.out.println("Error Message:" + e.getMessage());
        }
    }

    public static void printConcurrencyInfo(DatabaseMetaData dbmd) {
        try {
            boolean forwardOnlyReadOnly
                = dbmd.supportsResultSetConcurrency(TYPE_FORWARD_ONLY,
                    CONCUR_READ_ONLY);

            boolean forwardOnlyUpdatable
                = dbmd.supportsResultSetConcurrency(TYPE_FORWARD_ONLY,
                    CONCUR_UPDATABLE);

            boolean scrollSensitiveReadOnly
                = dbmd.supportsResultSetConcurrency(
                    TYPE_SCROLL_SENSITIVE,
                    CONCUR_READ_ONLY);

            boolean scrollSensitiveUpdatable
                = dbmd.supportsResultSetConcurrency(
                    TYPE_SCROLL_SENSITIVE,
                    CONCUR_UPDATABLE);

            boolean scrollInsensitiveReadOnly
                = dbmd.supportsResultSetConcurrency(
                    TYPE_SCROLL_INSENSITIVE,
                    CONCUR_READ_ONLY);

            boolean scrollInsensitiveUpdatable
                = dbmd.supportsResultSetConcurrency(
                    TYPE_SCROLL_INSENSITIVE,
                    CONCUR_UPDATABLE);
```

```java
                System.out.println("Scroll Forward-Only and " +
                        "Concurrency Read-Only: " +
                        forwardOnlyReadOnly);

                System.out.println("Scroll Forward-Only and " +
                        "Concurrency Updatable: " +
                        forwardOnlyUpdatable);

                System.out.println("Scroll Sensitive and " +
                        "Concurrency Read-Only: " +
                        scrollSensitiveReadOnly);

                System.out.println("Scroll Sensitive and " +
                        "Concurrency Updatable: " +
                        scrollSensitiveUpdatable);

                System.out.println("Scroll Insensitive and " +
                        "Concurrency Read-Only: " +
                        scrollInsensitiveReadOnly);

                System.out.println("Scroll Insensitive and " +
                        "Concurrency Updatable: " +
                        scrollInsensitiveUpdatable);
            }
            catch (SQLException e) {
                System.out.println("Could not get concurrency information.");
                System.out.println("Error Message:" + e.getMessage());
            }
        }

    public static void printHoldabilityInfo(DatabaseMetaData dbmd) {
        try {
                boolean holdOverCommit
                    = dbmd.supportsResultSetHoldability(
                            HOLD_CURSORS_OVER_COMMIT);

                boolean closeAtCommit
                    = dbmd.supportsResultSetHoldability(
                            CLOSE_CURSORS_AT_COMMIT);

                System.out.println("Hold Over Commit: " + holdOverCommit);
                System.out.println("Close At Commit: " + closeAtCommit);
            }
            catch (SQLException e) {
                System.out.println("Could not get concurrency information.");
                System.out.println("Error Message:" + e.getMessage());
            }
        }
    }
```

```
Supported result set scrollability.
Forward-Only: true
Scroll-Sensitive: false
Scroll-Insensitive: true

Supported result set concurrency.
Scroll Forward-Only and Concurrency Read-Only: true
Scroll Forward-Only and Concurrency Updatable: true
Scroll Sensitive and Concurrency Read-Only: false
Scroll Sensitive and Concurrency Updatable: false
Scroll Insensitive and Concurrency Read-Only: true
Scroll Insensitive and Concurrency Updatable: true

Supported result set holdability.
Hold Over Commit: true
Close At Commit: true
```

Getting a ResultSet

You can get a result set from a database using a Statement, a PreparedStatement, or a CallableStatement. In simple cases, you call executeQuery() method of a Statement object or a PreparedStatement object with a SELECT statement that will return a ResultSet. Here is a typical way to get a forward-only scrollable result set:

```
Connection conn = JDBCUtil.getConnection();
Statement stmt = conn.createStatement();
String sql = "select person_id, first_name, last_name, dob, income " +
             "from person";

// Execute the query to get the result set
ResultSet rs = stmt.executeQuery(sql);

// Process the result set using the rs variable
```

The returned ResultSet from the executeQuery() method is already open, and it is ready to be looped through to get the associated data. In the beginning, the cursor points before the first row in the result set. You must move the cursor to a valid row before you can access the column's values for that row. The next() method of the ResultSet is used to move the cursor to the next row. When the next() method is called for the first time, it moves the cursor to the first row in the result set.

It is very important to consider the return value of the next() method. It returns a boolean value. It returns true if the cursor is positioned to a valid row. Otherwise, it returns false. If you call the next() method on an empty ResultSet object for the first time, it will return false, because there is no valid row to move to. If the current row is the last row in the result set, calling the next() method will position the cursor after the last row and it will return false. A typical snippet of code for processing a forward-only scrollable ResultSet object is as follows:

```
ResultSet rs = get a result set object;

// Move the cursor to the next row by calling the next() method
while(rs.next()) {
        // Process the current row in rs here
}
// Done with the ResultSet
```

When a cursor is positioned after the last row in a forward-only scrollable ResultSet object, you cannot do anything with it, except close it using its close() method. A forward-only scrollable object is like a create-use-and-throw item. You cannot reopen a ResultSet either. To iterate through the result set data again, you must re-execute the query and obtain a new ResultSet. However, things are different for a bidirectional scrollable ResultSet, which lets you iterate through the rows as many times as you want. You will look at a bidirectional scrollable ResultSet object shortly.

After the program exits the while-loop, the cursor points to the row after the last row in the result set. What is the row after the last row and before the first row? They are just two imaginary rows. They do not exist in reality. These two positions of the cursor of the ResultSet object let you make decisions when you want to loop through the result set multiple times or when you get a ResultSet object as an argument in your method. When you do not create the ResultSet, you must know the cursor position correctly in order to process the rows in a specific order. The following four methods of the ResultSet interface let you know if the cursor is before the first row, on the first row, on the last row, or after the last row.

- `boolean isBeforeFirst() throws SQLException`

- `boolean isFirst() throws SQLException`

- `boolean isLast() throws SQLException`

- `boolean isAfterLast() throws SQLException`

The method names are self-explanatory. Support for these methods is optional for a forward-only scrollable ResultSet. Typically, you do not need to use these methods for a forward-only scrollable ResultSet.

A ResultSet object lets you read the value of a column from its current row using one of its getXxx() method, where Xxx is the data type of the column. There is one getXxx() method for each Xxx data type supported by JDBC. For example, to read an int, double, String, Object, and Blob value from a column, you can use the getInt(), getDouble(), getString(), getObject(), and getBlob() methods of the ResultSet interface, respectively. You must specify the index or name of the column in the getXxx() method whose value you want to read. The getXxx() methods are overloaded. One version accepts an int parameter, which lets you use the column index and another version accepts a String parameter, which lets you use the column label. If the column label is not specified in the query, you can specify the column name. The first column in the result set has an index of 1. Suppose you have the following ResultSet of a query:

```
select person_id as "Person ID", first_name, last_name from person
```

In the ResultSet, the person_id column has a column index of 1, the first_name column has a column index of 2, and the last_name column has a column index of 3. You have specified Person ID as the column label for the person_id column. You have not specified the column labels for the first_name and last_name columns. To get the value of the person_id column, you need to use either getInt(1) or getInt("PERSON ID"). To get the value of the first_name column, you need to use either getString(2) or getString("first_name").

■ **Tip**   Using a column label or name in the getXxx() methods is case-insensitive. That is, you can use getInt("person id") or getInt("PERSON ID") to get the value of a person_id column. I will use the term "column name" in this chapter to refer to the column label or name.

The following snippet of code shows how to read column's values of the current row in a result set:

```
Connection conn = JDBCUtil.getConnection();
Statement stmt = conn.createStatement();
String SQL = "select person_id, first_name, last_name, dob, income " +
             "from person";
ResultSet rs = stmt.executeQuery(SQL);
```

```
// Move the cursor to the next row one by one
while(rs.next()) {
        // Process the current row in rs
        int personId = rs.getInt("person_id");
        String firstName = rs.getString("first_name");
        String lastName = rs.getString("last_name");
        java.sql.Date dob = rs.getDate("dob");
        double income = rs.getDouble("income");

        // Do something with column values
}
```

You can rewrite the code inside the while-loop using the column indexes.

```
while(rs.next()) {
        // Process the current row in rs
        int personId = rs.getInt(1);
        String firstName = rs.getString(2);
        String lastName = rs.getString(3);
        java.sql.Date dob = rs.getDate(4);
        double income = rs.getDouble(5);

        // Do something with column values
}
```

It is a matter of personal preference whether to use a column index or a column name in a getXxx() method of the ResultSet. Sometimes you may not know the name of the columns in advance, such as when the user passes you a query to execute, and you have to use the data from the result set. When you do not know the column names, you should use the column indexes. You can get the names of columns in a ResultSet object using the ResultSetMetaData object. Please refer to the "ResultSetMetaData" section for more details.

In a ResultSet, when a column has a null value, the getXxx() method returns the default value for the Xxx data type. For example, for numeric data types (int, double, byte, etc.), the getXxx() method returns zero when the column has a null value. The reason behind returning the default value for the data type instead of returning a null is that a primitive data type cannot have a null value in Java. A getXxx() method returns false for the boolean data type when the column has a null value. The getXxx() returns null if Xxx is a reference type. If you want to know whether the column value, which you read using a getXxx() method, is null, you need to call the wasNull() method immediately after calling the getXxx() method. If the wasNull() method returns true, the column value is null in the result set. If the wasNull() method returns false, the column value is not null in the result set. Note that the wasNull() method does not accept any parameter and it returns null value status of the last read column using a getXxx() method. Here is a snippet of code to demonstrate the null value check for a column:

```
ResultSet rs = get a result set object;
java.sql.Date dob = rs.getDate("dob");
if (rs.wasNull()) {
        System.out.println("DOB is null");
}
else {
        System.out.println("DOB is " + dob);
}
```

444

The getDate() method of the ResultSet object returns a java.sql.Date object. The toString() method of the java.sql.Date class returns a string in a yyyy-mm-dd format. If you need the date value converted to any other format, you need to work with an object of the java.text.SimpleDateFormat class to format your date value. The getTime() and getTimestamp() methods of a ResultSet return a java.sql.Time object and a java.sql.Timestamp object, respectively. The toString() method of the java.sql.Time class returns a string in an hh:mm:ss format. The toString() method of the java.sql.Timestamp class returns a string in a yyyy-mm-dd hh:mm:ss.fffffffff format.

Let's look at a complete example of processing a ResultSet using a Statement object and a PreparedStatement object. Listing 6-11 demonstrates how to execute a query in a database and process the results.

Listing 6-11. Getting and Processing a ResultSet Using a Statement and a PreparedStatement

```java
// QueryPersonTest.java
package com.jdojo.jdbc;

import java.sql.Connection;
import java.sql.PreparedStatement;
import java.util.Date;
import java.sql.ResultSet;
import java.sql.SQLException;
import java.sql.Statement;
import java.text.SimpleDateFormat;

public class QueryPersonTest {
        // Will be used to format dates
        private static final SimpleDateFormat sdf =
                            new SimpleDateFormat("MM/dd/yyyy");

        public static void main(String[] args) {
                Connection conn = null;
                try {
                        conn = JDBCUtil.getConnection();

                        System.out.println("Using Statement Object...");
                        displayPersonUsingStatement(conn, 101);
                        displayPersonUsingStatement(conn, 102);

                        System.out.println("Using PreparedStatement Object...");
                        displayPersonUsingPreparedStatement(conn, 101);
                        displayPersonUsingPreparedStatement(conn, 102);

                        // Commit the transaction
                        JDBCUtil.commit(conn);
                }
                catch (SQLException e) {
                        System.out.println(e.getMessage());
                        JDBCUtil.rollback(conn);
                }
                finally {
                        JDBCUtil.closeConnection(conn);
                }
        }
```

```java
    public static void displayPersonUsingStatement(Connection conn,
                int inputPersonId) throws SQLException {
        String SQL = "select person_id, first_name, last_name, " +
                    " gender, dob, income from person " +
                    " where person_id = " + inputPersonId;

        Statement stmt = null;
        ResultSet rs = null;
        try {
                stmt = conn.createStatement(
                            ResultSet.TYPE_SCROLL_SENSITIVE,
                            ResultSet.CONCUR_UPDATABLE);
                rs = stmt.executeQuery(SQL);
                printResultSet(rs);
        }
        finally {
                // Closing the Statement closes the associated ResultSet
                JDBCUtil.closeStatement(stmt);
        }
    }

    public static void displayPersonUsingPreparedStatement(
                Connection conn, int inputPersonId) throws SQLException {

        String SQL = "select person_id, first_name, last_name, " +
                    " gender, dob, income from person " +
                    " where person_id = ?";

        PreparedStatement pstmt = null;
        ResultSet rs = null;
        try {
                pstmt = conn.prepareStatement(SQL);

                // Set the IN parameter for person_id
                pstmt.setInt(1, inputPersonId);

                // Execute the query
                rs = pstmt.executeQuery();
                printResultSet(rs);
        }
        finally {
                // Closing the Statement closes the ResultSet
                JDBCUtil.closeStatement(pstmt);
        }
    }

    public static void printResultSet(ResultSet rs) throws SQLException {
        while (rs.next()) {
                int personId = rs.getInt("person_id");
                String firstName = rs.getString("first_name");
                String lastName = rs.getString("last_name");
```

```
                        String gender = rs.getString("gender");
                        Date dob = rs.getDate("dob");
                        boolean isDobNull = rs.wasNull();

                        double income = rs.getDouble("income");
                        boolean isIncomeNull = rs.wasNull();

                        // Format the dob in MM/dd/YYYY format
                        String formattedDob = null;
                        if (!isDobNull) {
                                formattedDob = formatDate(dob);
                        }

                        System.out.print("Person ID:" + personId);
                        System.out.print(", First Name:" + firstName);
                        System.out.print(", Last Name:" + lastName);
                        System.out.print(", Gender:" + gender);

                        if (isDobNull) {
                                System.out.print(", DOB:null");
                        }
                        else {
                                System.out.print(", DOB:" + formattedDob);
                        }

                        if (isIncomeNull) {
                                System.out.println(", Income:null");
                        }
                        else {
                                System.out.println(", Income:" + income);
                        }
                }
        }

        public static String formatDate(Date dt) {
                if (dt == null) {
                        return "";
                }

                String formattedDate = sdf.format(dt);
                return formattedDate;
        }
}
```

The displayPersonUsingStatement() method accepts a Connection object and a person id as parameters. It uses a Statement object to retrieve the person details in a ResultSet. It calls the printResultSet() method to print all rows in the ResultSet. Your ResultSet will have a maximum of one row, because person_id is a primary key in your person table, and you are using it in the where clause of the query. Look at the details of how the cursor is moved in a while-loop, and each column's value is read using an appropriate getXxx() method in the printResultSet() method. The value for the dob column is formatted in the mm/dd/yyyy format before printing it.

The displayPersonUsingPreparedStatement() method uses a PreparedStatement object to execute the query. Note that you must use a setXxx() method on a PreparedStatement to set the input parameter for the query. The code uses pstmt.setInt(1, inputPersonId) to set the person id value in the where clause of the query.

The main() method calls both of these methods to print the details of the same person id. In this example, you are not benefiting from precompilation of the PreparedStatement object, because you are calling this method separately for each person id. If you want to execute the same PreparedStatement with different inputs multiple times, you store the reference of the PreparedStatement in your program and reuse it. The intent of this example is to show you how to use a PreparedStatement to process a query, and I tried to keep the program logic as simple as possible.

Getting the Number of Rows in a ResultSet

How would you know the number of rows in a ResultSet? The simple answer is that a ResultSet does not know how many rows it contains. There is no method in the ResultSet interface that returns the number of rows in the result set.

The ResultSet interface contains a getRow() method that returns the current row number in the ResultSet. It returns zero if there is no current row, such as when the cursor is before the first row or after the last row. The support for the getRow() method is optional in a forward-only scrollable ResultSet. You can say that the getRow() method is of no help in determining the number of rows in a ResultSet object. You will need to apply some custom logic to get the number of rows in a result set. The following are some of the methods you can use to get the number of rows in a result set. None of them are without disadvantages.

Scrolling Through All Rows

This method applies a logic that loops through all rows using the next() method after getting the ResultSet. It maintains a counter variable, which is incremented by one for each loop-iteration. After exiting the loop, the counter variable contains the number of rows in the ResultSet. The following snippet of code shows this logic:

```
ResultSet rs = get a result set object;

// Initialize rowCount to 0
int rowCount = 0;

while(rs.next()) {
        // Increment rowCount by 1
        rowCount++;

        // Process the result set data for the current row
}

// Now, the rowCount variable contains the number of rows in rs
System.out.println("Row Count: " + rowCount);
```

If you need the number of rows in a result set before you process its rows, this logic will force you to get the result set twice: once for getting the number of rows and once for processing the rows. Between the time when you get the first result set and when you get the second result set, the data in the database might change, which will make the row count from the first execution invalid. This method is foolproof only if you need the number of rows in the result set after you have looped through all the rows.

Executing a Separate Query

This method executes a separate query to get the number of rows in a result set. Suppose you want to know the number of rows returned in a result set by executing a query, as shown:

```
select person_id, first_name, last_name, gender, dob, income
  from person
 where dob > {d '1970-01-25'}
```

To get the number of rows returned by this query, you may execute a query as follows:

```
select count(*)
  from person
 where dob > {d '1970-01-25'}
```

The value for the first column of the first row in the result set will give you the number of rows returned from your main query. However, this method suffers from the same drawback that rows in the database may change between the executions of the two queries.

Using a Bidirectional Scrollable ResultSet

In this method, you will need to create a ResultSet object that can scroll in both directions, forward and backward. You can specify the scrollable property of a ResultSet when you create a Statement object. Please refer to the next section for more details on creating a scrollable ResultSet object that can scroll in both directions. Make sure that your JDBC driver supports a ResultSet that can scroll in both directions. After you get the ResultSet, call its last() method to move its cursor to the last row in the result set. Call the getRow() method when the cursor is at the last row. The getRow() method will return the row number of the last row, which will be the number of rows in the result set. If you want to process the result set after getting the number of rows, you can call its beforeFirst() method to scroll the cursor before the first row and start a while-loop to process the rows in the result set again.

A JDBC driver may not support a ResultSet object that can scroll in both directions. In such cases, it may return a forward-only scrollable ResultSet object. After getting a ResultSet object, it is very important to check if it supports bidirectional scrolling before you call the last() method on it. A forward-only ResultSet object will throw a SQLException if you call the last() method. You can get the scrollable property of a ResultSet object by calling its getType() method. Listing 6-12 demonstrates this approach to get the number of rows in a result set.

Listing 6-12. Getting the Number of Rows in a Bidirectional Scrollable ResultSet

```java
// ResultSetRowCountTest.java
package com.jdojo.jdbc;

import java.sql.Connection;
import java.sql.ResultSet;
import java.sql.SQLException;
import java.sql.Statement;
import static java.sql.ResultSet.CONCUR_READ_ONLY;
import static java.sql.ResultSet.TYPE_SCROLL_INSENSITIVE;

public class ResultSetRowCountTest {
        public static void main(String[] args) {
                Connection conn = null;
                Statement stmt = null;
```

```
            try {
                    // Get a Connection
                    conn = JDBCUtil.getConnection();

                    // Request a bi-directional scrollable ResultSet
                    stmt = conn.createStatement(TYPE_SCROLL_INSENSITIVE,
                                            CONCUR_READ_ONLY);
                    String SQL = "select person_id, first_name, last_name, dob, " +
                                "income from person";

                    // Execute the query
                    ResultSet rs = stmt.executeQuery(SQL);

                    // Make sure you got a bi-directional ReseutSet
                    int cursorType = rs.getType();
                    if (cursorType == ResultSet.TYPE_FORWARD_ONLY) {
                            System.out.println("JDBC driver returned a " +
                                                "forward - only cursor.");
                    }
                    else {
                            // Move the cursor to the last row
                            rs.last();

                            // Get the last row number, which is the row count
                            int rowCount = rs.getRow();
                            System.out.println("Row Count: " + rowCount);

                            // Place the cursor before the first row to
                            // process all rows again
                            rs.beforeFirst();
                    }

                    // Process the result set
                    while (rs.next()) {
                            System.out.println("Person ID: " + rs.getInt(1));
                    }
            }
            catch (SQLException e) {
                    e.printStackTrace();
            }
            finally {
                    JDBCUtil.closeStatement(stmt);
                    JDBCUtil.commit(conn);
                    JDBCUtil.closeConnection(conn);
            }
    }
}
```

Bidirectional Scrollable ResultSets

You can request a JDBC driver for a bidirectional scrollable ResultSet by specifying the scrollability property when you create a Statement, prepare a PreparedStatement, or prepare a CallableStatement using different methods of the Connection interface. The following is the list of methods of the Connection interface that implicitly or explicitly let you specify the scrollability property of a ResultSet object. The throws clause from the methods declarations has been excluded. They all throw a SQLException.

- Statement createStatement()

- Statement createStatement(int scrollability, int concurrency)

- Statement createStatement(int scrollability, int concurrency, int holdability)

- PreparedStatement prepareStatement(String SQL)

- PreparedStatement prepareStatement(String SQL, int scrollability, int concurrency)

- PreparedStatement prepareStatement(String SQL, int scrollability, int concurrency, int holdability)

- CallableStatement prepareCall(String SQL)

- CallableStatement prepareCall(String SQL, int scrollability, int concurrency)

- CallableStatement prepareCall(String SQL, int scrollability, int concurrency, int holdability)

Not all JDBC drivers support all three types of scrollability properties for a result set. However, all drivers will support at least the forward-only result set. The default value of the scrollability of a ResultSet object is TYPE_FORWARD_ONLY. When you specify a result set's scrollability in one of these methods and if the JDBC driver does not support that type of scrollability, the driver will not generate an error. Rather, it will return a result set with the scrollability type that closely matches the requested scrollability type. If you specify a scrollability of a ResultSet other than forward-only, it is good practice to check the scrollability type of the returned ResultSet object using the getType() method. The following snippet of code shows how to test for the scrollability property of a ResultSet object:

```
Connection conn = JDBCUtil.getConnection();

// Request a bi-directional change insensitive ResultSet
Statement stmt = conn.createStatement(ResultSet.TYPE_SCROLL_INSENSITIVE,
                                      ResultSet.CONCUR_READ_ONLY);

String SQL = "your select statement goes here";

// Get a result set
ResultSet rs = stmt.executeQuery(SQL);

// Let's see what type of result set the JDBC driver returned
int cursorType = rs.getType();

if (cursorType == ResultSet.TYPE_FORWARD_ONLY) {
        System.out.println("ResultSet is TYPE_FORWARD_ONLY");
}
else if (cursorType == ResultSet.TYPE_SCROLL_SENSITIVE) {
        System.out.println("ResultSet is TYPE_SCROLL_SENSITIVE");
}
```

```
else if (cursorType == ResultSet.TYPE_SCROLL_INSENSITIVE) {
        System.out.println("ResultSet is TYPE_SCROLL_INSENSITIVE");
}
```

The default value for the concurrency of a ResultSet is read-only, as indicated by the constant ResultSet.CONCUR_READ_ONLY. You can only read data from a ResultSet that has read-only concurrency. If you want to update data using a ResultSet such as change a column's value, insert new rows, or delete existing rows, you must have a ResultSet whose concurrency is ResultSet.CONCUR_UPDATABLE. Not all JDBC drivers support the updatable concurrency. You may request a JDBC driver that you want a ResultSet object with an updatable concurrency. If a JDBC driver does not support it, it will return a read-only ResultSet object. You can check for the concurrency of a ResultSet object as follows:

```
Connection conn = JDBCUtil.getConnection();

// Request a bidirectional change insensitive ResultSet
// with concurrency as CONCUR_UPDATABLE
Statement stmt = conn.createStatement(ResultSet.TYPE_SCROLL_INSENSITIVE,
                                      ResultSet.CONCUR_UPDATABLE);

String SQL = "your select statement goes here";

// Get a result set
ResultSet rs = stmt.executeQuery(SQL);

// Let's see what type of concurrency the JDBC driver returned
int concurrency = rs.getConcurrency();

if (concurrency == ResultSet.CONCUR_READ_ONLY) {
        System.out.println("ResultSet is CONCUR_READ_ONLY");
}
else if (concurrency == ResultSet.CONCUR_UPDATABLE) {
        System.out.println("ResultSet is CONCUR_UPDATABLE");
}
```

The JDBC driver determines the default value for the holdability of a ResultSet. Different JDBC drivers have different default values for this property. You can check for the holdability of a ResultSet using the getHoldability() method of the ResultSet. You can also use the getHoldability() method of the Connection to get this property of a ResultSet object. Here is how you check the holdability of a ResultSet:

```
Connection conn = JDBCUtil.getConnection();

// Request a bidirectional change insensitive ResultSet with concurrency
// as CONCUR_UPDATABLE and holdability of HOLD_CURSORS_OVER_COMMIT
Statement stmt = conn.createStatement(ResultSet.TYPE_SCROLL_INSENSITIVE,
                                      ResultSet.CONCUR_UPDATABLE,
                                      ResultSet.HOLD_CURSORS_OVER_COMMIT);

String SQL = "your select statement goes here";

// Get a result set
ResultSet rs = stmt.executeQuery(SQL);
```

```
// Let's see what type of holdability the JDBC driver returned
int holdability = conn.getHoldability(); // Java 1.4 and later
//int holdability = rs.getHoldability(); // Java 6 and later

if (holdability == ResultSet.HOLD_CURSORS_OVER_COMMIT) {
        System.out.println("ResultSet is HOLD_CURSORS_OVER_COMMIT");
}
else if (holdability == ResultSet.CLOSE_CURSORS_AT_COMMIT) {
        System.out.println("ResultSet is CLOSE_CURSORS_AT_COMMIT");
}
```

■ **Tip**   The getType(), getConcurrency(), and getHoldability() methods throw a SQLException that you will have to handle in your code.

Scrolling Through Rows of a ResultSet

There are many methods in the ResultSet interface that let you move the cursor position to a row in the result set. There are two sets of rows that a cursor may point to. One set of rows consists of two imaginary rows–one before the first row and one after the last row. Another set of rows consists of the rows that match the query. Table 6-7 shows the rows and column structure of a ResultSet. The cursor in a ResultSet is positioned before the first row when it is created as shown by > in the table.

Table 6-7. *Rows and Column Structures of a ResultSet*

	Column 1	Column 2	Column 3	Column 4	Column 5	Column 6
Before First Row >			An imaginary row			
Row 1	101	John	Jacobs	M	01/01/1970	45000.00
Row 2	102	Donna	Duncan	F	01/01/1960	35000.00
Row 3	102	Buddy	Rice	M	01/01/1965	25000.00
After Last Row			An imaginary row			

The table shows three rows in the result set with data that match the query criteria. Note that a ResultSet does not retrieve all rows for a query at once. The number of rows a ResultSet will retrieve from the database is JDBC driver-dependent. It may choose to retrieve one row at a time from a database. You can give a hint to the JDBC driver using the setFetchSize(int fetchSize) method of the ResultSet object to fetch a specified number of rows from the database whenever more rows are needed. When does a ResultSet need to fetch more rows from the database? A ResultSet needs to fetch more rows if you position its cursor to a row that is not in its cache. For example, calling the next() method of a ResultSet may trigger a fetch from the database. Suppose a ResultSet fetches 10 records at a time. If you call the next() method the first time, it will fetch and cache 10 records and, for nine subsequent calls to its next() method, it will give you rows from its cache. Fetching and caching rows for a ResultSet is dependent on a JDBC driver and the underlying DBMS.

You can use the getRow() method of the ResultSet interface to get the row number of the row at which the cursor is currently positioned. If the cursor is positioned before the first row or after the last row, the getRow() method returns zero.

If you have a ResultSet object that has its scrollability set to forward-only, you can only use its next() method to move the cursor, which moves its cursor one row in the forward direction. Once the cursor is pointing after the last row, calling the next() method has no effect. The next() method returns true if it is pointing to a row that was returned from the query. Otherwise, it returns false.

If a ResultSet has a bidirectional scrollability, you have many methods to change its cursor position. The next() method can also be used in this type of ResultSet to move the cursor one row forward from its current position. All cursor movement methods can be put into two categories:

- Relative cursor movement methods

- Absolute cursor movement methods

The relative cursor movement methods move the cursor in the forward or backward direction relative to the current position of the cursor. You have two types of methods in this category: one that moves the cursor one row forward or backward from the current position, and one that moves the cursor forward or backward a specified number of rows. An example of this type of cursor movement is moving the cursor to the next/previous row from the current position. Table 6-8 lists relative cursor movement methods whose categories are shown as Relative.

Table 6-8. *The Cursor Movement Methods of the ResultSet Interface*

Method	Category	Description
boolean next()	Relative	Moves the cursor one row forward from its current position. It returns true if the cursor is positioned to a valid row in the result set. It returns false if the cursor is positioned after the last row. It may throw an exception or return false if you call it when cursor is already positioned after the last row. This behavior is JDBC driver-dependent.
boolean previous()	Relative	It is the counterpart of the next() method. It moves the cursor one row backward from its current position. It returns true if the cursor is positioned to a valid row in the result set. It returns false if the cursor is positioned before the first row.
boolean relative(int rows)	Relative	Moves the cursor forward or backward by the specified number of rows from its current position. A positive value for rows such as relative(5) moves the cursor forward. A negative value for rows such as relative(-5) moves the cursor backward. Calling relative(0) has no effect. Calling relative(1) and relative(-1) has the same effect as calling next() and previous(), respectively. If the number of specified rows to move is beyond the range of rows (including before the first row and after the last row), the cursor will be positioned before the first row or after the last row depending on the direction of the specified movement. It returns true if the cursor is positioned to a valid row. Otherwise, it returns false. Some JDBC drivers throw a SQLException when you call this method and the cursor is not positioned to a valid row, for example, when it is positioned before the first or after the last row. Some JDBC drivers just return false in such cases.

(continued)

Table 6-8. (*continued*)

Method	Category	Description
boolean first()	Absolute	Moves the cursor to the first row in the result set. It returns true if the cursor is positioned to the first row. It returns false if the result set is empty.
boolean last()	Absolute	Moves the cursor to the last row in the result set. It returns true if the cursor is positioned to the last row. It returns false if the result set is empty.
void beforeFirst()	Absolute	Positions the cursor before the first row. Calling this method has no effect on an empty result set.
void afterLast()	Absolute	Positions the cursor after the last row. Calling this method has no effect on an empty result set.
boolean absolute(int row)	Absolute	Moves the cursor to the specified row number. It accepts a positive as well as a negative row number. If a positive row number is specified, the row is counted from the beginning. If a negative row number is specified, the row number is counted from the end. Suppose there are 10 rows in a result set. Calling absolute(1) will position the cursor to the first row. Calling absolute(2) will position the cursor to the second row. Calling absolute(-1) will position the cursor to the first row from the end, which would be the last row. Calling absolute(-2) will position the cursor to the second-last row. Calling absolute(8) and absolute(-3) will have the same effect as positioning the cursor on the eighth row in a 10-row result set. Calling absolute(0) positions the cursor before the first row. It returns true if the cursor is positioned to a valid row. Otherwise, it returns false. Any attempt to move the cursor beyond the valid row range will position the cursor either before the first row or after the last row depending on the direction of the movement. Calling absolute(1) is same as calling first(). Calling absolute(-1) is same as calling last().

The absolute cursor movement methods move the cursor to a specific row irrespective of the current cursor position. You have two types of methods in this category: one that accepts a row number to move the cursor to that row such as the row number 8 and another that moves the cursor to a known position such as to the last row. Examples of this type of cursor movement are moving the cursor to the eighth row, the first row, the last row, before the first row, or after the last row, etc. Table 6-8 lists the absolute cursor movement methods whose categories are shown as Absolute. All methods in the table throw a SQLException.

■ **Tip** You can only use the next() method to move the cursor in a forward-only scrollable ResultSet. Using any other methods on a forward-only scrollable ResultSet will throw an exception. All cursor movement methods can be used with a bidirectional scrollable ResultSet object. Use the last() method with caution. This method call will force the JDBC driver to retrieve all rows from the database. If a DBMS does not support a bidirectional scrollable cursor, a JDBC driver will have to cache all rows on the client. For a very large result set, it may affect the performance of the application adversely.

Knowing the Cursor Position in a ResultSet

The five methods in the ResultSet interface let you know where the cursor is currently positioned. Four methods return a boolean value of true if cursor is at the specific position. These methods are isBeforeFirst(), isFirst(), isLast(), and isAfterLast(). The method names are self-explanatory. They return false if they are called on an empty result set. The fifth method, called getRow(), returns the current row number as an int. It returns 0 If the cursor is positioned before the first row, after the last row, or result set is empty.

Closing a ResultSet

You can close a ResultSet object by calling its close() method. Calling the close() method on an already closed ResultSet has no effect.

```
ResultSet rs = get a result set object;

// Process the rs object...

// Close the result set
rs.close();
```

Closing the ResultSet object frees the resources associated with it. A ResultSet object can also be closed implicitly in the following situations:

- When the Statement object that produces the ResultSet object is closed, it automatically closes the ResultSet object.

- When a Statement object is re-executed, its previously opened ResultSet object is closed.

- If a Statement object produces multiple result sets, retrieving the next result set closes the previously retrieved ResultSet.

- If it is a forward-only scrollable ResultSet, a JDBC driver may choose to close it when its next() method returns false as the part of optimization. Once the next() method returns false for a forward-only scrollable ResultSet, you cannot do anything with that ResultSet anyway.

You cannot perform any activities on a closed ResultSet, except calling its close() or isClosed() method. Calling any other methods will throw a SQLException. However, all is not lost when a ResultSet object is closed. You can still get to the following pieces of information on a closed ResultSet:

- If you have accessed a Blob, Clob, NClob, or SQLXML object from a result set when it was open, those objects are still valid after the ResultSet has been closed. They are valid at least until the duration of the transaction.

- If you have a ResultSetMetaData object from a ResultSet object when it was open, you can still use it to get metadata information about the result set. The following snippet of code shows the correct and incorrect sequence of statements:

```
ResultSet rs = get a result set object;
ResultSetMetaData rsmd = rs.getMetaData();
rs.close(); // rs is closed

// You can still use rsmd object to get info about rs
System.out.println("Column Count:" + rsmd.getColumnCount());

// Can use only isClosed() and close() method on rs because it is closed.
ResultSetMetaData rsmd = rs.getMetaData(); // An error
```

Making Changes to a ResultSet

You can use a ResultSet to perform insert, update, and delete operations on database tables. The concurrency for the ResultSet object must be ResultSet.CONCUR_UPDATABLE in order to perform updates on the ResultSet. Inserting a new row and updating an existing row in a ResultSet is a two-step process, whereas deleting a row is a one-step process. In the two-step process, you need to make changes in the ResultSet object first and then call one of its methods to send changes to the database. In the one-step process, changes to the ResultSet are propagated to the database automatically.

Inserting a Row Using a ResultSet

So far, you are aware of only two imaginary rows in a result set. They were rows before the first row and after the last row. However, there is one more imaginary row that exists in a ResultSet and that is called an *insert row*. You can think of this row as an empty new row, which acts as a staging area for a new row that you want to insert. You can position the cursor to the insert row using the ResultSet object's moveToInsertRow() method. When the cursor moves to the insert row, it remembers its previous position. You can call the moveToCurrentRow() method to move the cursor from the insert row back to the previously current row. So, the first step in inserting a new row is to move the cursor to the insert row.

```
// Move the cursor to an insert row to add a new row
rs.moveToInsertRow();
```

At this point, a new row has been inserted in the staging area and all columns have undefined values. Calling a getXxx() method to read column values may throw an exception at this point. Once the cursor is positioned at the insert-row, you need to set the values for all the columns (at least for non-nullable columns) using one of the updateXxx() methods of the ResultSet interface, where Xxx is the data type of the column. The first argument to an updateXxx() method is either the column index or the column name, and the second argument is the column value. If you want to insert a new row in the person table using a ResultSet, your updateXxx() method call will look as follows:

```
// Leave dob and income unset to use null values for them
rs.updateInt("person_id", 501);
rs.updateString("first_name", "Richard");
rs.updateString("last_name", "Castillo");
rs.updateString("gender", "M");
```

Once you update the value for a column, you can use a getXxx() method to retrieve the new values from the ResultSet.

You are not done yet with the new row. You must send the changes to the database before your new row becomes part of the ResultSet. You can send the newly inserted row to the database by calling the insertRow() method of the ResultSet interface as shown:

```
// Send changes to the database
rs.insertRow();
```

The call to the insertRow() method may or may not make the inserted row a permanent row in the database. If the auto-commit mode is enabled for the Connection, the insertRow() call will also commit your transaction. In that case, the new row becomes part of the database permanently. If the auto-commit mode is disabled for the Connection, you can make the insert permanent by committing the transaction, or cancel the insert by rolling back the transaction. Note that committing or rolling back a transaction will commit or rollback all pending activities, not only the newly inserted row.

Once you have sent your inserted row to the database, you can move to the previously current row by calling the moveToCurrentRow() method. Moving to another row before calling the insertRow() method after calling the moveToInsertRow() method discards the new row.

Listing 6-13 demonstrates how to use a ResultSet to insert a new row. After getting the ResultSet object in the addRow() method, it checks if it is updatable. If the ResultSet object is not updatable, it prints a message to indicate that and does not do anything. In the end, it prints all rows in the result set. The printed records also include the new row. Note that you do not update the values for dob and income columns for new rows and the JDBC driver will use null values for them when it inserts a new row in the person table. If you run the program more than once in the same database, an error message is printed because the program will attempt to insert a person record with the same person_id again causing a duplicate row in the table.

Listing 6-13. Inserting a New Row Using a ResultSet

```
// ResultSetInsert.java
package com.jdojo.jdbc;

import java.sql.Connection;
import java.sql.ResultSet;
import java.sql.SQLException;
import java.sql.Statement;
import static java.sql.ResultSet.CONCUR_UPDATABLE;
import static java.sql.ResultSet.TYPE_FORWARD_ONLY;

public class ResultSetInsert {
        public static void main(String[] args) {
                Connection conn = null;
```

```
        try {
                conn = JDBCUtil.getConnection();

                // Add a new row
                addRow(conn);

                // Commit the transaction
                JDBCUtil.commit(conn);
        }
        catch (SQLException e) {
                System.out.println(e.getMessage());
                JDBCUtil.rollback(conn);
        }
        finally {
                JDBCUtil.closeConnection(conn);
        }
}

public static void addRow(Connection conn) throws SQLException {
        String SQL = "select person_id, first_name, "
                        + "last_name, gender, dob, income  "
                        + "from person";

        Statement stmt = null;
        try {
                stmt = conn.createStatement(TYPE_FORWARD_ONLY,
                                        CONCUR_UPDATABLE);

                // Get the result set
                ResultSet rs = stmt.executeQuery(SQL);

                // Make sure your resultset is updatable
                int concurrency = rs.getConcurrency();

                if (concurrency != ResultSet.CONCUR_UPDATABLE) {
                        System.out.println("The JDBC driver does not " +
                                "support updatable result sets.");
                        return;
                }

                // First insert a new row to the ResultSet
                rs.moveToInsertRow();
                rs.updateInt("person_id", 501);
                rs.updateString("first_name", "Richard");
                rs.updateString("last_name", "Castillo");
                rs.updateString("gender", "M");

                // Send the new row to the database
                rs.insertRow();

                // Move back to the current row
                rs.moveToCurrentRow();
```

```
                              // Print all rows in the result set
                              while (rs.next()) {
                                      System.out.print("Person ID: " +
                                              rs.getInt("person_id") +
                                              ", First Name: " +
                                              rs.getString("first_name") +
                                              ", Last Name: " +
                                              rs.getString("last_name"));
                                      System.out.println();
                              }
                      }
                      finally {
                              JDBCUtil.closeStatement(stmt);
                      }
              }
      }
}
```

Updating a Row Using a ResultSet

Here are the steps involved in updating an existing row in a ResultSet object.

1. Move the cursor to a valid row in the result set. Note that you can update data only for an existing row. It is obvious that the cursor should not be positioned before the first row or after the last row if you want to update the data in a row.

2. Call an updateXxx() method for a column to update the column's value.

3. If you do not want to go ahead with the changes made using updateXxx() method calls, you need to call the cancelRowUpdates() method of the ResultSet to cancel the changes.

4. When you are done updating all the column's values for the current row, call the updateRow() method to send the changes to the database. If the auto-commit mode is enabled for the Connection, changes will be committed. Otherwise, you need to commit the changes to the database.

5. If you move the cursor to a different row before calling the updateRow(), all your changes made using the updateXxx() method calls will be discarded.

6. There is another way to lose your updates to columns in a row. If you call the refreshRow() method after calling updateXxx(), but before calling updateRow(), your changes will be lost because the JDBC driver will refresh the row's data from the database.

Listing 6-14 demonstrates how to update a row using a ResultSet object. It increases the income of every person with non-null income by 10%. If a person's income is null, it updates the income to 10000.00.

Listing 6-14. Updating Data Using a ResultSet

```
// ResultSetUpdate.java
package com.jdojo.jdbc;

import java.sql.Connection;
import java.sql.ResultSet;
import static java.sql.ResultSet.CONCUR_UPDATABLE;
import static java.sql.ResultSet.TYPE_FORWARD_ONLY;
```

```java
import java.sql.SQLException;
import java.sql.Statement;

public class ResultSetUpdate {
        public static void main(String[] args) {
                Connection conn = null;
                try {
                        conn = JDBCUtil.getConnection();

                        // Give everyone a 10% raise
                        giveRaise(conn, 10.0);

                        // Commit the transaction
                        JDBCUtil.commit(conn);
                }
                catch (SQLException e) {
                        System.out.println(e.getMessage());
                        JDBCUtil.rollback(conn);
                        e.printStackTrace();
                }
                finally {
                        JDBCUtil.closeConnection(conn);
                }

        }

        public static void giveRaise(Connection conn,
                                double raise) throws SQLException {
                String SQL = "select person_id, first_name, last_name, " +
                        "income from person";

                Statement stmt = null;

                try {
                        stmt = conn.createStatement(TYPE_FORWARD_ONLY,
                                                CONCUR_UPDATABLE);

                        // Get the result set
                        ResultSet rs = stmt.executeQuery(SQL);

                        // Make sure our resultset is updatable
                        int concurrency = rs.getConcurrency();

                        if (concurrency != CONCUR_UPDATABLE) {
                                System.out.println("The JDBC driver does not "+
                                        "support updatable result sets.");
                                return;
                        }

                        // Give everyone a raise
                        while (rs.next()) {
                                double oldIncome = rs.getDouble("income");
                                double newIncome = 0.0;
```

```
                        if (rs.wasNull()) {
                                // null income starts at 10000.00
                                oldIncome = 10000.00;
                                newIncome = oldIncome;
                        }
                        else {
                                // Increase the income
                                newIncome =
                                oldIncome + oldIncome * (raise / 100.0);
                        }

                        // Update the income column with the new value
                        rs.updateDouble("income", newIncome);

                        // Print the details about the changes
                        int personId = rs.getInt("person_id");
                        String firstName = rs.getString("first_name");
                        String lastName = rs.getString("last_name");

                        System.out.println(firstName + " " + lastName +
                                " (person id=" + personId +
                                ") income changed from " +
                                oldIncome + " to " + newIncome);

                        // Send the changes to the database
                        rs.updateRow();
                }
        }
        finally {
                JDBCUtil.closeStatement(stmt);
        }
    }
}
```

Deleting a Row Using a ResultSet

Deleting a row from a ResultSet is easier than updating and inserting a row. Here are the steps to delete a row.

1. Position the cursor at a valid row.

2. Call the deleteRow() method of the ResultSet to delete the current row.

The deleteRow() method deletes the row from the ResultSet object and, at the same time, it deletes the row from the database. There is no way to cancel the delete operation except by rolling back the transaction. If the auto-commit mode is enabled on the Connection object, deleteRow() will permanently delete the row from the database.

Typical code for deleting a row from a ResultSet object is as follows:

```
ResultSet rs = get an updatable result set object;

// Scroll to the row you want to delete, say the first row
rs.next();
```

```
// Delete the current row
rs.delete(); // Row is deleted from the result set and the database

// Commit or rollback changes depending on your processing logic
```

Handling Multiple Results from a Statement

Sometimes executing a SQL statement may return multiple results. Typically, you get multiple results by executing a stored procedure. The results include the update counts and result sets. For example, if you execute a stored procedure that updates some records and returns a result set, you get two results. The first one will be the update count and the second will be the result set. Some DBMSs let you suppress sending back the update counts. For example, you can use SET NOCOUNT ON and SET NOCOUNT OFF options inside your stored procedure in SQL Server DBMS to disable or enable the update count results. Consult your DBMS documentation for the options that are available to suppress the update count results.

Use the execute() method of the Statement object if it may return multiple results. You need to work with four things to process multiple results. You may or may not know the order in which the results are returned. The first thing you need to consider is the return value of the execute() method. You need to work with the following three methods of the Statement interface to access all results:

- getMoreResults()

- getUpdateCount()

- getResultSet()

The execute() method may generate many results or no results. You must read one result at a time. You must first scroll to a result before you can read it. The execute() method scrolls to the first result, if there is one. If the first result is a ResultSet, the execute() method returns true. If the first result is an update count or there is no result, it returns false. You can retrieve a ResultSet result by calling the Statement object's getResultSet() method. You can retrieve an update count by calling its getUpdateCount() method.

You can scroll to the next result by calling the getMoreResults() method of a Statement. The getMoreResults() method returns true if it scrolls to a ResultSet result. It returns false if it scrolls to an update count result or there are no more results.

Aren't the rules to process multiple results confusing? So, what criteria determine that you do have more results to process? It is a little tricky to tell. You will need to write a few lines of code to process multiple results returned by executing a statement. The following snippet of code puts the logic together. It uses a CallableStatement object. You can also use a Statement or PreparedStatement object. The following logic does not depend on the order or the count of the multiple results:

```
Callable cstmt = get a callable statement object;
boolean hasResultSet = cstmt.execute();
int updateCount = cstmt.getUpdateCount();

while (hasResultSet || updateCount != -1) {
        if (hasResultSet) {
                // The cursor is pointing to a ResultSet object
                ResultSet rs = cstmt.getResultSet();

                // Process the result set here
                System.out.println("Got a result set");
        }
```

```
        else {
                System.out.println("Got an update Count: " + updateCount);
        }

        // Move the cursor to the next result
        hasResultSet = cstmt.getMoreResults();

        // Get the new update count
        updateCount = cstmt.getUpdateCount();
}

// When we get to this point, all results have been processed.
```

■ **Tip** When you call the getMoreResults() method, the ResultSet that was previously obtained by using the getResultSet() method is closed. If you want to keep the previously accessed ResultSet, you can use another version of the getMoreResults() method that accepts an argument, which lets you specify what to do with the open ResultSet objects. As usual, closing the Statement object will close all ResultSets.

Getting a ResultSet from a Stored Procedure

I have covered a great deal of details on processing result sets that are produced by executing a SELECT statement (see Listing 6-11). A stored procedure can also produce a result set. Producing a result set in a stored procedure is easy in most of the databases. It is just a matter of writing a SELECT statement inside a stored procedure. The following is an example of creating a stored procedure in Adaptive Server Anywhere DBMS that returns a result set. The name of the stored procedure is get_person_details. It accepts one parameter, which is of type integer and is the value for person_id. To return a result set, it simply selects columns from the person table for the person_id that is passed in.

```
-- Adaptive Server Anywhere 9.0
create procedure get_person_details(@person_id integer)
as
begin
  select person_id, first_name, last_name, gender, dob, income
    from person
   where person_id = @person_id
end
```

Producing a result set inside a stored procedure in Oracle database is a little different. You need to work with a REF CURSOR type in an Oracle database to produce a result set. First, you work with an example of dealing with result sets produced by a stored procedure by a DBMS other than Oracle. Please refer to your DBMS and its JDBC documentation on how it supports producing a result set inside a stored procedure. At the end of this section, you will see an example of producing a result set in a stored procedure using Oracle DBMS.

This section contains the database script to create a get_person_details stored procedure in some DBMSs. If you are working with one of these DBMSs, you need to run the script for your DBMS before you can run the examples in this section. If your DBMS is not listed, you can duplicate the logic and create a get_person_details stored procedure in your DBMS, which produces a result set.

If your stored procedure produces only one result set, it is straightforward to process that result set. Here are the steps to process one result set from a stored procedure:

- Construct the stored procedure call in a string format using the JDBC standard syntax.

  ```
  String sql = "{call get_person_details(?)}";
  ```

- Prepare a CallableStatement using the SQL syntax created in the previous step.

  ```
  CallableStatement cstmt = conn.prepareCall(sql);
  ```

- Set any IN parameters that need to be passed to the stored procedure. In your case, you will pass a person_id to the stored procedure and you need to set a person_id as the IN parameter.

  ```
  cstmt.setInt(1, 101);
  ```

- Call the executeQuery() method of the CallableStatement object, which will return the result set produced by the stored procedure as a ResultSet.

  ```
  ResultSet rs = cstmt.executeQuery();
  ```

- Process the ResultSet object as usual by looping through its rows and using the getXxx() methods to read the columns values.

■ **Tip** If your stored procedure returns multiple result sets, you need to use the execute() method of the CallableStatement interface instead of the executeQuery() method. Please refer to the "Handling Multiple Results from a Statement" section for more details on how to handle multiple result sets produced by a stored procedure.

The following are the database scripts for creating the get_person_details stored procedure in different DBMSs.

MySQL Database

```
DELIMITER $$

DROP PROCEDURE IF EXISTS get_person_details $$

CREATE PROCEDURE get_person_details(in person_id_param int)
BEGIN
 select person_id, first_name, last_name, gender, dob, income
   from person
  where person_id = person_id_param;
END $$

DELIMITER ;
```

Adaptive Server Anywhere Database

```
create procedure get_person_details(@person_id integer)
as
begin
  select person_id, first_name, last_name, gender, dob, income
    from person
    where person_id = @person_id
end
```

Oracle Database

```
CREATE OR REPLACE
PACKAGE JDBC_TEST_PKG
AS
 type person_cursor_type is ref cursor;
END JDBC_TEST_PKG;

create or replace PROCEDURE GET_PERSON_DETAILS
( person_id_param IN NUMBER,
  person_cursor OUT jdbc_test_pkg.person_cursor_type
)
AS
BEGIN
  open person_cursor for
  select person_id, first_name, last_name, gender, dob, income
    from person
  where person_id = person_id_param;
END GET_PERSON_DETAILS;
```

SQL Server Database

```
-- Drop stored procedure if it already exists
IF EXISTS (
  SELECT *
    FROM INFORMATION_SCHEMA.ROUTINES
   WHERE SPECIFIC_SCHEMA = N'dbo'
     AND SPECIFIC_NAME = N'get_person_details'
)
   DROP PROCEDURE dbo.get_person_details
GO

CREATE PROCEDURE dbo.get_person_details
      @person_id int
AS
BEGIN
    SELECT person_id, first_name, last_name, gender, dob, income
      FROM person
     WHERE person_id = @person_id;
END;
GO
```

DB2 Database

```sql
create procedure get_person_details(in person_id_param int)
result sets 1
language sql
begin
    declare c1 cursor with return for
     select person_id, first_name, last_name, gender, dob, income
       from person
      where person_id = person_id_param;
    open c1;
end
@
```

The @ sign is used as the statement terminator in the above syntax.

Java DB Database

For the Java DB database, you need to write the stored procedure as a method in a Java class as shown in Listing 6-15.

Listing 6-15. The Java Code for the get_person_details Stored Procedure in Java DB

```java
// JavaDBGetPersonDetailsSp.java
package com.jdojo.jdbc;

import java.sql.Connection;
import java.sql.DriverManager;
import java.sql.PreparedStatement;
import java.sql.ResultSet;
import java.sql.SQLException;

public class JavaDBGetPersonDetailsSp {
        public static void getPersonDetails(int personId,
                        ResultSet[] personDetailRs) throws SQLException {

                // Must use the following URL to get the reference of
                // the Connection object in whose context this method
                // is called.
                String dbURL = "jdbc:default:connection";
                Connection conn = DriverManager.getConnection(dbURL);

                String sql = "select person_id, first_name, " +
                        "last_name, gender, dob, income " +
                        "from person " +
                        "where person_id = ?";
```

```
            PreparedStatement pstmt = conn.prepareStatement(sql);
            pstmt.setInt(1, personId);
            ResultSet rs = pstmt.executeQuery();
            personDetailRs[0] = rs;

            /* Do not close pstmt or rs here. They are meant to be
               procssed and closed by the caller of this stored
               procedure.
            */
        }
}
```

The command to create the get_person_details stored procedure in the Java DB database is as follows. For more details on working with stored procedures in Java DB, please refer to Listing 6-8 and the related steps in the section containing this listing.

```
-- Command to create the stored procedure
CREATE PROCEDURE get_person_details(IN person_id integer)
PARAMETER STYLE JAVA
LANGUAGE JAVA
READS SQL DATA
DYNAMIC RESULT SETS 1
EXTERNAL NAME 'com.jdojo.jdbc.JavaDBGetPersonDetailsSp.getPersonDetails';
```

Listing 6-16 contains the complete code that executes a stored procedure and processes the result set produced by the stored procedure. It uses the printResultSet() static method of the QueryPersonTest class (see Listing 6-11) to print a person's details. This program is valid for a database that has native support for a result set on the server side. Please refer to the example later in this section to process a result set produced by a stored procedure in an Oracle database.

Listing 6-16. Processing a ResultSet Produced by a Stored Procedure

```
// StoredProcedureResultSetTest.java
package  com.jdojo.jdbc;

import java.sql.CallableStatement;
import java.sql.Connection;
import java.sql.ResultSet;
import java.sql.SQLException;

public class StoredProcedureResultSetTest {
        public static void main(String[] args) {
                Connection conn = null;
                try {
                        conn = JDBCUtil.getConnection();

                        // Print details for person_id 101
                        printPersonDetails(conn, 101);

                        JDBCUtil.commit(conn);
                }
```

```
                catch (SQLException e) {
                        System.out.println(e.getMessage());
                        JDBCUtil.rollback(conn);
                }
                finally {
                        JDBCUtil.closeConnection(conn);
                }
        }

    public static void printPersonDetails(Connection conn,
            int personId) throws SQLException {
            String SQL = "{ call get_person_details(?) }";
            CallableStatement cstmt = null;
            try {
                    cstmt = conn.prepareCall(SQL);

                    // Set the IN parameters
                    cstmt.setInt(1, personId);
                    ResultSet rs = cstmt.executeQuery();

                    // Process the result set
                    QueryPersonTest.printResultSet(rs);
            }
            finally {
                    JDBCUtil.closeStatement(cstmt);
            }
        }
}
```

Now, it is time to work with an Oracle database only. Here are the steps that you will need to use to process a result set produced by a stored procedure in an Oracle database.

1. Construct the stored procedure call in a string format using the JDBC standard syntax. You will have an additional OUT parameter for an Oracle stored procedure. In an Oracle database, the stored procedure will pass back the reference of a REF CURSOR type in that OUT parameter. In your case, the first parameter is of the IN type and it will be used to pass a person_id. The second parameter is an OUT parameter of type oracle.jdbc. OracleTypes.CURSOR. Note that you must have the JAR file(s) for the Oracle JDBC driver included in the CLASSPATH to use the oracle.jdbc.OracleTypes.CURSOR interface.

   ```
   String sql = "{call get_person_details(?, ?)}";
   ```

2. Prepare a CallableStatement using the SQL syntax created in the previous step.

   ```
   CallableStatement cstmt = conn.prepareCall(sql);
   ```

3. Set any IN parameters that need to be passed to the stored procedure. In your case, you will pass a person_id to the stored procedure and you need to set that person_id as an IN parameter. Register the OUT parameter as oracle.jdbc.OracleTypes.CURSOR type.

   ```
   cstmt.setInt(1, 101);
   cstmt.registerOutParameter(2, oracle.jdbc.OracleTypes.CURSOR);
   ```

4. Call the execute() method of the CallableStatement object.

    ```
    cstmt.execute();
    ```

5. Get the ResultSet object, which is passed back in the second OUT parameter using the getObject() method and cast it as ResultSet.

    ```
    ResultSet rs = (ResultSet)cstmt.getObject(2);
    ```

6. Process the ResultSet object as usual by looping through its rows and using its getXxx() methods to read the column values.

Listing 6-17 contains the complete code that executes the get_person_details stored procedure in an Oracle database and processes the result set produced by the stored procedure. Make sure that you have the JDBCUtil.getConnection() method (see Listing 6-1) that returns a connection to an Oracle database. You must also compile the necessary package and procedure in the Oracle database as listed in this section for Oracle before you can run the program in Listing 6-17. Note that you will need to uncomment the following statement that appears inside the printPersonDetails() method:

```
//cstmt.registerOutParameter(2, oracle.jdbc.OracleTypes.CURSOR);
```

I have commented it so the entire class will compile. You will need to add the Oracle JDBC driver JAR file in CLASSPATH to compile the class, after uncommenting this statement.

Listing 6-17. Processing a ResultSet from a Stored Procedure in Oracle Database

```java
// OracleStoredProcedureResultSetTest.java
package com.jdojo.jdbc;

import java.sql.CallableStatement;
import java.sql.Connection;
import java.sql.ResultSet;
import java.sql.SQLException;

public class OracleStoredProcedureResultSetTest {
    public static void main(String[] args) {
        Connection conn = null;
        try {
            conn = JDBCUtil.getConnection();

            // Print details for person_id 101
            printPersonDetails(conn, 101);

            JDBCUtil.commit(conn);
        }
        catch (SQLException e) {
            System.out.println(e.getMessage());
            JDBCUtil.rollback(conn);
        }
        finally {
            JDBCUtil.closeConnection(conn);
        }
    }
```

```
    public static void printPersonDetails(Connection conn,
                    int personId) throws SQLException {
        String sql = "{ call get_person_details(?, ?) }";
        CallableStatement cstmt = null;
        try {
                cstmt = conn.prepareCall(sql);

                // Set the IN parameters
                cstmt.setInt(1, personId);


                /* Uncomment the following statement after you have
                   the Oracle JDBC driver in CLASSPATH.
                   Register the second parameter as an OUT parameter
                   which will return the REF CURSOR (the ResultSet) */
                //cstmt.registerOutParameter(2,
                //        oracle.jdbc.OracleTypes.CURSOR);

                // Execute the stored procedure
                cstmt.execute();

                // Get the result set from the OUT parameter
                ResultSet rs = (ResultSet) cstmt.getObject(2);

                // Process the result set
                QueryPersonTest.printResultSet(rs);
        }
        finally {
                JDBCUtil.closeStatement(cstmt);
        }
    }
}
```

Many databases support the REF CURSOR type. Java 8 has added direct support for REF CURSOR data type in the JDBC API by adding the JDBCType.REF_CURSOR enum constant that represents REF CUSROR data type in Java. Using this JDBC type, you will be able to work with the REF CURSOR type without using proprietary JDBC classes in your Java program. For example, you will be able to register the OUT parameter of the REF CURSOR database type in the printPersonDetails() method as follows:

```
cstmt.registerOutParameter(2, JDBCType.REF_CURSOR);
```

■ **Tip** At the time of this writing, the JDBCType.REF_CURSOR type has not been implemented in the Oracle JDBC driver. If you use this type to register a REF CURSOR database type, you will get a runtime error with an error message that this data type has not been implemented yet. Use the supportsRefCursors() method of the DatabaseMetaData interface, which was added in Java 8, to know if the database supports REF CURSOR.

ResultSetMetaData

A ResultSet object contains the rows of data returned by executing a query and detailed information about the columns. The information that it contains about the columns in the result set is called the *result set metadata*. An object of the ResultSetMetaData interface represents the result set metadata. You can get a ResultSetMetaData object by calling the getMetaData() method of the ResultSet interface.

```
ResultSet rs = get result set object;
ResultSetMetaData rsmd = rs.getMetaData();
```

A ResultSetMetaData contains a lot of information about all columns in a result set. All of the methods, except getColumnCount(), in the ResultSetMetaData interface accept a column index in the result set as an argument. It contains the table name, name, label, database data type, class name in Java, nullability, precision, etc. of a column. It also contains the column count in the result set. Its getTableName() method returns the table name of a column; the getColumnName() method returns the column's name; the getColumnLabel() method returns the column's label; the getColumnTypeName() method returns the column type in database; and the getColumnClassName() method returns Java class used to represent the data for the column. Its getColumnCount() method returns the number of columns in the result set.

The column label is a nice printable text that is used in a query after the column name. The following query uses "Person ID" as the column label for the person_id column. The first_name column does not have a specified label.

```
select person_id as "Person ID", first_name from person
```

The getColumnLabel(1) method call will return "Person ID", whereas getColumnName(1) will return person_id if the above query is used for a result set. If the column label is not specified in a query, the getColumnLabel() method returns the column name.

Listing 6-18 demonstrates how to use a ResultSetMetaData object to know more about a result set. The output is shown for Java DB. You may get a different output when you use a different JDBC driver because database-column-type-to-JDBC-column-type mapping depends on the JDBC driver.

Listing 6-18. Using a ResultSetMetaData Object to Get Information About a ResultSet

```
// ResultSetMetaDataTest.java
package  com.jdojo.jdbc;

import java.sql.Connection;
import java.sql.ResultSet;
import java.sql.ResultSetMetaData;
import java.sql.SQLException;
import java.sql.Statement;

public class ResultSetMetaDataTest {
        public static void main(String[] args) {
                Connection conn = null;
                try {
                        conn = JDBCUtil.getConnection();
                        String SQL = "select person_id as \"Person ID\", " +
                                "first_name as \"First Name\", " +
                                "gender as Gender, " +
                                "dob as \"Birth Date\", " +
                                "income as Income " +
                                "from person";
```

```
                // Print the reSult set matadata
                printMetaData(conn, SQL);

                JDBCUtil.commit(conn);
        }
        catch (SQLException e) {
                System.out.println(e.getMessage());
                JDBCUtil.rollback(conn);
        }
        finally {
                JDBCUtil.closeConnection(conn);
        }
    }
    public static void printMetaData(Connection conn, String SQL)
                throws SQLException {
        Statement stmt = conn.createStatement();
        try {
                ResultSet rs = stmt.executeQuery(SQL);
                ResultSetMetaData rsmd = rs.getMetaData();
                int columnCount = rsmd.getColumnCount();
                System.out.println("Column Count:" + columnCount);

                for (int i = 1; i <= columnCount; i++) {
                        System.out.println("Index:" + i +
                                ", Name:" + rsmd.getColumnName(i) +
                                ", Label:" + rsmd.getColumnLabel(i) +
                                ", Type Name:" + rsmd.getColumnTypeName(i) +
                                ", Class Name:" + rsmd.getColumnClassName(i));
                }
        }
        finally {
                JDBCUtil.closeStatement(stmt);
        }
    }
}
```

```
Index:1, Name:Person ID, Label:Person ID, Type Name:INTEGER, Class Name:java.lang.Integer
Index:2, Name:First Name, Label:First Name, Type Name:VARCHAR, Class Name:java.lang.String
Index:3, Name:GENDER, Label:GENDER, Type Name:CHAR, Class Name:java.lang.String
Index:4, Name:Birth Date, Label:Birth Date, Type Name:DATE, Class Name:java.sql.Date
Index:5, Name:INCOME, Label:INCOME, Type Name:DOUBLE, Class Name:java.lang.Double
```

If you have to write generic code to process any or an unknown result set, you will find a ResultSetMetaData object indispensable. For example, suppose you want to develop a Swing application that will let the user enter in a query and you will display the query data in a JTable. To construct the JTable, you must know the number of columns in the result set. You can use the getColumnCount() method of a ResultSetMetaData object to know the number of columns in a result set. You can use many other methods available in this object to construct an appropriate JTable.

Using RowSets

An instance of the RowSet interface is a wrapper for a result set. The RowSet interface inherits from the ResultSet interface. In simple terms, a RowSet is a Java object that contains a set of rows from a tabular data source. The tabular data source could be a database, a flat file, a spreadsheet, etc. The RowSet interface is in the javax.sql package. The following are the advantages of the RowSet over the ResultSet:

- A RowSet makes JDBC programming simpler. When you use a ResultSet object, you must deal with the Connection and Statement objects at the same time. A RowSet hides the complexities of using the Connection and Statement objects from the developers. All you have to work with is only one object, which is a RowSet object.

- A ResultSet is not Serializable and therefore, it cannot be sent over the network or saved to the disk for later use. A RowSet is Serializable. It can be sent over the network or saved to a disk for later use.

- A ResultSet is always connected to a data source. A RowSet object does not need to be connected to its data source all the time. It can connect to the database when needed such as to retrieve/update data in the data source.

- A RowSet is by default scrollable and updatable.

- The two properties of a RowSet, serialization and connectionlessness, makes it very useful in a thin client environment such as a mobile device or a web application. A thin client does not need to have a JDBC driver. It may get the data in a disconnected RowSet from a middle tier. It may modify the data and send the modified RowSet to the middle tier, which can connect to the data source and update the data. You can use this technique in an applet or a web page. You can have a servlet that can connect to a database, retrieve data in a disconnected RowSet, and pass it to an applet. The applet can modify the data and send the modified RowSet to the servlet, which can connect to the database to update the data. This way, an applet does not need to use a JDBC driver or anything related to database connectivity at all. There is also a RowSet type available for web usage that works with XML data.

- A ResultSet uses a database as its data source. You are not restricted to using only a database as a data source with a RowSet. You can implement a RowSet to use any tabular data source.

- A RowSet follows the JavaBeans model for properties setting and events notifications, which makes it possible to develop a RowSet using a visual tool that supports the JavaBeans development.

- A RowSet also supports filtering of data after the data has been retrieved. Filtering of data is not possible in a ResultSet. You must use a WHERE clause in a query to filter data in the database itself if you use a ResultSet.

- A RowSet makes it possible to join two or more data sets based on their column's values after they have been retrieved from their data sources. One data set can be retrieved from a database and another from a flat file. This is simply not possible when you use a ResultSet. When you use a ResultSet, joining multiple data sets is possible using SQL joins in the query that fills the ResultSet.

You also need to be aware of a few disadvantages of using a RowSet.

- A specific RowSet implementation may cache data in memory. You need to be careful when using such type of RowSets. You should not fetch large volumes of data using these RowSets. Otherwise, it may slow down the application.

- With cached data in a RowSet, there are more possibilities of data inconsistency between the data in the RowSet and data in the data source, when changes are applied to the data source.

The following interfaces in the `javax.sql.rowset` package define five types of rowsets:

- `JdbcRowSet`
- `CachedRowSet`
- `WebRowSet`
- `FilteredRowSet`
- `JoinRowSet`

Each type of rowset has features that are suitable for specific needs. All these rowset interfaces inherit, directly or indirectly, from the RowSet interface. The RowSet interface is inherited from the ResultSet interface. Therefore, all methods in the ResultSet interface are also available in all types of rowsets. Figure 6-7 depicts a class diagram for rowset interfaces.

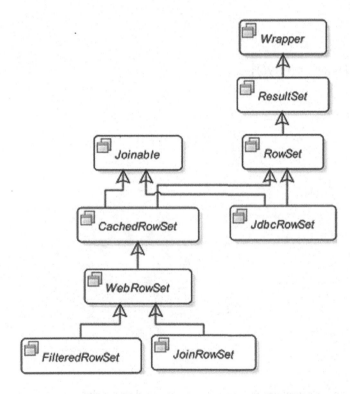

Figure 6-7. *A class diagram for the interfaces defining rowsets*

Who provides the implementation classes for the rowsets interfaces? Typically, database vendors are supposed to provide implementation classes for rowsets. They may provide them as part of their JDBC driver or as a separate bundle. Third parties can also provide rowset implementation classes. As a developer, you can also provide rowset implementations to suit specific needs.

Creating a RowSet

An instance of the RowSetFactory interface lets you create different types of RowSet objects without caring about the rowset implementation classes. To get a RowSetFactory, you need to use the newFactory() static method of the RowSetProvider class. The RowSetFactory interface has five methods to create five types of rowsets. Those methods are named as createXxxRowSet(), where Xxx can be Cached, Filtered, Jdbc, Join, and Web. For example, you will use the createJdbcRowSet() method of a RowSetFactory to create a JdbcRowSet. The following snippet of code shows how to create a JdbcRowSet:

```
import java.sql.SQLException;
import javax.sql.rowset.JdbcRowSet;
import javax.sql.rowset.RowSetFactory;
import javax.sql.rowset.RowSetProvider;
...

JdbcRowSet jdbcRs = null;
try {
        // Get the RowSetFactory implementation
        RowSetFactory rsFactory = RowSetProvider.newFactory();

        // Create a JdbcRowSet object
        jdbcRs = rsFactory.createJdbcRowSet();

        // Work with jdbcRs here
}
catch (SQLException e) {
        e.printStackTrace();
}
finally {
        if (jdbcRs != null) {
                try {
                        // Close the RowSet
                        jdbcRs.close();
                }
                catch (SQLException e) {
                        e.printStackTrace();
                }
        }
}
```

The newFactory() method of the RowSetProvider class searches for the implementation class for the RowSetFactory interface as follows:

- It looks for the value of the javax.sql.rowset.RowSetFactory system property. You can specify this property value on the command line. The following command sets this property value to the com.jdojo.MyRowSetFactoryImpl class when running the com.jdojo.jdbc.Test class:

  ```
  java -Djavax.sql.rowset.RowSetFactory=com.jdojo.MyRowSetFactoryImpl com.jdojo.jdbc.Test
  ```

- The service provider API looks for a class name in all available JAR files to the runtime under META-INF/services/javax.sql.rowset.RowSetFactory.

- It looks for the platform's default implementation for the RowSetFactory interface.

The RowSetProvider class has another static method called newFactory(String factoryClassName, ClassLoader cl) that lets you specify the class name of the RowSetFactory implementation to use. This method is useful when multiple RowSetFactory providers are available at runtime and you want to use a specific one. Suppose you have created a class com.jdojo.jdbc.MyRowSetFactory that implements the RowSetFactory interface. The following snippet of code shows how to use this version of the newFactory() method to use your own implementation of the RowSetFactory class:

```
String factoryClassName = "com.jdojo.jdbc.MyRowSetFactory";

// Use null as the second argument to use the current Thread's context classLoader
RowSetFactory factory = RowSetProvider.newFactory(factoryClassName, null);

// Create a JdbcRowSet
JdbcRowSet jdbcRs = factory.createJdbcRowSet();
```

Setting RowSet Connection Properties

A RowSet is a JavaBeans component. You can set its properties at design time using a visual development tool. You can also set its properties at runtime. Typically, a RowSet will need to connect to a data source to retrieve and update data. You can set the database connection properties for a RowSet in terms of a JDBC URL or a data source name. When you use a JDBC URL, the RowSet will use a JDBC driver to connect to the database registered with the DriverManager class. You can set the JDBC connection properties for a RowSet object as follows:

```
// Register the JDBC driver with the DriverManager here

// Create a RowSet
RowSet rs = create a RowSet;

// Set the conection properties for the RowSet
rs.setUrl("jdbc:derby:beginningJavaDB");
rs.setUsername("root");
rs.setPassword("chanda");
```

You do not need to establish a connection to the database. The RowSet will take care of establishing connection when it is needed.

Alternatively, you can set a data source name for the RowSet object. It will look up the data source name using a JNDI service to get a DataSource object for connecting to the database.

```
RowSet rs = create a RowSet;
rs.setDataSourceName("jdbc/myTestDB");
```

You need to set either a data source name or a JDBC URL. If you set both, the most recently set non-null value will be used to connect to the database.

Not all RowSets connect to a database. For example, if you use a RowSet to send data over the network, you do not need to set its connection properties. However, if a RowSet object needs to interact with a database, you must set these properties before you call any methods of that RowSet needing a database connection.

Setting a Command for a RowSet

You learned in the previous section that you do not need to worry about a Connection object to use a RowSet. The benefits of using a RowSet do not stop there. When you work with a RowSet, you do not need to worry about Statement, PreparedStatement, and CallableStatement objects either. However, you must specify a command that will generate the result set for the RowSet object. The command will be in a string in the form of a SQL SELECT statement or a stored procedure call. You can use a question mark as a placeholder for any parameter that you would like to pass to your command at runtime. To set a parameter value at runtime, you need to use one of setXxx(int paramIndex, Xxx paramValue) methods of the RowSet interface. Working with parameters in a command for a RowSet is the same as working with parameters for a PreparedStatement. The following snippet of code contains some examples of setting a command for a RowSet object:

```
RowSet rs = create a RowSet;

/* Example 1 */
// Command to select all rows from the person table
String sqlCommand = "select person_id, first_name, last_name from person";

// Set the command to the RowSet object
rs.setCommand(sqlCommand);

/* Example 2 */
// Command to select rows from the person table with two parameters that
// will be the range of the income
String sqlCommand = "select person_id, first_name, last_name, income " +
                    "from person " +
                    "where income between ? and ?;

// Set the command to the RowSet object
rs.setCommand(sqlCommand);

// Set the range of income between 20000.0 and 30000.0
rs.setDouble(1, 20000.0);
rs.setDouble(2, 30000.0);

/* Example 3 */
// Command to execute a stored procedure that accepts two parameters that will //be the
// range of the income. The getPersons() stored procedure produces a result set
String sqlCommand = "{call getPersons(?, ?)}";

// Set the command to the RowSet object
rs.setCommand(sqlCommand);

// Set the range of income between 20000.0 and 30000.0
rs.setDouble(1, 20000.0);
rs.setDouble(2, 30000.0);
```

Populating a RowSet with Data

A RowSet may be populated with data in many ways:

- By executing a command such as a SQL SELECT or a stored procedure
- By supplying it with a ResultSet in which it will read all its data from the supplied ResultSet
- By reading XML data into it
- By using any other custom methods

If you want to populate a RowSet with data by executing its command, you need to call its execute() method as shown:

```
// Execute its command to populate the RowSet
rs.execute();
```

After the execute() method is executed, the RowSet has the data in it and you need to scroll to a row to read/update its column's value. Other methods of populating a RowSet depend on the type of the RowSet. I will discuss an example of each type shortly in the section that describes the specific types of RowSets.

Scrolling Through Rows of a RowSet

In simple terms, a RowSet is a wrapper for a ResultSet. It inherits all cursor movement methods from the ResultSet interface. By default, all RowSet objects are bidirectional scrollable and updateable. However, check the implementation documentation for your RowSet to see if it imposes any restrictions on scrollability or updatability. The following snippet of code shows a typical while-loop that is used to scroll through all rows and read some column values from rows. It is the same as what you have been using to scroll through a ResultSet object.

```
RowSet rs = create a RowSet;
...
while(rs.next()) {
        // Read values for person_id and first_name from the current row
        int personID = rs.getInt("person_id");
        String firstName = rs.getString("first_name");

        // Perform other processing here
}
```

Updating Data in a RowSet

Updating data in a RowSet is similar to updating data in a ResultSet. To update a column's value, you need to move the cursor to a row, use one of the updateXxx() methods to set the new value for a column, and call the updateRow() method of the RowSet to make the changes permanent in the RowSet.

To insert a new row, you need to move the cursor to the insert row by calling the moveToInsertRow() method of the RowSet. You need to set values for columns in the insert row using one of updateXxx() methods. Finally, you call the insertRow() method of the RowSet.

To delete a row, you need to move the cursor to the row you want to delete and call the deleteRow() method of the RowSet.

How and when the changes made to a RowSet object are propagated to the database depends on the type of the RowSet. I will discuss updating different types of RowSet in the next few sections.

■ **Tip** You can make a RowSet read-only by calling its setReadOnly(true) method.

The RowSetUtil Class

You need to use repetitive code in examples in using rowsets such as to supply database connection properties, to get a RowSetFactory instance, and to print rows of a RowSet. Listing 6-19 contains the complete code for a RowSetUtil class that you will use in this section. Its setConnectionParameters() method loads a JDBC driver and sets its connection parameters. Its getRowSetFactory() method returns a RowSetFactory instance. Its printPersonRecord() method prints records from a RowSet, assuming that the RowSet contains at least person_id, first_name, and last_name columns from the person table.

Listing 6-19. A Utility Class to Help Working With a RowSet

```java
// RowSetUtil.java
package com.jdojo.jdbc;

import java.sql.Driver;
import java.sql.DriverManager;
import java.sql.SQLException;
import javax.sql.RowSet;
import javax.sql.rowset.RowSetFactory;
import javax.sql.rowset.RowSetProvider;

public class RowSetUtil {
        private static boolean driverLoaded = false;

        public static void setConnectionParameters(RowSet rs) throws SQLException {
                // Register the JDBC driver only once for your database
                if (!driverLoaded) {
                        // Change the JDBC driver class for your database
                        Driver derbyEmbeddedDriver =
                                new org.apache.derby.jdbc.EmbeddedDriver();
                        DriverManager.registerDriver(derbyEmbeddedDriver);

                        driverLoaded = true;
                }

                // Set the rowset database connection properties
                String dbURL = "jdbc:derby:beginningJavaDB;create=true;";
                String userId = "root";
                String password = "chanda";
                rs.setUrl(dbURL);
                rs.setUsername(userId);
                rs.setPassword(password);
        }
```

```java
    public static RowSetFactory getRowSetFactory() {
        try {
            RowSetFactory factory = RowSetProvider.newFactory();
            return factory;
        }
        catch (SQLException e) {
            throw new RuntimeException(e);
        }
    }

    // Print person id and name for each person record
    public static void printPersonRecord(RowSet rs) throws SQLException {
        while (rs.next()) {
            int personId = rs.getInt("person_id");
            String firstName = rs.getString("first_name");
            String lastName = rs.getString("last_name");
            System.out.println("Row #" + rs.getRow() + ":" +
                               " Person ID:" + personId +
                               ", First Name:" + firstName +
                               ", Last Name:" + lastName);
        }

        System.out.println();
    }
}
```

JdbcRowSet

A JdbcRowSet is also called a *connected rowset* because it always maintains a database connection. You can think of a JdbcRowSet as a thin wrapper for a ResultSet. As a ResultSet always maintains a database connection, so does a JdbcRowSet. It adds some methods that let you configure the connection behaviors. You can use its setAutoCommit() method to enable or disable the auto-commit mode for the connection. You can use its commit() and rollback() methods to commit or rollback changes made to its data.

A JDBC driver or underlying database may not support a bidirectional scrollable and updatable result set. In such cases, a JdbcRowSet implementation may provide such features. Listing 6-20 uses a JdbcRowSet to read records for all person_id in a specified range from the person table. Note that the code attempts to print the number of rows retrieved by using the last() method of the RowSet. At the end, it uses the printPersonRecord() method of the RowSetUtil class to print the records in the rowset.

Listing 6-20. Using a JdbcRowSet to Read Records from a Table

```java
// JdbcRowSetTest.java
package com.jdojo.jdbc;

import java.sql.SQLException;
import javax.sql.rowset.JdbcRowSet;
import javax.sql.rowset.RowSetFactory;

public class JdbcRowSetTest {
    public static void main(String[] args) {
        RowSetFactory factory = RowSetUtil.getRowSetFactory();
```

```
                    // Use a try-with-resources block
                    try (JdbcRowSet jdbcRs = factory.createJdbcRowSet()) {
                            // Set the connection parameters
                            RowSetUtil.setConnectionParameters(jdbcRs);

                            // Set the command and input parameters
                            String sqlCommand = "select person_id, first_name, " +
                                              "last_name from person " +
                                              "where person_id between ? and ?";

                            jdbcRs.setCommand(sqlCommand);
                            jdbcRs.setInt(1, 101);
                            jdbcRs.setInt(2, 301);

                            // Retrieve the data
                            jdbcRs.execute();

                            // Scroll to the last row to get the row count It may throw an
                            // exception if the underlying JdbcRowSet implementation
                            // does not support a bi-directional scrolling result set.
                            try {
                                    jdbcRs.last();
                                    System.out.println("Row Count: " + jdbcRs.getRow());

                                    // Position the cursor before the first row
                                    jdbcRs.beforeFirst();
                            }
                            catch(SQLException e) {
                                    System.out.println("JdbcRowSet implementation" +
                                            " supports forward-only scrolling");
                            }

                            // Print the records in the rowset
                            RowSetUtil.printPersonRecord(jdbcRs);
                    }
            catch (SQLException e) {
                    e.printStackTrace();
            }
        }
}
```

Updating data using a JdbcRowSet is similar to updating data using a ResultSet. Make sure that you set the auto-commit mode for the rowset appropriately. In case of a JdbcRowSet, all methods will be used on a JdbcRowSet object instead of a ResultSet object.

Listing 6-21 contains the complete code that retrieves a person record and updates its income to 65000.00. Note that you must call the updateRow() method of the JdbcRowSet after updating the column's value and before you scroll to another row. Otherwise, your changes will be lost as it is lost in the case of updating data in a ResultSet. In case of JdbcRowSet, you do not have a direct access to the Connection object. You need to use JdbcRowSet object's commit() and rollback() methods to commit and rollback changes to the database.

Listing 6-21. Updating Data in a JdbcRowSet

```java
// JdbcRowSetUpdateTest.java
package com.jdojo.jdbc;

import java.sql.SQLException;
import javax.sql.rowset.JdbcRowSet;
import javax.sql.rowset.RowSetFactory;

public class JdbcRowSetUpdateTest {
    public static void main(String[] args) {
        RowSetFactory factory = RowSetUtil.getRowSetFactory();

        // Use a try-with-resources block
        try (JdbcRowSet jdbcRs = factory.createJdbcRowSet()) {
            // Set the connection parameters
            RowSetUtil.setConnectionParameters(jdbcRs);

            // Set the auto-commit mode to false
            jdbcRs.setAutoCommit(false);

            // Set the command and input parameters
            String sqlCommand = "select person_id, first_name, " +
                                "last_name, income from person " +
                                "where person_id = ?";
            jdbcRs.setCommand(sqlCommand);
            jdbcRs.setInt(1, 101);

            // Retrieve the data
            jdbcRs.execute();

            // If a row is retrieved, update the first row's income
            // column to 65000.00
            if (jdbcRs.next()) {
                int personId = jdbcRs.getInt("person_id");
                jdbcRs.updateDouble("income", 65000.00);
                jdbcRs.updateRow();

                // Commit the changes
                jdbcRs.commit();

                System.out.println("Income has been set to " +
                        "65000.00 for person_id=" + personId);
            }
            else {
                System.out.println("No person record was found.");
            }
        }
        catch (SQLException e) {
            e.printStackTrace();
        }
    }
}
```

CachedRowSet

A CachedRowSet is also called a *disconnected rowset* because it is disconnected from a database when it does not need a database connection. It keeps the database connection open only for the duration it needs to interact with the database. Once it is done with the connection, it disconnects. For example, it connects to a database when it needs to retrieve or update data.

It retrieves all data generated by the command and caches the data in memory. Care should be taken not to retrieve a large volume of data in a CachedRowSet. Otherwise, it may degrade the performance of the application. It provides a new feature called *paging*, which lets you deal with large volume of data in chunks. You will see an example of paging in this section.

A CachedRowSet is always serializable, scrollable, and updatable. You can save it to a disk or send it over the network. Not all CachedRowSet will need a connection to a data source. For example, you can retrieve data in a CachedRowSet and send its copy to another application, say an applet running in a web browser. In this case, the applet can read/update the data in the CachedRowSet without needing a database connection. When the applet is done working with the CachedRowSet, it can send the updated rowset to the server. The CachedRowSet does not need to have a database connection while it is being used in an applet. You can use one of the following four methods to populate data in a CachedRowSet object:

- void execute() throws SQLException

- void execute(Connection conn) throws SQLException

- void populate(ResultSet data) throws SQLException

- void populate(ResultSet rs, int startRow) throws SQLException

If you have set the database connection properties for a CachedRowSet, you can use the execute() method. It will connect to the database using the connection properties, which were already set, and execute the command for the rowset to populate it with the data. Another version of the execute() method accepts a Connection, which will be used to populate the CachedRowSet with the data. Use the populate() method to populate a CachedRowSet with data from a ResultSet. Another version of the populate() method accepts a starting row number from where it reads the rows from the ResultSet into the CachedRowSet.

You need to be aware of some restrictions when using the populate() method of the CachedRowSet. This method uses a ResultSet object, which supplies the data. Before you pass the ResultSet to this method, you might move the cursor to a specific row. For example, suppose the cursor is on the tenth row in the ResultSet when you pass it to the populate() method. What would happen when you call the first version the populate() method? Would it try to read all rows in the ResultSet object or would it read the data from the eleventh row? What would happen when you call the second version of the populate() method starting at row 5 when the current row is 10? Java documentation for these methods in the CachedRowSet interface does not provide any information for these situations. It is up to the implementation class to decide the details. However, if you just retrieve the ResultSet object and pass it to either versions of the populate() method, it will behave as expected.

You can obtain the number of rows in a CachedRowSet using its size() method. Note that for a JdbcRowSet, you need to move the cursor to the last row and call its getRow() method to get the number of rows in it. Since a CachedRowSet caches all its rows in memory, it can provide you a count of all rows any time. Note that the size() method is not available for a JdbcRowSet.

```
// Get the row count in a CachedRowSet
int rowCount = myCachedRowSet.size();
```

Listing 6-22 demonstrates how to use a CachedRowSet to retrieve rows from a database. It is similar to using a JdbcRowSet except that you are able to use its size() method to get the number of rows retrieved. A CachedRowSet is always bidirectional scrollable.

Listing 6-22. Retrieving Data Using a CachedRowSet

```java
// CachedRowSetTest.java
package com.jdojo.jdbc;

import java.sql.SQLException;
import javax.sql.rowset.CachedRowSet;
import javax.sql.rowset.RowSetFactory;

public class CachedRowSetTest {
        public static void main(String[] args) {
                RowSetFactory factory = RowSetUtil.getRowSetFactory();

                // Use a try-with-resources block
                try (CachedRowSet cachedRs = factory.createCachedRowSet()) {
                        // Set the connection parameters
                        RowSetUtil.setConnectionParameters(cachedRs);

                        String sqlCommand = "select person_id, first_name, last_name " +
                                            "from person " +
                                            "where person_id between 101 and 501";

                        cachedRs.setCommand(sqlCommand);
                        cachedRs.execute();

                        // Print the records in cached rowset
                        System.out.println("Row Count: " + cachedRs.size());
                        RowSetUtil.printPersonRecord(cachedRs);
                }
                catch (SQLException e) {
                        e.printStackTrace();
                }
        }
}
```

A CachedRowSet provides an additional feature called *paging* to let you retrieve rows generated by a command in chunks. The chunk of rows that is retrieved at one time is called a *page*. You can think of a page as a set of rows, where you decide the number of rows in the set. The maximum number of rows in a page is called the *page size*. The CachedRowSet lets you set the page size by calling its setPageSize(int size) method. Suppose a command for a CachedRowSet generates 500 rows. By calling its setPageSize(90), it will retrieve a maximum of 90 rows at a time. When you call its execute() method, it will retrieve the first 90 rows. To retrieve the next 90 rows, you need to call its nextPage() method. When it has retrieved five pages (450 rows), calling the nextPage() will retrieve the remaining 50 rows. It also provides a previousPage() method to retrieve the previous page. You can use the nextPage() and previousPage() methods of a CachedRowSet to retrieve and process a large result set in chunks. Both methods return true if there are more pages to retrieve. Otherwise, they return false. Typically, you use a do-while loop and a while-loop when you use the paging feature. The outer do-while loop will scroll through pages and the inner while-loop will scroll through the rows in the current page. The following snippet of code shows the typical processing logic for a CachedRowSet using paging:

```
CachedRowSet cachedRs = create and set properties for a cached rowset here;
```

```
// Set the page size to 90
cachedRs.setPagesize(90);

// Retrieves the first page
cachedRs.execute();

do {
        // Process each row in the page
        while(cachedRs.next()) {
                // Process a row here...
        }

        // Retrieve the next page of rows
}
while (cachedRs.nextPage());
```

Listing 6-23 contains the complete code for demonstrating the paging feature of a CachedRowSet. It retrieves all records from the person table a page at a time using a page size of 2. Typically, you do not retrieve all rows from a table in your program. The person table has only a few rows. I have done it only for demonstration purpose to keep the code simpler and smaller.

Listing 6-23. Using Paging Feature of a CachedRowSet

```
// CachedRowSetPagingTest.java
package com.jdojo.jdbc;

import java.sql.SQLException;
import javax.sql.rowset.CachedRowSet;
import javax.sql.rowset.RowSetFactory;

public class CachedRowSetPagingTest {
        public static void main(String[] args) {
                RowSetFactory factory = RowSetUtil.getRowSetFactory();

                // Use a try-with-resources block
                try (CachedRowSet cachedRs = factory.createCachedRowSet()) {
                        // Set the connection parameters
                        RowSetUtil.setConnectionParameters(cachedRs);

                        // Set the command and teh page size
                        String sqlCommand = "select person_id, first_name, last_name " +
                                            "from person";
                        cachedRs.setCommand(sqlCommand);
                        cachedRs.setPageSize(2); // page size is 2

                        // Execute the command
                        cachedRs.execute();

                        int pageCounter = 1;
```

```
                        // Retrieve and print person records one page at a time
                        do {
                                System.out.println("Page #" + pageCounter +
                                        " (Row Count=" + cachedRs.size() + ")");

                                // Print the record in the current page
                                RowSetUtil.printPersonRecord(cachedRs);

                                // Increment the page count by 1
                                pageCounter++;
                        }
                        while (cachedRs.nextPage());
                }
                catch (SQLException e) {
                        e.printStackTrace();
                }
        }
}
```

You can update the data in a CachedRowSet and save the changes back to the database. The process of saving changes to the database for a CachedRowSet is different from that of a JdbcRowSet. There are two main reasons to keep the save process a little different for a CachedRowSet. First, it is disconnected and you do not want to connect to the database often. Second, the updated data may have conflicts with the data stored in the database.

The process of inserting, updating, and deleting rows in a CachedRowSet is the same as in a JdbcRowSet. After changing the values for the current row, you need to call the updateRow() method. Unlike a JdbcRowSet, a CachedRowSet does not send the changes to the database when you call the updateRow() method. You use the insertRow() and deleteRow() methods the same way as you do with a ResultSet or a JdbcRowSet. These methods do not send changes to the database when used with a CachedRowSet.

After you make changes to a CachedRowSet, you can send changes to the database by calling its acceptChanges() method that may commit the changes if you have set the commit-on-accept-change value to true. You need to refer to the implementation details of the CachedRowSet on how it lets you set the commit-on-accept-change value. If it is set to false, you need to use the commit() or rollback() method of the CachedRowSet interface to commit or rollback changes.

A CachedRowSet has to deal with conflicts that may exist between the data in it and the data in the database. For example, you might have retrieved a row from the database, changed the data, and kept the changes in the CachedRowSet for a long time. When you are ready to save your changes, another user might have changed the values for the same rows before you. A CachedRowSet uses a synchronization provider object to synchronize the changes with the database. It uses another object, a synchronization resolver, to resolve any conflicts that it detects during the synchronization process. When conflicts are detected during the acceptChanges() method call, it throws a SyncProviderException. You can get the synchronization resolver object that is an instance of the SyncResolver interface, using the getSyncResolver() method of the SyncProviderException object. A SyncResolver object lets you navigate through all conflicts and change the values in the rows with conflicts to new resolved values. You need to use the setResolvedValue() method of a SyncResolver object to set the resolved value when a conflict is detected.

Listing 6-24 demonstrates how to update a CachedRowSet. It does not set a resolved value for a data element when it detects a conflict. Rather, it just prints the details about the conflict.

Listing 6-24. Updating and Detecting Conflicts in a CachedRowSet

```java
// CachedRowSetUpdateTest.java
package com.jdojo.jdbc;

import java.sql.SQLException;
import javax.sql.rowset.CachedRowSet;
import javax.sql.rowset.RowSetFactory;
import javax.sql.rowset.spi.SyncProviderException;
import javax.sql.rowset.spi.SyncResolver;
import static javax.sql.rowset.spi.SyncResolver.DELETE_ROW_CONFLICT;
import static javax.sql.rowset.spi.SyncResolver.INSERT_ROW_CONFLICT;
import static javax.sql.rowset.spi.SyncResolver.UPDATE_ROW_CONFLICT;

public class CachedRowSetUpdateTest {
    public static void main(String[] args) throws SQLException {
        RowSetFactory factory = RowSetUtil.getRowSetFactory();
        CachedRowSet cachedRs = factory.createCachedRowSet();

        try {
            // Set the connection parameters for the CachedRowSet
            RowSetUtil.setConnectionParameters(cachedRs);

            String sqlCommand = "select person_id, first_name, last_name, "
                    + "gender, dob, income "
                    + "from person "
                    + "where person_id between 101 and 301";

            cachedRs.setKeyColumns(new int[]{1});

            cachedRs.setCommand(sqlCommand);
            cachedRs.execute();

            // Print the records in the cached rowset
            System.out.println("Before Update");
            System.out.println("Row Count: " + cachedRs.size());
            RowSetUtil.printPersonRecord(cachedRs);

            // Update income to 23000.00 for the first row
            if (cachedRs.size() > 0) {
                updateRow(cachedRs, 1, 23000.00);
            }

            // Insert a new row
            insertNewRow(cachedRs);

            // Send changes to the database
            cachedRs.acceptChanges();

            System.out.println("After Update");
            System.out.println("Row Count: " + cachedRs.size());
            cachedRs.beforeFirst();
            RowSetUtil.printPersonRecord(cachedRs);
        }
```

```
            catch (SyncProviderException spe) {
                    // When acceptChanges() detects some conflicts
                    SyncResolver resolver = spe.getSyncResolver();

                    // Print the details about the conflicts
                    printConflicts(resolver, cachedRs);
            }
            catch (SQLException e) {
                    e.printStackTrace();
            }
            finally {
                    if (cachedRs != null) {
                            try {
                                    cachedRs.close();
                            }
                            catch (SQLException e) {
                                    e.printStackTrace();
                            }
                    }
            }
    }

    public static void insertNewRow(CachedRowSet cachedRs) throws SQLException {
            // Move cursor to the insert-row
            cachedRs.moveToInsertRow();

            // Set the values for columns in the new row
            cachedRs.updateInt("person_id", 751);
            cachedRs.updateString("first_name", "Mason");
            cachedRs.updateString("last_name", "Baker");
            cachedRs.updateString("gender", "M");
            cachedRs.updateDate("dob", java.sql.Date.valueOf("2006-01-02"));
            cachedRs.updateDouble("income", 0.00);

            // Insert the new row in the rowset. It is not sent to the
            // database, until the acceptChanges() method is called
            cachedRs.insertRow();

            // Must move back to the current row
            cachedRs.moveToCurrentRow();
    }

    public static void updateRow(CachedRowSet cachedRs, int row, double newIncome)
            throws SQLException {
            // Set the values for columns in the new row
            cachedRs.absolute(row);
            cachedRs.updateDouble("income", newIncome);
            cachedRs.updateRow();
    }
```

```
        public static void printConflicts(SyncResolver resolver, CachedRowSet cachedRs) {
            try {
                while (resolver.nextConflict()) {
                    int status = resolver.getStatus();
                    String operation = "None";
                    if (status == INSERT_ROW_CONFLICT) {
                        operation = "insert";
                    }
                    else if (status == UPDATE_ROW_CONFLICT) {
                        operation = "update";
                    }
                    else if (status == DELETE_ROW_CONFLICT) {
                        operation = "delete";
                    }

                    // Get person_id from the database
                    Object oldPersonId
                            = resolver.getConflictValue("person_id");

                    // Get person ID from the cached rowset
                    int row = resolver.getRow();
                    cachedRs.absolute(row);
                    Object newPersonId = cachedRs.getObject("person_id");

                    // Use setResolvedValue() method to set resolved value
                    // for a column
                    // resolver.setResolvedValue(columnName,resolvedValue);
                    System.out.println("Conflict detected in row #"
                            + row
                            + " during " + operation + " operation."
                            + " person_id in database is " + oldPersonId
                            + " and person_id in rowset is " + newPersonId);
                }
            }
            catch (SQLException e) {
                e.printStackTrace();
            }
        }
    }
}
```

WebRowSet

The WebRowSet interface inherits from the CachedRowSet interface. It adds two more features to the CachedRowSet: reading data and metadata from an XML document, and exporting data and metadata to an XML document. The two methods that it adds to provide XML support are readXML() and writeXML(). Both of them are overloaded. They accept either a stream-based or a character-based source/sink. Use the readXML() method to read XML data, properties, and metadata from a source (a java.io.InputStream or a java.io.Reader) into a WebRowSet, and use the writeXML() method to write the data, properties, and metadata from a WebRowSet object to a destination, which could be a java.io.OutputStream or a java.io.Writer. The following snippet of code shows how to export the contents and properties of a WebRowSet to a string:

```
WebRowSet webRs = get a web rowset with data...;

// Create a StringWriter object to hold the exported XML
StringWriter sw = new StringWriter();

// Write the XML representation of webRs into sw
webRs.writeXml(sw);

// Get the String object from sw
String webRsXML = sw.toString();
```

At this point, the webRsXML contains the XML representation of the webRs object. You can pass it to another module of your application, where you would be able to recreate the WebRowSet with the same data, properties, and metadata. The following snippet of code shows how to import an XML document into a WebRowSet:

```
// Create a StringReader object from an XML string
StringReader sr = new StringReader(webRsXML);

// Create an empty WebRowSet object
RowSetFactory factory = RowSetUtil.getRowSetFactory();
WebRowSet newWebRs = factory.createWebRowSet();

// Import (or read) the XML contents into the new, empty WebRowSet
newWebRs.readXml(sr);
```

At this point, webRs and newWebRs are in the same state. A WebRowSet makes it easy to export its contents as XML and import an XML document into it. You can use these processes to get an XML document and to send it to another application, say an applet, which does not need to have JDBC connectivity to a database. When the applet is done making changes to the WebRowSet, it can export it as an XML document and pass it to another application that has a JDBC connectivity to synchronize the changes with the database.

The exported XML from a WebRowSet contains three sets of information: properties, metadata, and data. The properties refer to the properties that are set for the rowset. The metadata contains information about columns in the rowset such as the column count, column name, column data type, etc. The data section in the XML contains the original and changed data from the rowset.

Listing 6-25 demonstrates how to export a WebRowSet object as XML. You will find three elements in the output for this listing: <properties>, <metadata>, and <data>. The program changes the last name of the first row that was retrieved in the rowset. You may observe that the rowset keeps track of the changes that are made in its data, as shown by the presence of a <updateRow> element for the first row. You may get a different output when you run this program. The output depends on the data you have in the person table.

Listing 6-25. Exporting State of a WebRowSet as an XML Document

```
// WebRowSetXMLTest.java
package com.jdojo.jdbc;

import java.io.StringWriter;
import java.sql.SQLException;
import javax.sql.rowset.RowSetFactory;
import javax.sql.rowset.WebRowSet;
```

```java
public class WebRowSetXMLTest {
        public static void main(String[] args) {
                RowSetFactory factory = RowSetUtil.getRowSetFactory();

                // Use a try-with-resources block
                try (WebRowSet webRs = factory.createWebRowSet()) {
                        // Set the connection parameters for the WebRowSet
                        RowSetUtil.setConnectionParameters(webRs);

                        String sqlCommand = "select person_id, first_name, last_name " +
                                            "from person " +
                                            "where person_id between ? and ?";

                        webRs.setCommand(sqlCommand);
                        webRs.setInt(1, 101);
                        webRs.setInt(2, 102);
                        webRs.execute();

                        // Change the last name for the first record
                        if (webRs.first()) {
                                webRs.updateString("last_name", "Who knows?");
                        }

                        // Get the XML representation of of the WebRowSet
                        StringWriter sw = new StringWriter();
                        webRs.writeXml(sw);
                        String webRsXML = sw.toString();

                        // Print the exported XML from the WebRowSet
                        System.out.println(webRsXML);
                }
                catch (SQLException e) {
                        e.printStackTrace();
                }
        }
}
```

```xml
<?xml version="1.0"?>
<webRowSet xmlns="http://java.sun.com/xml/ns/jdbc" xmlns:xsi="http://www.w3.org/2001/
  XMLSchema-instance"
xsi:schemaLocation="http://java.sun.com/xml/ns/jdbc http://java.sun.com/xml/ns/jdbc/webrowset.xsd">
  <properties>
    <command>select person_id, first_name, last_name from person where person_id between ? and
      ?</command>
    <concurrency>1008</concurrency>
    <datasource><null/></datasource>
    <escape-processing>true</escape-processing>
    <fetch-direction>1000</fetch-direction>
    <fetch-size>0</fetch-size>
    <isolation-level>2</isolation-level>
    <key-columns>
    </key-columns>
```

```xml
    <map>
    </map>
    <max-field-size>0</max-field-size>
    <max-rows>0</max-rows>
    <query-timeout>0</query-timeout>
    <read-only>true</read-only>
    <rowset-type>ResultSet.TYPE_SCROLL_INSENSITIVE</rowset-type>
    <show-deleted>false</show-deleted>
    <table-name>person</table-name>
    <url>jdbc:derby:beginningJavaDB;create=true;</url>
    <sync-provider>
      <sync-provider-name>com.sun.rowset.providers.RIOptimisticProvider</sync-provider-name>
      <sync-provider-vendor>Oracle Corporation</sync-provider-vendor>
      <sync-provider-version>1.0</sync-provider-version>
      <sync-provider-grade>2</sync-provider-grade>
      <data-source-lock>1</data-source-lock>
    </sync-provider>
  </properties>
  <metadata>
    <column-count>3</column-count>
    <column-definition>
      <column-index>1</column-index>
      <auto-increment>false</auto-increment>
      <case-sensitive>false</case-sensitive>
      <currency>false</currency>
      <nullable>0</nullable>
      <signed>true</signed>
      <searchable>true</searchable>
      <column-display-size>11</column-display-size>
      <column-label>PERSON_ID</column-label>
      <column-name>PERSON_ID</column-name>
      <schema-name>ROOT</schema-name>
      <column-precision>10</column-precision>
      <column-scale>0</column-scale>
      <table-name>PERSON</table-name>
      <catalog-name></catalog-name>
      <column-type>4</column-type>
      <column-type-name>INTEGER</column-type-name>
    </column-definition>
    <column-definition>
      <column-index>2</column-index>
      <auto-increment>false</auto-increment>
      <case-sensitive>true</case-sensitive>
      <currency>false</currency>
      <nullable>0</nullable>
      <signed>false</signed>
      <searchable>true</searchable>
      <column-display-size>20</column-display-size>
      <column-label>FIRST_NAME</column-label>
      <column-name>FIRST_NAME</column-name>
      <schema-name>ROOT</schema-name>
      <column-precision>20</column-precision>
      <column-scale>0</column-scale>
```

```
        <table-name>PERSON</table-name>
        <catalog-name></catalog-name>
        <column-type>12</column-type>
        <column-type-name>VARCHAR</column-type-name>
      </column-definition>
      <column-definition>
        <column-index>3</column-index>
        <auto-increment>false</auto-increment>
        <case-sensitive>true</case-sensitive>
        <currency>false</currency>
        <nullable>0</nullable>
        <signed>false</signed>
        <searchable>true</searchable>
        <column-display-size>20</column-display-size>
        <column-label>LAST_NAME</column-label>
        <column-name>LAST_NAME</column-name>
        <schema-name>ROOT</schema-name>
        <column-precision>20</column-precision>
        <column-scale>0</column-scale>
        <table-name>PERSON</table-name>
        <catalog-name></catalog-name>
        <column-type>12</column-type>
        <column-type-name>VARCHAR</column-type-name>
      </column-definition>
    </metadata>
    <data>
      <currentRow>
        <columnValue>101</columnValue>
        <columnValue>John</columnValue>
        <columnValue>Jacobs</columnValue>
        <updateRow>Who knows?</updateRow>
      </currentRow>
      <currentRow>
        <columnValue>102</columnValue>
        <columnValue>Donna</columnValue>
        <columnValue>Duncan</columnValue>
      </currentRow>
    </data>
</webRowSet>
```

Who decides the format of the XML that a WebRowSet implementation should understand? If all implementations of the WebRowSet use different XML formats, the XML exported from a WebRowSet using one implementation cannot be imported into a WebRowSet object that uses another implementation. To avoid this kind of portability issues, Oracle provides an XML schema for the format of the standard WebRowSet XML. The schema is available at http://java.sun.com/xml/ns/jdbc/webrowset.xsd. A standard WebRowSet implementation should use this schema to export and import a WebRowSet implementation to ensure portability with other implementations.

FilteredRowSet

The FilteredRowSet interface inherits from the WebRowSet interface. It provides filtering capability to a rowset at the client side. You can apply a filter to the rowset by using a where clause in its SQL command, which is executed in a database. A FilteredRowSet lets you filter the rows of a rowset after it has retrieved the data from a database. You can think of a FilteredRowSet as a rowset that lets you view its rows based on a set of criteria, which is called a *filter*. Setting a filter to a rowset does not delete the rows from the rowset. Rather, it lets you access only those rows that meet the filter criteria. The filter also applies to inserting, updating, and deleting the rows in the rowset. You can only read, insert, update, and delete rows that meet the filter criteria. You can reset the filter any time you want to view all rows of a rowset. A filter is an object of a class that implements the javax.sql.rowset.Predicate interface. The following is the declaration of the Predicate interface:

```
public interface Predicate {
        boolean evaluate(RowSet rs);
        boolean evaluate(Object value, int colIndex) throws SQLException;
        boolean evaluate(Object value, String colName) throws SQLException;
}
```

If the evaluate() method returns true for a row, it is visible. Otherwise, it is filtered out and you cannot access it. All of the three versions of the evaluate() methods are called internally. The reference implementation for the rowset by Oracle does not supply an implementation for the Predicate interface. I will discuss an implementation of the Predicate interface in this section.

The FilteredRowSet interface adds two methods, one to set a filter and one to get the filter:

- Predicate getFilter()

- void setFilter(Predicate filter) throws SQLException

The setFilter() method sets a filter to the rowset. Setting null as a filter resets (or removes) the filter from a FilteredRowSet and makes all rows accessible. You can set a filter to a FilteredRowSet as follows:

```
// Create a FilteredRowSet
FilteredRowSet filteredRs = create a filtered row set;

// Set properties and retrieve data in the rowset

// Create a Filter
Predicate filter = create a filter object;

// Set the filter
filteredRs.setFilter(filter);

// Work with the filtered rowset here

// Remove the filter
filteredRs.setFilter(null);
```

Listing 6-26 contains the code that implements a range filter. It is based on a range of a numeric column.

Listing 6-26. An Implementation of the Predicate Interface

```
// RangeFilter.java
package com.jdojo.jdbc;

import java.sql.SQLException;
import javax.sql.RowSet;
import javax.sql.rowset.Predicate;
```

```java
public class RangeFilter implements Predicate {
        private final int columnIndex;
        private final String columnName;
        private final double min;
        private final double max;

        public RangeFilter(int columnIndex, String columnName,
                double min, double max) {
                this.columnIndex = columnIndex;
                this.columnName = columnName;
                this.min = min;
                this.max = max;
        }

        @Override
        public boolean evaluate(RowSet rs) {
                // Make sure we have a good row number to evaluate
                try {
                        if (rs.getRow() <= 0) {
                                return false;
                        }
                }
                catch (SQLException e) {
                        e.printStackTrace();
                }

                boolean showRow = false;
                Object value = null;

                try {
                        value = rs.getObject(columnName);
                        if (value instanceof Number) {
                                double num = ((Number) value).doubleValue();
                                showRow = (num >=min && num <= max);
                        }
                }
                catch (SQLException e) {
                        showRow = false;
                        e.printStackTrace();
                        throw new RuntimeException(e);
                }
                return showRow;
        }

        @Override
        public boolean evaluate(Object value, int columnIndex) {
                boolean showRow = false;
                if (columnIndex == this.columnIndex
                        && value instanceof Number) {
                        double num = ((Number) value).doubleValue();
                        showRow = (num >=min && num <= max);
                }
```

```
                return showRow;
        }

        @Override
        public boolean evaluate(Object value, String columnName) {
                boolean showRow = false;
                if (this.columnName.equalsIgnoreCase(columnName)
                        && value instanceof Number) {
                        double num = ((Number)value).doubleValue();
                        showRow = (num >=min && num <= max);
                }
                return showRow;
        }
}
```

Suppose person_id is the first column in your rowset and you want to see only rows that have person_id between 101 and 501. You can set a filter for the rowset using an object of the RangeFilter class as follows:

```
FilteredRowSet filteredRs = get a filtered row set...;
Predicate filter = new RangeFilter(1, "person_id", 101, 501);
filteredRs.setFilter(filter);
```

The RangeFilter class is a simple implementation of the Predicate interface. You need to have a little more sophisticated implementation that can be used in a production environment. For example, you may allow a filter criteria based on multiple columns.

Listing 6-27 demonstrates how to use a FilteredRowSet. The output of this program will depend on the data in the person table. A FilteredRowSet is not an alternative to using a filter in a SQL SELECT (using a WHERE clause). You should not retrieve a large number of rows in a FilteredRowSet and set a filter. It may degrade your application performance. You should use it when you get a disconnected (or cached) rowset in your program and you do not have control over its retrieval process. It is also useful if your FilteredRowSet is not representing rows from a database table such as if you are retrieving data from a flat file.

Listing 6-27. Using a FilteredRowSet

```
// FilteredRowSetTest.java
package com.jdojo.jdbc;

import java.sql.SQLException;
import javax.sql.rowset.Predicate;
import javax.sql.rowset.FilteredRowSet;
import javax.sql.rowset.RowSetFactory;

public class FilteredRowSetTest {
        public static void main(String[] args) {
                RowSetFactory factory = RowSetUtil.getRowSetFactory();

                // Use a try-with-resources block
                try (FilteredRowSet filteredRs
                        = factory.createFilteredRowSet()) {
                        // Set the connection parameters
                        RowSetUtil.setConnectionParameters(filteredRs);
```

```
                        // Prepare, set, and execute the command
                        String sqlCommand= "select person_id, first_name, last_name " +
                                        "from person";
                        filteredRs.setCommand(sqlCommand);
                        filteredRs.execute();

                        // Print the retrieved records
                        System.out.println("Before Filter - Row count: " +
                                filteredRs.size());
                        RowSetUtil.printPersonRecord(filteredRs);

                        // Set a filter
                        Predicate filter = new RangeFilter(1, "person_id", 101, 102);
                        filteredRs.setFilter(filter);

                        // Print the retrieved records
                        System.out.println("After Filter - Row count: " +
                                filteredRs.size());
                        filteredRs.beforeFirst();
                        RowSetUtil.printPersonRecord(filteredRs);
                }
                catch (SQLException e) {
                        e.printStackTrace();
                }
        }
}
```

JoinRowSet

The JoinRowSet interface inherits from the WebRowSet interface. It provides the ability to combine (or join) two or more disconnected rowsets into one rowset. Rows from two or more tables are joined in a query using a SQL JOIN. A JoinRowSet lets you have a SQL JOIN between two or more rowsets without using a SQL JOIN in a query.

Using a JoinRowSet is easy. You retrieve data in multiple rowsets: CachedRowSet, WebRowSet, or FilteredRowSet. Create an empty JoinRowSet and add all rowsets to it by calling its addRowSet() method. The first rowset that is added to the JoinRowSet becomes the reference rowset for establishing the joins when more rowsets are added. You can specify the JOIN columns in a rowset individually or when you add a rowset to a JoinRowSet.

There are five standard types of SQL JOIN:

- INNER_JOIN

- LEFT_OUTER_JOIN

- RIGHT_OUTER_JOIN

- FULL_JOIN

- CROSS_JOIN

A JoinRowSet lets you establish all of the above-mentioned SQL JOINs between rowsets. Except for CROSS_JOIN, which gives you a Cartesian product of rows in the rowsets, all other joins are based on matching columns in the joined rowsets. There are two ways to specify matching columns:

- If a rowset that is participating in the JOIN implements the Joinable interface, you can use one of its setMatchColumn() methods to specify the JOIN columns. The Joinable interface defines multiple versions of the setMatchColumn() method and other methods to work with JOIN columns.

- You can set the JOIN columns when you add a rowset to a JoinRowSet using one of its addRowSet() methods.

An implementation of the JoinRowSet interface may not support all five types of JOINs. You can use the following five methods of the JoinRowSet interface to check if an implementation supports a specific SQL JOIN type:

- boolean supportsInnerJoin()

- boolean supportsLeftOuterJoin()

- boolean supportsRightOuterJoin()

- boolean supportsFullJoin()

- boolean supportsCrossJoin()

You can specify a JOIN type in a JoinRowSet using its setJoinType() method, which accepts one of the five JOIN constants: INNER_JOIN, LEFT_OUTER_JOIN, RIGHT_OUTER_JOIN, FULL_JOIN, and CROSS_JOIN. By default, it uses INNER_JOIN, which is based on equality of matching columns.

You must have at least two rowsets to work with a JoinRowSet. It does not make sense to have a JoinRowSet to hold rows from only one rowset. Its name, "Join," itself implies that it represents a JOIN between at least two rowsets. The names or indexes of the columns in the joined rowsets do not have to be the same. The data types of the join columns need not be the same. However, data types of the join columns must be such that their values can be compared.

You have only been working with the person table in the previous examples. You can still work with only one table to form a SQL JOIN based on person_id column. Your first rowset will select person_id and first_name from the person table. The second rowset will select person_id and last_name from the person table. You will join the two rowsets based on person_id using INNER_JOIN, which is the default for a JoinRowSet. Listing 6-28 shows how to achieve this using a JoinRowSet.

Listing 6-28. Establishing SQL JOINs Using a JoinRowSet

```java
// JoinRowSetTest.java
package com.jdojo.jdbc;

import java.sql.SQLException;
import javax.sql.rowset.CachedRowSet;
import javax.sql.rowset.JoinRowSet;
import javax.sql.rowset.RowSetFactory;

public class JoinRowSetTest {
    public static void main(String[] args) {
        RowSetFactory factory = RowSetUtil.getRowSetFactory();

        // Use a try-with-resources block
        try (CachedRowSet cachedRs1 = factory.createCachedRowSet();
                CachedRowSet cachedRs2 = factory.createCachedRowSet();
                JoinRowSet joinRs = factory.createJoinRowSet() ) {
            // Set the connection parameters
            RowSetUtil.setConnectionParameters(cachedRs1);
            RowSetUtil.setConnectionParameters(cachedRs2);
```

```
                    String sqlCommand1 = "select person_id, first_name " +
                                         "from person " +
                                         "where person_id in (101, 102)";

                    String sqlCommand2 = "select person_id, last_name " +
                                         "from person " +
                                         "where person_id in (101, 102, 103)";

                    cachedRs1.setCommand(sqlCommand1);
                    cachedRs2.setCommand(sqlCommand2);

                    cachedRs1.execute();
                    cachedRs2.execute();

                    // Create a JoinRowSet for cachedRs1 and cachedRs2
                    // joining them based on the person_id column
                    joinRs.addRowSet(cachedRs1, "person_id");
                    joinRs.addRowSet(cachedRs2, "person_id");

                    System.out.println("Row Count: " + joinRs.size());
                    RowSetUtil.printPersonRecord(joinRs);
            }
            catch (SQLException e) {
                    e.printStackTrace();
            }
        }
}
```

You can add only a non-empty rowset to a JoinRowSet. Adding an empty rowset to a JoinRowSet throws a SQLException. The JoinRowSet can implement the SQL JOIN based on multiple columns. There is no limit on the number of rowsets added to a JoinRowSet. However, care should be taken not to add too many rowsets with a large number of rows to a JoinRowSet. This may slow down the application because of the processing needed to perform the JOIN operation on large number of rows.

The toCachedRowSet() method of the JoinRowSet returns a CachedRowSet that represents the rows based on the JOIN established in it. The returned CachedRowSet does not contain any changes made to the data through the JoinRowSet. You can make modifications to the data in a JoinRowSet and apply the changes back to the database, as you would do with a CachedRowSet. Make sure that you set the required properties for the JoinRowSet before you call the acceptChanges() method. For example, you will need to set its database connection properties, its command, etc., so it will have the required pieces of information to apply the changes to the database.

Working with a Large Object (LOB)

The JDBC API has support for working with large objects stored in a database. The type of a large object could be one of the following.

- Binary Large Object (Blob)
- Character Large Object (Clob)
- National Character Large Object (NClob)

The data for LOB columns is usually not stored in a database table itself. The database stores the data for a LOB at some other location. It stores a reference (or pointer) to the data location in the table. The reference for a LOB stored in the table is also called a *locator*. Whether a LOB column's data is stored with the table or at other location is determined by the DBMS based on some criteria. For example, a DBMS may decide that if the size of a LOB is smaller than 10k, it will store it in the table and if it grows bigger, it will be stored at some other location and the table will store a locator instead. When you retrieve the data for a column of a LOB type, usually a JDBC driver retrieves only the locator for the LOB. When you need the actual data, you need to perform some more operations on the locator to fetch the data. Usually a locator for a LOB has more information about the data than just being a pointer to the actual data, such as it knows the length of the data.

A Blob is used to store binary data. A Clob is used to store character data. An NClob is used to store Unicode character data. Consult your DBMS documentation about the data type name that it uses for Blob, Clob, and NClob types of LOBs. Oracle DBMS has the same names as Blob, Clob, and NClob, as data types that you can use to define columns in a table. The JDBC API lets you work with Blob, Clob, and NClob using the java.sql.Blob, java.sql.Clob, and java.sql.NClob interfaces, respectively.

You will work through an example of using Blob and Clob data types. The example will use a Java DB database. Java DB supports Blob and NClob types for LOBs through its Blob and Clob database data types, respectively.

Let's create a table named person_detail, which is used to store a person's picture as Blob and his text-only resume in a Clob column. The following is the script to create the table in Java DB:

```
create table person_detail (
        person_detail_id integer not null,
        person_id integer not null,
        picture blob,
        resume clob,
        primary key (person_detail_id),
        foreign key (person_id) references person(person_id)
);
```

You can run the program in Listing 6-29 to create the person_detail table in a Java DB database, assuming that the JDBCUtil.getConnection() method is configured to return a Connection to a Java DB database. If you are using a DBMS other than Java DB, please change the CREATE TABLE script of the program in Listing 6-29 to match the syntax of your database.

Listing 6-29. Create the person_detail Table in Java DB

```java
// CreatePersonDetailTable.java
package com.jdojo.jdbc;

import java.sql.Connection;
import java.sql.SQLException;
import java.sql.Statement;

public class CreatePersonDetailTable {
        public static void main(String[] args) {
                Connection conn = null;
                try {
                        conn = JDBCUtil.getConnection();

                        // Create a SQL string
                        String SQL = "create table person_detail( " +
                                "person_detail_id integer not null, " +
                                "person_id integer not null, " +
```

```
                                "picture blob, " +
                                "resume clob, " +
                                "primary key (person_detail_id), " +
                                "foreign key (person_id) references person(person_id))";

                Statement stmt = null;
                try {
                        stmt = conn.createStatement();
                        stmt.executeUpdate(SQL);
                }
                finally {
                        JDBCUtil.closeStatement(stmt);
                }

                // Commit the transaction
                JDBCUtil.commit(conn);
                System.out.println("Person table created successfully.");
        }
        catch (SQLException e) {
                System.out.println(e.getMessage());
                JDBCUtil.rollback(conn);
        }
        finally {
                JDBCUtil.closeConnection(conn);
        }
    }
}
```

Retrieving LOB Data

You can retrieve Blob, Clob and NClob column's data from a result set using the getBlob(), getClob(), and getNClob() methods of the ResultSet interface, respectively. These methods return an object of the java.sql.Blob, java.sql.Clob, and java.sql.NClob interfaces, respectively. These interfaces include many methods that let you query the LOB object and manipulate the data they represent. The following snippet of code reads rows from the person_detail table for the person_detail_id equal to 1001:

```
Connection conn = JDBCUtil.getConnection();
String SQL = "select person_id, picture, resume " +
             "from person_detail " +
             "where person_detail_id = ?";

PreparedStatement pstmt = null;
pstmt = conn.prepareStatement(SQL);
pstmt.setInt(1, 1001);
ResultSet rs = pstmt.executeQuery();

while(rs.next()) {
        int personId = rs.getInt("person_id");
        Blob pictureBlob = rs.getBlob("picture");
        Clob resumeClob = rs.getClob("resume");
}
```

After you get a Blob or Clob object from the ResultSet, you will need to read the data. Blob and Clob interfaces contain a length() method, which returns the number of bytes in a Blob object and the number of characters in a Clob object. The NClob interface inherits the Clob interface. The discussion for the Clob interface also applies to the NClob interface. If you want to read a Blob's data in a byte array and the Clob's data in a String object, here is how you do it. Note that the length() method of the Blob and Clob interfaces returns long.

```
// Read picture in a byte array
int pictureLength = (int)pictureBlob.length();
byte[] pictureData = pictureBlob.getBytes(1, pictureLength);

// Read resume in a string
int resumeLength = (int)resumeClob.length();
String resume = resumeClob.getSubString(1, resumeLength);
```

In the getBytes(int start, int length) method of the Blob interface, the first parameter is the starting position of the byte in the Blob object from where you want to start, and the second parameter is the number of bytes you want to read. The position of the first byte in a Blob object is 1, not 0. Similarly, the getSubString(int start, int length) method of the Clob interface accepts the starting position of the character in a Clob object and the number of characters to return. The position of the first character in a Clob object is 1, not 0.

▪ **Tip** Be careful when using the starting position in any context in JDBC programs. In the JDBC API, things start at position 1, and in other parts of Java such as arrays, things start at position 0.

Most of the time, you will not read the Blob's and Clob's data in an array or a String object. They may contain big amounts of data. The Blob and Clob interfaces let you read their data in chunks using an InputStream and a Reader, respectively. Typically, you would read the data from Blob and Clob objects and store them in a file on a disk. Here is how you do it. The Blob interface contains a getBinaryStream() method, which returns an InputStream. You can use that InputStream to read data contained in the Blob object. Similarly, the Clob interface contains a getCharacterStream() method, which returns a Reader. You can use that Reader object to read characters contained in the Clob object.

```
// Read picture data and save it to a file
String pictureFilePath = "c:\\mypicture.bmp";
FileOutputStream fos = new FileOutputStream(pictureFilePath);
InputStream in = pictureBlob.getBinaryStream();
int b = -1;

while((b = in.read()) != -1) {
        fos.write((byte)b);
}

fos.close();

// Read resume data and save it to a file
String resumeFilePath = "c:\\myresume.txt";
FileWriter fw = new FileWriter(resumeFilePath);
Reader reader = resumeClob.getCharacterStream();
```

```
int b = -1;
while((b = reader.read()) != -1) {
        fw.write((char)b);
}

fw.close();
```

Creating a LOB Data

In the previous section, you learned how to read LOB data from the database into a Java program. In this section, you will learn how to create a LOB in a Java program and send the LOB data to the database to store it in a table's column. The Connection interface contains three methods to create a LOB:

- Blob createBlob() throws SQLException

- Clob createClob() throws SQLException

- NClob createNClob() throws SQLException

You can use one of the methods to create an empty LOB of a specific type. For example, to store a picture and resume in a database, you would create a Blob object and a Clob object as follows:

```
Connection conn = JDBCUtil.getConnection();
Blob pictureBlob = conn.createBlob();
Clob resumeClob = conn.createClob();
```

Once you get the Blob and Clob objects, there are two ways to write data to them. You can write data to a Blob object using its setBytes() method, which accepts the position in the Blob object where you want to write, and the data in a byte array. You can also write data to a Blob object using an OutputStream. You need to call its setBinaryStream() method, which accepts the starting position for writing the data and returns an OutputStream. You need to use that OutputStream to write data to the Blob. Here are the two method's signatures:

- int setBytes(long pos, byte[] bytes) throws SQLException

- OutputStream setBinaryStream(long pos) throws SQLException

The following snippet of code shows how to write data to a Blob. It reads data from a file, which stores a picture, and writes all bytes to a Blob object. The while-loop reads one byte at a time from the file to keep the code simple and readable. In real-world programs, you will read and write a bigger chunk of data at a time.

```
// Get the output stream of the Blob object to write the picture data to it.
int startPosition = 1; // start writing from beginning
OutputStream out = pictureBlob.setBinaryStream(startPosition);

// Get ready to read from a file
String picturePath = "picture.jpg";
FileInputStream fis = new FileInputStream(picturePath);

// Read from the file and write to the Blob object
int b = -1;
while ((b = fis.read()) != -1) {
        out.write(b);
}
fis.close();
out.close();
```

The Clob interface provides the following three methods to write data to a Clob object:

- `int setString(long pos, String str) throws SQLException`
- `int setString(long pos, String str, int offset, int len) throws SQLException`
- `Writer setCharacterStream(long pos) throws SQLException`

The setString() method lets you write a String to it at a specified position. The second version of the setString() method lets you specify the offset into the source string to start reading and the number of characters to be read from the source string. The setCharacterStream() method returns a Writer, which you can use to write data in Unicode characters to the Clob. The Clob interface also contains a setAsciiStream() method, which returns an OutputStream that you can use to write the ASCII-encoded characters.

The following snippet of code shows how to write data to a Clob. It reads data from a file, which stores a resume in a text format and writes all characters to a Clob object. The while-loop reads one character at a time from the file to keep the code simple and readable. In real-world programs, you will read and write a bigger chunk of characters at a time.

```
// Get the Character output stream of the Clob object to write the resume data to it.
int startPosition = 1; // start writing from beginning
Writer writer = resumeClob.setCharacterStream(startPosition);

// Get ready to read from a file
String resumePath = "resume.txt";
FileReader fr = new FileReader(resumePath);

// Read from the file and write to the Clob object
int b = -1;
while ((b = fr.read()) != -1) {
        writer.write(b);
}
fr.close();
writer.close();
```

Finally, it is time to write the LOB's data to a database. You can use the setBlob() and setClob() methods of the PreparedStatement interface to set the Blob and Clob data as shown:

```
Connection conn = JDBCUtil.getConnection();
String SQL = "insert into person_detail " +
             "(person_detail_id, person_id, picture, resume) " +
             "values " +
             "(?, ?, ?, ?)";

PreparedStatement pstmt = null;
pstmt = conn.prepareStatement(SQL);
pstmt.setInt(1, 1);   // set person_detail_id
pstmt.setInt(2, 101); // Set person_id

Blob pictureBlob = conn.createBlob();

// Write data to pictureBlob object here

pstmt.setBlob(3, pictureBlob);
```

```
Clob resumeClob = conn.createClob();

// Write data to resumeClob object here

pstmt.setClob(4, resumeClob);

// Insert the record into the database
pstmt.executeUpdate();
```

The ResultSet interface also includes the updateBlob() and updateClob() methods, which you can use to update Blob and Clob objects through a ResultSet object. Blob and Clob objects may require a lot of resources. Once you are done with them, you need to free the resources held by them by calling their free() method.

■ **Tip**   Another way to set a Blob object's data in a PreparedStatement is to use its setBinaryStream() and setObject() methods. Another way to set Clob object's data in a PreparedStatement is to use its setAsciiStream(), setCharacterStream(), or setObject() method.

Listing 6-30 contains the complete code that shows how to insert a record in a table that contains Blob and Clob columns. It has been tested in Java DB. It reads the data of a picture from a file named picture.jpg and a resume from a file named resume.txt. Both files are assumed to be in the current directory. If the files do not exist, the program prints a message with their expected full path. Please change the file paths in the main() method if you want to use different files. The program inserts a record in the person_detail table and retrieves the same data and saves it to the local disk in the current directory. Running the program more than once will print an error message because it will try inserting a duplicate record in the person_detail table. Person details will be retrieved every time you run the program.

Listing 6-30. Reading and Writing Blob and Clob Data Database Columns

```java
// LOBTest.java
package com.jdojo.jdbc;

import java.io.FileInputStream;
import java.io.FileNotFoundException;
import java.io.FileOutputStream;
import java.io.FileReader;
import java.io.FileWriter;
import java.io.IOException;
import java.io.InputStream;
import java.io.OutputStream;
import java.io.Reader;
import java.io.Writer;
import java.nio.file.Files;
import java.nio.file.Path;
import java.nio.file.Paths;
import java.sql.Blob;
import java.sql.Clob;
import java.sql.Connection;
import java.sql.PreparedStatement;
import java.sql.ResultSet;
import java.sql.SQLException;
```

```java
public class LOBTest {
    public static void main(String[] args) {
        Connection conn = null;
        try {
            conn = JDBCUtil.getConnection();

            // Insert a record in the person_detail table. Files
            // picture.jpg and resume.txt are assumed to be in
            // the working directory
            String inPicturePath = "picture.jpg";
            String inResumePath = "resume.txt";

            // Make sure that the files exist
            ensureFileExistence(inPicturePath);
            ensureFileExistence(inResumePath);

            try {
                // Insert a person_detail record
                insertPersonDetail(conn, 1, 101,
                        inPicturePath, inResumePath);

                // Commit the transaction
                JDBCUtil.commit(conn);

                System.out.println(
                        "Inserted person details successfully");
            }
            catch(SQLException e) {
                System.out.print("Inserting person details failed: ");
                System.out.println(e.getMessage());
                JDBCUtil.rollback(conn);
            }

            // These files will be created in the current directory
            String outPicturePath = "out_picture.jpg";
            String outResumePath = "out_resume.txt";

            try {
                // Read the person_detail record
                retrievePersonDetails(conn, 1,
                        outPicturePath, outResumePath);

                // Commit the transaction
                JDBCUtil.commit(conn);

                System.out.println(
                "Retrieved and saved person details successfully.");
            }
            catch(SQLException e) {
                System.out.print("Retrieving person details failed: ");
                System.out.println(e.getMessage());
```

```
                                    JDBCUtil.rollback(conn);
                        }
                }
                catch (Exception e) {
                        System.out.println(e.getMessage());
                        JDBCUtil.rollback(conn);
                }
                finally {
                        JDBCUtil.closeConnection(conn);
                }
        }

        public static void insertPersonDetail(Connection conn,
                int personDetailId,
                int personId,
                String pictureFilePath,
                String resumeFilePath)
                throws SQLException {

                String SQL = "insert into person_detail " +
                        "(person_detail_id, person_id, picture, resume) " +
                        "values " +
                        "(?, ?, ?, ?)";

                PreparedStatement pstmt = null;
                try {
                        pstmt = conn.prepareStatement(SQL);
                        pstmt.setInt(1, personDetailId);
                        pstmt.setInt(2, personId);

                        // Set the picture data
                        if (pictureFilePath != null) {
                                // We need to create a Blob object first
                                Blob pictureBlob = conn.createBlob();
                                readInPictureData(pictureBlob, pictureFilePath);
                                pstmt.setBlob(3, pictureBlob);
                        }

                        // Set the resume data
                        if (resumeFilePath != null) {
                                // We need to create a Clob object first
                                Clob resumeClob = conn.createClob();
                                readInResumeData(resumeClob, resumeFilePath);
                                pstmt.setClob(4, resumeClob);
                        }

                        pstmt.executeUpdate();
                }
                catch (IOException | SQLException e) {
                        throw new SQLException(e);
                }
```

```java
        finally {
                JDBCUtil.closeStatement(pstmt);
        }
}

public static void retrievePersonDetails(Connection conn,
        int personDetailId,
        String picturePath,
        String resumePath) throws SQLException {

        String SQL = "select person_id, picture, resume " +
                    "from person_detail " +
                    "where person_detail_id = ?";

        PreparedStatement pstmt = null;
        try {
                pstmt = conn.prepareStatement(SQL);
                pstmt.setInt(1, personDetailId);
                ResultSet rs = pstmt.executeQuery();

                while (rs.next()) {
                        int personId = rs.getInt("person_id");
                        Blob pictureBlob = rs.getBlob("picture");
                        if (pictureBlob != null) {
                                savePicture(pictureBlob, picturePath);
                                pictureBlob.free();
                        }

                        Clob resumeClob = rs.getClob("resume");
                        if (resumeClob != null) {
                                saveResume(resumeClob, resumePath);
                                resumeClob.free();
                        }
                }
        }
        catch (IOException | SQLException e) {
                throw new SQLException(e);
        }
        finally {
                JDBCUtil.closeStatement(pstmt);
        }
}

public static void readInPictureData(Blob pictureBlob,
        String pictureFilePath)
        throws FileNotFoundException, IOException, SQLException {

        // Get the output stream of the Blob object to write
        // the picture data to it.
        int startPosition = 1; // start writing from the beginning
        OutputStream out = pictureBlob.setBinaryStream(startPosition);
```

```
            FileInputStream fis = new FileInputStream(pictureFilePath);

            // Read from the file and write to the Blob object
            int b = -1;
            while ((b = fis.read()) != -1) {
                    out.write(b);
            }

            fis.close();
            out.close();
    }

    public static void readInResumeData(Clob resumeClob,
            String resumeFilePath)
            throws FileNotFoundException, IOException, SQLException {

            // Get the character output stream of the Clob object
            // to write the resume data to it.
            int startPosition = 1; // start writing from the beginning
            Writer writer = resumeClob.setCharacterStream(startPosition);
            FileReader fr = new FileReader(resumeFilePath);

            // Read from the file and write to the Clob object
            int b = -1;
            while ((b = fr.read()) != -1) {
                    writer.write(b);
            }
            fr.close();
            writer.close();
    }

    public static void savePicture(Blob pictureBlob, String filePath)
            throws SQLException, IOException {
            FileOutputStream fos = new FileOutputStream(filePath);
            InputStream in = pictureBlob.getBinaryStream();

            int b = -1;
            while ((b = in.read()) != -1) {
                    fos.write((byte) b);
            }

            fos.close();
    }

    public static void saveResume(Clob resumeClob, String filePath)
            throws SQLException, IOException {
            FileWriter fw = new FileWriter(filePath);
            Reader reader = resumeClob.getCharacterStream();

            int b = -1;
            while ((b = reader.read()) != -1) {
```

```
                fw.write((char) b);
            }

            fw.close();
    }

    public static void ensureFileExistence(String filePath) {
            Path path = Paths.get(filePath);
            if (!Files.exists(path)) {
                    throw new RuntimeException("File " +
                            path.toAbsolutePath() + " does not exist");
            }
    }
}
```

Batch Updates

You saw examples of using the Statement, PreparedStatement, and CallableStatement interfaces that let you send one SQL command (or stored procedure call) at a time to the database. The JDBC API includes a batch update feature that lets you send multiple update commands to a database in a batch (in one bundle) for execution. A batch update greatly improves performance. The update commands that you can use in a batch update are SQL INSERT, UPDATE, DELETE, and stored procedures. A command in a batch should not produce a result set. Otherwise, the JDBC driver will throw a SQLException. A command should generate an update count that will indicate the number of rows affected in the database by the execution of that command.

If you are using a Statement to execute a batch of commands, you can have heterogeneous commands in the same batch. For example, one command could be a SQL INSERT statement and another could be a SQL UPDATE statement.

If you are using a PreparedStatement or CallableStatement to execute a batch of commands, you will execute one command with multiple set of input parameters. A CallableStatement used in a batch update must return an update count and it should not produce a result set. Otherwise, the JDBC driver will throw a SQLException.

■ **Tip** Batch update is an optional feature that may be provided by a JDBC driver. If a JDBC driver supports a batch update, the supportsBatchUpdates() method of the DatabaseMetaData object will return true. You can get the DatabaseMetaData object using the getMetaData() method of a Connection object. You should turn off the auto-commit mode when executing batch updates, so you should be able to commit or rollback the entire batch. If the auto-commit mode is turned on, the commit behavior depends on the JDBC driver implementation when an error occurs executing one of the commands in the batch.

How do you execute multiple commands in a batch? It is a multi- step process.

1. Create a Statement, a PreparedStatement, or a CallableStatement by using an appropriate method of a Connection object. At this point, there is no difference between executing one command and using a batch of commands.

2. Use the addBatch() method to add a command to the batch. Each type of statement object maintains a list of batch commands internally. The addBatch() method adds the command to the internal list of batch commands. You need to call the addBatch() method once for each command in the batch that you want to bundle together for execution.

3.   If you want to clear the list of batch commands without executing them, you can call the clearBatch() method of the Statement interface to do so.

4.   Use the executeBatch() method to send the batch of commands to the database for execution in one go.

It is important to understand the behavior of the executeBatch() method of the Statement interface. It returns an array of int if all commands in the batch are executed successfully. The array contains as many elements as the number of commands in the batch. Each element in the array contains the update count that is returned from the command. The order of the element in the array is the same as the order of commands in the batch. Sometimes, a command in a batch may execute without an error, but the JDBC driver was not able to get the update count value. In such a case, a value of Statement.SUCCESS_NO_INFO is returned in the array.

■ **Tip**   Java 8 has added an executeLargeBatch() method to the Statement interface that works the same as the executeBatch method, except that it returns a long[] instead of an int[]. Use this method when you expect the update counts of any commands in the batch to exceed Integer.MAX_VALUE.

A JDBC driver throws a BatchUpdateException if a command in the batch fails to execute successfully. It is up to the JDBC driver whether it continues to execute the subsequent commands in the batch upon failure or stops the batch execution upon the first failure. How do you know which command failed in a batch? When a BatchUpdateException is thrown, you can use its getUpdateCounts(), which returns an array of int. The update count array contains the update counts of the commands that were executed in the batch. If a JDBC driver executes all commands in a batch irrespective of a failure, the returned array will contain as many elements as the number of commands in the batch. If a command failed, its corresponding value in the array will be Statement.EXECUTE_FAILED. If the getUpdateCounts() method of BatchUpdateException object returns fewer number of elements than the number of commands in the batch, it means that the JDBC driver stopped processing any commands after the first failure.

The following snippet of code shows how to use a Statement object to execute a batch update:

```
Connection conn = JDBCUtil.getConnection();
Statement stmt = conn.createStatement();

// Add batch update commands
stmt.addBatch("insert into t1...);
stmt.addBatch("insert into t2...);
stmt.addBatch("update t3 set...);
stmt.addBatch("delete from t4...);

// Execute the batch updates
int[] updateCount = null;

try {
        updatedCount = stmt.executeBatch();
        System.out.println("Batch executed successfully.");
}
catch (BatchUpdateException e) {
        System.out.println("Batch failed.");
}
```

The following snippet of code shows how to use a `PreparedStatement` object to execute a batch update. The logic will be the same if you use a `CallableStatement`, except for the construction of the SQL in the string format. The `addBatch()` method in the `PreparedStatement` interface does not accept any parameter.

```java
String sql = "delete from person where person_id = ?";

Connection conn = JDBCUtil.getConnection();
PreparedStatement pstmt = conn.prepareStatement(sql);

// Add two commands to the batch.
// Command #1: Set the input parameter and add it to the batch.
pstmt.setInt(201);
pstmt.addBatch();

// Command #1: Set the input parameter and add it to the batch.
pstmt.setInt(301);
pstmt.addBatch();

// Execute the batch update
int[] updateCount = null;

try {
        updatedCount = pstmt.executeBatch();
        System.out.println("Batch executed successfully.");
}
catch (BatchUpdateException e) {
        System.out.println("Batch failed.");
}
```

Listing 6-31 contains the complete code to demonstrate how to use a batch update. It also shows how to handle the results of a batch update returned from the executeUpdate() method and from a BatchUpdateException. The insertPersonStatement() and insertPersonPreparedStatement() methods do the same work: the first one uses a Statement and the second one uses a PreparedStatement. In the main() method, the call to the insertPersonPreparedStatement() method is commented. You need to use one of these methods, but not both.

Listing 6-31. Using the Batch Update Feature of the JDBC API

```java
// BatchUpdateTest.java
package com.jdojo.jdbc;

import java.sql.Connection;
import java.sql.SQLException;
import java.sql.Statement;
import java.sql.BatchUpdateException;
import java.sql.PreparedStatement;
import java.sql.Types;
import java.sql.Date;

public class BatchUpdateTest {
        public static void main(String[] args) {
                Connection conn = null;
```

```
            try {
                    conn = JDBCUtil.getConnection();

                    // Prepare the data
                    int[] personIds = {801, 901};
                    String[] firstNames = {"Matt", "Greg"};
                    String[] lastNames = {"Flower", "Rice"};
                    String[] genders = {"M", "M"};
                    String[] dobString = {"{d '1960-04-01'}",
                                          "{d '1962-03-01'}"};
                    double[] incomes = {56778.00, 89776.00};

                    // Use batch update using the Statement objects
                    insertPersonStatement(conn, personIds, firstNames,
                            lastNames, genders, dobString, incomes);

                    // Use batch update using the PreparedStatement objects
                    /*
                     java.sql.Date[] dobDate = {Date.valueOf("1960-04-01"),
                     Date.valueOf("1962-03-01") };
                     insertPersonPreparedStatement(conn, personIds,
                     firstNames,lastNames, genders, dobDate, incomes);
                     */

                    // Commit the transaction
                    JDBCUtil.commit(conn);
            }
            catch (SQLException e) {
                    System.out.println(e.getMessage());
                    JDBCUtil.rollback(conn);
            }
            finally {
                    JDBCUtil.closeConnection(conn);
            }
    }

    public static void insertPersonStatement(Connection conn,
            int[] personId,
            String[] firstName, String[] lastName,
            String[] gender, String[] dob,
            double[] income) throws SQLException {

        int[] updatedCount = null;
        Statement stmt = null;

        try {
                stmt = conn.createStatement();
                for (int i = 0; i < personId.length; i++) {
                        String SQL = "insert into person " +
                                "(person_id, first_name, last_name," +
                                " gender, dob, income) " +
```

```
                        "values " +
                        "(" + personId[i] + ", " +
                        "'" + firstName[i] + "'" + ", " +
                        "'" + lastName[i] + "'" + ", " +
                        "'" + gender[i] + "'" + ", " +
                        dob[i] + ", " +
                        income[i] + ")";

                // Add insert command to the batch
                stmt.addBatch(SQL);
        }

        // Execute the batch
        updatedCount = stmt.executeBatch();
        System.out.println("Batch executed successfully.");
        printBatchResult(updatedCount);
    }
    catch (BatchUpdateException e) {
        // Let us see how many commands were successful
        updatedCount = e.getUpdateCounts();

        System.out.println("Batch failed.");
        int commandCount = personId.length;
        if (updatedCount.length == commandCount) {
                System.out.println(
                        "JDBC driver continues to execute all"
                        + " commands in a batch after a failure.");
        }
        else {
                System.out.println(
                        "JDBC driver stops executing subsequent"
                        + " commands in a batch after a failure.");
        }

        // Re-throw the exception
        throw e;
    }
    finally {
        JDBCUtil.closeStatement(stmt);
    }
}

public static void insertPersonPreparedStatement(
        Connection conn, int[] personId,
        String[] firstName, String[] lastName,
        String[] gender, java.sql.Date[] dob,
        double[] income) throws SQLException {

    int[] updatedCount = null;
    String SQL = "Insert into person " +
            "(person_id, first_name, last_name, gender, dob," +
```

```
                          " income) " +
                          " values " +
                          "(?, ?, ?, ?, ?, ?)";

            PreparedStatement pstmt = null;
            try {
                    pstmt = conn.prepareStatement(SQL);

                    for (int i = 0; i < personId.length; i++) {
                            // Set input parameters
                            pstmt.setInt(1, personId[i]);
                            pstmt.setString(2, firstName[i]);
                            pstmt.setString(3, lastName[i]);
                            pstmt.setString(4, gender[i]);
                            if (dob[i] == null) {
                                    pstmt.setNull(5, Types.DATE);
                            }
                            else {
                                    pstmt.setDate(5, dob[i]);
                            }

                            pstmt.setDouble(6, income[i]);

                            // Add insert command with current input parameters
                            pstmt.addBatch();
                    }

                    // Execute the batch
                    updatedCount = pstmt.executeBatch();
                    System.out.println("Batch executed successfully.");
                    printBatchResult(updatedCount);
            }
            catch (BatchUpdateException e) {
                    // Let us see how many commands were successful
                    updatedCount = e.getUpdateCounts();
                    System.out.println("Batch failed.");
                    int commandCount = personId.length;
                    if (updatedCount.length == commandCount) {
                            System.out.println(
                                    "JDBC driver continues to execute all" +
                                    "commands in a batch after a failure.");
                    }
                    else {
                            System.out.println(
                                    "JDBC driver stops executing subsequent" +
                                    "commands in a batch after a failure.");
                    }

                    // Re-throw the exception
                    throw e;
            }
```

```
        finally {
                JDBCUtil.closeStatement(pstmt);
        }
    }

    public static void printBatchResult(int[] updateCount) {
            System.out.println("Batch Results...");
            for (int i = 0; i < updateCount.length; i++) {
                    int value = updateCount[i];
                    if (value >=0) {
                            System.out.println("Command #" + (i + 1)
                                    + ": Success. Update Count=" + value);
                    } else if (value >=Statement.SUCCESS_NO_INFO) {
                            System.out.println("Command #" + (i + 1)
                                    + ": Success. Update Count=Unknown");
                    } else if (value >=Statement.EXECUTE_FAILED) {
                            System.out.println("Command #" + (i + 1) + ": Failed");
                    }
            }
    }
}
```

Savepoints in a Transaction

A database transaction consists of one or more changes as a unit of work. A savepoint in a transaction is like a marker that marks a point in a transaction so that, if needed, the transaction can be rolled back (or undone) up to that point. Let's take an example of inserting five records in the person table, like so:

```
Connection conn = JDBCUtil.getConnection();
Statement stmt = conn.createStatement();
stmt.execute("insert into person..."); // insert 1
stmt.execute("insert into person..."); // insert 2
stmt.execute("insert into person..."); // insert 3
stmt.execute("insert into person..."); // insert 4
stmt.execute("insert into person..."); // insert 5
```

At this point, you have only two choices: either you commit the transaction, which will insert all five records in the person table, or you roll back the transaction, so that none of the five records will be inserted. You can perform a commit or rollback as

```
conn.commit(); // Save all five records
```

or

```
conn.rollback(); // Do not save any of the five records
```

A savepoint will let you set a marker in between any of the above two INSERT statements. An object of the Savepoint interface represents a savepoint in a transaction. To mark a savepoint in a transaction, you simply call the setSavepoint() method of the Connection. The setSavepoint() method is overloaded. One version accepts no argument and another accepts a string, which is the name of the savepoint. The setSavepoint() method returns a Savepoint object, which is your marker and you must keep it for future use. Let's rewrite the above logic using a savepoint after every INSERT statement.

```
Connection conn = JDBCUtil.getConnection();
Statement stmt = conn.createStatement();
stmt.execute("insert into person...");      // insert 1
Savepoint sp1 = conn.setSavepoint();        // savepoint 1
stmt.execute("insert into person...");      // insert 2
Savepoint sp2 = conn.setSavepoint();        // savepoint 2
stmt.execute("insert into person...");      // insert 3
Savepoint sp3 = conn.setSavepoint();        // savepoint 3
stmt.execute("insert into person...");      // insert 4
Savepoint sp4 = conn.setSavepoint();        // savepoint 4
stmt.execute("insert into person...");      // insert 5
```

At this point, you have finer control on the transaction if you want to undo any of the above five inserts into the person table. Now you can use another version of the rollback() method of the Connection object, which accepts a Savepoint object. If you want to undo all changes that were made after savepoint 4, you can do so as follows:

```
// Rolls back insert 5 only
conn.rollback(sp4);
```

If you want to undo all changes that were made after savepoint 2, you can do so as follows:

```
// Rolls back inserts 3, 4, and 5
conn.rollback(sp2);
```

If you roll back up to save point 1, only the first insert will remain in the transaction. Can you change your mind after you have rolled back to a save point? Suppose, after you call conn.rollback(sp2), you realize that you have made a mistake and you wanted to roll back insert 4, and 5 only, and not insert 3. The call to conn.rollback(sp2) will rollback three inserts: 3, 4, and 5. Do you have any choice to go back only up to savepoint 3 after you have gone back to save point 2? No. You do not have any choice in such cases. Once you roll back up to a savepoint (say, spx), all savepoints that were created after the savepoint spx are released and you cannot refer to them again. If you refer to a released savepoint, the JDBC driver will throw a SQLException. The following snippet of code will throw a SQLException:

```
conn.rollback(sp2); // Will release sp3, and sp4
conn.rollback(sp3); // Will throw an exception. sp3 is already released.
```

Note that when you roll back a transaction to a savepoint, that savepoint itself is not released. When you call conn.rollback(sp2), savepoint sp2 remains valid. You can add more savepoints afterwards and roll back up to savepoint sp2 again.

You can also release a savepoint explicitly by calling releaseSavepoint(Savepoint sp) method of a Connection object. Releasing a savepoint also releases all subsequent savepoints that were created after this savepoint. For example, calling conn.releaseSavepoint(sp2) will release savepoints sp2, sp3, and sp4. All savepoints in a transaction are released when the transaction is committed or rolled back entirely. A JDBC driver will throw a SQLException if you use the savepoint that has been released by any of the above-described means. Listing 6-32 shows how to use a savepoint in a transaction.

Listing 6-32. Using Savepoints in a Transaction

```java
// SavePointTest.java
package com.jdojo.jdbc;

import java.sql.Connection;
import java.sql.SQLException;
import java.sql.PreparedStatement;
import java.sql.Savepoint;

public class SavePointTest {
    public static void main(String[] args) {
        Connection conn = null;
        try {
            // Connect to the database
            conn = JDBCUtil.getConnection();
            conn.setAutoCommit(false);

            // SQL Statement
            String SQL = "update person " +
                            "set income = ? " +
                            "where person_id = ?";

            PreparedStatement pstmt = conn.prepareStatement(SQL);
            pstmt.setDouble(1, 20000);
            pstmt.setInt(2, 101);
            pstmt.execute();

            // Set a save point
            Savepoint sp1 = conn.setSavepoint();

            // Change the income to 25000 and execute the SQL again
            pstmt.setDouble(1, 25000);
            pstmt.execute();

            // Set a save point
            Savepoint sp2 = conn.setSavepoint();

            // Perform some more database changes here
            // Roll back the transaction to the save point sp1,
            // so that income for person_id 101 will remain set
            // to 20000 and not the 25000
            conn.rollback(sp1);

            // Commit the transaction
            JDBCUtil.commit(conn);
        }
        catch (SQLException e) {
            System.out.println(e.getMessage());
            JDBCUtil.rollback(conn);
        }
```

```
            finally {
                    JDBCUtil.closeConnection(conn);
            }
    }
}
```

■ **Tip** You can check if a JDBC driver supports savepoints by using the `supportsSavepoints()` method of the `DatabaseMetaData` object.

Using a DataSource

You need a `Connection` to communicate with a database. So far, you have been obtaining a `Connection` using the `DriverManager` class. You need to register the database driver with the `DriverManager` and specify the details of the database connection properties. All these things have to be done in the Java code that resides with the main application logic. If anything related to the database connectivity changes, you must change your code that deals with establishing the database connection.

The JDBC API provides another way to obtain a `Connection` in a Java application. You can use the `javax.sql.DataSource` interface to get a connection to a database. In this alternative way of working with database connections, things are separated into two logical modules: connection management and connection consumption.

- One module is responsible for configuring and deploying the `DataSource` objects on a server that allows lookup using a Java Naming and Directory Interface (JNDI) service. The configuration involves setting the properties for the `DataSource` object, which it will use to establish a connection to the database such as server name, port number, network protocol, etc. The deployment involves storing the configured `DataSource` object on a JNDI server by giving it a logical name. The deployment is also known as binding, because a `DataSource` object is bound to a logical name. Usually, a system administrator performs this step. The logical name that is given to a `DataSource` object is announced to the developers who need to look up the `DataSource` object. Typically, you use a `DataSource` in an application server, which uses J2EE technology. The application server provides you with a GUI tool to configure and deploy `DataSource` objects.

- The Java application, which needs an instance of a `Connection` object, performs a lookup using the JNDI API using the logical name of a `DataSource`. The lookup operation returns an instance of the `DataSource` interface. You can get a `Connection` object from a `DataSource` object using its `getConnection()` method. The `getConnection()` method is overloaded. One version accepts no parameter and another version accepts `userId` and `password` as parameters. The `getConnection()` method works similar to the `getConnection()` method of the `DriverManager` class. A developer performs this step.

Usually, you configure and deploy a `DataSource` on a server, which is available using a JNDI service. The following is a sample snippet of code that you can use to configure and deploy a `DataSource` programmatically. It creates a `DataSource` provided by MYSQL JDBC driver.

```
import com.mySQL.jdbc.jdbc2.optional.MySQLDataSource;
import javax.naming.InitialContext;
import javax.naming.Context;
...
// Create a DataSource object
MySQLDataSource mds = new MySQLDataSource();
mds.setServerName("localhost");
```

```
mds.setPortNumber(3306);
mds.setUser("root");
mds.setPassword("chanda");

// Get the initial context
Context ctx = new InitialContext();

// Bind (or register) the DataSource object under a logical name "jdbc/mydb"
ctx.bind("jdbc.mydb", mds);
```

The Java application that needs a connection to a database will perform a lookup using the logical name of the DataSource that was given to it at the time of binding. Here is a typical snippet of Java code that you need to write when you need a Connection object:

```
import javax.sql.DataSource;
import java.sql.Connection;
import javax.naming.InitialContext;
import javax.naming.Context;
...
// Get the initial context
Context ctx = new InitialContext();

// Perform a lookup for the DataSource using its logical name "jdbc/mydb"
DataSource ds = (DataSource)ctx.lookup("jdbc/mydb");

// Get a Connection object from the DataSource object
Connection conn = ds.getConnection();

// Perform other database related tasks...

// Close the connection
conn.close()
```

The JDBC API provides two other types of data source interfaces: javax.sql.ConnectionPoolDataSource and javas.sql.XADataSource. The ConnectionPoolDataSource interface contains a getPooledConnection() method, which returns an instance of the PooledConnection interface. The XADataSource interface contains a getXAConnection() method, which returns an instance of the XAConnection interface.

An implementation of the ConnectionPoolDataSource interface provides the connection pooling feature to improve the application's performance. The basic DataSource implementation connects when a Connection object is obtained from it and disconnects from the database when the Connection object is closed. A ConnectionPoolDataSource implementation maintains a pool of database connections. When a database connection is needed, it gives a connection from its pool. When a database connection is closed, it does not disconnect the Connection object from the database physically. Rather, it returns the connection object to the pool for reuse. Establishing a database connection is a time-consuming process. By using a connection pool in an application using a ConnectionPoolDataSource, you improve your application's performance greatly. The connection pooling mechanism is also useful when the number of connections you can establish to a database is limited. In such cases, you can maintain a pool of limited number of connections and users will take turns using these connections.

The implementation of the XADataSource interface provides support for distributed transactions, which involve multiple databases. A transaction manager is used to manage a distributed transaction in conjunction with a XADataSource object. Typically, a XADataSource also supports connection pooling.

521

Retrieving SQL Warnings

Sometimes, a DBMS issues a SQL warning instead of throwing an exception. A SQL warning indicates that the database interaction has been completed; however, everything was not right. The JDBC API lets you retrieve SQL warnings signaled by a DBMS using a java.sql.SQLWarning object. The SQLWarning class inherits from the SQLException class. A SQLWarning stores chains of SQL warnings. A SQL warning may be issued on a Connection, a Statement (including PreparedStatement and CallableStatement), or a ResultSet. You can retrieve the first warning object associated with any of these objects using their getWarnings() methods. If there are no warnings reported in an object, the method returns null. Once you call the getWarnings() method on these objects, their warnings are cleared. You can also clear their warnings by calling their clearWarnings() method. Note that these objects must be open to access warnings reported on them. Once you execute or re-execute a Statement object, its warnings are reset. The following snippet of code may be used to print warnings details reported on any object—Connection, Statement or ResultSet:

```
// Check for warnings.
// Here xxx is either a Connection, Statement or ResultSet object
SQLWarning warning = xxx.getWarnings();
while(warning != null) {
        int errorCode = warning.getErrorCode();
        String sqlState = warning.getSQLState();
        String warningMsg = warning.getMessage();

        // Print the details
        System.out.println("Warning: " + warningMsg +
                        "SQL State: " + sqlState +
                        "Error Code:" + errorCode);

        // Get the next warning
        warning = warning.getNextWarning();
}
```

Enabling JDBC Trace

You can enable JDBC tracing that will log JDBC activities to a PrintWriter object. You can use the setLogWriter(PrintWriter out) static method of the DriverManager to set a log writer if you are using the DriverManager to connect to a database. If you are using a DataSource, you can use its setLogWriter(PrintWriter out) method to set a log writer. Setting null as a log writer disables the JDBC tracing. The following snippet of code sets a log writer to a C:\jdbc.log file on Windows:

```
// Sets the log writer to a file c:\jdbc.log
PrintWriter pw = new PrintWriter("C:\\jdbc.log");
DriverManager.setLogWriter(pw);
```

When you call the setLogWriter() method of the DriverManager class with the Java security enabled, Java checks for a java.sql.SQLPermission. You can grant this permission to an executing code in a security policy file. The following is an example of an entry in a security policy file that grants a permission to execute the setLogWriter() method on the DriverManager:

```
grant {
        permission java.sql.SQLPermission "setLog";
};
```

Summary

The JDBC API provides a standard database-independent interface to interact with any tabular data source, including a relational database management system (RDBMS) such as Oracle, SQL Server, DB2, Java DB, MySQL, etc. JDBC drivers facilitate connection to a database in Java programs. The JRE does not include any JDBC drivers. JDBC drivers are supplied by the DBMS vendors. Classes and interfaces in the JDBC API are in the java.sql and javax.sql packages.

The DriverManager class facilitates registration of JDBC drivers to connect to different types of databases. When passed in database connection properties such as the server location, protocol, database names, user id, password, etc., the DriverManager uses the registered JDBC drivers to connect to the database and returns an object of the Connection interface that represents a connection to the database.

You can use the getMetaData() method for a Connection object to get a DatabaseMetaData object. A DatabaseMetaData object contains information about the database such as the features are supported by the database, all tables in the database, etc.

The JDBC API provides mappings between SQL types and Java types. JDBC drivers perform the translation between the two types. This hides the differences in data type names and their internal representations in different databases. For example, you can use a java.sql.Date object to represent a SQL date value in your Java program irrespective of the DBMS you are using. The JDBC driver will take care of converting the value in the java.sql.Date to the DBMS-specific date value and vice versa.

A Statement is used to execute SQL statements in string forms from a Java program. The result set returned by a SQL statement is made available in the Java program as an object of the ResultSet interface.

A PreparedStatement is used to execute SQL statement with parameters. The SQL statement is pre-compiled to provide a faster execution on repeated use of the same SQL statement with different parameters. Using input parameters in the SQL statement as placeholders also prevents attacks from hackers that use SQL injections.

A CallableStatement is used to call a SQL stored procedure or a function in a database. Different DBMSs use different syntax to call stored procedures and functions. The JDBC API provides a DBMS-independent syntax to call stored procedures and functions using a CallableStatement.

A ResultSet represents tabular data defined in terms of rows and columns. Typically, you get a ResultSet by executing a SQL statement that returns a result set from the database. A ResultSet may scroll only in the forward direction or in both forward and backward directions. All JDBC drivers will support at least a forward-only ResultSet. A ResultSet may also be used to update data in the database.

A RowSet is a wrapper for a ResultSet. A RowSet hides the complexities that are involved in working with a ResultSet. A JdbcRowSet, which is also known as a connected rowset, maintains a database connection all the time. A CachedRowSet, which is also called a disconnected rowset, uses a database connection only for the duration it is needed. A WebRowSet is a CachedRowSet that supports importing data from an XML document and exporting its data to an XML document. A FilteredRowSet is a WebRowSet that provides filtering capability at the client side. A JoinRowSet is a WebRowSet that provides the ability to combine (or join) two or more disconnected rowsets into one rowset.

The JDBC provides support for working with database large objects, typically called, Blob, Clob, and NClob.

For a better performance, you can send multiple SQL commands to the database in one shot using the batch update feature of the JDBC API. Batch updates are supported through the Statement, PreparedStatement, and CallableStatement interfaces. The addBatch() method of the Statement object is used to add a SQL command to the batch. The executeBatch() method sends all SQL commands in the batch to the database for execution.

A database transaction consists of one or more changes as a unit of work. A savepoint in a transaction is a marker that marks a point in a transaction so that, if needed, the transaction can be rolled back up to the marked point. An instance of the Savepoint interface represents a savepoint. You can create a savepoint in a transaction using the setSavepoint() method of the Connection object. You can specify a savepoint in the rollback() method of the Connection object to roll back the transaction to the specified savepoint.

A DBMS may issue SQL warnings instead of throwing an exception. An instance of the SQLWarning class represents a set of SQL warnings. SQL warnings are nested in one SQLWarning object. Use the getWarnings() method of the Connection, Statement, or ResultSet objects to get SQL warnings associated with them. Use the getNextWarning() method of the SQLWarning class to retrieve the next SQL warning from the set.

You can enable JDBC tracing that will log JDBC activities to a PrintWriter object. You can use the setLogWriter(PrintWriter out) static method of the DriverManager to set a log writer.

CHAPTER 7

■ ■ ■

Java Remote Method Invocation

In this chapter, you will learn

- What Java Remote Method Invocation (RMI) is and the RMI architecture
- How to develop and package RMI server and client applications
- How to start the rmiregistry, RMI server, and client applications
- How to troubleshoot and debug RMI applications
- Dynamic class downloading in an RMI application
- Garbage collections of remote objects in RMI applications

What Is Java Remote Method Invocation?

Java supports a variety of application architectures that determine how and where the application code is deployed and executed. In the simplest application architecture, all Java code resides on a single machine and one JVM manages all Java objects and the interaction among them. This is an example of a standalone application, where all that is needed is a machine that can launch a JVM. Java also supports a distributed application architecture in which the application's code and execution can be distributed among multiple machines.

In Chapter 4, you saw Java applets where Java classes are deployed on a web server. The applet classes are downloaded to the client machine by the web browser and executed inside a JVM that runs on the client machine. In the case of an applet, the Java code is still executed inside one JVM. In Chapter 5, you learned network programming in Java that involves at least two JVMs running on different machines that execute the Java code for the client and server sockets. Typically, sockets are used to transfer data between two applications. In socket programming, it is possible for the client program to send a message to the server program. The server program creates a Java object, invokes a method on that object, and returns the result of the method invocation to the client program. Finally, the client program reads the result using sockets. In such cases, the client is able to invoke a method on a Java object that resides in a different JVM. This possibility opens up doors for new application architectures, called distributed programming, in which an application may utilize multiple machines, running multiple JVMs to process the business logic. Although it is possible to invoke a method on an object that resides in a different JVM (possibly on a different machine too) using socket programming, it is not easy to code. To achieve this, Java provides a separate mechanism called Java Remote Method Invocation (Java RMI).

Java RMI enables a Java application to invoke a method on a Java object in a remote JVM. I will use the term "remote object" to refer to a Java object that is created and managed by a JVM, other than the JVM that manages the Java code that calls methods on that "remote object." Typically, a remote object also implies that it is managed by a JVM that runs on a machine other than the machine from which it is accessed. However, it is not a requirement for a Java object to be a remote object that it should exist in a JVM on a different machine. For learning purposes, you will use one machine to deploy the remote object in one JVM and launch another application in a different JVM to access the remote object. RMI lets you treat the remote object as if it is a local object. Internally, it uses sockets to handle access to the remote object and to invoke its methods.

An RMI application consists of two programs, a client and a server, that run in two different JVMs. The server program creates a number of Java objects and makes them accessible to the remote client programs to invoke methods on those objects. The client program needs to know the location of the remote objects on the server, so it can invoke methods on them. The server program creates a remote object and registers (or binds) its reference to an RMI registry. An RMI registry is a name service that is used to bind a remote object reference to a name, so a client can get the reference of the remote object using a name-based lookup in the registry. An RMI registry runs in a separate process from the server program. It is supplied as a tool called `rmiregistry`. When you install a JDK/JRE on your machine, it is copied in the `bin` subdirectory under the JDK/JRE installation directory.

After the client program gets the remote reference of a remote object, it invokes methods using that reference as if it were a reference to a local object. RMI technology takes care of the details of invoking the methods on the remote reference in the server program running on a different JVM on a different machine. In an RMI application, Java code is written in terms of interfaces. The server program contains implementations for the interfaces. The client program uses interfaces along with the remote object references to invoke methods on the remote object that exists in the server's JVM. All Java library classes supporting Java RMI are in the `java.rmi` package and its subpackages.

The RMI Architecture

Figure 7-1 shows the RMI architecture in a simplified form. A rectangular box in the figure represents a component in an RMI application. An arrow line shows a message sent from one component to another in the direction of the arrow. The ovals showing numbers from 1 to 11 represent the sequence of steps that take place in a typical RMI application. I will discuss all steps in detail in this section.

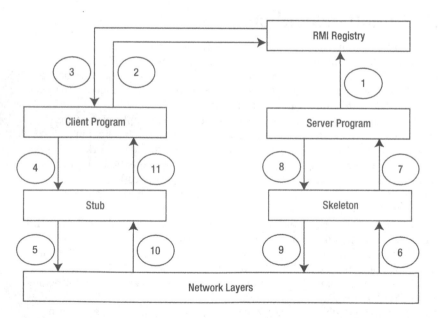

Figure 7-1. *The RMI architecture*

Let's assume that you have developed all Java classes and interfaces that are needed for an RMI application to run. In this section, you will walk through all the steps that are involved when you run an RMI application. You will develop the Java code that is needed for each step in the next few sections.

The first step involved in an RMI application is to create a Java object in the server. The object will be used as the remote object. There is an additional step that needs to be performed to make an ordinary Java object a remote object. The step is known as *exporting* the remote object. When an ordinary Java object is exported as a remote object, it becomes ready to receive/handle calls from remote clients. The export process produces a remote object reference (also called a stub). The remote reference knows the details about the exported object such as its location and methods that can be called remotely. This step is not labeled in Figure 7-1. It happens inside the server program. When this step finishes, the remote object has been created in the server and is ready to receive a remote method invocation.

The next step is performed by the server to register (or bind) the remote reference with an RMI registry. The server chooses a unique name for each remote reference it registers with an RMI registry. A remote client will need to use the same name to look up the remote reference in the RMI registry. This is labeled as #1 in Figure 7-1. When this step finishes, the RMI registry has registered the remote object reference and a client interested in invoking a method on the remote object may ask for its reference from the RMI registry.

■ **Tip**   For security reasons, an RMI registry and the server must run on the same machine so that a server can register the remote references with the RMI registry. If this restriction is not imposed, a hacker may register his own harmful Java objects to your RMI registry from his machine.

This step involves interaction between a client and an RMI registry. Typically, a client and an RMI registry run on two different machines. The client sends a lookup request to the RMI registry for a remote reference. The client uses a name to look up the remote reference in the RMI registry. The name is the same as the name that was used by the server to bind the remote reference in the RMI registry in step #1. The lookup step is labeled as #2 in Figure 7-1. The RMI registry returns the remote reference (or stub) to the client labeled as step #3 in Figure 7-1. If a remote reference is not bound in the RMI registry with the name used by the client in the lookup request, the RMI registry throws a NotBoundException. If this step finishes successfully, the client has received the remote reference (or stub) of the remote object running in the server.

In this step, the client invokes a method on the stub. It is shown as step #4 in Figure 7-1. At this point, the stub connects to the server and transmits the information required to invoke the method on the remote object, such as the name of the method, the method's arguments, etc. The stub knows about the server location and the details about how to contact the remote object on the server. This step is labeled as step #5 in Figure 7-1. Many different layers at the network level are involved in transmitting information emanating from stub to the server.

A skeleton is the server side counterpart of a stub on the client side. Its job is to receive the data sent by the stub. This is shown as step #6 in Figure 7-1. After a skeleton receives the data, it reassembles it into a more meaningful format and invokes the method on the remote object, which is shown as step #7 in Figure 7-1. Once the remote method call is over on the server, the skeleton receives the result of the method call (step #8) and transmits the information back to the stub (step #9) through the network layers. The stub receives the result of the remote method invocation (step #10), reassembles the result, and passes the result to the client program (step #11).

The steps #4 through #11 may be repeated to call the same or different methods on the same remote object. If a client wants to call a method on a different remote object, it will have to first perform steps #2 and #3 before initiating a remote method call.

It is typical in an RMI application that a client contacts an RMI registry to get the stub of a remote object in the beginning. If the client needs the stub of another remote object running in the server, it may get it by calling a method on the stub that it already has. Note that a remote object's method can also return a stub to a remote client. This way, a remote client may perform a lookup in the RMI registry only once at startup. The Java code that you write for an RMI application is no different from that of a non-RMI application, except for looking up for a remote object reference in the RMI registry.

Developing an RMI Application

This section will walk you through the steps to write the Java code to develop an RMI application. You will develop a remote utility RMI application that will let you perform three things: echo a message from the server, get the current date and time from the server, and add two integers. The following steps are involved in writing an RMI application:

- Writing a remote interface.

- Implementing the remote interface in a class. An object of this class serves as the remote object.

- Writing a server program. It creates an object of the class that implements the remote interface and registers it with the RMI registry.

- Writing a client program that accesses the remote object on the server.

Writing the Remote Interface

A remote interface is like any other Java interface whose methods are meant to be called from a remote client running in a different JVM. It has four special requirements:

- It must extend the Remote interface. The Remote interface is a marker interface that does not declare any methods.

- All methods in a remote interface must throw a RemoteException or an exception, which is its superclass such as IOException or Exception. The RemoteException is a checked exception. A remote method can also throw any number of other application-specific exceptions.

- A remote method may accept the reference of a remote object as a parameter. It may also return the reference of a remote object as its return value. If a method in a remote interface accepts or returns a remote object reference, the parameter or return type must be declared of the type Remote rather than of the type of the class that implements the Remote interface.

- A remote interface may only use three data types in its method's parameters or return value. It could be a primitive type, a remote object, or a serializable non-remote object. A remote object is passed by reference, whereas a non-remote serializable object is passed by copy. An object is serializable if its class implements the java.io.Serializable interface.

You will name your remote interface RemoteUtility. Listing 7-1 contains the code for the RemoteUtility remote interface. It contains three methods called echo(), getServerTime(), and add(), which provide your three intended functionalities.

Listing 7-1. A RemoteUtility Interface

```java
// RemoteUtility.java
package com.jdojo.rmi;

import java.rmi.Remote;
import java.rmi.RemoteException;
import java.time.ZonedDateTime;

public interface RemoteUtility extends Remote {
        // Echoes a string message back to the client
        String echo(String msg) throws RemoteException;

        // Returns the current date and time to the client
        ZonedDateTime getServerTime() throws RemoteException;

        // Adds two integers and returns the result to the client
        int add(int n1, int n2) throws RemoteException;
}
```

Implementing the Remote Interface

This step involves creating a class that implements the remote interface. You will name the class RemoteUtilityImpl.
It will implement the RemoteUtility remote interface and will provide implementations for three methods: echo(),
getServerTime(), and add(). You can have any number of other methods in this class. The only thing you must
do is provide implementations for all methods defined in the RemoteUtility remote interface. The remote client
will be able to call only remote methods of this class. If you define methods in this class other than those defined
in the remote interface, those methods are not available for remote method invocations. However, you can use the
additional methods to implement the remote methods. Listing 7-2 contains the code for the RemoteUtilityImpl class.

Listing 7-2. An Implementation Class for the RemoteUtility Remote Interface

```java
// RemoteUtilityImpl.java
package com.jdojo.rmi;

import java.time.ZonedDateTime;

public class RemoteUtilityImpl implements RemoteUtility {
        public RemoteUtilityImpl() {
        }

        @Override
        public String echo(String msg) {
                return msg;
        }

        @Override
        public ZonedDateTime getServerTime() {
                return ZonedDateTime.now();
        }

        @Override
        public int add(int n1, int n2) {
                return n1 + n2;
        }
}
```

The remote object implementation class is very simple. It implements the RemoteUtility interface and provides implementations for three methods of the interface. Note that these methods in the RemoteUtilityImpl class do not declare that they throw a RemoteException. The requirement to declare that all remote methods throw a RemoteException is for the remote interface, not the class implementing the remote interface.

There are two ways to write your implementation class for a remote interface. One way is to inherit it from the java.rmi.server.UnicastRemoteObject class. Another way is to inherit it from no class or any class other than the UnicastRemoteObject class. Listing 7-2 took the latter approach. It did not inherit the RemoteUtilityImpl class from any class.

What difference does it make if the implementation class for a remote interface inherits from the UnicastRemoteObject class or some other class? The implementation class of a remote interface is used to create remote objects whose methods are invoked remotely. The object of this class must go through an export process, which makes it suitable for a remote method invocation. The constructors for the UnicastRemoteObject class export the object automatically for you. So, if your implementation class inherits from the UnicastRemoteObject class, it will save you one step in the entire process later. Sometimes your implementation class must inherit from another class and that will force you not to inherit it from the UnicastRemoteObject class. One thing you need to note is that the constructors for the UnicastRemoteObject class throw a RemoteException. If you inherit the remote object implementation class from the UnicastRemoteObject class, the implementation class's constructor must throw a RemoteException in its declaration. Listing 7-3 rewrites RemoteUtilityImpl class by inheriting it from the UnicastRemoteObject class. There are two new things in this implementation—it uses the extends clause in the class declaration and it uses a throws clause in the constructor declaration. Everything else remains the same. I will discuss the difference in using the implementation of the RemoteUtilityImpl class shown in Listing 7-2 and Listing 7-3 when you write the server program later in this chapter.

Listing 7-3. Rewriting the RemoteUtilityImpl Class by Inheriting It from the UnicastRemoteObject Class

```java
// RemoteUtilityImpl.java
package com.jdojo.rmi;

import java.rmi.RemoteException;
import java.rmi.server.UnicastRemoteObject;
import java.time.ZonedDateTime;

public class RemoteUtilityImpl extends UnicastRemoteObject implements RemoteUtility {
        // Must throw RemoteException
        public RemoteUtilityImpl() throws RemoteException {
        }

        @Override
        public String echo(String msg) {
                return msg;
        }

        @Override
        public ZonedDateTime getServerTime() {
                return ZonedDateTime.now();
        }

        @Override
        public int add(int n1, int n2) {
                return n1 + n2;
        }
}
```

Writing the RMI Server Program

The responsibility of a server program is to create the remote object and make it accessible to remote clients. A server program performs the following things:

- Installs the security manager.

- Creates and exports the remote object.

- Registers the remote object with the RMI registry application.

The subsequent sections discuss these steps in detail.

Installing the Security Manager

You need to make sure that the server code is running under a security manager. An RMI program cannot download Java classes from remote locations if it is not running with a security manager. Without a security manager, it can only use local Java classes. In both RMI servers and RMI clients, programs may need to download class files from remote locations. You will look at examples of downloading Java classes from remote locations shortly. When you run a Java program under a security manager, you must also control access to the privileged resources through a Java policy file. The following snippet of code shows how to install a security manager if it is not already installed. You can use an object of the java.lang.SecurityManager class or java.rmi.RMISecurityManager class to install a security manager.

```
SecurityManager secManager = System.getSecurityManager();
if (secManager == null) {
        System.setSecurityManager(new SecurityManager());
}
```

A security manager controls the access to privileged resources through a policy file. You will need to set appropriate permissions to access the resources used in a Java RMI application. For this example, you will give all permissions to all code. However, you should use a properly controlled policy file in a production environment. The entry that you need to make in the policy file to grant all permissions is as follows:

```
grant {
        permission java.security.AllPermission;
};
```

Typically, a Java policy file resides in the user's home directory on a computer and it is named .java.policy. Note that the file name starts with a dot.

Creating and Exporting the Remote Object

The next step the RMI server program performs is to create an object of the class that implements the remote interface, which will serve as a remote object. In your case, you will create an object of the RemoteUtilityImpl class.

```
RemoteUtilityImpl remoteUtility = new RemoteUtilityImpl();
```

You need to export a remote object so remote clients can invoke its remote methods. If your remote object class (RemoteUtility class in this case) inherits from the UnicastRemoteObject class, you do not need to export it. It is exported automatically when you create it. If your remote object's class does not inherit from the

UnicastRemoteObject class, you need to export it explicitly using one of the exportObject() static methods of the UnicastRemoteObject class. When you export a remote object, you can specify a port number where it can listen for a remote method invocation. By default, it listens at port 0, which is an anonymous port. The following statement exports a remote object:

```
int port = 0;
RemoteUtility remoteUtilityStub =
    (RemoteUtility)UnicastRemoteObject.exportObject(remoteUtility, port);
```

The exportObject() method returns the reference of the exported remote object, which is also called a stub or a remote reference. You need to keep the reference of the stub, so you can register it with an RMI registry.

Registering the Remote Object

The final step that the server program performs is to register (or bind) the remote object reference with an RMI registry using a name. An RMI registry is a separate application that provides a name service. To register a remote reference with an RMI registry, you must first locate it. An RMI registry runs on a machine at a specific port. By default, it runs on port 1099. Once you locate the registry, you need to call its bind() method to bind the remote reference. You can also use its rebind() method, which will replace an old binding if it already exists for the specified name. The name used is a String. You will use the name MyRemoteUtility as the name for your remote reference. It is better to follow a naming convention for binding a reference object in the RMI registry to avoid name collisions.

```
Registry registry = LocateRegistry.getRegistry("localhost", 1099);
String name = "MyRemoteUtility";
registry.rebind(name, remoteUtilityStub);
```

That is all needed to write a server program. Listing 7-4 contains the complete code for the RMI server. It assumes that the RemoteUtilityImpl class does not inherit from the UnicastRemoteObject class as listed in Listing 7-2.

Listing 7-4. An RMI Remote Server Program

```
// RemoteServer.java
package com.jdojo.rmi;

import java.rmi.RemoteException;
import java.rmi.registry.LocateRegistry;
import java.rmi.registry.Registry;
import java.rmi.server.UnicastRemoteObject;

public class RemoteServer {
        public static void main(String[] args) {
                SecurityManager secManager = System.getSecurityManager();
                if (secManager == null) {
                        System.setSecurityManager(new SecurityManager());
                }

                try {
                        RemoteUtilityImpl remoteUtility = new RemoteUtilityImpl();
```

```
                // Export the object as a remote object
                int port = 0; // an anonymous port
                RemoteUtility remoteUtilityStub
                        = (RemoteUtility) UnicastRemoteObject.exportObject(
                                remoteUtility, port);

                // Locate the registry
                Registry registry = LocateRegistry.getRegistry("localhost", 1099);

                // Bind the exported remote reference in the registry
                String name = "MyRemoteUtility";
                registry.rebind(name, remoteUtilityStub);

                System.out.println("Remote server is ready...");
            }
            catch (RemoteException e) {
                e.printStackTrace();
            }
        }
}
```

If you use the implementation of the RemoteUtilityImpl class as listed in Listing 7-3, you will need to modify the code in Listing 7-4. The code in the try-catch block will change to the code as follows. All other code will remain the same.

```
RemoteUtilityImpl remoteUtility = new RemoteUtilityImpl();

// No need to export the object

// Locate the registry
Registry registry = LocateRegistry.getRegistry("localhost", 1099);

// Bind the exported remote reference in the registry
String name = "MyRemoteUtility";
registry.rebind(name, remoteUtility);

System.out.println("Remote server is ready...");
```

You are not ready to start your server program yet. I will discuss how to start an RMI application in the sections to follow.

For security reasons, you can bind a remote reference to an RMI registry only from the RMI server program that is running on the same machine as the RMI registry. Otherwise, a hacker may be able to bind any arbitrary and potentially harmful remote references to your RMI registry. By default, the getRegistry() static method of the LocateRegistry class returns a stub for a registry that runs on the same machine at port 1099. You may just use the following code to locate a registry in the server program.

```
// Get a registry stub for a local machine at port 1099
Registry registry = LocateRegistry.getRegistry();
```

Note that the call to the `LocateRegistry.getRegistry()` method does not try to connect to a registry application. It just returns a stub for the registry. It is the subsequent call on this stub, `bind()`, `rebind()` or any other method call that attempts to connect to the registry application.

Writing the RMI Client Program

The RMI client program calls the methods on remote objects, which exist on the remote server. The first thing that a client program must do is to know the location of the remote object. It is the RMI server program that creates and knows the location of the remote object. It is the responsibility of the server program to publish the location details of the remote object so a client can locate it and use it. The server program publishes the remote object's location details by binding it with an RMI registry and gives it a name, which is `MyRemoteUtility` in your case. The client program contacts the RMI registry and performs a name-based lookup to get the remote reference. After getting the remote reference, the client program calls methods on the remote reference, which are executed in the server. Typically, the RMI client program performs the following:

- It makes sure that it is running under a security manager.

```
SecurityManager secManager = System.getSecurityManager();
if (secManager == null) {
  System.setSecurityManager(new SecurityManager());
}
```

It locates the registry where the remote reference has been bound by the server. You must know the machine name or IP address, and the port number at which the RMI registry is running. In a real-world RMI program, you would not be using `localhost` in the client program to locate the registry. Rather, an RMI registry will be running on a separate machine. For your example, you will run all three programs—RMI registry, server, and client—on the same machine.

```
// Locate the registry
Registry registry = LocateRegistry.getRegistry("localhost", 1099);
```

- It performs the lookup in the registry using the `lookup()` method of the `Registry` interface. It passes the name of the bound remote reference to the `lookup()` method and gets back the remote reference (or stub). Note that the `lookup()` method must use the same name that was used to bind/rebind a remote reference by the server. The `lookup()` method returns a `Remote` object. You must cast it to the type of your remote interface. The following snippet of code casts the returned remote reference from the `lookup()` method to the `RemoteUtility` interface type:

```
String name = "MyRemoteUtility";
RemoteUtility remoteUtilStub = (RemoteUtility)registry.lookup(name);
```

- It calls methods on the remote reference (or stub). The client program treats the `remoteUtilStub` reference as if it is a reference to a local object. Any method call made on it is sent to the server for execution. All remote methods throw a `RemoteException`. You must handle the `RemoteException` when you call any remote method.

```
// Call the echo() method
String reply = remoteUtilStub.echo("Hello from the RMI client.");
```

Listing 7-5 contains the complete code for your client program. Do not run this program yet. You will go through the step-by-step process in the next few sections to run your RMI application. You may notice that writing RMI code is not complex. It is the plumbing of different components in RMI that is complex.

Listing 7-5. An RMI Remote Client Program

```java
// RemoteClient.java
package com.jdojo.rmi;

import java.rmi.NotBoundException;
import java.rmi.RemoteException;
import java.rmi.registry.LocateRegistry;
import java.rmi.registry.Registry;
import java.time.ZonedDateTime;

public class RemoteClient {
    public static void main(String[] args) {
        SecurityManager secManager = System.getSecurityManager();
        if (secManager == null) {
            System.setSecurityManager(new SecurityManager());
        }

        try {
            // Locate the registry
            Registry registry =
                LocateRegistry.getRegistry("localhost", 1099);

            String name = "MyRemoteUtility";
            RemoteUtility remoteUtilStub =
                (RemoteUtility) registry.lookup(name);

            // Echo a message from the server
            String msg = "Hello";
            String reply = remoteUtilStub.echo(msg);
            System.out.println("Echo Message: " + msg +
                                ", Echo reply: " + reply);

            // Get the server date and time with the zone info
            ZonedDateTime serverTime = remoteUtilStub.getServerTime();

            System.out.println("Server Time: " + serverTime);

            // Add two integers
            int n1 = 101;
            int n2 = 207;
            int sum = remoteUtilStub.add(n1, n2);
            System.out.println(n1 + " + " + n2 + " = " + sum);
        }
        catch (RemoteException | NotBoundException e) {
            e.printStackTrace();
        }
    }
}
```

Separating the Server and Client Code

It is important that you separate the code for the server and client programs in an RMI application. The server program needs to have the following three components:

- The remote interface
- The implementation class for the remote interface
- The server program

The client program needs to have the following two components.

- The remote interface
- The client program

The client program should not know about the implementation class that implements the remote interface. Having this class accessible to the client program defeats the purpose of developing an RMI application. You can have additional classes accessible to server and client programs, which are needed to run them.

For your example, you can separate the server and client class files, either in two directory structures, or in two JAR files. You will package the class files for the server and the client programs in `utilserver.jar` and `utilclient.jar`, respectively. The files in the `utilserver.jar` file are

- `RemoteUtility.class`
- `RemoteUtilityImpl.class`
- `RemoteServer.class`

The files in the `utilclient.jar` file are

- `RemoteUtility.class`
- `RemoteClient.class`

Generating Stub and Skeleton

RMI needs a stub class when a remote object is exported using the `UnicastRemoteObject` class. You can do one of the following two things:

- You can use the `UnicastRemoteObject` class to inherit your remote interface implementation class, which will export your remote object automatically.
- You can use the `exportObject()` method of the `UnicastRemoteObject` class to export the remote object explicitly.

In either case, when a remote object is exported, RMI needs a stub class. Prior to Java 5, you need to perform one extra step to generate the stub class for your remote interface implementation class. It is done by using an `rmic` command that is included in the `bin` subdirectory of your JDK installation folder. You run this command, passing the fully qualified name of the remote interface implementation class as shown:

```
rmic com.jdojo.rmi.RemoteUtilityImpl
```

You may need to set the `CLASSPATH` environment variable appropriately so that `rmic` will be able to find the class you specify as its argument. The above command will generate the following two class files in the same folder where the `RemoteUtilityImpl.class` file resides.

- `RemoteUtilityImpl_Stub.class`
- `RemoteUtilityImpl_Skel.class`

You need to include these two class files in the `utilserver.jar` file. Note that this step is needed only if you are using Java version prior to Java 5. You also need to perform this step if you have a client program that is running Java version prior to Java 5 and your server is running on Java 5 or later. If you are interested in looking at the Java source code that is generated for these two class files, you can use the -keep (or -keepgenerated) option with the `rmic` command, which will generate the Java source files for these classes. The following command will generate four files, two `.class` files and two `.java` files.

```
rmic -keep com.jdojo.chapter5.RemoteUtilityImpl
```

Running the RMI Application

You need to start all programs involved in an RMI application in the following specific sequence:

- Run the RMI registry.
- Run the RMI server program.
- Run the RMI client program.

Please refer to the "Troubleshooting an RMI Application" section later in this chapter if you have any problem in running any of the programs.

Your server and client programs use security managers. You must have your java policy file properly configured before you can run the RMI application successfully. You can grant all security permissions to an RMI application for learning purposes. You can do so by creating a text file named `rmi.policy` (you can use any other file name you want) and entering the following content, which grants all permissions to all code:

```
grant {
        permission java.security.AllPermission;
};
```

When you run the RMI client or server program, you need to set the `rmi.policy` file as your Java security policy file using the `java.security.policy` JVM option. It is assumed that you have saved the `rmi.policy` file in the `C:\` folder on Windows.

```
java -Djava.security.policy=file:/c:/rmi.policy <other-options>
```

This approach of setting a Java policy file is temporary. It should be only used for learning purposes. You will need to set a fine-grained security in a production environment.

Running the RMI Registry

The RMI registry application is supplied with the JDK/JRE installation. It is copied in the `bin` subfolder of the respective installation main folder. On the Windows platform, it is the `rmiregistry.exe` executable file. You can run the RMI registry by starting the `rmiregistry` application using a command prompt. It accepts a port number on which it will run. By default, it runs on port 1099. The following command starts it at port 1099 using a command prompt on Windows:

```
C:\java8\bin> rmiregistry
```

The following command starts the RMI registry at port 8967:

```
C:\java8\bin> rmiregistry 8967
```

The rmiregistry application does not print any startup message on the prompt. Usually, it is started as a background process.

Most likely, the command is not going to work on your machine. Using this command, you will be able to start the rmiregistry successfully. However, you will get ClassNotFoundException when you run the RMI server application in the next section. The rmiregistry application needs access to some of the classes (the registered ones) used in the RMI server application. There are three ways to make the classes available to rmiregistry:

- Set the CLASSPATH appropriately.

- Set the java.rmi.server.codebase JVM property to the URL that contains the classes needed by the rmiregistry.

- Set the JVM property named java.rmi.server.useCodebaseOnly to false. From JDK 7u21 (also in JDK 6u45 and JDK 5u45), this property is set to true by default. Earlier it was set to false by default. If this property is set to false, the rmiregistry can download the needed class files from the server.

The following command adds the serverutil.jar file to the CLASSPATH, before starting the rmiregistry:

```
C:\java8\bin> SET CLASSPATH=C:\utilserver.jar
C:\java8\bin> rmiregistry
```

Instead of setting the CLASSPATH to make classes available to the rmiregistry, you can also set the java.rmi.server.codebase JVM property that is a space-separated list of URLs, as shown:

```
rmiregistry -J-Djava.rmi.server.codebase=file:/C:/utilserver.jar
```

The following command resets the CLASSPATH and sets the java.rmi.server.useCodebaseOnly property for the JVM to false so the rmiregistry will download any class files needed from the RMI server. Your example will work using this command:

```
C:\java8\bin> SET CLASSPATH=
C:\java8\bin> rmiregistry -J-Djava.rmi.server.useCodebaseOnly=false
```

Running the RMI Server

The RMI registry must be running before you can run the RMI server. Recall that the server runs under a security manager that requires you to grant permissions to perform certain actions in a Java policy file. Make sure that you have entered the required grants in a policy file. You can use the following command to run the server program. The command text is entered in one line; it has been shown in multiple lines for clarity. Each part in the command text should be separated by a space, not a new line. In the command, you will need to change the path to the JAR and policy files that will reflect their paths on your machine.

```
java -cp C:\utilserver.jar
     -Djava.rmi.server.codebase=file:/C:/utilserver.jar
     -Djava.security.policy=file:/c:/rmi.policy
     com.jdojo.rmi.RemoteServer
```

The -cp option sets the CLASSPATH to utilserver.jar file. If you do not want to use a JAR file to package server-related class files, you can use any other CLASSPATH settings, so that the server program may run. If you have already set the appropriate CLASSPATH, you can remove the -cp option and the CLASSPATH value from the command text.

You need to set a java.rmi.server.codebase property. This is used by an RMI registry and a client program if they need to download class files that they do not have. The value of this property is a URL, which can point to a local file system, a web server, a FTP server, or any other resource. The URL may point to a JAR file, as it does in this case, or it can point to a directory. If it points to a directory, the URL must end with a forward slash. The following command uses a folder as its codebase. If an RMI registry and a client need any class files, they will attempt to download the class files from the URL file/C:/myrmi/classes/.

```
java -cp C:\utilserver.jar
    -Djava.rmi.server.codebase=file:/C:/myrmi/classes/
    com.jdojo.rmi.RemoteServer
```

You can also set a java.rmi.server.codebase property to point to a web server, where you can store your necessary class files as shown:

```
java -cp C:\utilserver.jar
    -Djava.rmi.server.codebase=http://www.jdojo.com/rmi/classes/
    com.jdojo.rmi.RemoteServer
```

If you store class files at multiple locations, you can specify all locations separated by a space as follows:

```
java -cp C:\utilserver.jar
    -Djava.rmi.server.codebase="http://www.jdojo.com/rmi/classes/
    ftp://www.jdojo.com/rmi/some/classes/c.jar"
    com.jdojo.rmi.RemoteServer
```

It specifies one location as a directory and another as a JAR file. One uses the http protocol and another ftp. The two values are separated by a space and they are on one line, not on two lines as shown. A ClassNotFoundException may occur when you run the server or client program, which is most likely caused by an incorrect setting for the java.rmi.server.codebase property, or by not setting this property at all.

Running an RMI Client Program

After the RMI registry and server applications are started successfully, it is time to start the RMI client application. You can use the following command to run the client program:

```
java -cp C:\utilclient.jar
    -Djava.rmi.server.codebase=file:/C:/utilclient.jar
    -Djava.security.policy=file:/c:/rmi.policy
    com.jdojo.rmi.RemoteClient
```

You do not have to include a java.rmi.server.codebase option when you run the above command. The client program can also be run with the following command. You should be able to see an output on the console when the client program runs successfully. You may get a different output when you run the program because it prints the current date and time with the zone information for the server machine running the server application.

```
java -cp C:\utilclient.jar
    -Djava.security.policy=file:/c:/rmi.policy
    com.jdojo.rmi.RemoteClient
```

```
Echo Message: Hello, Echo reply: Hello
Server Time: 2014-06-22T13:11:31.790-05:00[America/Chicago]
101 + 207 = 308
```

Troubleshooting an RMI Application

It is very likely that you will get many exceptions before you will be able to run the RMI application the very first time. This section will list a few exceptions that you may receive. It will also list some possible causes for those exceptions and some possible solutions. It is not possible to list all possible errors that you might get when you attempt to run an RMI application. You should be able to figure out most of the errors by looking at the stack prints of the exceptions.

java.rmi.StubNotFoundException

You get a StubNotFoundException when you try to run a server program. The exception stack trace will be similar to the following:

```
java.rmi.StubNotFoundException: Stub class not found: com.jdojo.rmi.RemoteUtilityImpl_Stub;
nested exception is:
java.lang.ClassNotFoundException: com.jdojo.rmi.RemoteUtilityImpl_Stub
 at sun.rmi.server.Util.createStub(Util.java:292)...
```

This exception could occur because of many reasons. Here are some of the reasons you could look for and fix:

- You may be running the server program using a Java version prior to Java 5. You must create the stub and skeleton using the rmic command and make them accessible to the JVM when you run the server program. Please refer to the "Generating Stub and Skeleton" section for more details.

- You may get this error when you are exporting a remote object and not passing a port number:

  ```
  RemoteUtility remoteUtilityStub =
      (RemoteUtility)UnicastRemoteObject.exportObject(remoteUtility);
  ```

  If you do not pass a port number to the exportObject() method of the UnicastRemoteObject class to export a remote object, you must generate the stub and skeleton using the rmic command first. Please refer to the "Generating Stub and Skeleton" section for more details. Another way to resolve this is to pass a port number to the exportObject() method. The port number 0 (zero) means an anonymous port.

  ```
  RemoteUtility remoteUtilityStub =
      (RemoteUtility)UnicastRemoteObject.exportObject(remoteUtility,0);
  ```

java.rmi.server.ExportException

You get an ExportException when you try to run the rmiregistry application or the server application. The exception stack trace will be similar to the one shown if you get this exception when you attempt to run the rmiregistry application.

```
java.rmi.server.ExportException:Port already in use: 1099; nested exception is:
java.net.BindException: Address already in use: JVM_Bind...
```

It states that the port number 1099 (may be a different number in your case) is already in use. Maybe you have already started the rmiregistry application at port 1099 (which is the default port number for an rmiregistry application) or some other application is using the port 1099. You can do one of the following two things to fix this problem:

- You can stop the application that is using the port 1099 and start the rmiregistry application at port 1009.

- You can start the rmiregistry application at a port other than 1099.

If you get an `ExportException` when you run the server program, it is caused by the failure of the export process of the remote object. There are many reasons for the export process to fail. The following exception stack trace (partial trace is shown) is caused by exporting the same remote object twice:

```
java.rmi.server.ExportException: object already exported
 at sun.rmi.transport.ObjectTable.putTarget(ObjectTable.java:189)
 at sun.rmi.transport.Transport.exportObject(Transport.java:92)...
```

Check your server program and make sure that you are exporting your remote object only once. It is a common mistake to inherit the remote object implementation class from the `UnicastRemoteObject` class and also use the `exportObject()` method of the `UnicastRemoteObject` class to export the remote object. When you inherit the remote object's implementation class from the `UnicastRemoteObject` class, the remote object, which you create, is exported automatically. If you try to export it again using the `exportObject()` method, you will get this exception. I have stressed this point a few times when discussing the remote interface implementation class. When you are developing an RMI application, remember the saying, "To err is programmer, to punish Java." Even a little mistake in the setup of an RMI program may cost you hours of your time to detect and fix.

java.security.AccessControlException

You get this exception when your Java policy file does not have `grant` entries that are necessary to run the RMI application. The following is the partial stack trace of an exception, which is caused when you attempt to run the server program, and it attempts to bind a remote object to the RMI registry:

```
java.security.AccessControlException: access denied (java.net.SocketPermission 127.0.0.1:1099
connect,resolve)...
```

Communications among registry, server, and client are performed using sockets. You must grant appropriate socket permission in the Java policy file for security, so that the three components of your RMI application may be able to communicate. Most of the security-related exceptions can be fixed by granting appropriate permissions in the Java policy file.

java.lang.ClassNotFoundException

You get a `ClassNotFoundException` exception when a class file that is needed by Java runtime is not found. You must have received this exception many times by now. Most of the time, you receive this exception when the `CLASSPATH` is not appropriately set. In an RMI application, this exception may be the cause for another exception.
The following stack trace shows that the `java.rmi.ServerException` exception was thrown, which has its cause in a `ClassNotFoundException` exception:

```
java.rmi.ServerException: RemoteException occurred in server thread; nested exception is:
        java.rmi.UnmarshalException: error unmarshalling arguments; nested exception is:
        java.lang.ClassNotFoundException: com.jdojo.rmi.RemoteUtility
...
Caused by: java.lang.ClassNotFoundException: com.jdojo.rmi.RemoteUtility
        at java.net.URLClassLoader$1.run(URLClassLoader.java:220)
        at java.net.URLClassLoader$1.run(URLClassLoader.java:209)
```

This type of exception is thrown when the `java.rmi.server.codebase` option is not set properly or not set at all when you run the server or the client application.

This exception was thrown when the server program was started without using the java.rmi.server.codebase option and the rmiregistry application was run without setting the CLASSPATH. When you try to bind/rebind a remote reference with an rmiregistry application, the server application sends the remote reference to the rmiregistry application. The rmiregistry application must load the class before it can represent the remote reference as a Java object in its JVM. At this time, the rmiregistry will try to download the required class files from the location that was specified at the server startup using the java.rmi.server.codebase property.

If you get this exception when you run the client program, make sure you have set the java.rmi.server. codebase property when you run the client program.

Please check the CLASSPATH and java.rmi.server.codebase property when you run the server and the client program to avoid this exception.

You get a ClassNotFoundException when you run the client program because the server was not able to find some class definitions that were required in unmarshalling the client call on the server side. The sample partial stack trace of the exception is shown:

```
java.rmi.ServerException: RemoteException occurred in server thread; nested exception is:
java.rmi.UnmarshalException: error unmarshalling arguments; nested exception is:
java.lang.ClassNotFoundException: com.jdojo.rmi.Square
  at sun.rmi.server.UnicastServerRef.dispatch(UnicastServerRef.java:336)
  at sun.rmi.transport.Transport$1.run(Transport.java:159)...
```

A remote method defined in a remote interface may accept a parameter, which may be of an interface or a class type. The client may pass an object of a class that implements the interface or an object of a subclass of type defined in the remote interface's method signature. If the class definition does not exist on the server, the server will attempt to download the class using the java.rmi.server.codebase property that was set in the client application. You need to make sure the class for which you are getting this error (exception stack trace shows com.jdojo.rmi.Square as class name) is either in the CLASSPATH of the server JVM or set the java.rmi.server.codebase property when you run the remote client, so that this class can be downloaded by the sever.

Debugging an RMI Application

You can turn on RMI logging for an RMI server application by setting the JVM property named java.rmi.server. logCalls to true. By default, it is set to false. The following command launches your RemoteServer application setting the java.rmi.server.logCalls property to true:

```
java -cp C:\utilserver.jar
    -Djava.rmi.server.logCalls=true
    -Djava.rmi.server.codebase="http://www.myurl.com/rmiclasses"
    com.jdojo.rmi.RemoteServer
```

When the java.rmi.server.logCalls property for the server JVM is set to true, all incoming calls to the server and stack trace of any exceptions that are thrown during execution of an incoming call are logged to the standard error.

The RMI runtime also lets you log the incoming calls in a server application to a file, irrespective of the value set for the java.rmi.server.logCalls property for the server JVM. You can log all incoming call details to a file using the setLog(OutputStream out) static method of java.rmi.server.RemoteServer class. Typically, you set the file output stream for logging in the beginning of the server program code such as the very first statement in the main() method of your com.jdojo.rmi.RemoteServer class. The following snippet of code enables the calls logging in a remote server application to a C:\rmi.log file. You can disable call logging by using null as the OutputStream in the setLog() method.

```
try {
        java.io.OutputStream os = new java.io.FileOutputStream("C:\\rmi.log");
        java.rmi.server.RemoteServer.setLog(os);
}
catch (FileNotFoundException e) {
        System.err.println("Could not enable incoming calls logging.");
        e.printStackTrace();
}
```

When a security manager is installed on the server, the running code, which enables logging to a file, must have a java.util.logging.LoggingPermission with permission target as "control". The following grant entry in the Java policy file will grant this permission. You will also have to grant the "write" permission to the log file (C:\rmi.log in this example) in the Java policy file.

```
grant {
        permission java.io.FilePermission "c:\\rmi.log", "write";
        permission java.util.logging.LoggingPermission "control";
};
```

If you want to get debugging information about an RMI client application, set a non-standard sun.rmi.client.logCalls property to true when you launch the RMI client application. It will display the debugging information on the standard error. Since this property is not the part of a public specification, it may be removed in future releases. You need to refer to the RMI specification for more details on debugging options.

Dynamic Class Downloading

The JVM loads the class definition before it can create an object of a class. It uses a class loader to load a class at runtime. A class loader is an instance of the java.lang.ClassLoader class. A class loader must locate the byte codes for a class before it can load its definition into the JVM. A Java class loader is capable of loading the byte codes of a class from any location such as a local file system, a network, etc. There could be multiple class loaders in one JVM and they could be system or custom defined.

The JVM creates a class loader at startup, which is called a *bootstrap* class loader. The bootstrap class loader is responsible for loading initial classes required for basic JVM functions. Class loaders are organized in a tree-like structure based on a parent-child relationship. The bootstrap class loader has no parent. All other class loaders have the bootstrap class loader as their direct or indirect parent. In a typical class loading process, when a class loader is asked to load the bytecode for a class, it asks its parent to load the class, which in turn asks its parent and so on, until the bootstrap class loader gets the request to load the class. If none of the parent class loaders are able to load the class, the class loader that received the initial request to load the class will attempt to load the class.

The RMI runtime uses a special RMI class loader that is responsible for loading the classes in an RMI application. When an object is being passed around in an RMI application from one JVM to another, the sending JVM has to serialize and marshal the object, and the receiving JVM has to deserialize and unmarshal it. The sending JVM adds the value of the property java.rmi.server.codebase to the object's serialized stream. When the object stream is received at other end, the receiving JVM must load the class definition of the object using a class loader before it can convert the object stream into a Java object. The JVM instructs the RMI class loader to load the class definition of the object, which it has received in a stream form. The class loader attempts to load the class definition from its JVM CLASSPATH. If the class definition is not found using the CLASSPATH, the class loader uses the value of the java.rmi.server. codebase property from the object's stream to load the class definition.

Note that the java.rmi.server.codebase property is set in one JVM and it is used to download the class definition in another JVM. This property can be set when you run the RMI server or client program. When one side (server or client) transmits an object to another side, which does not have the bytecode to represent the class definition for the object being received, the sending side must have set the java.rmi.server.codebase property at the time of sending the object, so that the receiving end can download the class bytecode using this property. The value for the java.rmi.server.codebase property is a space-separated list of URLs.

Downloading code from an RMI server to the client may be fine from a security point of view. Sometimes it may not be considered safe to download code from a client to the server. By default, downloading the classes from remote JVMs is disabled. RMI lets you enable/disable this feature by using a java.rmi.server.useCodebaseOnly property. By default, it is set to true. If it is set to true, the JVM's class loader will load classes only from local CLASSPATH or locally set java.rmi.server.codebase property. That is, if it is set to true, the class loader will not read the value of java.rmi.server.codebase from the received object's stream to download the class definition. Rather, it will look for the class definition in its JVM CLASSPATH and use URLs that are set as the value of the java.rmi.server.codebase property for its own JVM. That is, when the java.rmi.server.useCodebaseOnly property is set to true, the RMI class loader ignores the value for the codebase that is sent from the sending JVM in an object's stream. The property name useCodebaseOnly seems to be a misnomer. It could have conveyed its meaning better had it been named useLocallySetCodebaseOnly. Here is how you can set this property when you run the RMI server:

```
java -cp C:\utilserver.jar
    -Djava.rmi.server.codebase="http://www.myurl.com/rmiclasses"
    -Djava.rmi.server.useCodebaseOnly=true
    com.jdojo.rmi.RemoteServer
```

■ **Tip** Starting in JDK 7u21 (also in JDK 6u45 and JDK 5u45), the default value for the java.rmi.server.codebase property is set to true. Its default value used to be false. It means, by default, the application is not allowed to download classes from other JVMs.

There are two implications of setting the java.rmi.server.useCodebaseOnly property to true:

- If the server needs a class as part of a remote call from a client, it will always look in its CLASSPATH or it will use the value of java.rmi.server.codebase that you set for the server program. In the above example, all classes in the server must be found in its CLASSPATH or at the URL http://www.myurl.com/rmiclasses.

- If a client needs to use a new class type in a remote method call, the new class type must be known to the server in advance because the server will never use the client's instruction (set by using java.rmi.server.codebase property at the client side) about the location from where to download the required new classes. This means that you must make the new classes that will be used by a remote client available in server's CLASSPATH or at the URLs specified as the java.rmi.server.codebase property for the server. This situation may arise when a remote method accepts an interface type and the client sends an object of a class that implements that interface. In this case, the server may not have the same definition of the new implementation of the interface as the client.

The above argument applies to running an RMI client application as well if you set the java.rmi.server.useCodebaseOnly property to true for the JVM running the RMI client application. If this property is set to true for the client application, you must make all required classes available to the client either by placing them in its CLASSPATH or placing them at URLs and setting the URLs as the value for the java.rmi.server.codebase property at the client side.

Garbage Collection of Remote Objects

In an RMI application, remote objects are created in the JVM on the server. The RMI registry and remote clients keep references of the remote objects. Does a remote object ever get garbage collected? And, if it does get garbage collected, when does it happen and how does it happen? Garbage collection of a local object is easy. A local object is created and referenced in the same JVM. It is an easy task for a garbage collector to determine that a local object is no longer referenced in the JVM.

In an RMI application, you need a garbage collector that can keep track of the references of a remote object in remote JVMs. Suppose an RMI server creates a remote object of RemoteUtilityImpl class and five clients get its remote reference. An RMI registry is also a client that gets the remote reference as part of the bind/rebind process. When and how does the server garbage collect the lone object of the RemoteUtilityImpl class, which is being referenced by five clients?

The JVM on the server, which has the remote object, and the five JVMs at five different clients must interact, so the remote object in the server's JVM can be garbage collected when it is no longer used by any remote clients. Let's ignore the local references of the remote object in the server JVM for this discussion. The interaction between a remote client and an RMI server depend on many unreliable factors. For example, the network may go down and a remote client may not be able to communicate with the server. The second consideration is who initiates the interaction between the remote client and the server? Is it the server that keeps asking a remote client if it has a live remote reference? Is it the remote client who keeps telling the server that it still has a live remote reference? The responsibility of interaction between client and server is shared by both. The remote client needs to update the server about the aliveness of its remote references. If the server does not hear from any clients for a specific period of time, it takes a unilateral decision to make the remote object a candidate for a future garbage collection.

The RMI garbage collector is based on reference count. A reference count has an associated lease. A lease has a time period for which it is valid. When a remote client (including an RMI registry) gets a reference to a remote object, it sends a message to the RMI runtime on the server requesting a lease for that remote object reference. The server grants a lease for a specified time period to that client. The server increments the reference count for that remote object by one and sends back the lease to the client. By default, an RMI server grants a lease for 10 minutes for a remote object. Now, the following are some possibilities:

- The client may be done with the remote object reference within the time period for which it had acquired the lease from the server.

- The client may want to renew the lease for another extended time period.

- The client crashes. The server does not receive any message from the client, and the lease period for a remote reference that was acquired by the client expires.

Let's look at each possibility. A client sends messages to the server on three different occasions. It sends a message the very first time it receives a remote reference. It tells the server that it has a reference of the remote object. The second time, it sends a message to the server when it wants to renew the lease for a remote reference. The third time, it sends a message to the server when it is done with the remote reference. In fact, when a remote reference is garbage collected in a client application, it sends a message to the server that it is done with the remote object. Internally, there are only two types of messages that a remote client sends to a server: dirty and clean. The *dirty* message is sent to get a lease and the *clean* message is sent to remove/cancel the lease. These two messages are sent from a remote client to a server using the dirty() and clean() methods of the java.rmi.dgc.DGC interface. As a developer, you do not have any control over these messages (sending or receiving) except that you can customize the lease time period. The lease time period controls the frequency of these messages sent to the server.

When a client is done with a remote object reference, it sends a message to the server that it is done with it. The message is sent when the remote reference in the client's JVM is garbage collected. Therefore, it is important that you set the remote reference in the client program code to null as soon as you are done with it. Otherwise, the server will keep holding on to the remote object, even if it is no longer used by the remote client. You do not have any control on the timing of this message, which is sent from the remote client to the server. All you can do to expedite this message sending is to set the remote object reference in the client code to null, so the garage collector will attempt to garbage collect it and send a clean message to the server.

The RMI runtime keeps track of the leases for remote references in a remote client JVM. When a lease is half-way through its expiration period, the remote client sends a lease renewal request to the server and gets the lease renewed. When a lease for a remote client is renewed for a remote reference, the server keeps track of the lease expiration time and it will not garbage collect the remote object. It is important that you understand the importance of setting the lease period for a remote reference. If it is too small, a significant amount of network bandwidth will be used for renewing the lease frequently. If it is too large, the server will keep the remote object alive for a longer time in case a client is done with its remote reference and it does not inform the server to cancel the lease. I will discuss shortly how to set a lease period value in an RMI application.

If the server does not hear anything from a remote client about the lease of a remote reference that the client had acquired, after the expiration of the lease period, it simply cancels the lease and decrements the reference count for that remote object by one. This unilateral decision that is made by the server is important to handle the cases of ill-behaved remote clients (not telling the server that it is done with a remote reference) or any network/system hiccups that may prevent the remote client from communicating with the server.

When all clients are done with a remote reference of a remote object, its reference count in the server will go down to zero. A remote client is considered done with a remote reference when either its lease is expired or it has sent a clean message to the server. In this case, the RMI runtime will reference the remote object using a *weak reference*, so if there is no local reference to the remote object, it may be garbage collected.

By default, the lease period is set for 10 minutes. You can set the lease period using the java.rmi.dgc.leaseValue property when you start the RMI server. The value for the lease period is specified in milliseconds. The following command starts the server program with a lease period set to 5 minutes (300000 milliseconds). The command text is entered on one line with two parts separated by a space, not by a newline as shown; I have used a newline to separate the parts of the command for clarity.

```
java -cp C:/utilserver.jar
    -Djava.rmi.dgc.leaseValue=300000
    -Djava.rmi.server.codebase=file:/C:/utilserver.jar
    com.jdojo.rmi.RemoteServer
```

Except for setting the lease time period, everything is handled by the RMI runtime. The RMI runtime gives you one more piece of information about the garbage collection of a remote object. It can tell you when the reference count of the remote object has gone down to zero. It is important to get this notification if a remote object holds some resources that you would like to free when no remote client is referencing it. It is easy to get this notification. All you have to do is to implement the java.rmi.server.Unreferenced interface in your remote object implementation class. Its declaration is as follows:

```
public interface Unreferenced {
        void unreferenced()
|
```

The unreferenced() method is called when the remote reference count for a remote object becomes zero. If you want to get a notification in your example for the RemoteUtility remote object, you need to modify the declaration of the RemoteUtilityImpl class, as shown in Listing 7-6.

Listing 7-6. A Modified Version of the RemoteUtilityImpl Class That Implements the Unreferenced Interface

```java
// RemoteUtilityImpl.java
package com.jdojo.rmi;

import java.rmi.server.Unreferenced;
import java.time.ZonedDateTime;

public class RemoteUtilityImpl implements RemoteUtility, Unreferenced {
        public RemoteUtilityImpl() {
        }

        @Override
        public String echo(String msg) {
                return msg;
        }

        @Override
        public ZonedDateTime getServerTime() {
                return ZonedDateTime.now();
        }

        @Override
        public int add(int n1, int n2) {
                return n1 + n2;
        }

        @Override
        public void unreferenced() {
                System.out.println("RemoteUtility unreferenced at: " +
                                ZonedDateTime.now());
        }
}
```

You may notice that, this time, the RemoteUtilityImpl class implements the Unreferenced interface and provides implementation for the unreferenced() method, which prints a message on the standard output with the time when its reference count becomes zero. The unreferenced() method will be called by the RMI runtime. To test that the unreferenced() method is called, you can start the RMI registry application, and then start the RMI server application. The RMI registry will keep renewing the lease for the remote object. As long as an RMI registry is running, you will never see the unreferenced() method being called. You need to shut down the RMI registry application and wait for the remote object reference's lease to expire or to be cancelled by the RMI registry when you shut it down. After the RMI registry is shut down, you will see the message on the standard output for the server program that will be printed by the unreferenced() method.

An RMI registry should be used just as a bootstrap means to start the remote client. Later on, the remote client can receive a remote object's reference as a method call to another remote object. If a remote client receives a remote object reference by a remote method call on a remote object, that remote object's reference need not be registered with the RMI registry. In this case, after the last remote client is finished with the remote reference, the server will garbage collect the remote object instead of keeping it in memory when it is bound to an RMI registry.

Summary

Java Remote Method Invocation (RMI) allows a program running in one JVM to invoke methods on Java objects running in another JVM. RMI provides an API to develop distributed applications using the Java programming language.

An RMI application involves three applications running in three JVMs: the rmiregistry application, a server application, and a client application. The rmiregistry application is shipped with the JDK. You are responsible for developing the server and client applications. The server application creates Java objects called remote objects and registers them with the rmiregistry for later name lookup by clients. The client application looks up the remote object in the rmiregistry using a logical name and gets back a reference of the remote object. The client application invokes methods on the remote object reference that is sent to the server application for execution of the method on the remote object The results of the method execution is sent back from the server application to the client application.

An RMI application must follow a few rules to develop the classes and interfaces involved the remote communication. You need to create an interface (called remote interface) that must inherit from the Remote interface. All methods in the interface must include a throws clause that throws at least the RemoteException. The class for the remote object must implement the remote interface. The server application creates an object of the class implementing the remote interface, exports the object to give a status of a real remote object, and registers it with the rmiregistry. The client application needs only the remote interface.

If any of the three applications needs classes that are not locally available, they can download them dynamically at runtime. For a JVM to download classes dynamically, the java.rmi.server.useCodebaseOnly property must be set to false. By default, it is set to true, which disables dynamic downloading of the classes in a JVM. Along with a remote object reference, the JVM also receives the value of a property named java.rmi.server.codebase, which is the URLs from where the JVM may download (if permitted by its own java.rmi.server.useCodebaseOnly property setting) the classes needed to work with the remote object reference.

There are several components working together in an RMI application that make it hard to debug. You can log all calls to the RMI server by running it with the JVM property java.rmi.server.logCalls set to true. All calls to the server will be logged to a standard error. You can also log RMI server calls to a file.

RMI provides automatic garbage collection for remote objects running in the RMI server. The garbage collection of remote objects is based on reference counts and leases. When the client application gets the reference of the remote object, it also obtains a lease for the remote object from the server application. The lease is valid for a period. The client application keeps renewing the lease periodically as long it keeps the remote object reference. The server application keeps track of the reference count and the leases for the remote objects. When the client application is done with the remote reference, it sends a message to the server application and the server application reduces the reference count for the remote object by 1. When the reference count of the remote object reduces to zero in the server application, the remote object is garbage collected.

CHAPTER 8

■ ■ ■

Java Native Interface

In this chapter, you will learn

- What the Java Native Interface (JNI) is
- How to write Java programs that uses native methods
- How to write C++ programs to implement native methods
- How to create a shared library on Windows and Linux for the native implementation of methods used in Java
- The data type mapping between Java types and JNI types
- How to work with Java strings and arrays in native code
- How to create Java objects, and access fields and methods of those objects in native code
- Exception handling in native code
- How to embed the JVM in native code
- How to handle thread synchronization using the JNI in native code

What Is the Java Native Interface?

The Java Native Interface (JNI) is a programming interface that facilitates interaction between Java code and code written in native languages such as C, C++, FORTRAN, etc. The JNI supports calling C and C++ functions directly from Java. If you need to use native code written in any other language such as FORTRAN, you can use a C/C++ wrapper function to call it from Java. Interaction can take place both ways. Java code can call native code and vice versa, as shown in Figure 8-1.

Figure 8-1. *The JNI architecture*

Java calls native code using native methods. A native method in a Java context is a method that is declared in Java and implemented in a native language such as C/C++. The native method implementation is compiled into a *shared library*, which is loaded by the JVM. A shared library is called a dynamic link library (DLL) on Windows, and a shared object (SO) on UNIX. In Java code, you call a Java method and a native method the same way. A Java program is compiled into a platform-independent format called byte code. Native code is compiled into a platform-dependent format. Therefore, if a Java application uses native code, it is no longer portable to other platforms unless you develop the same shared library on all platforms. Sometimes you may access platform-specific features inside the native code, which is used from the Java application; in that case, you should be aware that your Java application cannot be run on other platforms.

Why would someone use the JNI when Java provides a rich set of features through its class libraries? It may be necessary to use the JNI to access native code in Java for the following reasons:

- If a Java application needs to implement some platform-specific features that are not possible to implement using the Java APIs.

- You may already have legacy code written in native languages and you want to reuse it in your Java application.

- You are developing a time-critical Java application where Java code does not perform as fast as expected. You can move the time-critical section of your Java code to native code.

You should consider using the JNI in a Java application as a last resort. You must explore all possibilities of implementing the needed features using the Java APIs. Using the JNI also changes the skill set that is required to develop an application. Either the developers who are working on Java application are trained in the native language (C/C++) or new developers are brought into the team who know the native language. Using native code in a Java application makes the application less stable and prone to security risks because the native code is run outside the JVM.

I will use C++ to implement native methods in this chapter. You can use the C language instead. All code examples in C++ listed in this chapter can be moved to the C language with minor changes. I will specify the differences between C++ code and C code whenever you need to make changes in C++ code to convert it to C.

System Requirements

You need a C or C++ compiler that can create a shared library. You also need a JDK installed on your computer to generate C/C++ header files. The native code referenced in this chapter has been developed using NetBeans 8.0 with Cygwin as the C++ compiler on the Windows platform. Java 8 was used to compile and run the Java code. However, using Cygwin as the C++ compiler is not a requirement to run any examples. You can use any other C/C++ compiler to create a shared library on your platform. Please visit `https://netbeans.org/kb/trails/cnd.html` for more details on how to configure NetBeans to use C++.

Getting Started with the JNI

Developing a Java application that uses the JNI involves the following steps:

- Writing the Java program

- Compiling the Java program

- Creating a C/C++ header file

- Writing a C/C++ program

- Creating a shared library

- Running the Java program

Subsequent sections discuss each step in detail.

Writing the Java Program

A Java program that uses the JNI differs from a Java-only program only in two aspects:

- Loading the shared library

- Declaring the native method

The shared library that contains the native method implementation must be loaded before Java can call the native method. A shared library is loaded using the loadLibrary(String libraryNameWithoutExtension) static method of the java.lang.System class as shown:

```
// Load a shared library named beginningjava
System.loadLibrary("beginningjava");
```

You can also load a shared library using the loadLibrary() method of the java.lang.Runtime class. Internally, the loadLibrary() method of the System class calls the loadLibrary() method of the Runtime class. The above code can be rewritten as follows:

```
// Load the shared library
Runtime.getRuntime().loadLibrary("beginningjava");
```

Note that you need to pass a shared library name without any platform-specific prefix and file extension to the loadLibrary() method. For example, if your shared library file name is beginningjava.dll on Windows or beginningjava.so on UNIX, you need to use beginningjava as the shared library name. The loadLibrary() method will append the file extension to find the shared library. This way, you do not need to change your Java code, which loads the shared library if you intend to run the same Java code on different platforms.

You can also load a shared library using the load() method of the System or Runtime class. The load() method accepts the absolute path of the shared library with the file extension. If a beginningjava.dll file on Windows platforms is in the C:\myjni directory, the call to the load() method will look as follows:

```
// Load the shared library
System.load("C:\\myjni\\beginningjava.dll");
```

Note that using the load() method forces you to use the absolute path and the file extension of the shared library, which makes your Java code non-portable to other platforms. You will use the loadLibrary() method of the System class to load shared library in your examples in this chapter. The load() and loadLibrary() methods throw a java.lang.UnsatisfiedLinkError if the specific library cannot be loaded.

How does the loadLibrary() method find the shared library file in the file system by just knowing the library name? You have two ways to let the JVM know about the location of your shared library:

- Include the directory that contains the shared library into the PATH environment variable on Windows and LD_LIBRARY_PATH environment variable on UNIX.

- Specify the directory (or directories, separated by semicolon) that contains the shared library using the java.library.path JVM property as a command line option. The following command assumes that the beginningjava shared library is placed in the C:\myjni\lib directory:

```
java -Djava.library.path=C:\myjni\lib your-class-name-to-run
```

A native method that is used in Java does not have a body written in Java because its implementation exists in the native code. However, you need to declare the native method in Java before you can use it. It is declared using the native keyword. A native method declaration in Java code ends with a semicolon. The following snippet of code declares a native method named hello(), which has no parameters and returns void.

```
public class Test {
        // Declare a native method called hello()
        public native void hello();
}
```

Calling a native method in Java code is the same as calling any other Java methods.

```
Test test = new Test();
test.hello();
```

You can declare a native method to have public, private, protected, or package-level scope. A native method can be declared static or non-static. You can have as many native methods in a Java class as you want.

You cannot declare a native method as abstract. This implies that an interface cannot have a native method because all methods declared in an interface are abstract if they are not declared static or default. An abstract method means that the method's implementation is missing and it will be implemented in Java, whereas native method means that the method's implementation is missing and it is implemented in native code. Declaring a method as native and abstract at the same time will be confusing as to where to look for the implementation of the method—in the Java code or in the native code. This is the reason why a method declaration cannot use the combination of the two modifiers abstract and native.

The native keyword must be used only to declare methods. You cannot declare a field as native. The following snippet of code declares two classes named WillCompile and WontCompile. Class WillCompile contains valid uses of the native keyword, whereas class WontCompile demonstrates the invalid uses of the native keyword.

```
public class WillCompile {
        public native void m1();
        private native void m2();
        protected native void m3();
        native void m4();

        public static native void m5();

        public native int m6(String str);
```

```
        // A non-native method (Java-only method)
        public int add(int a, int b) {
                return a + b;
        }
}

// Sample of Illegal use of native keyword in a Java class
public class WontCompile {
        // A field cannot be native
        private native String name;

        // A method cannot be abstract as well as native
        public abstract native String getName();
}
```

Now you are ready to write Java code to call your first native method. You will name your native method hello(). It does not accept any parameters and does not return any value. You will implement it in C++ later and it will print a message, Hello JNI, on the standard output. Listing 8-1 has the complete code for the HelloJNI class.

Listing 8-1. A HelloJNI Class That Uses a Native Method Named hello( )

```
// HelloJNI.java
package com.jdojo.jni;

public class HelloJNI {
        static {
                // Load the shared library using its name only
                System.loadLibrary("beginningjava");
        }

        // Declare the native method
        public native void hello();

        public static void main(String[] args) {
                // Create a HelloJNI object
                HelloJNI helloJNI = new HelloJNI();

                // Call the native method
                helloJNI.hello();
        }
}
```

The HelloJNI class performs three things:

- It loads a beginningjava shared library (beginningjava.dll on Windows and beginningjava.so on UNIX-like OS) in the static initializer. Note that you do not need to have the beginningjava shared library when you write and compile the HelloJNI class. The shared library is required when you run the HelloJNI class.

```
static {
    System.loadLibrary("beginningjava ");
}
```

- It declares a native method named hello(), which will be implemented in C++ code later.

```
public native void hello();
```

The Java compiler will compile the HelloJNI class with the hello() native method declaration without having the native code that implements the method. The implementation of the method will be required when it is called at runtime.

- It creates an object of the HelloJNI class in the main() method and calls the hello() method on the object.

```
HelloJNI helloJNI = new HelloJNI();
helloJNI.hello();
```

The code for the HelloJNI class is simple. There is nothing extraordinary that you have to do inside the Java code to use a native method. You cannot run this class yet, because when you run it, it will look for a beginningjava shared library with the native code for the hello() method, which you have not written yet.

Compiling the Java Program

Compiling a Java program that uses native methods is the same as compiling any other Java programs. There is no special setting that you need to apply when you compile the HelloJNI class. You can compile it using the javac command, like so:

```
javac HelloJNI.java
```

This command will generate a HelloJNI.class file, which will contain the class definition of the HelloJNI class, whose fully qualified name is com.jdojo.jni.HelloJNI. Make sure that you have the HelloJNI.class file available because it is necessary to perform the next step.

Creating the C/C++ Header File

Before you start writing the code for a native method in C/C++, you need to generate a header file that will contain the declaration of your method in C/C++. You will use this header file when you write the implementation of your hello() native method. The method signature for the hello() method in Java and C/C++ differs significantly.

You do not need to worry about the details about how to write the signature of a method in C/C++, which will be used by the Java code. The JDK provides a tool called javah that generates all required header files for you. The javah tool is located in the JDK_HOME\bin folder, where JDK_HOME is the installation folder for the JDK. For example, if you have installed the JDK in the C:\java8 directory on Windows, the javah tool is in C:\java8\bin. The tool accepts the fully qualified class name of a Java class and generates a header file with extension .h that contains the method signature for all native methods declared in the specified class. The following command will generate a C/C++ header file for all native methods declarations in the HelloJNI class:

```
javah com.jdojo.jni.HelloJNI
```

The javah tool will look for the HelloJNI class in the CLASSPATH. If it is not in the CLASSPATH, you can specify CLASSPATH using a –classpath or -cp command line option as follows:

```
javah -cp C:\myclasses com.jdojo.jni.HelloJNI
```

This command will generate a header file named com_jdojo_jni_HelloJNI.h in the current directory. By default, the generated file name is based on the fully qualified name of the class. A dot in the class name is replaced with an underscore and the file has an .h extension. You can also specify the header file name that the javah command will generate by using an -o option. You can look at other options supported by the javah command by executing a javah -help command. The contents of the com_jdojo_jni_HelloJNI.h file are shown in Listing 8-2.

Listing 8-2. Contents of the com_jdojo_jni_HelloJNI.h File

```
/* DO NOT EDIT THIS FILE - it is machine generated */
#include <jni.h>
/* Header for class com_jdojo_jni_HelloJNI */

#ifndef _Included_com_jdojo_jni_HelloJNI
#define _Included_com_jdojo_jni_HelloJNI
#ifdef __cplusplus
extern "C" {
#endif
/*
 * Class:      com_jdojo_jni_HelloJNI
 * Method:     hello
 * Signature: ()V
 */
JNIEXPORT void JNICALL Java_com_jdojo_jni_HelloJNI_hello
  (JNIEnv *, jobject);

#ifdef __cplusplus
}
#endif
#endif
```

You do not need to worry about the details in the header file. You only need the method signature that is generated for your native hello() method. The method signature void hello() in the Java code has been translated into the following method signature for the C/C++ code:

```
JNIEXPORT void JNICALL Java_com_jdojo_jni_HelloJNI_hello (JNIEnv *, jobject);
```

JNIEXPORT and JNICALL are two macros. The keyword void denotes that the native method does not return any value. The javah command uses a rule to generate the name of the native method in the header file. In this case, the method name is Java_com_jdojo_jni_HelloJNI_hello. I will discuss the details of the naming rules used by the javah tool later. Although the method declaration of the hello() method in the Java code does not accept any parameters, the native method declaration in the header file accepts two parameters. Take it as a rule that all native method declarations in a native language will accept two additional parameters than the number of parameters declared in the Java code. The additional parameters are added as the first and second parameters for the method in the native language. The first parameter is a pointer to a JNIEnv type object, which is a table of function pointers to facilitate interaction between the native environment and Java environment. The second parameter is of type either jobject or jclass. If the native method is declared non-static in the Java code, the second parameter is of type jobject, which is a reference to the Java object on which the native method is called. It is similar to the this reference that is available inside every non-static method in Java. Since the native hello() method in Java has been declared non-static, the second parameter type is of type jobject. If the native method is declared as static in Java, the second parameter will be of type jclass and it will be the reference to the class object in the JVM on which the native method is called.

At the end of this step, you should have a header file named com_jdojo_jni_HelloJNI.h with the contents shown as in Listing 8-2.

Writing the C/C++ Program

Listing 8-3 shows the C/C++ code that you need to write for the hello() native method. The next section describes the step-by-step process to set up a project and write the C++ code using the NetBeans IDE. The source code file for C++ is named hellojni.cpp. In this case, the code will be the same if you choose to use the C language instead. Note that hello is the name of your native method in Java code, whereas in C/C++ it is named Java_com_jdojo_jni_HelloJNI_hello.

Listing 8-3. A C/C++ Implementation for the hello() Native Method

```
// hellojni.cpp
#include <stdio.h>
#include <jni.h>
#include "com_jdojo_jni_HelloJNI.h"

JNIEXPORT void JNICALL Java_com_jdojo_jni_HelloJNI_hello(JNIEnv *env, jobject obj) {
    printf("Hello JNI\n");
    return;
}
```

Here are the things that this program does. It uses three C/C++ compiler preprocessor include directives to include three header files: stdio.h, jni.h, and com_jdojo_jni_HelloJNI.h. It includes stdio.h to use the standard Input/Output functionalities, jni.h to use the JNI-related functionalities, and com_jdojo_jni_HelloJNI.h to include functionalities related to your hello() native method.

The jni.h file is copied to JDK_HOME\include directory when you install the JDK. For example, if you installed the JDK in C:\java8, the jni.h file will be in the C:\java8\include directory. There is a subdirectory that is created under the JDK_HOME\include directory. The subdirectory name is platform-dependent. It is named win32 on Windows, linux on Linux, etc.. You need to use the following two directoroes as an include-path option when you compile the hellojni.cpp file:

- C:\java8\include

- C:\java8\include\win32

These inlcude paths are for Windows. Please change them according to your platform.

You can place the com_jdojo_jni_HelloJNI.h file in any directory on your machine. You will need to include the directory that contains this file in the include-path option when you compile the hellojni.cpp file.

The function signature is copied from the com_jdojo_jni_HelloJNI.h header file. You have named the two parameters as env and obj. It does not matter what name you use for these parameters in your code.

```
JNIEXPORT void JNICALL Java_com_jdojo_jni_HelloJNI_hello
(JNIEnv *env, jobject obj)
```

You have provided the implementation for the native method by adding two statements. The first statement uses the printf() function to print a message, Hello JNI, on the standard output, and the second one returns from the function, as shown:

```
printf("Hello JNI\n");
return;
```

Creating a Shared Library

In this section, you will compile the `hellojni.cpp` file into a shared library named `beginningjava`. The shared library will be a file named `beginningjava.dll` on Windows and `beginningjava.so` on a UNIX-like OS. Your operating system may use a different file extension for a shared library. Many compilers are available that can be used to create a shared library from C/C++ code. This section explains how to create a shared library on

- Windows using a GNU C++ compiler named g++, known as a MinGW compiler (**Min**imalist **G**NU for **W**indows).

- On Fedora Linux using a GNU C++ compiler named g++.

To create a shared library, you can use the C/C++ compiler on a command prompt or an IDE such as Microsoft Visual Studio on Windows or NetBeans on Windows and Linux. Note that NetBeans does not ship with a C/C++ compiler. You will need to download a compiler such as MinGW or Cygwin to use the NetBeans IDE to create a shared library.

Creating a Shared Library on Windows

The following sections describe how to install the MinGW C++ compiler called g++ on Windows and how to use it via the command prompt to create the shared library named `beginningjava.dll`.

Installing MinGW C/C++ Compiler

Follow these steps to install the MinGW compiler:

- Download the MinGW compiler from `http://sourceforge.net/projects/mingw` and install it on your machine.

- Assume that you have installed MinGW in the `C:\MinGW` directory. You need to install the following packages of MinGW: mingw-developer-toolkit, migw32-base, mingw32-gcc-g++, and msys-base. If you have installed MinGW in another directory, please replace this directory path with your installation directory path in the following discussions in this section.

- Add the `C:\MinGW\bin` directory to the system `PATH` environment variable. If you do not set the system PATH environment variable, you will be able to work with MinGW by setting the PATH environment variable on the command prompt.

- Verify that the `C:\MinGw\bin\g++.exe` file exists on your machine. g++ is the C++ compiler and `gcc` is the C compiler used by MinGW. You will use C++ code in this chapter and the g++ compiler to compiler the C++ code.

Using the g++ Command

You need to use the g++ command to create a shared library. You will need two types of files to create the shared library:

- The C++ source file that contains the C++ code. In this case, you have named it `hellojin.cpp` as shown in Listing 8-3.

- The `com_jdojo_jni_HelloJNI.h` header file shown in Listing 8-2.

- The JNI-related header files that are located in JDK_HOME\include and JDK_HOME\include\ win32 directories where JDK_HOME is the directory in which you have installed the JDK.

You can pass several options to the g++ compiler. The following command shows the minimum options needed to create your shared library:

```
g++ -Wl,--kill-at -shared -I<include-dir> -o <output-file> <source-files>
```

Here,

- The -Wl,<option> is used to pass options to the linker. The <option> is a comma-separated list of linker options. In this command, you are passing the --kill-at option to the linker to strip the stdcall suffixes (@nn) from symbols before they are exported. If you do not specify this option, you will get a java.lang.UnsatisfiedLinkError when you run the Java program that uses the shared library.

- The –shared option indicates that you want to create a shared library.

- The –I<include-dir> option is used to pass the directory that contains the header files (.h files). You can repeat this option once for each directory.

- The –o <output-file> option specifies the output file name. In your case, you will use the output file named beginningjava.dll.

- The <source-files> is a space-separated list of C++ source files.

To simplify the command syntax to generate the shared library, I will assume that the following directories and files on your machine exist:

- C:\dll\hellojni.cpp

- C:\dll\com_jdojo_jni_HelloJNI.h

- C:\java8\include

- C:\java8\include\win32

The following command will generate the beginingjava.dll file in the C:\dll directory. Each part of the command is shown in a separate line for clarity; you will enter the entire command in one line.

```
C:\> g++ -Wl,--kill-at -shared
    -IC:/java8/include -IC:/java8/include/win32 -IC:/dll
    -o C:/dll/beginningjava.dll
    C:/dll/hellojni.cpp
```

Note the use of the forward slashes in file paths. With the g++ command on Windows, you can use either a forward slash or a backslash as the path separator. Please change the path in the command to match the paths of these files and directories on your machine.

If you have not set the PATH environment variable to the C:\MinGW\bin directory, you may get the following error when you run the g++ command:

```
'g++' is not recognized as an internal or external command,operable program or batch file
```

■ **Note**   On Windows, if you want to use NetBeans IDE with MinGW, please refer to the following link for the setup instruction: https://netbeans.org/community/releases/80/cpp-setup-instructions.html.

Creating a Shared Library on Linux

The following sections describe how to install the GNU C++ compiler called g++ on Fedora Linux and how to use it on a terminal to create the shared library named beginningjava.so.

Installing MinGW C/C++ Compiler

Installing the g++ compiler on Linux is easy. Running the following command on a terminal in Linux will install the g++ compiler:

```
$ yum install gcc-c++
```

When you run the command, you may get the following message:

```
$ yum install gcc-c++
You need to be root to perform this command.
$
```

If you get this message, you need to log in as root to install the compiler. Use the su – command to login as root, enter the root password when prompted, and then run the yum command.

```
$ su -
Password: Enter Your Password Here
# yum install gcc-c++
```

During the installation, the yum command will prompt you several times to confirm downloads of the compiler setup files. You need to answer yes when you get those prompts. If the g++ compiler is already installed on your machine, the yum command will print a message to that effect.

That's all it takes install the g+= compiler on Linux.

Using the g++ Command

You need to use the g++ command to create a shared library. You will need two types of files to create the shared library:

- The C++ source file that contains the C++ code. In this case, you have named it hellojni.cpp as shown in Listing 8-3.

- The com_jdojo_jni_HelloJNI.h header file shown in Listing 8-2.

- The JNI-related header files that are located in JDK_HOME/include and JDK_HOME/include/ win32 directories where JDK_HOME is the directory in which you have installed the JDK.

You can pass several options to the g++ compiler. The following command shows the minimum options needed to create your shared library:

```
g++ -shared –I<include-dir> -o <output-file> <source-files>
```

Here,

- The shared option indicates that you want to create a shared library.

- The -I<include-dir> option is used to pass the directory that contains the header files (.h files). You can repeat this option once for each directory.

- The -o <output-file> option specifies the output file name. In your case, you will use the output file name of beginningjava.so.

- The <source-files> is a space-separated list of C++ source files.

To simplify the command syntax to generate the shared library, I will assume that the following directories and files on your machine exist:

- /home/ksharan/slib/hellojni.cpp

- /home/ksharan/slib/com_jdojo_jni_HelloJNI.h

- /home/ksharan/java8/include

- /home/ksharan/java8/include/linux

The following command will generate the beginingjava.so file in the /home/ksharan/slib directory. Each part of the command is shown in a separate line for clarity; you will enter the entire command in one line.

```
$ g++ -shared
 -I/home/ksharan/java8/include -I/home/ksharan/java8/include/linux -I/home/ksharan/slib
 -o /home/ksharan/slib/beginningjava.so
 /home/ksharan/slib/hellojni.cpp
```

Please change the path in the command to match the paths of these files and directories on your machine.

■ **Note**   On Linux, if you want to use NetBeans IDE with the g++ compiler, please refer to the following link for the setup instruction: https://netbeans.org/community/releases/80/cpp-setup-instructions.html.

Running the Java Program

Before proceeding to run the Java class, please make sure that you were able to create the shared library (the beginningjava.dll file on Windows and beginningjava.so file on a UNIX-like OS). If you were not able to create the shared library, you can use the shared libraries provided with the source code for this book. The shared libraries are located in a directory named cplusplus.

Now you are ready to run your HelloJNI Java class as shown in Listing 8-1. Suppose you have placed the beginningjava shared library file in the C:\myjni\lib directory. Run the HelloJNI class using the following command:

```
C:\> java -Djava.library.path=C:\myjni\lib com.jdojo.jni.HelloJNI
```

The -Djava.library.path=C:\myjni\lib option instructs the JVM to look for shared libraries in the C:\myjni\lib directory. If the above command runs successfully, it will print a message, Hello JNI, on the standard output. Alternatively, you can also add the directory that contains the shared library to the PATH environment variable and the Java runtime will find it. Windows will also find the shared library without setting the java.library.path option if the shared library is in the current directory. The following commands show how to set the PATH environment variable (on Windows) for the current session and run the class:

```
C:\> SET PATH=C:\myjni\lib;%PATH%
C:\> java com.jdojo.jni.HelloJNI
```

Native Function Naming Rules

The javah command uses a naming rule, which is based on name mangling, to generate native method names in the C/C++ header file. The Java runtime uses the same rule to resolve the Java native method name to the native function name in a shared library. The name mangling rule is used so that the name generated for the native function is a valid C/C++ name without a name collision. You can think of name mangling as simply replacing invalid characters with characters that make up a valid function name. The native function name is generated based on the following parts, which are concatenated using an underscore:

- The method name starts with the word Java.

- The mangled fully qualified name of the package of the Java class that contains the native method's declaration. An underscore is used as a package/sub-package separator.

- The native method name in Java.

- For an overloaded native method, two underscores followed by the mangled method's signature

Java runtime uses two names for a native function—a short name and a long name. The short name does not use two underscores followed by the mangled method's signature. The Java runtime searches the shared library for the short name first. If it does not find a function using the short name, it searches with the long name. The mangled name uses a conversion table shown in Table 8-1.

Table 8-1. *The Escape Sequence Used in the Name-Mangling Process*

Original Character	Substituted Character
Any non-ASCII Unicode character	_0xxxx
	Note that alphabets used in _0xxxx are all lowercase such as _0abcd
_ (an underscore)	_1
; (a semi-colon)	_2
[(a beginning square bracket)	_3

Characters such as a semicolon and beginning with a square bracket may occur as part of a method's parameter signature that is used internally by Java. Table 8-2 shows few examples of method declarations in .Java code and the method signature used internally by Java.

Table 8-2. *Examples of Java Method's Declaration and Internally Used Method Signatures*

Method Declaration	Internally Used Method Signature
public static void javaPrintMsg(java.lang.String)	(Ljava/lang/String;)V
public void javaCallBack()	()V
public static void main(java.lang.String[])	([Ljava/lang/String;)V

If you declare a parameter of type java.lang.String, it is used internally as Ljava/lang/String;. To know about the signature of a method that is used internally by Java, you need to use the javap command with a -s option. The following command will print the method signatures for all methods in the com.jdojo.jni.HelloJNI class. You can use a -private option to print signatures of all methods including the private ones.

```
javap -s -private com.jdojo.jni.HelloJNI
```

If you are required to use a method signature of a Java method inside a JNI function in native code, you should run the javap command to get the signatures instead of entering them by hand. You can learn the rules used to make up the method signature that is used internally by Java. However, using the javap command makes it easy to get this information. Let's consider the declaration of some native methods in a class Test as shown in Listing 8-4.

Listing 8-4. A Test Class with Some Native Method Declarations

```
package com.jdojo.jni;

public class Test {
        private native void sayHello();
        private native void printMsg(String msg);
        private native int[] increment(int[] num, int incrementValue);
        private native double myMethod(int i, String s[], String ss);
        private native double myMethod(double i, String s[], String ss);
        private native double myMethod(short i, String s[], String ss);
}
```

If you compile the Test class and run the command

```
javah com.jdojo.jni.Test
```

you get a com_jdojo_jni_Test.h header file that has the contents shown in Listing 8-5.

Listing 8-5. The Header File Generated for the Class com.jdojo.jni.Test

```
/* DO NOT EDIT THIS FILE - it is machine generated */
#include <jni.h>
/* Header for class com_jdojo_jni_Test */

#ifndef _Included_com_jdojo_jni_Test
#define _Included_com_jdojo_jni_Test
#ifdef __cplusplus
extern "C" {
#endif
/*
 * Class:     com_jdojo_jni_Test
 * Method:    sayHello
 * Signature: ()V
 */
JNIEXPORT void JNICALL Java_com_jdojo_jni_Test_sayHello
  (JNIEnv *, jobject);

/*
 * Class:     com_jdojo_jni_Test
 * Method:    printMsg
 * Signature: (Ljava/lang/String;)V
 */
JNIEXPORT void JNICALL Java_com_jdojo_jni_Test_printMsg
  (JNIEnv *, jobject, jstring);
```

```
/*
 * Class:     com_jdojo_jni_Test
 * Method:    increment
 * Signature: ([II)[I
 */
JNIEXPORT jintArray JNICALL Java_com_jdojo_jni_Test_increment
  (JNIEnv *, jobject, jintArray, jint);

/*
 * Class:     com_jdojo_jni_Test
 * Method:    myMethod
 * Signature: (I[Ljava/lang/String;Ljava/lang/String;)D
 */
JNIEXPORT jdouble JNICALL Java_com_jdojo_jni_Test_myMethod__I_3Ljava_lang_String_2Ljava_lang_
String_2
  (JNIEnv *, jobject, jint, jobjectArray, jstring);

/*
 * Class:     com_jdojo_jni_Test
 * Method:    myMethod
 * Signature: (D[Ljava/lang/String;Ljava/lang/String;)D
 */
JNIEXPORT jdouble JNICALL Java_com_jdojo_jni_Test_myMethod__D_3Ljava_lang_String_2Ljava_lang_
String_2
  (JNIEnv *, jobject, jdouble, jobjectArray, jstring);

/*
 * Class:     com_jdojo_jni_Test
 * Method:    myMethod
 * Signature: (S[Ljava/lang/String;Ljava/lang/String;)D
 */
JNIEXPORT jdouble JNICALL Java_com_jdojo_jni_Test_myMethod__S_3Ljava_lang_String_2Ljava_lang_
String_2
  (JNIEnv *, jobject, jshort, jobjectArray, jstring);

#ifdef __cplusplus
}
#endif
#endif
```

You can look at the native function names that are generated for different native method's declarations. Do not worry about the data types used for the function's parameters. I will cover data type mapping between Java and native language in the next section.

Data Type Mapping

The JNI defines mapping between data types used in Java and native functions. Table 8-3 lists the mapping for primitive data types between Java and native C/C++ language. Note that all you have to do is to add a j in front of the name of a primitive data type in Java and you get the equivalent data type name in C/C++. JNI also defines a data type named jsize, which is used to store the length, such as the length of an array or a string.

Table 8-3. *The Mapping Between Java Primitive Data Types and JNI Native Data Types*

Java Primitive Types	Native Primitive Type	Description
boolean	jboolean	Unsigned 8 bits
byte	jbyte	Signed 8 bits
char	jchar	Unsigned 16 bits
double	jdouble	64 bits
float	jfloat	32 bits
int	jint	Signed 32 bits
long	jlong	Signed 64 bits
short	jshort	Signed 16 bits
void	void	N/A

The JNI defines reference type equivalents for Java reference types. It is not possible to define a separate type in the JNI for all reference types that can be created in Java. All Java reference types can be mapped to the JNI reference type called jobject. You have some specialized JNI reference types that represent commonly used reference types in Java, such as jstring in JNI represents java.lang.String in Java. Table 8-4 lists the reference type mapping between Java and the JNI.

Table 8-4. *The Reference Type Mapping Between Java and JNI*

Java Reference Type	JNI Type
Any Java object	jobject
java.lang.String	jstring
java.lang.Class	jclass
java.lang.Throwable	jthrowable

The JNI defines separate reference types to represent Java arrays. The type jarray is a generic array type that represents any Java array type. There is a specialized array type for each type of array in Java. In JNI, an array type is named like jxxxArray, where xxx could be object, boolean, byte, char, double, float, int, long, and short. For example, jintArray in C/C++ represents an int array in Java. Note that all reference type arrays in Java are represented by jobjectArray type in C/C++.

While working with C/C++ code using the JNI, you will come across another type called jvalue. It is a union type defined in C/C++ as follows:

```
typedef union jvalue {
        jboolean z;
        jbyte    b;
        jchar    c;
        jshort   s;
        jint     i;
        jlong    j;
```

```
        jfloat   f;
        jdouble  d;
        jobject  l;
} jvalue
```

Note that the jvalue union type does not have an equivalent type in Java. Typically, the jvalue type is defined as a parameter type in built-in functions that are part of the JNI API.

Using JNI Functions in C/C++

JNI functions let you access the JVM data structures and objects in native code. Sometimes they let you convert the data in a particular format that is passed between Java and the native environments. All native functions have their first parameter, which is always a pointer to JNIEnv, which in turn is a pointer to a table of all JNI function pointers.

There are always two versions of functions that you can call on type JNIEnv: one for C and one for C++. The C version of the function accepts a pointer to JNIEnv as the first parameter, and C++ will not have that first parameter. The two versions of the same methods, C and C++, are called differently. The following snippet of code shows the difference in calling a JNI function in C and C++, assuming FuncXxx is the function name and env is a pointer to JNIEnv type:

```
// C style
(*env)->FuncXxx(env, list-of-arguments...);

// C++ style
env->FuncXxx(list-of-arguments...);
```

This chapter uses the C++ way of calling JNI functions. You can convert the code to C style easily by using the above snippet of code as a reference.

As a concrete example, the following are the function signatures for the GetStringUTFChars() JNI function that let you convert a Java string to a UTF-8 string format:

```
// C Version of the GetStringUTFChars() JNI function
const char * GetStringUTFChars(JNIEnv *env, jstring string, jboolean *isCopy);

// C++ Version of the GetStringUTFChars() JNI function
const char * GetStringUTFChars(jstring string, jboolean *isCopy);
```

If you want to call this function in C or C++, your code will look as follows:

```
// C Code
const char *utfMsg = (*env)->GetStringUTFChars(env, msg, iscopy);

// C++ Code
const char *utfMsg = env->GetStringUTFChars(msg, iscopy);
```

Working with Strings

Strings are represented differently in Java and C/C++. In Java, a string is represented as a sequence of 16-bit Unicode characters, whereas in C/C++ a string is a pointer to a sequence of null-terminated characters. The jstring reference type in the native code represents an instance of the java.lang.String class, which is a sequence of 16-bit Unicode characters. The JNI has functions to convert a Java string to a native string and vice versa. One set of string functions works with UTF-8 strings and the other set works with Unicode strings. When Java passes a string to the native code, you must convert the string in native code to native format (UTF-8 or Unicode) before using it. The same logic goes for returning a string from native code to Java. You must convert the native string to an instance of jstring before it can be returned to Java.

Let's start with an example in which you will pass a string from Java code to C/C++ code. The C/C++ code will convert the Java string to a native UTF-8 format and print it on the standard output using the printf() function. The native methods' declaration in Java would be as follows:

- public native void printMsg(String msg);

- public native String getMsg();

The printMsg() method accepts a Java string and its native function will print it on the standard output. The getMsg() method returns a native string to Java and Java will print it on the standard output. Listing 8-6 contains the Java code that declares these two native methods. Note that the static initialize loads the shared library named beginningjava that you had created in the previous section. This time, you will need to include the C++ code for the new native method in the shared library.

Listing 8-6. Passing Strings from Java to a Native Function and Vice Versa

```
// JNIStringTest.java
package com.jdojo.jni;

public class JNIStringTest {
        static {
                System.loadLibrary("beginningjava");
        }

        public native void printMsg(String msg);
        public native String getMsg();

        public static void main(String[] args) {
                JNIStringTest stringTest = new JNIStringTest();

                String javaMsg = "Hello from Java to JNI";
                stringTest.printMsg(javaMsg);

                String nativeMsg = stringTest.getMsg();
                System.out.println(nativeMsg);
        }
}
```

The following are the native function declarations for printMsg() and getMsg() in C/C++:

- JNIEXPORT void JNICALL Java_com_jdojo_jni_JNIStringTest_printMsg(JNIEnv *env, jobject obj, jstring msg);

- JNIEXPORT jstring JNICALL Java_com_jdojo_jni_JNIStringTest_getMsg(JNIEnv *env, jobject obj);

Note that the first two parameters in the native functions are of type JNIEnv and jobject. The printMsg() function contains a third parameter of type jstring and its return type is void. The getMsg() function contains only two standard parameters and it returns a jstring.

To convert a jstring to a UTF-8 native string, you need to use the GetStringUTFChars() JNI function that you can access using a JNIEnv reference. The GetStringUTFChars() JNI function has two versions: one for C and one for C++.

The GetStringUTFChars() function converts a Java string (in a jstring in C/C++ code) to a UTF-8 format and returns a pointer to the converted UTF-8 string. If it fails, it returns NULL. The GetStringUTFChars() function may have to make a copy of the original Java string object in memory for converting it to UTF-8 format. The isCopy parameter to the functions, which is a pointer to a boolean variable, can be used to check if this function had to copy the original Java string. If isCopy is not NULL, it is set to JNI_TRUE if a copy of the Java string was made. Otherwise, it is set to JNI_FALSE. Once you are done with the returned value of this function, you must call the ReleaseStringUTFChars() method to release the memory. The C and C++ style signatures of this method are as follows:

```
// C Style
void ReleaseStringUTFChars(JNIEnv *env, jstring string, const char *utf);

// C++ Style
void ReleaseStringUTFChars(jstring string, const char *utf);
```

Listing 8-7 contains the implementations for the printMsg() and getMsg() native methods in C++. The code is in the jnistringtest.cpp file in the source code for this book. The code for getMsg() is simple. It uses the NewStringUTF() JNI function to get a Java string from the native string.

Listing 8-7. Contents of the jnistringtest.cpp File

```cpp
// jnistringtest.cpp
#include <stdio.h>
#include <jni.h>
#include "com_jdojo_jni_JNIStringTest.h"

JNIEXPORT void JNICALL Java_com_jdojo_jni_JNIStringTest_printMsg
(JNIEnv *env, jobject obj, jstring msg) {
    const char *utfMsg;
    jboolean *iscopy = NULL;

    // Get the UTF string
    utfMsg = env->GetStringUTFChars(msg, iscopy);
    if (utfMsg == NULL) {
        printf("Could not convert Java string to UTF-8 string.\n");
        return;
    }

    // Print the message on the standard output
    printf("%s\n", utfMsg);

    // Release the memory
    env->ReleaseStringUTFChars(msg, utfMsg);
}

JNIEXPORT jstring JNICALL Java_com_jdojo_jni_JNIStringTest_getMsg
(JNIEnv *env, jobject obj) {
    const char *utfMsg = "Hello from JNI to Java";
    jstring javaString = env->NewStringUTF(utfMsg);
    return javaString;
}
```

Run the javah command for the JNIStringTest class to create the com_jdojo_jni_JNIStringTest.h C++ header file.

```
javah com.jdojo.jni.JNIStringTest
```

To include the C++ contents of the hellojni.cpp and jnistringtest.cpp files in the same shared library named beginningjava, you need to pass both files as the source files to the g+= command. The following is the command on Windows, assuming that you have placed the header files for both source files in the C:\dll directory.

```
C:\> g++ -Wl,--kill-at -shared
    -IC:/java8/include -IC:/java8/include/win32 -IC:/dll
    -o C:/dll/beginningjava.dll
    C:/dll/hellojni.cpp C:/dll/jnistringtest.cpp
```

Please refer to the "Creating a Shared Library on Linux" section for creating the shared library with both C++ source files on Linux.

Now you are ready to run the JNIStringTest class as listed in Listing 8-6. It will generate the following output:

```
Hello from JNI to Java
Hello from Java to JNI
```

You can use the GetStringUTFLength(jstring string) JNI function to get the length of a jstring in bytes to represent it in UTF-8 format. The JNI also has functions that let you work with Unicode native strings. The Unicode string functions are named UTF string functions without the word "UTF". For example, to get the length of a jstring in terms of Unicode characters, you have a GetStringLength() function as opposed to the GetStringUTFLength() function. To construct a new Java String (a jstring) from Unicode characters, you have a NewString() JNI function as opposed to the NewStringUTF() JNI function, which creates a Java string from a UTF-8 native string. Sometimes you may need to convert a Java String in jstring to a native encoding and vice versa. You can use the java.lang.String class, which has a rich set of constructors and methods that let you convert string in one encoding to byte array and vice versa. I will cover how to access Java classes in the native code in a later section.

Working with Arrays

The JNI lets you pass an array of primitive or reference types from Java to native code and vice versa. You cannot access or work with Java arrays directly in native code. You will need to use JNI functions to work with Java arrays in native code. The JNI provides a different set of functions for primitive and reference arrays. Some functions are common to both types. All array-related methods used in this section use the C++ version. Add JNIEnv *env as the first parameter to them to get the corresponding C version.

The GetArrayLength() method returns the length of an array of a primitive or reference type. Its declaration is

```
jsize GetArrayLength(jarray array)
```

You can use the New<Xxx>Array() method to create an array of a primitive type, where <Xxx> is one of the primitive types of Boolean, Byte, Char, Double, Float, Int, Long, or Short. You need to pass the length of the primitive type array as a parameter to this method. It returns NULL if an array could not be created. The following snippet of code creates an int array and a double array each of length 10:

```
jintArray iArray = env->NewIntArray(10);
jdoubleArray dArray = env->NewDoubleArray(10);
```

You can use Get<Xxx>ArrayElements() to get the contents of a primitive array, where <Xxx> is one of the primitive types of Boolean, Byte, Char, Double, Float, Int, Long, or Short. It is declared as follows:

```
<RRR> *Get<Xxx>ArrayElements(<AAA> array, jboolean *isCopy)
```

Here, <RRR> is the JNI native data type such as jint or jdouble, and <AAA> is a JNI array type such as jintArray, jdoubleArray, etc. The isCopy parameter indicates if the returned array elements are copies of the original array. If isCopy is not NULL, it is set to JNI_TRUE if a copy of original array was made. It is set to JNI_FALSE if a copy of original array was not made. You can also make changes to the array elements in the native code that will be reflected to the original array. You need to release the elements, which you get using this method after you are done with them. You need to use the Release<Xxx>ArrayElements() method to release the array elements, which is declared as follows:

```
void Release<Xxx>ArrayElements(<AAA> array, <RRR> *elems, jint mode)
```

The last parameter mode in the Release<Xxx>ArrayElements() function indicates how the buffer, which was used in native code for array elements, is released. Its value can be 0, JNI_COMMIT, or JNI_ABORT. 0 means copy back the content and free the elems buffer; JNI_COMMIT means copy back the content, but do not free the elems buffer; and JNI_ABORT means free the buffer without copying back the possible changes. The following snippet of code accesses an int Java array in native code and prints all of its element values on the standard output:

```
jintArray num = get a Java array...;
const jsize count = env->GetArrayLength(num);
jboolean isCopy;
jint *intNum = env->GetIntArrayElements(num, &isCopy);

for (jsize i = 0; i < count; i++) {
        printf("%i\n", intNum[i]);
}

// Release the intNum buffer without copying back any changes made to the array elements
env->ReleaseIntArrayElements(num, intNum, JNI_ABORT);
```

Reference type Java arrays in the native code are treated differently. You can use the NewObjectArray() function to create a new reference type array. The method is declared as follows:

```
jobjectArray NewObjectArray(jsize length, jclass elementClass, jobject initialElement)
```

Note that you need to use the array element's class type object to create a reference array. The last parameter is the initial element with which all elements of the array will be initialized.

Unlike primitive type arrays, you do not need to get array elements for reference type arrays to access them. You can access one element at a time using the GetObjectArrayElement() function. You can use the SetObjectArrayElement() function to set the value of an array element of a reference type. These methods are declared as follows:

- `jobject GetObjectArrayElement(jobjectArray array, jsize index)`
- `void SetObjectArrayElement(jobjectArray array, jsize index, jobject value)`

Let's look at examples of using arrays in a JNI application. Listing 8-8 contains the Java code that declares three native methods using arrays.

Listing 8-8. An Example of Accessing and Manipulating Arrays in Native Code

```java
// JNIArrayTest.java
package com.jdojo.jni;

import java.util.Arrays;

public class JNIArrayTest {
        static {
                System.loadLibrary("beginningjava");
        }

        // Three native method declarations
        public native int sum(int[] num);
        public native String concat(String[] str);
        public native int[] increment(int[] num, int incrementBy);

        public static void main(String[] args) {
                JNIArrayTest test = new JNIArrayTest();

                int[] num = {1, 2, 3, 4, 5};
                String[] str = {"One", "Two", "Three", "Four", "Five" } ;

                System.out.println("Original Number Array: " + Arrays.toString(num));

                System.out.println("Original String Array: " + Arrays.toString(str));
                int sum = 0;
                sum = test.sum(num);
                System.out.println("Sum: " + sum);

                String concatenatedStr = test.concat(str);
                System.out.println("Concatenated String: " + concatenatedStr);

                int increment = 5;
                int[] incrementedNum = test.increment(num, increment);
                System.out.println("Increment By: " + increment);
                System.out.println("Incremented Number Arrays: " +
                                        Arrays.toString(incrementedNum));
        }
}
```

The sum() native method accepts an int array and returns the sum of all its elements as int. Be careful not to pass big numbers in the int array when you call the sum() method. Otherwise, the result may overflow. The concat() native method accepts a String array. It concatenates all elements in the array and returns a String object. The increment() native method accepts an int array and an int number. It returns a new int array, which contains all elements of the original array that are incremented by the specified number. The main() method contains the code to test the three native methods.

Run the javah command for the JNIArrayTest class to create the com_jdojo_jni_JNIArrayTest.h C++ header file.

```
javah com.jdojo.jni.JNIArrayTest
```

Listing 8-9 contains the C++ implementation of the three native methods in the jniarraytest.cpp file. The concat() method's implementation assumes that the length of all elements in String array will not exceed 500 bytes. Please refer to the previous section on how to include the C+= source file in the shared library.

Listing 8-9. Contents of the jniarraytest.cpp File with the C++ Implementation of the sum( ), concat( ), and increment( ) Native Methods

```cpp
// jniarraytest.cpp
#include <jni.h>
#include <cstring>
#include "com_jdojo_jni_JNIArrayTest.h"

JNIEXPORT jint JNICALL Java_com_jdojo_jni_JNIArrayTest_sum
(JNIEnv *env, jobject obj, jintArray num) {
    jint sum = 0;
    const jsize count = env->GetArrayLength(num);

    jboolean isCopy;
    jint *intNum = env->GetIntArrayElements(num, &isCopy);

    for (jsize i = 0; i < count; i++) {
        sum += intNum[i];
    }

    // Release the intNum buffer without copying back any changes made to the array elements
    env->ReleaseIntArrayElements(num, intNum, JNI_ABORT);

    return sum;
}

JNIEXPORT jstring JNICALL Java_com_jdojo_jni_JNIArrayTest_concat
(JNIEnv *env, jobject obj, jobjectArray strArray) {
    const int MAX_LENGTH = 500;
    char dest[MAX_LENGTH];

    for (int i = 0; i < MAX_LENGTH; i++) {
        dest[i] = (char)NULL;
    }

    const jsize count = env->GetArrayLength(strArray);

    for (jsize i = 0; i < count; i++) {
        // Get the string object from the array
        jstring strElement =
                (jstring) env->GetObjectArrayElement(strArray, i);
        const char *tempStr = env->GetStringUTFChars(strElement, NULL);

        if (tempStr == NULL) {
            printf("Could not convert Java string to UTF-8 string.\n");
            return NULL;
        }
```

```
        // Concatenate tempStr to dest
        strcat(dest, tempStr);

        // Release the memory used by tempStr
        env->ReleaseStringUTFChars(strElement, tempStr);

        // Delete the local reference of jstring
        env->DeleteLocalRef(strElement);
    }

    jstring returnStr = env->NewStringUTF(dest);
    return returnStr;
}

JNIEXPORT jintArray JNICALL Java_com_jdojo_jni_JNIArrayTest_increment
(JNIEnv *env, jobject obj, jintArray num, jint incrementBy) {

    const jsize count = env->GetArrayLength(num);

    jboolean isCopy;
    jint *intNum = env->GetIntArrayElements(num, &isCopy);

    jintArray modifiedNumArray = env->NewIntArray(count);
    jboolean isNewArrayCopy;
    jint *modifiedNumElements =
            env->GetIntArrayElements(modifiedNumArray, &isNewArrayCopy);

    for (jint i = 0; i < count; i++) {
        modifiedNumElements[i] = intNum[i] + incrementBy;
    }

    if (isCopy == JNI_TRUE) {
        env -> ReleaseIntArrayElements(num, intNum, JNI_COMMIT);
    }

    if (isNewArrayCopy == JNI_TRUE) {
        env -> ReleaseIntArrayElements(modifiedNumArray,
                modifiedNumElements,
                JNI_COMMIT);
    }

    return modifiedNumArray;
}
```

Running the JNIArrayTest class as shown in Listing 8-8 will produce the following output:

```
Original Number Array: [1, 2, 3, 4, 5]
Original String Array: [One, Two, Three, Four, Five]
Sum: 15
Concatenated String: OneTwoThreeFourFive
Increment By: 5
Incremented Number Arrays: [6, 7, 8, 9, 10]
```

Accessing Java Objects in Native Code

You can use Java objects in native code in different ways: You can

- Create Java objects in native code.

- Access Java objects and classes existing in the JVM from the native code.

- Access/modify fields of a Java object inside the native code.

- Invoke a Java instance and static methods of Java objects from the native code.

The following sections describe the steps needed to use Java objects in native code.

Getting a Class Reference

An instance of the jclass type represents a class object in native code. If you invoke a native function, which is declared as static and native in a Java class, your native function always gets the reference of the class object as the second parameter. Sometimes you may have a reference of a Java object in the jobject type and you want to get its class object reference. You need to use the GetObjectClass() JNI function to get the reference of the class object of a Java object as shown:

```
jobject obj = get the reference to a Java object;
jclass cls = env->GetObjectClass(obj);
```

Use the FindClass() JNI function to get the reference of a class object using the class name. You need to use the fully qualified name of the class in the FindClass() method by replacing a dot in the package name with a forward slash. If you are trying to get the reference of a class object for an array, you need to use the array class signature. To get the reference of the class object for the java.lang.String class, you need to use java/lang/String as the class name. To get the class object reference for int[], you need to use [I as the class name. To know the correct signature for the class of an array type, you can declare a field in a class of that array type and use the javap command with the -s and -private options. The following snippet of code demonstrates how to get the reference of the class object for some Java reference types:

```
jclass cls;

// Get the reference of the java.lang.String class object
cls = env->FindClass("java/lang/String");

// Get the reference of the int[] array class object
cls = env->FindClass("[I");

// Get the reference of the int[][] array class object
cls = env->FindClass("[[I");

// Get the reference of the String[] array class object. Note a semi-colon in signature
cls = env->FindClass("[Ljava/lang/String;");
```

Accessing Fields and Methods of a Java Object/Class

Before you can access the fields of a Java object/class in native code, you must get the field ID. You need to use the GetFieldID() JNI function to get the field ID of an instance field and the GetStaticFieldID() JNI function to get the field ID for a static field. The signatures of these two methods are as follows:

- jfieldID GetFieldID(jclass cls, const char *name, const char *sig)

- jfieldID GetStaticFieldID(jclass cls, const char *name, const char *sig)

The cls parameter is the reference of the class object, which defines the instance/static field. The name parameter is the name of the field. The sig parameter is the signature of the field. You need to use the javap command with the -s and -private options to get the signature of a field defined in a class.

You need to use a Get<Xxx>Field() JNI function to get the value of an instance field and a GetStatic<Xxx>Field() JNI function to get the value of a static field, where <Xxx> is the type of field whose value can be Boolean, Byte, Char, Double, Float, Int, Long, Short, or Object. The Set<Xxx>Field() and SetStatic<Xxx>Field() JNI functions let you set the value of instance and static fields, respectively. The declaration for these methods are as follows where <RRR> is a native data type, for example, if <Xxx> is int, <RRR> is jint:

- <RRR> Get<Xxx>Field(jobject obj, jfieldID fieldID)

- <RRR> GetStatic<Xxx>Field(jclass clazz, jfieldID fieldID)

- void Set<Xxx>Field(jobject obj, jfieldID fieldID, <RRR> value)

- void SetStatic<Xxx>Field(jclass clazz, jfieldID fieldID, <RRR> value)

Suppose obj is an instance of jobject (that is, a Java object reference) and cls is its class reference. There are two fields, num and count, of type int in the class represented by cls. The num field is an instance field and count field is a static field. The following snippet of code shows how to access these two fields in native code and increment their values by 1:

```
// Get the field ID of num and count fields
jfieldID numFieldId = env->GetFieldID(cls, "num", "I");
jfieldID countFieldId = env->GetStaticFieldID(cls, "count", "I");

// Get the field values
jint numValue = env->GetIntField(obj, numFieldId);
jint countValue = env->GetStaticIntField(cls, countFieldId);

// Increment the values by 1 and set them back to the fields
numValue = numValue + 1;
countValue = countValue + 1;
env->SetIntField(obj, numFieldId, numValue);
env->SetStaticIntField(cls, countFieldId, countValue);
```

The steps to use a method of Java object/class in native code are similar to using their fields. You need to get the method ID of a method before you can access the method. You can use GetMethodID() and GetStaticMethodID() JNI functions to get the method ID for an instance method and a static method, respectively. Their declarations are as follows:

- jmethodID GetMethodID(jclass clazz, const char *name, const char *sig)

- jmethodID GetStaticMethodID(jclass clazz, const char *name, const char *sig)

The name of the method is its simple name, and its signature can be obtained using the javap command with the -s and -private options. The following snippet of code shows how to get the method ID from a few methods of a Java class assuming that cls represents the class object reference:

```
jmethodID methodID

// Method is "void objectCallBack()"
methodID = env->GetMethodID(cls, "objectCallBack", "()V");

// Method is "static void classCallBack()"
methodID = env->GetStaticMethodID(cls, "classCallBack", "()V");

// Method is "int getLength(String str)"
methodID = env->GetMethodID(cls, "getLength", "(Ljava/lang/String;)I");

// Method is "int[] increment(int[], int)"
methodID = env->GetMethodID(cls, "increment", "([II)[I");
```

Calling an instance or static method is easy. You need to use an object/class, the method ID, and method arguments, if any, to call a method. You can use any of the following methods to call an instance method of an object:

- <RRR> Call<Xxx>Method(jobject obj, jmethodID methodID, arg1, arg2...)
- <RRR> Call<Xxx>MethodA(jobject obj, jmethodID methodID, const jvalue *args)
- <RRR> Call<Xxx>MethodV(jobject obj, jmethodID methodID, va_list args)

Here, <Xxx> in the method name is the return type of the method and it could be Boolean, Byte, Char, Double, Float, Int, Long, Short, Object, or Void. The <RRR> is the return type of the method and it could be jboolean, jbyte, jchar, jdouble, jfloat, jint, jlong, jshort, jobject, or void depending on the corresponding <Xxx> value. The difference between Call<Xxx>Method(), Call<Xxx>MethodA(), and Call<Xx>MethodV() is how you want to pass the arguments to the method. The Call<Xxx>Method() method lets you pass arguments to a method as a comma-separated list. The Call<Xxx>MethodA() method lets you pass arguments to a method as an array of jvalue type. The Call<Xxx>MethodV() method lets you pass arguments to a method as va_list. The following snippet of code shows how to call an instance method assuming that obj is a reference of jobject type and the method ID is methodID:

```
// Method is "void m1()"
env->CallVoidMethod(obj, methodID);

// Method is "void m2(int a)"
env->CallVoidMethod(obj, methodID, 109);

// Method is "int m2(double a)"
jint value = env->CallIntMethod(obj, methodID, 109.23);
```

Calling a static method is similar to calling an instance method. You need to use a class object reference to call a static method. You need to use one of the following JNI functions to call a static method. Note that the JNI function names, which are used to call static methods, contain the word Static.

- <RRR> CallStatic<Xxx>Method(jclass cls, jmethodID methodID, arg1, arg2...)
- <RRR> CallStatic<Xxx>MethodA(jclass cls, jmethodID methodID, jvalue *args)
- <RRR> CallStatic<Xxx>MethodV(jclass cls, jmethodID methodID, va_list args)

The JNI lets you call an instance method on an object from any class in its class hierarchy. When you use a Call<Xxx>Method() function, it uses the object's class to call the method. Consider the following class hierarchy:

```java
// A.java
package com.jdojo.jni;

public class A {
        public int m1() {
                return 1;
        }
}

// B.java
package com.jdojo.jni;

public class B extends A {
        @Override
        public int m1() {
                return 3;
        }
}

// C.java
package com.jdojo.jni;

public class C extends B {
        @Override
        public int m1() {
                return 3;
        }
}
```

Classes B and C override the m1() method. If you use CallIntMethod() to call the m1() method of an object of class C, it will call m1() method in class C and it returns 3. The JNI lets you call the m1() method in class A or class B using an object of class C. To call a method on an object from its superclass, you need to use one of the following JNI methods:

- <RRR> CallNonvirtual<Xxx>Method(jobject obj, jclass cls, jmethodID methodID, arg1, arg2...)

- <RRR> CallNonvirtual<Xxx>MethodA(jobject obj, jclass cls, jmethodID methodID, const jvalue *args)

- <RRR> CallNonvirtual<Xxx>MethodV(jobject obj, jclass cls, jmethodID methodID, va_list args)

You need to use the reference of the object and its class in these versions of the methods. The methodID must be obtained using the class from which the method needs to be called. For example, the following snippet of code calls the m1() method from class B on an object of class C. The code also creates an object of class C.

```
// Get the class references for B and C
jclass bCls = env->FindClass("com/jdojo/jni/B");
jclass cCls = env->FindClass("com/jdojo/jni/C");
```

```
// Get method ID for the constructor of class C
jmethodID cConstrctorID = env->GetMethodID(cCls, "<init>", "()V");

// Create an object of class C
jobject cObject = env->NewObject(cCls, cConstrctorID);

// Get the method ID for the m1() method in class B
jmethodID bMethodID = env->GetMethodID(bCls, "m1", "()I");

// Call the m1() method in class B using an object of class C
jint h = env->CallNonvirtualIntMethod(cObject, bCls, bMethodID);

// will print 2, which is returned from m1() in class B
printf("%i\n", h);
```

Let's look at a complete example of accessing fields and methods of a Java object in native code. Listing 8-10 contains the Java code in which a class named JNIJavaObjectAccessTest contains two fields named num and count. It also contains two methods named objectCallBack() and classCallBack(). You will access the fields and methods in native code. It has a native method called callBack(). The callBack() native method increments the num and count fields by 1 and calls the objectCallBack() and classCallBack() methods. Before you can run the JNIJavaObjectAccessTest class, you will need to generate the com_jdojo_jni_JNIJavaObjectAccessTest.h C++ header file and the shared library including the contents from the jnijavaobjectaccesstest.cpp file as shown in Listing 8-11.

Listing 8-10. Accessing Fields and Methods of Java Objects/Classes from Native Code

```
// JNIJavaObjectAccessTest.java
package com.jdojo.jni;

public class JNIJavaObjectAccessTest {
        static {
                System.loadLibrary("beginningjava");
        }

        private int num = 10;
        private static int count = 1001;

        public void objectCallBack() {
                System.out.println("Inside objectCallBack() method.");
        }

        public static void classCallBack() {
                System.out.println("Inside classCallBack() method.");
        }

        public native void callBack();

        public int hashCode() {
                return -9999;
        }

        public static void main(String[] args) {
                JNIJavaObjectAccessTest test = new JNIJavaObjectAccessTest();
```

```
                    System.out.println("Before calling native method...");
                    System.out.println("num = " + test.num);
                    System.out.println("count = " + count);

                    // Call native method
                    test.callBack();

                    System.out.println("After calling native method...");
                    System.out.println("num = " + test.num);
                    System.out.println("count = " + count);
            }
}
```

```
Before calling native method...
num = 10
count = 1001
Inside objectCallBack() method.
Inside classCallBack() method.
After calling native method...
num = 11
count = 1002
```

Listing 8-11. Contents of the the jnijavaobjectsaccesstest.cpp File That Contains the C++ Implementation of the callBack( ) Native Methods Declared in JNIJavaObjectAccessTest Class

```cpp
// jnijavaobjectaccesstest.cpp
#include <stdio.h>
#include <jni.h>
#include "com_jdojo_jni_JNIJavaObjectAccessTest.h"

JNIEXPORT void JNICALL Java_com_jdojo_jni_JNIJavaObjectAccessTest_callBack
(JNIEnv *env, jobject obj) {
    jclass cls;

    // Get the class reference for the object
    cls = env->GetObjectClass(obj);
    if (cls == NULL) {
        return;
    }

    // Access the fields
    jfieldID numFieldId = env->GetFieldID(cls, "num", "I");
    jfieldID countFieldId = env->GetStaticFieldID(cls, "count", "I");

    jint numValue = env->GetIntField(obj, numFieldId);
    jint countValue = env->GetStaticIntField(cls, countFieldId);

    numValue = numValue + 1;
    countValue = countValue + 1;
```

```
env->SetIntField(obj, numFieldId, numValue);
env->SetStaticIntField(cls, countFieldId, countValue);

// Call the instance method
jmethodID instanceMethodID = env->GetMethodID(cls,
        "objectCallBack",
        "()V");
if (instanceMethodID != 0) {
    env->CallVoidMethod(obj, instanceMethodID);
}

// Call the static method
jmethodID staticMethodID = env->GetStaticMethodID(cls,
        "classCallBack",
        "()V");
if (staticMethodID != 0) {
    env->CallStaticVoidMethod(cls, staticMethodID);
}

return;
}
```

Creating Java Objects

The JNI lets you create Java objects in native code without invoking any constructor or by invoking a specific constructor. You need to use the AllocObject() JNI function to allocate memory for a Java object without invoking any of its constructors. Note that all instance fields will have their default values according to their data types. Instance fields will not be initialized when you use AllocObject() JNI function and no instance initializer will be invoked either. Here is the snippet of code to allocate memory for an object of a class in Java:

```
jclass cls = get the class reference;
jobject obj = env->AllocObject(cls);
if (obj == NULL) {
        // The object could not be created. Handle the error condition.
}
```

You can create a Java object by invoking a specific constructor of a Java class using one of the following JNI functions. The functions differ only in how to pass the parameters for a constructor.

- jobject NewObject(jclass clazz, jmethodID methodID, arg1, arg2...)

- jobject NewObjectA(jclass clazz, jmethodID methodID, const jvalue *args)

- jobject NewObjectV(jclass clazz, jmethodID methodID, va_list args)

The methodID parameter is the method ID of the constructor that you want to invoke. There is a special string that is used for a method name when you want to get the method ID for a constructor of a class. You need to use <init> or $init$ as the method name for a constructor. Consider the code for a class named IntWrapper as shown in Listing 8-12.

Listing 8-12. A Sample Class to Demonstrate the Java Object Creation in Native Code

```
// IntWrapper.java
package com.jdojo.jni;

public class IntWrapper {
        private int value = -1;

        public IntWrapper() {
        }

        public IntWrapper(int value) {
                this.value = value;
        }

        public int getValue() {
                return value;
        }
}
```

You can get the reference of the IntWrapper class in native C++ code as shown:

```
jclass wrapperCls = env->FindClass("com/jdojo/jni/IntWrapper");
```

The following C++ code allocates memory for an IntWrapper object without invoking a constructor:

```
jobject wrapperObject = env->AllocObject(wrapperCls);
```

At this point, wrapperObject exists in memory and its instance field value still has the default value of 0. If you call the getValue() method on wrapperObject at this point, it will return 0 and not –1, as you might expect.

You need to use the NewObject() JNI function if you want to create an object of a Java class by invoking one of its constructors. The following snippet of code creates an object of the IntWrapper class by invoking its no-args constructor. The signature for a constructor depends on the number and type of parameters it accepts. For the no-args constructor, the signature is ()V. If a constructor accepts an int parameter, its signature would be (I)V. You can get the signature of a constructor of a class by using the javap command with the –s option. Use the –private option with javap if you also want to include the private member's signatures.

```
// Get the method ID for the default constructor of class IntWrapper
jmethodID mid = env->GetMethodID(wrapperCls, "<init>", "()V");

// Create an object of class IntWrapper using the default constructor
jobject wrapperObject = env->NewObject(wrapperCls, mid);
```

At this point, if you call the getValue() method on wrapperObject, it will return -1, which is the initial value of the value instance field. When a constructor is called, all instance fields are initialized.

The following snippet of code calls the second version of the constructor of the IntWrapper class, which accepts an int parameter. It passes 999 as the value for the parameter for the constructor IntWrapper(int value).

```
// Get the method ID for the constructor for class IntWrapper
jmethodID wrapperConstrctorID = env->GetMethodID(wrapperCls, "<init>","(I)V");
```

```
// Create an object of class IntWrapper passing 999 to the constructor
jobject wrapperObject = env->NewObject(wrapperCls, wrapperConstrctorID, 999);
```

At this point, if you call the getValue() method on abcObject, it will return 999, which is set in its constructor during its creation.

■ **Tip** The AllocObject() and NewObject() JNI functions can be used only to create objects of a non-array reference type. You need to use the NewObjectArray() JNI function to create an array of a specific type.

Exception Handling

The JNI lets you handle exceptions in native code. Native code can detect and handle exceptions that are thrown in the JVM as a result of calling a JNI function. Native code can also throw an exception that can be propagated to Java code. The exception handling mechanism in the native code differs from that of the Java code. When an exception is thrown in Java code, the control is transferred immediately to the nearest catch block that can handle the exception. When an exception is thrown during native code execution, the native code keeps executing and the exception remains pending until the control returns to the Java code. Once an exception is pending, you should not execute any other JNI functions except the ones that free native resources. There are two ways to detect if an exception has occurred as a result of a JNI function call in the native code:

- By checking for the special return value from the function
- By checking if an exception has occurred after the function returns

Some JNI functions return a special value if an exception occurs. For example, if you call the FindClass() JNI function and the class is not found, any one of the four exceptions may be thrown: ClassFormatError, ClassCircularityError, NoClassDefFoundError, or OutOfMemoryError. The FindClass() JNI function returns NULL as a special value if any of the four exceptions is thrown. You should check for NULL as a return value just after a call to the FindClass() JNI function and write code to handle the exception. Typically, you return the control to the caller so that the caller can handle the exception as shown:

```
jclass cls = env->FindClass("abc/xyz/NonExistentClass");
if (cls == NULL) {
        /* Here, free up any resources you had held and return. Exception is pending at
           this time. It will be thrown when the control returns to the Java code.
        */
        return;
}
```

In some cases, it is not possible to return a special value from a JNI function to indicate that an exception has occurred. Suppose you are accessing a Java array in native code and you have exceeded the array's boundary. In this case, an exception of type ArrayIndexOutOfBoundsException is thrown by the JVM. You may call a method of a Java object where an exception occurs. In such cases, you need to use either ExceptionOccurred() or ExceptionCheck() JNI function immediately after such JNI function call to check if an exception has occurred. These functions have the following signatures:

- jthrowable ExceptionOccurred()
- jboolean ExceptionCheck()

If an exception occurred during a function call, the ExceptionOccurred() function returns the reference of that exception object. Otherwise, it returns NULL. If an exception occurred during the function call, the ExceptionCheck() function returns JNI_TRUE. Otherwise, it returns JNI_FALSE. The following snippet of code demonstrates how to use these functions. You only need to use one of the two functions, not both at the same time.

```
// Using method ExceptionOccurred()

// Call a JNI function, which may throw an exception

jthrowable e = env->ExceptionOccurred();
if (e != NULL) {
        /* Free up any resources that you had held and return. Exception is pending at this
           time. It will be thrown when the control returns to the Java code.
        */
        return;
}

// Using method ExceptionCheck()

// Call a JNI function, which may throw an exception

jboolean gotException = env->ExceptionCheck();

if (gotException) {
        /* Free up any resources that you had held and return. Exception is pending at
           this time. It will be thrown when the control returns to the Java code.
        */
        return;
}
```

Once you have detected an exception that has occurred in native code, you have three options:

- Clear the exception and handle it in native code.

- Return the control to Java code and let the Java code handle the exception.

- Clear the exception, handle it in native code, and throw a new exception from native code that Java code can handle.

The following sections explain the three ways of handling the exceptions.

Handle the Exception in Native Code

You can clear the exception and handle the exceptional condition in the native code. Use the ExceptionClear() JNI function to clear a pending exception, as shown:

```
// Call a JNI function, which may throw an exception

jboolean gotException = env->ExceptionCheck();
if (gotException) {
        // Clear the exception
        env->ExceptionClear();

        // Write some code to take care of the exceptional condition
}
```

Once you clear the exception, that exception is not pending anymore.

Handling the Exception in Java Code

You can return the control to the caller by using a return statement and let the caller handle the exception as shown:

```
// Call a JNI function, which may throw an exception

jboolean gotException = env->ExceptionCheck();
if (gotException) {
        /* Free up any resources that you had held and return. Exception  is pending at this time.
           It will be thrown when the control returns to the caller.
        */
        return;
}
```

Throwing a New Exception from Native Code

You can handle the exception in the native code, clear the exception, and throw a new exception. Note that throwing an exception from the native code does not transfer the control back to the Java code. You must write code such as a return statement to transfer the control back to the Java code, so the exception you throw is handled in Java. You can throw an exception in the native code using either of the following two JNI functions. Both functions return zero on success and a negative integer on failure.

- jint Throw(jthrowable obj)
- jint ThrowNew(jclass clazz, const char *message)

The Throw() function accepts a jthrowable object. The ThrowNew() function accepts the exception's class reference and a message. The following snippet of code shows how to throw a java.lang.Exception using the ThrowNew() function:

```
if (someErrorConditionIsTrue) {
        jclass cls = env->FindClass("java/lang/Exception");

        // Check for exception here (omitted)
        env->ThrowNew(cls, "your error message goes here");
        return;
}
```

■ **Tip** If you want to print the stack trace of an exception in the native code, you can use the ExceptionDescribe() JNI function. It prints an exception stack trace on the standard error. If you want to raise a fatal error from the native code, you can use the FatalError(const char *msg) JNI function. The FatalError() function does not return and the JVM will not recover from this error either. A native method declared in Java code can also use a throws clause the same way as a Java non-native method can. The following is a valid native method declaration inside a Java class:

```
public native int myMethod() throws Exception;
```

Creating an Instance of the JVM

So far, you have seen Java applications using native code. Now you are ready to see the reverse. That is, a native application using Java code. Why would you use Java code from a native application? You may want to use Java code from a native application for the following reasons:

- You may already have an application coded in Java and you want to use the existing code.

- Java provides a rich set of class libraries. You may want to take advantage of Java class libraries in your native application.

The part of the JNI API that lets you create and load a JVM in native code is known as the *Invocation API*. The JNI lets you embed a JVM inside a native application. That is, you can create a JVM from a native application and use Java classes as you use them in a Java application. It takes just a few lines of code to create a JVM in native code. All you need to do is to prepare the initial arguments that you want to pass to a JVM and call the JNI_CreateJavaVM() Invocation API function to create the JVM.

The initial argument that is passed to a JVM is a JavaVMInitArgs structure that is defined as follows:

```
typedef struct JavaVMInitArgs {
        jint version;
        jint nOptions;
        JavaVMOption *options;
        jboolean ignoreUnrecognized;
} JavaVMInitArgs;
```

The version field indicates the JNI version and it must be set to at least JNI_VERSION_1_2. The nOptions field is set to the number of options you want to pass to a JVM. The options field is an array of a JavaVMOption structure, which is defined as follows:

```
typedef struct JavaVMOption {
        char *optionString;
        void *extraInfo;
} JavaVMOption;
```

If ignoreUnrecognized is set to JNI_TRUE, the JNI_CreateJavaVM() function will ignore the unrecognized options. If it is set to JNI_FALSE, the JNI_CreateJavaVM() function will return JNI_ERR as soon as it encounters an unrecognized option.

The optionString field in the JavaVMOption structure is a string that is the value for the option to a JVM in the default platform encoding.

The extraInfo field is used for special kinds of JVM arguments. It represents a function hook for redirecting a JVM message, a JVM exit hook, or a JVM abort hook. The type of hook the extraInfo field represents depends on the value for the optionString field. If the optionString field has the value of vfprintf, exit, or abort, the extraInfo field represents a JVM message redirection hook, a JVM exit hook, or a JVM abort hook, respectively. Note that vfprintf hook redirects only the JVM message to the hook. It does not redirect the System.out and System.err messages to the hook. If you have set a vsprintf hook in native code and used one of the print()/println() methods of System.out/System.err in Java code, those messages would not be redirected to your vfprintf hook. You need to use the setOut() and setErr() methods of the System class to redirect System.out and System.err messages. The exit hook for a JVM is called upon a normal termination of the JVM such as by calling the System.exit(int exitCode) method in Java code. The abort hook for a JVM is called upon abnormal termination of the JVM. The following snippet of code shows how to populate the extraInfo field with a different VM hook. First, three functions are defined that will serve as the three types of hooks. Note that the functions must have the same signatures as shown in the following snippet of code:

```
jint JNICALL jvmMsgRedirection_hook(FILE *stream, const char *format, va_list args) {
        // You can log the VM message here.
        // Let us just print the VM message on the standard output.
        return vfprintf(stdout, format, args);
}

void JNICALL jvmExit_hook(jint code) {
        // You can do some cleanup work here

        printf("VM exited with exit code %i\n", code);
}

void JNICALL jvmAbort_hook() {
        printf("VM was aborted\n");
}

JavaVMOption jvmOption[3];

// Add JVM hooks
options[0].optionString = "vfprintf";
options[0].extraInfo = jvmMsgRedirection_hook;

options[1].optionString = "exit";
options[1].extraInfo = jvmExit_hook;

options[2].optionString = "abort";
options[2].extraInfo = jvmAbort_hook;
```

The following snippet of code shows how to populate a JavaVMInitArgs structure with initial arguments for the JVM. It sets only two arguments, java.class.path and java.lib.path. You can set more JVM arguments if you need to.

```
// Populate the JVM options in JavaVMOption structure
const jint MAX_OPTIONS = 2; // will pass two arguments to the JVM

JavaVMOption options[MAX_OPTIONS];

// Our first argument is java.class.path (CLASSPATH for JVM)
options[0].optionString = "-Djava.class.path=.;c:\\myjni\\classes";

// Our second argument is java.library.path (PATH to find a shared library)
options[1].optionString = "-Djava.library.path=c:\\myjni\\libs";
```

```
// Populate JavaVMInitArgs structure with options details
JavaVMInitArgs vm_args;
vm_args.version = JNI_VERSION_1_2;
vm_args.nOptions = MAX_OPTIONS;
vm_args.options = options;
vm_args.ignoreUnrecognized = true;
```

Once you have the JVM arguments ready in a `JavaVMInitArgs` structure, you are just one JNI function call away from creating a JVM in your native code. The `JNI_CreateJavaVM()` JNI function accepts three arguments. The first argument is a pointer to a `JavaVM` structure that represent the JVM. The second argument is a pointer to a `JNIEnv` structure, which is the JNI interface. The third argument is the initial argument to the JVM. The following snippet of code shows how to create a JVM in native code. You need to check for any errors that the `JNI_CreateJavaVM()` function might return. It returns `JNI_ERR` if cannot create a JVM.

```
JNIEnv *env;
JavaVM *jvm;
long status;
status = JNI_CreateJavaVM(&jvm, (void**)&env, &vm_args);

if (status == JNI_ERR) {
  printf("Could not create VM. Exiting application...\n");
  return 1;
}
```

Once you get the `JNIEnv` structure, you can use it to find a class, create an object of that class, and execute any methods on that object. In fact, it lets you access the entire JVM using JNI.

After you are done with the JVM, you need to destroy it.

```
// Destroy JVM
jvm->DestroyJavaVM();
```

Listing 8-13 contains the code for a `EmbeddedJVMJNI` class with a `printMsg()` static method to print a message on the standard output. Later, you will create a JVM in native code, and call the `printMsg()` method.

Listing 8-13. An EmbeddedJVMJNI Java Class

```
// EmbeddedJVMJNI.java
package com.jdojo.jni;

public class EmbeddedJVMJNI {
        public static void printMsg(String msg) {
                System.out.println(msg);
        }
}
```

The C++ console application listed in Listing 8-14 creates a JVM and calls the `printMsg()` method of the `EmbeddedJVMJNI` class. The book's source code contains the C++ code in `createjvm.cpp` file. The program lets you specify the CLASSPATH as the command line argument. If you do not specify the CLASSPATH, it uses the current directory as the CLASSPATH.

Listing 8-14. Contents of the createjvm.cpp File That Creates a JVM in a Native Application

```cpp
// createjvm.cpp
#include <jni.h>
#include <iostream>
#include <string>

int main(int argc, char **argv) {
    std::string classpath("");

    if (argc < 2) {
        std::cout << "You did not pass the classpath."
                  << " Using the current directory as the classpath.\n";
        classpath = ".";
    }
    else {
        classpath = argv[1];
    }

    std::string classpathOption("-Djava.class.path=");

    classpathOption = classpathOption + classpath;

    // Pass the classpath as an argument to the JVM
    const jint MAX_OPTIONS = 1;
    JavaVMOption options[MAX_OPTIONS];
    options[0].optionString = (char *)(classpathOption.c_str());;

    // Prepare the JVM initial arguments
    JavaVMInitArgs vm_args;
    vm_args.version = JNI_VERSION_1_2;
    vm_args.nOptions = MAX_OPTIONS;
    vm_args.options = options;
    vm_args.ignoreUnrecognized = true;

    // Create the JVM
    JavaVM *jvm;
    JNIEnv *env;
    long status = JNI_CreateJavaVM(&jvm, (void**) &env, &vm_args);
    if (status == JNI_ERR) {
        std::cout << "Could not create VM. Exiting application...\n";
        return 1;
    }

    const char *className = "com/jdojo/jni/EmbeddedJVMJNI";
    jclass cls = env->FindClass(className);
    if (cls == NULL) {
        // Print exception stack trace and destroy the JVM
        env->ExceptionDescribe();
        jvm->DestroyJavaVM();
        return 1;
    }
```

```
        if (cls != NULL) {
            jmethodID mid = env->GetStaticMethodID(cls, "printMsg",
                    "(Ljava/lang/String;)V");
            if (mid != NULL) {
                jstring m = env->NewStringUTF("Hello from C++...\n");
                env->CallStaticVoidMethod(cls, mid, m);
                if (env->ExceptionCheck()) {
                    env->ExceptionDescribe();
                    env->ExceptionClear();
                }
            }
        }

    // Destroy JVM
    jvm->DestroyJavaVM();
    return 0;
}
```

You will need to compile the createjvm.cpp file into an executable. When you compile this program, you need to provide the path of the jvm.lib file, which is installed in the JAVA_HOME\lib directory on Windows. Assuming that you have installed the JDK in C:\java8 on Windows, you can use the following command to create the createjvm.exe file on Windows:

```
C:> g++ -IC:/java8/include -IC:/java8/include/win32
        -o createjvm
        createjvm.cpp
        C:/java8/lib/jvm.lib
```

The command is entered on one line, but it is shown on multiple lines for readability. The first two lines in the command are the same as you were using to create the shared libraries before. The -o option is used to specify the executable output file name, which is createjvm in this case. The last option is the path of the library called jvm.lib that needs to be statically linked.

The following command will create a createjvm executable file on Linux, assuming that you have installed the JDK in the /home/ksharan/java8 directory:

```
$ g++ -I/home/ksharan/java8/include -I/home/ksharan/java8/include/linux
    -o createjvm
    createjvm.cpp
    /home/ksharan/java8/jre/lib/i386/client/libjvm.so
```

On Windows, when you run the createjvm.exe application, it will look for the jvm.dll shared library, which is found in JRE_HOME\bin\client directory. You need to include the directory that contains the jvm.dll file in the PATH environment variable.

```
C:\> SET PATH=C:\java8\bin\client;%PATH%
C:\> createjvm C:\myclasses
Hello from C++...
```

When you run the `createjvm.exe` file, you may get the following error:

```
Exception in thread "main" java.lang.NoClassDefFoundError: com/jdojo/jni/EmbeddedJVMJNI
Caused by: java.lang.ClassNotFoundException: com.jdojo.jni.EmbeddedJVMJNI
...
```

The error indicates that the CLASSPATH was not set properly and the JVM was not able to find the EmbeddedJVMJNI class. Using the above command, the class is searched in the `C:\myclasses` directory. To fix this error, either run the `createjvm` application with correct argument for the CLASSPATH or move the `com\jdojo\jni\EmbeddedJVMJNI.class` file into the `C:\myclasses` directory.

On Linux, you will need to set the LD_LIBRARY_PATH, so the `libjvm.so` file is loacted when the createjvm aplication is run. You can set this as follows:

```
$ export LD_LIBRARY_PATH=/home/ksharan/java8/jre/lib/i386/client
```

Now you are ready to run the createjvm application as shown:

```
$ ./createjvm /home/ksharan/myclasses
Hello from C++...
```

The command will search for the `com/jdojo/jni/EmbeddedJVMJNI.class` in the `/home/ksharan/myclasses` directory.

Synchronization in Native Code

The JNI provides two functions called `MonitorEnter()` and `MonitorExit()` to synchronize access to native code in a multithreaded environment. These functions are used in tandem and their use is equivalent to using the synchronized keyword in Java code. These functions are declared as follows:

- `jint MonitorEnter(jobject obj)`
- `jint MonitorExit(jobject obj)`

Both functions return 0 (`JNI_OK` is defined as 0 in the `jni.h` header file) on success and a negative number on failure. You must check their return values to handle the code synchronization properly. Here is the sample Java code that uses synchronization:

```
Object someObject = get the reference of a java object;

// Other logic goes here

synchronized(someObject) {
      // Synchronized code goes here
}
```

The equivalent native code is as follows:

```
jobject someObject = get the reference of a java object;

// Other logic goes here
```

```
jint enterStatus = env->MonitorEnter(someObject);
if (enterStatus != JNI_OK) {
        // Handle the error condition here
}

// Synchronized code goes here

jint exitStatus = env->MonitorExit(someObject);
if (exitStatus != JNI_OK ) {
        // Handle the error condition here
}
```

There are no equivalent JNI functions for Java wait() and notify() to aid in thread synchronization. However, you can always invoke these two Java methods from native code.

Summary

The Java Native Interface (JNI) is a programming interface that facilitates interaction between Java programs and programs written in native languages such as C, C++, FORTRAN, etc. The JNI makes it possible to use a method in Java code and to implement that method in a native language such as C or C++. The JNI also makes it possible to embed the JVM in a native application that can access the Java class libraries.

The method used in Java but implemented in a native language is called a native method, and it is declared using the keyword native. The native method in Java does not have a body. Its body is represented by a semicolon. The implementation of the native method is written in a native language and compiled into a shared library. The shared library is made available to the Java runtime using the java.library.path JVM option or they are located in the PATH environment variable.

The javah command is used to generate the required header file for the native language. It takes the fully qualified class name of the class containing the native method as an argument.

The JNI defines mapping between data types used in Java and native code. For example, jboolean, jchar, jint, etc. are the native equivalent of the boolean, char, int, etc. primitive data types in Java. The jclass, jobject, and jstring types in native code are mapped to the Class, Object, and String classes in Java.

The JNI provides functions to facilitate the conversion between the Java and native representation of strings. It also provides special functions to access the length of Java arrays and array elements.

The JNI also lets you create Java objects inside the native code. You can also access the fields and methods of the Java objects inside the native code.

The Throwable type in Java is mapped to the type jthrowable in native code. The JNI lets you handle exceptions in native code. Native code can detect and handle exceptions that are thrown in the JVM as a result of calling a JNI function. Native code can also throw an exception that can be propagated to Java code. When an exception is thrown during native code execution, the native code keeps executing and the exception remains pending until the control returns to the Java code.

The JNI lets you embed the JVM in a native application giving full access to the rich Java class library to them. The part of the JNI API that lets you create and load a JVM in native code is known as the Invocation API. The JVM is created in native code using the JNI_CreateJavaVM() method of provided by the Invocation API.

In a multithreaded environment, it is possible to synchronize access to a critical section in native code by using the two JNI functions called MonitorEnter() and MonitorExit(). These functions are used in tandem and their use is equivalent to using the synchronized keyword in Java code.

CHAPTER 9

■ ■ ■

Introduction to JavaFX

In this chapter, you will learn

- What JavaFX is
- How to write simple JavaFX programs
- Properties, bindings, and observable collections in JavaFX
- Event handling
- Using layout panes, controls, 2D shapes, and drawing on a canvas
- Applying effects, transformations, and animations
- Using FXML to build UIs in JavaFX applications
- Printing nodes in JavaFX

JavaFX is a vast topic and it deserves a book by itself. This is an introductory chapter to show you the features offered by JavaFX. None of these topics are covered comprehensively.

What Is JavaFX?

JavaFX is an open source Java-based GUI framework for developing rich client applications. It is comparable to other frameworks on the market such as Adobe Flex and Microsoft Silverlight. JavaFX is also seen as the successor of Swing in the arena of GUI development technology in the Java platform. The JavaFX library is available as a public Java API. JavaFX contains several features that make it a preferred choice for developing rich client applications:

- JavaFX is written in Java, enabling you to take advantage of all Java features such as multithreading, generics, lambda expressions, etc. You can use any Java editor of your choice, such as NetBeans, to author, compile, run, debug, and package your JavaFX application.
- JavaFX supports data binding through its libraries.
- JavaFX code can be written using any JVM-supported scripting languages such as Visage, Groovy, Scala, Nashorn, etc.
- JavaFX offers two ways to build a UI: using Java code and using FXML. FXML is an XML-based scriptable markup language to define a UI declaratively. Oracle provides a tool called Scene Builder that is a visual editor for building FXML.
- JavaFX provides a rich set of multimedia support such as playing back audios and videos. It takes advantage of available codecs on the platform.

- JavaFX lets you embed web content in applications.

- JavaFX provides out-of-the-box support for applying effects and animations, which are important for developing gaming applications. In JavaFX, you can achieve sophisticated animations by writing just a few lines of code.

The JavaFX platform consists of the following components to take advantage of the Java native libraries and the available hardware and software on the platform. The arrangement of those components is shown in Figure 9-1.

- JavaFX Public API

- Quantum Toolkit

- Prism

- Glass Windowing Toolkit

- Media Engine

- Web Engine

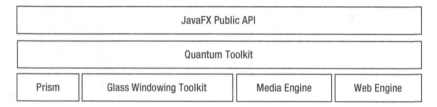

Figure 9-1. *Components making up the JavaFX platform*

The GUI in JavaFX is constructed as a *scene graph*. A scene graph is a collection of visual elements called nodes that are arranged in a tree-like hierarchy. A scene graph is built using the public JavaFX API. Nodes in a scene graph can handle user inputs and gestures. They can have effects, transformations, and states. Types of nodes in a scene graph include simple user interface (UI) controls such as buttons, text fields, 2D and 3D shapes, images, media (audios and videos), web content, charts, etc.

Prism is a hardware accelerated graphics pipeline used for rendering the scene graph. If hardware-accelerated rendering is not available on the platform, Java 2D is used as the fallback rendering mechanism. For example, before using Java 2D for rendering, JavaFX will try using DirectX on Windows and OpenGL on Mac, Linux, and embedded platforms.

The *Glass Windowing Toolkit* provides graphics and windowing services such as windows and the timer using the native operating system. The toolkit is also responsible for managing event queues. In JavaFX, event queues are managed by a single, operating system level thread called *JavaFX Application Thread*. All user input events are dispatched on the JavaFX Application Thread. JavaFX requires that a live scene graph must be modified only on the JavaFX Application Thread.

Prism uses a separate thread, other than the JavaFX Application Thread, for the rendering purpose. It accelerates the rendering process by rendering a frame while the next frame is being processed. When a scene graph is modified, for example, by entering text in a text field, Prism needs to re-render the scene graph. Synchronizing the scene graph with Prism is accomplished using an event called a *pulse* event. A pulse event is queued on the JavaFX Application Thread when the scene graph is modified and it needs to be re-rendered. A pulse event is an indication that the scene graph is not in sync with the rendering layer in Prism and the latest frame at the Prism level should be rendered. Pulse events are throttled at 60 frames per second maximum.

The media engine is responsible for providing media support in JavaFX, for example, playing back audios and videos. It takes advantage of the available codecs on the platform. The media engine uses a separate thread to process media frames and the JavaFX Application Thread to synchronize the frames with the scene graph. The media engine is based on *GStreamer*, which is an open source multimedia framework.

The web engine is responsible for processing web content (HTML) embedded in the scene graph. Prism is responsible for rendering the web content. The web engine is based on *Webkit*, which is an open source web browser engine. It supports HTML5, Cascading Style Sheets (CSS), JavaScript, and Document Object Model (DOM).

The *Quantum* toolkit is an abstraction over the low-level components such as Prism, Glass, Media Engine, and Web Engine. It also facilitates coordination between low-level components.

The History of JavaFX

JavaFX was originally developed by Chris Oliver at Seebeyond and it was called F3 (Form Follows Function). F3 was a Java scripting language for easily developing GUI applications. It offered declarative syntax, static typing, type inference, data binding, animation, 2D graphics, Swing components, etc. Seebeyond was bought by Sun Microsystems, and F3 was named as JavaFX in 2007. Oracle acquired Sun Microsystem in 2010. Oracle open sourced JavaFX in 2013.

The first version of JavaFX was released in the fourth quarter of 2008. The current release for JavaFX is version 8.0. The version number of JavaFX jumped from 2.2 to 8.0. From Java 8, the version numbers of Java SE and JavaFX will be the same. In future, the major versions of Java SE and JavaFX will be released at the same time and their versions will be kept in sync. For example, JavaFX 9 will be released with Java SE 9, JavaFX 10 will be released with Java SE 10, and so on.

Table 9-1 contains the list of releases of JavaFX. Starting with the release of Java SE 8, JavaFX is part of the Java SE runtime library and you do not need to perform any additional setup to compile and run your JavaFX programs.

***Table 9-1.** JavaFX Releases*

Release Date	Version	Comments
Q4, 2008	JavaFX 1.0	It was the initial release of JavaFX. It used a declaration language called *JavaFX Script* to write the JavaFX code.
Q1, 2009	JavaFX 1.1	Support for JavaFX Mobile was introduced.
Q2, 2009	JavaFX 1.2	
Q2, 2010	JavaFX 1.3	
Q3, 2010	JavaFX 1.3.1	
Q4, 2011	JavaFX 2.0	Support for JavaFX script and JavaFX Mobile was dropped. It used the Java programming language to write the JavaFX code.
Q2, 2012	JavaFX 2.1	Support for Mac OS for desktop only was introduced.
Q3, 2012	JavaFX 2.2	
Q1, 2014	JavaFX 8.0	JavaFX version jumped from 2.2 to 8.0. JavaFX and Java SE versions will match from Java 8.

System Requirements

To use the examples in this chapter, you need to have JDK8 installed. It is not necessary to have the NetBeans IDE to compile and run the programs in this book. However, the NetBeans IDE has special features for creating, running, and packaging JavaFX applications that makes developing JavaFX applications using NetBeans easier. You can use any other IDE such as Eclipse, JDeveloper, IntelliJ IDEA, etc. or just use the command prompt to compile and run JavaFX programs.

The JavaFX Runtime Library

All JavaFX classes are packaged in a JAR file named jfxrt.jar that is located in the JRE_HOME\lib\ext directory where JRE_HOME is the installation directory for the JRE.

If you compile and run JavaFX programs on the command line, you do not need to worry about setting the JavaFX runtime JAR file in the CLASSPATH. Java 8 compiler (the javac command) and launcher (the java command) automatically include the JavaFX runtime JAR file in the CLASSPATH.

The NetBeans IDE automatically includes the JavaFX runtime JAR file in the CLASSPATH when you create a Java or JavaFX project. If you are using an IDE other than NetBeans, you may need to include jfxrt.jar in the IDE CLASSPATH to compile and run a JavaFX application from inside the IDE.

JavaFX Source Code

Experienced developers sometimes prefer to look at the source code of the JavaFX library to learn how things are implemented behind the scenes. Oracle provides the JavaFX source code. The Java 8 installation copies the source in the JDK home directory. The file name is javafx-src.zip. Unzip the file in a directory and use your favorite Java editor to open the source code.

Your First JavaFX Application

Your first JavaFX application will display the text Hello JavaFX in a window. You will take an incremental step-by-step approach to developing your first JavaFX application by adding as few lines of code as possible and learning what the code does and why it is needed.

Creating the HelloJavaFX Class

A JavaFX application is a class that must inherit from the Application class. The Application class is in the javafx.application package. You will name your class HelloFXApp and it will be stored in the com.jdojo.jfx package.

```
// HelloFXApp.java
package com.jdojo.jfx;

import javafx.application.Application;

public class HelloFXApp extends Application {
        // Application logic goes here
}
```

The program includes a package declaration, an import statement, and the class declaration. There is nothing like JavaFX in the code. It looks like any other Java code. However, you have fulfilled one requirement of the JavaFX application by inheriting the HelloFXApp class from the Application class. The HelloFXApp class will not compile at this point.

Overriding the start() Method

If you try compiling the HelloFXApp class, it will result in the following compile-time error:

```
HelloFXApp is not abstract and does not override abstract method start(Stage) in Application
```

The error is stating that the Application class contains an abstract start(Stage stage) method, which has not been overridden in the HelloFXApp class. As a Java developer, you know what to do next: you either declare the HelloJavaFX class as abstract or provide an implementation for the start() method. You need to provide an implementation for the start() method in this class. The start() method in the Application class is declared as follows:

- public abstract void start(Stage stage) throws java.lang.Exception

The following is the revised code for your application:

```
// HelloFXApp.java
package com.jdojo.jfx;

import javafx.application.Application;
import javafx.stage.Stage;

public class HelloFXApp extends Application {
        @Override
        public void start(Stage stage) {
                // The logic for starting the application goes here
        }
}
```

In the revised code, you have incorporated two things:

- You have added one more import statement to import the Stage class from the javafx.stage package.

- You implemented the start() method. The throws clause for the method is dropped, which is fine by the rules for overriding methods in Java.

The start() method is the entry point for a JavaFX application. It is called by the JavaFX application launcher. Notice that the start() method is passed an instance of the Stage class, which is known as the *primary stage* of the application. You can create more stages as necessary in your application. However, the primary stage is always created by the JavaFX runtime for you.

■ **Tip** Every JavaFX application class must inherit from the Application class and provide the implementation for the start(String stage) method.

Showing the Stage

Similar to a stage in the real world, a JavaFX stage is used to display a scene. A scene has visuals—such as text, shapes, images, controls, animations, effects, etc.—with which the user may interact, as is the case with all GUI-based applications.

In JavaFX, the primary stage is a container for a scene. The stage look-and-feel is different depending on the environment your application is run in. You do not need to take any action based on the environment because the JavaFX runtime takes care of all the details for you. For example, if the application runs as a desktop application, the primary stage will be a window with a title bar and an area to display the scene; if the application is run in a web browser as an applet, the primary stage will be an embedded area in the browser window.

The primary stage created by the application launcher does not have a scene. You will create a scene for your stage in the next section.

You must show the stage to see the visuals contained in its scene. Use the show() method to show the stage. Optionally, you can set a title for the stage using the setTitle() method. The revised code for the HelloFXApp class is as follows:

```java
// HelloFXApp.java
package com.jdojo.jfx;

import javafx.application.Application;
import javafx.stage.Stage;

public class HelloFXApp extends Application {
        @Override
        public void start(Stage stage) {
                // Set a title for the stage
                stage.setTitle("Hello JavaFX Application");

                // Show the stage
                stage.show();
        }
}
```

Launching the Application

You are ready to run your first JavaFX application. You can use one of the following two options to run a JavaFX application:

- It is not necessary to have a main() method in the class to start a JavaFX application. When you run a Java class that inherits from the Application class, the java command launches the JavaFX application if the class being run does not contain the main() method.

- Include a main() method in the JavaFX application class. Inside the main() method, call the launch() static method of the Application class to launch the JavaFX application. The launch() method takes a String array as an argument, which is the parameters passed to the JavaFX application.

If you are using the first option, you do not need to write any additional code for the HelloJavaFX class. If you are using the second option, the revised code for the HelloFXApp class with the main() method will be as shown in Listing 9-1.

Listing 9-1. A JavaFX Application Without a Scene

```
// HelloFXApp.java
package com.jdojo.jfx;

import javafx.application.Application;
import javafx.stage.Stage;

public class HelloFXApp extends Application {
        public static void main(String[] args) {
                // Launch the JavaFX application
                Application.launch(args);
        }

        @Override
        public void start(Stage stage) {
                stage.setTitle("Hello JavaFX Application");
                stage.show();
        }
}
```

The main() method calls the launch() method, which will do some setup work and call the start() method of the HelloFXApp class. Your start() method sets the title for the primary stage and shows the stage.

Compile the HelloFXApp class using the following command:

```
javac com/jdojo/intro/HelloFXApp.java
```

Run the HelloFXApp class using the following command:

```
java com.jdojo.jfx.HelloFXApp
```

A window with a title bar as shown in Figure 9-2 is displayed.

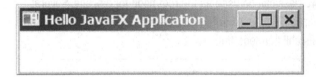

Figure 9-2. A JavaFX stage without a scene

The main area of the window is empty. This is the content area in which the stage will show its scene. Because you do not have a scene for your stage yet, you see an empty area. The title bar shows the title that you have set in the start() method.

You can close the application using the Close menu option in the window title bar. Use Alt + F4 to close the window on Windows. You can use any other option to close the window as provided by your platform.

■ **Tip** The launch() method of the Application class does not return until all windows are closed or the application exits using the Platform.exit() method. The Platform class is in the javafx.application package.

You have not seen anything exciting in JavaFX yet. You need to wait for that until you create a scene in the next section.

Adding the main() Method

As described in the previous section, the Java 8 launcher (the java command) does not require a main() method to launch a JavaFX application. If the class that you want to run inherits from the Application class, the java command launches the JavaFX application by automatically calling the Application.launch() method for you.

If you are using NetBeans IDE to create the JavaFX project, you do not need to have a main() method to launch your JavaFX application if you run the application by running the JavaFX project. However, the NetBeans IDE requires you to have a main() method when you run the JavaFX application class as a file, for example, by selecting the HelloFXApp file, right-clicking it, and selecting the Run File option from the menu.

Some IDEs still require the main() method to launch a JavaFX application. All examples in this chapter will include the main() method that will launch the JavaFX applications.

Adding a Scene to the Stage

An instance of the Scene class, which is in the javafx.scene package, represents a scene. A stage contains one scene. A scene contains visual contents.

The contents of the scene are arranged in a tree-like hierarchy. At the top of the hierarchy is the *root* node. The root node may contain child nodes, which in turn may contain their child nodes, and so on. You must have a root node to create a scene. You will use a VBox as the root node. VBox stands for vertical box, which arranges its children vertically.

```
VBox root = new VBox();
```

■ **Tip** Any node that inherits from the javafx.scene.Parent class can be used as the root node for a scene. Several nodes, known as layout panes or containers, for example, VBox, HBox, Pane, FlowPane, GridPane, TilePane, etc., can be used as a root node. Group is a special container that groups its children together.

A node that can have children provides a getChildren() method that returns an ObservableList of its children. To add a child node to a node, simply add the child node to the ObservableList. The following snippet of code adds a Text node to a VBox:

```
// Create a VBox node
VBox root = new VBox();

// Create a Text node
Text msg = new Text("Hello JavaFX");

// Add the Text node to the VBox as a child node
root.getChildren().add(msg);
```

The Scene class contains several constructors. You will use the one that lets you specify the root node and the size of the scene. The following statement creates a scene with the VBox as the root node, 300px width, and 50px height:

```
// Create a scene
Scene scene = new Scene(root, 300, 50);
```

You need to set the scene to the stage by calling the setScene() method of the Stage class.

```
// Set the scene to the stage
stage.setScene(scene);
```

That's it. You have completed your first JavaFX program with a scene. Listing 9-2 contains the complete program. The program displays a window as shown in Figure 9-3.

Listing 9-2. A JavaFX Application with a Scene Having a Text Node

```java
// HelloFXApp.java
package com.jdojo.jfx;

import javafx.application.Application;
import javafx.scene.Scene;
import javafx.scene.layout.VBox;
import javafx.scene.text.Text;
import javafx.stage.Stage;

public class HelloFXApp extends Application {
        public static void main(String[] args) {
                Application.launch(args);
        }

        @Override
        public void start(Stage stage) {
                Text msg = new Text("Hello JavaFX");
                VBox root = new VBox();
                root.getChildren().add(msg);

                Scene scene = new Scene(root, 300, 50);
                stage.setScene(scene);
                stage.setTitle("Hello JavaFX Application");
                stage.show();
        }
}
```

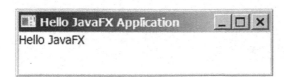

Figure 9-3. *A JavaFX application with scene having a Text node*

Improving the HelloFX Application

JavaFX is capable of doing much more than you have seen so far. Let's enhance the first program and add some more user interface elements such as buttons and text fields. This time, the user will be able to interact with the application. Use an instance of the Button class to create a button as shown:

```
// Create a button with "Exit" text
Button exitBtn = new Button("Exit");
```

When a button is clicked, an ActionEvent is fired. You can add an ActionEvent handler to handle the event. Use the setOnAction() method to set an ActionEvent handler for the button. The following statement sets an ActionEvent handler for the button. The handler terminates the application. You can use a lambda expression or an anonymous class to set the ActionEvent handler. The following snippet of code shows both approaches:

```
// Using a lambda expression
exitBtn.setOnAction(e -> Platform.exit());

// Using an anonymous class
import javafx.event.ActionEvent;
import javafx.event.EventHandler;
...
exitBtn.setOnAction(new EventHandler<ActionEvent>() {
        @Override
        public void handle(ActionEvent e) {
                Platform.exit();
        }
});
```

The program in Listing 9-3 shows how to add more nodes to the scene. The program uses the setStyle() method of the Label class to set the fill color of the Label to blue. I will discuss using CSS in JavaFX briefly later.

Listing 9-3. Interacting with Users in a JavaFX Application

```
// ImprovedHelloFXApp.java
package com.jdojo.jfx;

import javafx.application.Application;
import javafx.application.Platform;
import javafx.scene.Scene;
import javafx.scene.control.Button;
import javafx.scene.control.Label;
import javafx.scene.control.TextField;
import javafx.scene.layout.VBox;
import javafx.stage.Stage;

public class ImprovedHelloFXApp extends Application {
        public static void main(String[] args) {
                Application.launch(args);
        }
```

```java
@Override
public void start(Stage stage) {
        Label nameLbl = new Label("Enter your name:");
        TextField nameFld = new TextField();

        Label msg = new Label();
        msg.setStyle("-fx-text-fill: blue;");

        // Create buttons
        Button sayHelloBtn = new Button("Say Hello");
        Button exitBtn = new Button("Exit");

        // Add the event handler for the Say Hello button
        sayHelloBtn.setOnAction(e -> {
                String name = nameFld.getText();
                if (name.trim().length() > 0) {
                        msg.setText("Hello " + name);
                }
                else {
                        msg.setText("Hello there");
                }
        });

        // Add the event handler for the Exit button
        exitBtn.setOnAction(e -> Platform.exit());

        // Create the root node
        VBox root = new VBox();

        // Set the vertical spacing between children to 5px
        root.setSpacing(5);

        // Add children to the root node
        root.getChildren().addAll(nameLbl, nameFld, msg, sayHelloBtn, exitBtn);

        Scene scene = new Scene(root, 350, 150);
        stage.setScene(scene);
        stage.setTitle("Improved Hello JavaFX Application");
        stage.show();
    }
}
```

The improved HelloFX program displays a window as shown in Figure 9-4. The window contains two labels, a text field, and two buttons. A VBox is used as the root node for the scene. Enter a name in the text field and click the Say Hello button to see a hello message. Clicking the Say Hello button without entering a name displays the message Hello there. The application displays a message in a Label control. Click the Exit button to exit the application.

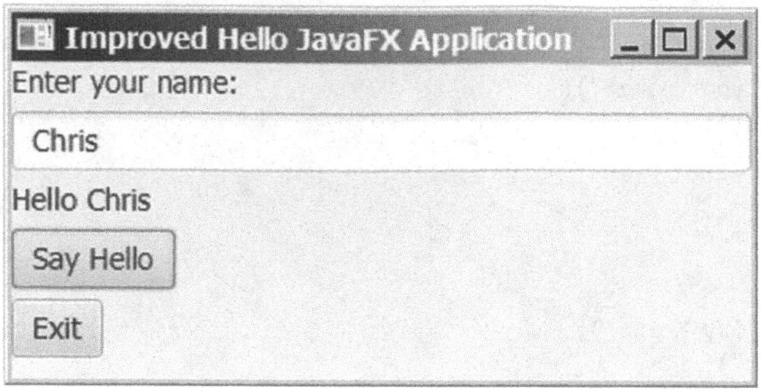

Figure 9-4. A JavaFX Application with two labels, a text field, and two buttons

The Life Cycle of a JavaFX Application

JavaFX runtime creates several threads that are used to perform different tasks at different stages in the application. In this section, you are interested in only those threads that are used to call methods of the Application class during its life cycle. The JavaFX runtime creates, among other threads, two threads named

- JavaFX-Launcher
- JavaFX Application Thread

The launch() method of the Application class create these threads. During the lifetime of a JavaFX application, the JavaFX runtime calls the following methods of the JavaFX application class in order:

- The no-args constructor
- The init() method
- The start() method
- The stop() method

The JavaFX runtime creates the instance of the specified application class on the JavaFX Application Thread.

The JavaFX-Launcher thread calls the init() method of the application class. The init() method implementation in the Application class is empty. You can override this method in your application class. It is not allowed to create a Stage or a Scene on the JavaFX-Launcher thread. They must be created on the JavaFX Application Thread. Therefore, you cannot create a Stage or a Scene inside the init() method. Attempting to do so throws a runtime exception. It is fine to create UI controls, for example, buttons, shapes, etc. in the init() method.

The JavaFX Application Thread calls the start(Stage stage) method of the application class. Note that the start() method in the Application class is declared abstract, and you must override this method in your application class.

At this point, the launch() method waits for the JavaFX application to finish.

When the application finishes, the JavaFX Application Thread calls the stop() method of the application class. The default implementation of the stop() method is empty in the Application class. You will have to override this method in your application class to perform your logic when your application stops.

The program in Listing 9-4 illustrates the life cycle of a JavaFX application. It displays a stage an Exit button. You will see the first three lines of the output when the stage is shown. You will need to close the stage by clicking the Exit button to see the last line of the output.

Listing 9-4. The Life Cycle of a JavaFX Application

```java
// FXLifeCycleApp.java
package com.jdojo.jfx;

import javafx.application.Application;
import javafx.application.Platform;
import javafx.scene.Group;
import javafx.scene.Scene;
import javafx.scene.control.Button;
import javafx.stage.Stage;

public class FXLifeCycleApp extends Application {
        public FXLifeCycleApp() {
                String name = Thread.currentThread().getName();
                System.out.println("FXLifeCycleApp() constructor: " + name);
        }

        public static void main(String[] args) {
                Application.launch(args);
        }

        @Override
        public void init() {
                String name = Thread.currentThread().getName();
                System.out.println("init() method: " + name);
        }

        @Override
        public void start(Stage stage) {
                String name = Thread.currentThread().getName();
                System.out.println("start() method: " + name);

                // Add an Exit button to the scene
                Button exitBtn = new Button("Exit");
                exitBtn.setOnAction(e -> Platform.exit());

                Scene scene = new Scene(new Group(exitBtn), 300, 100);
                stage.setScene(scene);
                stage.setTitle("JavaFX Application Life Cycle");
                stage.show();
        }

        @Override
        public void stop() {
                String name = Thread.currentThread().getName();
                System.out.println("stop() method: " + name);
        }
}
```

```
FXLifeCycleApp() constructor: JavaFX Application Thread
init() method: JavaFX-Launcher
start() method: JavaFX Application Thread
stop() method: JavaFX Application Thread
```

Terminating a JavaFX Application

A JavaFX application may be terminated explicitly or implicitly. You can terminate a JavaFX application explicitly by calling the Platform.exit() method. When this method is called, after or from within the start() method, the stop() method of the Application class is called, and then the JavaFX Application Thread is terminated. At this point, if there are only daemon threads running, the JVM will exit. If this method is called from the constructor or the init() method of the Application class, the stop() method may not be called.

■ **Tip** A JavaFX application may be run in web browsers. Calling Platform.exit() method in web environments may not have any effect.

A JavaFX application may be terminated implicitly when the last window is closed. This behavior can be turned on or turned off using the static setImplicitExit(boolean implicitExit) method of the Platform class. Passing true to this method turns this behavior on. Passing false to this method turns this behavior off. By default, this behavior is turned on. This is the reason that in most of the examples so far, your applications were terminated when you closed the windows. When this behavior is turned on, the stop() method of the Application class is called before terminating the JavaFX Application Thread. Terminating the JavaFX Application Thread does not always terminate the JVM. The JVM terminates if all running non-daemon threads terminate. If the implicit terminating behavior of the JavaFX application is turned off, you must call the exit() method of the Platform class to terminate the application.

What Are Properties and Bindings?

A property is a publicly accessible attribute of a class that affects its state, behavior, or both. Even though a property is publicly accessible, its use (read/write) invokes methods that hide the actual implementation to access the data. Properties are observable, so interested parties are notified when its value changes. A property can be read-only, write-only, or read-write. A read-only property has a getter, but no setter. A write-only property has a setter, but no getter. A read-write property has a getter and a setter.

Unlike other programming languages such as C#, properties in Java are not supported at the language level. Java support for properties comes through the JavaBeans API and design patterns. For more details on properties in Java, please refer to the JavaBeans specification, which can be downloaded from www.oracle.com/technetwork/java/javase/documentation/spec-136004.html.

In programming, the term *binding* is used in many contexts. Here, I want to define it in the context of *data binding*. Data binding defines a relationship between data elements (usually variables) in a program to keep them synchronized. In a GUI application, data binding is frequently used to synchronize the elements in the data model with the corresponding UI elements. Consider the following statement, assuming that x, y, and z are numeric variables:

```
x = y + z;
```

The statement defines a binding between x, y, and z. When the statement is executed, the value of x is synchronized with the sum of the values of y and z. A binding also has a time factor. In the above statement, the value of x is bound to the sum of y and z, and is valid at the time the statement is executed. The value of x may not be equal the sum of y and z before and after the statement is executed. Sometimes it is desired for a binding to hold over a period. Consider the following statement that defines a binding using listPrice, discounts, and taxes:

```
soldPrice = listPrice - discounts + taxes;
```

For this case, you would like to keep the binding valid forever, so the sold price is computed correctly whenever listPrice, discounts, or taxes change. In this binding, listPrice, discounts, and taxes are known as *dependencies*, and it is said that soldPrice is bound to listPrice, discounts, and taxes.

For a binding to work correctly, it is necessary that it is notified whenever its dependencies change. Programming languages that support binding provide a mechanism to register listeners with the dependencies. When dependencies become invalid or when they change, all listeners are notified. A binding may synchronize itself with its dependencies when it receives such notifications.

A binding may be an *eager binding* or a *lazy binding*. In an eager binding, the bound variable is recomputed immediately when the dependencies change. In a lazy binding, the bound variable is not recomputed when its dependencies change; it is recomputed when its value is read next time. A lazy binding performs better as compared to an eager binding.

A binding may be *unidirectional* or *bidirectional*. A unidirectional binding works only in one direction: changes in the dependencies are propagated to the bound variable. A bidirectional binding works in both directions in which the bound variable and the dependency keep their values synchronized with each other. Typically, a bidirectional binding is defined only between two variables. For example, a bidirectional binding, x = y and y = x, declares that the values of x and y are always the same.

Mathematically, it is not possible to define a bidirectional binding between multiple variables uniquely. In the above example, the sold price binding is a unidirectional binding. If you want to make it a bidirectional binding, it is not uniquely possible to compute the values of the list price, discounts, and taxes when the sold price is changed. There are an infinite number of possibilities in the other direction.

Applications with GUIs provide users with UI widgets such as text fields, check boxes, buttons, etc., to manipulate data. The data displayed in UI widgets has to be synchronized with the underlying data model and vice versa. In this case, a bidirectional binding is needed to keep the UI and the data model synchronized.

Properties and Bindings in JavaFX

JavaFX supports properties, events, and binding through *Properties and Binding* APIs. Support for properties in JavaFX is a huge leap forward from the JavaBeans properties. All properties in JavaFX are observable. They can be observed for invalidation and value changes. You can have read-write or read-only properties. All read-write properties support binding. A property in JavaFX can represent a value or a collection of values.

In JavaFX, properties are objects. There is a property class hierarchy for each type of property. For example, the IntegerProperty, DoubleProperty, and StringProperty classes represent properties of int, double, and String types, respectively. These classes are abstract. There are two types of implementation classes for them: one to represent a read-write property and one to represent a wrapper for a read-only property. For example, the SimpleDoubleProperty and ReadOnlyDoubleWrapper classes are concrete classes whose objects are used as read-write and read-only properties of type double, respectively. The following is an example of how to create an IntegerProperty with an initial value of 100:

```
IntegerProperty counter = new SimpleIntegerProperty(100);
```

Property classes provide two pairs of getter and setter methods:

- The get() and set() methods
- The getValue() and setValue() methods

The get() and set() methods get and set the value of the property, respectively. For primitive type properties, they work with primitive type values. For example, for IntegerProperty, the return type of the get() method and the parameter type of the set() method are int. The getValue() and setValue() methods work with object type; for example, their return type and parameter type are Integer for IntegerProperty.

For reference type properties, such as StringProperty and ObjectProperty<T>, both pairs of getter and setter work with object type. That is, both get() and getValue() methods of StringProperty return a String, and set() and setValue() methods take a String parameter. With auto-boxing for primitive types, it does not matter which version of getter and setter is used. The getValue() and setValue() methods exist to help you write generic code in terms of object types.

The following snippet of code uses an IntegerProperty, and its get() and set() methods. The counter property is a read-write property because it is an object of the SimpleIntegerProperty class.

```
IntegerProperty counter = new SimpleIntegerProperty(1);
int counterValue = counter.get();
System.out.println("Counter:" + counterValue);

counter.set(2);
counterValue = counter.get();
System.out.println("Counter:" + counterValue);
```

```
Counter:1
Counter:2
```

Working with read-only properties is a bit tricky. A ReadOnlyXxxWrapper class wraps two properties of Xxx type: one read-only and one read-write. Both properties are synchronized. Its getReadOnlyProperty() method returns a ReadOnlyXxxProperty object. The following snippet of code shows how to create a read-only Integer property:

```
// Create a read-only wrapper property
ReadOnlyIntegerWrapper idWrapper = new ReadOnlyIntegerWrapper(100);

// Get the read-only version of the read-only wrapper property object
ReadOnlyIntegerProperty id = idWrapper.getReadOnlyProperty();

System.out.println("idWrapper:" + idWrapper.get());
System.out.println("id:" + id.get());

// Change the value
idWrapper.set(101);

System.out.println("idWrapper:" + idWrapper.get());
System.out.println("id:" + id.get());
```

```
idWrapper:100
id:100
idWrapper:101
id:101
```

The idWrapper property is read-write, whereas the id property is read-only. When the value in idWrapper is changed, the value in id is changed automatically. To define a read-only property in a class, you declare the idWrapper as a private instance variable. If its value is needed outside the class, you return the id, so the outside world can read the value but cannot change it.

■ **Tip**   Typically, a wrapper property is used as a private instance variable of a class. The class can change the property internally. One of its methods returns the read-only property object of the wrapper class, so the same property is read-only for the outside world.

You can use seven types of properties that represent a single value. The base classes for those properties are named as XxxProperty, read-only base classes are named as ReadOnlyXxxProperty, and wrapper classes are named as ReadOnlyXxxWrapper. The values for Xxx for each type are listed in Table 9-2.

Table 9-2. *Property Classes That Wrap a Single Value*

Type	Xxx Value
int	Integer
long	Long
float	Float
double	Double
boolean	Boolean
String	String
Object	Object

A property object wraps three pieces of information:

- The reference of the bean that contains it
- A name
- A value

When you create a property object, you can supply all or none of the above three pieces of information. Concrete property classes, named like SimpleXxxProperty and ReadOnlyXxxWrapper, provide four constructors that let you supply combinations of the three pieces of information. The following are the constructors for the SimpleIntegerProperty class:

- SimpleIntegerProperty()
- SimpleIntegerProperty(int initialValue)
- SimpleIntegerProperty(Object bean, String name)
- SimpleIntegerProperty(Object bean, String name, int initialValue)

The default value for the initial value depends on the type of the property. It is zero for numeric types, false for boolean type, and null for reference types.

A property object may be part of a bean or it may be a standalone object. The specified bean is the reference to the bean object that contains the property. For a standalone property object, it can be null. Its default value is null.

The name of the property is its name. If not supplied, it defaults to an empty string.

The following snippet of code creates a property object as part of a bean and sets all three values. The first argument to the constructor of the SimpleStringProperty class is this, which is the reference of the Person bean; the second argument, "name", is the name of the property; and the third argument, "Li", is the value of the property.

```
public class Person {
        private StringProperty name = new SimpleStringProperty(this, "name", "Li");

        // More code for the Person goes here
}
```

Every property class contains the getBean() and getName() methods that return the bean reference and the property name, respectively.

Using Properties in JavaFX Beans

In the previous section, you saw the use of JavaFX properties as standalone objects. In this section, you will use them in classes to define properties. Let's create a Book class with three properties (ISBN, title, and price) that will be modeled using JavaFX properties classes.

In JavaFX, you do not declare the property of a class as one of the primitive types. Rather, you use one of the JavaFX property classes. The title property of the Book class will be declared as follows. It is declared private as usual.

```
public class Book {
        private StringProperty title =
                new SimpleStringProperty(this, "title", "Unknown");
}
```

You declare a public getter for the property, which is named, by convention, as XxxProperty, where Xxx is the name of the property. The getter returns the reference of the property. For your title property, the getter will be named titleProperty as shown:

```
public class Book {
        private StringProperty title =
                new SimpleStringProperty(this, "title", "Unknown");

        public final StringProperty titleProperty() {
                return title;
        }
}
```

The declaration of the Book class is fine to work with the title property as shown in the following snippet of code that sets and gets the title of a book:

```
Book beginningJava8 = new Book();
beginningJava8.titleProperty().set("Beginning Java 8");
String title = beginningJava8.titleProperty().get();
```

According to the JavaFX design patterns (not for any technical requirements), a JavaFX property has a getter and a setter that are similar to the getters and setters in JavaBeans. The return type of the getter and the parameter type of the setter are the same as the type of the property value. The getTitle() and setTitle() methods for the title property are declared as follows:

```
public class Book {
        private StringProperty title =
                new SimpleStringProperty(this, "title", "Unknown");

        public final StringProperty titleProperty() {
                return title;
        }

        public final String getTitle() {
                return title.get();
        }

        public final void setTitle(String title) {
                this.title.set(title);
        }
}
```

Note that the getTitle() and setTitle() methods use the title property object internally to get and set the title value.

■ **Tip**   In JavaFX, by convention, getters and setters for a property of a class are declared as final. Additional getters and setters, using JavaBeans naming convention, are added to make the class interoperable with the older tools and frameworks that use the old JavaBeans naming conventions to identify properties of a class.

The following snippet of code shows the declaration of a read-only ISBN property for the Book class:

```
public class Book {
        private ReadOnlyStringWrapper ISBN =
                            new ReadOnlyStringWrapper(this, "ISBN", "Unknown");

        public final String getISBN() {
                return ISBN.get();
        }

        public final ReadOnlyStringProperty ISBNProperty() {
                return ISBN.getReadOnlyProperty();
        }

        // More code for the Book class goes here
}
```

Note the following points about the declaration of the read-only ISBN property:

- It uses the ReadOnlyStringWrapper class instead of the SimpleStringProperty class.

- There is no setter for the property value. You may declare one; however, it must be private.

- The getter for the property value works the same as for a read-write property.

- The ISBNProperty() method uses ReadOnlyStringProperty as the return type, and not ReadOnlyStringWrapper. It obtains a read-only version of the property object from the wrapper object and returns the same.

For the users of the Book class, its ISBN property is read-only. However, it can be changed internally and the change will be reflected in the read-only version of the property object automatically. Listing 9-5 shows the complete code for the Book class.

Listing 9-5. A Book Class with a Read-Only and Two Read-Write Properties

```java
// Book.java
package com.jdojo.jfx;

import javafx.beans.property.DoubleProperty;
import javafx.beans.property.ReadOnlyStringProperty;
import javafx.beans.property.ReadOnlyStringWrapper;
import javafx.beans.property.SimpleDoubleProperty;
import javafx.beans.property.SimpleStringProperty;
import javafx.beans.property.StringProperty;

public class Book {
        private StringProperty title =
                new SimpleStringProperty(this, "title", "Unknown");
        private DoubleProperty price =
                new SimpleDoubleProperty(this, "price", 0.0);
        private ReadOnlyStringWrapper ISBN =
                new ReadOnlyStringWrapper(this, "ISBN", "Unknown");

        public Book() {
        }

        public Book(String title, double price, String ISBN) {
                this.title.set(title);
                this.price.set(price);
                this.ISBN.set(ISBN);
        }

        public final String getTitle() {
                return title.get();
        }

        public final void setTitle(String title) {
                this.title.set(title);
        }
```

```
        public final StringProperty titleProperty() {
                return title;
        }

        public final double getprice() {
                return price.get();
        }

        public final void setPrice(double price) {
                this.price.set(price);
        }

        public final DoubleProperty priceProperty() {
                return price;
        }

        public final String getISBN() {
                return ISBN.get();
        }

        public final ReadOnlyStringProperty ISBNProperty() {
                return ISBN.getReadOnlyProperty();
        }
}
```

Listing 9-6 tests the properties of the Book class. It creates a Book object, prints the details, changes some properties, and prints the details again. Note the use of the ReadOnlyProperty parameter type for the printDetails() method. All property classes implement, directly or indirectly, the ReadOnlyProperty interface.

The toString() methods of the property implementation classes return a well-formatted string that contains all relevant pieces of information for a property. I did not use the toString() method of the property objects because I wanted to show you the use of different methods of the JavaFX properties.

Listing 9-6. A BookPropertyTest Class to Test Properties of the Book Class

```
// BookPropertyTest.java
package com.jdojo.jfx;

import javafx.beans.property.ReadOnlyProperty;

public class BookPropertyTest {
        public static void main(String[] args) {
                Book book = new Book("Beginning Java 8", 49.99, "1430266619");

                System.out.println("After creating the Book object...");

                // Print Property details
                printDetails(book.titleProperty());
                printDetails(book.priceProperty());
                printDetails(book.ISBNProperty());
```

```
                // Change the book's properties
                book.setTitle("Harnessing JavaFX 8.0");
                book.setPrice(9.49);

                System.out.println("\nAfter changing the Book properties...");

                // Print Property details
                printDetails(book.titleProperty());
                printDetails(book.priceProperty());
                printDetails(book.ISBNProperty());
        }

        public static void printDetails(ReadOnlyProperty<?> p) {
                String name = p.getName();
                Object value = p.getValue();
                Object bean = p.getBean();
                String beanClassName =
                        (bean == null) ? "null" : bean.getClass().getSimpleName();
                String propClassName = p.getClass().getSimpleName();

                System.out.print(propClassName);
                System.out.print("[Name:" + name);
                System.out.print(", Bean Class:" + beanClassName);
                System.out.println(", Value:" + value + "]");
        }
}
```

```
After creating the Book object...
SimpleStringProperty[Name:title, Bean Class:Book, Value:Beginning Java 8]
SimpleDoubleProperty[Name:price, Bean Class:Book, Value:49.99]
ReadOnlyPropertyImpl[Name:ISBN, Bean Class:Book, Value:1430266619]
After changing the Book properties...

SimpleStringProperty[Name:title, Bean Class:Book, Value:Harnessing JavaFX 8.0]
SimpleDoubleProperty[Name:price, Bean Class:Book, Value:9.49]
ReadOnlyPropertyImpl[Name:ISBN, Bean Class:Book, Value:1430266619]
```

Handling Property Invalidation Events

A property generates an invalidation event when the status of its value changes from valid to invalid for the first time. Properties in JavaFX use lazy evaluation. When an already invalid property becomes invalid again because of the status of its value changed again, an invalidation event is not generated. An invalid property becomes valid when it is recomputed, such as by calling the get() or getValue() method of the property.

Listing 9-7 is the program to demonstrate when invalidation events are generated for properties. The program includes enough comments to help you understand the logic.

Listing 9-7. Testing Invalidation Events for JavaFX Properties

```java
// InvalidationTest.java
package com.jdojo.jfx;

import javafx.beans.Observable;
import javafx.beans.property.IntegerProperty;
import javafx.beans.property.SimpleIntegerProperty;

public class InvalidationTest {
    public static void main(String[] args) {
        // Create a property
        IntegerProperty counter = new SimpleIntegerProperty(100);

        // Add an invalidation listener to the counter property using a
        // method reference. The invalidated() method of thi class will
        // be called when the counter property becomes invalid..
        counter.addListener(InvalidationTest::invalidated);

        System.out.println("Before changing the counter value-1");
        counter.set(101);
        System.out.println("After changing the counter value-1");

        /*
         * At this point counter property is invalid and further changes
         * to its value will not generate any invalidation events.
         */
        System.out.println();
        System.out.println("Before changing the counter value-2");
        counter.set(102);
        System.out.println("After changing the counter value-2");

        // Make the counter property valid by calling its get() method
        int value = counter.get();
        System.out.println("Counter value = " + value);

        /* At this point the counter property is valid and further changes
           to its value will generate invalidation events.
         */

        // Try setting the same value
        System.out.println();
        System.out.println("Before changing the counter value-3");
        counter.set(102);
        System.out.println("After changing the counter value-3");

        // Try setting a different value
        System.out.println();
        System.out.println("Before changing the counter value-4");
        counter.set(103);
        System.out.println("After changing the counter value-4");
    }
```

```
        public static void invalidated(Observable prop) {
                System.out.println("Counter is invalid.");
        }
}
```

```
Before changing the counter value-1
Counter is invalid.
After changing the counter value-1

Before changing the counter value-2
After changing the counter value-2
Counter value = 102

Before changing the counter value-3
After changing the counter value-3

Before changing the counter value-4
Counter is invalid.
After changing the counter value-4
```

In the beginning, the program creates an IntegerProperty named counter and adds an invalidation listener to the property.

```
// Create the counter property
IntegerProperty counter = new SimpleIntegerProperty(100);

// Add an invalidation listener to the counter proeprty
counter.addListener(InvalidationTest::invalidated);
```

When you create a property object, it is valid. When you change the counter property to 101, it fires an invalidation event. At this point, the counter property becomes invalid. When you change its value to 102, it does not fire an invalidation event because it is already invalid. You use the get() method to read the counter value, which makes it valid again. Now, you set the same a value of 102 to the counter, which does not fire an invalidation event, as the value did not really change; its value was already 102. The counter property is still valid. At the end, you change its value to a different value, and sure enough, an invalidation event is fired.

■ **Tip**   You are not limited to adding only one invalidation listener to a property. You can add as many invalidation listeners as you need. If you do not need an invalidation listener anymore, make sure to remove it by calling the removeListener() method of the property; otherwise, it may lead to memory leaks.

Handling Property Change Events

You can register a ChangeListener to receive notifications about property change events. A property change event is fired every time the value of a property changes. The changed() method of a ChangeListener receives three values:

- The reference of the property object

- The old value of the property

- The new value of the property

You will run a similar test case for testing property change events as you did for invalidation events in the previous section. Listing 9-8 contains the program to demonstrate change events that are generated for properties.

Listing 9-8. Testing Change Events for JavaFX Properties

```java
// ChangeTest.java
package com.jdojo.jfx;

import javafx.beans.property.IntegerProperty;
import javafx.beans.property.SimpleIntegerProperty;
import javafx.beans.value.ObservableValue;

public class ChangeTest {
    public static void main(String[] args) {
        // Create a counter property
        IntegerProperty counter = new SimpleIntegerProperty(100);

        // Add a change listener to the counter property
        counter.addListener(ChangeTest::changed);

        System.out.println("Before changing the counter value-1");
        counter.set(101);
        System.out.println("After changing the counter value-1");

        System.out.println();
        System.out.println("Before changing the counter value-2");
        counter.set(102);
        System.out.println("After changing the counter value-2");

        // Try setting the same value
        System.out.println();
        System.out.println("Before changing the counter value-3");
        counter.set(102); // No change event will be fired.
        System.out.println("After changing the counter value-3");

        // Try setting a different value
        System.out.println();
        System.out.println("Before changing the counter value-4");
        counter.set(103);
        System.out.println("After changing the counter value-4");
    }
```

```
        public static void changed(ObservableValue<? extends Number> prop,
                                    Number oldValue,
                                    Number newValue) {
            System.out.print("Counter changed: ");
            System.out.println("Old = " + oldValue + ", new = " + newValue);
        }
}
```

```
Before changing the counter value-1
Counter changed: Old = 100, new = 101
After changing the counter value-1

Before changing the counter value-2
Counter changed: Old = 101, new = 102
After changing the counter value-2

Before changing the counter value-3
After changing the counter value-3

Before changing the counter value-4
Counter changed: Old = 102, new = 103
After changing the counter value-4
```

In the beginning, the program creates an IntegerProperty named counter.

```
// Create a counter property
IntegerProperty counter = new SimpleIntegerProperty(100);
```

It's little tricky to add a ChangeListener. The addListener() method in the IntegerPropertyBase class is declared as follows:

- void addListener(ChangeListener<? super Number> listener)

If you are using generics, the ChangeListener for an IntegerProperty must be written in terms of the Number class or a superclass of the Number class. Three ways to add a ChangeListener to the counter property are as follows. The code uses anonymous classes that I will translate to lambda expressions at the end.

```
// Method-1: Using generics and the Number class
counter.addListener(new ChangeListener<Number>() {
        @Override
        public void changed(ObservableValue<? extends Number> prop,
                            Number oldValue,
                            Number newValue) {
            System.out.print("Counter changed: ");
            System.out.println("Old = " + oldValue + ", new = " + newValue);
        }});

// Method-2: Using generics and the Object class
counter.addListener(new ChangeListener<Object>() {
        @Override
```

```
        public void changed(ObservableValue<? extends Object> prop,
                             Object oldValue,
                             Object newValue) {
            System.out.print("Counter changed: ");
            System.out.println("Old = " + oldValue + ", new = " + newValue);
    }});
```

```
// Method-3: Not using generics. It may generate compile-time warnings.
counter.addListener(new ChangeListener() {
        @Override
        public void changed(ObservableValue prop,
                             Object oldValue,
                             Object newValue) {
            System.out.print("Counter changed: ");
            System.out.println("Old = " + oldValue + ", new = " + newValue);
    }});
```

Listing 9-8 uses the first method that makes use of generics; as you can see, the signature of the changed() method in the ChangeTest class matches with the changed() method signature in method-1. You have used a lambda expression with a method reference to add a ChangeListener as shown:

```
// Add a change listener using a method reference
counter.addListener(ChangeTest::changed);
```

The output shows that a property change event is fired when the property value is changed. Calling the set() method with the same value does not fire a property change event.

Unlike generating invalidation events, a property uses an eager evaluation for its value to generate change events because it has to pass the new value to the property change listeners.

Property Bindings in JavaFX

In JavaFX, a binding is an expression that evaluates to a value. The binding consists of one or more observable values known as its dependencies. The binding observes its dependencies for changes and recomputes its value automatically when needed. JavaFX uses lazy evaluation for all bindings. When a binding is initially defined or when its dependencies change, its value is marked as invalid. The value of an invalid binding is computed when it is requested next time, usually using its get() or getValue() method. All property classes in JavaFX have built-in support for bindings.

Let's discuss a quick example of binding in JavaFX. Consider the following expression that represents the sum of two integers x and y:

```
x + y
```

The expression x + y represents a binding, which has two dependencies, x and y. You can give it a name sum as follows:

```
sum = x + y
```

To implement the above logic in JavaFX, you create two IntegerProperty variables, x and y:

```
IntegerProperty x = new SimpleIntegerProperty(100);
IntegerProperty y = new SimpleIntegerProperty(200);
```

617

The following statement creates a binding named sum that represents the sum of x and y:

```
NumberBinding sum = x.add(y);
```

A binding has an isValid() method that returns true, if it is valid; otherwise, it returns false. You can get the value of a NumberBinding using the methods intValue(), longValue(), floatValue(), and doubleValue() as int, long, float, and double, respectively. The program in Listing 9-9 shows how to create and use a binding.

Listing 9-9. Using a Simple Binding in JavaFX

```java
// BindingTest.java
package com.jdojo.jfx;

import javafx.beans.binding.NumberBinding;
import javafx.beans.property.IntegerProperty;
import javafx.beans.property.SimpleIntegerProperty;

public class BindingTest {
        public static void main(String[] args) {
                // Create two properties x and y
                IntegerProperty x = new SimpleIntegerProperty(100);
                IntegerProperty y = new SimpleIntegerProperty(200);

                // Create a binding: sum = x + y
                NumberBinding sum = x.add(y);

                System.out.println("After creating sum");
                System.out.println("sum.isValid(): " + sum.isValid());

                // Let us get the value of sum, so it computes its value and
                // becomes valid
                int value = sum.intValue();

                System.out.println();
                System.out.println("After requesting value");
                System.out.println("sum.isValid(): " + sum.isValid());
                System.out.println("sum = " + value);

                // Change the value of x
                x.set(250);

                System.out.println();
                System.out.println("After changing x");
                System.out.println("sum.isValid(): " + sum.isValid());

                // Get the value of sum again
                value = sum.intValue();

                System.out.println();
                System.out.println("After requesting value");
```

```
                    System.out.println("sum.isValid(): " + sum.isValid());
                    System.out.println("sum = " + value);
            }
}
```

```
After creating sum
sum.isValid(): false

After requesting value
sum.isValid(): true
sum = 300

After changing x
sum.isValid(): false

After requesting value
sum.isValid(): true
sum = 450
```

When the sum binding is created, it is invalid and it does not know its value. This is evident from the output. Once you request its value, using the sum.intValue() method, it computes its value and marks itself as valid. When you change one of its dependencies, it becomes invalid until you request its value again.

■ **Tip**   A binding, internally, adds invalidation listeners to all its dependencies. When any of its dependencies become invalid, it marks itself as invalid. An invalid binding does not mean that its value has changed. All it means is that it needs to recompute its value when the value is requested next time.

In JavaFX, you can also bind a property to a binding. Recall that a binding is an expression that is synchronized with its dependencies automatically. Using this definition, a bound property is a property whose value is computed based on an expression, which is automatically synchronized when the dependencies change. Suppose you have three properties called x, y, and z as follows:

```
IntegerProperty x = new SimpleIntegerProperty(10);
IntegerProperty y = new SimpleIntegerProperty(20);
IntegerProperty z = new SimpleIntegerProperty(60);
```

You can bind the property z to expression x + y, using the bind() method of the Property interface as follows:

```
// Bind z to x + y
z.bind(x.add(y));
```

Note that you cannot write z.bind(x + y) because the + operator does not know how to add values of two IntegerProperty objects. You need to use the binding API to create a binding expression.

Now, when x, y, or both change, the z property becomes invalid. The next time you request the value of z, it recomputes the expression x.add(y) to get its value.

You can use the unbind() method of the Property interface to unbind a bound property. Calling the unbind() method on an unbound or never bound property has no effect. You can unbind the z property as follows:

```
// Unbind the z proeprty
z.unbind();
```

After unbinding, a property behaves as a normal property, maintaining its value independently. In other words, unbinding a property breaks the link between the property and its dependencies. Listing 9-10 shows how to bind a property to an expression made up of other properties.

Listing 9-10. Binding a Property to an Expression

```java
// BoundProperty.java
package com.jdojo.jfx;

import javafx.beans.property.IntegerProperty;
import javafx.beans.property.SimpleIntegerProperty;

public class BoundProperty {
    public static void main(String[] args) {
        // Create three properties
        IntegerProperty x = new SimpleIntegerProperty(10);
        IntegerProperty y = new SimpleIntegerProperty(20);
        IntegerProperty z = new SimpleIntegerProperty(60);

        // Create the binding z = x + y
        z.bind(x.add(y));

        System.out.println("After binding z: Bound = " +
                z.isBound() + ", z = " + z.get());

        // Change x and y
        x.set(15);
        y.set(19);
        System.out.println("After changing x and y: Bound = " +
                z.isBound() + ", z = " + z.get());

        // Unbind z
        z.unbind();

        // Will not affect the value of z as it is not bound
        // to x and y anymore
        x.set(100);
        y.set(200);
        System.out.println("After unbinding z: Bound = " +
                z.isBound() + ", z = " + z.get());
    }
}
```

```
After binding z: Bound = true, z = 30
After changing x and y: Bound = true, z = 34
After unbinding z: Bound = false, z = 34
```

A binding has a direction, which is the direction in which changes are propagated. JavaFX supports two types of binding for properties: unidirectional binding and bidirectional binding. A unidirectional binding works only in one direction; changes in dependencies are propagated to the bound property, not vice versa. A bidirectional binding works in both directions; changes in dependencies are reflected in the property and vice versa.

The bind() method of the Property interface creates a unidirectional binding between a property and an ObservableValue, which could be a complex expression. The bindBidirectional() method creates a bidirectional binding between a property and another property of the same type.

The statement z.bind(x.add(y)) in the previous example create a unidirectional binding. In a unidirectional binding, the bound property cannot be changed. Its value is always computed using its dependencies. Attempting to change the value of a unidirectional bound property throws a RuntimeException.

A bidirectional binding works in both directions. It has some restrictions. It can only be created between properties of the same type. That is, a bidirectional binding can only be of the type x = y and y = x, where x and y are of the same type.

```
// Create two properties called x and y
IntegerProperty x = new SimpleIntegerProperty(10);
IntegerProperty y = new SimpleIntegerProperty(20);

// Create bidirectional binding between x and y
x.bindBidirectional(y);

// Now, both x and y are 20. The values and x and y are
// always the same when x or y is changed.

// Remove the bidirectional binding between x and y
x.unbindBidirectional(y);

// Now, x and y maintain their values independent of each other.
```

Bindings are used a lot in JavaFX application to bind properties of UI elements to properties of other UI elements or to the data model. Let's look at an example of a JavaFX GUI application that uses bindings. You will create a screen with a circle that will be centered on the screen. The circumference of the circle will touch the closer sides of the screen. If the width and height of the screen is the same, the circumference of circle will touch all four sides of the screen.

Attempting to develop the screen with a centered circle without bindings is a tedious task. The Circle class in the javafx.scene.shape package represents a circle. It has three properties, centerX, centerY, and radius of the DoubleProperty type. The centerX and centerY properties define the (x, y) coordinates of the center of the circle. The radius property defines the radius of the circle. By default, a circle is filled with black color. You create a circle with centerX, centerY, and radius set to the default value of 0.0 as follows:

```
Circle c = new Circle();
```

Next, add the circle to a group and create a scene with the group as its root node as shown:

```
Group root = new Group(c);
Scene scene = new Scene(root, 150, 150);
```

The following bindings will position and size the circle according to the size of the scene:

```
// The center of the circle is always in the center of the scene
c.centerXProperty().bind(scene.widthProperty().divide(2));
c.centerYProperty().bind(scene.heightProperty().divide(2));

// The radius of the circle will be always the half of the minimum
// of the width and height of the scene
c.radiusProperty().bind(Bindings.min(scene.widthProperty(), scene.heightProperty())
                            .divide(2));
```

The first two bindings bind the centerX and centerY of the circle to the middle of the width and height of the scene, respectively. The third binding binds the radius of the circle to the half (see divide(2)) of the minimum of the width and the height of the scene. That's it! The binding API does the magic of keeping the circle centered when the application is run.

Listing 9-11 contains the complete program. Figure 9-5 shows the screen when the program is initially run. Try resizing the window and you will notice that the center of the circle is always in the middle of the scene.

Listing 9-11. Using the Binding API to Keep a Circle Centered on a Scene

```
// CenteredCircle.java
package com.jdojo.jfx;

import javafx.application.Application;
import javafx.beans.binding.Bindings;
import javafx.scene.Group;
import javafx.scene.Scene;
import javafx.scene.shape.Circle;
import javafx.stage.Stage;

public class CenteredCircle extends Application {
        public static void main(String[] args) {
                Application.launch(args);
        }

        @Override
        public void start(Stage stage) {
                Circle c = new Circle();
                Group root = new Group(c);
                Scene scene = new Scene(root, 100, 100);

                // Bind circle's centerX, centerY, and radius
                // to scene's properties
                c.centerXProperty().bind(scene.widthProperty().divide(2));
                c.centerYProperty().bind(scene.heightProperty().divide(2));
                c.radiusProperty().bind(Bindings.min(scene.widthProperty(),
                                                scene.heightProperty())
                                        .divide(2));

                // Set the stage properties and make it visible
                stage.setTitle("A Centered Circle");
                stage.setScene(scene);
```

```
                stage.sizeToScene();
                stage.show();
        }
}
```

Figure 9-5. *A circle centered on the scene*

Observable Collections

Observable collections in JavaFX are an extension to collections in the Java programming language. The Collections framework in Java has the List, Set, and Map interfaces. JavaFX adds the following three types of observable collections that may be observed for changes in their contents:

- An observable list

- An observable set

- An observable map

JavaFX supports observable collections through the following three new interfaces:

- ObservableList

- ObservableSet

- ObservableMap

The three interfaces inherit List, Set, and Map from the java.util package. In addition to inheriting from the Java collection interfaces, JavaFX collection interfaces also inherit the Observable interface. All JavaFX observable collection interfaces and classes are in the javafx.collections package. Figure 9-6 shows a partial class diagram for the interfaces representing observable collections.

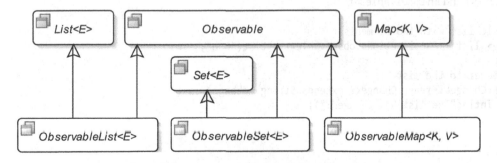

Figure 9-6. *A partial class diagram for observable collection interfaces in JavaFX*

The observable collections in JavaFX have two additional features:

- They support invalidation notifications as they are inherited from the Observable interface.

- They support change notifications. You can register change listeners that are notified when their contents change.

The FXCollections class is a utility class to work with JavaFX collections. It consists of all static methods. JavaFX does not expose the implementation classes of lists, sets, and maps. You need to use one of the factory methods in the FXCollections class to create objects of the ObservableList, ObservableSet, and ObservableMap interfaces. The following snippet of code shows how to create observable collections:

```
// Create an observable list with two elements
ObservableList<String> list = FXCollections.observableArrayList("One", "Two");

// Create an observable set with two elements
ObservableSet<String> set = FXCollections.observableSet("one", "two");

// Create an observable map and two key-value pairs
ObservableMap<String, Integer> map = FXCollections.observableHashMap();
map.put("one", 1);
map.put("two", 2);
```

You can add invalidation and change listeners to observable collections. Adding an InvalidationListener to observable collections is the same as adding an InvalidationListener to a property that you have seen in the previous section. Each type of observable collection has its own change listener type:

- An instance of the ListChangeListener interface represents a change listener for an ObservableList.

- An instance of the SetChangeListener interface represents a change listener for an ObservableSet.

- An instance of the MapChangeListener interface represents a change listener for an ObservableMap.

Use the addListener() method of the observable collections to add a change listener to them. All change listener interfaces for the observable collections declare a static inner class called Change that encapsulates the changes in the respective type of collections. For example, you have a ListChangeListener.Change static inner class to encapsulate changes in an ObservableList. The change listener is passed an instance of the Change class. You need to use the next() method of the Change class to iterate over all changes. The Change class contains several methods to provide the details of the changes made to the particular collection. The following snippet of code shows how to add a change listener to an ObservableList and an ObservableSet:

```
// Create an observable list with two elements
ObservableList<String> list = FXCollections.observableArrayList("One", "Two");

 // Add a change listener to the list
list.addListener((ListChangeListener.Change<? extends String> change) -> {
        System.out.println("The list has changed.");
});
```

```
// Create an observable set
ObservableSet<String> set = FXCollections.observableSet("one", "two");

// Add a change listener to the set
set.addListener((SetChangeListener.Change<? extends String> change) -> {
       System.out.println("The list has changed.");
});
```

Let's look at a detailed example of how to handle changes in an ObservableList. Observing an ObservableList for changes is a bit tricky. There could be several kinds of changes to a list. Some of the changes could be exclusive, whereas some can occur along with other changes. Elements of a list can be permutated, updated, replaced, added, and removed. You can add a change listener to an ObservableList using its addListener() method, which takes an instance of the ListChangeListener interface. The changed() method of the listeners is called every time a change occurs in the list. The following snippet of code shows how to add a change listener to an ObservableList<String>. The onChanged() method is simple; it prints a message on the standard output when it is notified of a change.

```
// Create an observable list
ObservableList<String> list = FXCollections.observableArrayList();

// Add a change listener to the list
list.addListener((ListChangeListener.Change<? extends String> change) -> {
       System.out.println("List has changed.");
});
```

Listing 9-12 contains a complete program that shows how to detect changes in an ObservableList. After adding a change listener, it manipulates the list and the listener is notified each time, as is evident from the output. This program is simplified to keep it short and readable. The ListChangeListener.Change object contains all details about the changes in the list such as the affected range, size of addition and removal, etc.

Listing 9-12. Detecting Changes in an ObservableList

```
// ObservableListTest.java
package com.jdojo.jfx;

import javafx.collections.FXCollections;
import javafx.collections.ListChangeListener;
import javafx.collections.ObservableList;

public class ObservableListTest {
       public static void main(String[] args) {
               // Create a list with some elements
               ObservableList<String> list =
                       FXCollections.observableArrayList("one", "two");

               System.out.println("After creating the list: " + list);

               // Add a ChangeListener tp teh list
               list.addListener(ObservableListTest::onChanged);

               // Add some more elements to the list
               list.addAll("three", "four");
               System.out.println("After addAll() - list: " + list);
```

```
                // We have four elements. Remove the middle two
                // from index 1 (inclusive) to index 3 (exclusive)
                list.remove(1, 3);
                System.out.println("After remove() - list: " + list);

                // Retain only the element "one"
                list.retainAll("one");
                System.out.println("After retainAll() - list: " + list);

                // Replace the first element in the list
                list.set(0, "ONE");
                System.out.println("After set() - list: " + list);
        }

        public static void onChanged(ListChangeListener.Change<? extends String> change) {
                while (change.next()) {
                        if (change.wasPermutated()) {
                                System.out.println("A permutation is detected.");
                        }
                        else if (change.wasUpdated()) {
                                System.out.println("An update is detected.");
                        }
                        else if (change.wasReplaced()) {
                                System.out.println("A replacement is detected.");
                        }
                        else {
                                if (change.wasRemoved()) {
                                        System.out.println("A removal is detected.");
                                }
                                else if (change.wasAdded()) {
                                        System.out.println("An addition is detected.");
                                }
                        }
                }
        }
}
```

```
After creating the list: [one, two]
An addition is detected.
After addAll() - list: [one, two, three, four]
A removal is detected.
After remove() - list: [one, four]
A removal is detected.
After retainAll() - list: [one]
A replacement is detected.
After set() - list: [ONE]
```

Event Handling

In general, the term *event* is used to describe an occurrence of interest. In a GUI application, an event is an occurrence of a user interaction with the application. Clicking of the mouse, pressing a key on the keyboard, etc. are examples of events in a JavaFX application.

An event in JavaFX is represented by an object of the javafx.event.Event class or any of its subclasses. Every event in JavaFX has three properties:

- An event source

- An event target

- An event type

When an event occurs, you typically perform some processing by executing a piece of code. The piece of code that is executed in response to an event is known as an *event handler* or an *event filter*. I will clarify the difference between an event handler and an event filter shortly. For now, think of both as a piece of code and I will refer to both of them as event handlers. When you want to handle an event for a UI element, you need to add event handlers to the UI element. When the UI element detects the event, it executes your event handlers.

The UI element that calls event handlers is the source of the event for those event handlers. When an event occurs, it passes through a chain of event dispatchers. The source of an event is the current element in the event dispatcher chain. The event source changes as the event passes through one dispatcher to another in the event dispatcher chain.

The event target is the destination of an event. The event target determines the route through which the event travels during its processing. Suppose a mouse click occurs over a Circle node. In this case, the Circle node is the event target of the mouse-clicked event.

The event type describes the type of the event that occurs. Event types are defined in a hierarchical fashion. Each event type has a name and a supertype.

The three properties that are common to all events in JavaFX are represented by objects of three different classes. Specific events define additional event properties; for example, the event class to represent a mouse event adds properties to describe the location of the mouse cursor, state of the mouse buttons, etc.

Table 9-3 lists the classes and interfaces involved in event processing. JavaFX has an event delivery mechanism that defines the details of the occurrence and processing of events.

Table 9-3. *The List of Classes Involved in Events Processing*

Name	Class/Interface	Description
Event	Class	An instance of this class represents an event. Several subclasses of the Event class exist to represent specific types of events.
EventTarget	Interface	An instance of this interface represents an event target.
EventType	Class	An instance of this class represents an event type, such as mouse pressed, mouse released. mouse moved, etc.
EventHandler	Interface	An instance of this interface represents an event handler or an event filter. Its handle() method is called when the event for which it has been registered occurs.

Event Processing Mechanism

When an event occurs, several steps are performed as part of the event processing:

- Event Target Selection
- Event Route Construction
- Event Route Traversal

Event Target Selection

The first step in the event processing is the selection of the event target. Recall that an event target is the destination node of an event. The event target is selected based on the event type. For mouse events, the event target is the node at the mouse cursor. Multiple nodes can be at the mouse cursor. For example, you can have a circle placed over a rectangle. The topmost node at the mouse cursor is selected as the event target.

The event target for key events is the node that has focus. How a node gets the focus depends on the type of the node. For example, a TextField may get focus by clicking the mouse inside it or using the focus traversal keys such as Tab or Shift-Tab on the Windows operating system. Shapes such as Circles, Rectangles, etc. do not get focus, by default. If you want them to receive key events, you can give them focus by calling the requestFocus() method of the Node class.

Event Route Construction

An event travels through event dispatchers in an event dispatch chain. The event dispatch chain is the *event route*. The initial and default route for an event is determined by the event target. The default event route consists of the container-children path starting at the stage to the event target node.

Suppose you have placed a Circle and a Rectangle in an HBox and the HBox is the root node of the Scene of a Stage. When you click on the Circle, the Circle becomes the event target. The Circle constructs the default event route, which is the path starting at the stage to the event target (the Circle).

In fact, an event route consists of event dispatchers that are associated with nodes. However, for all practical and understanding purposes, you can think of the event route as the path made up of the nodes. Typically, you do not deal with event dispatchers directly.

Figure 9-7 shows the event route for the mouse-clicked event. The nodes on the event route are shown in gray background fills. The nodes on the event route are connected by solid lines. Note that the Rectangle that is part of the scene graph is not part of the event path when the Circle is clicked.

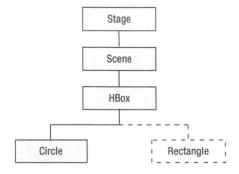

Figure 9-7. *Construction of the default event route for an event*

An event dispatch chain (or event route) has a *head* and a *tail*. In this case, the Stage and the Circle are the head and the tail of the event dispatch chain, respectively. The initial event route may be modified as the event processing progresses. Typically, but not necessarily, the event passes through all nodes in its route twice during the event traversal step as described in the next section.

Event Route Traversal

An event route traversal consists of two phases:

- Capture Phase
- Bubbling Phase

An event travels through each node in its route twice: once during capture phase and once during bubbling phase. You can register event filters and event handlers to a node for specific events types. The event filters are executed as the event passes through the node during the capture phase. The event handlers are executed as the event passes through the node during the bubbling phase. The event filters and handlers are passed in the reference of the current node as the source of the event. As the event travels from one node to another, the event source keeps changing. However, the event target remains the same from the start to the finish of the event route traversal.

During the route traversal, a node can consume the event in event filters or handlers, thus completing the processing of the event. Consuming an event is simply calling the consume() method on the event object. When an event is consumed, the event processing is stopped, even though some of the nodes in the route were not traversed at all.

Event Capture Phase

During the capture phase, an event travels from the head to tail of its event dispatch chain. Figure 9-8 shows the travelling of a mouse-clicked event for the Circle in this example in the capture phase. The down arrows in the figure denote the direction the event travels. As the event passes through a node, the registered event filters for the node are executed. Note that the event capture phase executes only event filters, not event handlers, for the current node.

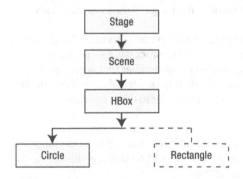

Figure 9-8. *The event capture phase*

In this example, the event filters for the Stage, Scene, HBox, and Circle are executed in order, assuming none of the event filters consumes the event.

You can register multiple event filters for a node. If the node consumes the event in one of its event filters, its other event filters, which have not been executed yet, are executed before the event processing stops. Suppose you have registered five event filters for the Scene in your example, and the first event filter that is executed consumes the event. In this case, the other four event filters for the Scene will still be executed. After executing the fifth event filter for the Scene, the event processing will stop, without the event travelling to the remaining nodes (HBox and Circle).

In the event capture phase, you can intercept events (and provide a generic response) that are targeted at the children of a node. For example, you can add event filters for the mouse-clicked event to the Stage in this example to intercept all mouse-clicked events for all its children. You can block events from reaching its target by consuming the event in event filters for a parent node. For example, if you consume the mouse-clicked event in a filter for the Stage, the event will not reach its target, say, the Circle.

Event Bubbling Phase

During the bubbling phase, an event travels from the tail to head of its event dispatch chain. Figure 9-9 shows the travelling of a mouse-clicked event for the Circle in your example, in the bubbling phase.

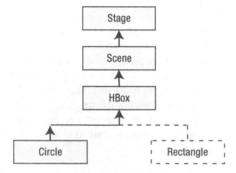

Figure 9-9. *The event bubbling phase*

The up arrows in the figure denote the direction of the event travel. As the event passes through a node, the registered event handlers for the node are executed. Note that the event bubbling phase executes event handlers for the current node, whereas the event capture phase executes the event filters.

In your example, the event handlers for the Circle, HBox, Scene, and Stage are executed in order, assuming none of the event filters consumes the event. Note that the event bubbling phase starts at the target of the event and travels up to the topmost parent in the parent-children hierarchy.

You can register multiple event handlers for a node. If the node consumes the event in one of its event handlers, its other event handlers, which have not been executed yet, are executed before the event processing stops. Suppose you have registered five event handlers for the Circle in your example, and the first event handler that is executed consumes the event. In this case, the other four event handlers for the Circle will still be executed. After executing the fifth event handler for the Circle, the event processing will stop without the event travelling to the remaining nodes (HBox, Scene, and Stage).

Typically, event handlers are registered to target nodes to provide specific response to events. Sometimes, event handlers are installed on parent nodes to provide a default event response for all its children. If an event target decides to provide a specific response to the event, it can do so by adding event handlers and consuming the event, thus blocking the event from reaching the parent nodes in the event bubbling phase.

Let's discuss a trivial example. Suppose you want to display a message box when the user clicks anywhere inside a window. You can register an event handler to the window to display the message box. When the user clicks inside a circle in the window, you want to display a specific message. You can register an event handler to the circle to provide the specific message and consume the event. This will provide a specific event response when the circle is clicked, whereas for other nodes, the window provides a default event response.

Creating Event Filters and Handlers

Creating event filters and handlers are as simple as creating objects of the class that implements the EventHandler interface. Before Java 8, you would use inner classes to create event filters and handlers.

```
EventHandler<MouseEvent> aHandler = new EventHandler<MouseEvent>() {
        @Override
        public void handle(MouseEvent e) {
                // Event handling code goes here
        }
};
```

From Java 8, using a lambda expression is the best choice for creating the event filters and handlers, as shown:

```
EventHandler<MouseEvent> aHandler = e -> {
        // Event handling code goes here
};
```

This chapter uses lambda expressions to create event filters and handlers. If you are not familiar with lambda expressions in Java 8, it is suggested that you learn at least the basics, so you can understand the event handling code. The following snippet of code creates a MouseEvent handler. It prints the type of the mouse event that occurs.

```
EventHandler<MouseEvent> mouseEventHandler =
        e -> System.out.println("Mouse event type: " + e.getEventType());
```

Registering Event Filters and Handlers

If a node is interested in processing events of specific types, you need to register event filters and handlers for those event types with the node. When the event occurs, the handle() method of the registered event filters and handlers for the node are called following the rules discussed in the previous sections. If the node is no longer interested in processing the events, you need to unregister the event filters and handlers from the node. Registering and unregistering event filters and handlers are also known as adding and removing event filters and handlers, respectively.

JavaFX provides two ways to register and unregister event filters and handlers with nodes:

- Using the addEventFilter(), addEventHandler(), removeEventFilter(), and removeEventHandler() methods

- Using the onXxx convenience properties

You can use the addEventFilter() and addEventHandler() methods to register event filters and handlers with nodes, respectively. These methods are defined in the Node class, Scene class, and Window class. Some classes such as MenuItem and TreeItem can be event targets; however, they are not inherited from the Node class.

- `<T extends Event> void addEventFilter(EventType<T> eventType, EventHandler<? super T> eventFilter)`

- `<T extends Event> void addEventHandler(EventType<T> eventType, EventHandler<? super T> eventHandler)`

These methods take two parameters. The first parameter is the event type and the second one is an object of the EventHandler interface.

You can handle mouse-clicked events for a Circle using the following snippet of code:

```
import javafx.scene.shape.Circle;
import javafx.event.EventHandler;
import javafx.scene.input.MouseEvent;
...
// Create a circle
Circle circle = new Circle (100, 100, 50);

// Create a MouseEvent filter
EventHandler<MouseEvent> mouseEventFilter =
        e -> System.out.println("Mouse event filter has been called.");

// Create a MouseEvent handler
EventHandler<MouseEvent> mouseEventHandler =
        e -> System.out.println("Mouse event handler has been called.");

// Register the MouseEvent filter and handler to the Circle
// for mouse-clicked events
circle.addEventFilter(MouseEvent.MOUSE_CLICKED, mouseEventFilter);
circle.addEventHandler(MouseEvent.MOUSE_CLICKED, mouseEventHandler);
```

The code creates two EventHandler objects, which print a message on the console. At this stage, they are not event filters or handlers. They are just two EventHandler objects. Note that giving the reference variables names and printing messages that use the words filter and handler does not make any difference in their status as filters and handlers. The last two statements register one of the EventHandler objects as an event filter and another as an event handler; both are registered for the mouse-clicked event.

The Node, Scene, and Window classes contain event properties to store event handlers of some selected event types. The property names use the event type pattern. They are named as onXxx. For example, the onMouseClicked property stores the event handler for the mouse-clicked event type, the onKeyTyped property stores the event handler for the key-typed event, and so on. You can use the setOnXxx() methods of these properties to register event handlers for a node. For example, use the setOnMouseClicked() method to register an event handler for the mouse-clicked event and use the setOnKeyTyped() method to register an event handler for the key-typed event, and so on. The setOnXxx() methods in various classes are known as convenience methods for registering event handlers.

You need to remember some points about the onXxx convenience properties:

- They only support the registration of event handlers, not event filters. If you need to register event filters, use the addEventFilter() method.

- They only support the registration of *one event handler* for a node. Multiple event handlers for a node may be registered using the addEventHandler() method.

- These properties exist only for the commonly used events for a node type. For example, the onMouseClicked property exists in the Node and Scene classes, but not the Window class; the onShowing property exists in the Window class, but not in the Node and Scene classes.

The following snippet of code shows how to use the convenience onMouseClicked property to set an event handler for a circle:

```
// Create a circle
Circle circle = new Circle (100, 100, 50);

// Create a MouseEvent handler
EventHandler<MouseEvent> eventHandler =
        e -> System.out.println("Mouse event handler has been called.");

// Register the handler using the setter method for the onMouseClicked
// convenience event property
circle.setOnMouseClicked(eventHandler);
```

The following snippet of code show how to add an ActionEvent handler to a Button using the setOnAction() convenience method of the Button class:

```
// Create a button
Button exitBtn = new Button("Exit");

// Add the event handler for the Exit button
exitBtn.setOnAction(e -> Platform.exit());
```

The convenience event properties do not provide a separate method to unregister the event handler. Setting the property to null unregisters the event handler that has already been registered.

```
// Unregister the mouse-clicked event handler for the circle
circle.setOnMouseClicked(null);
```

Classes that define the onXxx event properties also define getOnXxx() getter methods that return the reference of the registered event handler. If no event handler is set, the getter method returns null.

Listing 9-13 contains a program that shows the event routing and handling mechanisms. It also shows how to consume an event and its effect. Figure 9-10 shows the screen when you run the program.

Listing 9-13. Handling and Consuming Events

```
// EventHandling.java
package com.jdojo.jfx;

import javafx.application.Application;
import javafx.event.EventHandler;
import javafx.geometry.Insets;
import javafx.scene.Scene;
import javafx.scene.control.CheckBox;
import javafx.scene.input.MouseEvent;
import static javafx.scene.input.MouseEvent.MOUSE_CLICKED;
import javafx.scene.layout.HBox;
import javafx.scene.paint.Color;
import javafx.scene.shape.Circle;
import javafx.scene.shape.Rectangle;
import javafx.stage.Stage;
```

```java
public class EventHandling extends Application {
        private CheckBox consumeEventCbx =
                new CheckBox("Consume Mouse Click at Circle");

        public static void main(String[] args) {
                Application.launch(args);
        }

        @Override
        public void start(Stage stage) {
                Circle circle = new Circle(50, 50, 50);
                circle.setFill(Color.CORAL);

                Rectangle rect = new Rectangle(100, 100);
                rect.setFill(Color.TAN);

                HBox root = new HBox();
                root.setPadding(new Insets(20));
                root.setSpacing(20);
                root.getChildren().addAll(circle, rect, consumeEventCbx);

                Scene scene = new Scene(root);

                // Register mouse-clicked event handlers to all nodes,
                // except the rectangle and checkbox
                EventHandler<MouseEvent> handler = e -> handleEvent(e);
                EventHandler<MouseEvent> circleMeHandler =
                        e -> handleEventforCircle(e);

                stage.addEventHandler(MOUSE_CLICKED, handler);
                scene.addEventHandler(MOUSE_CLICKED, handler);
                root.addEventHandler(MOUSE_CLICKED, handler);
                circle.addEventHandler(MOUSE_CLICKED, circleMeHandler);

                stage.setScene(scene);
                stage.setTitle("Event Handling");
                stage.show();
        }

        public void handleEvent(MouseEvent e) {
                print(e);
        }

        public void handleEventforCircle(MouseEvent e) {
                print(e);
                if (consumeEventCbx.isSelected()) {
                        e.consume();
                }
        }
}
```

```java
public void print(MouseEvent e) {
        String type = e.getEventType().getName();
        String source = e.getSource().getClass().getSimpleName();
        String target = e.getTarget().getClass().getSimpleName();

        // Get coordinates of the mouse relative to the event source
        double x = e.getX();
        double y = e.getY();

        System.out.println("Type=" + type + ", Target=" + target +
                ", Source=" + source +
                ", location(" + x + ", " + y + ")");
    }
}
```

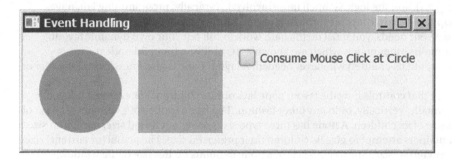

Figure 9-10. *Handling and consuming events*

The program adds a Circle, a Rectangle, and a CheckBox to an HBox. The HBox is a container that lays out its children horizontally on one row. The HBox is added to the scene as the root node. An event handler is added to the Stage, Scene, HBox, and Circle. Notice that you have a different event handler for the Circle just to keep the program logic simple. When the CheckBox is selected, the event handler for the Circle consumes the mouse-clicked event, thus preventing the event from travelling up to the HBox, Scene, and Stage. If the CheckBox is not selected, the mouse-clicked event on the Circle travels from the Circle to the HBox, Scene, and Stage. Run the program and using the mouse, click on the different areas of the scene to see the effect. Notice that the mouse-clicked event handler for the HBox, Scene, and Stage are executed, even if you click on a point outside the Circle, because they are in the event dispatch chain of the clicked nodes.

Clicking on the CheckBox does not execute the mouse-clicked event handlers for the HBox, Scene, and Stage, whereas clicking on the Rectangle does. Can you think of a reason for this behavior? The reason is simple. The CheckBox has a default event handler that takes a default action and consumes the event, preventing it from travelling up the event dispatch chain. The Rectangle does not consume the event, allowing it to travel up the event dispatch chain.

■ **Tip** Consuming an event by the event target in an event filter has no effect on the execution of any other event filters. However, it prevents the event bubbling phase from happening. Consuming an event in the event handlers of the topmost node, which is the head of the event-dispatch chain, has no effect on the event processing at all.

Layout Panes

You can use two types of layouts to arrange nodes in a scene graph:

- Static Layout

- Dynamic Layout

In a static layout, the position and size of nodes are calculated once and they stay the same as the window is resized. The user interface looks good when the window has the size for which the nodes were originally laid out.

In a dynamic layout, nodes in a scene graph are laid out every time a user action necessitates a change in their position, size, or both. Typically, changing the position or size of one node affects the position and size of other nodes in the scene graph. The dynamic layout forces recomputation of the position and size of some or all nodes as the window is resized.

Both static and dynamic layouts have advantages and disadvantages. A static layout gives developers full control over the design of the user interface. It lets you make use of the available space as you see fit. A dynamic layout requires more programming work and the logic is much more involved. Typically, programming languages supporting GUIs such as JavaFX support dynamic layouts through libraries. Libraries solve most of the use-cases for dynamic layouts. If they do not meet your needs, you must do the hard work to roll out your own dynamic layout.

A *layout pane* is a node that contains other nodes, which are known as its children (or child nodes). The responsibility of a layout pane is to lay out its children whenever needed. A layout pane is also known as a *container* or a *layout container*.

A layout pane has a *layout policy* that controls how the layout pane lays out its children. For example, a layout pane may lay out its children horizontally, vertically, or in any other fashion. The layout policy of a container is a set of rules to compute the position and size of its children. A node has three type sizes called preferred size, minimum size, and maximum size. Most of the containers attempt to give its children their preferred size. The actual (or current) size of a node may be different from its preferred size. The current size of a node depends on the size of the window, the layout policy of the container, and the expanding and shrinking policy for the node, etc.

JavaFX contains several container classes. Figure 9-11 shows a class diagram for the container classes. A container class is a subclass, direct or indirect, of the Parent class.

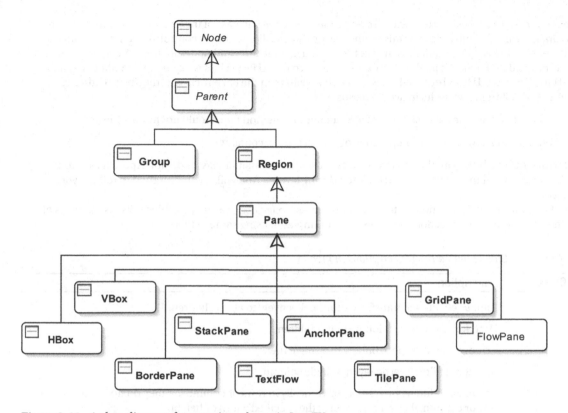

Figure 9-11. *A class diagram for container classes in JavaFX*

A Group lets you apply effects and transformations to all its children collectively. The Group class is in the javafx.scene package.

Subclasses of the Region class are used to lay out children. They can be styled with CSS. The Region class and most of its subclasses are in the javafx.scene.layout package.

It is true that a container needs to be a subclass of the Parent class. However, not all subclasses of the Parent class are containers. For example, the Button class is a subclass of the Parent class; however, it is a control, not a container. A node must be added to a container to be part of a scene graph. The container lays out its children according to its layout policy. If you do not want the container to manage the layout for a node, you need to set the managed property of the node to false.

A node can be a child node of only one container at a time. If a node is added to a container while it is already the child node of another container, the node is removed from the first container before being added to the second one. Often times, it is necessary to nest containers to create a complex layout. That is, you can add a container to another container as a child node.

The Parent class contains three methods to get the list of children of a container:

- `protected ObservableList<Node> getChildren()`

- `public ObservableList<Node> getChildrenUnmodifiable()`

- `protected <E extends Node> List<E> getManagedChildren()`

The getChildren() method returns a modifiable ObservableList of the child nodes of a container. If you want to add a node to a container, you add the node to this list. This is the most commonly used method of the container classes. You have been using this method to add children to containers like Group, HBox, VBox, etc. from the very first program.

Notice the protected access for the getChildren() method. If the subclass of the Parent class does not want to be a container, it will keep the access for this method as protected. For example, control-related classes such as Button and TextField keep this method as protected, so you cannot add child nodes to them. A container class overrides this method and makes it public. For example, the Group and Pane classes expose this method as public.

The getChildrenUnmodifiable() method is declared as public in the Parent class. It returns a read-only ObservableList of children. It is useful in two scenarios:

- You need to pass the list of children of a container to a method that should not modify the list.

- You want to know what makes up a control, which is not a container.

The getManagedChildren() method has the protected access. Container classes do not expose it as public. They use it internally to get the list of managed children during layouts. You will use this method to roll out your own container classes.

Table 9-4 contains brief descriptions of the container classes in JavaFX. It is not possible to discuss all types of containers in this chapter. In this section, I will show you examples of using some of them.

Table 9-4. *Container Classes with a Brief Descriptions in JavaFX*

Container Class	Description
Group	Applies effects and transformations collectively to all its children.
Pane	Used for absolute positioning of its children.
HBox	Arranges children horizontally in a single row.
VBox	Arranges children vertically in a single column.
FlowPane	Arranges children horizontally or vertically in rows or columns. If they do not fit in a single row or column, they are wrapped at the specified width or height.
BorderPane	Divides the layout area in the top, right, bottom, left, and center regions, and places each of its children in one of the five regions.
StackPane	Arranges children in a back-to-front stack.
TilePane	Arranges children in a grid of uniformly sized cells.
GridPane	Arranges children in a grid of variable sized cells.
AnchorPane	Arranges children by anchoring their edges to the edges of the layout area.
TextFlow	Lays out rich text whose contents may consist of several Text nodes.

A container is meant to contain children. You can add children to a container when you create the container object or after creating it. All container classes provide constructors that take a varargs Node type argument to add the initial set of children. Some containers provide constructors to add an initial set of children and set initial properties for the containers.

You can also add children to a container at any time after the container is created. Containers store their children in an observable list, which can be retrieved using the getChildren() method. Adding a node to a container is as simple as adding a node to that observable list. The following snippet of code shows how to add children to an HBox when it is created and after it is created.

```
// Create two buttons
Button okBtn = new Button("OK");
Button cancelBtn = new Button("Cancel");

// Create an HBox with two buttons as its children
HBox hBox1 = new HBox(okBtn, cancelBtn);

// Create an HBox with two buttons with 20px horizontal spacing between them
double hSpacing = 20;
HBox hBox2 = new HBox(hSpacing, okBtn, cancelBtn);

// Create an empty HBox, and afterwards add two buttons to it
HBox hBox3 = new HBox();
hBox3.getChildren().addAll(okBtn, cancelBtn);
```

■ **Tip** When you need to add multiple child nodes to a container, use the addAll() method of the ObservableList rather than using the add() method multiple times.

The program in Listing 9-14 shows how to use a BorderPane, a HBox, and a VBox to arrange UI elements as shown in Figure 9-12.

Listing 9-14. Using the BorderPane Container

```
// BorderPaneTest.java
package com.jdojo.jfx;

import javafx.application.Application;
import javafx.geometry.Insets;
import javafx.scene.Node;
import javafx.scene.Scene;
import javafx.scene.control.Button;
import javafx.scene.control.Label;
import javafx.scene.control.TextArea;
import javafx.scene.control.TextField;
import javafx.scene.layout.BorderPane;
import javafx.scene.layout.HBox;
import javafx.scene.layout.Priority;
import javafx.scene.layout.VBox;
import javafx.stage.Stage;

public class BorderPaneTest extends Application {
        public static void main(String[] args) {
                Application.launch(args);
        }

        public void start(Stage stage) {
                // Set the top and left child nodes to null
                Node top = null;
                Node left = null;
```

```java
            // Build the content nodes for the center region
            VBox center = getCenter();

            // Create the right child node
            Button okBtn = new Button("Ok");
            Button cancelBtn = new Button("Cancel");

            // Make the OK and cancel buttons the same size
            okBtn.setMaxWidth(Double.MAX_VALUE);
            VBox right = new VBox(okBtn, cancelBtn);
            right.setStyle("-fx-padding: 10;");

            // Create the bottom child node
            Label statusLbl = new Label("Status: Ready");
            HBox bottom = new HBox(statusLbl);
            BorderPane.setMargin(bottom, new Insets(10, 0, 0, 0));
            bottom.setStyle("-fx-background-color: lavender;" +
                            "-fx-font-size: 7pt;" +
                            "-fx-padding: 10 0 0 0;" );

            BorderPane root =
                    new BorderPane(center, top, right, bottom, left);
            root.setStyle("-fx-background-color: lightgray;");

            Scene scene = new Scene(root);
            stage.setScene(scene);
            stage.setTitle("Using a BorderPane");
            stage.show();
    }

    private VBox getCenter() {
            // A Label and a TextField in an HBox
            Label nameLbl = new Label("Name:");
            TextField nameFld = new TextField();
            HBox.setHgrow(nameFld, Priority.ALWAYS);
            HBox nameFields = new HBox(nameLbl, nameFld);

            // A Label and a TextArea
            Label descLbl = new Label("Description:");
            TextArea descText = new TextArea();
            descText.setPrefColumnCount(20);
            descText.setPrefRowCount(5);
            VBox.setVgrow(descText, Priority.ALWAYS);

            // Box all controls in a VBox
            VBox center = new VBox(nameFields, descLbl, descText);

            return center;
    }
}
```

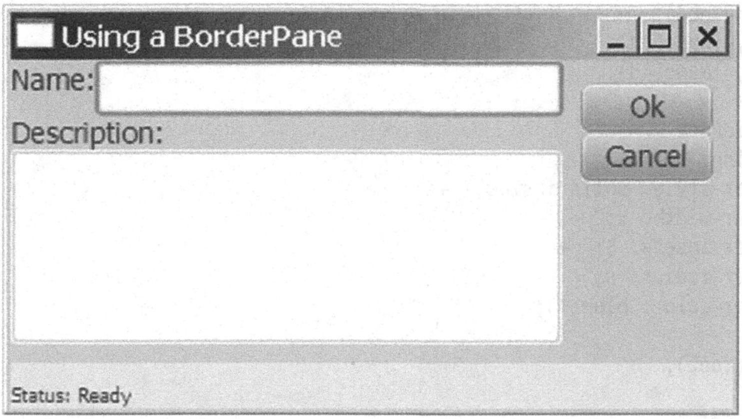

Figure 9-12. *A BorderPane using some controls in its top, right, bottom, and center regions*

Notice the use of the setStyle() method for the containers in Listing 9-14. You can customize the visual appearance of the containers and controls in JavaFX using CSS. The CSS attributes in JavaFX are named and work very similar to CSS attributes used to customize HTML contents in browsers. CSS attributes in JavaFX starts with -fx-; for example, the CSS attribute name for specifying the font size is -fx-font-size. You can also set styles to a JavaFX application using a CSS file. Listing 9-15 shows how to add padding and a rounded, blue border around the scene by adding a style to the root node of the scene. Figure 9-13 shows the resulting scene in a window.

Listing 9-15. Using CSS to to Add a Padding and a Rounded, Blue Border to a Scene

```java
// CSSTest.java
package com.jdojo.jfx;

import javafx.application.Application;
import javafx.scene.Scene;
import javafx.scene.control.Label;
import javafx.scene.control.TextField;
import javafx.scene.layout.GridPane;
import javafx.stage.Stage;

public class CSSTest extends Application {
        public static void main(String[] args) {
                Application.launch(args);
        }

        @Override
        public void start(Stage stage) {
                TextField fNameFld = new TextField();
                Label fNameLbl = new Label("First Name:");

                TextField lNameFld = new TextField();
                Label lNameLbl = new Label("Last Name:");
```

```
            GridPane root = new GridPane();
            root.addRow(0, fNameLbl, fNameFld);
            root.addRow(1, lNameLbl, lNameFld);

            // Set a CSS for the GridPane
            root.setStyle("-fx-padding: 10;" +
                          "-fx-border-style: solid inside;" +
                          "-fx-border-width: 2;" +
                          "-fx-border-insets: 5;" +
                          "-fx-border-radius: 5;" +
                          "-fx-border-color: blue;");

            Scene scene = new Scene(root);
            stage.setScene(scene);
            stage.setTitle("Using CSS");
            stage.show();
        }
}
```

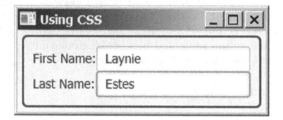

Figure 9-13. *Using CSS to add pading and a rounded, blue border around the scene*

Using CSS in JavaFX is a big topic. This chapter does not discuss CSS in JavaFX in detail. Please refer to the following web page for the CSS reference guide that lists all CSS attributes for all nodes that can be styled using CSS:

docs.oracle.com/javase/8/javafx/api/javafx/scene/doc-files/cssref.html

Controls

JavaFX lets you create applications using GUI components. An application with a GUI performs three tasks:

- Accepts inputs from the user through input devices such as a keyboard, a mouse, etc.
- Processes the inputs (or takes actions based on the input)
- Displays outputs

A user interface provides a means to exchange information in terms of input and output between an application and users. Entering text using a keyboard, selecting a menu item using a mouse, and clicking a button are examples of providing inputs to a GUI application. The application displays output on a computer monitor using text, charts, dialog boxes, etc.

Users interact with a GUI application using graphical elements called *controls* or *widgets*. Buttons, labels, text fields, text area, radio buttons, and checkboxes are a few examples of controls. Devices like a keyboard, a mouse, and a touch screen are used to provide input to controls. Controls can also display output to the users. Controls generate events that indicate occurrences of some kind of interaction between the user and the control. For example, pressing a button using a mouse or a spacebar generates an action event indicating that the user has pressed the button.

JavaFX provides a rich set of easy-to-use basic as well as advanced controls. Controls are typically added to layout panes that position and size them. It is not possible to discuss all controls. I will list most controls in JavaFX and provide a brief description of what they do.

Each control in JavaFX is represented by an instance of a class. If multiple controls share basic features, they inherit from a common base class. Control classes are in the `javafx.scene.control` package. A control class is a subclass, direct or indirect, of the `Control` class, which in turn inherits from the `Region`. Recall that the `Region` class inherits from the `Parent` class. Therefore, technically, a `Control` is also a `Parent`.

A `Parent` can have children. Typically, a control is composed of another node (sometimes, multiple nodes) that is its child node. Control classes do not expose the list of its children through the `getChildren()` method, and therefore you cannot add any children to them.

Control classes expose the list of their internal unmodifiable children through the `getChildrenUnmodifiable()` method, which returns an `ObservableList<Node>`. You are not required to know about the internal children of a control to use the control. However, if you need the list of their children, the `getChildrenUnmodifiable()` method will give you that.

Figure 9-14 shows a class diagram for classes of some commonly used controls. The list of control classes is a lot bigger than the one shown in the class diagram. Table 9-5 contains a list of most of the controls in JavaFX with their brief description.

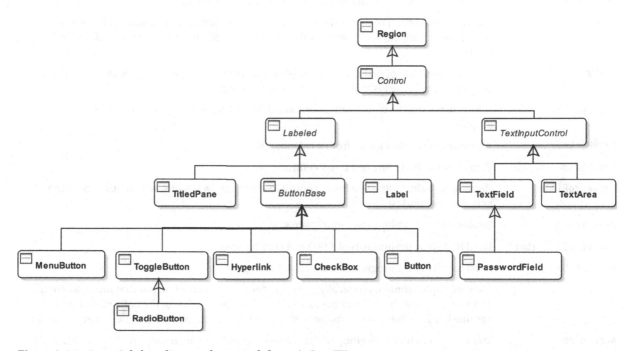

Figure 9-14. *A partial class diagram for control classes in JavaFX*

Table 9-5. *JavaFX Controls*

Control	Description
Label	A non-editable text control that is typically used to display the label for another control.
Button	Represents a command button control. It can display text and an icon. It generates an ActionEvent when it is activated.
Hyperlink	Represents a hyperlink control, which looks like a hyperlink in a webpage. It generates an ActionEvent when it is activated.
MenuButton	Looks like a button and behaves like a menu. When it is activated, it shows a list of options in the form of a pop-up menu. To execute a command when a menu option is selected, you need to add the ActionEvent handler to the MenuItems added to the MenuButton.
ToggleButton	Represents a two-state button control. The two states are *selected* and *unselected*.
RadioButton	Represents a radio button. It is used to provide a mutually exclusive choice from the list of choices.
CheckBox	Represents a three-state selection control. The three states are *checked*, *unchecked*, and *undefined*.
ChoiceBox	Allows users select an item from a small list of predefined items.
ComboBox	An advanced version of the ChoiceBox control. It has many features, such as the ability to be editable, changing appearance of the items in the list, etc., which are not offered by in ChoiceBox.
ListView	Provides users an ability to select multiple items from a list of items. Typically, all or more than one item in a list is visible to the user all the time.
ColorPicker	Allows users select a color from a standard color palette or define a custom color graphically.
DatePicker	Allows users to select a date from a calendar pop-up.
TextField	Represents a single-line text input control.
PasswordField	Represents a single-line text input control to enter passwords or sensitive text where the actual text is masked.
TextArea	Represents a multi-line text input control.
ProgressIndicator	Used to display the progress of a task in a circular area.
ProgressBar	Used to display the progress of a task in a rectangular area.
TitledPane	Used to display contents (typically, a group of controls) with a title bar that may contain title text and a graphic. It can be in the expanded or collapsed state. In the collapsed state, only the title bar is visible. In the expanded state, both the contents and the title bar are visible.
Accordion	Used as a container for a group of TitledPane controls in which only one TitledPane is visible at a time.
Pagination	Used to display a large single content by dividing it into smaller chunks called pages, such as the results of a search.
Tooltip	Used to show additional information about a control in a pop-up window for a short time when the mouse hovers over the control.

(continued)

Table 9-5. (*continued*)

Control	Description
ScrollBar	Used to add scrolling capability to a control.
ScrollPane	Provides a scrollable view of a node.
Separator	A horizontal or vertical line used to separate two groups of controls.
Slider	Used to select a numeric value from a numeric range graphically by sliding a thumb (or knob) along a track.
MenuBar	A horizontal bar that acts as a container for menus.
Menu	Contains a list of actionable items, which are displayed on demand, for example, by clicking it.
MenuItem	Represents an actionable option in a menu.
ContextMenu	A pop-up control that displays a list of menu items on request.
ToolBar	Used to display a group of nodes, which provide the commonly used action items on a screen.
TabPane	Displays multiple tab pages represented by instances of the Tab class. The contents of only one tab page are visible at a time.
Tab	Represents a tab page in a TabPane.
HTMLEditor	Provides rich text editing capability in JavaFX.
FileChooser	Allows you to select files from the file system graphically.
DirectoryChooser	Allows you to select directories using a platform-dependent directory dialog
TableView	Used to display and edit tabular data using rows and columns.
TreeView	Used to display and edit hierarchical data arranged in a tree-like structure.
TreeTableView	A combination of TableView and TreeView controls. Provides the ability to have a drill-down table.
WebView	Displays a web page.

Listing 9-16 creates a form using JavaFX controls to enter person details such as first name, last name, birth date, and gender as shown in Figure 9-15. Enter the data and click the Save button to display the entered data in the TextArea at the bottom of the window. The form uses the following controls:

- Two instances of the TextField control to enter the first and last names.
- A DatePicker control to enter the birth date.
- A ChoiceBox control to select a gender.
- A Button control to save the data.
- A Button control to close the window.
- A TextArea control to display the entered data when the Save button is clicked.

Listing 9-16. Creating a Form Using JavaFX Controls to Enter Person Details

```java
// PersonView.java
package com.jdojo.jfx;

import javafx.application.Application;
import javafx.scene.Scene;
import javafx.scene.control.Button;
import javafx.scene.control.ChoiceBox;
import javafx.scene.control.DatePicker;
import javafx.scene.control.Label;
import javafx.scene.control.TextArea;
import javafx.scene.control.TextField;
import javafx.scene.layout.GridPane;
import javafx.scene.layout.VBox;
import javafx.stage.Stage;

public class PersonView extends Application {
        // Labels
        Label fNameLbl = new Label("First Name:");
        Label lNameLbl = new Label("Last Name:");
        Label bDateLbl = new Label("Birth Date:");
        Label genderLbl = new Label("Gender:");

        // Fields
        TextField fNameFld = new TextField();
        TextField lNameFld = new TextField();
        DatePicker bDateFld = new DatePicker();
        ChoiceBox<String> genderFld = new ChoiceBox<>();
        TextArea dataFld = new TextArea();

        // Buttons
        Button saveBtn = new Button("Save");
        Button closeBtn = new Button("Close");

        public static void main(String[] args) {
                Application.launch(args);
        }

        @Override
        public void start(Stage stage) throws Exception {
                // Populate the gender choice box
                genderFld.getItems().addAll("Male", "Female", "Unknown");

                // Set the preferred rows and columns for the text area
                dataFld.setPrefColumnCount(30);
                dataFld.setPrefRowCount(5);

                GridPane grid = new GridPane();
                grid.setHgap(5);
                grid.setVgap(5);
```

```java
        // Place the controls in the grid
        grid.add(fNameLbl, 0, 0);  // column=0, row=0
        grid.add(lNameLbl, 0, 1);  // column=0, row=1
        grid.add(bDateLbl, 0, 2);  // column=0, row=2
        grid.add(genderLbl, 0, 3); // column=0, row=3

        grid.add(fNameFld, 1, 0);  // column=1, row=0
        grid.add(lNameFld, 1, 1);  // column=1, row=1
        grid.add(bDateFld, 1, 2);  // column=1, row=2
        grid.add(genderFld, 1, 3); // column=1, row=3
        grid.add(dataFld, 1, 4, 3, 2); // column=1, row=4, colspan=3, rowspan=3

        // Add buttons and make them the same width
        VBox buttonBox = new VBox(saveBtn, closeBtn);
        saveBtn.setMaxWidth(Double.MAX_VALUE);
        closeBtn.setMaxWidth(Double.MAX_VALUE);

        grid.add(buttonBox, 2, 0, 1, 2); // column=2, row=0, colspan=1, rowspan=2

        // Show the data in the text area when the Save button is clicked
        saveBtn.setOnAction(e -> showData());

        // Close the window when the Close button is clicked
        closeBtn.setOnAction(e -> stage.hide());

        // Set a CSS for the GridPane to add a padding and a blue border
        grid.setStyle("-fx-padding: 10;" +
                      "-fx-border-style: solid inside;" +
                      "-fx-border-width: 2;" +
                      "-fx-border-insets: 5;" +
                      "-fx-border-radius: 5;" +
                      "-fx-border-color: blue;");

        Scene scene = new Scene(grid);
        stage.setScene(scene);
        stage.setTitle("Person Details");
        stage.sizeToScene();
        stage.show();
    }

    private void showData() {
        String data = "First Name = " + fNameFld.getText() +
                      "\nLast Name=" + lNameFld.getText() +
                      "\nBirth Date=" + bDateFld.getValue() +
                      "\nGender=" + genderFld.getValue();
        dataFld.setText(data);
    }
}
```

Person Details

| | |
First Name: John Save
Last Name: Jacobs Close
Birth Date: 7/17/1985
Gender: Male ▼

First Name = John
Last Name=Jacobs
Birth Date=1985-07-17
Gender=Male

Figure 9-15. A form using JavaFX controls to enter person details

Using 2D Shapes

JavaFX offers variety nodes to draw different types of shapes, such as lines, circles, rectangles, etc. You can add shapes to a scene graph. You can draw 2D and 3D shapes. In this section, I will show you how to draw 2D shapes. Using 3D shapes in JavaFX has a learning curve. Because of space limitation, I will not discuss 3D shapes in this book. All 2D shape classes are in the javafx.scene.shape package. Classes representing 2D shapes are inherited from the abstract Shape class as shown in Figure 9-16.

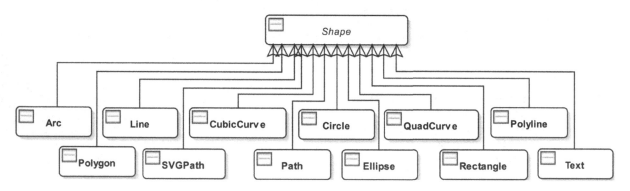

Figure 9-16. A class diagram for 2D shapes

A shape has a size and a position that are defined by its properties. For example, the width and height properties define the size of a rectangle; the radius property defines the size of a circle, the x and y properties define the position of the upper-left corner of a rectangle, the centerX and centerY properties define the center of a circle.

Shapes are not resized by their parents during layout. The size of a shape changes only when its size-related properties are changed. You may see a phrase like "JavaFX shapes are non-resizable." It means shapes are non-resizable by their parent during layout. They can be resized only by changing their properties.

Shapes have an interior and a stroke. All properties for defining the interior and stroke of a shape are declared in the Shape class. The fill property specifies the color to fill the interior of the shape. The default fill is Color.BLACK. The stroke property specifies the color for the outline stroke, which is null by default, except for Line, Polyline, and Path that have Color.BLACK as their default stroke color.

The Shape class contains a smooth property, which is true by default. Its true value indicates that an antialiasing hint should be used to render the shape. If it is set to false, the antialiasing hint will not be used, which may result in the edges of shapes being not crisp.

The program in Listing 9-17 creates a circle, a rectangle, a line, a polygon to represent a parallelogram, a polyline to represent a hexagon, and an arc with a chord. The shapes are shown in Figure 9-17. Note the following points about creating the shapes in this program:

- It creates a circle of radius 40px.

- It creates a rectangle of 100px width and 75px height.

- It creates a line from (0, 0) and (50, 50).

- It creates a polygon representing a parallelogram, by connecting four points: (30.0, 0.0), (130.0, 0.0), (100.00, 50.0), and (0.0, 50.0). The polygon is automatically closed by connecting the first and the last points.

- It creates a polyline representing a hexagon. A polyline is similar to a polygon, except that it is not closed automatically. Notice that the first point (100.0, 0.0) and the last point (100.0, 0.0) are the same in the polyline constructor, so it is closed.

- It creates an arc using the constructor Arc(double centerX, double centerY, double radiusX, double radiusY, double startAngle, double length) of the Arc class. An arc can be chord, round, or open. The program uses the arc type as ArcType.CHORD to connect the two extreme points on the arc by a straight line (a chord).

Listing 9-17. Using 2D Shapes in JavaFX

```
// ShapeTest.java
package com.jdojo.jfx;

import javafx.application.Application;
import javafx.scene.Scene;
import javafx.scene.layout.HBox;
import javafx.scene.paint.Color;
import javafx.scene.shape.Arc;
import javafx.scene.shape.ArcType;
import javafx.scene.shape.Circle;
import javafx.scene.shape.Line;
import javafx.scene.shape.Polygon;
import javafx.scene.shape.Polyline;
import javafx.scene.shape.Rectangle;
import javafx.stage.Stage;

public class ShapeTest extends Application {
        public static void main(String[] args) {
                Application.launch(args);
        }

        @Override
        public void start(Stage stage) {
                // Create a circle with an yellow fill and a black stroke of 2.0px
                Circle circle = new Circle(40);
                circle.setFill(Color.YELLOW);
                circle.setStroke(Color.BLACK);
                circle.setStrokeWidth(2.0);
```

```java
        // Create a rectangle
        Rectangle rect = new Rectangle(100, 75);
        rect.setFill(Color.RED);

        // Create a line
        Line line = new Line(0, 0, 50, 50);
        line.setStrokeWidth(5.0);
        line.setStroke(Color.GREEN);

        // Create a parallelogram
        Polygon parallelogram = new Polygon();
        parallelogram.getPoints().addAll(30.0, 0.0,
                                        130.0, 0.0,
                                        100.00, 50.0,
                                        0.0, 50.0);
        parallelogram.setFill(Color.AZURE);
        parallelogram.setStroke(Color.BLACK);

        // Create a hexagon
        Polyline hexagon = new Polyline(100.0, 0.0,
                                    120.0, 20.0,
                                    120.0, 40.0,
                                    100.0, 60.0,
                                    80.0, 40.0,
                                    80.0, 20.0,
                                    100.0, 0.0);
        hexagon.setFill(Color.WHITE);
        hexagon.setStroke(Color.BLACK);

        // A CHORD arc with no fill and a stroke
        Arc arc = new Arc(0, 0, 50, 100, 0, 90);
        arc.setFill(Color.TRANSPARENT);
        arc.setStroke(Color.BLACK);
        arc.setType(ArcType.CHORD);

        // Add all shapes to an HBox
        HBox root =
                new HBox(circle, rect, line, parallelogram, hexagon, arc);
        root.setSpacing(10);
        root.setStyle("-fx-padding: 10;" +
                    "-fx-border-style: solid inside;" +
                    "-fx-border-width: 2;" +
                    "-fx-border-insets: 5;" +
                    "-fx-border-radius: 5;" +
                    "-fx-border-color: blue;");

        Scene scene = new Scene(root);
        stage.setScene(scene);
        stage.setTitle("2D Shapes");
        stage.show();
    }
}
```

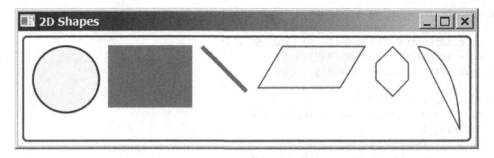

Figure 9-17. *Some 2D shapes in JavaFX*

The Path class, along with many other classes such as MoveTo, LineTo, HLineTo, and VLineTo, can be used to draw very complex shapes in JavaFX. JavaFX also supports Scalable Vector Graphics (SVG) using the SVGPath class from path data in an encoded string. The SVG specification is can be found at www.w3.org/TR/SVG. The detailed rules of constructing the path data in string format can be found at www.w3.org/TR/SVG/paths.html. JavaFX partially supports the SVG specification. This book does not cover creating 2D shapes using the Path and SVGPath class in detail. Listing 9-18 shows how to create triangles using the Path and SVGPath classes as shown in Figure 9-18. Please refer to the JavaFX API documentation for details on how to use these classes.

Listing 9-18. Using Path and SVGPath Classes to Create 2D Shapes

```
// PathTest.java
package com.jdojo.jfx;

import javafx.application.Application;
import javafx.scene.Scene;
import javafx.scene.layout.HBox;
import javafx.scene.paint.Color;
import javafx.scene.shape.LineTo;
import javafx.scene.shape.MoveTo;
import javafx.scene.shape.Path;
import javafx.scene.shape.SVGPath;
import javafx.stage.Stage;

public class PathTest extends Application {
    public static void main(String[] args) {
        Application.launch(args);
    }

    @Override
    public void start(Stage stage) {
        // Create a triangle using a Path
        Path pathTriangle = new Path(new MoveTo(50, 0),
                                     new LineTo(0, 50),
                                     new LineTo(100, 50),
                                     new LineTo(50, 0));

        pathTriangle.setFill(Color.LIGHTGRAY);
        pathTriangle.setStroke(Color.BLACK);
```

```
                // Create a triangle using a SVGPath
                SVGPath svgTriangle = new SVGPath();
                svgTriangle.setContent("M50, 0 L0, 50 L100, 50 Z");
                svgTriangle.setFill(Color.LIGHTGRAY);
                svgTriangle.setStroke(Color.BLACK);

                // Add all shapes to an HBox
                HBox root = new HBox(pathTriangle, svgTriangle);
                root.setSpacing(10);
                root.setStyle("-fx-padding: 10;" +
                              "-fx-border-style: solid inside;" +
                              "-fx-border-width: 2;" +
                              "-fx-border-insets: 5;" +
                              "-fx-border-radius: 5;" +
                              "-fx-border-color: blue;");

                Scene scene = new Scene(root);
                stage.setScene(scene);
                stage.setTitle("2D Shapes using Path and SVGPath Classes");
                stage.show();
        }
}
```

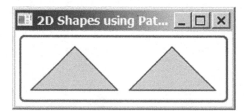

Figure 9-18. *Creating triangles using the Path and SVGPath classes*

Drawing on a Canvas

Through the `javafx.scene.canvas` package, JavaFX provides the Canvas API that offers a drawing surface to draw shapes, images, and text using drawing commands. The API also gives pixel-level access to the drawing surface where you can write any pixels on the surface. The API consists of the following two classes:

- Canvas
- GraphicsContext

A canvas is a bitmap image that is used as a drawing surface. An instance of the Canvas class represents a canvas. It inherits from the Node class. Therefore, a canvas is a node that can be added to a scene graph, and effects and transformations can be applied to it. A Canvas has a graphics context associated with it that is used to issue drawing commands to the Canvas. An instance of the GraphicsContext class represents a graphics context.

The Canvas class contains two constructors. The no-args constructor creates an empty Canvas. Later, you can set the size of the canvas using its width and height properties. The other constructor takes the width and height of the Canvas as parameters. The following snippet of code shows how to create canvases:

```
// Create a Canvas of zero width and height
Canvas canvas = new Canvas();

// Set the canvas size
canvas.setWidth(400);
canvas.setHeight(200);

// Create a 400X200 canvas
Canvas canvas = new Canvas(400, 200);
```

Once you create a Canvas, you need to get its graphics context using the get getGraphicsContext2D() method as shown:

```
// Get the graphics context of the canvas
GraphicsContext gc = canvas.getGraphicsContext2D();
```

All drawing commands are provided in the GraphicsContext class as methods. Drawings that fall outside the bounds of the Canvas are clipped. The Canvas uses a buffer. The drawing commands push necessary parameters to the buffer. It is important to note that you should use the graphics context from any one thread before adding the Canvas to the scene graph. Once the Canvas is added to the scene graph, the graphics context should be used only on the JavaFX Application Thread.

The program in Listing 9-19 shows how to draw a round rectangle, an oval, and text on a Canvas. Figure 9-19 shows the canvas with all drawings. The strokeRoundRect(double x, double y, double w, double h, double arcWidth, double arcHeight) method is used to draw a round rectangle; the fillOval(double x, double y, double w, double h) method is used to draw a filled oval. The strokeText(String text, double x, double y) method is used to draw text.

Listing 9-19. Drawing on a Canvas

```java
// CanvasTest.java
package com.jdojo.jfx;

import javafx.application.Application;
import javafx.scene.Scene;
import javafx.scene.canvas.Canvas;
import javafx.scene.canvas.GraphicsContext;
import javafx.scene.layout.Pane;
import javafx.scene.paint.Color;
import javafx.stage.Stage;

public class CanvasTest extends Application {
    public static void main(String[] args) {
        Application.launch(args);
    }
```

```
        @Override
        public void start(Stage stage) {
                // Create a canvas
                Canvas canvas = new Canvas(300, 100);

                // Get the graphics context of the canvas
                GraphicsContext gc = canvas.getGraphicsContext2D();

                // Set line width and fill color
                gc.setLineWidth(2.0);
                gc.setFill(Color.RED);

                // Draw a rounded rectangle
                gc.strokeRoundRect(10, 10, 50, 50, 10, 10);

                // Fill an oval
                gc.fillOval(70, 10, 50, 20);

                // Draw text
                gc.strokeText("Hello Canvas", 150, 20);

                Pane root = new Pane();
                root.getChildren().add(canvas);
                Scene scene = new Scene(root);
                stage.setScene(scene);
                stage.setTitle("Drawing on a Canvas");
                stage.show();
        }
}
```

Figure 9-19. *A rectangle, an ellipse, and text drawn on a canvas*

Applying Effects

An effect is a filter that accepts one or more graphical inputs, applies an algorithm on the inputs, and produces an output. Typically, effects are applied to nodes to create visually appealing user interfaces. Examples of effects are shadow, blur, warp, glow, reflection, blending, different types of lighting, etc. The JavaFX library provides several effect-related classes. An effect is a conditional feature. Effects applied to nodes will be ignored if they are not available on the platform. Figure 9-20 shows four Text nodes using the drop shadow, blur, glow, and bloom effects.

Figure 9-20. *Text nodes with different effects*

Applying effects to a node in JavaFX is easy. The Node class contains an effect property that specifies the effect applied to the node. By default, it is null. To apply an effect, create an object of the specific effect class and set it to the node using the setEffect() method. The following snippet of code applies a drop shadow effect to a Text node:

```
Text t1 = new Text("Drop Shadow");
t1.setFont(Font.font(24));
t1.setEffect(new DropShadow());
```

An instance of the Effect class represents an effect. The Effect class is the abstract base for all effect classes. All effect classes are in the javafx.scene.effect package.

The program in Listing 9-20 creates Text nodes and applies effects to them. The Text nodes look as shown in Figure 9-20.

Listing 9-20. Applying Effects to Nodes

```
// EffectTest.java
package com.jdojo.jfx;

import javafx.application.Application;
import javafx.scene.Scene;
import javafx.scene.effect.Bloom;
import javafx.scene.effect.BoxBlur;
import javafx.scene.effect.DropShadow;
import javafx.scene.effect.Glow;
import javafx.scene.layout.HBox;
import javafx.scene.layout.StackPane;
import javafx.scene.paint.Color;
import javafx.scene.shape.Rectangle;
import javafx.scene.text.Font;
import javafx.scene.text.FontWeight;
import javafx.scene.text.Text;
import javafx.stage.Stage;

public class EffectTest extends Application {
        public static void main(String[] args) {
                Application.launch(args);
        }

        @Override
        public void start(Stage stage) {
                Text t1 = new Text("Drop Shadow!");
                t1.setFont(Font.font(24));
                t1.setEffect(new DropShadow());
```

```
Text t2 = new Text("Blur!");
t2.setFont(Font.font(24));
t2.setEffect(new BoxBlur());

Text t3 = new Text("Glow!");
t3.setFont(Font.font(24));
t3.setEffect(new Glow());

Text t4 = new Text("Bloom!");
t4.setFont(Font.font("Arial", FontWeight.BOLD, 24));
t4.setFill(Color.WHITE);
t4.setEffect(new Bloom(0.10));

// Stack the Text node with bloom effect over a Reactangle
Rectangle rect = new Rectangle(100, 30, Color.GREEN);
StackPane spane = new StackPane(rect, t4);

HBox root = new HBox(t1, t2, t3, spane);
root.setSpacing(20);
root.setStyle("-fx-padding: 10;" +
              "-fx-border-style: solid inside;" +
              "-fx-border-width: 2;" +
              "-fx-border-insets: 5;" +
              "-fx-border-radius: 5;" +
              "-fx-border-color: blue;");

Scene scene = new Scene(root);
stage.setScene(scene);
stage.setTitle("Applying Effects");
stage.show();
    }
}
```

■ **Tip** An effect applied to a Group is applied to all its children. It is also possible to chain multiple effects where the output of one effect becomes the input for the next effect in the chain.

Applying Transformations

A transformation is a mapping of points in a coordinate space to themselves, preserving distances and directions between them. Several types of transformations can be applied to points in a coordinate space. JavaFX supports the following types of transformation:

- Translation
- Rotation
- Shear
- Scale
- Affine

An instance of the abstract `Transform` class represents a transformation in JavaFX. The `Transform` class contains common methods and properties used by all types of transformations on nodes. It contains factory methods to create specific types of transformations. Figure 9-21 shows a class diagram for the classes representing different types of transformations. The name of the classes match the type of transformation they provide. All classes are in the `javafx.scene.transform` package.

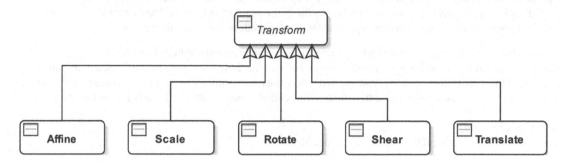

Figure 9-21. *A class diagram for transform-related classes*

An affine transformation is the generalized transformation that preserves the points, lines, and planes. The parallel lines remain parallel after the transformation. It may not preserve the angles between lines and the distances between points. However, the ratios of distances between points on a straight line are preserved. Translation, scale, homothetic transformation, similarity transformation, reflection, rotation, and shear are examples of the affine transformation.

An instance of the `Affine` class represents an affine transformation. The class is not easy to use for beginners. Its use requires advanced knowledge of mathematics such as matrix. If you need a specific type of transformation, use the specific subclasses such as `Translate`, `Shear`, etc. rather than using the generalized `Affine` class. You can also combine multiple individual transformations to create a more complex one.

Using transformations is easy. However, sometimes it is confusing because there are multiple ways to create and apply them. There are two ways to create a `Transform` instance:

- Use one of the factory methods of the `Transform` class, for example, the `translate()` method to create a `Translate` object, the `rotate()` method to create a `Rotate` object, etc.

- Use the specific class to create a specific type of transform, for example, the `Translate` class for a translation, the `Rotate` class for a rotation, etc.

Both of the following `Translate` objects represent the same translation:

```
double tx = 20.0;
double ty = 10.0;

// Using the factory method in the Transform class
Translate translate1 = Transform.translate(tx, ty);

// Using the Translate class constructor
Translate translate2 = new Translate(tx, ty);
```

There are two ways to apply a transformation to a node:

- Use the specific properties in the Node class. For example, use the translateX, translateY, and translateZ properties of the Node class to apply a translation to a node. Note that you cannot apply a shear transformation this way.

- Use the transforms sequence of a node. The getTransforms() method the Node class returns an ObservableList<Transform>. Populate this list with all the Transform objects. The Transforms will be applied in sequence. You can apply a shear transformation using only this method.

The two methods of applying Transforms work little differently. I will discuss the differences when I discuss the specific types of transformation. Sometimes it is possible to use both methods to apply transformations, and in that case, the transformations in the transforms sequence are applied before the transformation set on the properties of the node.

The following snippet of code applies three transformations called shear, scale, and translation to a Rectangle:

```
// Create a rectangle
Rectangle rect = new Rectangle(100, 50, Color.LIGHTGRAY);

// Apply transforms using the transforms sequence of the Rectangle
Transform shear = Transform.shear(2.0, 1.2);
Transform scale = Transform.scale(1.1, 1.2);
rect.getTransforms().addAll(shear, scale);

// Apply a translation using the translatex and translateY
// properties of the Node class
rect.setTranslateX(10);
rect.setTranslateY(10);
```

The shear and scale transformations are applied using the transforms sequence. The translation is applied using the translateX and translateY properties of the Node class. The transformations in the transforms sequence, shear and scale, are applied in sequence followed with the translation. Discussing all types of transformations is beyond the scope of this book. Please refer to the JavaFX API documentation for more details.

Listing 9-21 shows how to apply translate, rotate, scale, and shear transformations to a rectangle. It creates two rectangles of the same size and located at the same place. The rectangles use different fill colors to distinguish between them. Translate, rotate, scale, and shear transformations are applied to the rectangle with the yellow fill. No transformations are applied to the rectangle with the light gray fill. Figure 9-22 shows both rectangles.

Listing 9-21. Applying Transformations to Nodes

```
// TransformationTest.java
package com.jdojo.jfx;

import javafx.application.Application;
import javafx.scene.Scene;
import javafx.scene.layout.Pane;
import javafx.scene.paint.Color;
import javafx.scene.shape.Rectangle;
import javafx.scene.transform.Rotate;
import javafx.scene.transform.Scale;
import javafx.scene.transform.Shear;
import javafx.scene.transform.Translate;
import javafx.stage.Stage;
```

```java
public class TransformationTest  extends Application {
        public static void main(String[] args) {
                Application.launch(args);
        }

        @Override
        public void start(Stage stage) {
                Rectangle rect1 = new Rectangle(100, 50, Color.LIGHTGRAY);
                rect1.setStroke(Color.BLACK);

                Rectangle rect2 = new Rectangle(100, 50, Color.YELLOW);
                rect2.setStroke(Color.BLACK);

                // Apply a translation, rotate, scale and shear transformations
                // to rect2
                Translate translate = new Translate(50, 10);
                Rotate rotate = new Rotate(30, 0, 0);
                Scale scale = new Scale(0.5, 0.5);
                Shear shear = new Shear(0.5, 0.5);
                rect2.getTransforms().addAll(translate, rotate, scale, shear);

                Pane root = new Pane(rect1, rect2);
                root.setPrefSize(200, 100);
                Scene scene = new Scene(root);
                stage.setScene(scene);
                stage.setTitle("Applying Transformations");
                stage.show();
        }
}
```

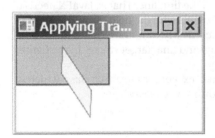

Figure 9-22. *Two rectangles, one with transformations and one without transformations*

Animation

In the real world, *animation* implies some kind of motion that is generated by displaying images in quick succession. For example, when you watch a movie, you are watching images that change so quickly that you get an illusion of motion.

In JavaFX, animation is defined as changing the property of a node over time. If the property that changes determines the location of the node, the animation in JavaFX will produce an illusion of motion as found in movies. Not all animations have to involve motion; for example, changing the fill property of a Shape over time is an animation in JavaFX that does not involve motion.

To understand how animation is performed, it is important to understand some key concepts:

- Timeline
- Key Frame
- Key Value
- Interpolator

Animation is performed over a period of time. A *timeline* denotes the progression of time during animation with an associated key frame at a given instant. A *key frame* represents the state of the node being animated at a specific instant on the timeline. A key frame has associated key values. A *key value* represents the value of a property of the node along with an interpolator to be used.

Suppose you want to move a circle in a scene from left to right horizontally in 10 seconds. Figure 9-23 shows the circle at few positions. The thick horizontal line represents a timeline. Circles with a solid outline represent the key frames at specific instants on the timeline. The key values associated with key frames are shown at the top line. For example, the value for `translateX` property of the circle for the key frame at the fifth second is 500, which is shown as tx=500 in the figure.

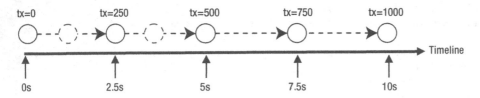

Figure 9-23. *Animating a circle along a horizontal line using a timeline*

Timeline, key frames, and key values are provided by the developer. In your example, you have five key frames. If JavaFX shows only five key frames at the five respective instants, the animation will look jerky. To provide a smooth animation, JavaFX needs to interpolate the position of the circle at any instant on the timeline. That is, JavaFX needs to create intermediate key frames between two consecutive key frames. JavaFX does this with the help of an *interpolator*. By default, it uses a *linear interpolator* that changes the property being animated linearly with time. That is, if the time on the timeline passes x%, the value of the property will be x% between the initial and final target values. In the figure, circles with the dashed outline are created by JavaFX using an interpolator.

Classes providing animation in JavaFX are in the `javafx.animation` package, except the `Duration` class, which is in the `javafx.util` package. Figure 9-24 shows a class diagram for the animation-related classes.

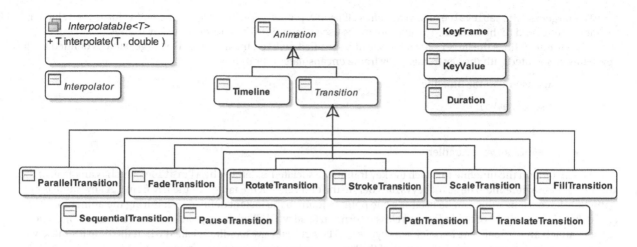

Figure 9-24. *A class diagram for core classes used in animation*

The abstract Animation class represents an animation. It contains common properties and methods used by all types of animations. JavaFX supports two types of animations:

- Timeline Animations

- Transitions

In a timeline animation, you create a timeline and add key frames to it. JavaFX creates the intermediate key frames using an interpolator. An instance of the Timeline class is represented by a timeline animation. This type of animation requires more coding on your part, but it gives you more control.

Several types of animations are commonly performed, for example, moving a node along a path, changing the opacity of a node over time, etc. These types of animations are known as *transitions*. They are performed using an internal timeline. An instance of the Transition class represents a transition animation. Several subclasses of the Transition class exist to support specific types of transitions. For example, the FadeTransition class implements a fading effect animation by changing the opacity of a node over time. You create an instance of one of the subclasses of the Transition class, specify the initial and final values for the property to be animated, and the duration for the animation. JavaFX takes care of creating the timeline and performing the animation. This type of animation is easier to use.

Sometimes you may want to perform multiple transitions sequentially or simultaneously. The SequentialTransition and ParallelTransition classes let you perform a set of transitions sequentially and simultaneously, respectively.

The Duration class is in the javafx.util package. It represents a duration of time in milliseconds, seconds, minutes, and hours. It is an immutable class. A Duration represents the amount of time for each cycle of an animation. A Duration can represent a positive or negative duration.

An instance of the KeyValue class represents a key value that is interpolated for a particular interval during animation. It encapsulates three things:

- A target

- An end value for the target

- An interpolator

The target is a `WritableValue`, which qualifies all JavaFX properties to be a target. The end value is the value for the target at the end of the interval. The interpolator is used to compute the intermediate key frames.

A key frame defines the target state of a node at a specified point on the timeline. The target state is defined by the key values associated with the key frame. A key frame encapsulates four things:

- An instant on the timeline
- A set of `KeyValues`
- A name
- An `ActionEvent` handler

The instant on the timeline to which the key frame is associated is defined by a `Duration`, which is an offset of the key frame on the timeline. The set of `KeyValues` define the end value of the target for the key frame. A key frame may optionally have a name that can be used as a cue point to jump to the instant defined by it during the animation. The `getCuePoints()` method of the `Animation` class returns an `ObservableMap` of cue points on the `Timeline`. Optionally, you can attach an `ActionEvent` handler to a `KeyFrame`. The `ActionEvent` handler is called when the time for the key frame arrives during animation. An instance of the `KeyFrame` class represents a key frame.

Using the Timeline Animation

A timeline animation is used for animating any properties of a node. An instance of the `Timeline` class represents a timeline animation. Using a timeline animation involves the following steps:

- Construct key frames
- Create a `Timeline` object with key frames
- Set the animation properties
- Use the `play()` method to run the animation

You can add key frames to a `Timeline` at the time of creating it or after. The `Timeline` instance keeps all key frames in an `ObservableList<KeyFrame>` object. The `getKeyFrames()` method returns the reference of the list. You can modify the list of key frames at any time. If the timeline animation is already running, you need to stop and restart it to pick up the modified list of key frames.

The `Timeline` class contains several constructors:

- `Timeline()`
- `Timeline(double targetFramerate)`
- `Timeline(double targetFramerate, KeyFrame... keyFrames)`
- `Timeline(KeyFrame... keyFrames)`

The no-args constructor creates a `Timeline` with no key frames with animation running at the optimum rate. Other constructors let you specify the target frame rate for the animation, which is the number of frames per second, and the key frames. Note that the order in which the key frames are added to a `Timeline` is not important. The timeline will order them based on their time offset.

The program in Listing 9-22 starts a timeline animation that scrolls a text horizontally from right to left across the scene forever. Figure 9-25 shows a screenshot of the animation.

Listing 9-22. Scrolling a Text Node Using a Timeline Animation

```java
// ScrollingText.java
package com.jdojo.jfx;

import javafx.animation.KeyFrame;
import javafx.animation.KeyValue;
import javafx.animation.Timeline;
import javafx.application.Application;
import javafx.geometry.VPos;
import javafx.scene.Scene;
import javafx.scene.layout.Pane;
import javafx.scene.text.Font;
import javafx.scene.text.Text;
import javafx.stage.Stage;
import javafx.util.Duration;

public class ScrollingText extends Application {
        public static void main(String[] args) {
                Application.launch(args);
        }

        @Override
        public void start(Stage stage) {
                Text msg = new Text("JavaFX animation is cool!");
                msg.setTextOrigin(VPos.TOP);
                msg.setFont(Font.font(24));

                Pane root = new Pane(msg);
                root.setPrefSize(500, 70);
                Scene scene = new Scene(root);

                stage.setScene(scene);
                stage.setTitle("Scrolling Text");
                stage.show();

                /* Set up a Timeline animation */
                // Get the scene width and the text width
                double sceneWidth = scene.getWidth();
                double msgWidth = msg.getLayoutBounds().getWidth();

                // Create the initial and final key frames
                KeyValue initKeyValue =
                                new KeyValue(msg.translateXProperty(), sceneWidth);
                KeyFrame initFrame = new KeyFrame(Duration.ZERO, initKeyValue);

                KeyValue endKeyValue =
                        new KeyValue(msg.translateXProperty(), -1.0 * msgWidth);
                KeyFrame endFrame =
                        new KeyFrame(Duration.seconds(3), endKeyValue);
```

```
                // Create a Timeline object
                Timeline timeline = new Timeline(initFrame, endFrame);

                // Let the animation run forever
                timeline.setCycleCount(Timeline.INDEFINITE);

                // Start the animation
                timeline.play();
        }
}
```

Figure 9-25. *Scrolling text using a timeline animation*

The logic to perform the animation is in the start() method. The method starts with creating a Text object, a Pane with the Text object, and setting up a scene for the stage. After showing the stage, it sets up an animation. First, it gets the width of the scene and the Text object.

```
double sceneWidth = scene.getWidth();
double msgWidth = msg.getLayoutBounds().getWidth();
```

Two key frames are created: one for time = 0 seconds and one for time = 3 seconds. The animation uses the translateX property of the Text object to change its horizontal position to make it look scroll. At zero seconds, the Text is positioned at the scene width, so it is invisible. At 3 seconds, it is placed to the left of the scene at a distance equal to its length, so again it is invisible.

```
KeyValue initKeyValue = new KeyValue(msg.translateXProperty(), sceneWidth);
KeyFrame initFrame = new KeyFrame(Duration.ZERO, initKeyValue);

KeyValue endKeyValue = new KeyValue(msg.translateXProperty(), -1.0 * msgWidth);
KeyFrame endFrame = new KeyFrame(Duration.seconds(3), endKeyValue);
```

A Timeline object is created with two key frames.

```
Timeline timeline = new Timeline(initFrame, endFrame);
```

By default, the animation will run only one time. That is, the Text will scroll from right to left once and the animation will stop. You can set the cycle count for an animation, which is the number of times the animation needs to run. You run your animation forever by setting the cycle count to Timeline.INDEFINITE as follows:

```
timeline.setCycleCount(Timeline.INDEFINITE);
```

Finally, the animation is started by calling the play() method.

```
timeline.play();
```

This example has a flaw. The scrolling text does not update its initial horizontal position when the width of the scene changes. You can rectify this problem by updating the initial key frame whenever the scene width changes. Append the following statement to the start() method of Listing 9-22. It adds a ChangeListener for the scene's width that updates key frames and restarts the animation.

```
scene.widthProperty().addListener( (prop, oldValue , newValue) -> {
        KeyValue kv = new KeyValue(msg.translateXProperty(), scene.getWidth());
        KeyFrame kf = new KeyFrame(Duration.ZERO, kv);
        timeline.stop();
        timeline.getKeyFrames().clear();
        timeline.getKeyFrames().addAll(kf, endFrame);
        timeline.play();
});
```

It is possible to create a Timeline animation with only one key frame. The key frame is treated as the last key frame. The Timeline synthesizes an initial key frame (for time = 0 seconds) using the current values for the property being animated. To see the effect, replace the statement

```
Timeline timeline = new Timeline(initFrame, endFrame);
```

in Listing 9-22 with the following statement

```
Timeline timeline = new Timeline(endFrame);
```

The Timeline will create an initial key frame with the current value of translateX property of the Text object, which is 0.0. This time, the Text scrolls differently. The scrolling starts by placing the Text at 0.0 and scrolling it to the left, so it goes beyond the scene.

FXML

FXML is an XML-based language for building a user interface for JavaFX applications. You can use FXML to build an entire scene or part of a scene. FXML allows application developers to separate the logic for building the UI from the business logic. If the UI part of the application changes, you do not need to recompile the JavaFX code; you can change the FXML using a text editor and rerun the application. You still use JavaFX to write business logic using the Java programming language. An FXML document is an XML document. A basic knowledge of XML is required to understand FXML.

A JavaFX scene graph is a hierarchical structure of Java objects. The XML format is well suited for storing information representing some kind of hierarchy. Therefore, using FXML to store the scene graph is very intuitive.

It is common to use FXML to build a scene graph in a JavaFX application. However, the use of FXML is not limited to building only scene graphs. It can build a hierarchical object graph of Java objects. In fact, it can be used to create just one object, for example, an object of a Person class.

Let's get a quick preview of what an FXML document looks like. You want to create a simple UI. It consists of a VBox with a Label and a Button. Listing 9-23 contains the JavaFX code to build the UI, which is familiar to you. Listing 9-24 contains the FXML version for building the same UI.

Listing 9-23. Building an Object Graph in JavaFX

```java
import javafx.scene.layout.VBox;
import javafx.scene.control.Label;
import javafx.scene.control.Button;

VBox root = new VBox();
root.getChildren().addAll(new Label("FXML is cool"),
                          new Button("Say Hello"));
```

Listing 9-24. Building an Object-Graph in FXML

```xml
<?xml version="1.0" encoding="UTF-8"?>

<?import javafx.scene.layout.VBox?>
<?import javafx.scene.control.Label?>
<?import javafx.scene.control.Button?>

<VBox>
        <children>
                <Label text="FXML is cool"/>
                <Button text="Say Hello"/>
        </children>
</VBox>
```

The first line in FXML is the standard XML declaration that is used by XML parsers. It is optional in FXML. If it is omitted, the version and encoding are assumed to be 1 and UTF-8, respectively. The next three lines are import statements that correspond to the import statements in Java code. Elements representing UI (for example, VBox, Label, and Button) have the same name as the name of JavaFX classes. The `<children>` tag specifies the children of the VBox. The text property for the Label and Button are specified using the text attributes of the respective elements.

An FXML document is simply a text file. Typically, the file name has a .fxml extension such as hello.fxml. For example, you can use Notepad to create an FXML document on Windows. If you have used XML, you know that it is not easy to edit a large XML document in a text editor. Oracle provides a visual editor called *Scene Builder* for editing FXML documents. Scene Builder is open source. You can download its latest version from www.oracle.com/technetwork/java/javase/downloads/javafxscenebuilder-info-2157684.html. Scene Builder can also be integrated into NetBeans IDE, so you can edit FXML documents using Scene Builder from inside the NetBeans IDE. Using Scene Builder is not discussed in this book.

In this section, I will cover the basics of FXML. You will develop a simple JavaFX application using FXML. The application consists of the following:

- A VBox

- A Label

- A Button

The spacing for the VBox is set to 10px. The text properties for the Label and Button are set to FXML is cool! and Say Hello. When the Button is clicked, the text in the Label changes to Hello from FXML!. Figure 9-26 shows two instance of the window displayed by the application.

Figure 9-26. *Two instances of a window whose scene graph is created using FXML*

The program in Listing 9-25 is the JavaFX implementation of this example application using the Java programming language to build the UI.

Listing 9-25. The JavaFX Version of the FXML Example Application

```java
// SayHelloFX.java
package com.jdojo.jfx;

import javafx.application.Application;
import javafx.event.ActionEvent;
import javafx.scene.Scene;
import javafx.scene.control.Button;
import javafx.scene.control.Label;
import javafx.scene.layout.VBox;
import javafx.stage.Stage;

public class SayHelloFX extends Application {
        private Label msgLbl = new Label("FXML is coll!");
        private Button sayHelloBtn = new Button("Say Hello");

        public static void main(String[] args) {
                Application.launch(args);
        }

        @Override
        public void start(Stage stage) {
                // Set the preferred width of the lable
                msgLbl.setPrefWidth(150);

                // Set the ActionEvent handler for the button
                sayHelloBtn.setOnAction(this::sayHello);

                VBox root = new VBox(10);
                root.getChildren().addAll(msgLbl, sayHelloBtn);
                root.setStyle("-fx-padding: 10;" +
                                "-fx-border-style: solid inside;" +
                                "-fx-border-width: 2;" +
                                "-fx-border-insets: 5;" +
                                "-fx-border-radius: 5;" +
                                "-fx-border-color: blue;");
```

```
            Scene scene = new Scene(root);
            stage.setScene(scene);
            stage.setTitle("Hello FXML");
            stage.show();
    }

    public void sayHello(ActionEvent e) {
            msgLbl.setText("Hello from FXML!");
    }
}
```

Now let's build another version of the program in Listing 9-25 in which the UI will be built using FXML. Create an FXML file sayhello.fxml with the contents shown in Listing 9-26. Listing 9-26 is the FXML document for your example. It will create the root element for the scene shown in Figure 9-26. Save the sayhello.fxml file in the resources/fxml directory where the parent directory of the resources directory is included in the CLASSPATH for the application. Suppose, on Windows, you have added C:\myjavafx in the CLASSPATH; the path of sayhello.fxml will be

```
C:\myjavafx\resources\fxml\sayhello.fxml
```

Listing 9-26. The Contents of the sayhello.fxml File

```xml
<?xml version="1.0" encoding="UTF-8"?>
<?language javascript?>
<?import javafx.scene.Scene?>
<?import javafx.scene.layout.VBox?>
<?import javafx.scene.control.Label?>
<?import javafx.scene.control.Button?>

<VBox spacing="10" xmlns:fx="http://javafx.com/fxml">
        <Label fx:id="msgLbl" text="FXML is cool!" prefWidth="150"/>
        <Button fx:id="sayHelloBtn" text="Say Hello" onAction="sayHello()"/>
        <style>
                -fx-padding: 10;
                -fx-border-style: solid inside;
                -fx-border-width: 2;
                -fx-border-insets: 5;
                -fx-border-radius: 5;
                -fx-border-color: blue;
        </style>
        <fx:script>
                function sayHello() {
                        msgLbl.setText("Hello from FXML!");
                }
        </fx:script>
</VBox>
```

You have set the spacing property for the VBox, the fx:id attribute for the Label and Button controls. You have set the style property of the VBox using a <style> property element. You had an option to set the style using a style attribute or a property element. You used a property element because the style value is a big string and it is more readable if entered on multiple lines. The <fx:script> element defines a script block with one function, sayHello(). The function sets the text property of the Label identified by the msgLbl fx:id attribute. You have set the sayHello() function as the onAction attribute of the Button, so when the Button is clicked, the sayHello() function is executed.

To build the UI from an FML, you need to load it into the JavaFX program. Loading an FXML is performed by an instance of the FXMLLoader class, which is in the javafx.fxml package.

The FXMLLoader class provides several constructors that let you specify the location, charset, resource bundle, etc. to be used for loading the document. You need to specify at least the location of the FXML document, which is a URL. The class contains a load() method to perform the actual loading of the document. The following snippet of code loads an FXML document from a local file system in Windows:

```
// Build the URL to locate the FXMl file
String fxmlDocUrl = "file:///C:/resources/fxml/test.fxml";
URL fxmlUrl = new URL(fxmlDocUrl);

// Create an FXMLLoader object and set its location that is the URL of the
// FML contents
FXMLLoader loader = new FXMLLoader();
loader.setLocation(fxmlUrl);

// Load the FXML that will return a VBox
VBox root = loader.<VBox>load();
```

The load() method is has a generic return type. In the above snippet of code, you made your intention clear in the call to the load() method (loader.<VBox>load()) that you are expecting a VBox instance from the FXML document. If you prefer, you may omit the generic parameter as shown:

```
// The return type of the load() method will be inferred as VBox
VBox root = loader.load();
```

The FXMLLoader class supports loading an FXML document using an InputStream. The following snippet of code loads the same FXML document using an InputStream:

```
FXMLLoader loader = new FXMLLoader();
String fxmlDocPath = "C:\\resources\\fxml\\test.fxml";
FileInputStream fxmlStream = new FileInputStream(fxmlDocPath);
VBox root = loader.<VBox>load(fxmlStream);
```

Internally, the FXMLLoader reads the document using streams, which may throw an IOException. All versions of the load() method in FXMLLoader class throws an IOException. I have omitted the exception handling in these snippets of code to keep the simple. In your application, you will need to handle the exception.

What do you do next after loading an FXML document? At this point, the role of FXML is over and your JavaFX code should take over.

The program in Listing 9-27 contains the JavaFX code for the example. It loads the FXML document stored in the sayhello.fxml file. The program loads the document from the CLASSPATH. The loader returns a VBox, which is set as the root for the scene. Rest of the code is the same you have used before. Note one difference in the declaration of the start() method. The method declares that it may throw an IOException, which you have to add because you have called the load() method of the FXMLLoader inside the method. When you run the program, it displays a window as shown in Figure 9-26. Click the button and the text for the Label will change.

Listing 9-27. Using FXML to Build the GUI

```java
// SayHelloFXML.java
package com.jdojo.jfx;

import javafx.application.Application;
import javafx.fxml.FXMLLoader;
import java.io.IOException;
import java.net.URL;
import javafx.scene.Scene;
import javafx.scene.layout.VBox;
import javafx.stage.Stage;

public class SayHelloFXML extends Application {
        public static void main(String[] args) {
                Application.launch(args);
        }

        @Override
        public void start(Stage stage) throws IOException {
                // Construct a URL for the FXML document
                URL fxmlUrl = this.getClass()
                        .getClassLoader()
                        .getResource("resources/fxml/sayhello.fxml");

                // Load the FXML document
                VBox root = FXMLLoader.<VBox>load(fxmlUrl);
                Scene scene = new Scene(root);
                stage.setScene(scene);
                stage.setTitle("Hello FXML");
                stage.show();
        }
}
```

FXML offers a lot more than what you have seen in this example. Using FXML, you can bind the UI elements to variables in JavaFX, data binding, and event handling, create custom controls, etc. Discussing these features is beyond the scope of this book.

Printing

JavaFX 8 has added support for printing nodes through the Print API in the `javafx.print` package. The API consists of the following classes and a number of enums (not listed):

- `Printer`
- `PrinterAttributes`
- `PrintResolution`
- `PrinterJob`
- `JobSettings`
- `Paper`

- PaperSource

- PageLayout

- PageRange

Instances of these classes represent different components of the printing process. For example, a Printer represents a printer that can be used for printing jobs; a PrinterJob represents a print job that can be sent to a Printer for printing; a Paper represents the paper sizes available on printers, etc.

The Print API provides support for printing nodes that may or may not be attached to a scene graph. It is a common requirement to print the contents of a web page, not the WebView node that contains the web page. The javafx.scene.web.WebEngine class contains a print(PrinterJob job) method that prints the contents of the web page, not the WebView node.

If a node is modified during the printing process, the printed node may not appear correct. Note that the printing of a node may span multiple pulse events, resulting in a concurrent change in the content being printed. To ensure correct printing, make sure that the node being printed is not modified during the print process.

Nodes can be printed on any thread including the JavaFX Application Thread. It is recommended that a large, time-consuming print job be submitted on a background thread to keep the UI responsive.

Classes in the Print API are final as they represent existing printing device properties. Most of them do not provide any public constructors as you cannot make up a printing device. Rather, you obtain their references using factory methods in the classes.

The Printer.getAllPrinters() static method returns an observable list of installed printers on the machine. Note that the list of printers returned by the method may change over time as new printers are installed or old printers removed. Use the getName() method of the Printer to get the name of the printer represented by the Printer. The following snippet of code lists all installed printers on the machine running the code. You may get a different output.

```
import javafx.collections.ObservableSet;
import javafx.print.Printer;
...
ObservableSet<Printer> allPrinters = Printer.getAllPrinters();
for(Printer p : allPrinters) {
        System.out.println(p.getName());
}
```

```
ImageRight Printer
Microsoft XPS Document Writer
PDF995
Sybase DataWindow PS
\\pro-print1\IS-HP4000
\\pro-print1\IS-HP4650(Color)
```

The Printer.getDefaultPrinter() method returns the default Printer. The method may return null if no printer is installed. The default printer may be changed on a machine. Therefore, the method may return different printers from call to call, and the printer returned may not be valid after some time. The following snippet of code shows how to get the default printer:

```
Printer defaultPrinter = Printer.getDefaultPrinter();
if (defaultPrinter!= null) {
        String name = defaultPrinter.getName();
        System.out.println("Default printer name: " + name);
}
```

```
else {
        System.out.println("No printers installed.");
}
```

Printing a node is easy: create a `PrinterJob` and call its `printPage()` method passing the node to be printed. Printing a node using the default printer with all default settings takes only three lines of code:

```
PrinterJob printerJob = PrinterJob.createPrinterJob();
printerJob.printPage(myNode); // myNode is the node to be printed
printerJob.endJob();
```

In a real-world application, you want to handle the errors, and the above code is rewritten as follows:

```
// Create a printer job for the default printer
PrinterJob printerJob = PrinterJob.createPrinterJob();
if (printerJob!= null) {
        // Print the node
        boolean printed = printerJob.printPage(node);
        if (printed) {
                // End the printer job
                printerJob.endJob();
        }
        else {
                System.out.println("Printing failed.");
        }
}
else {
        System.out.println("Could not create a printer job.");
}
```

You can use the `createPrinterJob()` static method of the `PrinterJob` class to create a printer job. The method is overloaded as shown:

- `static PrinterJob createPrinterJob()`

- `static PrinterJob createPrinterJob(Printer printer)`

The method with no-args creates a printer job for the default printer. You can use the other version of the method to create a printer job for the specified printer.

You can change the printer for a `PrinterJob` by calling its `setPrinter()` method. If the current printer job settings are not supported by the new printer, the settings are reset automatically for the new printer.

```
// Set a new printer for the printer job
printerJob.setPrinter(myNewPrinter);
```

Setting `null` as the printer for the job will use the default printer. Use one of the following `printPage()` methods of the `PrinterJob` class to print a node:

- `boolean printPage(Node node)`

- `boolean printPage(PageLayout pageLayout, Node node)`

The first version of the method takes only the node to be printed as the parameter. It uses the default page layout for the job for printing. The second version lets you specify a page layout for printing the node. The method returns true if the printing was successful. Otherwise, it returns false.

When you are done printing, call the endJob() method. The method returns true if the job can be successfully spooled to the printer queue. Otherwise, it returns false, which may indicate that the job could not be spooled or it was already completed. After a successful completion of the job, the job can no longer be reused.

You can cancel a print job using the cancelJob() method of the PrinterJob. The printing may not be cancelled immediately, for example, when a page is in the middle of printing. The cancellation occurs as soon as possible. The method does not have any effect if

- The job has already been requested to be cancelled.

- The job is already completed.

- The job has error.

The PrinterJob class contains a read-only jobStatus property that indicates the current status of the print job. The status is defined by one of the following constants of the PrinterJob.JobStatus enum:

- NOT_STARTED

- PRINTING

- CANCELED

- DONE

- ERROR

The NOT_STARTED status indicates a new job. In this status, the job can be configured and printing can be initiated. The PRINTING status indicates that the job has requested to print at least one page and it has not terminated printing. In this status, the job cannot be configured.

The other three statuses, CANCELED, DONE, and ERROR, indicate terminated state of the job. Once the job is in one of these statuses, it should not be reused. There is no need to call the endJob() method when the status goes to CANCELED or ERROR. The DONE status is entered when the printing was successful and the endJob() method was called.

The program in Listing 9-28 shows how to print nodes. It displays a TextArea where you can enter text. Two Buttons are provided: one prints the TextArea node and the other the entire scene. When printing is initiated, the print job status is displayed in a Label. The code in the print() method is the same code you have seen in the examples. The method includes the logic to display the job status in the Label. The program displays a window as shown in Figure 9-27. Run the program, enter text in the TextArea, and click one of the two buttons to print.

Listing 9-28. Printing Nodes

```java
// PrintingNodes.java
package com.jdojo.jfx;

import javafx.application.Application;
import javafx.print.PrinterJob;
import javafx.scene.Node;
import javafx.scene.Scene;
import javafx.scene.control.Button;
import javafx.scene.control.Label;
import javafx.scene.control.TextArea;
import javafx.scene.layout.HBox;
import javafx.scene.layout.VBox;
import javafx.stage.Stage;
```

```java
public class PrintingNodes extends Application {
        private Label jobStatus = new Label();

        public static void main(String[] args) {
                Application.launch(args);
        }

        @Override
        public void start(Stage stage) {
                VBox root = new VBox(5);

                Label textLbl = new Label("Text:");
                TextArea text = new TextArea();
                text.setPrefRowCount(10);
                text.setPrefColumnCount(20);
                text.setWrapText(true);

                // Button to print the TextArea node
                Button printTextBtn = new Button("Print Text");
                printTextBtn.setOnAction(e -> print(text));

                // Button to print the entire scene
                Button printSceneBtn = new Button("Print Scene");
                printSceneBtn.setOnAction(e -> print(root));

                HBox jobStatusBox =
                        new HBox(5, new Label("Print Job Status:"), jobStatus);
                HBox buttonBox = new HBox(5, printTextBtn, printSceneBtn);

                root.getChildren().addAll(textLbl, text, jobStatusBox, buttonBox);
                Scene scene = new Scene(root);
                stage.setScene(scene);
                stage.setTitle("Printing Nodes");
                stage.show();
        }

        private void print(Node node) {
                jobStatus.textProperty().unbind();
                jobStatus.setText("Creating a printer job...");

                // Create a printer job for teh default printer
                PrinterJob job = PrinterJob.createPrinterJob();
                if (job != null) {
                        // Show the printer job status
                        jobStatus.textProperty().bind(job.jobStatusProperty().asString());

                        // Print the node
                        boolean printed = job.printPage(node);
                        if (printed) {
                                // End the printer job
                                job.endJob();
                        }
```

```
            else {
                    jobStatus.textProperty().unbind();
                    jobStatus.setText("Printing failed.");
            }
        }
        else {
                jobStatus.setText("Could not create a printer job.");
        }
    }
}
```

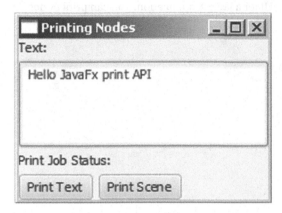

Figure 9-27. *A window letting the user print text in a TextArea and the scene*

The Printing API provides more printing features, such as displaying the print dialog. Please refer to the JavaFX API documentation for classes in the `javafx.print` package for more details.

Summary

JavaFX is an open source Java-based GUI framework for developing rich client applications. It is the successor of Swing in the arena of GUI development technology in the Java platform.

The GUI in JavaFX is shown in a stage. A stage is an instance of the `Stage` class. A stage is a window in a desktop application and an area in the browser in a web application. A stage contains a scene. A scene contains a group of nodes (graphics) arranged in a tree-like structure.

A JavaFX application inherits from the `Application` class. The JavaFX runtime creates the first stage called the primary stage and calls the `start()` method of the application class, passing the reference of the primary stage. The developer needs to add a scene to the stage and make the stage visible.

JavaFX supports property classes whose instances are used to represent properties of classes. Properties support unidirectional and bidirectional bindings. If a property is bound to an expression, the property value is synchronized automatically with the value of the expression. Properties support invalidation and change notifications. Interested parties can register for these notifications. They are notified when the properties become invalid or its value changes. A property becomes invalid when its dependencies change.

JavaFX provides observable list, set, and map that are instances of the `ObservableList`, `ObservableSet`, and `ObservableMap` interfaces. They can be observed for invalidation and changes. The `FXCollections` class contains factory methods to create instances of such observable collections.

JavaFX supports event-handling for UI elements. You can register event handlers for UI elements. When the event occurs, your registered event handlers are executed.

JavaFX provides layout panes that are containers for nodes. They arrange the nodes in a particular way. For example, the HBox layout pane arranges nodes by placing them horizontally in one row whereas the VBox layout pane arranges nodes by placing them vertically in one column. JavaFX provides a rich set of controls such as Button, Label, ChoiceBox, ComboBox, TextField, DatePicker, etc. The HTMLEditor control provides the editing capability to edit rich text. The WebView node is used to display the contents of a webpage.

JavaFX provides extensive support for drawing 2D and 3D shapes. It provides the Canvas API to draw 2D shapes on a canvas using the drawing commands. The Canvas API also lets you access (read and write) pixels on the canvas surface.

You can apply effects, transformations, and animations to nodes in a scene by writing a few lines of code. JavaFX supports FXML, an XML-based markup language for building the GUI for a JavaFX application. You can print nodes and the contents of a web page using the Printing API.

CHAPTER 10

■ ■ ■

Scripting in Java

In this chapter, you will learn

- What scripting in Java is

- How to execute scripts from Java and how to pass parameters to scripts

- How the ScriptContext is used in executing scripts

- How to use the Java programming language in scripts

- How to implement a script engine

- How to use the jrunscript and jjs command-line tools to execute scripts

What Is Scripting in Java?

Some believe that the Java Virtual Machine (JVM) can execute programs written only in the Java programming language. However, that is not true. The JVM executes language-neutral bytecode. It can execute programs written in any programming language, if the program can be compiled into Java bytecode.

A *scripting language* is a programming language that provides you with the ability to write *scripts* that are evaluated (or interpreted) by a runtime environment called a *script engine* (or an interpreter). A script is a sequence of characters that is written using the syntax of a scripting language and used as the source for a program executed by an interpreter. The interpreter parses the scripts, produces intermediate code, which is an internal representation of the program, and executes the intermediate code. The interpreter stores the variables used in a script in data structures called *symbol tables*.

Typically, unlike in a compiled programming language, the source code (called a script) in a scripting language is not compiled, but is interpreted at runtime. However, scripts written in some scripting languages may be compiled into Java bytecode that can be run by the JVM.

Java 6 added scripting support to the Java platform that lets a Java application execute scripts written in scripting languages such as Rhino JavaScript, Groovy, Jython, JRuby, Nashorn JavaScript, etc. Two-way communication is supported. It also lets scripts access Java objects created by the host application. The Java runtime and a scripting language runtime can communicate and make use of each other's features.

Support for scripting languages in Java comes through the Java Scripting API. All classes and interfaces in the Java Scripting API are in the javax.script package.

Using a scripting language in a Java application provides several advantages:

- Most scripting languages are dynamically typed, which makes it simpler to write programs.

- They provide a quicker way to develop and test small applications.

- Customization by end users is possible.

- A scripting language may provide domain-specific features that are not available in Java.

Scripting languages have some disadvantages as well. For example, dynamic typing is good to write simpler code; however, it turns into a disadvantage when a type is interpreted incorrectly and you have to spend a lot of time debugging it.

Scripting support in Java lets you take advantage of both worlds: it allows you to use the Java programming language for developing statically typed, scalable, and high-performance parts of the application and use a scripting language that fits the domain-specific needs for other parts.

I will use the term *script engine* frequently in this chapter. A *script engine* is a software component that executes programs written in a particular scripting language. Typically, but not necessarily, a script engine is an implementation of an interpreter for a scripting language. Interpreters for several scripting languages have been implemented in Java. They expose programming interfaces so a Java program may interact with them.

JDK 7 was co-bundled with a script engine called Rhino JavaScript. JDK 8 replaced the Rhino JavaScript engine with a lightweight, faster script engine called Nashorn JavaScript. This chapter discusses Nashorn JavaScript, not Rhino JavaScript. Please visit www.mozilla.org/rhino for more details on Rhino JavaScript documentation. If you want to migrate programs written with Rhino JavaScript to Nashorn, please visit the *Rhino Migration Guide* at https://wiki.openjdk.java.net/display/Nashorn/Rhino+Migration+Guide. If you are interested in using Rhino JavaScript with JDK 8, visit the page at https://wiki.openjdk.java.net/display/Nashorn/Using+Rhino+JSR-223+engine+with+JDK8.

Java includes a command-line shell called jrunscript that can be used to run scripts in an interactive mode or a batch mode. The jrunscript shell is scripting-language-neutral; the default language is Rhino JavaScript in JDK 7 and Nashorn in JDK 8. I will discuss the jrunscript shell in detail later in this chapter. JDK 8 includes another command-line tool called jjs that invokes the Nashorn engine and offers Nashorn-specific command-line options. If you are using Nashorn, you should use the jjs command-line tool over jrunscript. I will discuss the jjs command-line tool later in this chapter.

Java can execute scripts in any scripting language that provides an implementation for a script engine. For example, Java can execute scripts written in Nashorn JavaScript, Rhino JavaScript, Groovy, Jython, JRuby, etc. Examples in this chapter use Nashorn JavaScript language.

In this chapter, the terms "Nashorn," "Nashorn Engine," "Nashorn JavaScript," "Nashorn JavaScript Engine," "Nashorn Scripting Language," and "JavaScript" have been used synonymously.

Executing Your First Script

In this section, you will use Nashorn to print a message on the standard output. The same steps can be used to print a message using any other scripting languages, with one difference: you will need to use the scripting language-specific code to print the message. You need to perform the following three steps to run a script in Java:

- Create a script engine manager.

- Get an instance of a script engine from the script engine manager.

- Call the eval() method of the script engine to execute a script.

A script engine manager is an instance of the ScriptEngineManager class.

```
// Create an script engine manager
ScriptEngineManager manager = new ScriptEngineManager();
```

An instance of the ScriptEngine interface represents a script engine in a Java program. The getEngineByName(String engineShortName) method of a ScriptEngineManager is used to get an instance of a script engine. To get an instance of the Nashorn engine, use JavaScript as the short name of the engine as shown:

```
// Get the reference of a Nashorn engine
ScriptEngine engine = manager.getEngineByName("JavaScript");
```

■ **Tip**   The short name of a script engine is case-sensitive. Sometimes a script engine has multiple short names. Nashorn engine has the following short names: nashorn, Nashorn, js, JS, JavaScript, javascript, ECMAScript, ecmascript. You can use any of the short names of an engine to get its instance using the getEngineByName() method of the ScriptEngineManager class.

In Nashorn, the print() function prints a message on the standard output and a string literal is a sequence of characters enclosed in single or double quotes. The following snippet of code stores a script in a String object that prints Hello Scripting! on the standard output:

```
// Store a Nashorn script in a string
String script = "print('Hello Scripting!')";
```

If you want to use double quotes to enclose the string literal in Nashorn, the statement will look as shown:

```
// Store a Nashorn script in a string
String script = "print(\"Hello Scripting!\")";
```

To execute the script, you need to pass it to the eval() method of the script engine. A script engine may throw a ScriptException when it runs a script. For this reason, you need to handle this exception when you call the eval() method of the ScriptEngine. The following snippet of code executes the script stored in the script variable:

```
try {
        engine.eval(script);
}
catch (ScriptException e) {
        e.printStackTrace();
}
```

Listing 10-1 contains the complete code for the program to print a message on the standard output.

Listing 10-1. Printing a Message on the Standard Output Using Nashorn

```
// HelloScripting.java
package com.jdojo.script;

import javax.script.ScriptEngine;
import javax.script.ScriptEngineManager;
import javax.script.ScriptException;

public class HelloScripting {
        public static void main(String[] args) {
                // Create a script engine manager
                ScriptEngineManager manager = new ScriptEngineManager();

                // Obtain a Nashorn script engine from the manager
                ScriptEngine engine = manager.getEngineByName("JavaScript");
```

```
            // Store the script in a String
            String script = "print('Hello Scripting!')";

            try {
                    // Execute the script
                    engine.eval(script);
            }
            catch (ScriptException e) {
                    e.printStackTrace();
            }
        }
}
```

```
Hello Scripting!
```

Using Other Scripting Languages

It is very simple to use a scripting language, other than Nashorn, in a Java program. You need to perform only one task before you can use a script engine: include the JAR files for a particular script engine in your application CLASSPATH. Implementers of script engines provide those JAR files.

Java uses a discovery mechanism to list all script engines whose JAR files have been included in the application CLASSPATH. An instance of the ScriptEngineFactory interface is used to create and describe a script engine. The provider of a script engine provides an implementation for the ScriptEngineFactory interface. The getEngineFactories() method of the ScriptEngineManager returns a List<ScriptEngineFactory> of all available script engines factories. The getScriptEngine() method of the ScriptEngineFactory returns an instance of the ScriptEngine. Several other methods of the factory return metadata about the engine.

Listing 10-2 shows how to print details of all available script engines. The output shows that the script engine for Groovy, Jython, and JRuby are available. They are available because I have added the JAR files for their engines to the CLASSPATH on my machine. This program is helpful when you have included the JAR files for a script engine in the CLASSPATH and you want to know the short name of the script engine. You may get a different output when you run the program.

Listing 10-2. Listing All Available Script Engines

```
// ListingAllEngines.java
package com.jdojo.script;

import java.util.List;
import javax.script.ScriptEngineFactory;
import javax.script.ScriptEngineManager;

public class ListingAllEngines {
        public static void main(String[] args) {
                ScriptEngineManager manager = new ScriptEngineManager();

                // Get the list of all available engines
                List<ScriptEngineFactory> list = manager.getEngineFactories();
```

```
            // Print the details of each engine
            for (ScriptEngineFactory f : list) {
                    System.out.println("Engine Name:" + f.getEngineName());
                    System.out.println("Engine Version:" +
                            f.getEngineVersion());
                    System.out.println("Language Name:" + f.getLanguageName());
                    System.out.println("Language Version:" +
                            f.getLanguageVersion());
                    System.out.println("Engine Short Names:" + f.getNames());
                    System.out.println("Mime Types:" + f.getMimeTypes());
                    System.out.println("--------------------------");
            }
        }
}
```

```
Engine Name:jython
Engine Version:2.5.3
Language Name:python
Language Version:2.5
Engine Short Names:[python, jython]
Mime Types:[text/python, application/python, text/x-python, application/x-python]
--------------------------
Engine Name:JSR 223 JRuby Engine
Engine Version:1.7.0.preview1
Language Name:ruby
Language Version:jruby 1.7.0.preview1
Engine Short Names:[ruby, jruby]
Mime Types:[application/x-ruby]
--------------------------
Engine Name:Groovy Scripting Engine
Engine Version:2.0
Language Name:Groovy
Language Version:2.0.0-rc-2
Engine Short Names:[groovy, Groovy]
Mime Types:[application/x-groovy]
--------------------------
Engine Name:Oracle Nashorn
Engine Version:1.8.0_05
Language Name:ECMAScript
Language Version:ECMA - 262 Edition 5.1
Engine Short Names:[nashorn, Nashorn, js, JS, JavaScript, javascript, ECMAScript, ecmascript]
Mime Types:[application/javascript, application/ecmascript, text/javascript, text/ecmascript]
--------------------------
```

Table 10-1 lists details on how to install script engines before you can use them in your Java application. The list of web sites and instructions are valid at the time of this writing; they may become invalid at the time of reading. However, they show you how a script engine for a scripting language is installed. If you are interested in using Nashorn, you do not need to install anything on your machine. Nashorn is available in JDK 8

Table 10-1. *Installation Details for Installing Some Script Engines*

Script Engine	Version	Website	Installation Instructions
Groovy	2.3	groovy.codehaus.org	Download the installation file for Groovy; it's a ZIP file. Unzip it. Look for a JAR file named groovy-all-2.0.0-rc-2.jar in the embeddable folder. Add this JAR file to the CLASSPATH.
Jython	2.5.3	www.jython.org	Download the Jython installer file that is a JAR file. Extract the jython.jar file and add it to the CLASSPATH.
JRuby	1.7.13	www.jruby.org	Download the JRuby installation file. You have an option to download a ZIP file. Unzip it. In the lib folder, you will find a jruby.jar file that you need to include in the CLASSPATH.

Listing 10-3 shows how to print a message on the standard output using JavaScript, Groovy, Jython, and JRuby. If a script engine is not available, the program prints a message to that effect.

Listing 10-3. Printing a Message on the Standard Output Using Different Scripting Languages

```
// HelloEngines.java
package com.jdojo.script;

import javax.script.ScriptEngine;
import javax.script.ScriptEngineManager;
import javax.script.ScriptException;

public class HelloEngines {
    public static void main(String[] args) {
        // Get the script engine manager
        ScriptEngineManager manager = new ScriptEngineManager();

        // Try executing scripts in Nashorn, Groovy, Jython, and JRuby
        execute(manager, "JavaScript", "print('Hello JavaScript')");
        execute(manager, "Groovy", "println('Hello Groovy')");
        execute(manager, "jython", "print 'Hello Jython'");
        execute(manager, "jruby", "puts('Hello JRuby')");
    }

    public static void execute(ScriptEngineManager manager,
                               String engineName,
                               String script) {
        // Try getting the engine
        ScriptEngine engine = manager.getEngineByName(engineName);
        if (engine == null) {
            System.out.println(engineName + " is not available.");
            return;
        }

        // If we get here, it means we have the engine installed.
        // So, run the script
```

```
        try {
                engine.eval(script);
        }
        catch (ScriptException e) {
                e.printStackTrace();
        }
    }
}
```

```
Hello JavaScript
Hello Groovy
Hello Jython
Hello JRuby
```

Sometimes you may want to play with a scripting language just for fun, and you do not know the syntax that is used to print a message on the standard output. The ScriptEngineFactory class contains a method named getOutputStatement(String toDisplay) that you can use to find the syntax for printing text on the standard output. The following snippet of code shows how to get the syntax for Nashorn:

```
// Get the script engine factory for Nashorn
ScriptEngineManager manager = new ScriptEngineManager();
ScriptEngine engine = manager.getEngineByName("JavaScript");
ScriptEngineFactory factory = engine.getFactory();

// Get the script
String script = factory.getOutputStatement("\"Hello JavaScript\"");
System.out.println("Syntax: " + script);

// Evaluate the script
engine.eval(script);
```

```
Syntax: print("Hello JavaScript")
Hello JavaScript
```

For other scripting languages, use their engine factories to get the syntax.

Exploring the javax.script Package

The Java Scripting API in Java consists of a small number of classes and interfaces. They are in the javax.script package. This chapter contains a brief description of classes and interfaces in this package. I will discuss their usage in subsequent chapters.

The ScriptEngine and ScriptEngineFactory Interfaces

The ScriptEngine interface is the main interface of the Java Scripting API whose instances facilitate the execution of scripts written in a particular scripting language.

The implementer of the ScriptEngine interface also provides an implementation of the ScriptEngineFactory interface. A ScriptEngineFactory performs two tasks:

- It creates instances of the script engine.

- It provides information about the script engine such as engine name, version, language, etc.

The AbstractScriptEngine Class

The AbstractScriptEngine class is an abstract class. It provides a partial implementation for the ScriptEngine interface. You will not use this class directly unless you are implementing a script engine.

The ScriptEngineManager Class

The ScriptEngineManager class provides a discovery and instantiation mechanism for script engines. It also maintains a mapping of key-value pairs as an instance of the Bindings interface storing state that is shared by all script engines that it creates.

The Compilable Interface and the CompiledScript Class

The Compilable interface may optionally be implemented by a script engine that allows compiling scripts for their repeated execution without recompilation.

The CompiledScript class is an abstract class. It is extended by the providers of a script engine. It stores a script in a compiled form, which may be executed repeatedly without recompilation. Note that using a ScriptEngine to execute a script repeatedly causes the script to recompile every time, thus slowing down the performance.

A script engine is not required to support script compilation. It must implement the Compilable interface if it supports script compilation.

The Invocable Interface

The Invocable interface may optionally be implemented by a script engine that may allow invoking procedures, functions, and methods in scripts that have been compiled previously.

The Bindings Interface and the SimpleBindings Class

An instance of a class that implements the Bindings interface is a mapping of key-value pairs with a restriction that a key must be non-null, non-empty String. It extends the java.util.Map interface. The SimpleBindings class is an implementation of the Bindings interface.

The ScriptContext Interface and the SimpleScriptContext Class

An instance of the ScriptContext interface acts as a bridge between the Java host application and the script engine. It is used to pass the execution context of the Java host application to the script engine. The script engine may use the context information while executing a script. A script engine may store its state in an instance of a class that implements the ScriptContext interface, which may be accessible to the Java host application.

The SimpleScriptContext class is an implementation of the ScriptContext interface.

The ScriptException Class

The ScriptException class is an exception class. A script engine throws a ScriptException if an error occurs during the execution, compilation, or invocation of a script. The class contains three useful methods called getLineNumber(), getColumnNumber(), and getFileName(). These methods report the line number, the column number, and the file name of the script in which the error occurs. The ScriptException class overrides the getMessage() method of the Throwable class and includes the line number, column number, and the file name in the message that it returns.

Discovering and Instantiating ScriptEngines

You can create a script engine using a ScriptEngineFactory or ScriptEngineManager. Who is actually responsible for creating a script engine: ScriptEngineFactory, ScriptEngineManager, or both? The short answer is that a ScriptEngineFactory is always responsible for creating instances of a script engine. The next question is "What is the role of a ScriptEngineManager?"

A ScriptEngineManager uses the service provider mechanism to locate all available script engine factories. It searches all JAR files in the CLASSPATH and other standard directories. It looks for a resource file, which is a text file named javax.script.ScriptEngineFactory under a directory named META-INF/services. The resource file consists of the fully qualified names of the classes implementing the ScriptEngineFactory interface. Each class name is specified in a separate line. The file may include comments that start with a # character. A sample resource file may have the following contents that include class names for two script engine factories:

```
#Java Kishori Script Engine Factory class
com.jdojo.script.JKScriptEngineFactory

#Another factory class
com.jdojo.script.FunScriptFactory
```

A ScriptEngineManager locates and instantiates all available ScriptEngineFactory classes. You can get a list of instances of all factory classes using the getEngineFactories() method of the ScriptEngineManager class. When you call a method of the manager to get a script engine based on a criterion such as the getEngineByName(String shortName) method to get an engine by name, the manager searches all factories for that criterion and returns the matching script engine reference. If no factories are able to provide a matching engine, the manager returns null. Please refer to Listing 10-2 for more details on listing all available factories and describing script engines that they can create.

Now you know that a ScriptEngineManager does not create instances of a script engine. Rather, it queries all available factories and passes the reference of a script engine created by the factory back to the caller.

To make the discussion complete, let's add a twist to the ways a script engine can be created. You can create an instance of a script engine in three ways:

- Instantiate the script engine class directly.

- Instantiate the script engine factory class directly and call its getScriptEngine() method.

- Use one of the getEngineByXxx() methods of the ScriptEngineManager class.

It is advised to use the ScriptEngineManager class to get instances of a script engine. This method allows all engines created by the same manager to share a state that is a set of key-value pairs stored as an instance of the Bindings interface. The ScriptEngineManager instance stores this state.

■ **Tip** It is possible to have more than one instance of the ScriptEngineManager class in an application. In that case, each ScriptEngineManager instance maintains a state common to all engines that it creates. That is, if two engines are obtained by two different instances of the ScriptEngineManager class, those engines will not share a common state maintained by their managers unless you make it happen programmatically.

Executing Scripts

A ScriptEngine can execute a script in a String and a Reader. Using a Reader, you can execute a script stored on the network or in a file. One of the following versions of the eval() method of the ScriptEngine interface is used to execute a script:

- Object eval(String script)

- Object eval(Reader reader)

- Object eval(String script, Bindings bindings)

- Object eval(Reader reader, Bindings bindings)

- Object eval(String script, ScriptContext context)

- Object eval(Reader reader, ScriptContext context)

The first argument of the eval() method is the source of the script. The second argument lets you pass information from the host application to the script engine that can be used during the execution of the script.

In Listing 10-1, you saw how to use a String object to execute a script using the first version of the eval() method. In this section, you will store your script in a file and use a Reader object as the source of the script, which will use the second version of the eval() method. The next section discusses the other four versions of the eval() method. Typically, a script file is given a .js extension.

Listing 10-4 shows the contents of a file named helloscript.js. It contains only one statement in Nashorn that prints a message on the standard output.

Listing 10-4. The Contents of the helloscript.js File

```
// Print a message
print('Hello from JavaScript!');
```

Listing 10-5 has the Java program that executes the script stored in the helloscript.js file, which should be stored in the current directory. If the script file is not found, the program prints the full path of the helloscript.js file where it is expected. If you have trouble executing the script file, try using the absolute path in the main() method such as C:\scripts\helloscript.js on Windows, assuming that the helloscript.js file is saved in the C:\scripts directory.

Listing 10-5. Executing a Script Stored in a File

```
// ReaderAsSource.java
package com.jdojo.script;

import java.io.IOException;
import java.io.Reader;
import java.nio.file.Files;
import java.nio.file.Path;
import java.nio.file.Paths;
```

```java
import javax.script.ScriptEngine;
import javax.script.ScriptEngineManager;
import javax.script.ScriptException;

public class ReaderAsSource {
        public static void main(String[] args) {
                // Construct the script file path
                String scriptFileName = "helloscript.js";
                Path scriptPath = Paths.get(scriptFileName);

                // Make sure the script file exists. If not, print the full path of
                // the script file and terminate the program.
                if (! Files.exists(scriptPath) ) {
                        System.out.println(scriptPath.toAbsolutePath() +
                                " does not exist.");
                        return;
                }

                // Get the Nashorn script engine
                ScriptEngineManager manager = new ScriptEngineManager();
                ScriptEngine engine = manager.getEngineByName("JavaScript");

                try {
                        // Get a Reader for the script file
                        Reader scriptReader = Files.newBufferedReader(scriptPath);

                        // Execute the script in the file
                        engine.eval(scriptReader);
                }
                catch (IOException | ScriptException e) {
                        e.printStackTrace();
                }
        }
}
```

```
Hello from JavaScript!
```

In a real-world application, you should store all scripts in files that allow modifying scripts without modifying and recompiling your Java code. You will not follow this rule in most of the examples in this chapter; you will store your scripts in String objects to keep the code short and simple.

Passing Parameters

The Java Scripting API allows you to pass parameters from the host environment (Java application) to the script engine and vice versa. In this section, you will see the technical details of parameter passing mechanisms between the host application and the script engine.

Passing Parameters from Java Code to Scripts

A Java program may pass parameters to scripts. A Java program may also access global variables declared in a script after the script is executed. Let's discuss a simple example of this kind where a Java program passes a parameter to a script. Consider the program in Listing 10-6 that passes a parameter to a script.

Listing 10-6. Passing Parameters From a Java Program to Scripts

```
// PassingParam.java
package com.jdojo.script;

import javax.script.ScriptEngine;
import javax.script.ScriptEngineManager;
import javax.script.ScriptException;

public class PassingParam {
        public static void main(String[] args) {
                // Get the Nashorn engine
                ScriptEngineManager manager = new ScriptEngineManager();
                ScriptEngine engine = manager.getEngineByName("JavaScript");

                // Store the script in a String. Here, msg is a variable
                // that we have not declared in the script
                String script = "print(msg)";

                try {
                        // Store a parameter named msg in the engine
                        engine.put("msg", "Hello from Java program");

                        // Execute the script
                        engine.eval(script);
                }
                catch (ScriptException e) {
                        e.printStackTrace();
                }
        }
}
```

```
Hello from Java program
```

The program stores a script in a String object as follows:

```
// Store a Nashorn script in a String object
String script = "print(msg)";
```

In the statement, the script is

```
print(msg)
```

Note that msg is a variable used in the print() function call. The script does not declare the msg variable or assign it a value. If you try to execute the above script without telling the engine what the msg variable is, the engine will throw an exception stating that it does not understand the meaning of the variable msg. This is where the concept of passing parameters from a Java program to a script engine comes into play.

You can pass a parameter to a script engine in several ways. The simplest way is to use the put(String paramName, Object paramValue) method of the script engine, which accepts two arguments:

- The first argument is the name of the parameter, which needs to match the name of the variable in the script.

- The second argument is the value of the parameter.

In your case, you want to pass a parameter named msg to the script engine and its value is a String. The call to the put() method is

```
// Store the value of the msg parameter in the engine
engine.put("msg", "Hello from Java program");
```

Note that you must call the put() method of the engine before calling the eval() method. In your case, when the engine attempts to execute print(msg), it will use the value of the msg parameter that you passed to the engine.

Most script engines let you use the parameter names that you pass to it as the variable name in the script. You saw this kind of example when you passed the value of the parameter named msg and used it as a variable name in the script in Listing 10-6. A script engine may have a requirement for declaring variables in scripts, for example, a variable name must start with a $ prefix in PHP and a global variable name contains a $ prefix in JRuby. If you want to pass a parameter named msg to a script in JRuby, your code would be as shown:

```
// Get the JRuby script engine
ScriptEngineManager manager = new ScriptEngineManager();
ScriptEngine engine = manager.getEngineByName("jruby");

// Must use the $ prefix in JRuby script
String script = "puts($msg)";

// No $ prefix used in passing the msg parameter to the JRuby engine
engine.put("msg", "Hello from Java");

// Execute the script
engine.eval(script);
```

Properties and methods of Java objects passed to scripts can be accessed in scripts, as they are accessed in Java code. Different scripting languages use different syntax to access Java objects in scripts. For example, you can use the expression msg.toString() in the example shown in Listing 10-6 and the output will be the same. In this case, you are calling the toString() method of the variable msg. Change the statement that assigns the value to the script variable in Listing 10-6 to the following and run the program, which will produce the same output:

```
String script = "println(msg.toString())";
```

Passing Parameters from Scripts to Java Code

A script engine may make variables in its global scope available to Java code. The get(String variableName) method of a ScriptEngine is used to access those variables in Java code. It returns a Java Object. The declaration of a global variable is scripting-language-dependent. The following snippet of code declares a global variable and assigns it a value in JavaScript:

```
// Declare a variable named year in Nashorn
var year = 1969;
```

Listing 10-7 contains a program that shows how to access a global variable in Nashorn from Java code.

Listing 10-7. Accessing Script Global Variables in Java Code

```java
// AccessingScriptVariable.java
package com.jdojo.script;

import javax.script.ScriptEngine;
import javax.script.ScriptEngineManager;
import javax.script.ScriptException;

public class AccessingScriptVariable {
        public static void main(String[] args) {
                // Get the Nashorn engine
                ScriptEngineManager manager = new ScriptEngineManager();
                ScriptEngine engine = manager.getEngineByName("JavaScript");

                // Write a script that declares a global variable named year and
                // assign it a value of 1969.
                String script = "var year = 1969";

                try {
                        // Execute the script
                        engine.eval(script);

                        // Get the year global variable from the engine
                        Object year = engine.get("year");

                        // Print the class name and the value of the variable year
                        System.out.println("year's class:" +
                                year.getClass().getName());
                        System.out.println("year's value:" + year);
                }
                catch (ScriptException e) {
                        e.printStackTrace();
                }
        }
}
```

```
year's class:java.lang.Integer
year's value:1969
```

The program declares a global variable year in the script and assigns it a value of 1969 as shown:

```
String script = "var num = 1969";
```

When the script is executed, the engine adds the year variable to its state. In Java code, the get() method of the engine is used to retrieve the value of the year variable as shown:

```
Object year = engine.get("year");
```

When the year variable was declared in the script, you did not specify it data type. The conversion of a script variable value to an appropriate Java object is automatically performed. If you run the program in Java 7, your output will show java.lang.Double as the class name and 1960.0 as the value for the year variable. This is because Java 7 uses Rhino script engine that interprets 1969 as a Double whereas Java 8 uses Nashorn script engine that interprets it as an Integer.

Advanced Parameter Passing Techniques

To understand the details of the parameter passing mechanism, three terms must be understood clearly: bindings, scope, and context. These terms are confusing at first. This section explains the parameter passing mechanism using the following steps:

- First, it defines these terms.

- Second, it defines the relationship between these terms.

- Third, it explains how to use them in Java code.

Bindings

A Bindings is a set of key-value pairs where all keys must be non-empty, non-null Strings. In Java code, a Bindings is an instance of the Bindings interface. The SimpleBindings class is an implementation of the Bindings interface. A script engine may provide its own implementation of the Bindings interface.

■ **Tip** If you are familiar with the java.util.Map interface, it is easy to understand Bindings. The Bindings interface inherits the Map<String,Object> interface. Therefore, a Bindings is just a Map with a restriction that its keys must be non-empty, non-null Strings.

Listing 10-8 shows how to use a Bindings. It creates an instance of SimpleBindings, adds some key-value pairs to it, retrieves the values of the keys, removes a key-value pair, etc. The get() method of the Bindings interface returns null if the key does not exist or the key exists and its value is null. If you want to test if a key exists, you need to call its contains() method.

Listing 10-8. Using Bindings Objects

```java
// BindingsTest.java
package com.jdojo.script;

import javax.script.Bindings;
import javax.script.SimpleBindings;

public class BindingsTest {
        public static void main(String[] args) {
                // Create a Bindings instance
                Bindings params = new SimpleBindings();

                // Add some key-value pairs
                params.put("msg", "Hello");
                params.put("year", 1969);

                // Get values
                Object msg = params.get("msg");
                Object year = params.get("year");
                System.out.println("msg = " + msg);
                System.out.println("year = " + year);

                // Remove year from Bindings
                params.remove("year");
                year = params.get("year");

                boolean containsYear = params.containsKey("year");
                System.out.println("year = " + year);
                System.out.println("params contains year = " + containsYear);
        }
}
```

```
msg = Hello
year = 1969
year = null
params contains year = false
```

You will not use a Bindings by itself. Often, you will use it to pass parameters from Java code to a script engine. The ScriptEngine interface contains a createBindings() method that returns an instance of the Bindings interface. This method gives a script engine a chance to return an instance of the specialized implementation of the Bindings interface. You can use this method as shown:

```java
// Get the Nashorn engine
ScriptEngineManager manager = new ScriptEngineManager();
ScriptEngine engine = manager.getEngineByName("JavaScript");

// Instead of instantiating the SimpleBindings class, use the
// createBindings() method of the engine
Bindings params = engine.createBindings();

// Work with params as usual
```

Scope

Let's move to the next term, which is scope. A scope is used for a `Bindings`. The scope of a `Bindings` determines the visibility of its key-value pairs. You can have multiple `Bindings` occurring in multiple scopes. However, one `Bindings` may occur only in one scope. How do you specify the scope for a `Bindings`? I will cover this shortly.

Using the scope for a `Bindings` lets you define parameter variables for script engines in a hierarchical order. If a variable name is searched in an engine state, the `Bindings` with a higher precedence is searched first, followed by `Bindings` with lower precedence. The first found value of the variable is returned.

The Java Scripting API defines two scopes. They are defined as two `int` constants in the `ScriptContext` interface. They are

- `ScriptContext.ENGINE_SCOPE`

- `ScriptContext.GLOBAL_SCOPE`

The engine scope has higher precedence than the global scope. If you add two key-value pairs with the same key to two `Bindings` (one in engine scope and one in global scope), the key-value pair in the engine scope will be used whenever a variable with the same name as the key has to be resolved.

Understanding the role of the scope for a `Bindings` is so important that I will run through another analogy to explain it. Think about a Java class that has two sets of variables: one set contains all instance variables in the class and another contains all local variables in a method. These two sets of variables with their values are two `Bindings`. The type of variables in a `Bindings` defines the scope. Just for the sake of this discussion, I will define two scopes: instance scope and local scope. When a method is executed, a variable name is looked up in the local scope `Bindings` first because the local variables take precedence over instance variables. If a variable name is not found in the local scope `Bindings`, it is looked up in the instance scope `Bindings`. When a script is executed, `Bindings` and their scopes play a similar role.

Defining the Script Context

A script engine executes a script in a context. You can think of the context as the environment in which a script is executed. A Java host application provides two things to a script engine: a script and the context in which the script needs to be executed. An instance of the `ScriptContext` interface represents the context for a script. The `SimpleScriptContext` class is an implementation of the `ScriptContext` interface. A script context consists of four components:

- A set of `Bindings`, where each `Bindings` is associated with a different scope

- A `Reader` that is used by the script engine to read inputs

- A `Writer` that is used by the script engine to write outputs

- An error `Writer` that is used by the script engine to write error outputs

The set of `Bindings` in a context is used to pass parameters to the script. A reader and writers in a context control input source and output destinations of the script, respectively. For example, by setting a file writer as a writer, you can send all outputs from a script to a file.

Each script engine maintains a default script context, which it uses to execute scripts. So far, you have executed several scripts without providing script contexts. In those cases, script engines were using their default script contexts to execute scripts. In this section, I will cover how to use an instance of the `ScriptContext` interface by itself. In the next section, I will cover how an instance of the `ScriptContext` interface is passed to a `ScriptEngine` during script execution.

You can create an instance of the `ScriptContext` interface using the `SimpleScriptContext` class, like so:

```
// Create a script context
ScriptContext ctx = new SimpleScriptContext();
```

An instance of the SimpleScriptContext class maintains two instances of Bindings: one for engine scope and one for global scope. The Bindings in the engine scope is created when you create the instance of the SimpleScriptContext. To work with the global scope Bindings, you will need to create an instance of the Bindings interface.

By default, the SimpleScriptContext class initializes the input reader, the output writer, and the error writer for the context to the standard input System.in, the standard output System.out, and standard error output System.err, respectively. You can use the getReader(), getWriter(), and getErrorWriter() methods of the ScriptContext interface to get the references of the reader, writer, and the error writer from the ScriptContext, respectively. Setter methods are also provided to set a reader and writers. The following snippet of code shows how to obtain the reader and writers. It also shows how to set a writer to a FileWriter to write the script output to a file.

```
// Get the reader and writers from the script context
Reader inputReader = ctx.getReader();
Writer outputWriter = ctx.getWriter();
Writer errWriter = ctx.getErrorWriter();

// Write all script outputs to an out.txt file
Writer fileWriter = new FileWriter("out.txt");
ctx.setWriter(fileWriter);
```

After you create a SimpleScriptContext, you can start storing key-value pairs in the engine scope Bindings because an empty Bindings in the engine scope is created when you create the SimpleScriptContext object. The setAttribute() method is used to add a key-value pair to a Bindings. You must provide the key name, value, and the scope for the Bindings. The following snippet of code adds three key-value pairs.

```
// Add three key-value pairs to the engine scope bindings
ctx.setAttribute("year", 1969, ScriptContext.ENGINE_SCOPE);
ctx.setAttribute("month", 9, ScriptContext.ENGINE_SCOPE);
ctx.setAttribute("day", 19, ScriptContext.ENGINE_SCOPE);
```

If you want to add key-value pairs to a Bindings in global scope, you will need to create and set the Bindings first, like so:

```
// Add a global scope Bindings to the context
Bindings globalBindings = new SimpleBindings();
ctx.setBindings(globalBindings, ScriptContext.GLOBAL_SCOPE);
```

Now you can add key-value pairs to the Bindings in global scope using the setAttribute() method, like so:

```
// Add two key-value pairs to the global scope bindings
ctx.setAttribute("year", 1982, ScriptContext.GLOBAL_SCOPE);
ctx.setAttribute("name", "Boni", ScriptContext.GLOBAL_SCOPE);
```

At this point, you can visualize the state of the ScriptContext instance as shown in Figure 10-1.

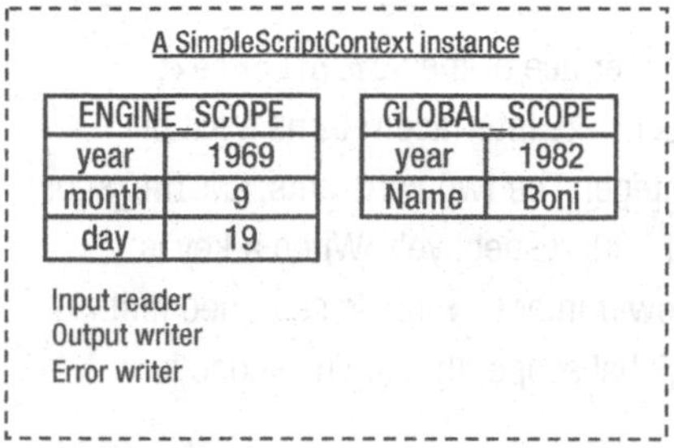

```
A SimpleScriptContext instance

ENGINE_SCOPE          GLOBAL_SCOPE
 year    1969          year    1982
 month    9            Name    Boni
 day     19

Input reader
Output writer
Error writer
```

Figure 10-1. *A pictorial view of an instance of the SimpleScriptContext class*

You can perform several operations on a ScriptContext. You can set a different value for an already stored key using the setAttribute(String name, Object value, int scope) method. You can remove a key-value pair using the removeAttribute(String name, int scope) method for a specified key and a scope. You can get the value of a key in the specified scope using the getAttribute(String name, int scope) method.

The most interesting thing that you can do with a ScriptContext is to retrieve a key value without specifying its scope using its getAttribute(String name) method. A ScriptContext searches for the key in the engine scope Bindings first. If it is not found in the engine scope, the Bindings in the global scope is searched. If the key is found in these scopes, the corresponding value from the scope, in which it is found first, is returned. If neither scope contains the key, null is returned.

In your example, you have stored the key named year in the engine scope as well as in the global scope. The following snippet of code returns 1969 for the key year from the engine scope as the engine scope is searched first. The return type of the getAttribute() method is Object.

```
// Get the value of the key year without specifying the scope.
// It returns 1969 from the Bindings in the engine scope.
int yearValue = (Integer)ctx.getAttribute("year");
```

You have stored the key named name only in the global scope. If you attempt to retrieve its value, the engine scope is searched first, which does not return a match. Subsequently, the global scope is searched and the value "Boni" is returned as shown:

```
// Get the value of the key named name without specifying the scope.
// It returns "Boni" from the Bindings in the global scope.
String nameValue = (String)ctx.getAttribute("name");
```

You can also retrieve the value of a key in a specific scope. The following snippet of code retrieves values for the key "year" from the engine scope and the global scope:

```
// Assigns 1969 to engineScopeYear and 1982 to globalScopeYear
int engineScopeYear = (Integer)ctx.getAttribute("year", ScriptContext.ENGINE_SCOPE);
int globalScopeYear = (Integer)ctx.getAttribute("year", ScriptContext.GLOBAL_SCOPE);
```

■ **Tip** The Java Scripting API defines only two scopes: engine and global. A subinterface of the `ScriptContext` interface may define additional scopes. The `getScopes()` method of the `ScriptContext` interface returns a list of supported scopes as a `List<Integer>`. Note that a scope is represented as an integer. The two constants, `ENGINE_SCOPE` and `GLOBAL_SCOPE` in the `ScriptContext` interface, are assigned values 100 and 200, respectively. When a key is searched in multiple `Bindings` occurring in multiple scopes, the scope with the lower integer value is searched first. Because the value 100 for the engine scope is lower than the value 200 for the global scope, the engine scope is searched for a key first when you do not specify the scope.

Listing 10-9 shows how to work with an instance of a class implementing the `ScriptContext` interface. Note that you do not use a `ScriptContext` in your application by itself. It is used by script engines during script execution. Most often, you manipulate a `ScriptContext` indirectly through a `ScriptEngine` and a `ScriptEngineManager`, which is discussed in detail in the next section.

Listing 10-9. Using an Instance of the ScriptContext Interface

```java
// ScriptContextTest.java
package com.jdojo.script;

import java.util.List;
import javax.script.Bindings;
import javax.script.ScriptContext;
import javax.script.SimpleBindings;
import javax.script.SimpleScriptContext;
import static javax.script.ScriptContext.ENGINE_SCOPE;
import static javax.script.ScriptContext.GLOBAL_SCOPE;

public class ScriptContextTest {
        public static void main(String[] args) {
                // Create a script context
                ScriptContext ctx = new SimpleScriptContext();

                // Get the list of scopes supported by the script context
                List<Integer> scopes = ctx.getScopes();
                System.out.println("Supported Scopes: " + scopes);

                // Add three key-value pairs to the engine scope bindings
                ctx.setAttribute("year", 1969, ENGINE_SCOPE);
                ctx.setAttribute("month", 9, ENGINE_SCOPE);
                ctx.setAttribute("day", 19, ENGINE_SCOPE);

                // Add a global scope Bindings to the context
                Bindings globalBindings = new SimpleBindings();
                ctx.setBindings(globalBindings, GLOBAL_SCOPE);

                // Add two key-value pairs to the global scope bindings
                ctx.setAttribute("year", 1982, GLOBAL_SCOPE);
                ctx.setAttribute("name", "Boni", GLOBAL_SCOPE);
```

```
            // Get the value of year without specifying the scope
            int yearValue = (Integer)ctx.getAttribute("year");
            System.out.println("yearValue = " + yearValue);

            // Get the value of name
            String nameValue = (String)ctx.getAttribute("name");
            System.out.println("nameValue = " + nameValue);

            // Get the value of year from engine  and global scopes
            int engineScopeYear = (Integer)ctx.getAttribute("year", ENGINE_SCOPE);
            int globalScopeYear = (Integer)ctx.getAttribute("year", GLOBAL_SCOPE);

            System.out.println("engineScopeYear = " + engineScopeYear);
            System.out.println("globalScopeYear = " + globalScopeYear);
        }
}
```

```
Supported Scopes: [100, 200]
yearValue = 1969
nameValue = Boni
engineScopeYear = 1969
globalScopeYear = 1982
```

Putting Them Together

In this section, I will show you how instances of Bindings and their scopes, ScriptContext, ScriptEngine, ScriptEngineManager, and the host application work together. The focus will be on how to manipulate the key-value pairs stored in Bindings in different scopes using a ScriptEngine and a ScriptEngineManager.

A ScriptEngineManager maintains a set of key-value pairs in a Bindings. It lets you manipulate those key-value pairs using the following four methods:

- void put(String key, Object value)

- Object get(String key)

- void setBindings(Bindings bindings)

- Bindings getBindings()

The put() method adds a key-value pair to the Bindings. The get() method returns the value for the specified key; it returns null if the key is not found. The Bindings for an engine manager can be replaced using the setBindings() method. The getBindings() method returns the reference of the Bindings of the ScriptEngineManager.

Every ScriptEngine, by default, has a ScriptContext known as its default context. Recall that, besides readers and writers, a ScriptContext has two Bindings: one in the engine scope and one in the global scope. When a ScriptEngine is created, its engine scope Bindings is empty and its global scope Bindings refers to the Bindings of the ScriptEngineManager that created it.

By default, all instances of the ScriptEngine created by a ScriptEngineManager share the Bindings of the ScriptEngineManager. It is possible to have multiple instances of ScriptEngineManager in the same Java application. In that case, all instances of ScriptEngine created by the same ScriptEngineManager share the Bindings of the ScriptEngineManager as their global scope Bindings for their default contexts.

The following snippet of code creates a `ScriptEngineManager`, which is used to create three instances of `ScriptEngine`:

```
// Create a ScriptEngineManager
ScriptEngineManager manager = new ScriptEngineManager();

// Create three ScriptEngines using the same ScriptEngineManager
ScriptEngine engine1 = manager.getEngineByName("JavaScript");
ScriptEngine engine2 = manager.getEngineByName("JavaScript");
ScriptEngine engine3 = manager.getEngineByName("JavaScript");
```

Now, let's add three key-value pairs to the `Bindings` of the `ScriptEngineManager` and two key-value pairs to the engine scope `Bindings` of each `ScriptEngine`.

```
// Add three key-value pairs to the Bindings of the manager
manager.put("K1", "V1");
manager.put("K2", "V2");
manager.put("K3", "V3");

// Add two key-value pairs to each engine
engine1.put("KE11", "VE11");
engine1.put("KE12", "VE12");
engine2.put("KE21", "VE21");
engine2.put("KE22", "VE22");
engine3.put("KE31", "VE31");
engine3.put("KE32", "VE32");
```

Figure 10-2 shows a pictorial view of the state of the `ScriptEngineManager` and three `ScriptEngines` after the snippet of code is executed. It is evident from the figure that the default contexts of all `ScriptEngines` share the `Bindings` of the `ScriptEngineManager` as their global scope `Bindings`.

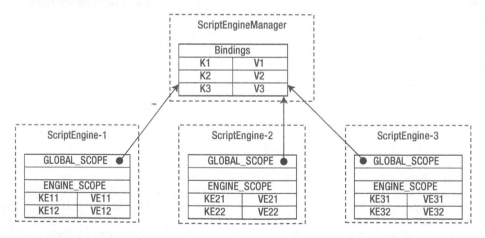

Figure 10-2. *A pictorial view of three ScriptEngines created by a ScriptEngineManager*

The Bindings in a ScriptEngineManager can be modified in the following ways:

- By using the put() method of the ScriptEngineManager

- By getting the reference of the Bindings using the getBindings() method of the ScriptEngineManager, and then using the put() and remove() method on the Bindings

- By getting the reference of the Bindings in the global scope of the default context of a ScriptEngine using its getBindings() method, and then using the put() and remove()method on the Bindings

When the Bindings in a ScriptEngineManager is modified, the global scope Bindings in the default context of all ScriptEngines created by this ScriptEngineManager are modified because they share the same Bindings.

The default context of each ScriptEngine maintains an engine scope Bindings separately. To add a key-value pair to the engine scope Bindings of a ScriptEngine, use its put() method as shown:

```
ScriptEngine engine1 = null; // get an engine

// Add an "engineName" key with its value as "Engine-1" to the
// engine scope Bindings of the default context of engine1
engine1.put("engineName", "Engine-1");
```

The get(String key) method of the ScriptEngine returns the value of the specified key from its engine scope Bindings. The following statement returns "Engine-1", which is the value for the engineName key.

```
String eName = (String)engine1.get("engineName");
```

It is a two-step process to get to the key-value pairs of the global scope Bindings in the default context of a ScriptEngine. First, you need to get the reference of the global scope Bindings using its getBindings() method as shown:

```
Bindings e1Global = engine1.getBindings(ScriptContext.GLOBAL_SCOPE);
```

Now you can modify the global scope Bindings of the engine using the e1Global reference. The following statement adds a key-value pair to the e1Global Bindings:

```
e1Global.put("id", 89999);
```

Because of the sharing of the global scope Bindings of a ScriptEngine by all ScriptEngines, the above snippet of code will add the key "id" with its value to the global scope Bindings of the default context of all ScriptEngines created by the same ScriptEngineManager that created engine1. Modifying the Bindings in a ScriptEngineManager using code as shown above is not recommended. You should modify the Bindings using the ScriptEngineManager reference instead, which makes the logic clearer to the readers of the code.

Listing 10-10 demonstrates the concepts discussed in this section. A ScriptEngineManager adds two key-value pairs with keys n1 and n2 to its Bindings. Two ScriptEngines are created; they add a key called engineName to their engine scope Bindings. When the script is executed, the value of the engineName variable in the script is used from the engine scope of the ScriptEngine. The values for variables n1 and n2 in the script are retrieved from the global scope Bindings of the ScriptEngine. After executing the script for the first time, each ScriptEngine adds a key called n2 with a different value to their engine scope Bindings. When you execute the script for the second time, the value for the n1 variable is retrieved from the global scope Bindings of the engine, whereas the value for the variable n2 is retrieved from the engine scope Bindings as shown in the output.

Listing 10-10. Using Global and Engine Scope Bindings of Engines Created by the Same ScriptEngineManager

```java
// GlobalBindings.java
package com.jdojo.script;

import javax.script.ScriptEngine;
import javax.script.ScriptEngineManager;
import javax.script.ScriptException;

public class GlobalBindings {
        public static void main(String[] args) {
                ScriptEngineManager manager = new ScriptEngineManager();

                // Add two numbers to the Bindings of the manager that will be
                // shared by all its engines
                manager.put("n1", 100);
                manager.put("n2", 200);

                // Create two JavaScript engines and add the name of the engine
                // in the engine scope of the default context of the engines
                ScriptEngine engine1 = manager.getEngineByName("JavaScript");
                engine1.put("engineName", "Engine-1");

                ScriptEngine engine2 = manager.getEngineByName("JavaScript");
                engine2.put("engineName", "Engine-2");

                // Execute a script that adds two numbers and prints the result
                String script = "var sum = n1 + n2; "
                        + "print(engineName + ' - Sum = ' + sum)";

                try {
                        // Execute the script in two engines
                        engine1.eval(script);
                        engine2.eval(script);

                        // Now add a different value for n2 for each engine
                        engine1.put("n2", 1000);
                        engine2.put("n2", 2000);

                        // Execute the script in two engines again
                        engine1.eval(script);
                        engine2.eval(script);
                }
                catch (ScriptException e) {
                        e.printStackTrace();
                }
        }
}
```

```
Engine-1 - Sum = 300
Engine-2 - Sum = 300
Engine-1 - Sum = 1100
Engine-2 - Sum = 2100
```

The story of the global scope Bindings shared by all ScriptEngines that are created by a ScriptEngineManager is not over yet. It is as complex, and confusing, as it can get! Now the focus will be on the effects of using the setBindings() method of ScriptEngineManager class and the ScriptEngine interface. Consider the following snippet of code:

```
// Create a ScriptEngineManager and two ScriptEngines
ScriptEngineManager manager = new ScriptEngineManager();
ScriptEngine engine1 = manager.getEngineByName("JavaScript");
ScriptEngine engine2 = manager.getEngineByName("JavaScript");

// Add two key-value pairs to the manager
manager.put("n1", 100);
manager.put("n2", 200);
```

Figure 10-3 shows the state of the engine manager and its engines after the above script is executed. At this point, there is only one Bindings stored in the ScriptEngineManager and two ScriptEngines are referring to it as their global scope Bindings.

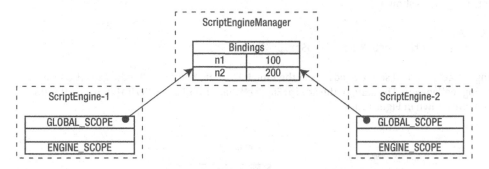

Figure 10-3. *Initial state of ScriptEngineManager and two ScriptEngines*

Let's create a new Bindings and set it as the Bindings for the ScriptEngineManager using its setBindings() method, like so:

```
// Create a Bindings, add two key-value pairs to it, and set it as the new Bindings
// for the manager
Bindings newGlobal = new SimpleBindings();
newGlobal.put("n3", 300);
newGlobal.put("n4", 400);
manager.setBindings(newGlobal);
```

Figure 10-4 shows the state of the ScriptEngineManager and two ScriptEngines after the code is executed. Notice that the ScriptEngineManager has a new Bindings and the two ScriptEngines are still referring to the old Bindings as their global scope Bindings.

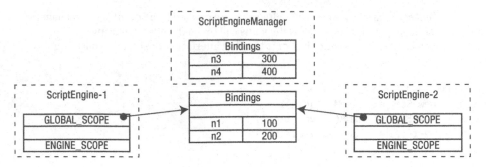

Figure 10-4. *State of ScriptEngineManager and two ScriptEngines after a new Bindings is set to the ScriptEngineManager*

At this point, any changes made to the `Bindings` of the `ScriptEngineManager` will not be reflected in the global scope `Bindings` of the two `ScriptEngines`. You can still make changes to the `Bindings` shared by the two `ScriptEngines` and both `ScriptEngines` will see the changes made by either of them.

Let's create a new `ScriptEngine` as shown:

```
// Create a new ScriptEngine
ScriptEngine engine3 = manager.getEngineByName("JavaScript");
```

Recall that a `ScriptEngine` gets a global scope `Bindings` at the time it is created and that `Bindings` is the same as the `Bindings` of the `ScriptEngineManager`. The state of the `ScriptEngineManager` and three ScriptEngines, after the above statement is executed, are shown in Figure 10-5.

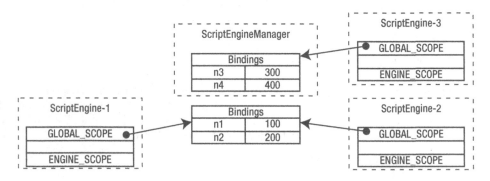

Figure 10-5. *State of ScriptEngineManager and three ScriptEngines after the third ScriptEngine is created*

Here is another twist to the so-called "globalness" of the global scope of `ScriptEngines`. This time, you will use the `setBindings()` method of a `ScriptEngine` to set its global scope `Bindings`. Figure 10-6 shows the state of the `ScriptEngineManager` and three ScriptEngines after the following snippet of code is executed:

```
// Set a new Bindings for the global scope of engine1
Bindings newGlobalEngine1 = new SimpleBindings();
newGlobalEngine1.put("n5", 500);
newGlobalEngine1.put("n6", 600);
engine1.setBindings(newGlobalEngine1, ScriptContext.GLOBAL_SCOPE);
```

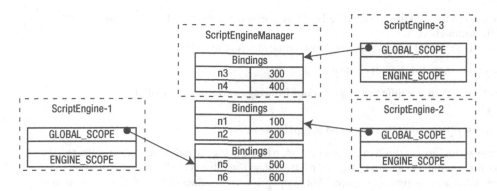

Figure 10-6. *State of ScriptEngineManager and Three ScriptEngines After a New Global Scope Bindings Is Set for engine1*

■ **Tip** By default, all ScriptEngines that a ScriptEngineManager creates share its Bindings as their global scope Bindings. If you use the setBindings() method of a ScriptEngine to set its global scope Bindings or if you use the setBindings() method of a ScriptEngineManager to set its Bindings, you break the "globalness" chain as discussed in this section. To keep the "globalness" chain intact, you should always use the put() method of the ScriptEngineManager to add key-value pairs to its Bindings. To remove a key-value pair from the global scope of all ScriptEngines created by a ScriptEngineManager, you need to get the reference of the Bindings using the getBindings() method of the ScriptEngineManager and use the remove() method on the Bindings.

Using a Custom ScriptContext

In the previous section, you saw that each ScriptEngine has a default script context. The get(), put(), getBindings(), and setBindings() methods of the ScriptEngine operate on its default ScriptContext. When no ScriptContext is specified to the eval() method of the ScriptEngine, the default context of the engine is used. The following two versions of the eval() method of the ScriptEngine use its default context to execute the script:

- Object eval(String script)
- Object eval(Reader reader)

You can pass a Bindings to the following two versions of the eval() method:

- Object eval(String script, Bindings bindings)
- Object eval(Reader reader, Bindings bindings)

These versions of the eval() method do not use the default context of the ScriptEngine. They use a new ScriptContext whose engine scope Bindings is the one passed to these methods and the global scope Bindings is the same as for the default context of the engine. Note that these two versions of the eval() method keep the default context of the ScriptEngine untouched.

You can pass a ScriptContext to the following two versions of the eval() method:

- Object eval(String script, ScriptContext context)
- Object eval(Reader reader, ScriptContext context)

These versions of the eval() method use the specified context to execute the script. They keep the default context of the ScriptEngine untouched.

The three sets of the eval() method let you execute scripts using different isolation levels:

- The first set lets you share the default context by all scripts.

- The second set lets scripts use different engine scope Bindings and share the global scope Bindings.

- The third set lets scripts execute in an isolated ScriptContext.

Listing 10-11 shows how scripts are executed in different isolation levels using the different version of the eval() method. The program uses three variables called msg, n1, and n2. It displays the value stored in the msg variable. The values of n1 and n2 are added and the sum is displayed. The script prints what values of n1 and n2 were used in computing the sum. The value of n1 is stored in the Bindings of ScriptEngineManager that is shared by the default context of all ScriptEngines. The value of n2 is stored in the engine scope of the default context and the custom contexts. The script is executed twice using the default context of the engine, once in the beginning and once in the end, to prove that using a custom Bindings or a ScriptContext in the eval() method does not affect the Bindings in the default context of the ScriptEngine. The program declares a throws clause in its main() method to keep the code shorter.

Listing 10-11. Using Different Isolation Levels for Executing Scripts

```java
// CustomContext.java
package com.jdojo.script;

import javax.script.Bindings;
import javax.script.ScriptContext;
import javax.script.ScriptEngine;
import javax.script.ScriptEngineManager;
import javax.script.ScriptException;
import javax.script.SimpleScriptContext;
import static javax.script.SimpleScriptContext.ENGINE_SCOPE;
import static javax.script.SimpleScriptContext.GLOBAL_SCOPE;

public class CustomContext {
        public static void main(String[] args) throws ScriptException {
                ScriptEngineManager manager = new ScriptEngineManager();
                ScriptEngine engine = manager.getEngineByName("JavaScript");

                // Add n1 to Bindings of the manager, which will be shared
                // by all engines as their global scope Bindings
                manager.put("n1", 100);

                // Prepare the script
                String script = "var sum = n1 + n2;" +
                            "print(msg + " +
                            "' n1=' + n1 + ', n2=' + n2 + " +
                            "', sum=' + sum);";

                // Add n2 to the engine scope of the default context of the engine
                engine.put("n2", 200);
                engine.put("msg", "Using the default context:");
                engine.eval(script);
```

```
            // Use a Bindings to execute the script
            Bindings bindings = engine.createBindings();
            bindings.put("n2", 300);
            bindings.put("msg", "Using a Bindings:");
            engine.eval(script, bindings);

            // Use a ScriptContext to execute the script
            ScriptContext ctx = new SimpleScriptContext();
            Bindings ctxGlobalBindings = engine.createBindings();
            ctx.setBindings(ctxGlobalBindings, GLOBAL_SCOPE);
            ctx.setAttribute("n1", 400, GLOBAL_SCOPE);
            ctx.setAttribute("n2", 500, ENGINE_SCOPE);
            ctx.setAttribute("msg", "Using a ScriptContext:", ENGINE_SCOPE);
            engine.eval(script, ctx);

            // Execute the script again using the default context to
            // prove that the default context is unaffected.
            engine.eval(script);
    }
}
```

```
Using the default context: n1=100, n2=200, sum=300
Using a Bindings: n1=100, n2=300, sum=400
Using a ScriptContext: n1=400, n2=500, sum=900
Using the default context: n1=100, n2=200, sum=300
```

Return Value of the eval() Method

The eval() method of the ScriptEngine returns an Object, which is the last value in the script. It returns null if there is no last value in the script. It is error prone, and confusing at the same time, to depend on the last value in a script. The following snippet of code shows some examples of using the return value of the eval() method for Nashorn. The comments in the code indicate the returned value from the eval() method.

```
Object result = null;

// Assigns 3 to result
result = engine.eval("1 + 2;");

// Assigns 7 to result
result = engine.eval("1 + 2; 3 + 4;");

// Assigns 6 to result
result = engine.eval("1 + 2; 3 + 4; var v = 5; v = 6;");

// Assigns 7 to result
result = engine.eval("1 + 2; 3 + 4; var v = 5;");

// Assigns null to result
result = engine.eval("print(1 + 2)");
```

It is better not to depend on the returned value from the eval() method. You should pass a Java object to the script as a parameter and let the script store the returned value of the script in that object. After the eval() method is executed, you can query that Java object for the returned value. Listing 10-12 contains the code for a Result class that wraps an integer. You will pass an object of the Result class to the script that will store the returned value in it. After the script finishes, you can read the integer value stored in the Result object in your Java code. The Result needs to be declared public so it is accessible to the script engine. The program in Listing 10-13 shows how to pass a Result object to a script that populates the Result object with a value. The program contains a throws clause in the main() method's declaration to keep the code short.

Listing 10-12. A Result Class That Wraps an Integer

```java
// Result.java
package com.jdojo.script;

public class Result {
        private int val = -1;

        public void setValue(int x) {
                val = x;
        }

        public int getValue() {
                return val;
        }
}
```

Listing 10-13. Collecting the Return Value of a Script in a Result Object

```java
// ResultBearingScript.java
package com.jdojo.script;

import javax.script.ScriptEngine;
import javax.script.ScriptEngineManager;
import javax.script.ScriptException;

public class ResultBearingScript {
        public static void main(String[] args) throws ScriptException {
                // Get the Nashorn engine
                ScriptEngineManager manager = new ScriptEngineManager();
                ScriptEngine engine = manager.getEngineByName("JavaScript");

                // Pass a Result object to the script. The script will store the
                // result of the script in the result object
                Result result = new Result();
                engine.put("result", result);

                // Store the script in a String
                String script = "3 + 4; result.setValue(101);";

                // Execute the script, which uses the passed in Result object to
                // return a value
                engine.eval(script);
```

```
        // Use the result object to get the returned value from the script
        int returnedValue = result.getValue(); // Will be 101

        System.out.println("Returned value is " + returnedValue);
    }
}
```

```
Returned value is 101
```

Reserved Keys for Engine Scope Bindings

Typically, a key in the engine scope Bindings represents a script variable. Some keys are reserved and they have special meanings. Their values may be passed to the engine by the implementation of the engine. An implementation may define additional reserved keys.

Table 10-2 contains the list of all reserved keys. Those keys are also declared as constants in the ScriptEngine interface. An implementation of a script engine is not required to pass all these keys to the engine in the engine scope bindings. As a developer, you are not supposed to use these keys to pass parameters from a Java application to a script engine.

Table 10-2. *The List of Reserved Keys for Engine Scope Bindings*

Key	Constant in ScriptEngine Interface	Meaning of the Value of the key
"javax.script.argv"	ScriptEngine.ARGV	Used to pass an array of Object to pass a set of positional argument.
"javax.script.engine"	ScriptEngine.ENGINE	The name of the script engine.
"javax.script.engine_version"	ScriptEngine.ENGINE_VERSION	The version of the script engine.
"javax.script.filename"	ScriptEngine.FILENAME	Used to pass the name of the file or the resource that the source of the script.
"javax.script.language"	ScriptEngine.LANGUAGE	The name of the language supported by the script engine.
"javax.script.language_version"	ScriptEngine.LANGUAGE_VERSION	The version of the scripting language supported by the engine.
"javax.script.name"	ScriptEngine.NAME	The short name of the scripting language.

Changing the Default ScriptContext

You can get and set the default context of a ScriptEngine using its getContext() and setContext() methods, respectively, as shown:

```
ScriptEngineManager manager = new ScriptEngineManager();
ScriptEngine engine = manager.getEngineByName("JavaScript");

// Get the default context of the ScriptEngine
ScriptContext defaultCtx = engine.getContext();
```

```
// Work with defaultCtx here

// Create a new context
ScriptContext ctx = new SimpleScriptContext();

// Configure ctx here

// Set ctx as the new default context for the engine
engine.setContext(ctx);
```

Note that setting a new default context for a ScriptEngine will not use the Bindings of the ScriptEngineManager as its global scope Bindings. If you want the new default context to use the Bindings of the ScriptEngineManager, you need set it explicitly as shown:

```
// Create a new context
ScriptContext ctx = new SimpleScriptContext();

// Set the global scope Bindings for ctx the same as the Bindings for the manager
ctx.setBindings(manager.getBindings(), ScriptContext.GLOBAL_SCOPE);

// Set ctx as the new default context for the engine
engine.setContext(ctx);
```

Sending Scripts Output to a File

You can customize the input source, output destination, and error output destination of a script execution. You need to set appropriate reader and writers for the ScriptContext that is used to execute a script. The following snippet of code will write the script output to a file named jsoutput.txt in the current directory:

```
// Create a FileWriter
FileWriter writer = new FileWriter("jsoutput.txt");

// Get the default context of the engine
ScriptContext defaultCtx = engine.getContext();

// Set the output writer for the default context of the engine
defaultCtx.setWriter(writer);
```

The code sets a custom output writer for the default context of the ScriptEngine that will be used during the execution of scripts that use the default context. If you want to use a custom output writer for a specific execution of a script, you need to use a custom ScriptContext and set its writer.

■ **Tip** Setting a custom output writer for a ScriptContext does not affect the destination of the standard output of the Java application. To redirect the standard output of the Java application, you need to use the System.setOut() method.

Listing 10-14 shows how to write output of a script execution to a file named jsoutput.txt. The program prints the full path of the output file on the standard output. You may get a different output when you run the program. You need to open the output file in a text editor to see the script's output.

Listing 10-14. Writing the Output of Scripts to a File

```java
// CustomScriptOutput.java
package com.jdojo.script;

import java.io.File;
import java.io.FileWriter;
import java.io.IOException;
import javax.script.ScriptContext;
import javax.script.ScriptEngine;
import javax.script.ScriptEngineManager;
import javax.script.ScriptException;

public class CustomScriptOutput {
        public static void main(String[] args) {
                // Get the Nashorn engine
                ScriptEngineManager manager = new ScriptEngineManager();
                ScriptEngine engine = manager.getEngineByName("JavaScript");

                // Print the absolute path of the output file
                File outputFile = new File("jsoutput.txt");
                System.out.println("Script output will be written to " +
                                outputFile.getAbsolutePath());

                FileWriter writer = null;

                try {
                        writer = new FileWriter(outputFile);

                        // Set a custom output writer for the engine
                        ScriptContext defaultCtx = engine.getContext();
                        defaultCtx.setWriter(writer);

                        // Execute a script
                        String script = "print('Hello custom output writer')";
                        engine.eval(script);
                }
                catch (IOException | ScriptException e) {
                        e.printStackTrace();
                }
                finally {
                        if (writer != null) {
                                try {
                                        writer.close();
                                }
```

```
                            catch (IOException e) {
                                e.printStackTrace();
                            }
                    }
                }
            }
}
```

```
Script output will be written to C:\jsoutput.txt
```

Invoking Procedures in Scripts

A scripting language may allow for creating procedures, functions, and methods. The Java Scripting API lets you invoke such procedures, functions, and methods from a Java application. I will use the term "procedure" to mean procedure, function, and method in this section. I will use the specific term when the context of the discussion requires it.

Not all script engines are required to support procedure invocation. The Nashorn JavaScript engine supports procedure invocation. If a script engine supports it, the implementation of the script engine class must implement the Invocable interface. It is the responsibility of the developer to check if a script engine implements the Invocable interface, before invoking a procedure. Invoking a procedure is a four-step process:

- Check if the script engine supports procedure invocation.

- Cast the engine reference to the Invocable type.

- Evaluate the script that contains the source code for the procedure.

- Use the invokeFunction() method of the Invocable interface to invoke procedures and functions. Use the invokeMethod() method to invoke methods of the objects created in a scripting language.

The following snippet of code performs the check that the script engine implementation class implements the Invocable interface:

```
// Get the Nashorn engine
ScriptEngineManager manager = new ScriptEngineManager();
ScriptEngine engine = manager.getEngineByName("JavaScript");

// Make sure the script engine implements the Invocable interface
if (engine instanceof Invocable) {
        System.out.println("Invoking procedures is supported.");
else
        System.out.println("Invoking procedures is not supported.");
}
```

The second step is to cast the engine reference to the Invocable interface type.

```
Invocable inv = (Invocable)engine;
```

The third step is to evaluate the script, so the script engine compiles and stores the compiled form of the procedure for later invocation. The following snippet of code performs this step:

```
// Declare a function named add that adds two numbers
String script = "function add(n1, n2) { return n1 + n2; }";

// Evaluate the function. Call to eval() does not invoke the function.
// It just compiles it.
engine.eval(script);
```

The last step is to invoke the procedure or function.

```
// Invoke the add function with 30 and 40 as the function's arguments.
// It is as if you called add(30, 40) in the script.
Object result = inv.invokeFunction("add", 30, 40);
```

The first argument to the invokeFunction() is the name of the procedure or function. The second argument is a varargs that is used to specify arguments to the procedure or function. The invokeFunction() method returns the value returned by the procedure or function.

Listing 10-15 shows how to invoke a function. It invokes a function written in Nashorn JavaScript.

Listing 10-15. Invoking a Function Written in Nashorn JavaScript

```
// InvokeFunction.java
package com.jdojo.script;

import javax.script.Invocable;
import javax.script.ScriptEngine;
import javax.script.ScriptEngineManager;
import javax.script.ScriptException;

public class InvokeFunction {
        public static void main(String[] args) {
                ScriptEngineManager manager = new ScriptEngineManager();
                ScriptEngine engine = manager.getEngineByName("JavaScript");

                // Make sure the script engine implements the Invocable interface
                if (!(engine instanceof Invocable)) {
                        System.out.println("Invoking procedures is not supported.");
                        return;
                }

                // Cast the engine reference to the Invocable type
                Invocable inv = (Invocable)engine;

                try {
                        String script = "function add(n1, n2) { return n1 + n2; }";

                        // Evaluate the script first
                        engine.eval(script);
```

```
                    // Invoke the add function twice
                    Object result1 = inv.invokeFunction("add", 30, 40);
                    System.out.println("Result1 = " + result1);

                    Object result2 = inv.invokeFunction("add", 10, 20);
                    System.out.println("Result2 = " + result2);
            }
            catch (ScriptException | NoSuchMethodException e) {
                    e.printStackTrace();
            }
        }
    }
}
```

```
Result1 = 70
Result2 = 30
```

An object-oriented or object-based scripting language may let you define objects and their methods. You can invoke methods of such objects using the invokeMethod() method of the Invocable interface, which is declared as follows:

```
Object invokeMethod(Object objectRef, String name, Object... args)
```

The first argument is the reference of the object, the second argument is the name of the method that you want to invoke on the object, and the third argument is a varargs argument that is used to pass arguments to the method being invoked.

Listing 10-16 demonstrates the invocation of a method on an object that is created in Nashorn JavaScript. Note that the object is created inside the Nashorn script. To invoke the method of the object from Java, you need to obtain the reference of the object through the script engine. The program evaluates the script that creates an object with an add() method and stores its reference in a variable named calculator. The engine.get("calculator") method returns the reference of the calculator object to the Java code.

Listing 10-16. Invoking a Method on an Object Created in Nashorn JavaScript

```
// InvokeMethod.java
package com.jdojo.script;

import javax.script.Invocable;
import javax.script.ScriptEngine;
import javax.script.ScriptEngineManager;
import javax.script.ScriptException;

public class InvokeMethod {
        public static void main(String[] args) {
                // Get the Nashorn engine
                ScriptEngineManager manager = new ScriptEngineManager();
                ScriptEngine engine = manager.getEngineByName("JavaScript");

                // Make sure the script engine implements the Invocable interface
                if (!(engine instanceof Invocable)) {
                        System.out.println("Invoking methods is not supported.");
                        return;
                }
```

```
        // Cast the engine reference to the Invocable type
        Invocable inv = (Invocable) engine;

        try {
                // Declare a global object with an add() method
                String script = "var calculator = new Object();" +
                    "calculator.add = function add(n1, n2){return n1 + n2;}";

                // Evaluate the script first
                engine.eval(script);

                // Get the calculator object reference created in the script
                Object calculator = engine.get("calculator");

                // Invoke the add() method on the calculator object
                Object result = inv.invokeMethod(calculator, "add", 30, 40);
                System.out.println("Result = " + result);
        }
        catch (ScriptException | NoSuchMethodException e) {
                e.printStackTrace();
        }
    }
}
```

Result = 70

■ **Tip**   Use the `Invocable` interface to execute procedures, functions, and methods repeatedly. Evaluation of the script, having procedures, functions, and methods, stores the intermediate code in the engine that results in performance gain on their repeated execution.

Implementing Java Interfaces in Scripts

The Java Scripting API lets you implement Java interfaces in a scripting language. Methods of the Java interface may be implemented in scripts using top-level procedures or instance methods of an object.

The advantage of implementing a Java interface in a scripting language is that you can use instances of the interface in Java code as if the interface was implemented in Java. You can pass instances of the interface as arguments to Java methods.

The `getInterface()` method of the `Invocable` interface is used to obtain the instances of a Java interface that is implemented in scripts. The method has two versions:

- `<T> T getInterface(Class<T> cls)`

- `<T> T getInterface(Object obj, Class<T> cls)`

The first version is used to obtain an instance of a Java interface whose methods are implemented as top-level procedures in scripts. The interface type is passed to this method as its argument. Suppose you have a `Calculator` interface, as declared in Listing 10-17, that has two methods called add() and subtract().

Listing 10-17. A Calculator Interface

```java
// Calculator.java
package com.jdojo.script;

public interface Calculator {
        int add (int n1, int n2);
        int subtract (int n1, int n2);
}
```

Consider the following two top-level functions written in JavaScript:

```javascript
function add(n1, n2) {
        return n1 + n2;
}

function subtract(n1, n2) {
        return n1 - n2;
}
```

The above two functions provide the implementations for the two methods of the `Calculator` interface. After the above functions are compiled by a JavaScript engine, you can obtain an instance of the `Calculator` interface as shown:

```java
// Cast the engine reference to the Invocable type
Invocable inv = (Invocable)engine;

// Get the reference of the Calculator interface
Calculator calc = inv.getInterface(Calculator.class);
if (calc == null) {
        System.err.println("Calculator interface implementation not found.");
}
else {
        // Use calc to call add() and subtract() methods
}
```

You can add two numbers as shown:

```java
int sum = calc.add(15, 10);
```

Listing 10-18 shows how to implement a Java interface using top-level procedures in Nashorn. Please consult the documentation of a scripting language to learn how it supports this functionality.

Listing 10-18. Implementing a Java Interface Using Top-Level Functions in Script

```java
// UsingInterfaces.java
package com.jdojo.script;

import javax.script.Invocable;
import javax.script.ScriptEngine;
import javax.script.ScriptEngineManager;
import javax.script.ScriptException;
```

```java
public class UsingInterfaces {
        public static void main(String[] args) {
                // Get the Nashorn engine
                ScriptEngineManager manager = new ScriptEngineManager();
                ScriptEngine engine = manager.getEngineByName("JavaScript");

                // Make sure the script engine implements Invocable interface
                if (!(engine instanceof Invocable)) {
                        System.out.println("Interface implementation in script"
                                + " is not supported.");
                        return;
                }

                // Cast the engine reference to the Invocable type
                Invocable inv = (Invocable) engine;

                // Create the script for add() and subtract() functions
                String script = "function add(n1, n2) { return n1 + n2; } "
                        + "function subtract(n1, n2) { return n1 - n2; }";

                try {
                        // Compile the script that will be stored in the engine
                        engine.eval(script);

                        // Get the interface implementation
                        Calculator calc = inv.getInterface(Calculator.class);
                        if (calc == null) {
                                System.err.println("Calculator interface " +
                                        "implementation not found.");
                                return;
                        }

                        int result1 = calc.add(15, 10);
                        System.out.println("add(15, 10) = " + result1);

                        int result2 = calc.subtract(15, 10);
                        System.out.println("subtract(15, 10) = " + result2);
                }
                catch (ScriptException e) {
                        e.printStackTrace();
                }
        }
}
```

```
add(15, 10) = 25
subtract(15, 10) = 5
```

The second version of the getInterface() method is used to obtain an instance of a Java interface whose methods are implemented as instance methods of an object. Its first argument is the reference of the object that is created in the scripting language. The instance methods of the object implement the interface type passed in as the second argument. The following code in Nashorn creates an object whose instance methods implement the Calculator interface:

```
// Create an object
var calc = new Object();

// Add add() and subtract() methods to the calc object
calc.add = function add(n1, n2) {
            return n1 + n2;
        };
calc.subtract = function subtract(n1, n2) {
                return n1 - n2;
            };
```

When instance methods of a script object implements methods of a Java interface, you need to perform an extra step. You need to get the reference of the script object before you can get the instance of the interface, as shown:

```
// Get the reference of the global script object obj
Object calc = engine.get("calc");

// Get the implementation of the Calculator interface
Calculator calculator = inv.getInterface(calc, Calculator.class);
```

Listing 10-19 shows how to implement methods of a Java interface as instance methods of an object using Nashorn.

Listing 10-19. Implementing Methods of a Java Interface as Instance Methods of an Object in a Script

```
// ScriptObjectImplInterface.java
package com.jdojo.script;

import javax.script.Invocable;
import javax.script.ScriptEngine;
import javax.script.ScriptEngineManager;
import javax.script.ScriptException;

public class ScriptObjectImplInterface {
    public static void main(String[] args) {
        // Get the Nashorn engine
        ScriptEngineManager manager = new ScriptEngineManager();
        ScriptEngine engine = manager.getEngineByName("JavaScript");

        // Make sure the engine implements the Invocable interface
        if (!(engine instanceof Invocable)) {
            System.out.println("Interface implementation in " +
                                "script is not supported.");
            return;
        }
```

```
        // Cast the engine reference to the Invocable type
        Invocable inv = (Invocable)engine;

        String script = "var calc = new Object(); " +
                "calc.add = function add(n1, n2) {return n1 + n2; }; " +
                "calc.subtract = function subtract(n1, n2) {return n1 - n2;};";

        try {
                // Compile and store the script in the engine
                engine.eval(script);

                // Get the reference of the global script object calc
                Object calc = engine.get("calc");

                // Get the implementation of the Calculator interface
                Calculator calculator = inv.getInterface(calc, Calculator.class);
                if (calculator == null) {
                        System.err.println("Calculator interface " +
                                                "implementation not found.");
                        return;
                }

                int result1 = calculator.add(15, 10);
                System.out.println( "add(15, 10) = " + result1);

                int result2 = calculator.subtract(15, 10);
                System.out.println("subtract(15, 10) = " + result2);
        }
        catch (ScriptException e) {
                        e.printStackTrace();
        }
    }
}
```

```
add(15, 10) = 25
subtract(15, 10) = 5
```

Using Compiled Scripts

A script engine may allow compiling a script and executing it repeatedly. Executing compiled scripts may increase the performance of an application. A script engine may compile and store scripts in the form of Java classes, Java class files, or in a language-specific form.

Not all script engines are required to support script compilation. Script engines that support script compilation must implement the Compilable interface. Nashorn engine supports script compilation. The following snippet of code checks if a script engine implements the Compilable interface:

```
// Get the script engine reference
ScriptEngineManager manager = new ScriptEngineManager();
ScriptEngine engine = manager.getEngineByName("YOUR_ENGINE_NAME");
```

```
if (engine instanceof Compilable) {
        System.out.println("Script compilation is supported.");
}
else {
        System.out.println("Script compilation is not supported.");
}
```

Once you know that a script engine implements the Compilable interface, you can cast its reference to a Compilable type as

```
// Cast the engine reference to the Compilable type
Compilable comp = (Compilable)engine;
```

The Compilable interface contains two methods:

- CompiledScript compile(String script) throws ScriptException

- CompiledScript compile(Reader script) throws ScriptException

The two versions of the method differ only in the type of the source of the script. The first version accepts the script as a String and the second one as a Reader.

The compile() method returns an object of the CompiledScript class. CompiledScript is an abstract class. The provider of the script engine provides the concrete implementation of this class. A CompiledScript is associated with the ScriptEngine that creates it. The getEngine() method of the CompiledScript class returns the reference of the ScriptEngine to which it is associated.

To execute a compiled script, you need to call one of the following eval() methods of the CompiledScript class:

- Object eval() throws ScriptException

- Object eval(Bindings bindings) throws ScriptException

- Object eval(ScriptContext context) throws ScriptException

The eval() method without any arguments uses the default script context of the script engine to execute the compiled script. The other two versions work the same as the eval() method of the ScriptEngine interface when you pass a Bindings or a ScriptContext to them.

Listing 10-20 shows how to compile a script and execute it. It executes the same compiled script twice with different parameters.

Listing 10-20. Using Compiled Scripts

```
// CompilableTest .java
package com.jdojo.script;

import javax.script.Bindings;
import javax.script.Compilable;
import javax.script.CompiledScript;
import javax.script.ScriptEngine;
import javax.script.ScriptEngineManager;
import javax.script.ScriptException;

public class CompilableTest  {
        public static void main(String[] args) {
                // Get the Nashorn engine
                ScriptEngineManager manager = new ScriptEngineManager();
```

```
        ScriptEngine engine = manager.getEngineByName("JavaScript");
        if (!(engine instanceof Compilable)) {
                System.out.println("Script compilation not supported.");
                return;
        }

        // Cast the engine reference to the Compilable type
        Compilable comp = (Compilable)engine;

        try {
                // Compile a script
                String script = "print(n1 + n2)";
                CompiledScript cScript = comp.compile(script);

                // Store n1 and n2 script variables in a Bindings
                Bindings scriptParams = engine.createBindings();
                scriptParams.put("n1", 2);
                scriptParams.put("n2", 3);
                cScript.eval(scriptParams);

                // Execute the script again with different values for n1 and n2
                scriptParams.put("n1", 9);
                scriptParams.put("n2", 7);
                cScript.eval(scriptParams);
        }
        catch (ScriptException e) {
                e.printStackTrace();
        }
    }
}
```

5
16

Using Java in Scripting Languages

Scripting languages allow using Java class libraries in scripts. Each scripting language has its own syntax for using Java classes. It is not possible, and is outside the scope of this book, to discuss the syntax of all scripting languages. In this section, I will discuss the syntax of using some Java constructs in Nashorn. For the complete coverage of the Nashorn language, please refer to the web site at https://wiki.openjdk.java.net/display/Nashorn/Main.

Declaring Variables

Declaring variables in a scripting language is not related to Java. Typically, scripting languages let you assign values to variables without declaring them. The types of variables are determined at runtime based on the types of the values they store.

In Nashorn, the keyword var is used to declare a variable. If you wish, you can omit the keyword var in a variable declaration. The following snippet of code declares two variables and assigns them a value:

```
// Declare a variable named msg using the var keyword
var msg = "Hello";

// Declare a variable named greeting without using the keyword var
greeting = "Hello";
```

Importing Java Classes

There are four ways to import Java classes in scripts in Nashorn:

- Using the Packages global object
- Using the type() function of the Java global object
- Using the importPackage() and importClass() functions
- Using a JavaImporter in a with clause

The following sections will describe the four ways of importing Java classes in script in detail.

Using the Packages Global Object

Nashorn defines all Java packages as properties of a global variable named Packages. For example, the java.lang and javax.swing packages may be referred to as Packages.java.lang and Packages.javax.swing, respectively. The following snippet of code uses the java.util.List and javax.swing.JFrame in Nashorn:

```
// Create a List
var list1 = new Packages.java.util.ArrayList();

// Create a JFrame
var frame1 = new Packages.javax.swing.JFrame("Test");
```

Nashorn declares java, javax, org, com, edu, and net as global variables that are aliases for Packages.java, Packages.javax, Packages.org, Packages.com, Packages.edu, and Packages.net, respectively. Class names in examples in this book start with the prefix com, for example, com.jdojo.script.Test. To use this class name inside the JavaScript code, you may use Packages.com.jdojo.script.Test or com.jdojo.script.Test. However, if a class name does not start with one of these predefined prefixes, you must use the Packages global variable to access it; for example, if your class name is p1.Test, you need to access it using Packages.p1.Test inside JavaScript code. The following snippet of code uses the java and javax aliases for Packages.java and Packages.javax:

```
// Create a List
var list2 = new java.util.ArrayList();

// Create a JFrame
var frame2 = new javax.swing.JFrame("Test");
```

Using the Java Global Object

Accessing packages as the properties of the Packages object was also supported in Rhino JavaScript in Java 7. Using the Packages object is slower and error-prone. Nashorn defines a new global object called Java that contains many useful functions to work with Java packages and classes. If you are using Java 8 or later, you should use the Java object over the Packages object. The type() function of the Java object imports a Java type into the script. You need to pass the fully qualified name of the Java type to import. In Nashorn, the following snippet of code imports the java.util.ArrayList class and creates its object:

```
// Import java.util.ArrayList type and call it ArrayList
var ArrayList = Java.type("java.util.ArrayList");

// Create an object of the ArrayList type
var list = new ArrayList();
```

In the code, you call the imported type returned from the Java.type() function as ArrayList that is also the name of the class that is imported. You do it to make the next statement read as if it was written Java. Readers of the second statement will know that you are creating an object of the ArrayList class. However, you can give the imported type any name you want. The following snippet of code imports java.util.ArrayList and calls it MyList:

```
// Import java.util.ArrayList type and call it MyList
var MyList = Java.type("java.util.ArrayList");

// Create an object of the MyList type
var list2 = new MyList();
```

Using the importPackage() and importClass() Functions

Rhino JavaScript allowed using the simple names of the Java types in script. Rhino JavaScript had two built-in functions called importPackage() and importClass() to import all classes from a package and a class from a package, respectively. For compatibility reasons, Nashorn keeps these functions. To use these functions in Nashorn, you need to load the compatibility module from mozilla_compat.js file using the load() function. The following snippet of code rewrites the above logic using these functions:

```
// Load the compatibility module. It is needed in Nashorn, not in Rhino.
load("nashorn:mozilla_compat.js");

// Import ArrayList class from the java.util package
importClass(java.util.ArrayList);

// Import all classes from the javax.swing package
importPackage(javax.swing);

// Use simple names of classes
var list1 = new ArrayList();
var frame1 = new JFrame("Test");
```

JavaScript does not import all classes from the java.lang package automatically because JavaScript classes with the same names, for example, String, Object, Number, etc., will conflict with class names in the java.lang package. To use a class from the java.lang package, you can import it or use the Packages or Java variable to use its fully qualified name. You cannot import all classes from the java.lang package. The following snippet of code generates an error because the String class name is already defined in JavaScript:

```
// Load the compatibility module. It is needed in Nashorn, not in Rhino.
load("nashorn:mozilla_compat.js");

importClass(java.lang.String); // An error
```

If you want to use the java.lang.String class, you need to use its fully qualified name. The following snippet of code uses the built-in JavaScript String class and the java.lang.String class:

```
var javaStr = new java.lang.String("Hello"); // Java String class
var jsStr = new String("Hello");             // JavaScript String class
```

If a class name in the java.lang package does not conflict with a JavaScript top-level class name, you can use the importClass() function to import the Java class. For example, you can use the following snippet of code to use the java.lang.System class:

```
// Load the compatibility module. It is needed in Nashorn, not in Rhino.
load("nashorn:mozilla_compat.js");

importClass(java.lang.System);

var jsStr = new String("Hello");
System.out.println(jsStr);
```

In the above snippet of code, jsStr is a JavaScript String that has been passed to the System.out.println() Java method that accepts a java.lang.String type. JavaScript takes care of the conversion from a JavaScript type to a Java type automatically in such cases.

Using the JavaImporter Object

In JavaScript, you can use the simple names of classes using a JavaImporter object reference in a with clause. The constructor of the JavaImporter class accepts a list of Java packages and classes. You can create a JavaImporter object as shown:

```
// Import all classes from the java.lang package
var langPkg = new JavaImporter(Packages.java.lang);

// Import all classes from the java.lang and java.util packages and the
// JFrame class from the javax.swing package
var pkg2 = JavaImporter(java.lang, java.util, javax.swing.JFrame);
```

Note the use of the new operator in the first statement. The second statement does not use the new operator. Both statements are valid in JavaScript.

The following snippet of code creates a JavaImporter object and uses it in a with clause:

```
// Create a Java importer for java.lang and java.util packages
var javaLangAndUtilPkg = JavaImporter(java.lang, java.util);

// Use the imported types in the with clause
with (javaLangAndUtilPkg) {
        var list = new ArrayList();
        list.add("one");
        list.add("two");
        System.out.println("Hello");
        System.out.println("List is " + list);
}
```

```
Hello
List is [one, two]
```

Creating and Using Java Objects

Use the new operator with a constructor to create a new Java object in scripts. The following snippet of code creates a String object in Nashorn:

```
// Create a Java String object
var javaString = new java.lang.String("A Java string");
```

Accessing methods and properties of Java objects is similar in most scripting languages. Some scripting languages let you invoke getter and setter methods on an object using the property name. The following snippet of code in Nashorn creates a java.util.Date object and accesses the object's method using both the property names and the method names:

```
var dt = new java.util.Date();
var year = dt.year + 1900;
var month = dt.month + 1;
var date = dt.getDate();
println("Date:" + dt);
println("Year:" + year + ", Month:" + month + ", Day:" + date);
```

```
Date:Wed Jul 09 00:35:31 CDT 2014
Year:2014, Month:7, Day:9
```

While using JavaScript, it is important to understand the different types of String objects. A String object may be a JavaScript String object or a Java java.lang.String object. JavaScript defines a length property for its String class, whereas Java has a length() method for its java.lang.String class. The following snippet of code shows the difference in creating and accessing the length of a JavaScript String and a Java java.lang.String objects:

```
// JavaScript String
var jsStr = new String("Hello JavaScript String");
print("JavaScript String: " + jsStr);
print("JavaScript String Length: " + jsStr.length);
```

```
// Java String
var javaStr = new java.lang.String("Hello Java String");
print("Java String: " + javaStr);
print("Java String Length: " + javaStr.length());
```

```
JavaScript String: Hello JavaScript String
JavaScript String Length: 23
Java String: Hello Java String
Java String Length: 17
```

Using Overloaded Java Methods

Java resolves an overloaded method call at compile time. That is, the Java compiler determines the signature of the method that will be called when the code is run. Consider the code for a PrintTest class shown in Listing 10-21. You may get a different output in the second line.

Listing 10-21. Using Overloaded Methods in Java

```
// PrintTest.java
package com.jdojo.script;

public class PrintTest {
        public void print(String str) {
                System.out.println("print(String): " + str);
        }

        public void print(Object obj) {
                System.out.println("print(Object): " + obj);
        }

        public void print(Double num) {
                System.out.println("print(Double): " + num);
        }

        public static void main(String[] args) {
                PrintTest pt = new PrintTest();
                Object[] list = new Object[]{"Hello", new Object(), 10.5};

                for(Object arg : list) {
                        pt.print(arg);
                }
        }
}
```

```
print(Object): Hello
print(Object): java.lang.Object@affc70
print(Object): 10.5
```

When the PrintTest class is run, all three calls to the print() method call the same version, print(Object) of the PrintTest class. When the code is compiled, the Java compiler sees the call pt.print(arg) as a call to the print() method with an Object type argument (which is the type of arg) and therefore binds this call to print(Object) method.

In a scripting language, the type of a variable is known at runtime, not at compile time. The interpreters of scripting languages resolve an overloaded method call appropriately depending on the runtime type of the arguments in a method call. The output of the following JavaScript code shows that the call to the print() method of the PrintTest class is resolved at runtime depending on the type of the argument:

```
// In JavaScript
var pt = new com.jdojo.script.PrintTest();
var list = ["Hello", new Object(), 10.5];
for (var i = 0; i < list.length; ++i) {
    pt.print(list[i]);
}
```

```
print(String): Hello
print(Object): [object Object]
print(Double): 10.5
```

JavaScript lets you select a specific version of the overloaded method explicitly. You can pass the signature of the overloaded method to be invoked with the object reference. The following snippet of code selects the print(Object) version:

```
// In JavaScript
var pt = new com.jdojo.script.PrintTest();
pt["print(java.lang.Object)"](10.5); // Calls print(Object)
pt["print(java.lang.Double)"](10.5); // Calls print(Double)
```

```
print(Object): 10.5
print(Double): 10.5
```

Using Java Arrays

The way Java arrays can be created in JavaScript differs in Rhino and Nashorn. In Rhino, you need to needed to create a Java array using the newInstance() static method of the java.lang.reflect.Array class. This syntax is also supported in Nashorn. The following snippet of code shows how to create and access Java arrays using the Rhino syntax:

```
// Create a java.lang.String array of 2 elements, populate it, and print the // elements
// Rhino you were able to use java.lang.String as the first argument, but in // Nashorn, you
// need to use java.lang.String.class instead.
var strArray = java.lang.reflect.Array.newInstance(java.lang.String.class, 2);
strArray[0] = "Hello";
strArray[1] = "Array";
for(var i = 0; i < strArray.length; i++) {
        print(strArray[i]);
}
```

```
Hello
Array
```

To create primitive type arrays such as int, double, etc., you need to use their TYPE constants for their corresponding wrapper classes as shown:

```
// Create an int array of 2 elements, populate it, and print the elements
var intArray = java.lang.reflect.Array.newInstance(java.lang.Integer.TYPE, 2);
intArray[0] = 100;
intArray[1] = 200;
for(var i = 0; i < intArray.length; i++) {
        print(intArray[i]);
}
```

```
100
200
```

Nashorn supports a new syntax to create Java arrays. First, create the appropriate Java array type using the Java.type() method, and then use the familiar new operator to create the array. The following snippet of code shows how to create a String[] of two elements in Nashorn:

```
// Get the java.lang.String[] type
var StringArray = Java.type("java.lang.String[]");

// Create a String[] array of 2 elements
var strArray = new StringArray (2);
strArray[0] = "Hello";
strArray[1] = "Array";
for(var i = 0; i < strArray.length; i++) {
        print(strArray[i]);
}
```

```
Hello
Array
```

Nashorn supports creating the arrays of primitive types the same way. The following snippet of code creates an int[] of two elements in Nashorn:

```
// Get the int[] type
var IntArray = Java.type("int[]");

// Create a int[] array of 2 elements
var intArray = new IntArray(2);
intArray[0] = 100;
intArray[1] = 200;
for(var i = 0; i < intArray.length; i++) {
        print(intArray[i]);
}
```

```
100
200
```

You can use a JavaScript array when a Java array is expected. JavaScript will perform the necessary conversion from a JavaScript array to a Java array. Suppose you have a `PrintArray` class, as shown in Listing 10-22, that contains a `print()` method that accepts a `String` array as an argument.

Listing 10-22. A PrintArray Class

```
// PrintArray.java
package com.jdojo.script;

public class PrintArray {
        public void print(String[] list) {
                System.out.println("Inside print(String[] list):");
                for(String s : list) {
                        System.out.println(s);
                }
        }
}
```

The following snippet of JavaScript code passes a JavaScript array to the `PrintArray.print(String[])` method. JavaScript takes care of converting the native array to a `String` array, as shown in the output.

```
// Create a JavaScript array and populate it with three strings
var names = new Array();
names[0] = "Rhino";
names[1] = "Nashorn";
names[2] = "JRuby";

// Create an object of the PrintArray class
var pa = new com.jdojo.script.PrintArray();

// Pass a JavaScript array to the PrintArray.print(String[] list) method
pa.print(names);
```

```
Inside print(String[] list):
Rhino
Nashorn
JRuby
```

Nashorn supports array type conversion between Java and JavaScript arrays using the `Java.to()` and `Java.from()` function. The `Java.to()` function converts a JavaScript array type to a Java array type. The function takes the array object as the first argument and the target Java array type as the second argument. The target array type can be specified as a string or a type object. The following snippet of code converts a JavaScript array to a Java `String[]`:

```
// Create a JavaScript array and populate it with three integers
var personIds = [100, 200, 300];

// Convert the JavaScript integer array to java String[]
var JavaStringArray = Java.to(personIds, "java.lang.String[]")
```

If the second argument in the Java.to() function is omitted, the JavaScript array is converted to a Java Object[].

The Java.from() function converts a Java array type to a JavaScript array. The function takes the Java array as an argument. The following snippet of code shows how to convert a Java int[] to a JavaScript array:

```
// Create a Java int[]
var IntArray = Java.type("int[]");
var personIds = new IntArray(3);
personIds[0] = 100;
personIds[1] = 200;
personIds[2] = 300;

// Convert the Java int[] array to a JavaScript array
var jsArray = Java.from(personIds);

// Print the elements in the JavaScript array
for(var i = 0; i < jsArray.length; i++) {
    print(jsArray[i]);
}
```

```
100
200
300
```

It seems that Nashorn is not able to convert a Java String[] to a JavaScript array. An attempt to do so in the following script results in the error shown:

```
// Create a Java String object
var str = new java.lang.String("Rhino,Nashorn,JRuby");
var strDelimiter = new java.lang.String(",");
var strArray = str.split(strDelimiter);

// Convert the Java String[] array to a JavaScript array
var jsArray = Java.from(strArray); // Nashorn throws an ScriptException here

// Print the elements in tje JavaScript array
for(var i = 0; i < jsArray.length; i++) {
    print(jsArray[i]);
}
```

```
javax.script.ScriptException: TypeError: Can only convert Java arrays and lists to
JavaScript arrays. Cant convert object of type {0}. in <eval> at line number 8...
```

■ **Tip**   It is possible to return a JavaScript array to Java code from a JavaScript function. You need to extract the elements of the native array in Java code, and therefore you need to use JavaScript-specific classes in Java. This approach is not advised. You should convert a JavaScript array to a Java array and return the Java array from a JavaScript function so the Java code deals only with Java classes.

Extending Java Classes Implementing Interfaces

JavaScript lets you extend Java classes and implement Java interfaces in JavaScript. The following sections describe different ways of achieving this.

Using a Script Object

You need to create a script object that contains implementations of the methods of the interface and pass it to the constructor of the Java interface using the new operator. In Java, an interface does not have a constructor and it cannot be used with the new operator. However, JavaScript lets you do that.

Let's implement the Calculator interface shown in Listing 10-17. The following statement creates a script object that implements the add() and subtract() methods. Note that the two method's implementations are separated by a comma. The method name and its implementation are separated by a colon.

```
var calFuncObj = {
                    add: function (n1, n2) {
                            return n1 + n2;
                    },
                    subtract: function (n1, n2) {
                            return n1 - n2;
                    }
                };
```

The following statement creates an implementation of the Calculator interface:

```
var calc = new com.jdojo.script.Calculator(calFuncObj);
```

Now you can start using the calc object as if it were an implementation of the Calculator interface as shown:

```
var n1 = 15;
var n2 = 10;
var result1 = calc.add(n1, n2);
var result2 = calc.subtract(n1, n2);
print(n1 + " + " + n2 + " = " + result1);
print(n1 + " - " + n2 + " = " + result2);
```

```
15 + 10 = 25
15 - 10 = 5
```

Using the Anonymous Class-like Syntax

This method uses a syntax that is very similar to the syntax of creating an anonymous class in Java. The following statement implements the Java Calculator interface and creates an instance of that implementation:

```
var calc = new com.jdojo.script.Calculator() {
                add: function (n1, n2) {
                        return n1 + n2;
                },
```

```
                subtract: function (n1, n2) {
                        return n1 - n2;
                }
        };
```

Now you can use the `calc` object the same way as you did before.

Using JavaAdapter Object and Java.extend() Function

JavaScript lets you implement multiple interfaces and extend a class using the `JavaAdapter` class. However, the Rhino JavaScript implementation that is bundled with JDK has overridden the implementation of `JavaAdapter`, which allows you to implement only one interface; it does not let you extend a class. The first argument to the `JavaAdapter` constructor is the interface to implement and the second argument is the script object that implements the methods. To use the `JavaAdapter` object in Nashorn, you need to load the Rhino compatibility module. The following snippet of code implements the `Calculator` interface using `JavaAdapter`:

```
// Need to load the compatibility module in Nashorn.
// You do not need to the following load() call in Rhino.
load("nashorn:mozilla_compat.js");

var calFuncObj =  {
                        add: function (n1, n2) {
                                return n1 + n2;
                        },
                        subtract: function (n1, n2) {
                                return n1 - n2;
                        }
                };

var calc = new JavaAdapter(com.jdojo.script.Calculator, calFuncObj);
```

Now you can use the `calc` object the same way as you did before.

Nashorn provides a better way that can let you extend a class and implement multiple interfaces using the `Java.extend()` function. In the `extend()` function, you can pass maximum one class type and multiple interface type. It returns a type that combines all passed in types. You need to use the previously discussed anonymous class-like syntax to provide the implementation for the abstract methods of the new type or override the existing method of the types being extended. The following snippet of code uses the `Java.extend()` method to implement the `Calculator` interface:

```
// Get the Calculator interface type
var CalculatorType = Java.type("com.jdojo.script.Calculator");

// Get a type that extends the Calculator type
var CalculatorExtender = Java.extend(CalculatorType);

// Implement the abstract methods in CalculatorExtender
// using an anonymous class like syntax
var calc = new CalculatorExtender() {
                        add: function (n1, n2) {
                                return n1 + n2;
                        },
```

```
                    subtract: function (n1, n2) {
                            return n1 - n2;
                    }
            };

var n1 = 15;
var n2 = 10;
var result1 = calc.add(n1, n2);
var result2 = calc.subtract(n1, n2);
print(n1 + " + " + n2 + " = " + result1);
print(n1 + " - " + n2 + " = " + result2);
```

```
15 + 10 = 25
15 - 10 = 5
```

Using a JavaScript Function

Sometimes a Java interface has only one method. In those cases, you can pass a JavaScript function object in place of an implementation of the interface. The Runnable interface in Java has only one method run(). When you need to use an instance of the Runnable interface in JavaScript, you can pass a JavaScript function object.

The following snippet of code shows how to create a Thread object and start it. In the constructor of the Thread class, a JavaScript function object myRunFunc is passed instead of an instance of the Runnable interface.

```
function myRunFunc() {
        print("A thread is running.");
}

// Call Thread(Runnable) constructor and pass the myRunFunc function object // that
// will serve as an implementation for the run() method of the Runnable    // interface.
var thread = new java.lang.Thread(myRunFunc);
thread.start();
```

```
A thread is running.
```

Using Lambda Expressions

JavaScript supports anonymous functions that can be used as lambda expressions. The following is an anonymous function that takes a number as an argument and returns its square:

```
function (n) {
        return n * n;
}
```

The following is an example of creating a Runnable object in JavaScript using an anonymous function as a lambda expression. The Runnable object is used in the constructor of the Thread class.

```
var Thread = Java.type("java.lang.Thread");

// Create a Thread using a Runnable object. The Runnable
// object is created using an anonymous function as a lambda expressions.
var thread = new Thread(function() {
                        print("Hello Thread");
                });

// Start the thread
thread.start();
```

The Java equivalent of the JavaScript code using a lambda expression is as follows:

```
// Create a Thread  using a Runnable object. The Runnable object is created using a
// lambda expressions.
Thread thread = new Thread(() -> {
        System.out.println("Hello Thread");
});

// Start the thread
thread.start();
```

Implementing a Script Engine

Implementing a full-blown script engine is no simple task and it is out of scope of this book. This section is meant to give you a brief, but complete, overview of the setup needed to implement a script engine. In this section, you will implement a simple script engine called the JKScript engine. It will evaluate arithmetic expressions with the following rules:

- It will evaluate an arithmetic expression that consists of two operands and one operator.

- The expression may have two number literals, two variables, or one number literal and one variable as operands. The number literals must be in decimal format. Hexadecimal, octal, and binary number literals are not supported.

- The arithmetic operations in an expression are limited to add, subtract, multiply, and divide.

- It will recognize +, -, *, and / as arithmetic operators.

- The engine will return a Double object as the result of the expression.

- Operands in an expression may be passed to the engine using global scope or engine scope bindings of the engine.

- It should allow executing scripts from a String object and a java.io.Reader object. However, a Reader should have only one expression as its contents.

- It will not implement the Invocable and Compilable interfaces.

Using these rules, some valid expressions for your script engine are as follows:

- `10 + 90`

- `10.7 + 89.0`

- `+10 + +90`

- `num1 + num2`

- `num1 * num2`

- `78.0 / 7.5`

You need to provide implementation for the following two interfaces when you implement a script engine:

- `javax.script.ScriptEngineFactory` interface.

- `javax.script.ScriptEngine` interface

As part of your implementation for the JKScript script engine, you will develop three classes as listed in Table 10-3. In the subsequent sections, you will develop these classes.

Table 10-3. *The List of Classes to be Developed for the JKScript Script Engine*

Class	Description
Expression	The `Expression` class is the heart of your script engine. It performs the work of parsing and evaluating an arithmetic expression. It is used inside the `eval()` methods of the `JKScriptEngine` class.

JKScriptEngine	An implementation of the `ScriptEngine` interface. It extends the `AbstractScriptEngine` class that implements the `ScriptEngine` interface. The `AbstractScriptEngine` class provides a standard implementation for several versions of the `eval()` methods of the `ScriptEngine` interface. You need to implement the following two versions of the `eval()` method:
	
	`Object eval(String, ScriptContext)`
	`Object eval(Reader, ScriptContext)`

JKScriptEngineFactory	An implementation of the `ScriptEngineFactory` interface.

The Expression Class

The `Expression` class contains the main logic for parsing and evaluating an arithmetic expression. Listing 10-23 contains the complete code for the `Expression` class.

Listing 10-23. The Expression Class That Parses and Evaluates an Arithmetic Expression

```
// Expression.java
package com.jdojo.script;

import java.util.regex.Matcher;
import java.util.regex.Pattern;
import javax.script.ScriptContext;
```

```java
public class Expression {
        private String exp;
        private ScriptContext context;

        private String op1;
        private char op1Sign = '+';

        private String op2;
        private char op2Sign = '+';

        private char operation;

        private boolean parsed;

        public Expression(String exp, ScriptContext context) {
                if (exp == null || exp.trim().equals("")) {
                        throw new IllegalArgumentException(this.getErrorString());
                }
                this.exp = exp.trim();

                if (context == null) {
                        throw new IllegalArgumentException("ScriptContext cannot be null.");
                }
                this.context = context;
        }

        public String getExpression() {
                return exp;
        }

        public ScriptContext getScriptContext() {
                return context;
        }

        public Double eval() {
                // Parse the expression
                if (!parsed) {
                        this.parse();
                        this.parsed = true;
                }

                // Extract the values for the operand
                double op1Value = getOperandValue(op1Sign, op1);
                double op2Value = getOperandValue(op2Sign, op2);

                // Evaluate the expression
                Double result = null;
                switch (operation) {
                        case '+':
                                result = op1Value + op2Value;
                                break;
```

```
                case '-':
                        result = op1Value - op2Value;
                        break;
                case '*':
                        result = op1Value * op2Value;
                        break;
                case '/':
                        result = op1Value / op2Value;
                        break;
                default:
                        throw new RuntimeException("Invalid operation:" + operation);
        }
        return result;
}

private double getOperandValue(char sign, String operand) {
        // Check if operand is a double
        double value;
        try {
                value = Double.parseDouble(operand);
                return sign == '-' ? -value : value;
        }
        catch (NumberFormatException e) {
                // Ignore it. Operand is not in a format that can be
                // converted to a double value.
        }

        // Check if operand is a bind variable
        Object bindValue = context.getAttribute(operand);
        if (bindValue == null) {
                throw new RuntimeException(operand + " is not found in the script context.");
        }

        if (bindValue instanceof Number) {
                value = ((Number) bindValue).doubleValue();
                return sign == '-' ? -value : value;
        }
        else {
                throw new RuntimeException(operand + " must be bound to a number.");
        }
}

public void parse() {
        // Supported expressiona are of the form v1 op v2, where v1 and v2
        // are variable names or numbers, and op could be +, -, *, or /

        // Prepare the pattern for the expected expression
        String operandSignPattern = "([+-]?)";
        String operandPattern = "([\\p{Alnum}\\p{Sc}_.]+)";
        String whileSpacePattern = "([\\s]*)";
        String operationPattern = "([+*/-])";
```

735

```java
                String pattern = "^" + operandSignPattern + operandPattern +
                        whileSpacePattern + operationPattern + whileSpacePattern +
                        operandSignPattern + operandPattern + "$";

                Pattern p = Pattern.compile(pattern);
                Matcher m = p.matcher(exp);
                if (!m.matches()) {
                        // The expression is not in the expected format
                        throw new IllegalArgumentException(this.getErrorString());
                }

                // Get operand-1
                String temp = m.group(1);
                if (temp != null && !temp.equals("")) {
                        this.op1Sign = temp.charAt(0);
                }
                this.op1 = m.group(2);

                // Get operation
                temp = m.group(4);
                if (temp != null && !temp.equals("")) {
                        this.operation = temp.charAt(0);
                }

                // Get operand-2
                temp = m.group(6);
                if (temp != null && !temp.equals("")) {
                        this.op2Sign = temp.charAt(0);
                }
                this.op2 = m.group(7);
        }

        private String getErrorString() {
                return "Invalid expression[" + exp + "]" +
                        "\nSupported expression syntax is: op1 operation op2" +
                        "\n where op1 and op2 can be a number or a bind variable" +
                        " , and operation can be +, -, *, and /.";
        }

        @Override
        public String toString() {
                return "Expression: " + this.exp + ", op1 Sign = " +
                        op1Sign + ", op1 = " + op1 + ", op2 Sign = " +
                        op2Sign + ", op2 = " + op2 + ", operation = " + operation;
        }
}
```

The Expression class is designed to parse and evaluate an arithmetic expression of the form

```
op1 operation op2
```

Here, op1 and op2 are two operands that can be numbers in decimal format or variables, and operation can be +, -, *, or /.

The suggested use of the Expression class is

```
Expression exp = new Expression(expression, scriptContext);
Double value = exp.eval();
```

Let's discuss important components of the Expression class in detail.

The Instance Variables

Instance variables exp and context are the expression and the ScriptContext to evaluate the expression, respectively. They are passed in to the constructer of this class.

The instance variables op1 and op2 represent the first and the second operands in the expression, respectively. The instance variables op1Sign and op2Sign represent signs, which could be '+' or '-', for the first and the second operands in the expression, respectively. The operands and their signs are populated when the expression is parsed using the parse() method.

The instance variable operation represents an arithmetic operation (+, -, *, or /)) to be performed on the operands.

The instance variable parsed is used to keep track of the fact whether the expression has been parsed or not. The parse() method sets it to true,

The Constructor

The constructor accepts an expression and a ScriptContext and makes sure that they are not null and stores them in the instance variables. It trims the leading and trailing whitespaces from the expression before storing it in the instance variable exp.

The parse() Method

The parse() method parses the expression into operands and operations. It uses a regular expression to parse the expression text. The regular expression expects the expression text in the following form:

- An optional sign + or - for the first operand

- The first operand that may consist of a combination of alphanumeric letters, currency signs, underscores, and decimal points

- Any number of whitespaces

- An operation sign that may be +, -, *, or /

- An optional sign + or - for the second operand

- The second operand that may consist of a combination of alphanumeric letters, currency signs, underscores, and decimal points

The regular expression ([+-]?) will match the optional sign for the operand. The regular expression ([\\p{Alnum}\\p{Sc}_.]+) will match an operand, which may be a decimal number or a name. The regular expression ([\\s]*) will match any number of whitespaces. The regular expression ([+*/-]) will match an operation sign. All regular expressions are enclosed in parentheses to form groups, so you can capture the matched parts of the expression.

If an expression matches the regular expression, the parse() method stores the matches parts into respective instance variables.

Note that the regular expression to match the operand is not perfect. It will allow several invalid cases, such as an operand having multiple decimal points, etc. However, for this demonstration purpose, it will do.

The getOperandValue() Method

This method is used during an expression evaluation after the expression has been parsed. If the operand is a double number, it returns the value by applying the sign of the operand. Otherwise, it looks up the name of the operand in the ScriptContext. If the name of the operand is not found in the ScriptContext, it throws a RuntimeException. If the name of the operand is found in the ScriptContext, it checks if the value is a number. It the value is a number, it returns the value after applying the sign to the value; otherwise, it throws a RuntimeException.

The getOperandValue() method does not support operands in hexadecimal, octal, and binary formats. For example, an expression like "0x2A + 0b1011" will not be treated as an expression having two operands with int literals. It is left to readers to enhance this method to support numeric literals in hexadecimal, octal, and binary formats.

The eval() Method

The eval() method evaluates the expression and returns a double value. First, it parses the expression if it has not already been parsed. Note that multiple calls to the eval() parses the expression only once.

It obtains values for both operands, performs the operation, and returns the value of the expression.

The JKScriptEngine Class

Listing 10-24 contains the implementation for the JKScript script engine. Its eval(String, ScriptContext) method contains the main logic.

```
Expression exp = new Expression(script, context);
Object result = exp.eval();
```

It creates an object of the Expression class. It calls the eval() method of the Expression object that evaluates the expression and returns the result.

The eval(Reader, ScriptContext) method reads all lines from the Reader, concatenates them, and passes the resulting String to the eval(String, ScriptContext) method to evaluate the expression. Note that a Reader must have only one expression. An expression may be split into multiple lines. Whitespaces in the Reader are ignored.

Listing 10-24. An Implementation of JKScript Script Engine

```
// JKScriptEngine.java
package com.jdojo.script;

import java.io.BufferedReader;
import java.io.IOException;
import java.io.Reader;
import javax.script.AbstractScriptEngine;
import javax.script.Bindings;
import javax.script.ScriptContext;
import javax.script.ScriptEngineFactory;
import javax.script.ScriptException;
import javax.script.SimpleBindings;
```

```java
public class JKScriptEngine extends AbstractScriptEngine {
        private ScriptEngineFactory factory;

        public JKScriptEngine(ScriptEngineFactory factory) {
                this.factory = factory;
        }

        @Override
        public Object eval(String script, ScriptContext context)
                        throws ScriptException {
                try {
                        Expression exp = new Expression(script, context);
                        Object result = exp.eval();
                        return result;
                }
                catch (Exception e) {
                        throw new ScriptException(e.getMessage());
                }
        }

        @Override
        public Object eval(Reader reader, ScriptContext context)
                        throws ScriptException {
                // Read all lines from the Reader
                BufferedReader br = new BufferedReader(reader);

                String script = "";
                String str = null;
                try {
                        while ((str = br.readLine()) != null) {
                                script = script + str;
                        }
                }
                catch (IOException e) {
                        throw new ScriptException(e);
                }

                // Use the String version of eval()
                return eval(script, context);
        }

        @Override
        public Bindings createBindings() {
                return new SimpleBindings();
        }

        @Override
        public ScriptEngineFactory getFactory() {
                return factory;
        }
}
```

The JKScriptEngineFactory Class

Listing 10-25 contains the implementation for the ScriptEngineFactory interface for the JKScript engine. Some of its methods return a "Not Implemented" string because you do not support features exposed by those methods. The code in the JKScriptEngineFactory class is self-explanatory. An instance of the JKScript engine may be obtained using ScriptEngineManager with a name of jks, JKScript, or jkscript as coded in the getNames() method.

Listing 10-25. A ScriptEngineFactory Implementation for JKScript Script Engine

```java
// JKScriptEngineFactory.java
package com.jdojo.script;

import java.util.ArrayList;
import java.util.Arrays;
import java.util.Collections;
import java.util.List;
import javax.script.ScriptEngine;
import javax.script.ScriptEngineFactory;

public class JKScriptEngineFactory implements ScriptEngineFactory {
        @Override
        public String getEngineName() {
                return "JKScript Engine";
        }

        @Override
        public String getEngineVersion() {
                return "1.0";
        }

        @Override
        public List<String> getExtensions() {
                return Collections.unmodifiableList(Arrays.asList("jks"));
        }

        @Override
        public List<String> getMimeTypes() {
                return Collections.unmodifiableList(
                        Arrays.asList("text/jkscript") );
        }

        @Override
        public List<String> getNames() {
                List<String> names = new ArrayList<>();
                names.add("jks");
                names.add("JKScript");
                names.add("jkscript");
                return Collections.unmodifiableList(names);
        }
```

```java
    @Override
    public String getLanguageName() {
            return "JKScript";
    }

    @Override
    public String getLanguageVersion() {
            return "1.0";
    }

    @Override
    public Object getParameter(String key) {
            switch (key) {
                    case ScriptEngine.ENGINE:
                            return getEngineName();
                    case ScriptEngine.ENGINE_VERSION:
                            return getEngineVersion();
                    case ScriptEngine.NAME:
                            return getEngineName();
                    case ScriptEngine.LANGUAGE:
                            return getLanguageName();
                    case ScriptEngine.LANGUAGE_VERSION:
                            return getLanguageVersion();
                    case "THREADING":
                            return "MULTITHREADED";
                    default:
                            return null;
            }
    }

    @Override
    public String getMethodCallSyntax(String obj, String m, String[] p) {
            return "Not implemented";
    }

    @Override
    public String getOutputStatement(String toDisplay) {
        return "Not implemented";
    }

    @Override
    public String getProgram(String[] statements) {
            return "Not implemented";
    }

    @Override
    public ScriptEngine getScriptEngine() {
            return new JKScriptEngine(this);
    }
}
```

Preparing for Deployment

Before you package the classes for the JKScript script engine, you need to perform one more step. Create a directory named META-INF. Under the META-INF directory, create a subdirectory named services. In the services directory, create a text file named javax.script.ScriptEngineFactory. Note the file name must be the way it is mentioned and it should not have any extension such as .txt.

Edit the javax.script.ScriptEngineFactory file and enter the contents as shown in Listing 10-26. The first line in the file is a comment that starts with a # sign. The second line is the fully qualified name of the JKScript script engine factory class.

Listing 10-26. Contents of the File Named javax.script.ScriptEngineFactory

```
#The factory class for the JKScript engine
com.jdojo.script.JKScriptEngineFactory
```

Why do you have to perform this step? You will package the javax.script.ScriptEngineFactory file along with the class files for the JKScript engine in a JAR file. The discovery mechanism for script engines searches for this file in the META-INF/services directory in all JAR files in the CLASSPATH. If this file is found, its contents are read and all script factory classes are instantiated and included in the list of script engine factory. Therefore, this step is necessary to make your JKScript engine auto-discoverable by the ScriptEngineManager.

Packaging the JKScript Files

You need to package all files for the JKScript script engine in a JAR file named jkscript.jar. You can name the file anything else as well. The following is the list of files with their directories. Note that an empty manifest.mf file will work in this case.

- com\jdojo\script\Expression.class
- com\jdojo\script\JKScriptEngine.class
- com\jdojo\script\JKScriptEngineFactory.class
- META-INF\manifest.mf
- META-INF\services\javax.script.ScriptEngineFactory

You can create the jkscript.jar file manually by copying all of the above listed files, except the manifest.mf file, in a directory, say C:\build on Windows, and then executing the following command from the C:\build directory:

```
C:\build> jar cf jkscript.jar com\jdojo\script\*.class META-INF\services\*.*
```

Using the JKScript Script Engine

It is time to test your JKScript script engine. The first and most important step is to include the jkscript.jar, which you created the previous section, to the application CLASSPATH. Once you have included the jkscript.jar file in your application CLASSPATH, using JKScript is no different from using any other script engines.

The following snippet of code creates an instance of the JKScript script engine using JKScript as its name. You can also use its other names, jks and jkscript.

```
// Create the JKScript engine
ScriptEngineManager manager = new ScriptEngineManager();
ScriptEngine engine = manager.getEngineByName("JKScript");
if (engine == null) {
        System.out.println("JKScript engine is not available. ");
        System.out.println("Add jkscript.jar to CLASSPATH.");
}
else {
        // Evaluate your JKScript
}
```

Listing 10-27 contains a program that uses the JKScript script engine to evaluate different types of expressions. Expressions stored in String objects and files are executed. Some expressions use numeric literals and some bind variables whose values are passed in bindings in engine scope and global scope of the default ScriptContext of the engine. Note that this program expects a file named jkscript.txt in the current directory that contains an arithmetic expression that can be understood by the JKScript script engine. If the script file does not exist, the program prints a message on the standard output with the path of the expected script file. You may get a different output in the last line.

Listing 10-27. Using the JKScript Script Engine

```
// JKScriptTest.java
package com.jdojo.script;

import java.io.FileNotFoundException;
import java.io.IOException;
import java.io.Reader;
import java.nio.file.Files;
import java.nio.file.Path;
import java.nio.file.Paths;
import javax.script.ScriptEngine;
import javax.script.ScriptEngineManager;
import javax.script.ScriptException;

public class JKScriptTest {
        public static void main(String[] args) throws FileNotFoundException, IOException {
                // Create JKScript engine
                ScriptEngineManager manager = new ScriptEngineManager();
                ScriptEngine engine = manager.getEngineByName("JKScript");
                if (engine == null) {
                        System.out.println("JKScript engine is not available. ");
                        System.out.println("Add jkscript.jar to CLASSPATH.");
                        return;
                }

                // Test scripts as String
                testString(manager, engine);

                // Test scripts as a Reader
                testReader(manager, engine);
        }
```

```java
    public static void testString(ScriptEngineManager manager,
                                            ScriptEngine engine) {
        try {
                // Use simple expressions with numeric literals
                String script = "12.8 + 15.2";
                Object result = engine.eval(script);
                System.out.println(script + " = " + result);

                script = "-90.0 - -10.5";
                result = engine.eval(script);
                System.out.println(script + " = " + result);

                script = "5 * 12";
                result = engine.eval(script);
                System.out.println(script + " = " + result);

                script = "56.0 / -7.0";
                result = engine.eval(script);
                System.out.println(script + " = " + result);

                // Use global scope bindings variables
                manager.put("num1", 10.0);
                manager.put("num2", 20.0);
                script = "num1 + num2";
                result = engine.eval(script);
                System.out.println(script + " = " + result);

                // Use global and engine scopes bindings. num1 from
                // engine scope and num2 from global scope will be used.
                engine.put("num1", 70.0);
                script = "num1 + num2";
                result = engine.eval(script);
                System.out.println(script + " = " + result);

                // Try mixture of number literal and bindings. num1 from
                // the engine scope bindings will be used
                script = "10 + num1";
                result = engine.eval(script);
                System.out.println(script + " = " + result);
        }
        catch (ScriptException e) {
                e.printStackTrace();
        }
    }

    public static void testReader(ScriptEngineManager manager,
                                            ScriptEngine engine) {
        try {
                Path scriptPath = Paths.get("jkscript.txt").toAbsolutePath();
```

```
                    if (!Files.exists(scriptPath)) {
                        System.out.println(scriptPath +
                                " script file does not exist.");
                        return;
                    }

                    try(Reader reader = Files.newBufferedReader(scriptPath);) {
                        Object result = engine.eval(reader);
                        System.out.println("Result of " +
                                scriptPath + " = " + result);
                    }
                }
            }
            catch(ScriptException | IOException e) {
                e.printStackTrace();
            }
        }
    }
}
```

```
12.8 + 15.2 = 28.0
-90.0 - -10.5 = -79.5
5 * 12 = 60.0
56.0 / -7.0 = -8.0
num1 + num2 = 30.0
num1 + num2 = 90.0
10 + num1 = 80.0
Result of C:\jkscript.txt - 190.0
```

The jrunscript Command-line Shell

The JDK includes a command-line script shell called jrunscript. It is script-engine-independent and it can be used to evaluate any script including your JKScript. You can find this shell in the JAVA_HOME\bin directory, where JAVA_HOME is the directory in which you have installed the JDK. IN this section, I will discuss how to use the jrunscript shell to evaluate script using different script engines.

The Syntax

The syntax to use the jrunscript shell is

jrunscript [options] [arguments]

Both [options] and [arguments] are optional. However, if both are specified, [options] must precede [arguments]. Table 10-4 lists all available options for the jrunscript shell.

Table 10-4. *The List of Options for the jrunscript shell*

Option	Description
-classpath <path>	Used to specify the CLASSPATH.
-cp <path>	The same as the option -classpath.
-D<name>=<value>	Sets a system property for Java runtime.
-J<flag>	Passes the specified <flag> to the JVM on which jrunscript is run.
-l <language>	Allows you to specify a scripting language that you want to use. By default, Rhino JavaScript is used in JDK 6 and JDK 7. In JDK 8, Nahsorn is the default. If you want to use a language other than JavaScript, say JKScript, you will need to use -cp or -classpath option to include the JAR file that contains the script engine.
-e <script>	Executes the specified script. Typically, it is used to execute a one-liner script.
-encoding <encoding>	Specifies the character encoding used while reading script files.
-f <script-file>	Evaluates the specified script-file in batch mode.
-f -	Allows you to evaluate scripts in interactive mode. It reads scripts from the standard input and executes.
-help	Outputs the help message and exits.
-?	Outputs the help message and exits.
-q	Lists all available script engines and exits. Note that script engines other than JavaScript are available only when you include their JAR files using the -cp or -classpath option.

The [arguments] part of the command is a list of arguments, which are interpreted depending on whether the -e or -f option is used or not. Arguments that are passed to the script are available inside the script as an array named arguments. Table 10-5 lists interpretations of the arguments when they are used with the -e or -f option.

Table 10-5. *Interpretation of [arguments] in Combination of the -e or -f Option*

-e or -f option	Arguments	Interpretation
Yes	Yes	If -e or -f option is specified, all arguments are passed to the script as script arguments.
No	Yes	If arguments are specified with no -e or -f option, the first argument is considered a script file to run. The rest of the arguments, if any, are passed to the script as script arguments.
No	No	If arguments and -e or -f option are missing, the shell works in interactive mode, where the shell executes the script entered in the standard input interactively.

Execution Modes of the Shell

You can use the jrunscript shell in the following three modes:

- One-liner mode
- Batch mode
- Interactive mode

One-liner Mode

The -e option lets you use the shell in one-liner mode. It executes one line of script. The following command prints a message on the standard output using Rhino JavaScript engine:

```
C:\>jrunscript -e "print('Hello Rhino Nashorn!')"
Hello Rhino Nashorn!
```

In one-liner mode, the entire script must be entered on one line. However, a one-liner script may contain multiple statements.

Batch Mode

The -f option lets you use the shell in batch mode. It executes a script file. Consider a script file named nashorntest.js as shown in Listing 10-28.

Listing 10-28. A nashorntest.js Script File Written in Nashorn JavaScript

```
// Print a message
print("Hello Nashorn!");

// Add two integers and print the value
var x = 10;
var y = 20;
var z = x + y;
print(x + " + " + y + " = " + z);
```

The following command runs the script in the nashorntest.js file in a batch mode. You may need to specify the full path of the nashorntest.js file if it is not in the current directory.

```
C:\>jrunscript -f nashorntest.js
Hello Nashorn!
10 + 20 = 30
```

Interactive Mode

In interactive mode, the shell reads and evaluates script as it is entered on the standard input. There are two ways to use the shell in interactive mode:

- Using no -e or -f option and no arguments
- Using "-f -" option

The following command uses no options and arguments to enter into interactive mode. Pressing the Enter key makes the shell evaluate the entered script.

```
c:\>jrunscript
nashorn> print("Hello Interactive mode!");
Hello Interactive mode!
nashorn> var num = 190;
nashorn> print("num is " + num);
num is 190
nashorn> exit();
```

Listing Available Script Engines

The jrunscript shell is a scripting-language-neutral shell. You can use it to run scripts in any scripting language for which the script engine JAR files are available. By default, the Nashorn JavaScript engine is available. To list all available script engines, you use the -q option as shown:

```
c:\>jrunscript -q
Language ECMAScript ECMA - 262 Edition 5.1 implementation "Oracle Nashorn" 1.8.0_05
```

Please refer to the next section on how to add a script engine to the shell.

Adding a Script Engine to the Shell

How do you make script engines other than the Nashorn JavaScript engine available to the shell? To make a script engine available to the shell, you need to provide the list of JAR files for the script engine using the -classpath or -cp option. The following command makes JKScript and jython script engines available to the shell by providing the list of JAR files for Jython and JKScript engines. Note that the Nashorn engine is always available by default. The command uses the -q option to list all available script engines.

```
c:\> jrunscript -cp C:\jython-standalone-2.5.3.jar;C:\jkscript.jar -q
Language python 2.5 implementation "jython" 2.5.3
Language ECMAScript ECMA - 262 Edition 5.1 implementation "Oracle Nashorn" 1.8.0_05
Language JKScript 1.0 implementation "JKScript Engine" 1.0
```

▪ **Tip** The CLASSPATH set using the -cp or -classpath option is effective only for the command in which the option is used. If you run the shell in interactive mode, the CLASSPATH is effective for the entire interactive session.

Using Other Script Engines

You can use other script engines by specifying the script engine name with the -l option. You must use the -cp or -classpath option to specify the JAR files for the script engine, so the shell has the access to the engine. The following command uses the JKScript engine in interactive mode:

```
C:\>jrunscript -cp C:\jkscript.jar -l JKScript
jks> 10 + 30
40.0
jks> +89.7 + -9.7
80.0
jks>
```

Passing Arguments to Scripts

The jrunscript shell allows passing arguments to scripts. The arguments are made available to the script in an array named arguments. You can access the arguments array inside the script in the language-specific way. The following command passes three arguments of 10, 20, and 30, and prints the value of the first argument.

```
C:\>jrunscript -e "print('First argument is ' + arguments[0])" 10 20 30
First argument is 10
```

Consider the Nashorn JavaScript file nashornargstest.js shown in Listing 10-29, which prints the number of arguments and their values that are passed to the script.

Listing 10-29. A nashornargstest.js File Written in Nashorn JavaScript to Print Command-Line Arguments

```
// nashornargstest.js
print("Number of arguments:" + arguments.length);
print("Arguments are ") ;
for(var i = 0; i < arguments.length; i++) {
        print(arguments[i]);
}
```

The following commands run the nashornargstest.js file using the jrunscript shell.

```
C:\>jrunscript nashornargstest.js
Number of arguments:0
Arguments are

C:\>jrunscript nashornargstest.js 10 20 30
Number of arguments:3
Arguments are
10
20
30
```

If you want to run the nashornargstest.js file from a Java application, you need to pass an argument named arguments to the engine. The argument named arguments is passed to the script by the shell automatically, not by a Java application.

The jjs Command-Line Tool

To work with the Nashorn script engine, JDK 8 includes a new command-line tool called jjs. The command is located in the JDK_HOME\bin directory. The command can be used to run scripts in files or scripts entered on the command-line in interactive mode. It can also be used to execute shell scripts. The syntax to invoke the command is

```
jjs <options> <script-files> <-- arguments>
```

Here,

- <options> are options for the jjs command. Two options are separated by spaces.

- <script-files> is the list of script files to be interpreted by the Nashorn engine.

- <-- arguments> is the list of arguments to be passed to the scripts or the interactive shell as arguments. Arguments are specified after double hyphens and they can be accessed using the arguments property.

Table 10-6 lists some of the commonly used options for the jjs tool. To print the list of all options, run the tool with the -xhelp option, like so:

```
jjs -xhelp
```

Table 10-6. *Options for the jjs Comand-line Tool*

Option	Description
-classpath \<path\> or -cp \<path\>	Used to specify the CLASSPATH.
-D\<name\>=\<value\>	Sets a system property for Java runtime. This option can be repeated to set multiple runtime properties values.
-J\<flag\>	Passes the specified \<flag\> to the JVM.
-scripting	Enabled shell scripting features.
-strict	Enables strict mode where the scripts are executed using the ECMAScript Edition 5.1 standards.
-fx	Launches the script as a JavaFX application.
-doe or –dump-on-error	When this is specified, a full stack trace of the error is printed. By default, a brief error message is printed.
-v or –version	Prints the version of the Nashorn engine.
-fv or –fullversion	Prints the full version of the Nashorn engine.
-t=\<timezone\> or –timezone=\<timezone\>	Sets the time zone for the script execution. The default time zone is Chicago/America.
-help or -h	Outputs the help message and exits.
-xhelp	Prints extended help.

If you run jjs without specifying any options or script files, it is run in interactive mode. The script is interpreted as you enter it. Strings in Nashorn can be enclosed in single quotes or double quotes. The following are some examples of using the jjs tool in interactive mode. It is assumed that you have included the path to the jjs tool in the PATH environment variable on your machine. If you have not done so, you can replace jjs with JDK_HOME\bin\jjs in the following command. You can execute the quit() or exit() function to exit the jjs tool.

```
c:\>jjs
jjs> "Hello Nashorn"
Hello Nashorn
jjs> "Hello".toLowerCase();
hello
jjs> var list = [1, 2, 3, 4, 5]
jjs> var sum = 0;
jjs> for each (x in list) { sum = sum + x};
15
jjs> quit()

c:\>
```

The following is an example of passing arguments to the jjs tool. The first five natural numbers are passed to the jjs tool as arguments and they are accessed using the arguments property later. Note that you must add a space between the two hyphens and the first argument.

```
c:\>jjs -- 1 2 3 4 5
jjs> for each (x in arguments) print(x)
1
2
3
4
5
jjs> quit()

c:\>
```

Consider the script in Listing 10-30. The script has been saved in a file named stream.js. The script works on a list of integers. The list can be passed to the script as the command-line arguments. If the list is not passed as arguments, it uses the first five natural numbers as the list. It computes the sum of the squares of odd integers in the list. It prints the list and the sum.

Listing 10-30. A Script to Compute the Sum of the Squares of Odd Integers in a List

```
// stream.js
var list;
if (arguments.length == 0) {
    list = [1, 2, 3, 4, 5];
}
else {
  list = arguments;
}

print("List of numbers: " + list);

var sumOfSquaredOdds = list.filter(function(n) {return n % 2 == 1;})
                           .map(function(n) {return n * n;})
                           .reduce(function(sum, n) {return sum + n;}, 0);

print("Sum of the squares of odd numbers: " + sumOfSquaredOdds);
```

Using the jjs tool, you can run the script in the stream.js file as follows. It is assumed that the stream.js file is in the current directory. Otherwise, you need to specify the full path of the file.

```
c:\>jjs stream.js
List of numbers: 1,2,3,4,5
Sum of the squares of odd numbers: 35

c:\>jjs stream.js -- 10 11 12 13 14 15
List of numbers: 10,11,12,13,14,15
Sum of the squares of odd numbers: 515

c:\>
```

The jjs tool can be invoked in scripting mode that allows you to run shell commands. You can start the jjs tool in scripting mode using the -scripting option. The shell commands are enclosed in back quotes. The following are examples of using the date and ls shell commands using the jjs tool in scripting mode:

```
c:\>jjs -scripting
jjs> `date`
Mon Jul 14 22:42:26 CDT 2014

stream.js
test.js

jjs> quit()

c:\>
```

You can capture the output of the shell command in a variable. Scripting mode allows for expression substitution in strings enclosed in double quotes. Note that the expression substitution feature is not available in strings enclosed in single quotes. The expression is enclosed in ${expression}. The following commands capture the value of the date shell command in a variable and embed the date value in a string using the expression substitution. Note that in the example, the expression substitution does not work when the string is enclosed in single quotes:

```
c:\>jjs -scripting
jjs> var today = `date`
jjs> "Today is ${today}"
Today is Mon Jul 14 22:48:26 CDT 2014

jjs> 'Today is ${today}'
Today is ${today}
jjs> quit()

c:\>
```

You can also execute the shell script stored in a file using the scripting mode, like so:

```
C:\> jjs -scripting myscript.js
```

The jjs tool supports heredocs in script files that can be run in scripting mode. A heredoc is also known as a here document, here-string, or here-script. It is a multiline string where whitespaces are preserved. A heredoc starts with a double angle brackets (<<) and a delimiting identifier. Typically, EOF or END is used as the delimiting identifier. However, you can use any other identifier that is not used as an identifier elsewhere in the script. The multiline string starts at the end line. The string is ended with the same delimiting identifier. The following is an example of using a heredoc in Nashorn:

```
var str = <<EOF
This is a multi-line string using the heredoc syntax.
Bye Heredoc!
EOF
```

Listing 10-31 contains the script that uses a heredoc in Nashorn. The $ARG property is defined only in scripting mode and its value is the arguments passed to the script using the jjs tool.

Listing 10-31. *The Contents of the heredoc.js File That Using Heredoc Style a Multiline String*

```
// heredoc.js
var str = <<EOF
This is a multiline string.
Number of arguments passed to this
script is ${$ARG.length}
Arguments are ${$ARG}

Bye Heredoc!
EOF

print(str);
```

You can execute the `heredoc.js` script file as shown:

```
c:\> jjs -scripting heredoc.js
This is a multi-line string.
Number of arguments passed to this
script is 0
Arguments are

Bye Heredoc!

c:\> jjs -scripting heredoc.js -- Kishori Sharan
This is a multi-line string.
Number of arguments passed to this
script is 2
Arguments are Kishori,Sharan

Bye Heredoc!
```

For more information on shell scripting in Nashorn, please refer to http://docs.oracle.com/javase/8/docs/technotes/guides/scripting/nashorn/shell.html.

JavaFX in Nashorn

The `jjs` command-line tool for Nashorn lets you use JavaFX from scripts. You need to create a `start()` function in JavaScript as you do to launch a JavaFX application in Java. Nashorn will take care of the rest. Optionally, you can also declare `init()` and `stop()` functions for your JavaFX application. You can use the fully qualified name of the JavaFX classes or import them using the `Java.type()` function. The following snippet of code shows the two approaches to create a `Label` in JavaFX:

```
// Using the fully qualified name of the Label class
var msg = new javafx.scene.control.Label("Hello JavaFX!");

// Using Java.type() function
var Label = Java.type("javafx.scene.control.Label");
var msg = new Label("Hello JavaFX!");
```

It may be cumbersome to type the fully qualified names of all JavaFX classes. Aren't scripts supposed to be shorter than Java code? Nashorn has a way to make your JavaFX script shorter. It includes several script files that import the JavaFX types as their simple names. You will need to load those script files using the load() method, and then you can use the simple names of JavaFX classes in your script. Nashorn includes a fx:controls.js script file that imports all JavaFX control classes as their simple class names. Table 10-7 contains the list of script files and the classes/packages they import.

Table 10-7. *The List of Nashorn Script Files and the Classes/Packages They Import*

Nashorn Script File	Imported Classes/Packages
fx:base.js	javafx.stage.Stage javafx.scene.Scene javafx.scene.Group javafx/beans javafx/collections javafx/events javafx/util
fx:graphics.js	javafx/animation javafx/application javafx/concurrent javafx/css javafx/geometry javafx/print javafx/scene javafx/stage
fx:controls.js	javafx/scene/chart javafx/scene/control
fx:fxml.js	javafx/fxml
fx:web.js	javafx/scene/web
fx:media.js	javafx/scene/media
fx:swing.js	javafx/embed/swing
fx:swt.js	javafx/embed/swt

The following snippet of code shows how to load this script file and use the simple name of the javafx.scene.control.Label class:

```
// Import all JavaFX control class names
load("fx:controls.js")

// Use the simple name of the Label control
var msg = new Label("Hello JavaFX!");
```

Listing 10-32 contains the code for a JavaFX application. Save the code in a file named hellojavafx.js.

Listing 10-32. A JavaFX Application Using Nashorn Script

```javascript
// hellojavafx.js

// Load Nashorn predefined scripts to import JavaFX specific classes and packages
load("fx:base.js")
load("fx:controls.js")
load("fx:graphics.js")

// Define the start() method of the JavaFX application class
function start(stage) {
        var nameLbl = new Label("Enter your name:");
        var nameFld = new TextField();
        var msg = new Label();
        msg.setStyle("-fx-text-fill: blue;");

        // Create buttons
        var sayHelloBtn = new Button("Say Hello");
        var exitBtn = new Button("Exit");

        // Add the event handler for the Say Hello button
        sayHelloBtn.onAction = function() {
                var name = nameFld.getText();
                if (name.trim().length() > 0) {
                        msg.text = "Hello " + name;
                }
                else {
                        msg.text = "Hello there";
                }
        };

        // Add the event handler for the Exit button
        exitBtn.onAction = function() {
                Platform.exit();
        };

        // Create the root node
        var root = new VBox();

        // Set the vertical spacing between children to 5px
        root.spacing = 5;

        // Add children to the root node
        root.children.addAll(nameLbl, nameFld, msg, sayHelloBtn, exitBtn);

        // Set the scene and title for the stage
        stage.scene = new Scene(root, 350, 150);
        stage.title = "Hello JavaFX from Nashorn";

        // Show the stage
        stage.show();
}
```

This is the Nashorn script equivalent of the JavaFX application defined as the ImprovedHelloFXApp Java class in Chapter 9. The Nashorn version of the code is little simpler to write. In the script, you are able to call the methods of the Java classes using their properties. For example, instead of writing

```
root.setSpacing(5);
```

in Java, you can write

```
root.spacing = 5;
```

in Nashorn JavaScript.

Adding the event handler for buttons is easier. You can set an anonymous function as the event handler for the buttons. Note that you are able to use onAction property to set the event handler rather than calling the setOnAction() method of the Button class. The following snippet of code shows how to set the ActionEvent handler for a button:

```
// Add the event handler for the Say Hello button
sayHelloBtn.onAction = function() {
        // Script code to handle the ActionEvent goes here
};
```

To run a JavaFX application, you need to start the jjs tool with a -fx option. The following command starts the JavaFX application that displays a window as shown in Figure 10-7. Enter a name and click the Say Hello button to see a message. Click the Exit button to exit the application.

```
C:\> jjs -fx hellojavafx.js
```

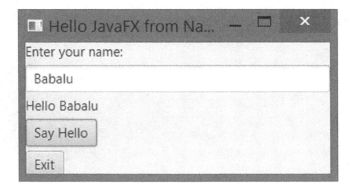

Figure 10-7. A JavaFX window created using Nashorn script

The jjs command-line tool makes it really easy to work with JavaFX applications. You can display a message in a JavaFX window in just one line of code. Nashorn creates a global variable named $STAGE that is the reference of the primary stage of the JavaFX application. Note that the $STAGE global variable is available in the script only when you use the jjs tool with the -fx option. Listing 10-33 shows the code for the simplest JavaFX application that displays a Label with a message in a JavaFX window. Save it in a file named simplestfxapp.js. Note that you do not have to create any function for the start() method any more. You do not need to even call the show() method on the $STAGE variable. Nashorn will show the stage automatically.

Listing 10-33. Using the $STAGE Global Variable in Nashorn Script

```
// simplestfxapp.js

$STAGE.scene = new javafx.scene.Scene(new javafx.scene.control.Label("Hello JavaFX Scripting"));
```

The following command will run the simplest JavaFX application that displays a window as shown in Figure 10-8.

Figure 10-8. *The simplest JavaFX application using Nashorn script*

Summary

A scripting language is a programming language that provides you the ability to write scripts that are evaluated (or interpreted) by a runtime environment called a script engine (or an interpreter). A script is a sequence of characters that is written using the syntax of a scripting language and used as the source for a program executed by an interpreter. The Java Scripting API allows you to execute scripts written in any scripting language that can be compiled to Java bytecode from the Java application. JDK 6 and 7 shipped with a script engine called Rhino JavaScript engine. In JDK 8, the Rhino JavaScript engine has been replaced with a script engine called Nashorn.

Scripts are executed using a script engine that is an instance of the ScriptEngine interface. The implementer of the ScriptEngine interface also provides an implementation of the ScriptEngineFactory interface whose job is to create instances of the script engine and provide details about the script engine. The ScriptEngineManager class provides a discovery and instantiation mechanism for script engines. A ScriptManager maintains a mapping of key-value pairs as an instance of the Bindings interface that is shared by all script engines that it creates.

You can execute scripts contained in a String or a Reader. The eval() method of the ScriptEngine is used execute the script. You can pass parameters to the script using the ScriptContext. Parameters passed can be local to a script engine, local to a script execution, or global to all script engines created by a ScriptManager. Using the Java Scripting API, you can also execute procedures and functions written in scripting languages. You can also pre-compile the scripts, if the script engine supports it, and execute the scripts repeated from Java to get a better performance.

You can implement your script engine using the Java Scripting API. You will need to provide the implementation for the ScriptEngine and the ScriptEngineFactory interfaces. You need to package your script engine code in a certain way so the engine can be discovered by the ScriptManager at runtime.

The Java 8 ships two command-line tools called jrunscript and jjs. They are located in the JDK_HOME\bin directory. They are used to run scripts on a command line. The jrunscript tool is script-language-neutral; it can be used to execute scripts in any script language such as Nashorn, JRuby, groovy, etc. The jjs tool is used to run Nashorn scripts and its extensions; you can run shell commands, scripts, and Java application using the jjs tool.

Index

■ A

Abstract Window Toolkit (AWT), 85
AccessControlException, 389
Action Interface, 148
Adaptive Server Anywhere
    database, 394, 399, 431, 466
addRow() method, 458
Applets, 249
    appletviewer command
        debug option, 262
        encoding option, 262
        Google Chrome browser, 261
        Jjavaoptions option, 262
        syntax, 260
    codebase attribute, 262–263
    definition, 249
    deployment
        <applet> tag, 252
        HTML document creation, 252
        JAR files, 254
        testing, 254
    development process, 250
    event-dispatching thread, 278
    getAppletContext() method, 274
    getAppletInfo() method, 270
    getAudioClip() method, 273
    getImage() method
        getDocumentBase() method, 272
        HTML content, 272–273
        URL, 272
    getParameterInfo() method, 269
    getParameter() method, 269
    HelloApplet class, 250–251
    HTML and JavaScript, 275
    JApplet class, 250
    Java code trusted
        codebase option, 283
        configuration file, 282
        file/directory path format, 284
        JVM option, 281
        partial error, 281
        policy files, 282
        SecurityTest class, 281
    Java Plug-in
        configuration, 257
        installation, 255
        Java Control Panel program, 256
    life cycle
        destroy() method, 265–266
        init() method, 264
        start() method, 264
        stop() method, 265
    list of attributes, <applet> tag, 270–271
    MAYSCRIPT attribute, 277
    package, 278
    paint() method, 280
    <param> tag, 266
    security restrictions for, 285
    signed document
        CA, 287
        HTML file creation, 289
        JAR file, 288
        jarsigner command, 287
        Java Plug-in setup, 289
        keytool command, 288
        manifest.mf file creation, 288
        ReadUserHomeApplet class, 287
    view, 260
Asynchronous socket channel
    client applications, 370
        Attachment class, 366
        ReadWriteHandler class, 366
    CompletionHandler class, 357
    server application, 359, 369
        AsyncEchoServerSocket class, 362
        Attachment class, 360
        CompletionHandler class, 360
        ReadWriteHandler class, 361
Auto-commit mode, 406

■ B

BatchUpdateException command, 512
Binary Large Object (Blob), 500
Bootstrap class loader, 543
Borders
    Bevel Border, 178, 194
    Compound Border, 178, 194
    Empty Border, 178, 194
    Etched Border, 178, 194
    Line Border, 178, 194
    Matte Border, 178, 194
    Soft Bevel Border, 178, 194
    Titled Border, 178, 194
ButtonGroup, 124

■ C

CachedRowSet
    acceptChanges() method, 487
    execute() method, 484
    paging, 484–487
    populate() method, 484
    size() method, 484
    updation and deletion, 488–490
CallableStatement interface, 425
    Adaptive Server Anywhere, 431
    DB2, 433–434
    INOUT parameters, 427–428
    IN parameters, 426
    Java DB, 434
    MySQL, 431
    Oracle, 432
    OUT parameters, 427
    return parameter, 428
    SQL server, 432–433
    stored procedure, 428
Certification Authority (CA), 287
Character Large Object (Clob), 500
Clean message, 545
close() method, 403, 424
Color Chooser, 172
commit() method, 406
Compilable interface, 717
compile() method, 718
ComponentEvent, 84
ComponentListener, 84
Connected rowset, 481
ConnectionPoolDataSource
        interface, 521
createBindings() method, 692
createJdbcRowSet() method, 476
Custom ScriptContext, 703

■ D

Data control language (DCL) statement, 414
Data definition language (DDL) statement, 414
Datagram channel
    binding, 372
    client application, 375
    close() method, 373
    echo server, 373
    multicast
        binding, 376
        close() method, 379
        creation, 376
        DGCMulticastClient class, 380
        DGCMulticastServer class, 381
        join() method, 378
        network interface, 377
        receive() method, 379
        send() method, 379
        setOption() method, 376
    open() method, 371
    receive() method, 373
    send() method, 372
    setOption() method, 371
Data manipulation language (DML) statement, 414
DataSource, 520
DB2 database, 394, 400, 433, 467
Derby.properties, 389
destroy() method, 265
Dirty message, 545
Disconnected rowset, 484
Document base attribute, 262
Drag and drop (DnD) mechanism, 219

■ E

EditorKit, 108
Engine scope bindings, 707
eval() method, 703, 705
evaluate() method, 495
Event handling
    classes and interfaces, 627
    dispatch chain, 628
    filters and handlers, 631
    route traversal
        bubbling phase, 630
        capture phase, 629
    source, 627
    target, 627, 628
    types, 627
execute() method, 416
executeQuery() method, 417
executeUpdate() method, 416

■ F

File Chooser, 172
FilteredRowSet, 494
FocusEvent, 84
FocusListener, 84
Font class, 181

■ G, H

getAppletContext() method, 274
getAppletInfo() method, 270
getApplet() method, 275
getAudioClip() method, 274
getBindings() method, 699
getCodeBase() method, 264
getConnection() method, 402
getDocumentBase() method, 264
getMetaData() method, 412
getParameterInfo() method, 269
getParameter() method, 266, 269
getScopes() method, 696
get(String key) method, 699
getTransactionIsolation() method, 409
getXxx() method, 411
give_raise stored procedure, 435

■ I

Implementing Remote Interface, 529
initApplet() method, 278
init() method, 251, 264
INOUT parameters, 427–428
IN parameters, 426
Interpreter, 677
Invocable interface, 710
Invocation API
    C++ console application, 586
    EmbeddedJVMJNI class, 586
    JavaVMInitArgs structure, 584–585
    JavaVMoption structure, 584
    printMsg() method, 586
    setout() and setErr() methods, 585
    version field, 584
invokeAndWait() method, 278
invokeLater() method, 278
IP address
    anycast, 304
    broadcast, 304
    definition, 297
    InetAddress class, 309
    Internet Assigned Numbers Authority (IANA), 297
    IPv4, 298

IPv6, 300
    loopback, 302
    machine address, 309
    multicast, 303
    Regional Internet Registry (RIR) organizations, 297
    unicast, 303
    unspecified, 304

■ J

Java data types, 409
Java DB database, 395, 401, 434
    configuration, 388
    embedded mode, 388
    installation files, 387
    NetBeans IDE, 391
    server mode, 388
Java.from() function, 728
JavaFX
    2D shapes
        class diagram, 648
        code implementation, 649
        path and SVGpath classes, 651
    animation, 659
        class diagram, 661
        interpolator, 660, 662
        key frame, 662
        keyvalue, 661
        timeline, 661–662
    binding, 604, 617
        bidirectional, 605
        eager binding, 605
        isValid() method, 618
        NumberBinding methods, 618
        unbind() method, 620
        unidirectional, 605
    canvas, drawing, 652
    components
        glass windowing toolkit, 592
        media engine, 592
        prism, 592
        Quantum toolkit, 593
        scene graph, 592
        web engine, 593
    container class (*see* Layout panes)
    controls, 642
    definition, 591
    effects, 654
    event handling
        classes and interfaces, 627
        dispatch chain, 628
        filters and handlers, 631
        route traversal, 629

JavaFX (*cont.*)
    source, 627
    target, 627, 628
    types, 627
  features, 591
  FXML, user interface, 665
  GuI components, 642
  HelloJavaFX class, 594
    getChildren() method, 598
    launch() method, 596
    main() method, 596, 598
    scene class, 598
    setOnAction() method, 600
    setScene() method, 599
    setStyle() method, 600
    setTitle() method, 596
    start() method, 595
    text node, 599
  history, 593
  layout panes
    BorderPane, 639
    class diagram, 637
    dynamic layout, 636
    parent class, 637
    setStyle() method, 641
    static layout, 636
    using CSS, 641
  lifecycle
    code implementation, 603
    init() method, 602
    launch() method, 602
    start() method, 602
    stop() method, 602
  new versions, 593
  observable collections
    addListener() method, 624–625
    changed() method, 625
    class diagram, 623
    FXCollections class, 624
    next() method, 624
    ObservableList, 623, 625
    ObservableMap, 623
    ObservableSet, 623–624
  printing nodes, 670
  properties, 604–605
    change events, 615
    counter property, 606
    get() and set() methods, 606
    getReadOnlyProperty() method, 606
    idWrapper property, 607
    IntegerProperty, 606
    invalidation event, 612
    ISBN property, book class, 609
    printDetails() method, 611
    removeListener() method, 614

    SimpleIntegerProperty, 607
    title property, book class, 608
    toString() methods, 611
  runtime library, 594
  source code, 594
  termination, 604
  timeline animation, 662
  transformations, 656
    Affine, 657
    class diagram, 657
    rotate class, 657
    scale class, 658
    shear class, 658
    translate class, 657
Java Interface implementation
  Calculator interface, 714
  getInterface() method, 713, 716
  instance methods, 716–717
java.lang.AutoCloseable interface, 403
java.lang.ClassNotFoundException, 541
Java Naming and Directory
    Interface (JNDI) service, 520
Java Native Interface (JNI), 549
  architecture, 550
  arrays, 568
  C/C++
    header file creation, 554
    program implementation, 556
  class libraries, 550
  compiling, 554
  definition, 549
  dynamic link library (DLL), 550
  exception handling
    Exceptioncheck() function, 582
    ExceptionClear() function, 582
    ExceptionOccurred() function, 582
    FatalError() function, 583
    FindClass() function, 581
    return statement, 583
    ThrowNew() function, 583
  functions, C/C++, 565
  JVM creation (*see* Invocation API)
  mapping
    primitive data types, 563
    reference type, 564
  naming rules
    header file, 562
    javah command, 561
    mangled method's signature, 561
    method's parameter signature, 561
    test class, 562
  objects (*see* Java objects)
  program implementation
    abstract method, 552
    loadLibrary() method, 551

load() method, 551
native method, 552–553
run command, 560
shared library creation
on Linux, 559
on Windows, 557
strings, 566
synchronization
MonitorEnter(), 589
MonitorExit(), 589
system requirements, 550
Java objects
class reference
FindClass() function, 573
GetObjectClass() function, 573
creation
AllocObject() function, 579
getValue() method, 580
methodID parameter, 579
wrapperObject, 580
field access
cls parameter, 574
GetField() function, 574
GetStaticField() function, 574
JNIJavaObjectAccessTest class, 577
methods
callIntMethod(), 576
CallMethod() function, 576
GetMethodID(), 574
GetStaticMethodID(), 574
instance method, 575
javap command, 575
static methods, 575
Java Plug-in
configuration, 257
installation, 255
Java Control Panel program, 256
Java Remote Method
Invocation (Java RMI)
architecture, 526
client and server, 526
client program, 536
debugging, 542
dynamic class downloading, 543
garbage collector, 545
remote interface
client program, 534
implementation, 529
requirements, 528
server program, 531
remote object, 525
RMI client program, 539
RMI registry application, 537
RMI server, 538
server program, 536

troubleshooting
java.lang.ClassNotFoundException, 541
java.rmi.server.ExportException, 540
java.rmi.StubNotFoundException, 540
java.security.AccessControlException, 541
UnicastRemoteObject class, 536
java.rmi.server.ExportException, 540
java.rmi.StubNotFoundException, 540
Java Runtime Environment (JRE), 255
java.security.AccessControlException, 541
Java.security.manager JVM option, 281
java.sql.Connection interface, 396
java.sql.SQLException, 402
Java.to() function, 728
Java.type() method, 726
Javax.script Package
AbstractScriptEngine class, 684
Bindings interface, 684
Compilable interface, 684
CompiledScript class, 684
getEngineFactories() method, 685
Invocable interface, 684
ScriptContext interface, 684
ScriptEngineFactory interface, 684
ScriptEngine interface, 683
ScriptEngineManager class, 684
ScriptException class, 685
JButton, 86
JCheckBox, 123
JColorChooser, 172, 176, 194
JComboBox, 125
JDBC
auto-commit mode, 406
batch updates
BatchUpdateException, 513
BatchUpdateException command, 512
CallableStatement interface, 511
coding implementation, 512–513
executeBatch() method, 512
multi-step process, 511
commit() method, 406
DatabaseMetaData, 412–413
data types, 409
driver
Adaptive Server Anywhere, 399
CLASSPATH setting up, 396
DB2, 400
getConnection() method, 402
Java DB, 401
java.sql.DriverManager class, 396–397
jdbc.drivers system property, 397
MySQL, 400
Oracle, 398
registerDriver() method, 397
SQL Server, 399

JDBC (*cont.*)
    types of, 386–387
    URL format, 398
  execute() method, 463
  getMoreResults() method, 463–464
  LOB (*see* Large object (LOB))
  result sets (*see* Result sets)
  rollback() method, 406
  RowSets (*see* RowSets)
  SQL statements (*see* SQL statements)
  SQL warning, 522
  table creation, 393
    Adaptive Server Anywhere, 394
    DB2, 394
    Java DB, 395
    MySQL, 395
    Oracle, 394
    SQL Server, 394
  transaction
    INSERT statement, 518
    person table creation, 517
    rollback() method, 518
    setSavepoint() method, 517
    SQLException, 518
    using savepoints, 519
  transaction isolation level
    dirty read, 407
    non-repeatable read, 407
    phantom read, 408–409
JDBC API, 385–386
JDBC-Native API driver, 387
JDBC-Net driver, 387
JDBC trace, 522
JEditorPane, 108
JFileChooser, 194
  accept() method, 175
  addChoosableFileFilter() method, 175
  dialog box, 174
  isAcceptAllFileFilterUsed() method, 176
  in JDialog, 172
  setCurrentDirectory() method, 173
  showDialog() method, 174
  showSaveDialog() method, 174
JFormattedTextField, 102
JFrame
  components
    add() method, 8–9
    BorderLayout, 11
    closeButton, 8, 11
    containment hierarchy, 8
    content pane, 7
    glass pane, 7
    Help button, 11
    JButton, 9–10
    layered pane, 7

    Layout Managers, 11
    pack() method, 10
    root pane, 7
    setBounds() method, 10
  creation
    program implementation, 4, 6
    resizing, 4–5
    setDefaultCloseOperation() method, 6
    setSize()method, 6
    setVisible () method, 3
    WindowsConstants interface, 5
  reusable creation
    initFrame() method, 68
    main() method, 67
jjs command-line tool
  $ARG property, 752–753
  EOF/END identifier, 752
  exit() function, 750
  ${expression}, 752
  JavaFX
    ActionEvent handler, 756
    classes/packages, 754
    fx option, 756
    hellojavafx.js, 755
    Label creation, 753
  scripting option, 752
    $STAGE global variable, 757
  stream.js, 751
  syntax, 749
  xhelp option, 749
JKScriptEngine class, 738
JKScriptEngineFactory class, 740
JLabel, 91
JList, 127
JMenuBar, 138
JMenuItem, 138
JoinRowSet, 498
JOptionPane, 166
JPanel, 90
JPasswordField, 101
JProgressBar, 135
JRadioButton, 123
jrunscript command-line shell, 678
  arguments array, 749
  arguments list, 746
  batch mode, 747
  cp/-classpath option, 748
  interactive mode, 747
  JKScript and jython script engines, 748
  one-liner mode, 747
  syntax, 745
  types of, 746
JScrollBar, 131
JScrollPane, 133
JSeparator, 137

JSlider, 136
JSpinner, 129
JSplitPane, 160
JTabbedPane, 160
JTable, 149
JTextArea, 105
JTextComponent, 95
JTextField, 97
JTextPane, 113
JToggleButton, 123
JToolBar, 146
JTree, 155
JWindow, 177

■ K

Keyboard indicator, 87
Keyboard shortcut, 87
KeyEvent, 85

■ L

Large object (LOB)
    Blob and Clob columns, 506–509
    Clob interface, 505
    Connection interface, 504
    data retrieval, 502–503
    OutputStream, 504
    PreparedStatement interface, 505
    table creation, Java DB, 501–502
    types, 500
Layout managers
    BorderLayout
        close button, 23
        code implementation, 21
        containers orientation, 22
        help button, 23
    BoxLayout
        code implementation, 26
        container alignment, 27
        filler, 28
        glue, 28–30
        rigid area, 28
        static methods, 27
        struct, 28
    CardLayout, 23
        actionPerformed() method, 25
        addActionListener() method, 25
        class methods, 24
        code implementation, 24
    FlowLayout
        code implementation, 16
        component orientation, 16
        JFrame buttons, 17
        nesting, 20

setAlignment() method, 17
setHgap() methods, 18
setVgap() methods, 18
GridBagConstraints, 32
    anchor constraint, 44
    gridx and gridy constraints, 34, 37, 41
    instance variables, 36
    ipadx constraints, 43
    ipady constraints, 43
GridBagLayout, 32
    code implementation, 33
    contentPane.add() method, 33
    fill constraint, 42
    insets constraint, 44
    weightx and weighty constraints, 47
GridLayout
    code implementation, 31
    constructors, 30
    containers, 31
GroupLayout, 56
    addComponent() method, 62
    addGap() method, 61
    grouping alignment, 58
    JFrame, 60
    leading alignment, 57
    linkSize() method, 65
    nested groups, 64
    ParallelGroup, 57, 58, 63
    sequential groups, 57, 63
    setVerticalGroup() method, 60
null, 66
snippet code, 33
SpringLayout
    code implementation, 50
    constants, 52
    constant() static method, 49
    pack() method, 51, 54
    putConstraint() method, 54–55
    scale() method, 50
    setting x and y constraints, 52
    strut, 49
    subtract() method, 49
    sum() method, 49
Layout panes
    BorderPane, 639
    class diagram, 637
    dynamic layout, 636
    parent class
        getChildren() method, 637
        getChildrenUnmodifiable()
            method, 638
        getManagedChildren() method, 638
    setStyle() method, 641
    static layout, 636
    using CSS, 641

length() method, 503, 723
Life cycle
    destroy() method, 265–266
    init() method, 264
    start() method, 264
    stop() method, 265
Live remote reference, 545
Locator, 501

■ M

main() method, 252
MAYSCRIPT attribute, 277
Menu, 137
META-INF/services directory, 685
MouseEvent, 85
MouseListener, 85
MouseMotionListener, 85
MouseWheelEvent, 85
MouseWheelListener, 85
MySQL database, 395, 400, 431, 465

■ N

National Character Large Object (NClob), 500
NetBeans IDE, 391
Network programming
    asynchronous socket channel, 357
        client applications, 365, 370
        server application, 359, 369
    blocking *vs.* non-blocking classes, 345
    campus area network (LAN), 294
    client-server paradigm, 305–306
    communication, 294
    datagram channel (*see* Datagram channel)
    data transmission, 294
    definition, 293
    host, 293
    internet, 294
    IP address, 297
        anycast, 303
        broadcast, 304
        InetAddress class, 309
        IPv4, 298
        IPv6, 300
        loopback, 302
        machine address, 309
        multicast, 303
        Regional Internet Registry (RIR)
          organizations, 297
        unicast, 303
        unspecified, 304
    local area network (LAN), 294
    metropolitan area network (MAN), 294
    network, 293

non-blocking socket, 345
    architecture, 346
    ByteBuffer object, 350
    echo server, 351
    operations, 347
    SelectionKey object, 349
    ServerSockeChannel, 347
packet switching networks, 295
port number
    application layer, 305
    IANA, 304
protocol suite
    application layer, 295
    internet layer, 296
    network interface layer, 296
    physical layer, 296
    transmission packets, 297
    transport layer, 296
socket
    accept primitive, 308
    bind primitive, 307
    close primitive, 309
    connectionless socket, 305–306
    connection-oriented socket, 305–306
    connect primitive, 308
    datagram socket, 307
    lifecycle, 306
    listen primitive, 307
    receive/receiveFrom primitive, 309
    security permissions, 356
    send/sendto primitive, 309
socket address, 311
topology, 294
transmission control protocol (TCP), 305
    client socket, 317, 319
    server socket, 312, 319
uniform resource identifier (URI)
    ASCII value, 331
    hierarchial syntax, 331
    http scheme, 330
    Java objects, 334
    rules, 332
    specifications, 332
uniform resource locator (URL), 330
    content reader, 338
    getContent() method, 339
    HTTP request method, 337
    Java objects, 335
    openConnection() method, 340
    Reader/Writer Class, 342
uniform resource name (URN), 330
user datagram protocol (UDP), 306
    connect() method, 327
    DatagramPacket, 320
    DatagramSocket, 320, 322

echo server, 322
    multicast sockets, 327
    sockets, 327
virtual connection, 305
wide area network (WAN), 294
newFactory() method, 476–477

O

Oracle database, 394, 398, 432, 466
OUT parameters, 427

P, Q

Paging, 484–487
paint() method, 280
parse() method, 737
Peer, 85
Plugin.jar file, 276
PreparedStatement interface, 414–415, 422
prepareStatement() method, 423
put() method, 689, 699

R

registerDriver() method, 397
Relational database management
        system (RDBMs), 385
Remote Interface, 528
Remote method Invocation, 525
Reserved keys, 707
ResultSetMetaData, 444, 472
Result sets
    absolute cursor movement, 455
    bidirectional scrollable
        getHoldability() method, 452
        getType() method, 449–451
        SQLException, 451
    close() method, 456–457
    Concurrency, 438
    deleteRow() method, 462
    displayPersonUsingPreparedStatement(), 448
    displayPersonUsingStatement(), 447
    executeQuery() method, 442
    getRow() method, 448
    getXxx() methods, 443
    Holdability, 438
    insertRow() method, 457
    next() method, 442, 448, 453
    PreparedStatement, 445–447
    query execution, 449
    relative cursor movement, 454–455
    rows and column, structures of, 453
    Scrollability, 438
    SELECT statement, 437

stored procedure (see Stored procedure)
toString() method, 445
try-catch block, 439–442
updateRow() method, 460
using while-loop, 444
wasNull() method, 444
Retrieving LOB Data, 502
Rhino JavaScript, 677
RMI architecture, 526
RMI client program, 534
RMI server program
    exportObject() method, 531
    rebind() method, 532
    security manager installation, 531
rollback() method, 406
RowSets
    advantages of, 474
    bidirectional scrollable and updateable, 479
    CachedRowSet
        acceptChanges() method, 487
        execute() method, 484
        paging, 484–487
        populate() method, 484
        size() method, 484
        updation and deletion, 488–490
    class diagram, 475
    command setting, 478
    creation, 476
    database connection properties, 477
    disadvantages of, 474
    FilteredRowSet, 494
    JdbcRowSet, 481
    JoinRowSet, 498
    RowSetUtil class, 480–481
    types of, 475
    updateRow() method, 479
    WebRowSet, 490

S

Scope, 693
Script context
    Bindings, 693
    FileWriter, 694
    getAttribute() method, 695
    global scope, 695
    interface, 696–697
    setAttribute() method, 694
    SimpleScriptContext class, 693, 695
Script engine, 677–678
    arithmetic expressions rules, 732
    Custom ScriptContext, 703
    Default ScriptContext, 707
    discovering and instantiating, 685
    eval() method, 686, 705

Script engine (*cont.*)
    Expression class, 733
        eval() method, 738
        getOperandValue() method, 738
        instance variables, 737
        parse() method, 737
    Groovy installation, 682
    helloscript.js, 686–687
    JKScriptEngine class, 738–739
    JKScriptEngineFactory class, 740–742
    JKScript script engine, 743–745
    JRuby installation, 682
    Jython installation, 682
    manifest.mf file, 742
Scripting language
    advantages, 677
    compiled scripts, 717
    definition, 677
    disadvantage, 678
    eval() method, 679
    getEngineFactories() method, 680–681
    Invocable interface, 710, 712
    invokeFunction() method, 711
    java in
        anonymous class creation, 729
        arrays, 725
        Calculator interface, 729
        global variable, 720
        importClass() function, 721–722
        importPackage() function, 721–722
        JavaAdapter object, 730
        Java.extend() method, 730
        lambda expressions, 731
        method overloading, 724–725
        Runnable interface, 731
        String object creation, 723
        type() function, 721
        variable declaration, 719
        with clause, 722–723
    java Interface (*see* Java Interface
        implementation)
    javax.script Package (*see* Javax.script Package)
    jrunscript shell, 678
    jsoutput.txt, 708–709
    Nashorn JavaScript, 712–713
    passing parameters
        bindings, 691–692
        java code to scripts, 688–689
        put() method, 697
        scope, 693
        script context (*see* Script context)
        ScriptEngineManager, 698, 700–703
        scripts to java code, 690–691
    print() function, 679
    ScriptEngineFactory class, 683
    ScriptEngineManager class, 678

Servlet, 249
setAsciiStream() method, 505
setBinaryStream() method, 504
setBindings() method, 701
setBytes() method, 504
setCharacterStream() method, 505
setFilter() method, 495
setJoinType() method, 499
setNull() method, 411
setString() method, 505
showDocument() method, 275
showStatus() method, 275
SQL Server database, 394, 399, 432–433, 466
SQL statements
    CallableStatement interface
        (*see* CallableStatement interface)
    DELETE, 421
    execute() method, 416
    executeQuery() method, 417
    executeUpdate() method, 416
    INSERT, 419–420
    person table creation, 418–419
    PreparedStatement interface, 414–415, 422
    statement object, 416
    time and timestamp escape sequences, 417
    UPDATE, 420–421
start() method, 264
stop() method, 265
Stored procedure, 464
    Adaptive Server Anywhere, 466
    DB2, 467
    Java DB
        coding implementation, 467
        JDBCUtil.getConnection() method, 470–471
        in Oracle database, 469
        printResultSet() static method, 468–469
    MySQL, 465
    Oracle, 466
    SQL server, 466
supportsStoredProcedures() method, 426
Swing, 1, 195
    character-based user interface, 2
    container, 2
    containment hierarchy, 2–3
    Dimension class, 13
    DnD
        canImport() and importData()
          methods, 224
        data transfer mechanism, 219
        drop modes, 221
        exportDone() method, 224
        JFrame, 226
        JList, 221
        myComponent, 220
        Transferable interface, 219–220
        TransferHandler class, 220

event handling, 4
    ActionEvent class, 69, 75
    Action listener, 72
    ActionListener interface, 70, 72
    event handler, 69
    event listener/eventhandler, 69
    EventListener interface, 72
    event source, 69
    getActionCommand() method, 75
    JButton, 70
    listener interface, 71
    triggering an event, 69
graphical user interface(GUI), 2
HTML, 195
Insets class, 13
JLayer, component decoration
    BlueBorderUI class, 232
    eventDispatched() method, 236
    event processing task, 235
    getView() and getUI() methods, 233
    JTextField components, 238
    paint() method, 233
    processFocusEvent() method, 236
    uninstallUI() method, 235
layout managers, 14
    BorderLayout, 21
    BoxLayout, 26
    CardLayout, 23
    FlowLayout, 16
    GridBagConstraints, 32
    GridBagLayout, 32
    GridLayout, 30
    GroupLayout, 56
    null, 66
    setLayout() method, 15
    SpringLayout, 49
MDI applications
    DesktopManager interface, 228
    JDesktopPane class, 227
    JFrame class, 228
    JInternalFrame class, 227
    on Windows, 228
mouse event handler
    ActionListener interface, 79
    adapter class, 78
    code implementation, 77
    JButton, 76
    methods, 76
    MouseListener interface, 76–77
pluggable look and feel, 205
Point class, 12
Rectangle class, 13
SDI applications, 227
shaped window, 245
simplest program (see JFrame)

Synth XML file
    buttonStyle style, 215
    CLASSPATH, 211
    <color> element, 216
    definition, 210
    <imageIcon> element, 216
    <imagePainter> element, 217
    JFrame, 212–213, 218
    key attribute, 214
    loading process, 210
    load() method, 211
    <property> element, 216
    painterCenter attribute, 217
    paintTextFieldBorder() and paintButtonBorder() methods, 217
    <state> element, 215
    <style> element, 214
    type attribute, 214
    using URL, 211
TDI applications, 227
threading mechanisms, 4
threading model
    JVM, 196
    SwingUtilities class, 197
    SwingWorker class, 199
Toolkit class, 230
translucent windows
    initFrame() method, 241
    JFrame, 242
    JPanel, 242
    per-pixel translucency, 244
    setOpacity(float opacity) method, 240
    translucent and opaque, 239
    transparent, 239
    WindowTranslucency enum, 239
user interface (UI), 1
Swing components, 122
    Border class
        bevel border, 181
        Bevel Border, 178
        compound border, 178, 181
        empty border, 178, 181
        etched border, 178, 181
        line border, 178, 181
        matte border, 178, 181
        Soft Bevel Border, 178
        Titled Border, 178
    color class, 177
    custom dialogs
        confirmation dialog, 162
        Input dialog, 162
        message dialog, 162
        modalities, 164
        Modal JDialog, 164
        Modeless JDialog, 164
        setModalityType() method, 164

Swing components (*cont.*)
   Double Buffering, 189
   drawing shapes, 184
      DrawingCanvas, 187
      getGraphics() method, 189
      Graphics class, methods of, 186
      paintComponent() method, 188
   font class
      Dialog, 182
      DialogInput, 182
      glyph, 181
      Monospace, 182
      object-oriented font, 182
      outline font, 182
      pitch, 182
      SansSerif, 182
      scalable font, 182
      Serif, 182
      setFont() method, 183
      typeface, 181
   Immediate Painting, 189
   JButton
      AbstractAction class, 88
      ActionListener interface, 87
      Action object, 88
      actionPerformed() method, 89
      constructors, 86
      ImageIcon class, 86
      keyboard mnemonic, 87
      methods, 88
      modifier key, 87
   JCheckBox, 123
   JColorChooser, 172, 176, 194
   JComboBox, 125
   JComponent class, 81
      accessibility, 82
      border, 82
      class hierarchy, 82
      events, 84
      heavyweight components, 85
      key binding, 82
      layout manager, 82
      lightweight components, 85
      look and feel, 82
      methods, 82
      on-screen painting, 82
      putClientProperty() and
         getClientProperty() methods, 82
      tool tip, 82
   JEditorPane
      EditorKit object, 108
      getEditPaneBox() method, 112
      getURLBox() method, 112
      go() method, 112
      HTML Browser, 109
      hyperlinkUpdate() method, 109
         main() method, 112
         read(InputStream in, Object description)
            method, 108
         setContentType(String contentType) method, 108
         setPage() method, 108
   JFileChooser, 172, 194
   JFormattedTextField
      advantages of, 105
      constructors, 102
      Default Formatter, 105
      Display Formatter, 105
      Edit Formatter, 105
      formatter factory, 103
      getValue() method, 105
      mask formatter, 104
      Null formatter, 105
      salaryField, 103
      setFormatterFactory() method, 105
   JFrame, 190
   JLabel
      constructors, 91
      setDisplayedMnemonic() method, 92
      setLabelFor() method, 92
      setText() method, 92
   JList, 127
      getSize() method, 128
      horizontal wrapping, 128
      methods, 129
      multiple interval selection, 128
      setSelectionMode() method, 128
      setVisibleRowCount() method, 128
      single interval selection mode, 128
      single selection mode, 128
      vertical argument, 128
      vertical wrapping, 128
   JMenu, 138
   JOptionPane
      arguments, 166
      CANCEL_OPTION, 167
      CLOSED_OPTION, 167
      Confirmation Dialog, 166
      createDialog() methods, 171
      Input dialog, 166
      Message dialog, 166
      NO_OPTION, 167
      OK_OPTION, 167
      Option dialog, 166
      showConfirmDialog() method, 168
      showInputDialog() method, 169–170
      showMessageDialog() methods, 168
      showOptionDialog() method, 170
      YES_OPTION, 167
   JPanel
      constructors, 90
      FlowLayout, 90
      with BorderLayout, 91

JPasswordField
    echo character, 101
    getText() and getPassword() method, 101
    setEchoChar() method, 102
JProgressBar, 135
JRadioButton, 123
JScrollBar, 131
JScrollPane
    four corners, 134
    JScrollBars, 133
    Row/Column headers, 133
    show always, 134
    show as needed, 134
    show never, 134
    viewport, 133, 135
JSeparator, 137
JSlider, 136
JSpinner
    components, 129
    JSpinner.DateEditor, 131
    JSpinner.ListEditor, 131
    JSpinner.NumberEditor, 131
    SpinnerDateModel, 130
    SpinnerListModel, 130–131
    SpinnerModel interface, 130
    SpinnerNumberModel, 130
JSplitPane, 160
JTabbedPane, 160
JTable
    AbstractTableModel class, 152
    addColumn() and addRow() methods, 150
    constructors, 151
    DefaultTableModel class, 152
    getColumnClass() method, 154
    getModel() method, 150
    getSelectedRowCount() method, 151
    getSelectedRow() method, 151
    getTableHeader() method, 151
    no-args constructor, 149
    setColumnIdentifiers() method, 150
    setValueAt() method, 151
    TableModel interface, 152
JTextArea, 105
    code implementation, 106
    constructors, 106
    JScrollPane, 108
    methods, 107
    setWrapStyleWord() method, 107
JTextComponent, 95
JTextField
    constructors, 97
    createDefaultModel() method, 100
    insertString() method, 100
    JFormattedTextField, 101
    LimitedCharDocument, 100

    named name and mirroredName, 98
    PlainDocument class, 99
JTextPane
    addStyle() method, 116
    attributes, 113
    buttons, 116
    dump() method, 120
    insertString() method, 119
    methods, 118
    plain document, 113
    root element, 113
    StyleContext object, 118
    styled document, 113
    StyledDocument interface, 113
    word processor, 119
    write() method, 119
JToggleButton, 123
JToolBar
    action interface, 148
    in JFrame, 146
JTree, 155
    branch node, 156
    DefaultMutableTreeNode, 158
    getPath() method, 158
    getRowCount() method, 157
    leaf node, 156
    MutableTreeNode, 156
    node, 156
    parent node, 156
    siblings, 156
    toString() method, 157
    tree-expansion event, 159
    TreeNode, 156
    TreePath, 158
    TreeSelectionListener, 159
    TreeSelectionModel interface, 158
    tree-will-expand event, 159
JWindow, 177
Menus, 137
    JMenuBar, 138
    JMenuItem, 138
    Nesting menus, 139
    pop-up menu, 138
    program, 142
    setAccelerator() method, 140
    setMnemonic() method, 140
    show() method, 141
Painting mechanism
    Graphics object, 185
    paintComponent() method, 185–186
    RepaintManager class, 184
    repaint() method, 184
text components
    class diagram, 93
    document interface, 94

Swing components (*cont.*)
    getDocument() method, 95
    JEditorPane and JTextPane, 94
    JTextArea, 94
    mutiline text component, 93
    MVC pattern, 94
    plain text component, 94
    single-line text component, 93
    styled text component, 94
  Validation
    invalidate() method, 184
    isValid() method, 183
    pack() method, 183
    revalidate() method, 184
    setVisible() method, 183
Symbol tables, 677
Synth, 210
System.setProperty() method, 397

■ T

Text Components, 93
Thread class, 731
toCachedRowSet() method, 500

Transaction Control Language (TCL) Statement, 414
Transaction isolation level
  dirty read, 407
  non-repeatable read, 407
  phantom read, 408–409
Transport Network Substrate(TNS), 398

■ U

updateXxx() method, 411

■ V

Validating text input
  setInputVerifier() method, 121
  verify() method, 121

■ W

WebRowSet, 490

■ X, Y, Z

XADataSource interface, 521

Get the eBook for only $10!

Now you can take the weightless companion with you anywhere, anytime. Your purchase of this book entitles you to 3 electronic versions for only $10.

This Apress title will prove so indispensible that you'll want to carry it with you everywhere, which is why we are offering the eBook in 3 formats for only $10 if you have already purchased the print book.

Convenient and fully searchable, the PDF version enables you to easily find and copy code—or perform examples by quickly toggling between instructions and applications. The MOBI format is ideal for your Kindle, while the ePUB can be utilized on a variety of mobile devices.

Go to www.apress.com/promo/tendollars to purchase your companion eBook.

Printed in the United States
By Bookmasters